JAZZ STYLES

History and Analysis

TENTH EDITION

MARK C. GRIDLEY

Heidelberg College
Tiffin, Ohio

PEARSON
Prentice
Hall

Upper Saddle River, New Jersey 07458

Library of Congress Cataloging-in-Publication Data

Gridley, Mark C., 1947—
  Jazz styles: history and analysis/Mark C. Gridley.—10th ed.
    p. cm.
  Includes bibliographical references and index.
ISBN 0-13-600589-6
  1. Jazz–Analysis, appreciation.   2. Style, Musical.   3. Jazz musicians.   I. Title.   ML3506.G74 2009
  781.65—dc22

                                    2007050313

Editor in Chief: *Sarah Touborg*
Executive Editor: *Richard Carlin*
Editorial Assistant: *Emma Gibbons*
Associate Marketing Manager: *Sasha Anderson-Smith*
Senior Managing Editor: *Mary Rottino*
Production Liaison: *Barbara Taylor-Laino*
Senior Operations Specialist: *Brian Mackey*
Operations Specialist: *Cathleen Peterson*
Composition/Project Management: *ICC Macmillan Inc.*
Art Director/Interior and Cover Design: *Ilze Lemesis*
Director, Image Resource Center: *Melinda Patelli*
Photo Research: *Mark Gridley*
Manager, Rights and Permissions: *Zina Arabia*
Rights and Permissions: *Mark Gridley*
Manager, Cover Visual Research & Permissions: *Karen Sanatar*
Image Permission Coordinator: *Ang'john Ferreri*
Printer/Binder: *Quad/Graphics Dubuque*
Cover Printer: *Phoenix Color Corporation*
Cover Photo: *Miles Davis, ©1988 Ebet Roberts*
Manager, Visual Research: *Beth Brenzel*
The book was set in *10.5/13 Goudy*

Portions of pages 77–78 originally appeared in *Jazz Educators Journal*, Vol. XVI (1984), No. 3, pp. 71–72, as
"Why Is Louis Armstrong So Important?" Portions of pages 363–368 originally appeared in *Popular Music and
Society*, Vol. IX (1983), No. 2, pp. 27–34, as "Clarifying Labels: Jazz, Rock, Funk and Jazz–Rock." Portions of
pages 43–51 originally appeared in *The Black Perspective in Music*, Vol. 12 (1984), No. 1, pp. 44–56, as "Towards
Identification of African Traits in Early Jazz." Portions of pages 191–97 originally appeared in *Popular Music and
Society*, Vol. IX (1984), No. 4, pp. 41–45, as "Why Have Modern Jazz Combos Been Less Popular Than Swing
Big Bands?" Portions of pages 203–04, 229–33 originally appeared in *Tracking: Popular Music Studies*, Vol. 2
(1990), Issue 2, pp. 8–16, as "Clarifying Labels: Cool Jazz, West Coast and Hard Bop." All of the above are
reproduced here by permission of their respective editors. The "(Meet the) Flintstones Theme" is used on the
Demonstration CD by permission of Barbera-Hanna Music (copyright 1960 and 1967), composed by William
Hanna, Joseph Barbera, and Hoyt Curtin. Reproduction and performance without permission of Barbera-Hanna
Music is forbidden.

Pearson Education Group   Pearson Education Canada Ltd.
Pearson Education, Ltd.   Pearson Educación de Mexico, S. A. de C.V.
Pearson Education Australia Pty. Limited   Pearson Education-Japan
Pearson Education Singapore, Pte. Ltd.   Pearson Education Malaysia, Pte. Ltd.
Pearson Education North Asia Ltd.

10 9 8 7 6 5 4
ISBN 0-13-600589-6   book alone

10 9 8 7 6 5 4 3 2 1
ISBN 0-205-69751-8   ala carte

CONTENTS

Preface   v
Acknowledgements   xiii

1   INTRODUCTION   2

PART I   Basics of Jazz

2   WHAT IS JAZZ?   6

3   APPRECIATING JAZZ IMPROVISATION   14

PART II   Premodern Jazz

4   ORIGINS OF JAZZ   34

5   EARLY JAZZ: COMBO JAZZ PRIOR TO THE MIDDLE 1930s   58

6   SWING: THE EARLY 1930s TO THE LATE 1940s   98

7   DUKE ELLINGTON   128

8   THE COUNT BASIE BANDS   148

PART III   Modern Jazz: The Early 1940s to the Early 1960s

9   BOP: THE EARLY 1940s TO THE EARLY 1950s   162

10   COOL JAZZ   202

11   HARD BOP   228

12   MILES DAVIS, HIS GROUPS & SIDEMEN   260

13   JOHN COLTRANE   288

PART IV Modern Jazz: The Early 1960s to the Present

14 1960s AND 1970s AVANT-GARDE AND "FREE" JAZZ   306

15 BILL EVANS, HERBIE HANCOCK, CHICK COREA, AND KEITH JARRETT   338

16 JAZZ-ROCK FUSION   362

17 1980 TO THE PRESENT   390

18 OTHER VOICES   428

Appendices

Appendix A: Brief Outline of Jazz Styles   444

Appendix B: Elements of Music   446

Appendix C: Strategies for Buying Recorded Music   471

Appendix D: A Small Basic Collection of Jazz Videos   478

Appendix E: Glossary   479

Appendix F: Supplementary Reading   483

Appendix G: Sources for Solo Transcriptions   488

Appendix H: For Musicians   490

Index   504

PREFACE

This book was written to help listeners increase their appreciation and enjoyment of jazz. The book and its accompanying *Demo CD* give readers a peek into how jazz musicians put together performances and how their methods have differed from style to style. There is discussion of how jazz originated, and the *Jazz Classics CDs* provide examples of the roots, the earliest recordings, and many major styles that developed later. Styles are described in ways that should help the reader get more out of listening to them. The music is presented in roughly chronological order, and the historically minded reader can use that order to examine major currents in the history of jazz. This particular book was intended, however, more as a description of the styles themselves rather than a decade-by-decade chronicle of the changing jazz scene.

This text was designed as a smorgasbord of information so readers would have a flexible reference source. Chapters can be skipped without doing serious damage to an introductory course in jazz appreciation or a single-semester course in jazz history. Numerous deletions and rearrangements in this book's contents have supplied workable sequences for hundreds of jazz courses since the first edition appeared in 1978.

Because of space limitations, this book deals almost exclusively with American instrumental jazz, and coverage is neither comprehensive nor encyclopedic. For more comprehensive coverage, see (a) "Supplementary Reading," (b) the books that are footnoted throughout the text, and (c) the bibliographies and discographies that appear in the *Instructor's Resource Manual for Jazz Styles, Tenth Edition* (write College Marketing, Prentice-Hall, 1 Lake Street, Upper Saddle River, NJ 07458) and *How to Teach Jazz History* (International Association for Jazz Education). With space limitations in mind, however, the book was designed to devote proportionally more pages to music that developed since 1940. This is because, since the first jazz recordings were not made until 1917, about three-fourths of recorded jazz history has occurred since 1940, and this is music that occupies the lion's share of available recording, nightclub, and concert fare encountered by today's readers. Another reason for this allocation of space is that much of the music discussed here in reference to the 1960s—John Coltrane and Chick Corea, for instance—provided foundations for the dominant styles of the 1970s, '80s, and '90s, as that which is discussed here regarding the 1930s—such as Count Basie and Lester Young, for instance—provided foundations for the dominant styles of the 1940s and 1950s.

No technical knowledge of music is required to understand the contents of this book, and the text's vocabulary has proven to be comprehensible for high school students as well as college students. Past editions have been used effectively in high schools and community colleges as well as universities. Many instructors have successfully taught their courses from this book without devoting any attention to technical terms. Other instructors have used Appendix B, "*Elements of Music,*" and the *Demo CD* to introduce basic technical concepts at the beginning of their course before they discuss selected jazz styles.

Though the book was originally conceived as a text for nonmusicians, previous editions have also been used as the basic text in jazz history courses for music majors. This occurred because of (a) the Appendix H, "For Musicians" that provides notations illustrating basic musical principles (chord changes, modes, comping, walking bass, ride rhythms, etc.) and because (b) the book is especially concerned with detailing the ways styles sound and how they can be differentiated in terms of preferred instruments, tone quality, melody, harmony, rhythm, and approaches to improvisation. Supplements of musical notation are referenced in footnotes throughout the text as well as in the sections devoted to technical references (see Appendices F and G).

CHANGES IN THIS TENTH EDITION

The order of chapters, the organization of topics within chapters, the appendices, and the facts in the ninth edition have all been retained for the convenience of professors who have geared their lectures and exams to them and want to use the tenth edition but continue using course syllabi and exams that are keyed to the earlier contents. Page numbers have changed, however.

At the request of professors and students who used previous editions of *Jazz Styles,* we have

1. added a third CD set of 17 historic recordings to satisfy requests for more music by:

    a. big bands (Andy Kirk, Stan Kenton, Carla Bley)

    b. recent styles (Keith Jarrett, Afro-Cuban—Paquito D'Rivera, Klezmer—Dave Douglas, polystylistic postmodern—Carla Bley, fusion and soul saxes—Brecker Brothers, neo-classical—Wynton Marsalis/Lincoln Center)

    c. Latin Jazz (Paquito D'Rivera)

    d. Charlie Parker ("Just Friends")

    e. Louis Armstrong ("Hotter Than That")

    f. singers (Ella Fitzgerald, Sarah Vaughan, Louis Armstrong)

    g. Lester Young (We restored "Lester Leaps In.")

    h. important musicians who were neglected in the previous 2CD *Jazz Classics* set:

    > Fats Waller, Coleman Hawkins, Mary Lou Williams, Dave Brubeck, Paul Desmond, Stan Kenton, Clifford Brown, Sonny Rollins, and Keith Jarrett

2. added new listening guides to accompany the selections on the new third CD

3. added a new Chapter 18, titled "Other Voices," to present Carla Bley, Joe Lovano, Paul Motian, Maria Schneider, and ECM Style

4. updated all of the footnotes to announce the most current availability of recordings and new readings (this entailed checking over three thousand CDs and many new books) and created new footnotes to help readers locate the sounds described by the new Chapter 18: Other Voices.

5. added new color performance photos

6. repackaged the *Listening to Jazz* demonstration video on DVD

Although not specific to this book, two new supplementary features are now available that will enhance student learning and aid classroom instruction. They are:

- the **Prentice Hall Jazz Video Collection,** with historic clips of Bessie Smith, Louis Armstrong, Duke Ellington, Charlie Parker, Billie Holiday, Miles Davis, and others in performance for student and classroom study. This video may be packaged with the main text at a discounted price, and is also available to any professor who adopts the main text.

- **Prentice Hall's MyJazzKit,** an online learning center, including a "starter kit" (basic theory, terms, a timeline), self-study aids (quizzes, flash cards, composer profiles, listening guides), interactive features (create your own jazz band and compositions), and audio and video resources. The web address is: *www.myjazzkit.com.*

HOW TO USE THIS BOOK

Music appreciation courses have been in existence far longer than jazz history courses. Since the 1960s, colleges have been extending the means by which nonmusician students can expand their appreciation of music. In addition to traditional approaches that teach listening skills by exposure to the forms and sounds of classical music, new courses also teach listening skills and multicultural awareness by introductory classes in jazz, rock, and world music. Some college curricula allow humanities elective credits to be earned by completing courses in jazz history. The *Jazz Styles* books, compact discs, and instructor's manuals are particularly useful for this type of course. With the *Demo CD* and the *Jazz Classics CDs*, the *Jazz Styles* textbook can serve as the core of a self-paced course of study in which the reader/listener becomes familiar with basic principles of music listening. The sights and sounds of jazz can be enjoyed apart from the presentations made by the instructor. The *Jazz Styles* materials can supplement and complement classroom experiences. Technical concepts that otherwise require lecture/demonstrations by professional musicians can be learned by pairing the CDs with the accompanying text pages. The contents of the *Demo CD* can be used as reinforcement of classroom lecture/demonstrations because they provide a handy source of review materials. Several professors have required that their students learn the contents of the *Demo CD* outside of class, thereby saving class time to use for other topics. No matter what approach is taken to using this textbook and its CDs, every individual and class is encouraged to listen to as much recorded and live jazz as possible. **The book will be an effective guide only if accompanied by repeated listening to pivotal selections and extensive listening to a variety of styles.**

In the margins of the book, you will notice callouts for where students can hear the music discussed in the text. These are available as supplements to the text. The following abbreviations are used:

JCCD1, 2, or *3:* The new 3CD *Jazz Classics* set

CCD1 or *2:* The 2CD set prepared for the *Concise Guide to Jazz,* 5th edition

Demo CD: The Demonstration Audio Disc for *Jazz Styles*

Demo DVD: Listening to Jazz demonstration DVD

For those who continue to use the *Smithsonian Collection of Classic Jazz,* we have offered some alternate performances, indicated by *SCCJ.*

Adapting the Book for Different Courses

This book was originally conceived in an omnibus format whose organization was intended to provide a flexible reference for learning about jazz. Sample syllabi for different class schedules and various approaches to introducing jazz are provided in the *Instructor's Resource Manual* that is available from Prentice-Hall sales representatives. The next five paragraphs outline approaches that have proven successful in schools where previous editions of this book have been required.

The text provides the essentials for a course titled **Understanding Jazz** if it is accompanied by several carefully conceived, in-class demonstrations by musicians plus a well chosen collection of recordings. A bare minimum collection might begin with this book's compact discs and a number of the albums footnoted in the text. The in-class demonstrations might follow the guidelines described in "Getting the Most from a Drumming Demonstration and Live Rhythm Section" in *How to Teach Jazz History* (Mark C. Gridley, IAJE Press, 1984/2005). Previous editions of the text have been used in this way at several colleges. These sections of the book provided the key components: "Elements of Music" (see Appendix B), Chapter 2 (What Is Jazz?), Chapter 3 (Appreciating Jazz Improvisation), and Chapter 4 (Origins of Jazz). Much emphasis was placed on the listening guides that appear throughout the text. Instructors usually supplemented that material with selected portions of styles chapters. The portions that give readers the most insight into how jazz is made are the nonbiographical units that appear at the beginnings of Chapters 5, 6, 9, 14, and 16.

The text provides the essentials for a historically organized course titled **Introduction to Jazz Styles.** Again, a basic collection of recordings is essential. The bare bones of such a collection could be taken from the *Jazz Classics CDs* for *Concise Guide to Jazz* (available from Prentice-Hall as ISBN 0-13-173332-X; *prenhall.com*) and the *Smithsonian Collection of Classic Jazz* (or *Ken Burns' Jazz: The Story of America's Music,* a 5CD set from Columbia Legacy C5K 61432. This is not the video from the television series.) The skeleton of the course is described in the "styles" chapters: Chapter 5 (Early Jazz), Chapter 6 (Swing), Chapter 9 (Bop), Chapter 10 (Cool Jazz), Chapter 11 (Hard Bop), Chapter 14 (1960s and 1970s Avant-Garde and "Free" Jazz), and Chapter 16 (Jazz-Rock Fusion). Instructors frequently preface their styles sequence with appendix materials (Elements of Music) and the introductory chapters (What Is Jazz; Appreciating Jazz Improvisation). They frequently supplement with more specialized chapters, such as those devoted to Duke Ellington and Miles Davis, for instance.

The text provides the essentials for a course concerned primarily with **Major Figures in Jazz:** Louis Armstrong (covered in Chapter 5), Duke Ellington (Chapter 7), Charlie Parker/Dizzy Gillespie (Chapter 9), Miles Davis (Chapters 12 and 16), and John Coltrane (Chapter 13). For those who wish to explore more than just the top five or six figures, the text also covers such other giants as Jelly Roll Morton (Chapter 5), Earl Hines (Chapter 5), Count Basie (Chapter 8), Lester Young (Chapter 8), Lennie Tristano (Chapter 10), Ornette Coleman (Chapter 14), Charles Mingus (Chapter 14), Bill Evans (Chapter 15), Sun Ra (Chapter 14), and Stan Kenton (Chapter 10), to name just a few.

For a course titled **History of Jazz,** the text can be used intact, though minor juggling of contents will make the final eight chapters more chronological. For example, the main treatment of Miles Davis (Chapter 12) runs from the 1950s to the late 1960s; so instructors may wish to postpone coverage of its second half until after covering parts of other chapters that deal with the early 1960s: John Coltrane (Chapter 13), Avant-Garde (Chapter 14), and Bill Evans (Chapter 15). Similarly, instructors may wish to postpone the final two-thirds of Chapter 15 (Bill Evans, Herbie Hancock, Chick Corea, and Keith Jarrett) until the 1970s have been covered, because the bulk of its material overlaps the same span and then spills into the 1980s with its updates on Herbie Hancock and Chick Corea. Before attempting to be perfectly chronological, instructors are encouraged to note that coverage of Charles Mingus in Chapter 14 runs from the 1940s to the 1970s, as does that of Sun Ra. Also note that Chapter 14's coverage for the Art Ensemble of Chicago, Anthony Braxton, and the World Saxophone Quartet overlaps the same time period as Chapter 16's coverage of jazz-rock. Incidentally, to do justice to the course title of "Jazz History," the instructor will need more than the brief recorded examples contained in the *Smithsonian Collection of Classic Jazz* (or the *Ken Burns' Jazz* 5 CD set), the *Jazz Classics CDs* for *Jazz Styles,* and the *Jazz Classics CDs* for the *Concise Guide to Jazz.* A good start would be a sampling of recordings that are footnoted for each chapter and/or the *Small Basic Collection* presented on page 5. If your library does not have them, perhaps you could request their ordering a few each budget year. Then eventually a suitable collection would be available for jazz history students.

Most single-semester jazz courses don't allow time for much attention to recent developments in jazz, but this book contains two optional chapters for instructors who make the time to introduce them and/or for students who want to investigate developments that are not addressed in class. Chapter 17 introduces new age, acid jazz, the soul saxes (discussing Michael Brecker with a 1992 recording and listening guide, Dave Sanborn, Kenny G, and their sources), smooth jazz, hip hop jazz, neo-swing, neo-classical jazz (including a 2001 Wynton Marsalis recording with listening guide), Klezmer jazz (Don Byron, John Zorn, and Dave Douglas with a 1994 recording and listening guide for a Douglas piece), and Latin Jazz (including a 1982 Paquito D'Rivera recording and listening guide). Note that teachers could cover Latin jazz as they cover each and every era if they had the appropriate recordings. The present book, however, focuses mostly on attention recently garnered by Afro-Cuban style in the United States.

Chapter 18 introduces Carla Bley (including a 1999 Bley recording and listening guide), Joe Lovano, Paul Motian, Maria Schneider, and ECM. The chapter presents such "Other Voices" in ways that a teacher could use in covering the present. The coverage of Bley and Schneider should also be helpful for teachers interested in big bands.

At several schools, jazz styles and history are introduced by instrument rather than by era. For example, the history of major influences on jazz styles of trumpet playing is treated separately from the history of major influences on piano styles. Each instrument is treated separately until all the instruments have been covered through all of jazz history. For the convenience of those schools, most of the era chapters in *Jazz Styles* are organized by instrument. Students need merely pull out the particular section of each chapter that deals with the instrument of the week. After all chapters have been scanned for that instrument, the next instrument can be investigated in a similar fashion. Some schools also have entire courses devoted to the study of styles for improvising on just one instrument. At least one professor requires *Jazz Styles* to be read by students in courses called "jazz trumpet," "jazz trombone," "jazz saxophone," "jazz piano," "jazz bass," and "jazz drums."

This text has also been used in courses called "American Music," "Contemporary Music," "Twentieth Century Music," "Popular Music in America," "African American Music," and "Black Music." The last third of the text is used in many courses called "Rock," "The History of Rock and Roll," and "Jazz/Rock Foundations." The "Elements of Music" appendix is used in numerous music appreciation courses. The "For Musicians" appendix is used in many courses in "Jazz Theory" and "Introduction to Jazz Styles," "Jazz Survey," and "Jazz Perspectives." Additionally, a number of band directors require their ensemble members to read the book, listen to the recordings, and learn where their own performance repertory fits in the large picture of jazz history.

Teaching Strategies

A number of professors have said that this book has too much information in it, and, in particular, that it is impossible for them to cover some chapters, such as Ellington and Coltrane, in a single-semester college course. These professors are correct. However, if they are unduly frustrated by this, they are overlooking two considerations. First is that **this book, like most good textbooks, is intended to be merely a resource, not a rigid syllabus for a particular course. It was never intended to be studied line-by-line, cover to cover by novice listeners in a single-semester jazz**

appreciation course. The second consideration is that part of **a teacher's job is to make judicious choices from the assortment of information offered in a textbook and then guide students to a comprehensible sampling that is suitable for them.**

Instructors need to be aware that students are often confused and frustrated in courses where professors do not routinely follow a detailed syllabus that tells what textbook pages, terms, and musicians the students are expected to learn. Textbooks tend to be overwhelming when students assume that they must learn everything in them. Helpful teachers tell their students what not to be overly concerned with. A few examples will clarify this. Whereas some teachers consider sideman names to be superfluous, others believe that familiarity with every musician in the Ellington chapter is essential for a minimum understanding of the music. Whereas some teachers feel that to know John Coltrane was an important post-Parker saxophonist is sufficient, other teachers consider an appreciation of Coltrane's McCoy Tyner-Jimmy Garrison-Elvin Jones rhythm section also to be essential. Some teachers want students to remember not only that Coltrane had roots in the styles of Coleman Hawkins, Lester Young, Charlie Parker, and Sonny Stitt, but also that Coltrane influenced such current giants as David Liebman and Joe Lovano. Some teachers believe that a basic introduction to jazz involves learning to discriminate soprano from tenor saxophone timbre. Other teachers feel that such a skill exceeds reasonable expectations for nonmusician students. Whereas some teachers feel that students should be able to recognize the sound of a 12-bar blues before receiving a passing grade in an introductory course, other teachers are more concerned that their students remember the birthplaces of famous musicians. Whereas some teachers believe that an immersion in the sounds of jazz is sufficient and students need not acquire knowledge about how it is made, other teachers believe that it is essential for students to appreciate the unwritten rules that musicians follow in putting together their performances. Regardless of a teacher's philosophy of jazz education, students benefit from being told what that philosophy is. They also welcome knowing what pages to read and what they will be expected to remember.

A number of instructors have said their students ask them what names are important among the many names appearing in *Jazz Styles*. Resourceful instructors tell their less-motivated students to learn approximately the ten to twenty names that receive the most page space. More-motivated students can do fine if they skip all but the boldfaced names. Jazz fans like to note new names to investigate further.

Here is a rule of thumb for *using a book that mentions a large number of important musicians*. Hold students responsible for familiarity with only the musicians whose work they have extended opportunity to hear. A single playing in class is not sufficient for a novice listener. If, however, students hear a musician in class and also own an example or two on recordings, it may be reasonable for a teacher to expect them to be able to identify that player's sound and describe his contributions. For example, if your music library or listening lab lacks the classic Miles Davis albums on Prestige that feature Philly Joe Jones, such as *Steamin'*, *Cookin'*, *Workin'*, *Relaxin'*, and the Columbia album *Milestones*, it would not be reasonable to hold students responsible for familiarity with Jones, even though he is discussed in the book. Conversely, it may be reasonable to expect students to recognize Lester Young's playing if the teacher plays several 1930s recordings in class by Lester Young, such as "Shoe Shine Boy" (*Ken Burns' Jazz CD2*) and "Lady Be Good" (*CCD1* Track 7), "Taxi War Dance," and "Lester Leaps In" (*JCCD1* Tracks 24 and 25). Late-period Young (1943–59), however, would be unreasonable to expect students to recognize because it differs so much from Young in the 1930s.

Students have reported several different *ways to use the tables of musician names* that appear in most styles chapters. One way is for keeping track of what is covered in class. Whenever the professor discusses a particular musician and plays examples of the music, students turn to the table and put a check mark next to that musician's name. Students also use the tables to help classify new musicians they hear on the radio, on friends' recordings, or see in concert. When they hear someone new, they look for that name in the book's tables. This helps them remember the new name and put the musician's style in perspective by classifying it. Pegging it in a familiar way helps organize what otherwise may be overwhelming new information. Students also benefit from access to the tables because they know that if they like the sound of one player, others named with him in that same table may also be enjoyable and worth seeking on recordings. **The names tables are presented merely as an optional reference source,** and a number of readers have reported using the book as a reference long after they complete the course. (The last thing any teacher should allow students to think is that they need to learn the names of all the musicians in all the tables.)

The name lists are also helpful in fleshing out stylistic concepts such as "hard bop." Such concepts are not sufficiently characterized by words, even by descriptions of style characteristics or by the profiles of the style's most eminent exponents. Greater understanding comes, for example, by listening to music by an assortment of artists who are not profiled in this book, but are listed as exemplars in the names table. Lee Morgan, Bobby Timmons, and Benny Golson, for instance, can be identified with the "hard bop" style by noticing their names in the hard bop musicians table. If a reader then listens to their recordings, the reader can come to a better understanding of what actually constitutes that style than would be afforded solely by listening to the Art Blakey and Clifford Brown recordings that come with the book.

The strategy that some professors use to choose textbooks is to seek one that will serve as a skeleton of knowledge to be fleshed out in lecture. This differs from the strategy of finding a book that can serve as a smorgasbord to be trimmed down. Instead of giving students a book having more than they will need, these professors prefer to give students a book having less than they need. These professors might wish to assign the *Concise Guide to Jazz,* the abridged version of *Jazz Styles.* By comparison with *Jazz Styles,* it contains about half the number of pages, 11 chapters instead of 18, a fifth the number of musician profiles, and about a fortieth the number of musician names and tune titles. It retains important appendix items from *Jazz Styles* such as the Elements of Music, Strategies for Buying Recorded Music, Glossary, and the optional For Musicians section of basic technical aspects of jazz. It also retains most of what is in the *Jazz Styles* chapters on What Is Jazz and Appreciating Jazz Improvisation. It comes with a *Demo CD* adapted from the *Jazz Styles Demo CD* and an optional 2 CDs containing 35 historic recordings that are analyzed in listening guides. The contents of the *Jazz Classics CDs* for the *Concise Guide to Jazz* are balanced across jazz history. However, they can also serve as a complement to the *Jazz Classics CDs* for *Jazz Styles* and the *Smithsonian Collection of Classic Jazz* because they duplicate only a few selections from those compilations.

A strategy that some professors use when choosing a textbook is to find a reference work that allows inquiring students to go beyond what can be covered in class. They want their students to have something to refer to whenever more information is sought about music they hear in class or on the radio. *Jazz Styles* is exhaustively indexed to serve precisely such a function. It also has tables listing the prominent names by style and era. Numerous footnotes steer the reader to the best sources for hearing the important musicians and reading about them.

Here is an example of the flexibility that *Jazz Styles* recently offered a professor who was willing to glean relevant material from the resources in the text rather than assuming the course must rigidly follow the book, page by page. For a one-semester course in jazz and rock that students took as a music appreciation elective, the instructor first introduced some "how to listen" ideas, by way of in-class demonstrations of instruments and analysis of song forms (as explained in the "Elements of Music" appendix and Chapter 3). Then an African retentions sequence (as explained in Chapter 4) was presented, moving smoothly to jazz-rock, because jazz-rock has more Africanisms than other jazz styles and because the course title was "Jazz and Rock." Joe Zawinul's "Birdland" was another handy point of departure because some students could connect it to the Count Basie riff band style they heard in "One O'Clock Jump." (These are found together on Tracks 5 and 6 on *Jazz Classics CD1*.) Then an assortment of pop music was presented (James Brown, Ray Charles, the Jacksons, and various Motown recording artists), and its African connections were outlined via Chapter 4 (Origins of Jazz) and Chapter 16 (Jazz-Rock Fusion). The explanations for African connections and origins of jazz/rock were keyed to the chart of parallel streams that appears in Chapter 16. Much of the sequence was done according to suggestions found in the "Demonstrating African Connections" chapter of *How to Teach Jazz History* (IAJE Press, 1984/2005). Then, for the remainder of the course, a few key jazz styles such as swing and bop were introduced, and discussion was offered for only a few essential figures (Louis Armstrong, Duke Ellington, Count Basie, Charlie Parker, Dizzy Gillespie, Miles Davis, and John Coltrane).

ACKNOWLEDGEMENTS

I remain deeply grateful to many people who took time out of their own busy schedules to provide ideas and feedback for past editions of this book and its abridged edition, the *Concise Guide to Jazz*. Since 1971, Harvey Pekar has been sharing his penetrating stylistic insights, historical perspective, and discographical knowledge. He was always willing to discuss controversies, direct me to new perspectives, and allow me to include his observations when I prepared my manuscripts. He provided historic recordings for almost every style. Every chapter in this text reflects his input. Since the very first manuscript in 1973, John Richmond has continued to be a source of counsel in my jazz history research, and he consulted in my preparation of the new listening guides for Ella Fitzgerald's "Perdido" and Fats Waller's "Handful of Keys." I also remain indebted to Chuck Braman for his help on the first five editions because the results survive in this new one, and he once again assisted with conceptualization of the new Chapter 17: "1980–2005" in the ninth edition and the listening guides for "Solar" and "Civilization Day".

I continue to appreciate the dedication to detail and accuracy in Bill Anderson's updating 552 footnotes of albums and books, updating the Small Basic Collection of CDs, the Small Basic Collection of Jazz Videos, the Supplementary Reading, and editing the 71-page discography in the *Instructor's Resource Manual*. He provided me with pivotal recordings and books for my research in the new sections and the discographical aspects of all the listening guides, not just the new ones. Over the years, Anderson's instant willingness to help in matters large and small has taken much of the pain out of my seemingly endless revision tasks.

This edition reflects extensive critiques performed on earlier editions by Morris Holbrook, Karl Koenig, Victor Schonfield, and Joel Simpson. Holbrook and Koenig allowed me to include their own words in my rewrites. Wallace Rave conceptualized the original analyses for Chapter 4's section on What Is African and What Is European About Jazz, as Koenig did for the brass bands origins of New Orleans jazz. A number of Joel Simpson's rephrasings from his editing of the *Concise Guide to Jazz* were borrowed to make the present book easier to read.

Many consultants were involved in the research, preparation, and editing of the new listening guides. The guide for "Express Crossing" was developed from a listening guide that David Cutler prepared for the piece's appearance on the *Prentice Hall Jazz Collection*. Cutler also provided the structural analyses for "Wolverine Blues," "Seven Come Eleven," "Misterioso," "Blue Rondo a la Turk," "Señor Blues," and "Fables of Faubus." Gridley expanded and edited all of Cutler's guides, with assistance from Wendy Raymaley. Guides for "Taxi War Dance" and "Harlem Airshaft" were substantially revised from previous editions for this new edition, based on the results of recent student testing. New guides for "Handful of Keys," "Above and Below," and "Baseball" were developed by Gridley from structural analyses provided by Bart Polot. Assistance for analysis of "Above and Below" also came from Jeff LeSueur and its composer Randy Brecker. George Foley and John Richmond also worked on the guide for "Handful of Keys." Richmond also consulted on "Perdido" and "Body and Soul." New guides for "Kiss and Run," "Hotter Than That," and "Miami" were developed from structural analyses provided by Paul Rinzler. Willard Jenkins commented on the listening guide for "Miami." The listening guide for "A Trumpet" was developed from a score prepared by Bob Morgan and from analysis that Morgan offered. The guide to

"Walkin' and Swingin'" was developed from a score prepared by David Berger and from highlights that Berger offered. Analysis of "Red Emma" was assisted by its composer Dave Douglas. The listening guide for "Sundial, Part 1" was developed from analyses provided by Marc Copland and Bob Fraser. All the new guides were tested and edited by Wendy Raymaley, Alissa Paolella, and Lacy Terry. Listening guides for "Baseball," "Above and Below," and "Handful of Keys" were additionally tested on other students by Bart Polot.

The new Chapter 18, titled "Other Voices," was conceptualized with the help of Bill Anderson, Rob Hoff, and Jim Szabo. Observations on Carla Bley were contributed by Jack Schantz, Judy Silvano, and Joe Lovano. Observations on Joe Lovano were contributed by Judy Silvano and Lovano himself. Observations on the Paul Motian Trio were contributed by Joe Lovano and Chuck Braman. The outline of coverage for Maria Schneider was contributed by Paul Ferguson, developed by Gridley, then proofed and edited by Schneider herself. The entire chapter was edited by Wendy Raymaley, who also edited rewrites for the What Is Jazz? chapter and the introduction to the Avant-Garde chapter.

This edition reflects research done for all previous editions and the kindness of hundreds of musicians who shared their observations, memories, and opinions with me. For a complete listing, see the Acknowledgements sections for the previous editions. The accuracy of coverage in this book is due in part to the cooperation of many musicians whose music is discussed on its pages. Unfortunately, several of them passed away before seeing the finished product. Over the past thirty years, the following players helped by means of conversations, proofreading, and/or correspondence: Benny Goodman, Stan Kenton, Bill Evans, Wayne Shorter, Joe Zawinul, Eric Gravatt, Herbie Hancock, Tony Williams, Joe Venuti, Al McKibbon, Dizzy Gillespie, Paul Smith, Richard Davis, Bob Curnow, Jimmy Heath, Jaco Pastorius, Red Rodney, Jimmy Giuffre, Andrew White, Bud Freeman, Gerry Mulligan, Maynard Ferguson, Billy Taylor, David "Fathead" Newman, George West, Paul Motian, Eddie "Cleanhead" Vinson, Ken McIntyre, William Parker, Barry Martyn, Don Sickler, Dave Berger, Richard Sudhalter, Val Kent, Mel Lewis, Ernie Krivda, Mike Lee, Bob Fraser, Fred Sharp, Chuck Wayne, Abe Laboriel, Gene Lees, Airto Moreira, Bill Kirchner, Gunnar Biggs, John Klayman, Mal Barron, Bill Dobbins, John Handy, and Harold Battiste.

I am grateful to the many professors and their students who took time to tell me how previous editions worked for their classes. A few evaluations came from:

Billy Barnard	*University of Minnesota at Duluth*
Gary Scott and Tom Horning	*Cuyahoga Community College*
Pete Ford	*Mercy College of Northwest Ohio*
Tim Powell	*Kent State University*
Norm Damschroder	*University of Toledo*
Jack Taylor	*University of Findlay*
Kent Engelhardt	*Youngstown State University*
Tom Everett	*Harvard University*
Jeff Stout	*Berklee College of Music*
Jeff Halsey	*Bowling Green State University*
Tom Knific	*Western Michigan University*
Richard Davis	*University of Wisconsin*
Michael Stephens	*Pasadena City College*
Michael Pagan	*University of Colorado*

Justin DiCiccio	*Manhattan School of Music*
Jeremy Yudkin	*Boston University*
Paul Murphy	*California State University at Channel Islands*
John Reid	*University of Calgary*
Andrew Speight	*San Francisco State University*
David Kay	*University School–Pepper Pike, Ohio*
Paul Ferguson	*Cleveland State University and Case Western Reserve University*
Lee Heritage	*University of Toledo*
Curt Wilson	*Texas Christian University*
Carroll Dashiell and George Broussard	*East Carolina University*
Terry Steele	*Slippery Rock State University*
John Joyce	*Tulane University*
Rick Helzer	*San Diego State University*
John Harding	*Coastal Carolina Community College*
Gerald Wilson	*UCLA*
Thomas Mason	*University of Southern California*
Howard Mandel	*New York University*

I am very grateful to Jim Schafer for the efficient computer services contributed to the production of photos that appear on these pages.

J azz includes many different streams of music. They can be played by almost any combination of instruments. They can evoke almost any mood. Some are light and happy. Some are heavy and serious. Some make you want to dance. Some make you think. Some are smooth and predictable. Some are agitated and full of surprises.

Jazz can be heard in many different places. It is often presented as serious music in concert halls. Some jazz is played in ballrooms for dancers. There is jazz in background music on the radio. Much jazz is played in night clubs where people listen while they drink and talk with their friends.

Jazz is unique for two very special aspects: (a) its provocative rhythms, technically known as "**syncopation**" and "**swing feeling,**" and (b) its insistence that performers create their parts as they play them, technically known as **improvisation.** Each jazz performance represents a new and original creation. Hearing live jazz is exciting not only for the way it makes us feel, but also for the realization that we are following the musical thinking of the musicians at the very moment they are inventing their music. They are taking us along with them while they make up fresh sounds. This is akin to the impossible situation of seeing a finished painting as we watch the artist apply paint to the canvas, *at the same time* as we watch one manufacturer produce the canvas and another manufacturer produce the paints themselves.

Guitarist Wes Montgomery
(Photo by Chuck Stewart)

Jazz has an impressive reputation. It is so interesting that it is played and analyzed in hundreds of colleges. Almost every high school and college has at least one jazz band. Though it originated in America, jazz is so compelling that musicians on every continent have played it, and today there is no city without it. The sounds of jazz have influenced the development of new styles in popular music and the work of symphonic composers. Jazz is so sturdy that the old styles are still being played, and new styles are always being developed. In fact, jazz is regarded as a fine art, not just a passing fad.

This book is organized historically, though it is not really about the history for its own sake so much as the styles themselves. The styles are presented chronologically because that is the easiest way to organize them. Since history and evolution of styles will be touched by your study, here are a few ideas to keep in mind. First of all, the central figures did not create their innovations entirely by themselves. Rather, their work reflects the influence of other players, as well as chance occurrences that were combined, modified, and developed in original ways. A stream of styles might emanate from the talent and hard work of a few musicians who devised the freshest approaches. However, jazz history cannot accurately be described as a single stream evolving from Dixieland directly to swing, and from swing directly to bop and so forth. Nor can approaches used in playing a given instrument be traced to a narrow line of innovators, each of whom is the sole influence on the next—a prominent saxophonist from the 1930s influencing his successor in the 1940s, who in turn influenced another successor in the 1950s, for example. There is no neat line of succession, with each subsequent style rendering the previous ones obsolete. Usually many different styles of jazz coexist, no matter which ones are in vogue with a particular audience at any given time.

Another idea to keep in mind when studying history is that the evolution of jazz cannot accurately be considered a series of "reactions," as though musicians became collectively angry and then suddenly fought a style by inventing another to oppose it. Many historians are fond of believing this. But the truth is that most musicians just find their own favorite way of playing. Often it is an existing style they like. They modify it to suit their tastes and capabilities. Sometimes they combine different approaches until the proportions please them. Many players stick with that style for good; others change their styles when they become bored with them.

Most of all, keep in mind that the more of jazz history you delve into, the more opportunities you have for discovering additional styles to enjoy. It is also good to know that the more we hear, the more skilled we will become as listeners. Then we can extract more pleasure from the sounds. Though some of the subtle aspects are not evident to us immediately, most are accessible after we exert some effort to find out what is going on. In other words, jazz offers a set of pleasures that deepen with understanding. The rewards are guaranteed—you will delight in the surprises that jazz improvisations offer. Incidentally, studying jazz can also lead you to other kinds of music you might enjoy. There is another advantage, too. As you become better at listening to jazz, you will also notice more of the subtle aspects in other kinds of music.

In the chapter notes, CDs are listed first with their recording date and second the most recent reissue, indicated by a small letter "c" before the year. For example, in this entry: "Miles Davis & the Modern Jazz Giants (Fantasy: OJC-347, 1954, c1989)," "1954" indicates the recording, and "c1989" the most recent reissue.

For a quick orientation to musical terms, see the "Elements of Music" appendix and the Demo CD.

Jazz Classics CD 1 & 2 for *Jazz Styles*. Prentice-Hall: ISBN 0-13-000561-6

Jazz Classics CD 1 & 2 for *Concise Guide to Jazz*. Prentice-Hall: ISBN 0-13-173332-X

(The above CDs are not available in stores; phone 800-947-7700 for mail order.)

Ken Burns' Jazz: The Story of America's Music. Columbia/Legacy: CSK 61432, 5CD set, 1917–92, c2000.

Louis Armstrong. *The Complete Hot Five and Hot Seven Recordings, Vol. 2*. Columbia: 87010, 1926, c2003.

Louis Armstrong. *The Complete Hot Five and Hot Seven Recordings, Vol. 3*. Columbia: 87011, 1927–28, c2003.

Sidney Bechet. *The Legendary Sidney Bechet*. RCA Bluebird: 6590, 1932–41, c1988.

Bix Beiderbecke. *Bix Beiderbecke, Vol. 1. Singin' the Blues*. Columbia: 45450, 1927, c1990.

Art Tatum. *Piano Starts Here*. Columbia: 64690, 1933, 1949, c1995.

Count Basie. *The Best of Early Basie*. Decca Jazz: 655, 1936–39, c1996.

Coleman Hawkins. *Body and Soul*. Victor Jazz: 68515, 1939–56, c1996.

Benny Goodman. *Benny Goodman at Carnegie Hall: Complete*. Columbia: C2K 65143, 2CD set, 1938, c1999.

Billie Holiday. *Billie Holiday + Lester Young: A Musical Romance*. Columbia/Legacy: 86635, 1937–41, 1958, c2002.

Charlie Christian. *The Genius of the Electric Guitar*. Columbia: 65564, 4CD set, 1939–41, c2002.

Duke Ellington. *Never No Lament: The Blanton-Webster Band*. RCA Bluebird: 50857, 3CD set, 1940–42, c2003.

Woody Herman. *Blowin' Up a Storm! The Columbia Years*. Columbia/Legacy: C2K 65646, 2CD set, 1945–47, c2001.

Dizzy Gillespie. *The Complete RCA Victor Recordings*. RCA Bluebird: 66528, 2CD set, 1937–1949, c1995.

Charlie Parker. *Yardbird Suite: The Ultimate Charlie Parker Collection*. Rhino: 72260, 2CD set, 1945–54, c1997.

Bud Powell. *Jazz Giant*. Verve: 314 543 832, 1949–50, c2001.

Thelonious Monk. *Best of Thelonious Monk: The Blue Note Years*. Blue Note: 95636, 1947–52, c1991.

Miles Davis. *Birth of the Cool*. Capitol: 30117, 1949–50, c2001.

Lee Konitz. *Subconscious-Lee*. Fantasy: OJC-186 (Prestige), 1949–50, c1991.

Stan Getz. *Complete Roost Recordings*. Blue Note: 59622, 3CD set, 1950–52, c1997.

Stan Kenton. *New Concepts of Artistry in Rhythm*. Capitol: 92865, 1952, c1989.

Dave Brubeck. *Jazz at Oberlin*. Fantasy: OJC-046, 1953, c1987.

Art Blakey. *A Night at Birdland, Vols. 1 & 2*. Blue Note: 32146/32147, 2CDs, 1954, c2001.

Sonny Rollins. *Sonny Rollins Plus 4*. Fantasy: OJC-243 (Prestige), 1956, c1987.

Charles Mingus. *Mingus Ah Um*. Columbia: 65512, 1959, c1998.

Ornette Coleman. *The Shape of Jazz to Come*. Atlantic: 1317, 1959, c1987.

Miles Davis. *Kind of Blue*. Columbia: 64935, 1959, c1997.

John Coltrane. *Giant Steps*. Rhino: 75203 (Atlantic 1311), 1959, c1998.

Bill Evans. *Sunday at the Village Vanguard*. Fantasy: OJC-140 (Riverside), 1961, c1987.

John Coltrane. *Live at Birdland*. Impulse!: 198, 1963, c1996.

Albert Ayler. *Spiritual Unity*. Get Back: 1001 (ESP-DISK 1002), 1964, c1998.

John Coltrane. *Interstellar Space*. Impulse!: 314 543 415, 1967, c2000.

Miles Davis. *Sorcerer*. Columbia: 65680, 1967, c1993.

Miles Davis. *Bitches Brew*. Columbia: C2K 65774, 2CD set, 1969–70, c1999.

Weather Report. *I Sing the Body Electric*. Columbia: 46107, 1971–72, c1990.

Chick Corea. *Now He Sings, Now He Sobs*. Blue Note: 38265, 1968, c2002.

Cecil Taylor. *Silent Tongues*. 1201 Music: 9017, 1974, c2000.

Keith Jarrett. *Staircase*. ECM: 422 827 337 (1090), 2CD set, 1976, c1994.

Many of these recordings may not be in your local CD store. See Appendix C for mail order sources.

Many different kinds of music have been called "jazz." So it is no surprise that people cannot agree about how to define it. Different people use different ways to decide whether a given performance should be called "jazz." Not all listeners focus on the same aspects. For example, some call it "jazz" if saxophones and drums are used. Some consider only how it makes them feel ("swinging"). Some decide it must be jazz if it is made by performers who have a reputation for jazz. Some won't call any music "jazz" unless they know that part of it is being composed as it is being performed. Another problem frequently occurs because people attempt to define jazz only by what they have heard called "jazz." Though it may include everything they themselves have heard called "jazz," this might omit other kinds of music that have been called "jazz" by different people. Moreover, some people use the term to designate all sorts of American popular music associated with the 1920s because that period was dubbed "The Jazz Age." Despite these problems, there are two elements that most jazz styles have in common—improvisation and jazz swing feeling.

Dizzy Gillespie, 1947
(Photo by William Gottlieb)

IMPROVISATION

To improvise is to compose and perform at the same time. Instead of saying "improvise," many people say *ad lib, ride,* or *jam.* This means that jazz musicians make up their music as they go along. A great deal of jazz is spontaneous. It is not written down or rehearsed beforehand. This is like the impromptu speaking all of us do every day when we talk "off the cuff." We use words and phrases we have used before. But now we improvise by using them in new ways and new orders that have not been rehearsed. A lot of originality can result. This is significant because being original is very important to jazz musicians. They try to be as spontaneous as possible. In fact, they try to never improvise the same way twice. Some of the spirit and vitality associated with jazz may be due to the spontaneity of improvisation. Several versions of a tune made during the same recording session may be entirely different because of this.

For most people, improvisation is an essential element of jazz, and musicians occasionally say "jazz" when they mean "improvise." For example, in a music publisher's brochure describing big band arrangements, a note might be included saying, "only the tenor saxophone part requires jazz." Or a musician's contractor might phone a player requesting that he play "jazz trumpet chair" in a big band, meaning the player will be the only trumpeter required to improvise.

If you are not very familiar with jazz, you might not be able to tell what has been written or memorized beforehand from what is being improvised. One clue is that if part of a performance sounds improvised, it quite often is. Improvised parts sometimes sound more casual and less organized than the written or memorized parts. The problem with using that clue, however, is that the best improvisations are so well constructed that they sound almost like written melodies.

Another clue comes from knowing about a routine that most jazz musicians use. The players begin with a tune they all know. First they play it once all the way through. The melody is played by the horns, the accompaniment by the piano, bass, and drums. Then the piano, bass, and drums continue to do what they did before. But this time, the horns make up and play new melodies of their own. They improvise their own melodies to the tune's accompaniment chords. The way the chords progress in that accompaniment guides the notes they choose for their new melodies, which we call improvisations. In other words, when the melody of the piece itself ends, what follows is improvised. Then it is all improvised until that same melody begins again. This kind of improvisation distinguishes jazz musicians from most pop musicians who merely decorate a tune by changing some of its rhythms or adding notes to it.

Even though improvisation is the main emphasis in jazz, not everything is spontaneous. Most jazz bands use arrangements of some sort. In large jazz ensembles where the players are seated with written arrangements in front of them, a player is usually improvising when he stands up to solo; otherwise, the music is coming from the written parts. And, of course, any lines played by several players in unison must have been prepared beforehand. In the next chapter, we will examine a few of the common practices that indicate what parts in a jazz performance are usually worked out in advance.

SWING FEELING

Next, we will consider different views regarding what jazz is. Some views allow music that bears no jazz swing feeling to be called jazz. Some views allow nonimprovised music to be called jazz. As a foundation for describing jazz swing feeling, let's discuss a few elements which contribute to swing feeling in performances of both jazz and non-jazz styles.

If music makes you want to dance, clap your hands, or tap your feet, it has the effect we call a swinging feeling. This effect can be created by almost any kind of music, not just jazz. Music that keeps a relatively steady beat and is performed with great spirit seems buoyant. In that sense, many nonjazz performances can be described as swinging. But to specify the unique ways in which an effective jazz performance swings, we must outline both the general characteristics of swinging and those characteristics specific to jazz swing feeling.

Swing is a rhythmic phenomenon which results from several easily defined factors and a few subtle, almost indefinable factors. This is solely a rhythmic concept. Musicians can play out of tune with each other yet still swing. For the sake of our discussion here, note also that the term "swing" should not be confused with its use as a label for an era in American popular music that began during the 1930s and continued until the late 1940s (swing era, swing bands, King of Swing, etc.). It is also not to be confused with its occasional use as a synonym for jazz itself.

Swing in the General Sense

One of the easily defined factors causing swing feeling is **constant tempo.** This helps us distinguish it from kinds of symphonic music where conductors are free to vary the tempo while playing a piece. A steady beat is nearly always kept in jazz pieces. It brings a certain momentum that is essential to swing feeling. Much of the excitement in jazz comes from musicians in the band tugging against this very solid foundation by playing notes slightly before or after the beat.

Another easily defined element of swing feeling is **cohesive group sound.** This is achieved when every member's playing is precisely synchronized with that of every other member. The different members need not be playing the same rhythms in unison, but each player must execute the rhythms of his part with great precision in relation to the beat and the sounds of the other instruments. A group cannot swing if its members are not playing closely together.

Saying that a performance swings means that the group is keeping a steady tempo and its rhythmic parts are synchronized. But to call music "swinging" also indicates that the performance conveys a **rhythmic lilt.** This property is also sometimes referred to as a good rhythmic groove. In fact, verbs derived from the nouns "swing" and "groove" are commonly applied to the sound of jazz: "The band is swinging tonight." "That pianist is really grooving." To a certain extent, swinging simply denotes pleasure. A swinging performance is like a swinging party. Both are very enjoyable.

The **spirit** with which a group plays contributes to swing feeling. Jazz has a reputation for being highly spirited music. In fact, the word "jazzy" is sometimes used instead of the word "spirited." To "jazz up" and to "liven up" are often used interchangeably, and some people call clothes "jazzy" if they are gaudy or extraverted.

Music that swings, then, has constant tempo, cohesive playing, and is performed with rhythmic lilt and spirit. Listeners may be inclined to describe a good performance of any kind of music as swinging if it conveys a feeling of life and energy that compels the listener to respond. This description of swinging applies not only to jazz, but also to lilting performances of polkas, waltzes, flamenco music, Gypsy music, marches, bluegrass, rock, and classical music. This general sense of swing can describe the feeling achieved by a good performance of almost any music that bears constant tempo, cohesive group sound, lilt, and spirit.

Swing in the Jazz Sense

For music to swing in the way peculiar to jazz, more conditions have to be met. One is **an abundance of syncopated rhythms.** "Syncopating" means accenting notes that occur just before or just after a beat. Think of syncopation as being off-beat accenting or the occurrence of stress where it is least expected. Jazz swing feeling requires precisely such off-beat accents. The tension generated by members of a band tugging at

Appendix B;
Demo CD
Track 20

opposite sides of the beat is essential to jazz swing feeling. Playing slightly after the beat can lend music a soulful or laid back feeling, and syncopations are especially good at providing this. Jazz musicians exaggerate this tendency more than classical musicians, and, if a classical musician were presented with a written syncopation, he would play it slightly earlier than would a jazz musician. Because rhythm is a matter of timing, we must remember that a player's degree of jazz swing feeling is tied to the success with which he times his syncopations. This means that when a player's quality of swing feeling is appraised, his sense of timing is valued more than his tone quality, note selection, and melodic imagination.

page 450; Demo CD *Track 43*

Another factor contributing to the special kind of swing feeling found in jazz is the **swing eighth-note pattern.** Here's a brief description of swing feeling: If you count beats as they go by "one, two, three, four," you are counting the "quarter notes." If you also say "and" after each number but fit it into the same amount of time, you are indicating two parts for each pulse, designating "eighth notes": "one and, two and, three and, four and." In most jazz, the eighth notes are uneven in their duration and their emphasis. The "ands" are shorter than the numbered pulses ("1, 2, 3, 4"), and they are louder, too. This makes them "swing eighth notes" instead of "straight eighth notes."

Another component of jazz swing feeling is not actually a rhythmic element. Jazz historian Harvey Pekar suggests that swing requires a continuous rising and falling motion or the alternation of more and less activity in a jazz line that provides **alternation of tension and relaxation in the listener.**

Swing in the jazz sense requires the properties that comprise swing in the general sense (constant tempo, cohesive playing, rhythmic lilt, and spirit) plus syncopation, swing eighth-note patterns, and the continuous alternation of tension and relaxation. As with swing in the general sense, jazz swing feeling exists in the ear of the beholder. **Listeners disagree about whether a given performance swings** at all, and, if so, how much. Note also that **there are several different types of jazz swing feeling.**

DEFINING JAZZ: FOUR VIEWS

1. For many people, music need only **be associated with the jazz tradition** to be called "jazz." According to this approach, the term "jazz" can be applied to almost any music that displays characteristics that have ever been associated with any music ever called "jazz." For example, music might be called "jazz" just because it has a bluesy flavor, or it uses instruments that have been associated with jazz, such as saxophones and drums, or has "jazzy rhythms," or it displays manipulations of pitch and tone quality associated with jazz. (See pages 48–50 for discussion of buzzings, roughnesses, blue notes, drops, doits, scoops, smears, and bends.) Defining jazz in this way is circular: If jazz is any music that has been called "jazz," then whatever has been called "jazz" defines the genre. In the view of some people, to know what jazz is, we merely go by how the word is used. This follows the position of many individuals who say that jazz cannot be defined. They just use the term, and then whatever they used it for becomes its meaning. This means that a given performance might fall into the jazz category even though it uses no improvisation and conveys no swing feeling. When people use the term that loosely, they rarely distinguish between jazz and other kinds of music to which we might best apply the term "jazz-like."[1]

2. For many other people, a performance need only **convey jazz swing feeling** in order to be called jazz. These people tend to say, "Jazz is a feeling more than anything else," or "Jazz is not *what* you play but *how* you play it."

3. For some people, a performance need only **be improvised** in order to qualify as jazz. Note, however, that if we define jazz this way, we overlook characteristics

that can distinguish jazz from other kinds of music that also employ improvisation, such as rock and some of the music of India and Africa.

4. The most common definition for jazz requires that a performance **contain improvisation and convey jazz swing feeling.**

Much music can be sorted according to the two categories of swing feeling (the general sense and the jazz sense) and the four approaches to defining jazz. The next few paragraphs illustrate these definitional approaches by highlighting kinds of music in which one or more of the critical properties are absent.

Applications of the Four Definitions

If we follow our fourth definition of jazz (i.e., it must be improvised and project jazz swing feeling), then what can be said about "jazz" performances in which the music doesn't seem to be improvised? For example, there are historically significant solos on alternate versions of the same record that differ very little from each other. This suggests that the later versions are not improvised, even if the first one was. Some concert music written and performed by famous jazz musicians also falls into this category. If we define jazz rigidly and insist that *some* improvisation is *always* required, then such performances can *not* be jazz. This may seem an odd conclusion in the case of pieces by bandleaders well known for performing jazz, but it is both logical and useful. In fact, a category for such works already exists: *swinging concert music*. And this term not only saves the marriage of jazz and improvisation, but it also creates a category for a musical tradition that, though *deriving* from jazz, might be kept *separate*. Yet for those of us who would be outraged to find someone calling our favorite "jazz" solo or "jazz" concert work anything other than "jazz," our first definition (association with the jazz tradition) is most appropriate because it would allow such improvisationless performances to be called "jazz."

Our fourth definition (it must be improvised and swing) is useful because it *excludes* music that does not swing and that jazz musicians do not ordinarily consider jazz, such as George Gershwin's symphonic piece "Rhapsody in Blue" even though it is bluesy and syncopated. This distinguishes it for those people who would consider the piece "jazz" merely because it has bluesy melodies and jazzy rhythms—see the first definition.

Controversy surrounds our fourth definition because it excludes some music that is called "jazz" by most listeners. Among the troublesome examples are (a) pieces you will study in the chapter called "1960s and 1970s Avant-Garde and 'Free' Jazz" because they do not convey jazz swing feeling, (b) some of the concert music mentioned in the Duke Ellington chapter because it is neither swinging nor largely improvised, and (c) recreations of jazz instrumentals, sung with lyrics by groups such as the Manhattan Transfer because, despite the swinging, the singers are not improvising. By our first definition (association with elements in the jazz tradition) and our second definition (jazz swing feeling), Manhattan Transfer's first recording of Joe Zawinul's "Birdland" would qualify as jazz because of its jazzy rhythms and swing feeling. However, Weather Report's original version of "Birdland" would qualify more clearly because of its improvisation and swing feeling (fourth definition) and because of its use of saxophone (an element associated with the jazz tradition, a criterion of our first definition).

"Ghosts: First Variation" JCCD3 *Track 2*

"Transblucency," JCCD1 *Track 22*

We could also apply this reasoning to classifying the very popular piano solos of George Winston. Most jazz musicians agree that Winston does not swing, and Winston himself refuses to call his music "jazz." However, his albums are often found in the "jazz" bins of music stores, and many listeners call him a "jazz pianist." Winston's music qualifies as jazz by our third definition (must be improvised), but not by our second (must swing) or our fourth (must swing and be improvised). Perhaps his music could be considered jazz in the same flexible sense of the term that is outlined in our first definition. This is the flexible sense that allows people to consider "jazz" the music in the famous movie with Al Jolson called *The Jazz Singer*, even though it is about a vaudeville singer who neither improvises nor swings (see page 401).

IS JAZZ POPULAR?

Now that we have considered a few definitions of jazz, let's examine five ways to answer the question of whether it is popular music.[2]

1. If "popular" means something liked by a large portion of the population, jazz does not qualify because jazz represents only about three percent of radio airplay and album sales.

2. If "popular" means "of the common people," jazz does not qualify as popular music. Unlike most folk musicians and blues players, jazz musicians represent a highly versatile and specially trained elite whose level of sophistication is not common to the population at large. We will learn more about this in the next chapter.

3. Some jazz is "popular music" in the sense that it is functional music or "utilitarian" because it constitutes dance music, film music, and party music. But for the most part, jazz fits none of those qualifications. It is not *primarily* utilitarian in nature. Instead, it is appreciated for its esthetic and intellectual rewards, and it is approached with some effort.

4. Some jazz can be considered "popular music" because it possesses an easy accessibility. But much jazz, especially the post-1930s styles, does not qualify in this way because it requires a cultivated taste.

5. The term "jazz" was once applied so loosely that it denoted syncopated popular music as a whole. We can find illustrations for this in the 1920s, when Al Jolson's movie about a vaudeville singer was titled *The Jazz Singer*. The confusion was furthered by the Neil Diamond remake of that movie. We must also remember that fiction writer F. Scott Fitzgerald dubbed the 1920s "The Jazz Age." So today many people think jazz is only music of "The Roaring Twenties," with musicians playing in speak-easies and wearing red-and-white striped clothing. Partly because of that situation, the term "jazz" is still frequently confused with popular music as a whole, long after it began acquiring a much narrower meaning. For instance, today many people still lump jazz with rock, and vice versa. Even now some people use the term "jazz" to designate almost every popular style that is not "classical" music. "Jazz" has been applied to the folk music of Peter, Paul & Mary, the folk-rock of Bob Dylan, the popular singing of Isaac Hayes, the written piano music of George Gershwin, and the minimalist compositions of Philip Glass and Steve Reich.

In summary, much jazz fails to qualify as popular music by any of the above definitions of the term "popular." It warrants the label of "art music." But to be prepared for arguments, we must remember that some jazz is popular music according to some conceptions of "popular music," and some jazz is popular music according to all of the above conceptions.

CHAPTER SUMMARY

1. Some people use the term "jazz" very loosely, applying it to anything they ever heard called jazz or anything that reminds them of anything they think it is.

2. Jazz involves improvisation and swing feeling.

3. Though most jazz groups use arrangements that are preset in some regard, a substantial portion of each performance is usually spontaneous.

4. Swing feeling is achieved by spirited performances of many different kinds of music which employ steady tempo.

5. Jazz swing feeling is like swing feeling in the general sense, but it also has an abundance of syncopated rhythms, swing eighth notes, and a continuous rise and fall of tension.

6. Some jazz is "popular music" because people use it as party music, film music, and dance music.

7. Jazz is not particularly popular by comparison with most other kinds of music, as evidenced by its three-percent market share.

8. For most people, jazz is a cultivated taste and not easily accessible. This makes it art music rather than popular music.

NOTES

1. See Mark C. Gridley, Robert Maxham, and Robert Hoff, "Three Approaches to Defining Jazz," *Musical Quarterly* 73, no. 4 (1989): 513–531; reprinted and updated in Lewis Porter, ed., *Jazz: A Century of Change: Readings and New Essays* (Schirmer, 1997) and in *jazzstyles.com/ ThreeApproach.html*.

2. See Mark C. Gridley, "Is Jazz Popular Music?" *The Instrumentalist*, 41, no. 8 (March 1987): 19–22, 25–26, 85; reprinted in *jazzstyles.com/ ArtorPop.html*.

Jazz can be a lot of fun to listen to. But some people miss that fun because they let themselves be intimidated. They think that to get more out of listening to jazz requires that they engage in a difficult learning process. They believe jazz can be enjoyed only by listeners who have deep technical knowledge. It is true that we get more out of listening if we know more about how jazz is made. But learning about jazz is not difficult. Some styles sound chaotic to everyone at first. They become more coherent each time we rehear them. Much of the real substance in jazz is subtle. We can enjoy it deeply once we begin noticing the subtleties. This book will point them out.

Studying from this book is very different from reading most other books. This book doesn't work if you merely read it. **This book works only if you combine your reading with a lot of jazz listening.** This book will not be very helpful unless you also attend concerts and listen to recordings. It works only if you find examples of what you are studying. **You are not really learning until you actually *hear* what the book is talking about.** A good rule of thumb is to never read more than about five paragraphs without listening to a corresponding recording. Choose your selections from the recordings that came with your book and the recordings that are cited in it. Visit a well-stocked record collection in your library or at a friend's place. Some college radio stations broadcast jazz, which can also help you. A few regions even have community public radio stations that broadcast jazz. Buying or borrowing recordings that are cited in this book's "Small Basic CD Collection" on page 5 also can be very useful. Having at least one good album for each chapter would be ideal.

Nat Adderley, Cannonball Adderley, Charles Lloyd, 1965
(Photo by Lee Tanner)

LISTENING TECHNIQUES

Study the *Demo CD*, the *DVD*, and Appendix B. The more jazz you hear, the more meaningful the demonstrations will be. The more familiar the demonstrations become to you, the more aspects you will recognize in the jazz that you hear. Don't try to absorb all of the Demo CD in one sitting. Try to space your listening sessions over several days. Some students have found that less than a half hour a day is enough to digest on the first time around.

Most of this chapter describes traditional approaches to making jazz. Therefore, it is helpful to have a few ways to find the sounds you are reading about. Here are three sources that should be easy to find on most campuses and in most libraries: *The Smithsonian Collection of Classic Jazz* (hereafter referred to as SCCJ), the *Jazz Classics CDs 1, 2,* and *3 for Jazz Styles* (your book; referred to as JCCD), and the *Jazz Classics CDs* for the abridged edition of this book, *Concise Guide to Jazz* (referred to as CCD). Selections that illustrate fairly well the techniques described in this chapter are: "Kiss and Run" by Sonny Rollins and Clifford Brown and "Cranky Spanky" by Art Blakey.

"Kiss and Run" and "Cranky Spanky," JCCD2 Tracks 6 and 7

Jazz fans use a number of different strategies when they listen. Try listening to one of these selections using each of these strategies:

Listen to the performance in a relaxed way first. Absorb the overall experience. Don't worry about trying to pick out anything in particular. It will still be there whenever you come back to listen again. Listen to the piece this way three or four times. Soon you will find that you are almost able to hum along with some of it.

Next, begin acquainting yourself with the basis of the music. The accompaniment is the best place to start. Pick out the sound of the bass. In traditional approaches to jazz combo playing, the bass part will be the steadiest. This makes it the easiest part to follow. Ignore the other sounds, and follow the bassist's part through the entire performance. You might want to do this several times. Like magic, the bass part will become clearer each time you rehear the performance.

After you have become good at finding and following the bass part, try to pick out the sound of the cymbals. Then try to follow the steady rhythm that is played on the cymbals and coordinated with the bass part. As you listen, you will begin to notice extra notes that come before and after the beat. Such decorations can be fascinating to follow. They make the music more exciting, and they give an accompanist's work a more personal touch. Listen to the performance several more times, focusing only on the bass and cymbals.

Once you have become accustomed to the music's steady foundation in the bass and cymbals, listen for the chords. These sounds may come from a piano or a guitar. You will notice that the chords are played in very rhythmic ways that prod the soloists and help make the band swing. Their harmonies help guide the improvisations.

By now, you already will have heard the solo lines several times, even if you were trying to ignore them. So it is time to consider the ways that many jazz fans rotate their attention among the various activities that are occurring in the combo performance.

1. **Hearing the improvised lines of a jazz soloist as melodies in themselves should help you enjoy much jazz.** Experienced listeners get as much pleasure from hearing their favorite improvisations as most people get from hearing their favorite songs. Many listeners pay close attention as the improvisations are unfolding. They want to notice when the line becomes particularly melodic. Then they can have the satisfaction of hearing a new song being composed. Some jazz improvisers strive to invent lines that are as catchy as the melodies in pop tunes and classical pieces. On the other hand, many improvisers tend toward more elaborate lines. Some passages in their improvisations are more melody-like

than others. There are gems of inspired melody hidden in many improvisations just waiting to be discovered by attentive listeners. We need to remember, however, that melody is more important in some styles than others. For instance, in some avant-garde and jazz-rock fusion performances, the music emphasizes instead the variations in mood, sound qualities, and rhythms. Sometimes the mood alone may be the most prominent aspect.

2. **One way a lot of jazz fans listen is to imagine layers of sound, one on top of another, all moving forward in time.** Each layer can represent the sound of a different instrument. Once you become skilled in visualizing separate sounds, you will begin to notice relationships between sounds. Try to imagine a graph of the solo line. The horizontal side of the graph represents time passing. The vertical dimension represents highness and lowness of pitch. Your graph can be embellished by colored shapes and textures representing the accompanying sounds of piano chords, drums, cymbals, bass, and so on. (See Figure 3.1 for possible visualizations of the ways tones change.)

3. **Some people hum the original tune to themselves while listening to the improvisations which are guided by its chord changes.** Try to synchronize the beginning of your humming with the beginning of a solo improvisation. Then keep the same tempo as the performer. Snatches of the original tune might turn up in the improvisation, and you will begin to recognize the chords in the accompaniment more clearly. You will also become aware of two compositions based on the same chord changes: the original tune and the improvised melody. As you become more aware of how they go together, your appreciation of jazz will deepen.

4. **Try listening to every note in a soloist's improvisation.** You might not be able to detect each note in fast passages, especially those of saxophonist John Coltrane or pianist Oscar Peterson. But with repeated listening and close concentration, eventually you should be able to hear every note. Do not be discouraged if this temporarily proves difficult. Even professional musicians need repeated listenings before they can account for every note in some improvisations. Your ears will get better and better the more you listen.

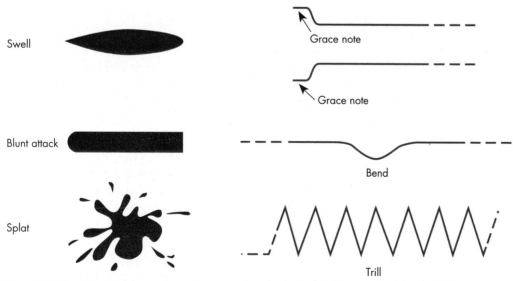

Figure 3.1 Possible visualizations of tone perceptions. In most, pitch and volume go up and down and time goes left to right.

CHORD PROGRESSIONS AND TUNE CONSTRUCTION

To improvise is to compose and perform at the same time. Jazz musicians make up their music as they go along. Much of this chapter outlines unwritten rules and guidelines that all jazz musicians know. These guide the improvisations in situations such as jam sessions where musicians do not know each other and have not rehearsed. They help musicians to piece together performances spontaneously. And they continue to guide improvisations long after rehearsals.

Most jazz is guided by musicians agreeing beforehand to maintain a given tempo, key, and progression of accompaniment chords. They then invent and play their own melodies and accompaniments in a way that is compatible with those chords. Frequently, the agreed-upon harmonies are borrowed from a familiar melody, and the melody itself is played before and after the improvisations. This is easy because jazz musicians tend to know many of the same tunes in the same keys. Though the original melody is often kept in mind by the improvisers, rarely are the improvised lines actually variations on the original melody. A progression of accompaniment chords is all that the improvised melodies and the original melody have in common. Performances are facilitated because standard chord changes for these tunes are followed, and traditions regarding the sequence of melody and improvisations are adhered to. In the next few paragraphs, we will examine those traditions.

Demo CD Track 33

Blues Chorus

When a jazz group plays a 12-bar blues, the melody is usually played twice. Then the soloists improvise over the progression of chords in its accompaniment. **One complete 12-bar progression of chords is called a blues chorus.** Each soloist usually improvises for several choruses. When one soloist ends an improvisation, another soloist takes over. (Listen to solos by Dave Brubeck and Paul Desmond on "Blue Rondo ala Turk" and Milt Jackson and Thelonious Monk on "Misterioso," both 12-bar blues.) The chords continue to progress in an unvarying cycle, even if a musician misses an entrance or overlaps into someone else's chorus. In that way, the whole group stays together. That particular progression of chords and the tempo at which it is played are the glue that holds the music together. After all the solos, the group concludes by playing the melody twice more.

Appendix B; Demo CD Track 19

"Misterioso," JCCD1 Track 29; "Blue Rondo ala Turk," JCCD2 Track 4

A-A-B-A

Some tunes are written in the form of four sections that are eight measures each. (The concept of "measure," also known as "bar," is explained in Appendix B.) This is called a 32-bar form. The most common arrangement for such pieces is comprised of two sections of music. One section is called the A-section. The other is called the B-section, bridge, release, inside, second strain, or channel. The A-section is played twice in succession. Then the B-section is inserted, followed by the A-section again. The sequence is **A-A-B-A**, and thousands of tunes have been organized this way. You might recall the format if you hum the melody to the Christmas carol "Deck the Halls" or the theme song for the "Flintstones" television program. The same format is used for "Cottontail," "Shaw Nuff," "Four Brothers," and "Things to Come."[1]

When jazz musicians play an A-A-B-A tune, they usually play its melody once before and once after the solo improvisations. Each solo adheres to the tune's chord progression. A repeating sequence of A-A-B-A is followed over and over again without interruption. The cycle continues A-A-B-A-A-A-B-A-A-A-B-A. What musicians signify by the term **chorus** is one playing through of a chord progression. The

Demo CD Track 33

"Cottontail," "Shaw Nuff," "Things to Come," and "Four Brothers," JCCD1 Tracks 20, 26, 27, 28

length of a solo is measured by the number of choruses that the soloist improvises. In a jam session, each soloist ends on the last measure of a given chorus and is immediately followed by another soloist starting on the first measure of the next chorus. If a soloist stops improvising in the middle of a chorus—usually at the end of an eight-measure section—another player immediately takes up where the previous player left off. The A-A-B-A form continues unchanged in its cycle.

Trading Fours, Trading Eights

Soloists sometimes alternate eight-measure sections with each other. One musician improvises on the first eight measures, another on the second eight, and so on. This is called *trading eights*. The same thing is done with four-measure sections and is called *trading fours*. Listen to the fourth chorus of "Lester Leaps In" (*JCCD1* Track 25 at 1'47"). Pianist Count Basie and tenor saxophonist Lester Young trade fours within the tune's 32-bar A-A-B-A construction. Sonny Rollins and Clifford Brown also do this ("Kiss and Run," *JCCD2* Track 6 at 5'41").

In jazz styles of the 1940s and 1950s, it is common for drummers to trade fours or eights with the rest of the group. A soloist, accompanied by the rhythm section, plays for four (or eight) bars. Then the entire band drops out while the drummer improvises alone for the same number of bars. This pattern repeats over and over so that various soloists are trading fours (or eights) with the drummer. The form of the tune and its tempo are maintained throughout that sequence, even though no chords or melodies are played during the drum solos. Adherence to that format allows the entire band to begin playing again, precisely after four (or eight) measures because each musician is silently counting the beats and thinking of the chords that are progressing while he is not playing. Sonny Rollins and Clifford Brown trade fours with drummer Max Roach at 5'00" in "Kiss and Run" (*JCCD2* Track 6),

Absence of Steady Tempo

When you are listening to improvisations and trying to detect the form of an underlying chord progression, watch for three different manipulations that might throw off your counting. First is an **absence of steady tempo.** This is not commonly found in jazz, but introductions and endings sometimes employ it. Ballad melodies sometimes also receive this treatment the first time they are played. (Miles Davis uses it for the beginning melody statement on his famous 1964 recording of "My Funny Valentine.") Jazz musicians use the term **rubato** to indicate such absence of steadiness in tempo.[2]

Aside from the infrequent occurrence of rubato, a passage within an improvisation might sound as though its tempo increased simply because of an increased amount of activity. Or, a passage might sound as though the tempo is decreasing simply because of a decreased amount of activity. Most of these situations can be deceiving because, after the theme statement, each chord is in effect for the same amount of time, yet it sounds like it is not. In other words, the chords change at the same rate. **Only the density of musical activity is changing,** not the tempo for the passage of the chords that guide improvisation. It is often difficult to differentiate a true rubato, in the jazz sense of the term, from an alteration in density (what you might call "pseudo rubato"), and some performers, notably post-1960 stylists, use both techniques. But it should not be too difficult to learn to detect two other manipulations: double-timing and half-timing.

Double-Timing

When a member of a band starts playing as though the tempo were double its original rate, we say that the musician is **double-timing.** (Double-timing is demonstrated on *JCCD1* Track 30 by Charlie Parker at the beginning of "Just Friends" and on *JCCD1*

Track 23 by Johnny Hodges at 3'18" on "Prelude to a Kiss." On *JCCD2* Track 8, it is demonstrated by Freddie Hubbard at 3'22" on "Maiden Voyage," on Track 1 by Lennie Tristano at 2'08" on "No Figs," and on Track 2 by Lee Konitz at 2'26" on "My Lady.") This results from doubling the rate of notes without doubling the amount of time each chord is in effect. To create double-time feeling, a soloist might switch from improvising eighth notes to improvising sixteenth notes. A bassist, for example, can create double-time feeling by playing eighth notes where he would ordinarily play quarter notes. He plays two notes on each beat instead of playing only one, and his walking bass pattern might now best be characterized as "running bass." The result is a feeling that the tempo has doubled, even though there is no change in the amount of time each chord's harmony is in effect. This can deceive the listener who is trying to follow the improvised solo line in relation to its underlying progression of accompaniment chords because twice as many sounds now occur on each beat. The solution is to concentrate harder on humming the original melody while listening to the improvisation. You might also tap your foot at the original tempo to help keep your place.

Demo CD Track 35

Half-Timing

The opposite of double-timing is **half-timing.** In half-timing, we halve the number of notes that are played without halving the rate at which the chords change. The tempo remains the same, but the note values become twice as long. The tempo seems to be slower, or it sounds half as fast as the absolute rate at which chords are passing. As with double-timing, the chords remain in effect for the same amount of time, regardless of the perceived pace.

Demo CD Track 36

Half-timing is rare, but double-timing is quite common. During the 1950s and 1960s, improvisations on ballads were often played in double-time. After the piece's melody was played once in its original tempo, solo improvisations followed, nearly always in double-time. It almost conveyed the impression that improvisers wanted to swing hard and were impatient with the slowness of the original tempo. Chords progressed in these performances at the same absolute rate during solos as during the tune itself, but the improvisations seemed twice as fast as the tune. Double-timing is common in Latin American jazz because the beat in that music is usually divided into eighth notes instead of quarter notes. The pulse often sounds twice as fast as it really is.

"Miami," JCCD3 *Track 10; Appendix B*

Quadruple-Timing

Rock music of the 1960s is often performed in double-time, and some is actually in quadruple-time. **In quadruple-time the beat is sounded in four equal parts (sixteenth notes).** Young dancers during the early 1960s often requested "fast music" when in fact they did not want up-tempo performances at all. They wanted music performed in a double-time or quadruple-time feeling. To the dancers, it was "fast."

"Above and Below," JCCD3 Track 8

Solo Breaks

The **solo break** is another manipulation that often leads the listener to believe mistakenly that the tempo has changed. It sounds as though the progression of accompaniment chords stops when all group members except the soloist stop playing. Actually, however, the tempo is maintained along with the amount of time each chord's harmonies are in effect. We perceive the tempo as suspended because everyone except the soloist has stopped playing.

Breaks are especially effective as springboards to launch solo choruses. Often, groups finish the opening melody statement with a two-measure break for the first soloist. On *JCCD2* Track 7, the saxophone solo at 0'32" is introduced in this way, as is the trumpet solo on *JCCD1* Track 27 at 0'40". Many tunes end with a long note

"After You're Gone," JCCD1 Track 16 at 0'24", 0'35", 1'28", and 1'44" and "Lester Leaps In," Track 25 at 1'30"

held for four or eight beats, and this "empty space" in the melody furnishes a good opportunity for a solo break. In other words, a combo might stop playing during the last two measures of a 32-bar tune, giving the soloist a two-measure break to launch an improvisation. If the piece is a 12-bar blues, the solo break takes place in the eleventh and twelfth measures.

| Demo CD *Track 34*

Beginning and Ending a Piece

Other standard alternatives are also available to aid unrehearsed performances. For example, if a band of horns (trumpet, saxophone, trombone) and rhythm section (piano, bass, and drums) wants to include an **introduction,** the performers have at least four stock alternatives:

1. Use the final four or eight measures of the tune, and let the rhythm section rework and play it without the horns.
2. Have the rhythm section play a common four- or eight-measure chord progression and improvise a line compatible with it. (Listen to Count Basie's four-measure introduction to "Lester Leaps In.")

| *"Lester Leaps In,"* | JCCD1 *Track 25*

3. Use an introduction that the entire group knows (from a famous recording of the tune, for example), thus including the horns in addition to the rhythm section.
4. Let the rhythm section play a one-, two-, or four-bar figure (called a *vamp*) over and over until the hornmen feel like starting the tune.

| *"Taxi War Dance,"* | JCCD1 *Track 24*

Endings are handled in similar ways. A few of the standard alternatives include:

1. End immediately at the end of the melody itself, with no extra notes.
2. Improvise a *ritard* for the last three or four bars, and then sustain the final chord. (Listen to the ending used by Louis Armstrong and Earl Hines on "Weather Bird" on *SCCJ.*)
3. Rest or sustain a chord while a soloist takes a *cadenza* (an improvisation out of context), then follow it with a sustained chord.
4. Repeat the last four bars of the tune, thus creating a tag, and then sustain the tune's final chord.
5. Use a well-known ending.
6. Let the rhythm section play a vamp followed by a final chord.
7. Have the rhythm section improvise some common progression and end with it.

Once a progression has begun, its chords and its tempo remain in charge of the situation. Even strangers can play with each other and be instantly compatible. Musicians from different style eras can also play with each other without much conflict because the tempo and chord progression hold things together.

Exceptions to the Rules

Although the tune is usually played as written, before and after the improvised solos, **jazz performers occasionally omit the melody statement.** For example, the 1945 Don Byas-Slam Stewart recording of "I Got Rhythm" (in *SCCJ*) does not have a return to the melody at the end. Charlie Parker does not completely state the melody in either one of his 1947 Dial recordings of "Embraceable You" (in *SCCJ*). Coleman Hawkins departs considerably from completing an opening melody statement in his 1939 recording of "Body and Soul" and never states the melody at the end, either. Miles Davis once recorded a 12-bar blues improvisation without a melody line and, quite understandably, called the piece "No Line."

| *"Body and Soul,"* | CCCD *Track 11*

| *Many examples are in* | the Demo CD.

During the 1960s and 1970s, much jazz departed from the tradition of improvising within fixed chord progressions and preset chorus lengths. Ornette Coleman and Cecil Taylor popularized such practices. Such music is often called "free jazz" because improvisers are free from the requirement to follow preset chord changes. Listen to the saxophone and bass solos on Albert Ayler's "Ghosts: First Variation" (JCCD3 Track 2) and the piano solo on Keith Jarrett's "Sundial, Part 1" (Track 5), and listen to the saxophone and trumpet solos on Ornette Coleman's "Civilization Day" (JCCD2 Track 12).

"The Promise," JCCD2 Track 11; *"Your Lady,"* CCD2 Track 3

Beginning in the 1960s, **John Coltrane and his disciples recorded pieces whose melodies had chord progressions in their accompaniment but whose improvisations were not based on those progressions.** These improvisations were accompanied by extensively repeated, two-chord patterns. Coltrane's improvisations on "My Favorite Things" exemplify this approach.

SKILLS POSSESSED BY THE IMPROVISER

Spontaneous music is not totally spontaneous creation. Extensive preparation is required. A musician must undergo much training before he can improvise coherent lines with jazz swing feeling. Some of this training is formal, but most is informal. Jazz players spend years practicing their instruments and learning tunes and the chord changes that accompany them.

Near-effortless command of an instrument is the constant goal of a jazz player because the ability to play any musical idea that comes to mind depends partly on instrumental proficiency. It is not unusual for a player to practice by himself for more than two hours a day, and some average more than four hours a day, five to six days per week. In other words, they play every spare minute. In addition to practicing scales and exercises, the jazz musician invents, collects, and develops phrases he might later use during improvisation. He tries out rhythmic variations of his favorite phrases. He practices to achieve fluency in different keys, in different registers of his instrument, and in different tempos and rhythmic styles.

To adequately respond to the harmonies produced by accompanists, **a jazz improviser must be well acquainted with harmony. Most jazz soloists know the piano well** because the piano keyboard provides a means for seeing and hearing relationships between melody and harmony at the same time.

To respond in a split second to his accompanists, the improvising soloist must have **an extremely quick and keen ear for pitch and rhythm.** This ability also helps him imagine a note or phrase and immediately play it. Jazz musicians are so quick to perceive and respond to subtle nuances in style and group direction that they can usually play a respectable performance the first time they work with an unfamiliar group.

Most jazz musicians have remarkably good memories for sounds. The average jazz improviser is able to hear a note or phrase once and then remember it and play it back. In fact, you can often hear an improviser incorporate phrases from the solo that immediately preceded his.

A jazz musician has to **remember hundreds of tunes and chord progressions.** He must be as familiar with pop tunes and jazz standards as he is with his native language, perhaps more so. The convenience of knowing many of the same tunes helps musicians play together without rehearsal.

Another helpful skill is that of **recognizing chord progressions** quickly. Many jazz musicians can play a tune from memory after hearing it only a few times, and they often improvise solos compatible with the tune's chord progression after hearing it only once or twice.

Even though improvisation is their primary skill, most jazz musicians can also read music. Basically, **the skills of reading and writing music** can be described as four levels:

1. The **ability to read music** accurately if allowed to practice or to look it over ahead of time: Many people call that "reading music."

2. The **ability to play a piece of music correctly the first time it is seen:** This is called "sight-reading." Musicians call it "reading." When musicians say someone "reads," they usually mean he is capable of sight reading. This skill is possessed by all symphony orchestra musicians and by most jazz musicians. It is not a common skill among pop singers or rock or country and western musicians. The ability to sight read saves rehearsal time because it is easier to learn a new piece by reading it than by trial and error ("by ear"). Some people go so far as to say that a player "is not a real musician unless he reads music." That latter attitude may be a bit severe, though, because there are players who are instrumentally proficient and compositionally creative but unable to sight-read music.

3. The **ability to make up an original tune and correctly notate it:** "writing music" or "composing." Actually, the act of making up a tune is "composing"; notation is more specialized. But the term "writing music" usually refers to the process of making up a tune, not necessarily to writing it down for musicians to play. Many people who are said to "write" music actually cannot write down their ideas. In other words, there are composers who cannot read or write music. Pop singers and rock musicians often make up songs and then pay a skilled musician to write them down for copyright, sales, and publication. (The singers and rock musicians often teach songs to each other by ear instead of placing sheet music in front of each other.)

4. The highest level of music reading and writing is **the ability to listen to someone else's music and then correctly notate it:** This skill is possessed by people who write down jazz solos they hear on records.

During the 1950s and 1960s, it was rare to find rock groups or country groups who could quickly notate their own work or sight-read someone else's. Some pop singers can read music, but most are unable to sight-read. But it is common for jazz musicians to both compose and notate their own tunes. **Nearly all jazz improvisers are also composers.** Most jazz musicians occasionally write down their improvisations in the form of tunes. Few of the tunes become famous in jazz history, but all serve as vehicles for improvisation. Some jazz players have written every tune on every album they have recorded. It is not unusual to find a jazz saxophonist or pianist who has written more than one hundred original tunes. Though many of them never write a memorable tune, some become so good at writing that they are more important as tune writers or band arrangers than as improvising players.

INSTRUMENT ROLES

To help follow the music in a jazz performance, you might try to divide the sounds into the functions they serve. For these reasons, we describe what the band members do in terms of solo roles and accompanying roles. The manner in which musicians fill these roles has been relatively standardized since the 1930s. Once you become familiar with them, you will appreciate how they sound within each style and era. With that frame of reference, you can also begin distinguishing innovations. Most of the chapters in this book describe styles by stressing departures that were made from the ways the musicians filled those roles. Particularly since 1960, certain jazz groups have made innovations in the use of instruments. So the best way to familiarize yourself

Figure 3.2 Ron Carter, Jaco Pastorius. String bass, also known as acoustic bass, bass viol, or upright bass (left). Electric bass guitar, also known as Fender bass or electric bass (right). Though it looks like a guitar, the electric bass can be differentiated from the solid body electric guitar by having four instead of six tuning pegs, one for each string.

with the basic roles is by listening to the selections that are cited in your reading, not by grabbing a jazz recording at random.

Jazz is partly an ensemble art. The soloist and accompanists combine to form an ensemble that attempts to play as a single unit. The soloist role can be assumed by any melody instrument, though saxophones and trumpets are the most common. The accompanists are usually classified as members of a *rhythm section*. This consists of musicians who play string bass or electric bass guitar (see Figure 3.2), drums (see Figure 3.3), and an instrument that plays chords, such as a piano or guitar.[3] The rhythm section is a group of players who improvise together to accompany and inspire the soloist. They provide a springboard for his lines and can make or break his effectiveness. The following discussion is intended to clarify the role of each instrument in the rhythm section.

Bass

Demo CD Tracks 23 and 32; DVD Tracks 20–35; "Cranky Spanky," JCCD2 Track 7 at 4′08″; Appendix H

The bassist improvises his part in the rhythm section by plucking a string once per beat and occasionally adding embellishments. Many bassists play the second and fourth of every four notes harder than the first and third. This helps create swing feeling. The bass pattern often rises and falls as though the music is walking up and down a staircase. This timekeeping style is called **walking bass.** Good walking bass lines make musical sense by themselves. In fact, some soloists consider walking bass to be the most essential sound in the rhythm section. They would play without drums or chording instrument before they would play without walking bass.

How does the bassist know what notes to play if he is improvising his part? The bassist selects his notes from important notes in the accompaniment chords that are guiding the solo improvisation. Sometimes the bassist's notes are not the same as the chord notes, but they lead into the chord notes or complement the chords. In other words, the bassist keeps the beat, provides a low-register component for the group sound, generates a bouyant quality in the effect of the music, and clarifies the progression of chords by playing its most important notes.

Some bassists employ a variety of techniques in their work. Occasionally a bassist will pluck two strings at the same time. That is called **double-stop.** Or he might strum his four bass strings as though a guitar. In symphony orchestras, the bass sound is usually extracted by a bow drawn across the strings similar to a saw cutting wood. This technique is called **arco,** not to be confused with plucking, which is called **pizzicato** ("pitts-a-cah-toe"). Though most jazz bassists are capable of it, they do not use the bow very often.

Demo CD *Tracks 21 and 22;* DVD *Track 22*

Some bassists fill in silences with musical remarks that sound almost like they were talking with the rest of the group. This technique is sometimes called "broken time." In some post-1960 groups, making these musical remarks became more important than stating the beat. In some bands, the bassist is often involved in intricate counterplay and musical conversations. Accompaniment rhythms also became more varied, once bassists were freed from playing exclusively walking style. Listen to Scott LaFaro on the first four choruses of "Solar." After the 1950s, bassists also played melody more often than they traditionally had. During the 1970s, it also became common for bassists to play written theme statements in unison with horns.

"Solar," JCCD3 *Track 3*

Piano

The pianist improvises chords in a syncopated fashion to provide harmonies and rhythms for complementing and supporting the soloist. These chords are usually played in the middle of the piano keyboard, creating notes in a pitch range that is easy to hear. (See Appendix H for transcriptions of typical piano accompaniments.) What the pianist is doing is called **comping.** This is short for ac**comp**anying. The pianist uses both hands to play the chorded rhythms behind a soloist. However, **when taking his own solo, he uses his left hand to comp while his right hand plays melodic lines:** Listen to Richie Powell comp for saxophone and trumpet solos on "Kiss and Run." Then listen to Chick Corea comp for himself in "Steps."

Demo CD *Tracks 20, 29, 31–33;* DVD *Tracks 36–39; "Kiss and Run,"* JCCD2 *Track 6; "Steps,"* JCCD3 *Track 4*

Comping is an improvised activity intended to enhance the solo line. Sometimes it inspires the soloist, suggesting chords and rhythms for his improvisation. Comping also involves responding instantaneously to changes in direction taken by a soloist. When the direction of a soloist's improvisation suggests a particular sequence of chords, the pianist must follow suit, even if that progression is not standard for the piece and was not discussed beforehand. The pianist has a very difficult task because he must be inventive when he comps, without getting in the soloist's way. Sometimes the pianist may stop playing if he feels that the soloist would sound better without piano accompaniment. Comping must not clash with the work of the bassist or conflict with the drummer's kicks and prods, either. The members of the rhythm section are providing an accompaniment for the ever-changing melodic and rhythmic directions of the soloist's improvisation. Ideally, the pianist and drummer will kick and prod the soloist in a fashion that is coordinated. They also underscore rhythms in written melodies and ensemble figures. Listen to drummer Art Blakey and pianist Sam Dockery on "Cranky Spanky."

"Cranky Spanky," JCCD2 *Track 7*

Drums

The drummer uses his right hand to play rhythms which provide both regular pulse and swing feeling. These rhythms are played on a cymbal suspended on the right side over the drum set (see Figures 3.3 and 3.4). Such a cymbal comes to occupy the role of *ride cymbal* if it is capable of producing a certain quality of "ping" and its sound sustains properly. The timekeeping rhythms played on it are called **ride rhythms.** Occasionally they consist of one stroke per beat (*ching, ching, ching, ching*), played in unison with the walking bass. But they are usually more complicated, for example, *ching chick a ching chick a ching chick a ching* OR *ching ching ching chick a ching* OR *ching chick a ching chick a ching chick a chick a ching,* etc. The drummer may play ride rhythms on other parts of his set, too. In fact, before the ride cymbal came into common use,

DVD *Track 9; "Seven Come Eleven,"* JCCD1 *Track 15; Appendix H*

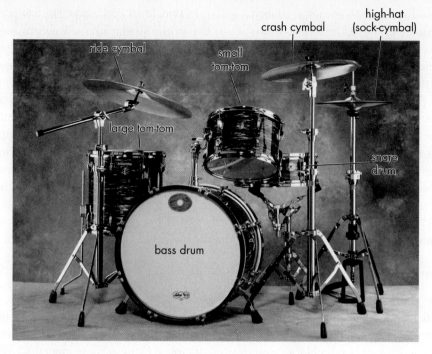

Figure 3.3 Audience view of drum set

ride rhythms were played on the snare drum and high-hat cymbals. Note also that the drummer might play ride rhythms on another cymbal suspended to his left, and the drummer's right hand is not limited to playing the ride cymbal. He can use it to play any of his instruments. The ride cymbal just gets more of its attention.

Demo CD *Track 4;*
DVD *Tracks 10
and 11*

Drummers frequently interrupt timekeeping patterns to make other, more colorful sounds. The *crash cymbal* is often struck by the drummer's right hand, after a fill, while ride rhythms are interrupted. By comparison with the ride cymbal, the crash cymbal makes a splashier tone color, and its sound disappears more quickly. A cymbal crash announces the saxophone solo (1'20" on *JCCD2* Track 8). Crashes are abundant in the drumming of Elvin Jones on "The Promise" and Tony Williams on "Masqualero" (*JCCD2* Tracks 11 and 10). Other colorations can be extracted from the *small tom tom*, suspended over the bass drum, and the *large tom tom*, sitting on the floor to the player's right.

Figures 3.3 and 3.4;
Demo CD *Tracks 6 and
7;* DVD *Track 5*

Figure 3.4 Aerial view photo of drummer at drum set

Figure 3.5   Open high-hat and closed high-hat

The drummer's left hand is free to accent and color the group sound by striking his *snare drum*, on a stand close to his lap (see Figure 3.4). The snare drum has a crisp, crackling sound. The sounds made by striking the snare drum are often called "fills" because they fill in a musical gap left by the soloist. In addition to "fills," the snare drum is used to provide an undercurrent of activity that seems to be "chattering" while the band is playing. Listen for these sounds from Roy Haynes on "Steps."

Demo CD *Tracks 5, 8, 31, and 32;* DVD *Track 2;* "Steps," JCCD3 *Track 4*

Accentuating the swing feeling achieved by the bassist's emphasis of the second and fourth beats in each measure, the drummer plays those same beats by pressing his left foot on a pedal which closes two cymbals together, making a "chick" sound. This apparatus is called a *high-hat* or *sock cymbal*. The high-hat will produce a "chick" sound if the pedal is depressed and held in closed position for a second. It can then be opened and closed again for another "chick" sound. A "ching" sound can be achieved by bringing the cymbals together just long enough for them to strike each other, and then releasing them to resonate (see Figure 3.5). All this is done by means of the high-hat's foot pedal. Sounds can also be extracted from the high-hat by sticks, wire brushes, or mallets. Each implement produces different sounds (see Figure 3.6). The high-hat cymbals can be struck when they are closed or open. Each cymbal in the unit can also be struck independently. Any part of any cymbal can be struck; each part produces a different sound.

Figure 3.5; DVD *Track 7;* Demo CD *Track 2;* "Cranky Spanky," JCCD2 *Track 7*

DVD *Track 10;* Demo CD *Tracks 3 and 4*

Sticks   Brushes   Mallets

Figure 3.6   Sticks, brushes, mallets.

Figure 3.7 Foot pedal for bass drum

DVD *Track 10* |

The drummer uses his right foot to press a pedal which, in turn, causes a mallet to strike the *bass drum* (see Figure 3.7). The drummer sometimes plays the bass drum lightly on every beat, and he also uses it for accents.

A drummer can be recognized on a record by the particular instruments he plays and the characteristic ways in which he strikes them. No two drummers have the same cymbal sound, and each drummer has his own personal way of tuning the drums and cymbals. By means of adjustment bolts, drummers tighten the striking surfaces of plastic or animal hide that are termed drumheads. In addition, some drummers attach gauze and tape to their drumheads to selectively deaden the sound. They tune cymbals by critical placement of tape on the underside. To produce a "sizzle" sound, they often drill holes in a cymbal and attach rivets. When the cymbal is struck, the rivets vibrate against the cymbal. Another technique that achieves a sustained hiss is to hang a large key chain across the top of the cymbal. When the cymbal is struck, the chain bounces and keeps vibrating.

Cymbals on a bandstand often appear old and dirty. This is because few drummers polish their cymbals. The cymbal's sound will be changed if any part of its surface is removed, whether it is dirt, corrosion, or the brass itself. Many drummers actually let new cymbals age to provide a desired tone quality.

Even though they are marketed in various brands, thicknesses, and diameters, cymbal manufacturing is not sufficiently standardized to guarantee perfect cymbals for every drummer. No two are alike, even among the same make and model. Drummers spend years searching for cymbals which give them the particular sound they desire. Many drummers collect cymbals, using certain ones for certain jobs, depending on the sound that is desired. When required to play on someone else's drum set, jazz drummers often remove its cymbals and use their own.

DVD *Track 10* |

DVD *Tracks 12–14* |

The drummer can create a huge variety of sounds, depending on what drum or cymbal he strikes, how hard he strikes it, and what part of the surface is struck. Striking the center of the cymbal creates a sound different from that produced by striking halfway to the edge which, in turn, is unlike striking the edge itself. The sound also varies according to what means are used to initiate it: sticks, wire brushes, mallets, and bare hands all produce different effects. Baby Dodds alternates between brushes and sticks in "Wolverine Blues" (*JCCD1* Track 8). Listen to drummer Max Roach in Charlie Parker's "Ko-Ko" (*SCCJ*). Roach plays snare drum with wire brushes for the introduction. Then he switches to playing ride cymbal with a drum stick for accompanying the solos. Roach can also be heard contributing spontaneous interjections by striking his snare drum with a drum stick and by striking the bass drum with a mallet that is mounted on a foot pedal.

"Kiss and Run," | JCCD2 *Track 6* |

We just summarized the basic drum set, "drum kit" or "set of traps." Most drummers also carry additional instruments such as extra cymbals, tom toms, and Latin American percussion instruments. Until the 1960s, many drummers also had a cowbell (without its clapper). Some also had a wood block.

Demo CD *Track 10;* *"Dixie Jazz Band One-Step,"* JCCD1 *Track 7 at 1'48"*

The public often considers drummers merely to be timekeepers for a band. Though this is true in some bands, throughout jazz history drummers have also added sounds and rhythms that make music more colorful and exciting. Many of these colorful sounds do make the tempo explicit. However, the point here is that much jazz percussion work does not consist merely of timekeeping patterns. It consists of decoration for the band's sound. In other words, **the drummer acts as a colorist in addition to acting as a timekeeper** (Listen to Tony Williams on "Maiden Voyage"). In fact, some bands have employed drummers exclusively for coloristic playing instead of timekeeping. Instead of "drummer," the designation "percussionist" is frequently used to describe that role.

JCCD2 *Track 8 at* *6'15"*

"Surucucu," JCCD3 *Track 6*

The drummer not only keeps time and colors the group sound, but he also **kicks and prods the soloist** in ways that relate to rhythms the pianist and bassist are using ("Cranky Spanky," *JCCD2* Track 7). The jazz drummer plays figures that underscore rhythms in the band arrangements. (Listen to Max Roach on "Kiss and Run," *JCCD2* Track 6.) By the mid-1960s, the conception of jazz drumming had changed so much that the sounds made by drummers in some groups were in the forefront as much as melody instruments. The amount of interplay between drummers and other group members began to equal the amount of interplay previously expected only among the other instruments ("The Promise," *JCCD2* Track 11; "Your Lady," *CCD2* Track 3).[4] In addition, **by his own playing, a drummer can control the loudness level, sound texture, and mood of a combo's performance,** much as a conductor does with a symphony orchestra ("Masqualero," *JCCD2* Track 10).[5]

The 1970s saw a large number of combos using two or more drummers.[6] In some performances, all the drummers would function as colorists. However, in most performances, one player would be explicitly stating the beats on a standard drum set while the other colored the sound using auxiliary percussion instruments.

"Surucucu," JCCD3 *Track 6*

Soloist

The jazz soloist learns to be aware of a number of important events while he is improvising. Although he cannot possibly be conscious of all of them all the time, he does manage to respond intuitively to most of them. Much successful jazz improvisation is largely the result of ultra-high-speed intuition. Here are **a few things the improvising soloist tries to do:**

1. *Remember the chord changes common to the tune he is playing.*[7]
2. *Create phrases compatible with the chord changes.*[8]
3. *Edit* his work so that each improvisation represents a clear musical statement.
4. *Think ahead* so that the phrases will fit together well.
5. *Remember what he has played* so that self-duplication does not occur.
6. *Swing* with the tempo of the piece. Incidentally, if you have been told that the rhythm section keeps time for the band, you might assume that steady tempo would not be maintained without a rhythm section. That is not true at all. Much jazz was originally dance music. So you might say that the rhythm section was keeping time to make the beat obvious for dancing. The improvising soloist keeps time to himself. The ability to keep perfect time enables a soloist to swing without a rhythm section or in spite of a bad one.
7. *Respond to the rhythmic figures of his accompanists* so that a creative interaction will occur instead of a monologue.

8. Keep loudness at a level which will *project* beyond the sound of the band and out to the audience.

9. *Play in tune and with the desired tone quality.*

10. *Remember how long he has been soloing* so that he can stop before he uses the time left for other soloists.

11. *Play in the mood of the piece.*

12. *Create something personal and original.*

This last point requires some clarification. An improviser's lines are not totally original in each and every performance. There are recurring themes in the improvisations of every jazz musician. In fact, these very themes combine with the player's own unique tone qualities and rhythmic feeling to help us identify his style. Using recurring themes is an accepted practice. Aspiring jazz musicians are advised to collect favorite "licks," those very themes and fragments which will later recur in their music and help us identify them. Most improvisers tend to play bits and pieces of lines they have played before, melodic figures they have practiced, and pet phrases of other improvisers. An improviser may actually play portions of a solo he remembers from another musician's recording. Sometimes an improviser will quote snatches of a pop tune or a classical piece. The bits and pieces that constitute a solo may not themselves be original, but the way in which they are combined often is.[9]

"Sundial, Part 1," JCCD3 *Track 5 at* 6′23″

Jazz improvisations can be very intimate, personal creations. This is especially obvious when a soloist uses his instrument almost as an extension or substitute for his own voice. This is apparent when drummers can be seen mouthing their rhythmic figures. It is also evident when pianists and guitarists can be heard humming the lines they are playing. Pianists Keith Jarrett and Oscar Peterson are known for this, often to the distraction of their listeners. Guitarist George Benson has intentionally incorporated such tendencies into his style. He sings the same notes he is playing on guitar, and makes certain that the audience hears the mixture of his voice and his guitar. The result is a unique and compelling sound that he adds to recordings that otherwise feature only his guitar or voice.

ALTERNATIVES AVAILABLE TO THE IMPROVISER

Describing what an improvising soloist does must take into account the actual playing situation. Let's examine a few alternatives suggested by three different situations: playing alone, playing with chord instruments, and playing according to chord changes and steady tempo. The following descriptions are separated only for the sake of clarity. The rules listed in each category are not binding, and they are not necessarily exclusive to that category. The player probably never thinks in these terms, either. He responds intuitively to the requirements of each situation. Consider these three situations as groups of requirements that build upon each other in the order presented here. In other words, the rules increase as the adherence to musical forms and roles increases and as the number of players increases. The first situation is what has become known as "free jazz," whereas the third situation typifies improvisatory practices running from the 1930s until now.

If he is playing alone and not required to follow chord changes or keep time, he is free to play anything that comes to mind:

1. He can organize his notes in a melodic sequence or

2. just place them in a haphazard way.

3. He can use notes common to a single key,

4. switch keys occasionally, or
5. play in no key at all.
6. He can group his notes in a way that implies a tempo, or
7. use no tempo of any sort, either stated or implied.
8. He can play loudly or softly at will.

If he is playing with chording instruments such as piano and guitar, but not necessarily improvising on a tune or chord changes:

1. He must play notes which are compatible and in tune with the other sounds.
2. His notes should not make the ensemble sound cluttered—they must have clarity and balance.
3. He must sequence his notes so that they fit with what preceded them and what is likely to follow. This means paying attention to both the construction of his own line and its relationship to the lines of the other performers.
4. He must adjust the loudness of his playing in response to the group sound, though he might suddenly play louder or softer for the sake of contrast.
5. He might play melodically with such strength that he surfaces to the forefront of the ensemble sound, or
6. He might choose, at any moment, to play notes and rhythms which are subsidiary to those of another group member. Those sounds might help create an ensemble texture instead of a solo line.

If an improviser is playing according to chord changes and constant tempo:

1. His lines must reflect the direction set by the chord progression.[10]
2. He must maintain the tempo of the piece, and
3. swing in that tempo, letting the steadiness of tempo give momentum to his improvisation.

CHAPTER SUMMARY

1. Unwritten rules are followed that enable jazz improvisers to piece together respectable performances without rehearsal.
2. Musicians know many of the same tunes, and they follow common practices when performing tunes having 12-bar blues and 32-bar A-A-B-A construction.
3. Jazz musicians play the melody before and after they play improvisations that are guided by a cycle of repetitions of its accompaniment.
4. It sometimes sounds like the musicians are playing twice as fast (double-time) when they double the density of their activity or half as fast (half-time) when they halve the density of their activity, even though accompaniment chords change at the same rate throughout the performance of a given piece.
5. Jazz musicians are thoroughly trained in methods of playing their instruments, and in reading and writing music, and they know so many tunes and chord progressions that they can instantaneously respond to what each other plays when improvising.
6. Walking bass style involves playing notes that serve to keep time for the band as well as outlining the chord progression being followed by the improvisers.

7. The jazz drummer uses snare drum, bass drum, ride cymbal, and high-hat cymbals to keep time for the band as well as contribute kicks and prods that communicate with the improvising soloist.

8. Comping is the accompaniment style in which the pianist feeds chords to the improvising soloist in a flexible and syncopated way.

9. The improvising soloist keeps many considerations in mind while performing—chord progressions, logical and original construction of the solo, communication with accompanists, etc.

NOTES

1. A few of the 32-bar A-A-B-A pieces found on *SCCJ* are "Body and Soul" (by Coleman Hawkins and by Benny Goodman), "I Got Rhythm" (by Don Byas and Slam Stewart), "Lester Leaps In" and "Taxi War Dance" (by Count Basie with Lester Young), "I Can't Believe That You're in Love with Me" (Benny Carter), "Willow Weep for Me" (Art Tatum), "The Man I Love" (Coleman Hawkins), "Moten Swing" (Bennie Moten), and "Smoke Gets in Your Eyes" (Thelonious Monk). If you do not have access to *SCCJ*, and you do not have examples of any 32-bar A-A-B-A compositions listed in Appendix B, find a recording of "Honeysuckle Rose," "Undecided," "Moose the Mooch," "Roseland Shuffle," "Jumpin' at the Woodside," "Off Minor," "There Is No Greater Love," "Polka Dots and Moonbeams," "Stompin' at the Savoy," "Give Me the Simple Life," or Mel Torme's "Christmas Song" ("Chestnuts roasting on an open fire…"). Note that the format followed by musicians recording these tunes might not be identical to the routine described above, but at least their solos will probably adhere to the chord progression of the tune. It should not take much time or thought to determine how the musicians are handling the form. Just listen for musical landmarks such as turnarounds and bridges as described in Appendix B and on the *Demo CD* Track 33.

2. Classical musicians, however, call that practice "free rhythmic style," and they reserve the term "rubato" for designating the situation in which the tempo remains steady but part of the time originally occupied by some notes is robbed from them and used to extend the sound of other notes. In other words, classical musicians use the term "rubato" to indicate that a passage is not played exactly as written and that the relative durations of the notes are adjusted at the discretion of the performer.

3. An organ can be substituted for both the chord instrument and the bass in a band because bass lines can be played on the organ by means of foot pedals. But despite this advantage, most jazz organists actually play bass lines with the left hand, using the foot pedals for assistance. This technique restricts the organist to a single hand for playing chords underneath the solos of others. It leaves no extra hand for chording behind their own right-hand solos. The poor pianos and poor sound systems often furnished by night clubs compel many groups to bring their own portable electric piano or electric organ. Incidentally, if a band carries an organist, they don't have to pay salary for a bassist because the organist can supply bass lines.

4. Listen to John Coltrane, *Live at Birdland* (Impulse!: 198, 1963, c1996); and *Sun Ship* (Impulse!: 167, 1965, c1995); or Miles Davis, *Miles Smiles* (Columbia/Legacy: 65682, 1966, c1998); and *Filles de Kilimanjaro* (Columbia/Legacy: 86555, 1968, c2002).

5. Listen to the drumming on "Masqualero" on Miles Davis, *Sorcerer* (Columbia/Legacy: 65680, 1967, c1998); or on *JCCD2*.

6. Listen to Weather Report, *I Sing the Body Electric* (Columbia: 46107, 1971–72, c1990); *Black Market* (Columbia/Legacy: 65169, 1976, c2002); and *Sweetnighter* (Columbia/Legacy: 64976, 1973, c1996); or Miles Davis, *Live-Evil* (Columbia/Legacy: C2K 65135, 1970, c1997); and *On the Corner* (Columbia/ Legacy: 63980, 1972, c2000).

7. Occasionally, when the improviser is at a jam session or sitting in with an unfamiliar group, he may not know the chord progressions of the tune being played. He might know the melody but be unsure of some of the progressions. Or he might be requested to play a tune he once knew but whose progressions he has forgotten. In these cases, he listens to the rhythm section and determines the chord changes while he improvises. He can usually guess some of the progressions because he knows certain patterns that recur in hundreds of tunes. He can also determine the chords by listening to other soloists use them. Note, however, that he cannot always predict the chord progressions the rhythm section will play, because a tune can be harmonized in many different ways. This practice of altering chord progressions, **reharmonization,** is very common in jazz.

8. The concept of compatibility is very broad. Both the particular style and the individual player determine what notes are "compatible" with the chord changes. For example, some notes that are compatible for modern jazz of the 1940s are not compatible for jazz of the 1920s.

9. To understand the mechanics of a sound that a musical model produces and the phrases that he prefers, developing jazz musicians usually analyze, memorize, and then imitate the model's work. Once the player has mastered the techniques required to produce whatever sounds and phrases he wants, he usually develops variations of the learned imitations and mixes them with his own original ideas. The process of artistic development starting with imitation is not exclusive to jazz musicians. It has been employed by painters, writers, and composers for centuries. It may seem curious to the outsider, but the musician's practice of analyzing, memorizing, and imitating is not usually viewed as plagiarism (stealing another's idea and calling it your own), but rather as a necessary first step in the elaborate training process which jazz musicians undergo. If, however, the player never moves beyond the imitation phase and ends up living out his career sounding much like his model, he frequently elicits the dismay of music critics and, to a lesser extent, the disappointment of fellow musicians. But there are exceptions to this. Some players may be so proficient or play with such beauty that they earn admiration despite their failure to develop beyond the imitation stage. Sometimes imitation

itself leads to innovation. For instance, tenor saxophonist Lester Young produced a tone quality that was unusual and highly influential for its time, partly because he was imitating the playing of Frankie Trumbauer, whose instrument was the smaller C-melody saxophone. Almost as important to jazz history as Young was trumpeter Roy Eldridge, who created an innovative style by imitating jazz saxophonists instead of trumpeters.

10. Though jazz musicians in this situation usually play notes that fit with the underlying chords, improvisers are free to initiate lines that deviate from an otherwise strictly defined chord progression. But if the line is to sound good, the improviser's accompanists must listen and instantly follow suit. Frequently a hornman initiates the deviation, and the pianist responds with appropriate chords. Or a pianist can suggest alterations in harmony by what he plays. Then the hornman picks up the direction, and the ensemble works together with the alteration. Soloists can also play notes that are incompatible with the underlying chords, while the rhythm section maintains the preset progression. This is called playing "against the changes" or playing "outside," and it is used effectively by some soloists, including many of the saxophonists who played on Miles Davis records during the 1970s and 1980s.

Jazz originated from pop music styles of the 1800s that were blended to satisfy social dancers. During the 1890s, jazz began to be recognizable as a style of its own. By the 1920s, it was fully formed and recorded in New York, Los Angeles, and Chicago. At least three essential **trends caused the birth of jazz:**

1. The practice of taking liberties with the melodies and accompaniments of tunes as they were being performed. This led to what we today call *improvisation*.

2. Taking liberties with tone qualities. For instance, musicians cultivated rough and raspy sounds to add to their collection of smooth tone qualities.

3. African Americans creating new kinds of music such as ragtime and the blues.

   Ragtime

   a. provided some of the *jazz repertory* and

   b. made *syncopated rhythms* popular.

   The blues

   a. provided another portion of jazz repertory,

   b. popularized the practice of *toying with a melody tone's pitch* to produce a soulful effect, and

   c. popularized the practice of manipulating the starting times for sung notes and phrases. Such delays are technically classified as *rhythmic displacement*.

The Superior Orchestra
(Photo courtesy of William Ransom Hogan Jazz Archive, Tulane University)

A glance back at the experiences of Africans in America will help us understand how these different kinds of music came together. When Africans were taken as slaves to the New World, they were not allowed to bring their musical instruments. They were not even grouped with their own families or members of the same language community who could help perpetuate their musical customs. Though slaves in some regions, especially New Orleans, were occasionally allowed to recreate their own music, such situations decreased over the centuries that slavery persisted, and slaves were expected to learn the music of their masters. Considering those situations, African musical tastes and performance practices could have simply died out, having been overpowered by the European musical tastes and performance practices of the majority culture. The African traditions were sufficiently robust, however, to be retained in new forms of music and creative alterations of European music. This may explain why European music often sounded different when played in the New World by musicians of African ancestry. For example, some slaves modified European church hymns, folk songs, and dance music to suit their own tastes and traditions.

There are numerous **ways in which African tastes and traditions were retained** in the New World despite their contrast with the musical tastes and traditions of the majority culture.

1. Some **children's games** were highly rhythmic and physical. A few used the player's own body as a drum. Patting juba is an example. Some children's activities involved highly syncopated songs, a few of which required interaction that cultivated the juggling of complicated rhythmic parts.

2. **African American church music** kept a few African musical traditions alive by practicing the modifications to European church hymns that slaves had incorporated, spicing them up by altering rhythms, adding pitch bends and new tone qualities. (See pages 48–50 and *Demo CD* Tracks 50–58.)

   They also made otherwise bland, non-swinging phrases more rhythmically emphatic in their execution. (These are illustrated in "One Day" on *JCCD1* Track 4.)

3. **Idiosyncrasies of speech patterns** used by African Americans who did not entirely assimilate Anglo-American models. The *rhythmic aspects* that reflect African retentions include emphasis on syllables that would not receive emphasis when spoken by Anglo-Americans and fusing words together that would otherwise be kept separate.

   Imaginative flexibility of pitch is also common. These practices were obvious in work songs and in creative ways called field hollers devised by workers for communicating in the fields. (This is illustrated by the cry of the blackberry vendor on *JCCD1* Track 1. We can notice such practices today in English-speaking citizens of Caribbean nations such as Jamaica and the Bahamas.)

4. Examples of **undiluted African music performed in public.** One tradition is the group of uninvited paraders who participate in the Mardi Gras celebration in New Orleans and appear on side streets after the officially sanctioned paraders pass. Though dressed as Native American Indians, these paraders are African Americans, and their music is essentially African. They are informally known as Mardi Gras Indians. The musicians and dancers in these groups represent members of social organizations that exist year-round and have managed to keep African music and dance traditions alive since at least as early as the 1880s. Their existence is made conspicuous during Mardi Gras, but Mardi Gras is not their reason for being.

5. The popularity of **blues singing** since the end of the 1800s made African musical practices continuously accessible.

6. The popularity of **music from Latin America and the Caribbean** has made available, since at least as early as the 1890s, most of the characteristics

discussed in this chapter because such music originated by fusing Spanish music with African music. (Some of the Latin American rhythms can be heard in "Señor Blues" [Track 5] and "Maiden Voyage" [Track 8] on *JCCD2*.)[1]

WHY DID JAZZ ORIGINATE IN NEW ORLEANS?

Before analyzing the features of jazz in greater depth, let's first examine the setting in which it was born. We will begin with the history of ethnic diversity in New Orleans. The next three paragraphs are paraphrased from the work of James Haskins in his book *The Creoles of Color of New Orleans* (Crowell, 1975).

Ethnic Diversity and Creoles of Color

France began building New Orleans in 1718, and 147 black slaves were brought there in 1719. There were free blacks there as early as 1722. In 1763 France gave the territory of Louisiana to Spain as a gift. But Spanish rule was not firmly established until 1769, and despite Spanish rule, the language and customs there remained primarily French. In 1801, Spain ceded Louisiana back to France, but Spain continued to rule the territory until the United States bought it from France in 1803.

Significant social patterns can be traced back to that period of Spanish rule. Marriage between the different ethnic groups in Louisiana occurred more frequently at that time. Furthermore, the Spanish freed many slaves, thereby increasing the number of free blacks (there were 1,147 by 1789). Under Spanish rule, **free people of color began to be regarded as a class that was separate from the whites and the slaves, with status closer to that of whites.** Many light-skinned women of color became mistresses to white men and were set up as second families to the men in separate houses. This was common where there were more white men than white women. Sex between blacks and whites prior to the mid-1800s led to a mixing of African and European traditions. The offspring from some of these unions were called *Creoles of Color*. Their ancestry was part African and part French. This distinguished them from the white Creoles, whose background was French and Spanish. Strictly speaking, Creole originally meant people speaking French and Spanish who were born in the New World. Creoles of Color were not referred to as Negro. That term was reserved for blacks who had little or no white ancestry.

Another event affected New Orleans Creoles at about this time. From 1791 to 1804, there was a slave revolt in Haiti against the white French and the Creole planters. This caused many free people of color from Haiti to move to New Orleans after, in 1809, being forced out of Cuba, where they had been given refuge. By 1810, the number of free people of color living in New Orleans had increased to 5,000. This made them the largest ethnic group there. The small white population reacted to their own minority status with fear. The whites captured business and governmental power. With that power, they began enacting laws ("black codes") and continued enacting laws for about one hundred years, which eroded the favored status of the Creoles of Color. These laws eventually placed Creoles of Color in the same position as Negroes. The process was slow. As late as 1830, Creoles of Color owned almost 2,500 slaves and continued to prosper in business. However, by the mid-1840s, life became so uncomfortable for them that many left New Orleans.

A sharp separation existed between the two groups of New Orleans residents who had African ancestry. Negroes lived in a racially mixed neighborhood, a large portion of which was uptown. They worked primarily as house servants and unskilled laborers. Many of the Creoles lived downtown in the area of New Orleans today known as the French Quarter. Creoles of Color were mostly well-educated, successful people—businessmen, physicians, landowners, and skilled craftsmen. They spoke French.

Many owned slaves, and often required their slaves to speak French, too. Children in Creole families often received high-quality musical training. Some even traveled to Paris for study at a conservatory. The Creoles maintained a resident symphony orchestra, and supported an opera house. This reinforced the intensely musical orientation of New Orleans, a city that had three opera houses, far more than any other American city of comparable size. By comparison with residents of other regions, they took the pleasures of music and dance more seriously.

The Blues

The vocal music of the uptown blacks in New Orleans included African American work songs, devised to ease the burden of laborers, and African American religious music that was a compromise between European church music and African vocal style. Another kind of black vocal music was the cry of the street vendor, a kind of music which capitalized on expressive variations in pitch and voice quality. (Listen to Track 1 on *JCCD1*.) These sounds had evolved into a new form of music by the first decade of the twentieth century. It began as an unaccompanied solo vocal style but eventually used guitar or banjo as accompaniment. The chords in this accompaniment were originally almost incidental to the melodic line—whatever chords the singer could play. The progression of chords was simple. Sometimes only two or three different chords were used in an entire song. Lyrics and melody lines were also simple, with brief pauses between phrases and much repetition. This was the form of music we now call *the blues*. (See Appendix B for a full explanation. Listen to *Demo CD* Tracks 17–19 for the accompaniment chord progression. Listen to Bessie Smith sing "Reckless Blues" on *CCD1* Track 3.)

This social history pertains to jazz because it helps us appreciate the origins of the intensely musical orientation of New Orleans. Creoles of Color, like the white Creoles, wholeheartedly favored European music, including French wind band and European concert traditions. Meanwhile, some music played by Negroes retained aspects of African musical practices. Though many Negro musicians received musical training in the European styles, their music was generally less refined than that of the Creoles. It may have included improvisation. In summary, many European concert traditions were absorbed and maintained by Creole music, and some African traditions were preserved in Negro music.

The Need for Live Music

To help us appreciate the setting in which jazz emerged, historian-musicologist Karl Koenig encourages us to envision life at the beginning of the twentieth century. Let's follow his observations, paraphrased in the next seven paragraphs from his writings.

To understand the effects of living in an age without the electronic devices we now possess, imagine trying to amuse yourself on a night in the New Orleans area. You could not listen to any radio or television programs, CDs, or tapes. You could not call anyone on the telephone or visit movie theaters or video arcades. Candlelight would be needed for reading. However, you could go to the town park or square, which would be illuminated by gas lamps. There you could buy flavored ices from a vendor, exchange pleasantries with your neighbors, and take a walk in the moonlight. You could also listen and dance to the local band. In other words, there almost had to be music, *live* music. A town without a band was a very dull place to be. The social and fraternal organizations knew this, as did the newspapers and commercial establishments. Therefore, sponsorship was provided for most of the local bands by churches (mostly Catholic), social and benevolent clubs, fraternal clubs (Elks, Masons, etc.), fire departments, townships, undertakers, and plantation owners.[2]

Brass Bands

The band was present at almost every social activity, most of which took place outdoors: picnics, sporting events, political speeches, or dramatic presentations at the town hall, and dances in the open-air pavilions. Dancing was the main social activity of the nineteenth century. The band played before the event and for the dance that followed. A large brass band was used so that the music could be heard in outdoor settings. Note that in the narrowest sense, a "brass band" has only brass instruments (such as cornet and trombone) plus drums and cymbals. But the early Louisiana bands also included a clarinet and later a saxophone. (These are technically known as "woodwinds," even when not constructed entirely of wood; see photographs on page 102.) When the social activity was held indoors, a large band was not needed. There the smaller "string band" was suitable. It was often composed of cornet, violin, guitar, bass, and piano, or some combination of those instruments.

There were bands in the New Orleans area long before the Civil War. Then, during the war, occupation by Union troops exposed the city to many more. About thirty different regimental bands of the occupying forces were stationed in and around New Orleans. They were very conspicuous. They played for the many military ceremonies and for concerts of patriotic and popular music. Their presence was an additional stimulus for the band tradition in New Orleans.

Ragtime

By the end of the 1800s, **ragtime** was very popular in New Orleans. The word "rag" refers to a kind of music that was put together like a military march and had rhythms borrowed from African American banjo music. You could tell ragtime music because many of the loud accents fell in between the beats. This is called syncopation. Musicians would use syncopation on all kinds of different tunes and say they were "ragging" those tunes. So the term "to rag" came to mean giving a piece of music a distinctly syncopated or ragged-time feeling. "Ragtime" ordinarily refers to a kind of written piano music that first appeared in the 1890s. The most famous composer of this style was Scott Joplin (1868–1917). (Listen to Joplin's "Maple Leaf Rag" in *SCCJ*.) The term has also been used to identify an entire era of music, not exclusively written piano music. For example, between the 1890s and the 1920s, there were ragtime bands, ragtime singers, ragtime banjo players, in addition to ragtime pianists. Many of the musicians we classify today as "jazz musicians" called themselves "ragtime" musicians. Because of this, some scholars consider ragtime to have been the first jazz style. However, ragtime was not a jazz style in the strict sense. It involved only limited improvisation, and it lacked what is today called jazz swing feeling. Instead, we can say that ragtime was a forerunner of jazz. It popularized using accents before and after the beat instead of always directly on it. Today jazz musicians play "around" the beat partly because ragtime made the practice popular.

Scott Joplin, the leading composer of ragtime piano music. His pieces and their syncopations influenced the development of early jazz playing styles.

(Photo courtesy of New York Public Library)

Combining Influences

During the 1890s, there were bands in almost every small town and settlement in Southern Louisiana. Their music reflected several influences. It combined march music and ragtime. Moreover, these two styles were interrelated. John Philip Sousa, the famous bandleader, had included ragtime pieces in his band concerts, and ragtime pianists often performed Sousa marches in a ragtime style. Another force was music of the Mexican bands that visited New Orleans. Musicians from these bands settled in and around New Orleans, and some became music teachers. Their music was respected and enjoyed so much that it influenced the styles of New Orleans trumpet players.

Band music influenced jazz quite directly. By the beginning of the twentieth century, New Orleanians were accustomed to hearing brass bands such as Sousa's and Arthur Pryor's, having already heard Patrick Gilmore's military bands of the Gulf Coast Command. Dances held in the middle 1800s were often provided with music by the military band that was stationed in the region. In fact, the march form was sometimes modified and used as dance music. Later a popular dance called the "two-step" was done to march-like music. Moreover, the way the themes were organized in ragtime pieces follows the pattern found in marches. Eventually roles of various instruments were transferred from marching band to jazz band. For instance, the flute and piccolo parts from march arrangements were imitated by jazz clarinetists. In the typical marching drum part, the bass drum played on beats one and three while the snare drum, with its sharper sound, played on beats two and four. In early jazz there is a correspondingly heavy emphasis on beats two and four. (See Appendix B for more explanation, and listen to the "Dixie Jazz Band One-Step" on *JCCD1* Track 7 and notice its similarity to march music.)

Party Atmosphere

Other factors besides the brass band movement made New Orleans an ideal setting for the birth of jazz. New Orleans was a center of commerce because of its nearness to the mouth of the Mississippi River, a flourishing trade route for America, the Caribbean, and Europe. Because the city was a seaport, it catered to travelers from all over the world, and New Orleans maintained a cosmopolitan party atmosphere. There were numerous taverns and dance halls. One aspect of the entertainment it provided was a famous prostitution district known as Storyville. It took its name from an alderman (city councilman), Sidney Story, who drafted legislation that sectioned off a portion of the town in 1897 and limited prostitution to that area. **The reason the party atmosphere of New Orleans is important to the beginning of jazz is that it generated so much work for musicians. There was so much demand for live music that there was a continuous need for fresh material. This caused musicians to stretch styles. They blended, salvaged, and continuously revised odd assortments of approaches and material. This ultimately became jazz.** Karl Koenig has offered this as the key explanation for the origin of jazz.

Dance Music

Now let's delve a bit more deeply into what probably occurred at the time jazz was born. Ordinarily jazz is thought to have derived from blues and rags that were popular in New Orleans. However, only a few pieces in the repertory of New Orleans brass bands were rags, and—at least between 1905 and 1915—12-bar blues pieces were not as common as we would expect if we designated these groups as "jazz" bands. In other words, our current notion of "jazz repertory" is not really reflected in the music of the first jazz musicians.

Unlike most of today's jazz, the earliest jazz was intended mostly for dancing, not just for listening. The music's beat, form, and spirit interested the dancers the most. The evolution of new dances and the overall popularity of dancing were big factors in the evolution of jazz. Dancers were not necessarily impressed by the wonders of collective improvisation or the inspirations of well-crafted solo improvis[...] responded more to new jazz rhythms.

The musicians who performed the first jazz have said that their reper[...] structed primarily to accompany dances such as the mazurka, schottisc[...] and one-step. These musicians, whom today we call "jazz players," w[...] specifically to play jazz.

At the beginning of the twentieth century, New Orleans parade ba[...] bands shared the same musicians and much of the same repertory. It [...] though the musicians walked directly from the street parade into the d[...] putting down a brass instrument and picking up a violin. The perform[...] accompanied dances were termed "string bands" or "orchestras"—vio[...] viol, and one or two wind instruments, played by the same musicians w[...] with trumpet and trombone. To satisfy the demands of dancers, these [...] combined music from different sources. Sometimes they ended u[...] sounds that were very compelling rhythmically. These approaches be[...] jazz style, and their manner of playing led to the idea that jazz is not *what* you pl[...] *how* you play it. In other words, **jazz was an outgrowth of treatments for many kinds of music being played on the demand of dancers.** Today we call these same musicians "jazz musicians," and their music "New Orleans jazz" or "Dixieland," though some people reserve the term "Dixieland" solely for the music of white bands. **Because their audiences liked ragtime so much, the musicians adapted repertory from many sources, often syncopating ("ragging") otherwise unsyncopated pieces, often lending rhythmic vitality to pieces that lacked it.**

In parades as well as dance halls, small bands were trying to perform music originally written for large bands. Their compromises led to what became standard Dixieland style and instrumentation. In trying to fill out the sound, more activity was required of each player, so musicians improvised parts to order. They got in the habit of improvising, and, as jazz evolved, this habit changed from a necessity into a choice. In essence, the musicians in New Orleans were combining diverse materials to please people who had a taste for special kinds of musical excitement. Jazz originated directly in the instrumentation, repertory, and musical practices of brass bands and string bands that were active before the 1920s.

To answer the question of why jazz originated in New Orleans, we can see that the city was highly musical at a time when ragtime and blues were popular and brass bands were at their peak of popularity. But other regions of America also had sizable entertainment districts and traditions for taking music and dance seriously. So what was a key difference about New Orleans? The *recent* history of publicly performed African music (as late as the 1850s), its subsequent and continuous vitality underground in social organizations there, and its annual emergence by way of "Indians" at Mardi Gras. This is what kept African practices alive and lent a distinct intensity, elasticity, and highly syncopated rhythmic character to most music, not just jazz, that came out of New Orleans. (Recall that Dr. John, the Neville Brothers, Fats Domino, and other nonjazz pop musicians also came from New Orleans and conveyed a similarly distinct rhythmic flavor.)

WHY DID JAZZ EMERGE NEAR THE BEGINNING OF THE TWENTIETH CENTURY?

There are several factors that might explain why jazz emerged when it did.

1. The **intensity of musical activity** in New Orleans was especially high at the beginning of the twentieth century.

> Rag = Music put together like a military march.
> - Scott Joplin (Maple leaf)
> - contained a jazz rag swing feeling.
> * Two step: - March like music
> - The center of music in New Orleans was Storyville.
> - Dixie lang: the music of white bands

2. As noted by Karl Koenig, the origin of jazz coincides with **the zenith of popularity for the brass concert band** in America.

3. Koenig reminds us that this was a **very fertile time** because there was (a) **so much work for musicians;** (b) so many bands; (c) plenty of motivation to play varied styles; and (d) almost all the musicians listened to each other's music.

4. Because of the **popularity of the ragtime style,** there was incentive to "rag" music from non-rag sources. This resulted in improvising syncopations into the performance of compositions that did not necessarily bear much syncopation.

5. Similarly, as the twentieth century began, the **popularity of blues** encouraged musicians to play band instruments in a bluesy way even when not playing a blues piece.

6. The cumulative effect of **social and legal changes in Louisiana** that gradually resulted in Creoles being consigned to the same low status the Negroes had. Remember that between the beginning of the 1800s and the beginning of the 1900s, distinctions between "pure" and "mixed" ancestry were more and more ignored. All citizens with any African ancestry were consigned to the same category. Creoles were forced to give up the status they had attained during the 1700s. They had to assume the status of Negroes and mix socially and occupationally with Negroes. Though the Creoles resented this, jazz was the ultimate benefactor because this readjustment further facilitated the blending of European traditions (as represented by the Creoles) with African traditions (as represented by the Negroes).

An African Heritage of Musical Tastes

Before beginning a more detailed examination of jazz elements, we must consider some important qualifications regarding the mixing of styles. When African American ragtime and blues began affecting the performance of other kinds of music, some observers contended that the race of the musician was responsible for the particular way the music was played. For example, many listeners felt that the highly rhythmic nature of African American forms reflected a rhythmic talent that came with the race of the musician. Yet these observers overlooked the fact that most musical preferences are probably learned, not genetic. Preferences for certain African techniques were indeed passed down from generation to generation by imitation and instruction. But slaves also learned European music that was available. For example, by the mid-1800s, there were highly accomplished concert artists in the European style who had slavery backgrounds. (Conversely, by the 1920s, there were highly accomplished jazz musicians whose backgrounds were strictly European and white.) It is not reasonable to expect all music played by blacks to sound African. No one inherits desires for music of any particular region; there is no "racial unconscious" that is transmitted genetically. Remember that in New Orleans, most black and Creole musicians played European types of dance music such as mazurkas, waltzes, polkas, and quadrilles. They had to, or they would not be hired. The fact that these New Orleans musicians had African ancestry was irrelevant to playing that music. So, as you consider the next few pages of analysis, keep in mind that (1) when we speak of African traditions, we are referring only to tastes for particular ways of making music, (2) these tastes were conveyed more by American Negro culture than by Creole culture, (3) the opportunity to alter established styles, and thereby season to taste, was capitalized upon by African Americans in such highly creative ways that the result was ragtime, blues, jazz, rock, and funk music; but (4) many Americans of African descent never had such preferences, and many whites did. Incidentally, by the 1980s, African American musical styles had become the most popular in the world, not just among people of African descent, but among all races in every geographic region.

WHAT IS AFRICAN AND WHAT IS EUR[...] ABOUT JAZZ?

Most innovators in jazz have been African American and, until rece[...]
tionately high percentage of jazz musicians has been African Ameri[...]
lead us to ask whether jazz contains characteristics of African music [...]
filtered into it through the African American culture that produce[...]
practitioners. The question is impossible to answer, however, becaus[...]
and European music have so many elements in common and because [...]
able as models when jazz was forming. But it remains interesting to c[...]
sibilities. So now we are going to examine eleven features of jazz, [...]
African and European sources.

[handwritten note: - Dance type: Mazurkas, waltzes, polkas, quadrilles — African Americans results — ragtimes — Blues — Jazz — rock — funk music]

FEATURES OF JAZZ

1. Improvisation
2. Syncopation
3. Harmony
4. Instruments
5. Role of percussion
6. Rough tone qualities
7. Repetition of brief patterns
8. Polyrhythms
9. Decorations of tone
10. Blue notes
11. Overlapping call and response

Joe "King" Oliver's Creole Jazz Band, 1923: Baby Dodds (drums), Honoré Dutrey (trombone), Oliver (cornet), Louis Armstrong (cornet), Bill Johnson (bass viol), Johnny Dodds (clarinet), Lil Hardin (piano)

(Photo courtesy of The Cleveland Press Collection/Cleveland State University Archives)

Handwritten margin note:

- <u>Improvisation</u>: The practice of spontaneously varying individual parts.
  ▫ Inventing elaborate melody lines, varying the timing, pitch, and timbre at it's beginning and ending.
  ▫ Toying with the rhythms of melodies.
  ▫ A given tone might be repeated several times

...tion

...ture of jazz we are going to examine is improvisation, the practice of ... **varying individual parts.** It has been an important element of music ...nning of time, and only recently in history was it difficult to find in ...cert music. Improvisation characterizes some African music and much ...gists are uncertain about the extent to which African American music ...ovisatory traditions from African music. Let's first consider improvisa-...of cultures that contributed slaves to the New World. For instance, in ...m ensemble of Ghana, the lead drummer is in charge of giving signals. ...e variable than any of the others, so it might be regarded as improvised. ...ka drum ensemble, the senior player has leeway to improvise more than ...t all members are allowed to slightly vary their parts as they play. Some ...g in leader-and-chorus format allows spontaneous variations in the ...o keep this in perspective, however, consider that these practices come ...the extent of improvisation that is found today in jazz. In the West ...g and the African American blues singing that evolved from it, impro-visations did not consist of inventing elaborate melody lines as eventually became common for jazz improvisers. Instead, these singers channeled their creativity into altering the sound of a single sustained tone, varying the timing, pitch, and timbre at its beginning and ending. They also improvised by toying with the rhythms of melodies. Tones would be started a bit earlier or later. Or a given tone might be repeated several times in succession instead of being sung only once. Similarly, a tone might be started, then softened, and then pushed again by an abrupt increase in volume. Sometimes whole phrases would be placed differently in relation to the underlying beat. This is known as *rhythmic displacement.* Incidentally, these techniques are still evident in performances of gospel music by African American singers and in gospel-influenced styles of pop music, such as the singing of Aretha Franklin and James Brown, particularly in the famous renditions of "Georgia on My Mind" and "America the Beautiful" by Ray Charles.

The reason we discuss singing at this point in a textbook about instrumental jazz is that these vocal practices are thought to have influenced the styles used by jazz musicians who played trumpet, trombone, clarinet, and saxophone. (That is why the beginning of *JCCD1* has an instrumental demonstration by Miles Davis directly following the cry of the African American street vendor.) Individual creativity and unorthodox means for learning how to play instruments have also been suggested as roots for pitch and timbre improvisation in horn work. Some musicologists believe that demand for live music was so great in New Orleans that many unpolished amateurs were called upon to perform as professionals, and the incomplete mastery these players had over their instruments gave us the collection of raw, unorthodox sounds we now associate with New Orleans jazz. Imitation of singing style, however, is the most popular explanation among musicologists. In addition, some scholars believe that the spirit of improvisation and the stress on individuality in jazz stem from African traditions. But these traits are also found in America within non-African folk music as well. So a striving for individuality among jazz musicians could be, but is not necessarily or exclusively, an extension of African preferences or what has been called "the black esthetic."

Now let's consider what European music could have contributed to the origins of improvisation in jazz. In America there was already a well-developed European tradition for improvising by the time jazz had begun. Improvised ornaments were common in pre-twentieth century concert music, and they have long been common in folk music and popular music. Within informal American music prior to the emergence of

"Street Cries,"
"Hunter's Dance," and
"One Day," JCCD1
Tracks 1, 3, and 4

jazz, there are also precedents for improvisation in the form of musi[c]
spontaneously varied entrances. Often singers start notes whenever th[ey]
instead of singing precisely in unison with the others. This is terme[d]
sounding to our ears like ensemble "sloppiness." It is also notable th[at]
variations were common parts of solo recital format for some keyboard
the 1800s, concert pianists often improvised within the encore numbe[r]
gram. And there existed a French and German keyboard tradition for
called *preluding*. Some early American musicians were even required
improvise a piece on demand, using phrases supplied by their audienc[e]
that the practice of making up music as you go along is precedented
African and European music. Both of these traditions could have infl[uenced]
of improvisation in jazz.

Now consider improvisation among New Orleans musicians at th[e]
the twentieth century. At least as late as 1923, the improvisational c
players was directed primarily at piecing together band routines. Some
ever, were spontaneously devised during performances, thereby qualifying as improvised. The skeletons for these routines were often provided by published arrangements
that were known among musicians as "stocks." For the first few run-throughs, many of
the parts were not fixed. Trombone counterlines, clarinet obbligatos, and trumpet
variations of the melody were sometimes invented and performed spontaneously. Accompaniments were improvised and varied by the more adventurous and creative
players. After a suitable set of parts had been worked out, the musicians frequently
remained relatively loyal to them. A striving for improvisation was not as central to a
jazz esthetic as it has become. The extent to which new melodies were freshly improvised during performance was limited. There was, however, a striving for personalization and individualization which did not require improvisation, at least in the sense
that the term is used here. Though the seeds were planted in New Orleans, it is possible that the kind and the extent of jazz improvisation known today did not first
emerge there.[3]

By the late 1920s, these improvisational tendencies had expanded to the extent of
improvisation we usually expect from most jazz today. Unfortunately, we do not know
why this change occurred. A few possibilities are (1) boredom with fixed routines; (2) a
need to learn new material without recourse to sheet music; (3) increased interest in
bravura solo excursions and emergence of the "star" system of players; (4) a continuation of European and/or African traditions for spontaneous alteration; (5) unbridled
creativity; (6) longer dances necessitating stretching out the numbers, that, in turn, led
to solos that give other hornmen time to rest their lips; and (7) a combination of these
reasons.

Syncopation

Next let's consider **syncopation,** a rhythmic phenomenon most easily understood as accents that don't occur on a main beat. (To hear the difference between unsyncopated
and syncopated playing, listen to the piano comping demonstrations on *Demo CD
Track 20.*) Syncopation is common in both African and European music, though
Africa is especially known for highly syncopated music. Some syncopation in jazz is
thought to derive from African American banjo music and ragtime. Some is thought to
stem from the heterophony discussed above. The taste for syncopation that exists
among jazz musicians might stem, in part, from musical preferences for *rhythmic contrast,* which musicologist Olly Wilson has shown to prevail among many African and
African American styles of music.

*Appendix B; Demo CD
Track 20*

[Handwritten margin notes:]
Syncopation: A rhythmic phenomenon most easily understood as accents that don't occur on a main beat

Harmony: Provided chord progression.

- Instruments: first ones that were used were trumpet, clarinet, trombone or sax

...ure of jazz is **harmony.** Though harmony is found in African music, the
...ssions in jazz are not common to native African music. European music
...rd progressions of the type that jazz uses.

...nts

...ure of jazz is the choice of instruments. Where did the earliest jazz groups
...**nstrumentation**? The European brass band provided the model that in-
...et, trombone, clarinet, saxophone, and tuba. The black and the white
...ds that were plentiful in New Orleans at the beginning of the twentieth
...brass band instrumentation, and they played marches and pop tunes for
...ics, dances, and funerals. The region of Africa that supplied slaves for
...ld did not have musical instruments that closely resembled the trumpet,
clarinet, trombone, or saxophone.

What about drums? The drums of West Africa can be found in some modern
jazz groups. The drums used in the earliest jazz, however, were from European-style
brass bands. (See illustrations in the previous chapter.) The wood block and cowbell, (heard on "Dixie Jazz Band One-Step") two other percussion instruments used
in the manner of drums, have been heard in jazz since the earliest recordings. They
are thought to have African ancestry, though China and Turkey have also contributed forerunners for many similar instruments in the New World. (Incidentally,
the way the ride cymbal is used in jazz is very similar to the way West African musicians play their atoke or karinyan, a slender, iron instrument, technically classed as
a clapperless bell.)

What about stringed instruments? The earliest jazz bands frequently employed
banjo (see Figure 4.1), an African American instrument that descended from the
African halam. They also employed guitar, which has a European ancestry. The bass
viol was also common in early jazz, and it too came from Europe.

Demo CD *Track 10;*
JCCD1 *Track 7*

Figure 4.1 Guitar and banjo (note that the guitar has six tuning pegs, one for each string, and the banjo has four). Guitars appear in a variety of shapes. Electric guitars are usually solid slabs of wood with electronic attachments embedded. Basically, a banjo has a guitar-like neck and strings attached to a body that consists of a wooden or metal hoop covered with a animal skin head. The banjo commonly used in early jazz had four strings.

Role of Percussion

A fifth feature of jazz is the **prominent role of percussion.** Most jazz groups include a drummer who plays a set of assorted instruments, providing almost continuous time-keeping sounds, thereby generating musical excitement. Drums are very important in much African music, too. And percussion is important in brass band music of European traditions as well as in some European folk dance music, such as Irish.

DVD *Tracks 2–19;* Demo CD *Tracks 1–15, pages 25–29*

A feature related to the role of percussion in jazz is playing melodic instruments in highly rhythmic or percussive ways. Nonpercussion instruments are used in these ways in many other kinds of music, too. But the extent to which melodic instruments are used this way is outstanding in jazz. It resembles the way melody instruments are employed in Africa. Musicologist Olly Wilson has called this *rhythmization*.

Roughenings, Buzzes, and Ringings

A sixth feature of jazz is the presence of **rough sounds, buzzes, and ringings.** Preferences for these kinds of sounds are thought to derive from African musical tastes and African traditions for improvising on tone quality. For instance, jazz drummers sometimes place a key chain atop the ride cymbal to create a sustained hiss or ringing sound. Some drummers insert rivets in a cymbal so that the vibration of the rivets against the cymbal creates a sizzle sound. Many jazz saxophonists cultivate a rasping tone quality. Saxophonist John Coltrane produced a wide range of sound qualities, from smooth to guttural, from full to shrieking. He can be heard in "So What" (*SCCJ*), "Flamenco Sketches," and "The Promise" (*JCCD2* Tracks 9 and 11). Listen for the raw tone qualities of soloists on Duke Ellington's "Harlem Airshaft" and the gruff tone quality of saxophonists Ben Webster on "Cottontail" and Coleman Hawkins on "Voodte" (*JCCD1* Tracks 21, 20, and 18). Compare this with the occasionally rough quality in the male lead singer's voice on "One Day" (*JCCD1* Track 4). On *JCCD1*, you can hear jazz trumpeters and trombonists play in a rough "growl" style: trumpeter Cootie Williams at the beginning of "Cottontail," and trombonist Joe Nanton on "Harlem Airshaft" (Track 21). Listen to the saxophone tone of Albert Ayler in "Ghosts: First Variation" (*JCCD3* Track 2). Other evidence of a taste for rough sounds and buzzes is the jazz brassman's preoccupation with the tone-altering potential of mutes (for example, on *SCCJ*, Joe Oliver's muted cornet solo on "Dippermouth Blues" and Cootie Williams's on "Concerto for Cootie").

DVD *Tracks 8–11*

Appendix B; Demo CD *Tracks 63–68*

Repetition of Brief Patterns

A seventh feature of jazz is the **extensive repetition of brief patterns.** Musicians use the term *ostinato* (from the Italian word for "obstinate") to describe the brief, repetitive patterns we are discussing. Ostinato is common in many different kinds of music, but it is a distinguishing trait of African music and jazz. One example is the ride rhythm (*Demo CD* Track 7; *JCCD1* Track 3). Another example of extensive repetition is the style of figure played by the left hand of the boogie-woogie pianist (*Demo CD* Track 38; Meade Lux Lewis, "Honky Tonk Train" on *SCCJ*). Other examples can be found in brief, repetitive bass figures common to jazz/rock fusion, as in recordings by Herbie Hancock and Weather Report from the 1970s and 1980s. There is extensive repetition of short phrases called *riffs* in some jazz styles of the 1930s and 1940s (*JCCD1* Track 5) as well as in jazz-rock of the 1970s and 1980s (*JCCD1* Track 6). These characteristics came from accompaniment rhythms in the folk music and march music that were popular in America at the same time. Some came from ragtime and military drumming. Using these musical devices contributes to swing feeling. The effect of these devices in African music is so similar to their effect in jazz that

"Chameleon," JCCD3 *Track 7*

...gists believe a taste for this effect was retained in African American culture, ...timately caused these practices to emerge in jazz. Though scholars are not ...us about this, most consider jazz swing feeling to be an African or an African ...n contribution to jazz.

...ythms

... feature of jazz is **the practice of sounding different rhythms at the same** ...articular is the sounding of some rhythms that have a basis of two pulses ...ding other rhythms that have a basis of three pulses, as though sounding a ...thm at the same time as a waltz rhythm. The combination is called a ...n. It contributes to the swing feeling and rhythmic excitement of jazz ...reates tensions within the listener who can neither resist following either ...pulses nor reconcile the two; examples include Louis Armstrong's scat ...Hotter Than That" (*JCCD1* Track 11); Richie Powell's piano comping in "Kiss and Run" (*JCCD2* Track 6); John Coltrane's "The Promise" (*JCCD* Track 11); and in Bill Evans's "Solar" (*JCCD3* Track 3).

"The Promise," JCCD2 | Track 11

Much of the polyrhythmic construction in jazz comes from the inventiveness of the musicians, not necessarily from the imitation of pre-existing models. We know this to be true, for example, in some work by drummers Max Roach and Elvin Jones. But some polyrhythms in early jazz are thought to be borrowed from combinations of rhythms found in ragtime. Note that polyrhythms are also employed in European folk music and concert music that were present in America before jazz originated. And they are prominent in African music. If derived from ragtime, these polyrhythms in jazz have a partly African ancestry because ragtime has roots in an African American banjo tradition and Cuban dance music of the 1800s. Musicologist Olly Wilson believes that jazz musicians' preference for polyrhythmic construction reflects *a tradition retained from African preference for rhythmic contrast.* However, we must not overlook its long use in European music, too, even though it seems somewhat less prominent there than in African music.

The Ways Tones Are Decorated

A ninth feature of jazz is the assortment of **ways in which tones are decorated.** Some of these came to us from practices in European classical, opera, and folk music. Some came by way of West African practices. Some originated in the New World from blending and expanding European and African tendencies. We have already discussed a preference for rough timbres as our sixth feature of jazz. Now let's examine alterations of pitch. Study Tracks 46–58 of the *Demo CD* to understand what is meant by "pitch bending," and "pitch manipulation." Listen until you can identify the occurrence of no vibrato, slow vibrato, fast vibrato, terminal vibrato, drop, scoop, smear, and doit. (See "Alterations of Pitch" on page 49.) Then study the first six minutes of the *JCCD1* set where many examples can be found. Notice them in the music of the street vendor ("Street Cries") letting pitch fall at the end of his notes, the male gospel singer ("One Day") who toys with the pitches at the beginnings of his notes, the clarinetist ("Dixie Jazz Band One-Step") who smears the pitches at the end of his notes, and Miles Davis ("Strawberries") using his horn to imitate the street vendor by placing pitch bends in the middle of his notes. Albert Ayler's "Ghosts: First Variation" (*JCCD3* Track 2) is rich with pitch bends. Listen to this music while you keep in mind the dimensions of sound that the jazz improviser can alter in his tone: duration, intensity, pitch (vibrato is a steady alternation of pitch), quality (roughness, for example), attack (how a note begins), and decay (how a note ends). Listen to the first four selections on the *JCCD1* several times. They go by quickly, but you will notice more decorations of tones each time you listen.

JCCD1 *Tracks 1–4; Demo* CD *Tracks 46–58*

Vibrato

To understand vibrato, imagine a sustained tone as a straight line.

Now imagine the pitch of that tone oscillating, that is, becoming alternately higher and lower. The up and down motion of the line represents the slight changes in pitch which constitute vibrato.

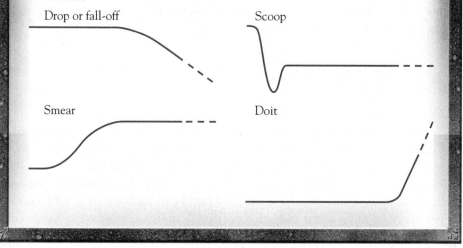 We often tend to take vibrato for granted, because it can be almost imperceptible. But if you listen carefully to sustained tones in the work of most singers, violinists, saxophonists, trombonists, and trumpeters, you will hear it.

Vibrato can be present or absent, fast or slow, regular or irregular. Many jazz singers and some jazz instrumentalists tend to start vibrato slowly and then increase its rate so that it is fastest at the end of the note.

This contrasts with the practice of musicians in symphony orchestras who tend to maintain an even rate of vibrato through a tone's complete duration. They employ different rates of vibrato for different styles of composition, however, and many use no vibrato at all.

Vibrato is considered an expressive device. It can also be a prime characteristic for differentiating styles. Early jazz players tended to use much quicker vibratos than modern jazz players. The fast vibrato was undoubtedly a characteristic contributing to the popular description of early jazz as "hot," while modern jazz of the 1940s and 50s with its slower vibrato was "cool." During the 1960s and 70s, many jazz saxophonists employed faster vibrato than was common during the 1940s and 50s. Saxophonists of the 1980s often used a regular rate of vibrato, rather than increasing it near the end of the tone. If you compare music from these periods, you will notice distinct differences in feeling, partly due to the vibrato rate.

Pitch Bends

Drop or fall-off

Scoop

Smear

Doit

Blue Notes

A tenth feature of jazz is the **blue note.** This is a concept best understood by listening to the examples on the *Demo CD* Tracks 54–58 and studying the discussion in Appendix B. A rough idea of what the term means can be gained by imagining the piano keyboard to represent the entire selection of pitches that musicians are allowed to draw upon. Then imagine how notes would sound if drawn from finer gradations of pitch, as though produced by piano keys existing in the cracks between the ordinary arrangement of keys. The notes that come out from "between the cracks" are blue notes. European music's pitch system, as represented by the piano's seven white keys and five black keys, does not provide all the intervals needed by West African music. Thus, sometimes when Africans performed European-style music, they sang using their own intervals. The sound of these intervals in reference to our ear's expectations was "blue." This is the area of musical performance we call *intonation*. This manner of toying with the pitch of notes is an expressive device that has become a jazz tradition. Though not used by all jazz musicians—they are impossible for pianists—blue notes are common in jazz horn playing. Some of these pitches, which in formal European music constitute "playing out of tune" or "off-key," are common in jazz. They are not ordinarily considered mistakes or the result of incomplete mastery of the musician's instrument. That such "out-of-tune" playing is prominent in so many styles of jazz reflects an esthetic of pitch flexibility more than any player's lack of ability to play "in tune." In other words, the kind of out-of-tune playing found in jazz is usually intentional, and it is used as a central element of the art. This might represent a retention of African or African American musical practices. However, such "neutral" pitches, as they are technically termed, were not exclusive to African traditions. They were also present in Anglo-American and Scotch-Irish folk music that was heard in early America.

Musicologists generally believe that approaches to pitch and tone quality among jazz horn players are not a direct imitation of African singing. They stem instead from imitating wide-ranging, imaginative sounds found in New World vocal idioms such as Negro field hollers, work songs, cries of street vendors, and the blues. The bluesy manipulations of pitch that are found in jazz horn work stem, in part, from imitating approaches to singing that were devised in the New World by blacks, as demonstrated in the first minute of *JCCD1*. In New Orleans, the most bluesy interpretations of dance music were frequently associated with black musicians.[4] Some of this was perpetuated in the humorous, novelty effects ("hokum" style) used by minstrel show musicians. The tendency to playfully vary the sounds of instruments might stem in part from African traditions. However, similar musical traditions also existed in other ethnic groups in New Orleans at the same time, so these practices do not necessarily reflect exclusively African American sources.

Call-and-Response

An eleventh feature of jazz is **call-and-response format.** One member or one section of the band offers a musical phrase that is like a question. Another member or section of the band then follows it with a new phrase that is like an answer. (At about 2'34" on "Cottontail," *JCCD1* Track 20, notice the "question" posed by the brass section and the "answer" offered by the sax section. Listen to the "call" of the bassist and the "response" of the horns in the theme statement of "So What" by Miles Davis in *SCCJ*.) This feature of jazz and African music receives considerable attention from musicologists but is not as common as most of the other features we have discussed. There is an interesting distinction, however, between the type of call and response used in West African music and that used in European music. In West African music, often the sound of the call is still in the air when the response begins. The two parts overlap. And sometimes the call begins again before the response is done, thereby overlapping once more. This causes rhythmic conflict and results in a provocative effect. It is the prominence of *overlapping* call and response, not merely call and response, that distinguishes West African and African American music from music elsewhere. (It is evident in the four excerpts sequenced together at the beginning of *JCCD1*: West African, American Gospel, swing-era riff style, and jazz-rock fusion. Nonoverlapping call and response formats can be found in some styles of band arrangements, as in "Taxi War Dance" and "Cottontail" on *JCCD1* Tracks 20 and 24.)

Handwritten note:
- Blues: Impossible for pianists
- Blue notes are common in jazz horn playing
- Call & Response: Begins with one member singing a question then there is a response back. * "so what" Miles Davis
* Street Cries of ↗ Charleston: fishermen, strawberry, Devil crab

Reissued on *The Riverside History of Cla...* ...en, Strawberry, and Devil Crab" is also on ... ...41, 1958, c1997).

This comparison illustrates traditions for ... ...can vocal and jazz instrumental styles. First is the ... ...the blackberries he is trying to sell. This recording ... ...on, South Carolina. Second is an excerpt from a pie... ...in-strumental version that Miles Davis made in 19... ...era was inspired by African American life in Cha... ...cal sounds of vendors pitching their wares. As a jazz ... ...al, very expressive tone qualities and inflections of ...

CD
TRACK

1	"Street Cries of Charleston" (male street vendor)
2	"Fishermen, Strawberry, and Devil Crab" (Miles Davis trumpet solo)

Call-and-response format is not necessarily a distinguishing feature of improvised combo jazz. What many believe to be a call-and-response kind of communication among group members is in many instances just solo and accompaniment in which the accompaniment follows its own patterns more than it spontaneously generates fresh responses to an improvising soloist. This is revealed when we examine recordings in which the solo line is missing and we discover comping almost identical to that which occurs in the presence of improvised solo lines. Also remember that comping ordinarily derives from a repertory of learned patterns, not necessarily from a spur-of-the-moment response evoked by the call of another musician's sound. (Prior to the Bill Evans Trio of 1961, heard on *JCCD3* Track 3, there was less spontaneous interaction among rhythm section members and less between accompanists and soloists than observers ordinarily believed.) In general, improvised lines are much more a "response" to the challenges of the chord progressions and the player's own ingenuity than to any "call" of another musician.

Some commentators have applied "call-and-response" to describe the function of the phrases that instrumentalists play to fill in a singer's pauses within the 12-bar blues (for example, in Bessie Smith's blues pieces in *SCCJ* or *CCD1* Track 3). However, careful listening reveals that the fills are not necessarily "responses" to the singer's phrases. They merely arrive in sequence with them. Often, they are just improvised lines inspired only by the player's own imagination. They frequently originate from attempts to reconcile horn lines with the underlying chord progressions more than from attempts to establish a musical dialog with the singer. The term "call-and-response" is therefore not always an appropriate designation.

Responsorial singing is a pervasive trait of African music, and it is common in European-derived church music found in America. Call-and-response patterns can be found in classical music and in folk music of many ethnic groups present in America. In summary, call-and-response format can be found in some jazz, and the model for it could reflect any or all of several available sources.

| *Appendix H*

"Hunter's Dance," a West African Folk Number
Reissued on *African Tribal Music & Dances* (Legacy International: 328, CD, 1952, c1993).

"One Day," an American Gospel Singing Number
Recorded for Okeh in 1951 by the Angelic Gospel Singers (four women), the Dixie Hummingbirds (five men), and a pianist; reissued on the anthology *The Gospel Sound* (Columbia/Legacy: C2K 57160, 2CD set, 1926–68, c1994).

"One O'Clock Jump," a Swing-Era Riff Band Number
Recorded for Okeh in 1942 by the Count Basie big band; reissued on Basie, *America's #1 Band* (Columbia/Legacy: C4K 87110, 4CD set, 1936–51, c2003).

"Birdland," a Jazz-Rock Fusion Number
Recorded in 1977 by Weather Report, on Oberheim Polyphonic Synthesizer (Joe Zawinul), soprano sax (Wayne Shorter), bass guitar (Jaco Pastorius), drums (Alex Acuna), and tambourine (Manolo Badrena); reissued on Weather Report, *Heavy Weather* (Columbia/Legacy: CK 65108, 1977, c1997).

These four pieces illustrate several properties that are common to West African music, African American gospel music, swing-era riff-band style, and jazz-rock fusion. Each piece demonstrates extensive repetition of brief patterns, much syncopation, an overlapping call-and-response format, and the capacity to evoke swing feeling in the listener. By the strictest definition, none of these truly qualifies as jazz because not much is improvised. The third and fourth pieces are usually called jazz, though, because they are played by jazz bands and because they swing.

Though call-and-response format is common in many kinds of music, not just African and African American styles, the format in which the response overlaps the call is particularly noticeable in African and African American music. The following examples therefore illustrate *overlapping* call-and-response format, not merely call-and-response.

"Hunter's Dance" is popular peasant music made by the people of Mali, also known as the Malinke people. To obtain this music, in 1952 ethnomusicologist Gilbert Rouget journeyed to Karala, a relatively isolated native village in the West African country of Guinea. The recording features a six-string harp-lute (dozo-konu), the voice of the man who plays it, a women's chorus accompanying him, a wooden whistle (fere), and a metal scraper (karinyan), which is a small tube of wrought iron that is slit down the middle. The karinyan is held in the left hand and struck with a nail held in the right hand, playing a rhythm similar to the jazz drummer's ride rhythm.

When listening to "Hunter's Dance," notice that the rhythms of the different parts are carefully calculated to achieve a provocative effect that is peculiarly African. Also notice how the music's excitement increases as the performance evolves and more layers of activity are added.

CD TRACK	ELAPSED TIME	"Hunter's Dance"
3	0'00"	repeating bass figure, obtained by plucking the strings of the dozo-konu; accompanied by a repeating rhythm on the metallic sounding karinyan
	0'15"	melody sung by the male voice
	0'20"	response sung by women's chorus
	0'23"	Before the response is complete, the male voice begins to sing again (thus the expression "overlapping call and response").

LISTENING GUIDE continued on next page

	0'27"	Women's chorus responds again.
	0'28"	whistle sounds
	0'30"	Male voice returns.

"One Day"

4

As in all the pieces of this African American sequence, the music's excitement increases over the course of the performance as more parts are layered on top of each other, each part's rhythms tugging at the others' in a provocative way. Tremendous spirit and exuberance are projected by this music. Ultimately the music sounds almost like it is going to break apart in wild abandon.

Here are a few highlights. The intensity and momentum are unrelenting, and they occur without the assistance of any bass or drums. Though highly rhythmic piano accompaniment is in the background, the manner in which the singers produce their rhythms is so compelling that they could probably swing without any accompaniment at all. Male voice is in the foreground, though its sound eases in and out of the sounds of background singers answering its phrases. Notice the tendency of the male lead singer to smear up into the pitch of the main notes. This gliding through the pitch range is a very expressive device he uses expertly. Also note the raspy timbre the male singer uses for one of his phrases. This is a preference that is also common to West African singers and musicians. The entrances of the lead singer are highly syncopated, and these syncopations are timed to evoke maximum swing feeling and rhythmic conflict. The responsorial chorus provides the repeating riff in this selection. Notice that the call-and-response pattern doubles in rate near the end, and finally a woman's voice soars high over the proceedings as one more element to tug at the beat and generate excitement. (A similar device is used at the end of "Birdland.")

"One O'Clock Jump"

5

This is a riff-band piece from the swing era. The original 1937 version of it was a big hit. Excerpted here are the ninth and tenth choruses in 12-bar blues form. Several different riffs are played against each other at the same time by different sections of the band: trombones, trumpets, and saxophones. This illustrates the principle of antiphony, literally "against sounds." Saxes play a syncopated figure, as though answering the trombone phrase. Trumpets play a different riff that is also syncopated, as though on the opposite end of a see-saw from the trombones. A timekeeping foundation is provided by piano, rhythm guitar, walking bass, and the drummer using sticks to play ride rhythms on opening and closing high hat. The overlapping of these parts generates rhythmic excitement.

"Birdland"

6

"Birdland" is in a style called jazz-rock fusion. This performance is excerpted from Weather Report's best-selling recording, a discotheque hit. For many years this piece continued to be copied and re-arranged by numerous ensembles, including the singing group Manhattan Transfer. Excerpted here is the chorus of the piece, the melody of which is played by sax, synthesizer, bass guitar, and voice. The chords in the accompaniment are provided by the synthesizer. Percussion accompaniment includes hand claps on beats two and four, tambourine providing steady eighth notes, and the sound of open high-hat cymbal struck with drum stick on upbeats, snapped shut on downbeats. In addition to doubling the melody, bass guitar fills in the gaps between the notes and phrases of the melody. A high-pitched male voice (bass guitarist Jaco Pastorius) sustains tones over the ensemble sound, offering a countermelody.

CHAPTER SUMMARY

1. Jazz originated in New Orleans around the beginning of the twentieth century.

2. New Orleans was the ideal site for the birth of jazz because it was an intensely musical city with a history of rich ethnic diversity, especially French and African.

3. Jazz emerged when brass bands were at a zenith of popularity and ragtime was in such high demand that brass bands and string bands were improvising rag-like syncopations into their pieces to please dancers.

4. African American forms of music such as the blues and ragtime blended with European dance music and church music.

5. Jazz has features that reflect African musical tastes that were retained in African American music—improvisation, syncopation, rough timbres, extensive repetition of brief patterns, polyrhythms, and overlapping call-and-response format.

6. Jazz reflects European music's instruments, chord progressions, and improvisation.

7. Blending of European and African practices resulted in blue notes and various decorations of a note by altering its pitch.

NOTES

1. Jazz originated in the blends of folk music, popular music, and light classical music that were current near the beginning of the twentieth century, especially in New Orleans. Collections that are useful for illustrating these styles include (items are compact discs unless otherwise indicated):

Come and Trip It: Instrumental Dance Music 1780s–1920s. New World: 80293, c1978.

Early Band Ragtime: Ragtime's Biggest Hits, 1899–1909. Smithsonian/Folkways: RBF 38, c1979.

Jazz. Vol. 1, *The South.* Smithsonian/Folkways: 2801, c1950.

Jazz. Vol. 2, *The Blues.* Smithsonian/Folkways: 2802, 1923–48, c1956.

Jazz: Some Beginnings. Smithsonian/Folkways: RF 31, 1914–26, c1977.

History of Classic Jazz. Riverside/Fantasy: 005, 3CD set, ca. 1900–1956, c1994 (Disc 1, Track 2).

The Sousa and Pryor Bands: Original Recordings, 1901–1926. New World: NW 282, LP, 1901–26, c1976 (out of print).

Steppin' on the Gas: Rags to Jazz. New World: NW 269, LP, 1913–27, c1978 (out of print) (side 1 only).

That's My Rabbit, My Dog Caught It: Traditional Southern Instrumental Styles. New World: NW 226, LP, 1925–77, c1978 (out of print).

Note: New World Records (Recorded Anthology of American Music) may be found in many college libraries; the Rockefeller Foundation donated sets to many educational institutions. Folkways records are in many music libraries. Liner notes for all New World albums are available at: *www.newworldrecords.org.*

Basic Texts on African Music

(The most useful texts for a jazz appreciation course are listed first.)

NKETIA, J.H. KWABENA. *The Music of Africa.* Norton, 1974.

NKETIA, J.H. KWABENA, and JACQUELINE COGGELL DJEDJE, ed. *Selected Reports in Ethnomusicology.* Vol. 5, *Studies in African Music.* Los Angeles, CA: Program in Ethnomusicology, Department of Music, Univ. of California, 1984.

BEBEY, FRANCIS. *African Music: A People's Art.* L. Hill, 1975.

KEBEDE, ASHENAFI. *Roots of Black Music: The Vocal, Instrumental, and Dance Heritage of Africa and Black America.* Prentice-Hall, 1982; Africa World Press, 1995.

JONES, A.M. *Studies in African Music.* Vols. 1 and 2. Oxford Univ., 1959, 1978.

ROBERTS, JOHN STORM. *Black Music of Two Worlds.* 2nd ed. Schirmer, 1998. Accompanying compact discs: *Black Music of Two Worlds,* Smithsonian/Folkways: 4602, 3CD set, c1977.

OLIVER, PAUL, et al. *Yonder Come the Blues: The Evolution of a Genre.* Cambridge, 2001. Reprints *Savannah Syncopators: African Retentions in the Blues* (Stein and Day, 1970) and two other books with added material. Accompanying 2-LP set: *Savannah Syncopators,* Columbia (UK): 52799.

CHERNOFF, JOHN MILLER. *African Rhythm and Sensibility: Aesthetics and Social Action in African Musical Idioms.* Univ. of Chicago, 1979, 1981. With accompanying audio cassette examples.

GAYLE, ADDISON. *The Black Aesthetic.* Doubleday, 1971.

Important Scholarly Papers About African Music

Many important insights and much of the most solid research data never find their way into full-length textbooks. Much scholarly thinking and data gathering are available only in papers read at professional conferences, rewritten for professional journals. A few of such works are included below. If your library does not carry these journals, ask your reference librarian to request the article via inter-library loan. Frequently a copy can be sent to you for free or a small fee from a library that holds the journal you seek.

(The most useful papers for a jazz appreciation course are listed first.)

WATERMAN, RICHARD A. "Hot Rhythm in Negro Music." *Journal of the American Musicological Society* 1 (1948): 24–37. Based on a paper delivered December 28, 1943.

____. "African Influence on the Music of the Americas." In *Anthropology and Art: Readings in Cross Cultural Aesthetics*. ed. Charlotte M. Otten, 227–44. Univ. of Texas, 1976. Reprinted from *Acculturation in the Americas: Proceedings and Selected Papers of the XXIX International Congress of Americanists*, ed. Sol Tax, Univ. of Chicago, 1952. Paper delivered in 1951.

____. "On Flogging a Dead Horse: Lessons Learned from the Africanisms Controversy." *Ethnomusicology* 7 (1963): 83–87.

EVANS, DAVID. "African Elements in Twentieth Century United States Black Folk Music." In *International Musicological Society, Report of the Twelfth Congress, Berkeley, 1977*, 54–66. Barenreiter, 1981.

TALLMADGE, WILLIAM. "Blue Notes and Blue Tonality." *The Black Perspective in Music* 12 (1984): 155–65.

KAUFMAN, ROBERT. "African Rhythm: A Reassessment" *Ethnomusicology* 24 (1980): 393–415.

EPSTEIN, DENA J. "The Folk Banjo." *Ethnomusicology* 19 (1975): 347–372.

GRIDLEY, MARK C., and WALLACE RAVE. "Towards Identification of African Traits in Early Jazz." *The Black Perspective in Music* 12 (1984): 44–56.

WILSON, OLLY. "The Significance of the Relationship Between Afro-American Music and West African Music." *The Black Perspective in Music* 2 (1974): 3–23.

____. "Black Music as an Art Form." *Black Music Research Journal* 3 (1983): 1–22.

Note: *Black Music Research Journal* is published by Center for Black Music Research, Columbia College Chicago, 600 South Michigan Ave, Chicago, IL 60605-1996.

WILLIAMS-JONES, PEARL. "Afro-American Gospel Music: A Crystallization of the Black Aesthetic." *Ethnomusicology* 19 (1975): 373–86.

HALL, GWENDOLYN MIDLO. *Africans in Colonial Louisiana: The Development of Afro-Creole Culture in the Eighteenth Century*. Louisiana State Univ., 1992.

HIRSCH, ARNOLD R., AND JOSEPH LOGSDON, ed. *Creole New Orleans: Race and Americanization*. Louisiana State Univ., 1992.

JACOBS, CLAUDE. "Benevolent Societies of New Orleans Blacks During the Late Nineteenth and Early Twentieth Centuries." *Louisiana History, Journal of the Louisiana Historical Association* 29, No. 1, 1988.

JOYAUX, GEORGE J., ed. "Forest's Voyage aux Etats-Unis de l'Amerique en 1831." *Louisiana Historical Quarterly* 39, No. 4, 1956.

LATROBE, BENJAMIN HENRY. *Impressions Respecting New Orleans, Diaries & Sketches 1818–1820*, ed. Sam Wilson, Jr. Columbia Univ., 1951.

FLOYD, SAMUEL A., JR., and MARTHA J. REISSER. "The Sources and Resources of Classic Ragtime Music." *Black Music Research Journal* 4 (1984): 22–59.

See above address for Center for Black Music Research.

EPSTEIN, DENA. "Black Spirituals: Their Emergence into Public Knowledge." *Black Music Research Newsletter* 8 (1986): 5–8. See above for address of Center for Black Music Research.

CRONBACH, LEE. "Structural Polytonality in Contemporary Afro-American Music." *Black Music Research Journal* 2 (1981–2): 15–33.

KOETTING, JAMES. "What Do We Know About African Rhythm?" *Ethnomusicology* 30 (1986): 58–63.

STONE, RUTH. "The Value of Local Ideas in Understanding West African Rhythm." *Ethnomusicology* 30 (1986): 54–57.

Early African American Culture and New Orleans

(The most useful items for a jazz appreciation course are listed first.)

EPSTEIN, DENA. "A White Origin for the Black Spiritual? An Invalid Theory and How It Grew." *American Music* 1 (1983): 53–59.

LOMAX, ALAN. *Mister Jelly Roll: The Fortunes of Jelly Roll Morton, New Orleans Creole and "Inventor of Jazz."* Duell, Sloan and Pearce, 1949; Univ. of California, 2001.

BERLIN, EDWARD A. *Reflections and Research on Ragtime*. I.S.A.M. Monographs, No. 24. Institute for Studies in American Music, Conservatory of Music, Brooklyn College, 1987.

GARST, JOHN F. "Mutual Reinforcement and the Origins of Spirituals." *American Music* 4 (1986): 390–406.

FOSTER, GEORGE M. *Pops Foster: The Autobiography of a New Orleans Jazzman as Told to Tom Stoppard*. Univ. of California, 1971.

SEALSFIELD, CHARLES. *The Americans as They Are: Described in a Tour Through the Valley of the Mississippi*. London: Hurst, Chance & Co., 1828; reprinted in Sealsfield, *The United States of North America as They Are. The Americans as They Are*. Olms Presse, 1972.

SCHAFER, WILLIAM, and RICHARD B. ALLEN. *Brass Bands and New Orleans Jazz*. Louisiana State Univ., 1977.

RIGHTOR, HENRY, ed. *Standard History of New Orleans, Louisiana, Giving a Description of the Natural Advantages, Natural History*. Chicago: Lewis Pub., 1900.

SHAPIRO, NAT, and NAT HENTOFF, ed. *Hear Me Talkin' to Ya: The Story of Jazz by the Men Who Made It*. Reinhart, 1955; Dover, 1966.

MARQUIS, DONALD M. *In Search of Buddy Bolden: First Man of Jazz*. Louisiana State Univ., 1978, 1993.

GUSHEE, LAWRENCE. *Pioneers of Jazz: The Story of the Creole Band*. Oxford Univ., 2005.

KOENIG, KARL. *Jazz in Print (1856–1929): An Anthology of Selected Early Readings in Jazz History*. Pendragon, 2002.

SMITH, MICHAEL. P. *Spirit World: Pattern in the Expressive Folk Culture of African-American New Orleans*. Gretna, LA: Pelican Pub. Co., 1992.

SMITH, MICHAEL P. *Mardi Gras Indians*. Gretna: Pelican Pub. Co., 1994.

SOUTHERN, EILEEN. *The Music of Black Americans: A History*. 3rd ed. Norton, 1997.

STERKX, H.E. *The Free Negro in Antebellum Louisiana*. Fairleigh Dickinson Univ., 1972.

EPSTEIN, DENA J. *Sinful Tunes and Spirituals: Black Folk Music to the Civil War*. Univ. of Illinois, 1977, 2003.

BLASSINGAME, JOHN W. *The Slave Community: Plantation Life in the Antebellum South*. rev. and enl. ed. Oxford, 1979.

KOENIG, KARL. "The Plantation Belt Brass Bands and Musicians." *The Second Line* 33 (1981): 24–40. Back issues of *The Second Line* are available from Hogan Jazz Archive, 304 Jones Hall, Tulane University, 6801 Freret Street, New Orleans, LA 70118; phone 504-865-5688; fax 504-865-5761; *www.tulane.edu/~lmiller/JazzHome.html*.

____. "Professor James B. Humphrey." *The Second Line* 34 (1982): 15–19.

____. "Chris Kelly, Blues King of New Orleans." *The Second Line* 35 (spring 1983): 4–26.

____. "Louisiana Brass Bands and History in Relation to Jazz History." *The Second Line* 35 (summer 1983): 7–15.

____. "John Philip Sousa's Impact on Jazz." *The Second Line* 35 (winter 1983): 39–41.

_____. "Jack Laine 'Papa.'" *The Mississippi Rag* (March 1984): 1–6. **Note:** *The Mississippi Rag* back issues are available from 9448 Lyndale Ave., S. Suite 120, Bloomington, MN 55420, phone 952-885-9918, fax 952-885-9943, web *www.mississippirag.com.*

Note: Informative summaries and bibliographies are included in H. Wiley Hitchcock and Stanley Sadie, ed., *The New Grove Dictionary of American Music* (Macmillan, 1986). See entries for New Orleans, Blues, Traditional Jazz, Spirituals, and Ragtime, as well as the entries for particular musicians.

Album Liner Notes That Summarize Pre-Jazz and Early Jazz Research

(Annotator's name is in parentheses. The most useful items for a jazz appreciation course are listed first. Items are compact discs unless otherwise stated.)

The Riverside History of Classic Jazz. (Charles Edward Smith). Riverside/Fantasy: 005, 3CD set, 1956, c1994.

The Roots of the Blues. (Alan Lomax). New World: 80252, c1977.

Steppin' on the Gas: Rags to Jazz 1913–1927. (Lawrence Gushee). New World: NW 269, LP, c1977 (out of print).

OLIVER, JOE "KING." *King Oliver's Jazz Band, 1923.* (Lawrence Gushee). Smithsonian: 2001, 2LP set, 1923, c1975 (out of print).

KEPPARD, FREDDIE. *Legendary New Orleans Cornet.* (Lawrence Gushee). Smithsonian: 2020, LP, 1924–1927, c1979 (out of print).

Roots of Black Music in America. (Samuel Charters). Smithsonian/Folkways: 2694, 2CD set, c1972.

Come and Trip It: Instrumental Dance Music 1780s–1920s. (Thorton Hagert). New World: 80293, c1978.

Georgia Sea Island Songs. (Alan Lomax). New World: 80278, c1977.

Note: Liner notes for all New World albums are available at their website: *www.newworldrecords.com.*

Recordings to Aid in Understanding African Music

Here is a brief compilation of available recordings that help connect jazz and African music. It is far from definitive, but it could get you started if you need materials for an ethnomusicologically oriented course in jazz or African American music. In pursuing the items on this list, note that ordinary record stores and most mail order houses do not sell these records, but you can get them from specialty houses and importers. Frequently it is best to order directly from mail order services. To obtain the French Ocora records, contact: Harmonia Mundi USA, 1117 Chestnut Street, Burbank, CA 91506; phone: 818-333-1500; web: *www.harmoniamundi.com.* If a large music library exists near you, it may be helpful to contact the reference librarian there for the names and addresses of dealers who service the library's ethnomusicology needs.

Many of the best recordings of African music and pre-jazz have been out of print for ages and are not listed here, though you might find them in libraries. One that is particularly worth seeking is *Anthology of Music of Black Africa* (Everest: 3254/3, 2LP set, c1969), half of which was originally issued in France as *Musique D'Afrique Occidentale* (Vogue: LVLX 193, LP, c[195?]), and reissued on CD: *African Tribal Music and Dances* (Legacy International: 328, 1952, c1993).

Note: If you choose illustrations not listed here, keep in mind that the music of Africa is very diverse, and that music from West Africa is the most relevant for your purposes. Stick to Gambia, Senegal, Guinea, Ivory Coast, Ghana, and Nigeria. Otherwise, you risk generalizing from music that may have had little or no influence

on jazz because the culture that produced it contributed few slaves to America.

These records are all interesting, and most contain informative notes:

Africa, South of the Sahara. Smithsonian/Folkways: 4503, 2CD set, c1957. (Compilation by Harold Courlander of numerous cultures, with richly detailed notes prepared by the eminent Africanist Alan P. Merriam; only some examples are from West Africa.)

Africa, the Dan. Anthology of World Music. Rounder: 5105 (Barenreiter Musicaphon BM 30 L 2301), 1966, c1998 (recorded by Hugo Zemp; people of Ivory Coast and Liberia).

African Journey: A Search for the Roots of the Blues. Sonet: SNTF 667 (Vanguard 73014/73015), 1974. (Compilation of various West African cultures visited by Samuel Charters and described in his travelogue: Charters, *The Roots of the Blues: An African Search* [Boston: M. Boyars, 1981; New York: DaCapo, 1991].)

Black Music of Two Worlds. Smithsonian/Folkways: 4602, 3CD set, c1977. (Contains music of Ghana, Sierra Leone, Liberia, as well as music from many areas of the New World; accompanies the book: John Storm Roberts, *Black Music of Two Worlds,* 2nd ed. [Schirmer, 1998].)

Cote d'Ivoire: Musique Des Baoule-Kode. Ocora: OCR 34, LP, 1961, c1982 (the Baule people of the Ivory Coast).

Drums of West Africa: Ritual Music of Ghana, Lyrichord: 7307, LP/AC, 1974–76 (music of the Ewe people). **Note:** Order from Lyrichord Discs, Inc., PO Box 1977, Old Chelsea Station, New York, NY 10011-1726; phone: 212-929-8234; fax: 212-929-8245; web: *www.lyrichord.com.*

The Griots: Ministers of the Spoken Word. Smithsonian/Folkways: 4178, 2CD set, 1974, c1975 (vocal music of Gambia, Senegal, and Mali collected by Samuel Charters).

Masques Dan: Cote d'Ivoire. Ocora: 580048 (OCR 52), 1965–1967, c1993 (music from Ivory Coast; French import distributed by Harmonia Mundi USA).

Music from Gambia. Vol. 1. Smithsonian/Folkways: 4521, 2CD set, 1971–72, c1978.

The Music of Nigeria: Hausa Music. UNESCO Collection, Anthology of African Music, Vol. 6. Barenreiter Musicaphon: BM 30 L 2306, LP, c1965 (the Hausa people of Nigeria).

Music of the Cameroons. Smithsonian/Folkways: 4372, 1959, c1961.

The Music of the Senufo. UNESCO Collection, Anthology of African Music, vol. 8. Barenreiter Musicaphon: BM 30 L 2308, LP, c1965 (people of Ivory Coast, Upper Volta, and Mali).

Musiques du Cameroun. Ocora: OCR 25, LP, 1965, c1965 (people of the Cameroons).

Roots of Black Music in America. Smithsonian/Folkways: 2694, 2CD set, c1972. (Wide range of African and African American music with lengthy and well-documented notes by Samuel Charters.)

Songs of War and Death from the Slave Coast: Abutia Kloe, Ewe, Ghana. Smithsonian/Folkways: 4258/4259, 2CD set, c1982 (music of the Ewe people of Ghana).

Togo: Music from West Africa. Rounder: 5004, 1978, c1991 (music of the Ewe people).

Wolof Music of Senegal and the Gambia. Smithsonian/Folkways: 4462, c1955.

2. Though the plantation system of labor was nonexistent in name, the plantations still operated with hired labor, and most of the plantations hired bandmasters/teachers to instruct these hired hands and to form bands. Many early jazz musicians received their musical training there.

3. The players may have done much without referring to written scores. However, the absence of notation in these situations should not be taken as evidence of improvisation any more than we would consider "improvised" the music of today's wedding bands and lounge acts that sometimes play fresh routines without notation. Research by Karl Koenig has shown that most early New Orleans jazz musicians could read music well enough to work out the notes and fingerings, though they could not necessarily sight read fast. Some could not read music, however, and most chose not to read pieces once they had been learned.

4. You might be able to detect blue notes in the Joe Oliver cornet solo on "Dippermouth Blues" in *SCCJ*. There are many Rex Stewart cornet solos which use blue notes on Duke Ellington records from the 1930s and 1940s. His "Boy Meets Horn" is the most famous example. Modern trumpeter Miles Davis is also particularly known for using blue notes. Listen to "Strawberries" on Davis, *Porgy and Bess* (Columbia/Legacy), excerpted on *JCCD1*, or "Solea" on Davis, *Sketches of Spain* (Columbia/Legacy). During the 1970s, Don Ellis played on a specially made trumpet that, by the addition of an extra valve, could produce quarter tones, those "notes in the cracks." Ordinarily, trumpeters had tried to achieve the same sound by depressing their trumpet key halfway, thereby leaving a cocked valve. However, they could not depend on obtaining this result consistently. The Ellis trumpet managed a similar effect, but much more reliably.

The earliest jazz musicians took liberties with the tunes and the accompaniments in their performances. Their new ideas and embellishments sometimes became more important to a performance than the tunes themselves. This trend evolved across the 1920s, and in some performances of the 1930s all that remained of the original was the tune's spirit and chord progressions. What is today called improvising was referred to by early jazz musicians as "messin' around," embellishing, "jassing," or "jazzing up."

The earliest jazz had roots in ragtime, blues, and brass band music. But after a few years, several important differences were heard:

1. Much of each performance was improvised.

2. Rhythmic feeling was looser and more relaxed, thus anticipating jazz swing feeling.

3. It generated some of its own repertory of compositions.

4. Its collectively improvised format created a more complex musical product than was typical in ragtime, blues, or brass band music.

5. The earliest jazz was even more exciting than ragtime, blues, or brass band music.

Original Dixieland Jazz Band
(Photo courtesy of William Ransom Hogan Jazz Archive, Tulane University)

TABLE 5.1   A Few of the Many Early Jazz Musicians

TRUMPET
Buddy Bolden
Freddie Keppard
Joe "King" Oliver
Louis Armstrong
Wingy Manone
Red Nichols
Bix Beiderbecke
Tommy Ladnier
Henry "Red" Allen
Joe Smith
Bubber Miley
Charlie Teagarden
Jabbo Smith
Nick LaRocca
Paul Mares
George Mitchell
Sidney DeParis
Muggsy Spanier
Phil Napoleon
Wild Bill Davidson
Mutt Carey

DRUMS
Baby Dodds
Papa Jack Laine
Paul Barbarin
Zutty Singleton
Sonny Greer
Dave Tough
George Wettling
Ben Pollack
Andrew Hilaire
Chauncey Morehouse
Gene Krupa
Vic Berton
Ray Bauduc
Tony Sbarbaro

COMPOSER-ARRANGER

Kid Ory
Jelly Roll Morton
W.C. Handy
Clarence Williams
Fats Waller

VIOLIN

Joe Venuti

BASS
Pops Foster
Wellman Braud
John Lindsay

TROMBONE
Kid Ory
J.C. Higginbotham
Miff Mole
Jack Teagarden
Fred Robinson
Charlie Green
Jimmy Harrison
Charlie Irvis
Joe "Tricky Sam"
    Nanton
George Brunis
Bill Rank
Tommy Dorsey
Glenn Miller
Wilbur DeParis
Eddie Edwards
Honore Dutrey

CLARINET AND SAXOPHONE
Johnny Dodds
Sidney Bechet
Jimmie Noone
Frank Teschemacher
Benny Goodman
Albert Nicholas
Barney Bigard
Omer Simeon
Alphonse Picou
Mezz Mezzrow
Jimmy Strong
Sidney Arodin
Darnell Howard
Leon Rappolo
Buster Bailey
Don Redman
Bud Freeman
Floyd Towne
Coleman Hawkins
Jimmy Dorsey
Hilton Jefferson
Stump Evans
Charlie Holmes
Larry Shields
Pee Wee Russell
Adrian Rollini
Don Murray
Tony Parenti
Izzy Friedman
Min Leibrook
Cecil Scott
Frankie Trumbauer
Edmond Hall
Gene Sedric
George Lewis

GUITAR AND BANJO
Lonnie Johnson
Johnny St. Cyr
Elmer Snowden
Eddie Lang
Eddie Condon

PIANO
James P. Johnson
Fate Marable
Jelly Roll Morton
Willie "The Lion"
    Smith
Fats Waller
Lil Hardin Armstrong
Pete Johnson
Clarence Williams
Meade Lux Lewis
Albert Ammons
Cripple Clarence
    Lofton
Cow Cow Davenport
Elmer Schoebel
Pinetop Smith
Jimmy Yancey
Earl Hines
Frank Signorelli
Fletcher Henderson
Joe Sullivan
Jimmy Blythe
Henry Ragas

Combo jazz began in New Orleans, and that city contributed several soloists of far-reaching significance. The best known were trumpeter Louis Armstrong and clarinetist-saxophonist Sidney Bechet. Jelly Roll Morton was the most significant composer-arranger from New Orleans, and his finest recordings were made during the 1920s in Chicago. New combinations of musicians in Chicago also made several

WHAT IS AFRICAN AND WHAT IS EUROPEAN ABOUT JAZZ?

Most innovators in jazz have been African American and, until recently, a disproportionately high percentage of jazz musicians has been African American. These facts lead us to ask whether jazz contains characteristics of African music that might have filtered into it through the African American culture that produced so many of its practitioners. The question is impossible to answer, however, because African music and European music have so many elements in common and because both were available as models when jazz was forming. But it remains interesting to consider the possibilities. So now we are going to examine eleven features of jazz, keeping in mind African and European sources.

FEATURES OF JAZZ

1. Improvisation
2. Syncopation
3. Harmony
4. Instruments
5. Role of percussion
6. Rough tone qualities

7. Repetition of brief patterns
8. Polyrhythms
9. Decorations of tone
10. Blue notes
11. Overlapping call and response

Joe "King" Oliver's Creole Jazz Band, 1923: Baby Dodds (drums), Honoré Dutrey (trombone), Oliver (cornet), Louis Armstrong (cornet), Bill Johnson (bass viol), Johnny Dodds (clarinet), Lil Hardin (piano)

(Photo courtesy of The Cleveland Press Collection/Cleveland State University Archives)

Improvisation

The first feature of jazz we are going to examine is improvisation, the practice of **spontaneously varying individual parts.** It has been an important element of music since the beginning of time, and only recently in history was it difficult to find in European concert music. Improvisation characterizes some African music and much jazz. Musicologists are uncertain about the extent to which African American music retained improvisatory traditions from African music. Let's first consider improvisation in music of cultures that contributed slaves to the New World. For instance, in the typical drum ensemble of Ghana, the lead drummer is in charge of giving signals. His part is more variable than any of the others, so it might be regarded as improvised. In the Mandinka drum ensemble, the senior player has leeway to improvise more than the others, but all members are allowed to slightly vary their parts as they play. Some African singing in leader-and-chorus format allows spontaneous variations in the leader's part. To keep this in perspective, however, consider that these practices come nowhere near the extent of improvisation that is found today in jazz. In the West African singing and the African American blues singing that evolved from it, improvisations did not consist of inventing elaborate melody lines as eventually became common for jazz improvisers. Instead, these singers channeled their creativity into altering the sound of a single sustained tone, varying the timing, pitch, and timbre at its beginning and ending. They also improvised by toying with the rhythms of melodies. Tones would be started a bit earlier or later. Or a given tone might be repeated several times in succession instead of being sung only once. Similarly, a tone might be started, then softened, and then pushed again by an abrupt increase in volume. Sometimes whole phrases would be placed differently in relation to the underlying beat. This is known as *rhythmic displacement.* Incidentally, these techniques are still evident in performances of gospel music by African American singers and in gospel-influenced styles of pop music, such as the singing of Aretha Franklin and James Brown, particularly in the famous renditions of "Georgia on My Mind" and "America the Beautiful" by Ray Charles.

The reason we discuss singing at this point in a textbook about instrumental jazz is that these vocal practices are thought to have influenced the styles used by jazz musicians who played trumpet, trombone, clarinet, and saxophone. (That is why the beginning of *JCCD1* has an instrumental demonstration by Miles Davis directly following the cry of the African American street vendor.) Individual creativity and unorthodox means for learning how to play instruments have also been suggested as roots for pitch and timbre improvisation in horn work. Some musicologists believe that demand for live music was so great in New Orleans that many unpolished amateurs were called upon to perform as professionals, and the incomplete mastery these players had over their instruments gave us the collection of raw, unorthodox sounds we now associate with New Orleans jazz. Imitation of singing style, however, is the most popular explanation among musicologists. In addition, some scholars believe that the spirit of improvisation and the stress on individuality in jazz stem from African traditions. But these traits are also found in America within non-African folk music as well. So a striving for individuality among jazz musicians could be, but is not necessarily or exclusively, an extension of African preferences or what has been called "the black esthetic."

Now let's consider what European music could have contributed to the origins of improvisation in jazz. In America there was already a well-developed European tradition for improvising by the time jazz had begun. Improvised ornaments were common in pre-twentieth century concert music, and they have long been common in folk music and popular music. Within informal American music prior to the emergence of

"Hunter's Dance," JCCD1 *Track 3*

"Street Cries," *"Hunter's Dance," and* *"One Day," JCCD1* *Tracks 1, 3, and 4*

jazz, there are also precedents for improvisation in the form of musicians making spontaneously varied entrances. Often singers start notes whenever they feel like it instead of singing precisely in unison with the others. This is termed *heterophony*, sounding to our ears like ensemble "sloppiness." It is also notable that improvised variations were common parts of solo recital format for some keyboard artists. During the 1800s, concert pianists often improvised within the encore number of their program. And there existed a French and German keyboard tradition for improvisation called *preluding*. Some early American musicians were even required to be able to improvise a piece on demand, using phrases supplied by their audience. So it is clear that the practice of making up music as you go along is precedented in both West African and European music. Both of these traditions could have influenced the use of improvisation in jazz.

Now consider improvisation among New Orleans musicians at the beginning of the twentieth century. At least as late as 1923, the improvisational creativity of the players was directed primarily at piecing together band routines. Some routines, however, were spontaneously devised during performances, thereby qualifying as improvised. The skeletons for these routines were often provided by published arrangements that were known among musicians as "stocks." For the first few run-throughs, many of the parts were not fixed. Trombone counterlines, clarinet obbligatos, and trumpet variations of the melody were sometimes invented and performed spontaneously. Accompaniments were improvised and varied by the more adventurous and creative players. After a suitable set of parts had been worked out, the musicians frequently remained relatively loyal to them. A striving for improvisation was not as central to a jazz esthetic as it has become. The extent to which new melodies were freshly improvised during performance was limited. There was, however, a striving for personalization and individualization which did not require improvisation, at least in the sense that the term is used here. Though the seeds were planted in New Orleans, it is possible that the kind and the extent of jazz improvisation known today did not first emerge there.[3]

By the late 1920s, these improvisational tendencies had expanded to the extent of improvisation we usually expect from most jazz today. Unfortunately, we do not know why this change occurred. A few possibilities are (1) boredom with fixed routines; (2) a need to learn new material without recourse to sheet music; (3) increased interest in bravura solo excursions and emergence of the "star" system of players; (4) a continuation of European and/or African traditions for spontaneous alteration; (5) unbridled creativity; (6) longer dances necessitating stretching out the numbers, that, in turn, led to solos that give other hornmen time to rest their lips; and (7) a combination of these reasons.

Syncopation

Next let's consider **syncopation,** a rhythmic phenomenon most easily understood as accents that don't occur on a main beat. (To hear the difference between unsyncopated and syncopated playing, listen to the piano comping demonstrations on *Demo CD Track 20*.) Syncopation is common in both African and European music, though Africa is especially known for highly syncopated music. Some syncopation in jazz is thought to derive from African American banjo music and ragtime. Some is thought to stem from the heterophony discussed above. The taste for syncopation that exists among jazz musicians might stem, in part, from musical preferences for *rhythmic contrast*, which musicologist Olly Wilson has shown to prevail among many African and African American styles of music.

Appendix B; Demo CD Track 20

Harmony

Appendix B; Demo CD
Tracks 16–19

A third feature of jazz is **harmony.** Though harmony is found in African music, the chord progressions in jazz are not common to native African music. European music provided chord progressions of the type that jazz uses.

Instruments

A fourth feature of jazz is the choice of instruments. Where did the earliest jazz groups derive their **instrumentation**? The European brass band provided the model that included trumpet, trombone, clarinet, saxophone, and tuba. The black and the white fraternal bands that were plentiful in New Orleans at the beginning of the twentieth century used brass band instrumentation, and they played marches and pop tunes for parades, picnics, dances, and funerals. The region of Africa that supplied slaves for the New World did not have musical instruments that closely resembled the trumpet, clarinet, trombone, or saxophone.

Demo CD Track 10;
JCCD1 Track 7

What about drums? The drums of West Africa can be found in some modern jazz groups. The drums used in the earliest jazz, however, were from European-style brass bands. (See illustrations in the previous chapter.) The wood block and cowbell, (heard on "Dixie Jazz Band One-Step") two other percussion instruments used in the manner of drums, have been heard in jazz since the earliest recordings. They are thought to have African ancestry, though China and Turkey have also contributed forerunners for many similar instruments in the New World. (Incidentally, the way the ride cymbal is used in jazz is very similar to the way West African musicians play their atoke or karinyan, a slender, iron instrument, technically classed as a clapperless bell.)

What about stringed instruments? The earliest jazz bands frequently employed banjo (see Figure 4.1), an African American instrument that descended from the African halam. They also employed guitar, which has a European ancestry. The bass viol was also common in early jazz, and it too came from Europe.

Figure 4.1 Guitar and banjo (note that the guitar has six tuning pegs, one for each string, and the banjo has four). Guitars appear in a variety of shapes. Electric guitars are usually solid slabs of wood with electronic attachments embedded. Basically, a banjo has a guitar-like neck and strings attached to a body that consists of a wooden or metal hoop covered with a animal skin head. The banjo commonly used in early jazz had four strings.

Role of Percussion

A fifth feature of jazz is the **prominent role of percussion.** Most jazz groups include a drummer who plays a set of assorted instruments, providing almost continuous time-keeping sounds, thereby generating musical excitement. Drums are very important in much African music, too. And percussion is important in brass band music of European traditions as well as in some European folk dance music, such as Irish.

DVD *Tracks 2–19;* Demo CD *Tracks 1–15, pages 25–29*

A feature related to the role of percussion in jazz is playing melodic instruments in highly rhythmic or percussive ways. Nonpercussion instruments are used in these ways in many other kinds of music, too. But the extent to which melodic instruments are used this way is outstanding in jazz. It resembles the way melody instruments are employed in Africa. Musicologist Olly Wilson has called this *rhythmization.*

Roughenings, Buzzes, and Ringings

A sixth feature of jazz is the presence of **rough sounds, buzzes, and ringings.** Preferences for these kinds of sounds are thought to derive from African musical tastes and African traditions for improvising on tone quality. For instance, jazz drummers sometimes place a key chain atop the ride cymbal to create a sustained hiss or ringing sound. Some drummers insert rivets in a cymbal so that the vibration of the rivets against the cymbal creates a sizzle sound. Many jazz saxophonists cultivate a rasping tone quality. Saxophonist John Coltrane produced a wide range of sound qualities, from smooth to guttural, from full to shrieking. He can be heard in "So What" (*SCCJ*), "Flamenco Sketches," and "The Promise" (*JCCD2* Tracks 9 and 11). Listen for the raw tone qualities of soloists on Duke Ellington's "Harlem Airshaft" and the gruff tone quality of saxophonists Ben Webster on "Cottontail" and Coleman Hawkins on "Voodte" (*JCCD1* Tracks 21, 20, and 18). Compare this with the occasionally rough quality in the male lead singer's voice on "One Day" (*JCCD1* Track 4). On *JCCD1*, you can hear jazz trumpeters and trombonists play in a rough "growl" style: trumpeter Cootie Williams at the beginning of "Cottontail," and trombonist Joe Nanton on "Harlem Airshaft" (Track 21). Listen to the saxophone tone of Albert Ayler in "Ghosts: First Variation" (*JCCD3* Track 2). Other evidence of a taste for rough sounds and buzzes is the jazz brassman's preoccupation with the tone-altering potential of mutes (for example, on *SCCJ*, Joe Oliver's muted cornet solo on "Dipper-mouth Blues" and Cootie Williams's on "Concerto for Cootie").

DVD *Tracks 8–11*

Appendix B; Demo CD *Tracks 63–68*

Repetition of Brief Patterns

A seventh feature of jazz is the **extensive repetition of brief patterns.** Musicians use the term *ostinato* (from the Italian word for "obstinate") to describe the brief, repetitive patterns we are discussing. Ostinato is common in many different kinds of music, but it is a distinguishing trait of African music and jazz. One example is the ride rhythm (*Demo CD* Track 7; *JCCD1* Track 3). Another example of extensive repetition is the style of figure played by the left hand of the boogie-woogie pianist (*Demo CD* Track 38; Meade Lux Lewis, "Honky Tonk Train" on *SCCJ*). Other examples can be found in brief, repetitive bass figures common to jazz/rock fusion, as in recordings by Herbie Hancock and Weather Report from the 1970s and 1980s. There is extensive repetition of short phrases called *riffs* in some jazz styles of the 1930s and 1940s (*JCCD1* Track 5) as well as in jazz-rock of the 1970s and 1980s (*JCCD1* Track 6). These characteristics came from accompaniment rhythms in the folk music and march music that were popular in America at the same time. Some came from ragtime and military drumming. Using these musical devices contributes to swing feeling. The effect of these devices in African music is so similar to their effect in jazz that

"Chameleon," JCCD3 *Track 7*

musicologists believe a taste for this effect was retained in African American culture, and it ultimately caused these practices to emerge in jazz. Though scholars are not unanimous about this, most consider jazz swing feeling to be an African or an African American contribution to jazz.

Polyrhythms

An eighth feature of jazz is **the practice of sounding different rhythms at the same time.** In particular is the sounding of some rhythms that have a basis of two pulses while sounding other rhythms that have a basis of three pulses, as though sounding a march rhythm at the same time as a waltz rhythm. The combination is called a **polyrhythm.** It contributes to the swing feeling and rhythmic excitement of jazz because it creates tensions within the listener who can neither resist following either division of pulses nor reconcile the two; examples include Louis Armstrong's scat singing in "Hotter Than That" (*JCCD1* Track 11); Richie Powell's piano comping in "Kiss and Run" (*JCCD2* Track 6); John Coltrane's "The Promise" (*JCCD* Track 11); and in Bill Evans's "Solar" (*JCCD3* Track 3).

"The Promise," JCCD2
Track 11

 Much of the polyrhythmic construction in jazz comes from the inventiveness of the musicians, not necessarily from the imitation of pre-existing models. We know this to be true, for example, in some work by drummers Max Roach and Elvin Jones. But some polyrhythms in early jazz are thought to be borrowed from combinations of rhythms found in ragtime. Note that polyrhythms are also employed in European folk music and concert music that were present in America before jazz originated. And they are prominent in African music. If derived from ragtime, these polyrhythms in jazz have a partly African ancestry because ragtime has roots in an African American banjo tradition and Cuban dance music of the 1800s. Musicologist Olly Wilson believes that jazz musicians' preference for polyrhythmic construction reflects *a tradition retained from African preference for rhythmic contrast.* However, we must not overlook its long use in European music, too, even though it seems somewhat less prominent there than in African music.

The Ways Tones Are Decorated

A ninth feature of jazz is the assortment of **ways in which tones are decorated.** Some of these came to us from practices in European classical, opera, and folk music. Some came by way of West African practices. Some originated in the New World from blending and expanding European and African tendencies. We have already discussed a preference for rough timbres as our sixth feature of jazz. Now let's examine alterations of pitch. Study Tracks 46–58 of the *Demo CD* to understand what is meant by "pitch bending," and "pitch manipulation." Listen until you can identify the occurrence of no vibrato, slow vibrato, fast vibrato, terminal vibrato, drop, scoop, smear, and doit. (See "Alterations of Pitch" on page 49.) Then study the first six minutes of the *JCCD1* set where many examples can be found. Notice them in the music of the street vendor ("Street Cries") letting pitch fall at the end of his notes, the male gospel singer ("One Day") who toys with the pitches at the beginnings of his notes, the clarinetist ("Dixie Jazz Band One-Step") who smears the pitches at the end of his notes, and Miles Davis ("Strawberries") using his horn to imitate the street vendor by placing pitch bends in the middle of his notes. Albert Ayler's "Ghosts: First Variation" (*JCCD3* Track 2) is rich with pitch bends. Listen to this music while you keep in mind the dimensions of sound that the jazz improviser can alter in his tone: duration, intensity, pitch (vibrato is a steady alternation of pitch), quality (roughness, for example), attack (how a note begins), and decay (how a note ends). Listen to the first four selections on the *JCCD1* several times. They go by quickly, but you will notice more decorations of tones each time you listen.

JCCD1 *Tracks 1–4;* Demo
CD *Tracks 46–58*

Vibrato

To understand vibrato, imagine a sustained tone as a straight line.

Now imagine the pitch of that tone oscillating, that is, becoming alternately higher and lower. The up and down motion of the line represents the slight changes in pitch which constitute vibrato.

We often tend to take vibrato for granted, because it can be almost imperceptible. But if you listen carefully to sustained tones in the work of most singers, violinists, saxophonists, trombonists, and trumpeters, you will hear it.

Vibrato can be present or absent, fast or slow, regular or irregular. Many jazz singers and some jazz instrumentalists tend to start vibrato slowly and then increase its rate so that it is fastest at the end of the note.

This contrasts with the practice of musicians in symphony orchestras who tend to maintain an even rate of vibrato through a tone's complete duration. They employ different rates of vibrato for different styles of composition, however, and many use no vibrato at all.

Vibrato is considered an expressive device. It can also be a prime characteristic for differentiating styles. Early jazz players tended to use much quicker vibratos than modern jazz players. The fast vibrato was undoubtedly a characteristic contributing to the popular description of early jazz as "hot," while modern jazz of the 1940s and 50s with its slower vibrato was "cool." During the 1960s and 70s, many jazz saxophonists employed faster vibrato than was common during the 1940s and 50s. Saxophonists of the 1980s often used a regular rate of vibrato, rather than increasing it near the end of the tone. If you compare music from these periods, you will notice distinct differences in feeling, partly due to the vibrato rate.

Pitch Bends

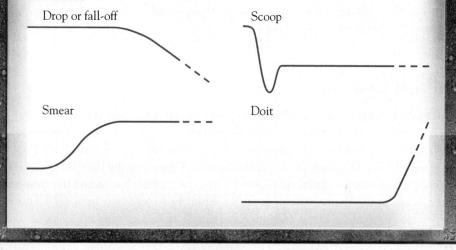

Drop or fall-off

Scoop

Smear

Doit

Blue Notes

A tenth feature of jazz is the **blue note.** This is a concept best understood by listening to the examples on the *Demo CD* Tracks 54–58 and studying the discussion in Appendix B. A rough idea of what the term means can be gained by imagining the piano keyboard to represent the entire selection of pitches that musicians are allowed to draw upon. Then imagine how notes would sound if drawn from finer gradations of pitch, as though produced by piano keys existing in the cracks between the ordinary arrangement of keys. The notes that come out from "between the cracks" are blue notes. European music's pitch system, as represented by the piano's seven white keys

and five black keys, does not provide all the intervals needed by West African music. Thus, sometimes when Africans performed European-style music, they sang using their own intervals. The sound of these intervals in reference to our ear's expectations was "blue." This is the area of musical performance we call *intonation*. This manner of toying with the pitch of notes is an expressive device that has become a jazz tradition. Though not used by all jazz musicians—they are impossible for pianists—blue notes are common in jazz horn playing. Some of these pitches, which in formal European music constitute "playing out of tune" or "off-key," are common in jazz. They are not ordinarily considered mistakes or the result of incomplete mastery of the musician's instrument. That such "out-of-tune" playing is prominent in so many styles of jazz reflects an esthetic of pitch flexibility more than any player's lack of ability to play "in tune." In other words, the kind of out-of-tune playing found in jazz is usually intentional, and it is used as a central element of the art. This might represent a retention of African or African American musical practices. However, such "neutral" pitches, as they are technically termed, were not exclusive to African traditions. They were also present in Anglo-American and Scotch-Irish folk music that was heard in early America.

Musicologists generally believe that approaches to pitch and tone quality among jazz horn players are not a direct imitation of African singing. They stem instead from imitating wide-ranging, imaginative sounds found in New World vocal idioms such as Negro field hollers, work songs, cries of street vendors, and the blues. The bluesy manipulations of pitch that are found in jazz horn work stem, in part, from imitating approaches to singing that were devised in the New World by blacks, as demonstrated in the first minute of *JCCD1*. In New Orleans, the most bluesy interpretations of dance music were frequently associated with black musicians.[4] Some of this was perpetuated in the humorous, novelty effects ("hokum" style) used by minstrel show musicians. The tendency to playfully vary the sounds of instruments might stem in part from African traditions. However, similar musical traditions also existed in other ethnic groups in New Orleans at the same time, so these practices do not necessarily reflect exclusively African American sources.

Call-and-Response

An eleventh feature of jazz is **call-and-response format.** One member or one section of the band offers a musical phrase that is like a question. Another member or section of the band then follows it with a new phrase that is like an answer. (At about 2′34″ on "Cottontail," *JCCD1* Track 20, notice the "question" posed by the brass section and the "answer" offered by the sax section. Listen to the "call" of the bassist and the "response" of the horns in the theme statement of "So What" by Miles Davis in *SCCJ*.) This feature of jazz and African music receives considerable attention from musicologists but is not as common as most of the other features we have discussed. There is an interesting distinction, however, between the type of call and response used in West African music and that used in European music. In West African music, often the sound of the call is still in the air when the response begins. The two parts overlap. And sometimes the call begins again before the response is done, thereby overlapping once more. This causes rhythmic conflict and results in a provocative effect. It is the prominence of *overlapping* call and response, not merely call and response, that distinguishes West African and African American music from music elsewhere. (It is evident in the four excerpts sequenced together at the beginning of *JCCD1*: West African, American Gospel, swing-era riff style, and jazz-rock fusion. Nonoverlapping call and response formats can be found in some styles of band arrangements, as in "Taxi War Dance" and "Cottontail" on *JCCD1* Tracks 20 and 24.)

Reissued on *The Riverside History of Classic Jazz* (Riverside: 005, 3CD set, c1994). "Fishermen, Strawberry, and Devil Crab" is also on Miles Davis, *Porgy and Bess* (Columbia/Legacy: 65141, 1958, c1997).

This comparison illustrates traditions for expressive inflections of pitch in both African American vocal and jazz instrumental styles. First is the call of an African American street vendor advertising the blackberries he is trying to sell. This recording was made early in the twentieth century in Charleston, South Carolina. Second is an excerpt from a piece called "Fishermen, Strawberry, and Devil Crab" in an instrumental version that Miles Davis made in 1958 of George Gershwin's opera, "Porgy and Bess." The opera was inspired by African American life in Charleston, including Gershwin's own scores for the musical sounds of vendors pitching their wares. As a jazz trumpeter, Davis is distinguished for his uniquely personal, very expressive tone qualities and inflections of pitch. His mastery of this tradition is conspicuous here.

CD
TRACK

1	"Street Cries of Charleston" (male street vendor)
2	"Fishermen, Strawberry, and Devil Crab" (Miles Davis trumpet solo)

Call-and-response format is not necessarily a distinguishing feature of improvised combo jazz. What many believe to be a call-and-response kind of communication among group members is in many instances just solo and accompaniment in which the accompaniment follows its own patterns more than it spontaneously generates fresh responses to an improvising soloist. This is revealed when we examine recordings in which the solo line is missing and we discover comping almost identical to that which occurs in the presence of improvised solo lines. Also remember that comping ordinarily derives from a repertory of learned patterns, not necessarily from a spur-of-the-moment response evoked by the call of another musician's sound. (Prior to the Bill Evans Trio of 1961, heard on *JCCD3* Track 3, there was less spontaneous interaction among rhythm section members and less between accompanists and soloists than observers ordinarily believed.) In general, improvised lines are much more a "response" to the challenges of the chord progressions and the player's own ingenuity than to any "call" of another musician.

| *Appendix H*

Some commentators have applied "call-and-response" to describe the function of the phrases that instrumentalists play to fill in a singer's pauses within the 12-bar blues (for example, in Bessie Smith's blues pieces in *SCCJ* or *CCD1* Track 3). However, careful listening reveals that the fills are not necessarily "responses" to the singer's phrases. They merely arrive in sequence with them. Often, they are just improvised lines inspired only by the player's own imagination. They frequently originate from attempts to reconcile horn lines with the underlying chord progressions more than from attempts to establish a musical dialog with the singer. The term "call-and-response" is therefore not always an appropriate designation.

Responsorial singing is a pervasive trait of African music, and it is common in European-derived church music found in America. Call-and-response patterns can be found in classical music and in folk music of many ethnic groups present in America. In summary, call-and-response format can be found in some jazz, and the model for it could reflect any or all of several available sources.

"Hunter's Dance," a West African Folk Number
Reissued on *African Tribal Music & Dances* (Legacy International: 328, CD, 1952, c1993).

"One Day," an American Gospel Singing Number
Recorded for Okeh in 1951 by the Angelic Gospel Singers (four women), the Dixie Hummingbirds (five men), and a pianist; reissued on the anthology *The Gospel Sound* (Columbia/Legacy: C2K 57160, 2CD set, 1926–68, c1994).

"One O'Clock Jump," a Swing-Era Riff Band Number
Recorded for Okeh in 1942 by the Count Basie big band; reissued on Basie, *America's #1 Band* (Columbia/Legacy: C4K 87110, 4CD set, 1936–51, c2003).

"Birdland," a Jazz-Rock Fusion Number
Recorded in 1977 by Weather Report, on Oberheim Polyphonic Synthesizer (Joe Zawinul), soprano sax (Wayne Shorter), bass guitar (Jaco Pastorius), drums (Alex Acuna), and tambourine (Manolo Badrena); reissued on Weather Report, *Heavy Weather* (Columbia/Legacy: CK 65108, 1977, c1997).

These four pieces illustrate several properties that are common to West African music, African American gospel music, swing-era riff-band style, and jazz-rock fusion. Each piece demonstrates extensive repetition of brief patterns, much syncopation, an overlapping call-and-response format, and the capacity to evoke swing feeling in the listener. By the strictest definition, none of these truly qualifies as jazz because not much is improvised. The third and fourth pieces are usually called jazz, though, because they are played by jazz bands and because they swing.

Though call-and-response format is common in many kinds of music, not just African and African American styles, the format in which the response overlaps the call is particularly noticeable in African and African American music. The following examples therefore illustrate *overlapping* call-and-response format, not merely call-and-response.

"Hunter's Dance" is popular peasant music made by the people of Mali, also known as the Malinke people. To obtain this music, in 1952 ethnomusicologist Gilbert Rouget journeyed to Karala, a relatively isolated native village in the West African country of Guinea. The recording features a six-string harp-lute (dozo-konu), the voice of the man who plays it, a women's chorus accompanying him, a wooden whistle (fere), and a metal scraper (karinyan), which is a small tube of wrought iron that is slit down the middle. The karinyan is held in the left hand and struck with a nail held in the right hand, playing a rhythm similar to the jazz drummer's ride rhythm.

When listening to "Hunter's Dance," notice that the rhythms of the different parts are carefully calculated to achieve a provocative effect that is peculiarly African. Also notice how the music's excitement increases as the performance evolves and more layers of activity are added.

CD TRACK	ELAPSED TIME	"Hunter's Dance"
3	0'00"	repeating bass figure, obtained by plucking the strings of the dozo-konu; accompanied by a repeating rhythm on the metallic sounding karinyan
	0'15"	melody sung by the male voice
	0'20"	response sung by women's chorus
	0'23"	Before the response is complete, the male voice begins to sing again (thus the expression "overlapping call and response").

LISTENING GUIDE continued on next page

0'27"   Women's chorus responds again.

0'28"   whistle sounds

0'30"   Male voice returns.

"One Day"

4

As in all the pieces of this African American sequence, the music's excitement increases over the course of the performance as more parts are layered on top of each other, each part's rhythms tugging at the others' in a provocative way. Tremendous spirit and exuberance are projected by this music. Ultimately the music sounds almost like it is going to break apart in wild abandon.

Here are a few highlights. The intensity and momentum are unrelenting, and they occur without the assistance of any bass or drums. Though highly rhythmic piano accompaniment is in the background, the manner in which the singers produce their rhythms is so compelling that they could probably swing without any accompaniment at all. Male voice is in the foreground, though its sound eases in and out of the sounds of background singers answering its phrases. Notice the tendency of the male lead singer to smear up into the pitch of the main notes. This gliding through the pitch range is a very expressive device he uses expertly. Also note the raspy timbre the male singer uses for one of his phrases. This is a preference that is also common to West African singers and musicians. The entrances of the lead singer are highly syncopated, and these syncopations are timed to evoke maximum swing feeling and rhythmic conflict. The responsorial chorus provides the repeating riff in this selection. Notice that the call-and-response pattern doubles in rate near the end, and finally a woman's voice soars high over the proceedings as one more element to tug at the beat and generate excitement. (A similar device is used at the end of "Birdland.")

"One O'Clock Jump"

5

This is a riff-band piece from the swing era. The original 1937 version of it was a big hit. Excerpted here are the ninth and tenth choruses in 12-bar blues form. Several different riffs are played against each other at the same time by different sections of the band: trombones, trumpets, and saxophones. This illustrates the principle of antiphony, literally "against sounds." Saxes play a syncopated figure, as though answering the trombone phrase. Trumpets play a different riff that is also syncopated, as though on the opposite end of a see-saw from the trombones. A timekeeping foundation is provided by piano, rhythm guitar, walking bass, and the drummer using sticks to play ride rhythms on opening and closing high hat. The overlapping of these parts generates rhythmic excitement.

"Birdland"

6

"Birdland" is in a style called jazz-rock fusion. This performance is excerpted from Weather Report's best-selling recording, a discotheque hit. For many years this piece continued to be copied and re-arranged by numerous ensembles, including the singing group Manhattan Transfer. Excerpted here is the chorus of the piece, the melody of which is played by sax, synthesizer, bass guitar, and voice. The chords in the accompaniment are provided by the synthesizer. Percussion accompaniment includes hand claps on beats two and four, tambourine providing steady eighth notes, and the sound of open high-hat cymbal struck with drum stick on upbeats, snapped shut on downbeats. In addition to doubling the melody, bass guitar fills in the gaps between the notes and phrases of the melody. A high-pitched male voice (bass guitarist Jaco Pastorius) sustains tones over the ensemble sound, offering a countermelody.

CHAPTER SUMMARY

1. Jazz originated in New Orleans around the beginning of the twentieth century.

2. New Orleans was the ideal site for the birth of jazz because it was an intensely musical city with a history of rich ethnic diversity, especially French and African.

3. Jazz emerged when brass bands were at a zenith of popularity and ragtime was in such high demand that brass bands and string bands were improvising rag-like syncopations into their pieces to please dancers.

4. African American forms of music such as the blues and ragtime blended with European dance music and church music.

5. Jazz has features that reflect African musical tastes that were retained in African American music—improvisation, syncopation, rough timbres, extensive repetition of brief patterns, polyrhythms, and overlapping call-and-response format.

6. Jazz reflects European music's instruments, chord progressions, and improvisation.

7. Blending of European and African practices resulted in blue notes and various decorations of a note by altering its pitch.

NOTES

1. Jazz originated in the blends of folk music, popular music, and light classical music that were current near the beginning of the twentieth century, especially in New Orleans. Collections that are useful for illustrating these styles include (items are compact discs unless otherwise indicated):

Come and Trip It: Instrumental Dance Music 1780s–1920s. New World: 80293, c1978.

Early Band Ragtime: Ragtime's Biggest Hits, 1899–1909. Smithsonian/Folkways: RBF 38, c1979.

Jazz. Vol. 1, *The South.* Smithsonian/Folkways: 2801, c1950.

Jazz. Vol. 2, *The Blues.* Smithsonian/Folkways: 2802, 1923–48, c1956.

Jazz: Some Beginnings. Smithsonian/Folkways: RF 31, 1914–26, c1977.

History of Classic Jazz. Riverside/Fantasy: 005, 3CD set, ca. 1900–1956, c1994 (Disc 1, Track 2).

The Sousa and Pryor Bands: Original Recordings, 1901–1926. New World: NW 282, LP, 1901–26, c1976 (out of print).

Steppin' on the Gas: Rags to Jazz. New World: NW 269, LP, 1913–27, c1978 (out of print) (side 1 only).

That's My Rabbit, My Dog Caught It: Traditional Southern Instrumental Styles. New World: NW 226, LP, 1925–77, c1978 (out of print).

Note: New World Records (Recorded Anthology of American Music) may be found in many college libraries; the Rockefeller Foundation donated sets to many educational institutions. Folkways records are in many music libraries. Liner notes for all New World albums are available at: *www.newworldrecords.org.*

Basic Texts on African Music

(The most useful texts for a jazz appreciation course are listed first.)

NKETIA, J.H. KWABENA. *The Music of Africa.* Norton, 1974.

NKETIA, J.H. KWABENA, and JACQUELINE COGGELL DJEDJE, ed. *Selected Reports in Ethnomusicology.* Vol. 5, *Studies in African Music.* Los Angeles, CA: Program in Ethnomusicology, Department of Music, Univ. of California, 1984.

BEBEY, FRANCIS. *African Music: A People's Art.* L. Hill, 1975.

KEBEDE, ASHENAFI. *Roots of Black Music: The Vocal, Instrumental, and Dance Heritage of Africa and Black America.* Prentice-Hall, 1982; Africa World Press, 1995.

JONES, A.M. *Studies in African Music.* Vols. 1 and 2. Oxford Univ., 1959, 1978.

ROBERTS, JOHN STORM. *Black Music of Two Worlds.* 2nd ed. Schirmer, 1998. Accompanying compact discs: *Black Music of Two Worlds,* Smithsonian/Folkways: 4602, 3CD set, c1977.

OLIVER, PAUL, et al. *Yonder Come the Blues: The Evolution of a Genre.* Cambridge, 2001. Reprints *Savannah Syncopators: African Retentions in the Blues* (Stein and Day, 1970) and two other books with added material. Accompanying 2-LP set: *Savannah Syncopators,* Columbia (UK): 52799.

CHERNOFF, JOHN MILLER. *African Rhythm and Sensibility: Aesthetics and Social Action in African Musical Idioms.* Univ. of Chicago, 1979, 1981. With accompanying audio cassette examples.

GAYLE, ADDISON. *The Black Aesthetic.* Doubleday, 1971.

Important Scholarly Papers About African Music

Many important insights and much of the most solid research data never find their way into full-length textbooks. Much scholarly thinking and data gathering are available only in papers read at professional conferences, rewritten for professional journals. A few of such works are included below. If your library does not carry these journals, ask your reference librarian to request the article via inter-library loan. Frequently a copy can be sent to you for free or a small fee from a library that holds the journal you seek.

(The most useful papers for a jazz appreciation course are listed first.)

WATERMAN, RICHARD A. "Hot Rhythm in Negro Music." *Journal of the American Musicological Society* 1 (1948): 24–37. Based on a paper delivered December 28, 1943.

____. "African Influence on the Music of the Americas." In *Anthropology and Art: Readings in Cross Cultural Aesthetics*. ed. Charlotte M. Otten, 227–44. Univ. of Texas, 1976. Reprinted from *Acculturation in the Americas: Proceedings and Selected Papers of the XXIX International Congress of Americanists*, ed. Sol Tax, Univ. of Chicago, 1952. Paper delivered in 1951.

____. "On Flogging a Dead Horse: Lessons Learned from the Africanisms Controversy." *Ethnomusicology* 7 (1963): 83–87.

EVANS, DAVID. "African Elements in Twentieth Century United States Black Folk Music." In *International Musicological Society, Report of the Twelfth Congress, Berkeley, 1977*, 54–66. Barenreiter, 1981.

TALLMADGE, WILLIAM. "Blue Notes and Blue Tonality." *The Black Perspective in Music* 12 (1984): 155–65.

KAUFMAN, ROBERT. "African Rhythm: A Reassessment" *Ethnomusicology* 24 (1980): 393–415.

EPSTEIN, DENA J. "The Folk Banjo." *Ethnomusicology* 19 (1975): 347–372.

GRIDLEY, MARK C., and WALLACE RAVE. "Towards Identification of African Traits in Early Jazz." *The Black Perspective in Music* 12 (1984): 44–56.

WILSON, OLLY. "The Significance of the Relationship Between Afro-American Music and West African Music." *The Black Perspective in Music* 2 (1974): 3–23.

____. "Black Music as an Art Form." *Black Music Research Journal* 3 (1983): 1–22.

Note: *Black Music Research Journal* is published by Center for Black Music Research, Columbia College Chicago, 600 South Michigan Ave, Chicago, IL 60605-1996.

WILLIAMS-JONES, PEARL. "Afro-American Gospel Music: A Crystallization of the Black Aesthetic." *Ethnomusicology* 19 (1975): 373–86.

HALL, GWENDOLYN MIDLO. *Africans in Colonial Louisiana: The Development of Afro-Creole Culture in the Eighteenth Century.* Louisiana State Univ., 1992.

HIRSCH, ARNOLD R., AND JOSEPH LOGSDON, ed. *Creole New Orleans: Race and Americanization.* Louisiana State Univ., 1992.

JACOBS, CLAUDE. "Benevolent Societies of New Orleans Blacks During the Late Nineteenth and Early Twentieth Centuries." *Louisiana History, Journal of the Louisiana Historical Association* 29, No. 1, 1988.

JOYAUX, GEORGE J., ed. "Forest's Voyage aux Etats-Unis de l'Amerique en 1831." *Louisiana Historical Quarterly* 39, No. 4, 1956.

LATROBE, BENJAMIN HENRY. *Impressions Respecting New Orleans, Diaries & Sketches 1818–1820*, ed. Sam Wilson, Jr. Columbia Univ., 1951.

FLOYD, SAMUEL A., JR., and MARTHA J. REISSER. "The Sources and Resources of Classic Ragtime Music." *Black Music Research Journal* 4 (1984): 22–59.

See above address for Center for Black Music Research.

EPSTEIN, DENA. "Black Spirituals: Their Emergence into Public Knowledge." *Black Music Research Newsletter* 8 (1986): 5–8. See above for address of Center for Black Music Research.

CRONBACH, LEE. "Structural Polytonality in Contemporary Afro-American Music." *Black Music Research Journal* 2 (1981–2): 15–33.

KOETTING, JAMES. "What Do We Know About African Rhythm?" *Ethnomusicology* 30 (1986): 58–63.

STONE, RUTH. "The Value of Local Ideas in Understanding West African Rhythm." *Ethnomusicology* 30 (1986): 54–57.

Early African American Culture and New Orleans

(The most useful items for a jazz appreciation course are listed first.)

EPSTEIN, DENA. "A White Origin for the Black Spiritual? An Invalid Theory and How It Grew." *American Music* 1 (1983): 53–59.

LOMAX, ALAN. *Mister Jelly Roll: The Fortunes of Jelly Roll Morton, New Orleans Creole and "Inventor of Jazz."* Duell, Sloan and Pearce, 1949; Univ. of California, 2001.

BERLIN, EDWARD A. *Reflections and Research on Ragtime.* I.S.A.M. Monographs, No. 24. Institute for Studies in American Music, Conservatory of Music, Brooklyn College, 1987.

GARST, JOHN F. "Mutual Reinforcement and the Origins of Spirituals." *American Music* 4 (1986): 390–406.

FOSTER, GEORGE M. *Pops Foster: The Autobiography of a New Orleans Jazzman as Told to Tom Stoppard.* Univ. of California, 1971.

SEALSFIELD, CHARLES. *The Americans as They Are: Described in a Tour Through the Valley of the Mississippi.* London: Hurst, Chance & Co., 1828; reprinted in Sealsfield, *The United States of North America as They Are. The Americans as They Are.* Olms Presse, 1972.

SCHAFER, WILLIAM, and RICHARD B. ALLEN. *Brass Bands and New Orleans Jazz.* Louisiana State Univ., 1977.

RIGHTOR, HENRY, ed. *Standard History of New Orleans, Louisiana, Giving a Description of the Natural Advantages, Natural History.* Chicago: Lewis Pub., 1900.

SHAPIRO, NAT, and NAT HENTOFF, ed. *Hear Me Talkin' to Ya: The Story of Jazz by the Men Who Made It.* Reinhart, 1955; Dover, 1966.

MARQUIS, DONALD M. *In Search of Buddy Bolden: First Man of Jazz.* Louisiana State Univ., 1978, 1993.

GUSHEE, LAWRENCE. *Pioneers of Jazz: The Story of the Creole Band.* Oxford Univ., 2005.

KOENIG, KARL. *Jazz in Print (1856–1929): An Anthology of Selected Early Readings in Jazz History.* Pendragon, 2002.

SMITH, MICHAEL. P. *Spirit World: Pattern in the Expressive Folk Culture of African-American New Orleans.* Gretna, LA: Pelican Pub. Co., 1992.

SMITH, MICHAEL P. *Mardi Gras Indians.* Gretna: Pelican Pub. Co., 1994.

SOUTHERN, EILEEN. *The Music of Black Americans: A History.* 3rd ed. Norton, 1997.

STERKX, H.E. *The Free Negro in Antebellum Louisiana.* Fairleigh Dickinson Univ., 1972.

EPSTEIN, DENA J. *Sinful Tunes and Spirituals: Black Folk Music to the Civil War.* Univ. of Illinois, 1977, 2003.

BLASSINGAME, JOHN W. *The Slave Community: Plantation Life in the Antebellum South.* rev. and enl. ed. Oxford, 1979.

KOENIG, KARL. "The Plantation Belt Brass Bands and Musicians." *The Second Line* 33 (1981): 24–40. Back issues of *The Second Line* are available from Hogan Jazz Archive, 304 Jones Hall, Tulane University, 6801 Freret Street, New Orleans, LA 70118; phone 504-865-5688; fax 504-865-5761; *www.tulane.edu/~lmiller/JazzHome.html*.

____. "Professor James B. Humphrey." *The Second Line* 34 (1982): 15–19.

____. "Chris Kelly, Blues King of New Orleans." *The Second Line* 35 (spring 1983): 4–26.

____. "Louisiana Brass Bands and History in Relation to Jazz History." *The Second Line* 35 (summer 1983): 7–15.

____. "John Philip Sousa's Impact on Jazz." *The Second Line* 35 (winter 1983): 39–41.

_____. "Jack Laine 'Papa.'" *The Mississippi Rag* (March 1984): 1–6.
Note: *The Mississippi Rag* back issues are available from 9448 Lyndale Ave., S. Suite 120, Bloomington, MN 55420, phone 952-885-9918, fax 952-885-9943, web *www.mississippirag.com.*

Note: Informative summaries and bibliographies are included in H. Wiley Hitchcock and Stanley Sadie, ed., *The New Grove Dictionary of American Music* (Macmillan, 1986). See entries for New Orleans, Blues, Traditional Jazz, Spirituals, and Ragtime, as well as the entries for particular musicians.

Album Liner Notes That Summarize Pre-Jazz and Early Jazz Research

(Annotator's name is in parentheses. The most useful items for a jazz appreciation course are listed first. Items are compact discs unless otherwise stated.)

The Riverside History of Classic Jazz. (Charles Edward Smith). Riverside/Fantasy: 005, 3CD set, 1956, c1994.

The Roots of the Blues. (Alan Lomax). New World: 80252, c1977.

Steppin' on the Gas: Rags to Jazz 1913–1927. (Lawrence Gushee). New World: NW 269, LP, c1977 (out of print).

OLIVER, JOE "KING." *King Oliver's Jazz Band, 1923.* (Lawrence Gushee). Smithsonian: 2001, 2LP set, 1923, c1975 (out of print).

KEPPARD, FREDDIE. *Legendary New Orleans Cornet.* (Lawrence Gushee). Smithsonian: 2020, LP, 1924–1927, c1979 (out of print).

Roots of Black Music in America. (Samuel Charters). Smithsonian/Folkways: 2694, 2CD set, c1972.

Come and Trip It: Instrumental Dance Music 1780s–1920s. (Thorton Hagert). New World: 80293, c1978.

Georgia Sea Island Songs. (Alan Lomax). New World: 80278, c1977.

Note: Liner notes for all New World albums are available at their website: *www.newworldrecords.com.*

Recordings to Aid in Understanding African Music

Here is a brief compilation of available recordings that help connect jazz and African music. It is far from definitive, but it could get you started if you need materials for an ethnomusicologically oriented course in jazz or African American music. In pursuing the items on this list, note that ordinary record stores and most mail order houses do not sell these records, but you can get them from specialty houses and importers. Frequently it is best to order directly from mail order services. To obtain the French Ocora records, contact: Harmonia Mundi USA, 1117 Chestnut Street, Burbank, CA 91506; phone: 818-333-1500; web: *www.harmoniamundi.com.* If a large music library exists near you, it may be helpful to contact the reference librarian there for the names and addresses of dealers who service the library's ethnomusicology needs.

Many of the best recordings of African music and pre-jazz have been out of print for ages and are not listed here, though you might find them in libraries. One that is particularly worth seeking is *Anthology of Music of Black Africa* (Everest: 3254/3, 2LP set, c1969), half of which was originally issued in France as *Musique D'Afrique Occidentale* (Vogue: LVLX 193, LP, c[195?]), and reissued on CD: *African Tribal Music and Dances* (Legacy International: 328, 1952, c1993).

Note: If you choose illustrations not listed here, keep in mind that the music of Africa is very diverse, and that music from West Africa is the most relevant for your purposes. Stick to Gambia, Senegal, Guinea, Ivory Coast, Ghana, and Nigeria. Otherwise, you risk generalizing from music that may have had little or no influence on jazz because the culture that produced it contributed few slaves to America.

These records are all interesting, and most contain informative notes:

Africa, South of the Sahara. Smithsonian/Folkways: 4503, 2CD set, c1957. (Compilation by Harold Courlander of numerous cultures, with richly detailed notes prepared by the eminent Africanist Alan P. Merriam; only some examples are from West Africa.)

Africa, the Dan. Anthology of World Music. Rounder: 5105 (Barenreiter Musicaphon BM 30 L 2301), 1966, c1998 (recorded by Hugo Zemp; people of Ivory Coast and Liberia).

African Journey: A Search for the Roots of the Blues. Sonet: SNTF 667 (Vanguard 73014/73015), 1974. (Compilation of various West African cultures visited by Samuel Charters and described in his travelogue: Charters, *The Roots of the Blues: An African Search* [Boston: M. Boyars, 1981; New York: DaCapo, 1991].)

Black Music of Two Worlds. Smithsonian/Folkways: 4602, 3CD set, c1977. (Contains music of Ghana, Sierra Leone, Liberia, as well as music from many areas of the New World; accompanies the book: John Storm Roberts, *Black Music of Two Worlds,* 2nd ed. [Schirmer, 1998].)

Cote d'Ivoire: Musique Des Baoule-Kode. Ocora: OCR 34, LP, 1961, c1982 (the Baule people of the Ivory Coast).

Drums of West Africa: Ritual Music of Ghana, Lyrichord: 7307, LP/AC, 1974–76 (music of the Ewe people). **Note:** Order from Lyrichord Discs, Inc., PO Box 1977, Old Chelsea Station, New York, NY 10011-1726; phone: 212-929-8234; fax: 212-929-8245; web: *www.lyrichord.com.*

The Griots: Ministers of the Spoken Word. Smithsonian/Folkways: 4178, 2CD set, 1974, c1975 (vocal music of Gambia, Senegal, and Mali collected by Samuel Charters).

Masques Dan: Cote d'Ivoire. Ocora: 580048 (OCR 52), 1965–1967, c1993 (music from Ivory Coast; French import distributed by Harmonia Mundi USA).

Music from Gambia. Vol. 1. Smithsonian/Folkways: 4521, 2CD set, 1971–72, c1978.

The Music of Nigeria: Hausa Music. UNESCO Collection, Anthology of African Music, Vol. 6. Barenreiter Musicaphon: BM 30 L 2306, LP, c1965 (the Hausa people of Nigeria).

Music of the Cameroons. Smithsonian/Folkways: 4372, 1959, c1961.

The Music of the Senufo. UNESCO Collection, Anthology of African Music, vol. 8. Barenreiter Musicaphon: BM 30 L 2308, LP, c1965 (people of Ivory Coast, Upper Volta, and Mali).

Musiques du Cameroun. Ocora: OCR 25, LP, 1965, c1965 (people of the Cameroons).

Roots of Black Music in America. Smithsonian/Folkways: 2694, 2CD set, c1972. (Wide range of African and African American music with lengthy and well-documented notes by Samuel Charters.)

Songs of War and Death from the Slave Coast: Abutia Kloe, Ewe, Ghana. Smithsonian/Folkways: 4258/4259, 2CD set, c1982 (music of the Ewe people of Ghana).

Togo: Music from West Africa. Rounder: 5004, 1978, c1991 (music of the Ewe people).

Wolof Music of Senegal and the Gambia. Smithsonian/Folkways: 4462, c1955.

2. Though the plantation system of labor was nonexistent in name, the plantations still operated with hired labor, and most of the plantations hired bandmasters/teachers to instruct these hired hands and to form bands. Many early jazz musicians received their musical training there.

3. The players may have done much without referring to written scores. However, the absence of notation in these situations should not be taken as evidence of improvisation any more than we would consider "improvised" the music of today's wedding bands and lounge acts that sometimes play fresh routines without notation. Research by Karl Koenig has shown that most early New Orleans jazz musicians could read music well enough to work out the notes and fingerings, though they could not necessarily sight read fast. Some could not read music, however, and most chose not to read pieces once they had been learned.

4. You might be able to detect blue notes in the Joe Oliver cornet solo on "Dippermouth Blues" in *SCCJ*. There are many Rex Stewart cornet solos which use blue notes on Duke Ellington records from the 1930s and 1940s. His "Boy Meets Horn" is the most famous example. Modern trumpeter Miles Davis is also particularly known for using blue notes. Listen to "Strawberries" on Davis, *Porgy and Bess* (Columbia/Legacy), excerpted on *JCCD1*, or "Solea" on Davis, *Sketches of Spain* (Columbia/Legacy). During the 1970s, Don Ellis played on a specially made trumpet that, by the addition of an extra valve, could produce quarter tones, those "notes in the cracks." Ordinarily, trumpeters had tried to achieve the same sound by depressing their trumpet key halfway, thereby leaving a cocked valve. However, they could not depend on obtaining this result consistently. The Ellis trumpet managed a similar effect, but much more reliably.

The earliest jazz musicians took liberties with the tunes and the accompaniments in their performances. Their new ideas and embellishments sometimes became more important to a performance than the tunes themselves. This trend evolved across the 1920s, and in some performances of the 1930s all that remained of the original was the tune's spirit and chord progressions. What is today called improvising was referred to by early jazz musicians as "messin' around," embellishing, "jassing," or "jazzing up."

The earliest jazz had roots in ragtime, blues, and brass band music. But after a few years, several important differences were heard:

1. Much of each performance was improvised.

2. Rhythmic feeling was looser and more relaxed, thus anticipating jazz swing feeling.

3. It generated some of its own repertory of compositions.

4. Its collectively improvised format created a more complex musical product than was typical in ragtime, blues, or brass band music.

5. The earliest jazz was even more exciting than ragtime, blues, or brass band music.

Original Dixieland Jazz Band
(Photo courtesy of William Ransom Hogan Jazz Archive, Tulane University)

TABLE 5.1 A Few of the Many Early Jazz Musicians

TRUMPET
Buddy Bolden
Freddie Keppard
Joe "King" Oliver
Louis Armstrong
Wingy Manone
Red Nichols
Bix Beiderbecke
Tommy Ladnier
Henry "Red" Allen
Joe Smith
Bubber Miley
Charlie Teagarden
Jabbo Smith
Nick LaRocca
Paul Mares
George Mitchell
Sidney DeParis
Muggsy Spanier
Phil Napoleon
Wild Bill Davidson
Mutt Carey

DRUMS
Baby Dodds
Papa Jack Laine
Paul Barbarin
Zutty Singleton
Sonny Greer
Dave Tough
George Wettling
Ben Pollack
Andrew Hilaire
Chauncey Morehouse
Gene Krupa
Vic Berton
Ray Bauduc
Tony Sbarbaro

COMPOSER-ARRANGER
Kid Ory
Jelly Roll Morton
W.C. Handy
Clarence Williams
Fats Waller

VIOLIN
Joe Venuti

BASS
Pops Foster
Wellman Braud
John Lindsay

TROMBONE
Kid Ory
J.C. Higginbotham
Miff Mole
Jack Teagarden
Fred Robinson
Charlie Green
Jimmy Harrison
Charlie Irvis
Joe "Tricky Sam"
   Nanton
George Brunis
Bill Rank
Tommy Dorsey
Glenn Miller
Wilbur DeParis
Eddie Edwards
Honore Dutrey

CLARINET AND SAXOPHONE
Johnny Dodds
Sidney Bechet
Jimmie Noone
Frank Teschemacher
Benny Goodman
Albert Nicholas
Barney Bigard
Omer Simeon
Alphonse Picou
Mezz Mezzrow
Jimmy Strong
Sidney Arodin
Darnell Howard
Leon Rappolo
Buster Bailey
Don Redman
Bud Freeman
Floyd Towne
Coleman Hawkins
Jimmy Dorsey
Hilton Jefferson
Stump Evans
Charlie Holmes
Larry Shields
Pee Wee Russell
Adrian Rollini
Don Murray
Tony Parenti
Izzy Friedman
Min Leibrook
Cecil Scott
Frankie Trumbauer
Edmond Hall
Gene Sedric
George Lewis

GUITAR AND BANJO
Lonnie Johnson
Johnny St. Cyr
Elmer Snowden
Eddie Lang
Eddie Condon

PIANO
James P. Johnson
Fate Marable
Jelly Roll Morton
Willie "The Lion"
   Smith
Fats Waller
Lil Hardin Armstrong
Pete Johnson
Clarence Williams
Meade Lux Lewis
Albert Ammons
Cripple Clarence
   Lofton
Cow Cow Davenport
Elmer Schoebel
Pinetop Smith
Jimmy Yancey
Earl Hines
Frank Signorelli
Fletcher Henderson
Joe Sullivan
Jimmy Blythe
Henry Ragas

Combo jazz began in New Orleans, and that city contributed several soloists of far-reaching significance. The best known were trumpeter Louis Armstrong and clarinetist-saxophonist Sidney Bechet. Jelly Roll Morton was the most significant composer-arranger from New Orleans, and his finest recordings were made during the 1920s in Chicago. New combinations of musicians in Chicago also made several

other figures important: Pittsburgh-born pianist Earl Hines; and Bix Beiderbecke, a Davenport, Iowa-born cornetist. Chicago was additionally the home of "The Austin High Gang," which, together with The New Orleans Rhythm Kings, created a white parallel of the New Orleans combo style that today is called "Dixieland." Another important part of early jazz was an East Coast piano tradition that evolved partly from New Jersey-born James P. Johnson and continued through Fats Waller to Count Basie. Let's examine these styles now.

THE CHICAGO SCENE

It was in Chicago that many black New Orleans musicians were first recorded in the early 1920s. What is usually referred to as New Orleans style is not the music that was played between 1900 and 1920 in New Orleans—we have never heard that music because it was not recorded—but rather the music recorded by New Orleans musicians in Chicago during the 1920s. We know from interviews and a few early records that the earliest forms of jazz were characterized by collective improvisation, with all group members playing at the same time. These early bands featured choruses in which every player was creating phrases which complemented every other player's phrases. For many listeners, the greatest appeal of early jazz is the activity of several horn lines sounding at the same time without clashing. Musicians managed to stay out of each others's way partly because they tended to fulfill set musical roles similar to those established for their instruments in brass bands. The trumpet often played the melody. The clarinet played busy figures with many notes. The clarinet part decorated the melody played by the

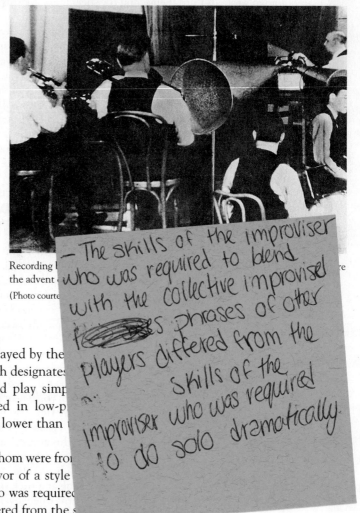

Recording [...] the advent [...] (Photo court[...]

handwritten note: — The skills of the improviser who was required to blend with the collective improvised phrases of other players differed from the skills of the improviser who was required to do solo dramatically

decoration is technically classified as an *obbligato*, which designates [...] that sounds in the background. The trombone would play simp[...] trombone's music outlined the chord notes and filled in low-p[...] notes. The trombone created motion in a pitch range lower than [...] trumpet.

The style of the black Chicago musicians, most of whom were fro[...] evolved away from a strictly collective approach in favor of a style [...] more improvised solos. The skills of the improviser who was require[...] the collectively improvised phrases of other players differed from the s[...] proviser who was required to solo dramatically. The delicate balance and sensitive interplay in collective improvisation which characterized the earliest form of jazz receded during the Chicago period of the New Orleans players. However, musicians who played Dixieland in subsequent eras tried to recapture the essence of those special skills which make successful collective improvisation possible.

The Original Dixieland Jazz Band

New Orleans jazz was first recorded in Chicago and New York, not in New Orleans. The **Original Dixieland Jazz Band (ODJB)** made the first recordings. This was a collection of white New Orleans musicians who organized a band in Chicago during 1916 and played in New York in 1917 (See photo on pages 58–59.). They used cornet,

Recorded for Victor on February 26, 1917, by Nick LaRocca (cornet), Larry Shields (clarinet), Eddie Edwards (trombone), Henry Ragas (piano), and Tony Spargo (drums).

This record was made in New York by a group of white New Orleans musicians who had come together in Chicago the preceding year. They called themselves the Original Dixieland Jass Band (ODJB). "Dixie Jazz Band One-Step" (also known as "Original Dixieland One-Step") was on the reverse side of "Livery Stable Blues," one of the most popular discs in the first decade of recorded jazz. The piece heard here originated from a combination of ideas contributed by all the band members, though ragtime composer Joe Jordan wrote its third theme, and the sheet music for this piece lists bandleader Nick LaRocca as composer. Worldwide sales of the record it was on are said to have reached about a million copies by the late 1930s.

This is the first instrumental jazz recording ever released, and music by the ODJB has continued to influence musicians, partly because this band made the first jazz records. However, there is controversy about what to call the music. First, the name for the style, as well as the piece itself, was originally "jass," not jazz. Second, the music on this recording might not qualify as jazz if we define jazz as music that has improvisation and swing feeling. We don't know whether any of the music was freshly improvised for this particular recording session, but we do know that most of the ODJB's music was worked out in advance, despite the spontaneity of its sound. For instance, the embellishments were recreated almost intact for most performances, though they are likely to have been improvised when this arrangement was first devised. Regarding its quality of swing, the feeling of this music does not have the easy rise and fall of tensions that we associate with swing feeling of later jazz. However, the ODJB's music is loaded with syncopations that evolved from ragtime, and it is highly spirited.

The roles that the different instruments assume on this recording were associated with what is known today as New Orleans, Chicago, or Dixieland style jazz. We can consider this record to be an example of music that was popular in New Orleans during this period because most of the fashions heard here were already common in New Orleans ragtime bands by 1917. So even though it was the first to be recorded, the ODJB was not necessarily the first or "The Original" band of its kind, as its name implies.

Though it often sounds as if a larger band is playing, this performance was constructed by only five instruments: cornet, clarinet, trombone, piano, and drums. The clarinet is most evident, and the piano is least evident, almost inaudible. The cornet and trombone sounds frequently blend so closely that you may have difficulty distinguishing them, though many trombone smears are conspicuous. As was typical for New Orleans drummers of the period, Spargo frequently switches instruments. At various moments he can be heard playing snare drum, wood block, and cowbell. He uses the cymbal sparingly, and a cymbal crash usually signifies a climactic moment in the music, as it does in nonjazz idioms.

To prepare yourself for following the various activities in this piece, it may help to keep three things in mind. First, the music goes by very fast. So you will need to count "1234 1234 . . . " almost as fast as you can to keep your place by counting beats. Second, you'll hear more each time you replay the recording. So don't get frustrated if it sounds like a blur the first time you listen to it. Third, the arrangement contains only three brief themes, and they are frequently repeated. So once you become acquainted with them, you will know almost all that is necessary to follow this arrangement.

Many of the different sounds are so close in their pitch range and rhythm that they blend together and disguise each other. But the more often you listen, the more distinct they will become. Your search for the separate instruments might resemble peering at a trick sketch on a comic book or cereal box. (Remember trying to identify a tiger hidden in jungle ferns where overlapping lines camouflaged its contours?) Repeated listening also allows you to get swept up in the excitement of this music. Then you can appreciate why this band was so popular.

You may find it helpful to think of the performance as a loud party in which people are talking to each other very energetically, sometimes agreeing, sometimes disagreeing, often interrupting each other. Once in a while an interrupter gets everyone's attention, and they stop to hear what he has to say. But they almost immediately return to chattering boisterously among themselves. Sometimes as one person speaks, others shout out their agreement with him, and a running commentary is happening most of the time.

To help get your counting synchronized with the music, note that the first two sounds in the performance indicate the first two beats. There is no sound on beat three or beat four. The musicians count these unsounded beats silently to themselves so they can restart their playing together on the first of the next group of four beats (henceforth termed "a measure"). Then the pattern repeats. This goes by very fast, but it is a dependable indication of the tempo for the entire piece. The third measure is occupied by a smear from the trombone that starts high, goes low, then goes back up high again, finishing on the first beat of the next measure.

LISTENING GUIDE *continued on next page*

The ODJB's roots in the brass band tradition are reflected in this piece's opening. The rhythm of the first four-measure sequence is called a "roll-off," a device usually played by a parade band's drummer to prepare musicians to march. Its effect is dramatic, as in a call to arms. The band stands at attention during the roll-off, then begins to march. By listening closely, you can hear the drummer playing the roll-off pattern underneath the horns. His rhythm is the same as theirs. The trombone smear in the third measure coincides with a drum roll. Like other march-style popular music of this period, this piece was also used to accompany a dance, in this case the dance was called the one-step.

The form of the performance is A - A′ - B - B′ - A - A′ - B - B′ - C - C′ - C - C′ - C - C′.

Terms to learn from the *DVD* and the *Demo CD* before listening: eighth notes, solo break, bass drum, snare drum, wood block, trombone smears, clarinet, and trumpet.

ELAPSED TIME

0'00″   **First Theme**

First Measure:	bang . . . . bang . . . . silence . . . . silence
numbered beats:	1 . . . . 2 . . . . 3 4
Second Measure:	bang . . . . bang . . . . silence . . . . silence
	1 . . . . 2 . . . . 3 4
Third Measure:	trombone smear . . . .
	1 . . . . 2 . . . . 3 4
Fourth Measure:	smear ends . . . . . silence . . . . .crash
	1 . . . . 2 . . . . 3 4

0'03″   *Fifth, Sixth, Seventh, and Eighth Measures:*
Band plays a new theme, with clarinet playing around the cornet and trombone parts. The drummer plays a military snare drum rhythm as a counteractivity to the rhythms of the horn lines.

0'07″   **Repeat of the First Theme** (A′, 8 measures)
We call this section A′ ("ay-prime") because it is the same as A, but the end differs.

0'15″   **Second Theme** (B, 8 measures)
In the final two beats of A′, the trombone begins to slide up until he reaches the first beat of the second theme, called "B." The entire band joins it on that beat. Then every instrument but clarinet immediately goes silent, and all we hear is clarinet slurring from note to note during beats 2, 3, and 4. This continues through another measure and is called a "stop-time." Then the clarinetist is joined by his bandmates, all playing different lines for an additional six measures (24 beats).

0'23″   **Repeat of the Second Theme** (B′; "bee-prime," 8 measures)
The beginning of this eight-measure section resembles the beginning of the preceding section, but the music goes in a different direction for its final four measures, conveying a more resolved quality than the first B. For that reason we designate this strain as B′ rather than B.

0'30″   **A-A′-B-B′** (32 measures)
This repetition occurs with only minor alterations. Follow the listening guide from the beginning.

1'00″   **Third Theme** (C, 16 measures)
"That Teasin' Rag" composed by Joe Jordan.

Trombone exchanges with clarinet in a call-and-response fashion, playfully trading descending smears; "clickety-clacking" of the drummer's sticks sound military rhythms on the wood block for the first eight measures, then alternately striking wood block and cowbell.

Trombone plays descending smears in unison with piano as a "call." Cornet and clarinet harmonize a bobbing little figure of eighth notes as a "response." This section ends with the horn parts going in different directions. A robust, authoritative trombone part emerges with a repeating figure near the end. Intensity builds and then culminates with a high-pitched, descending clarinet smear.

LISTENING GUIDE *continued on next page*

1'16" **C'** (16 measures)

Note: Every other time C occurs, it ends differently. So these alternate renditions are designated C' ("see-prime").

First beat is played by the drummer striking his cymbal for a crash. Then he plays wood block and cowbell. The trombone then briefly carries a melody of its own in the final eight measures, using a style similar to the tuba parts of march arrangements. The cornet chimes in with a sustained tone on an offbeat in the second to last measure.

1'32" **C** (16 measures)

Drummer begins this section emphasizing his cowbell and uses wood block less than before. Notice the descending trombone smears. A quick, high-pitched clarinet smear ends the section.

1'48" **C'** (16 measures)

Drummer begins the section with a cymbal crash, then plays patterns on wood block. He interrupts his pattern during the middle of this section and strikes the bass drum twice in succession.

2'03" **C** (16 measures)

If you listen closely during the last half of this section, you will hear the piano pounding out bass patterns. This section ends with a descending clarinet smear played more hurriedly than in the first C.

2'18" **C'** (16 measures)

2'26" *Final Eight Measures*

Drummer is playing snare drum instead of wood block and cowbell. Then he ties up the piece with a cymbal crash.

---

clarinet, trombone, piano, and drums. Under the leadership of cornetist **Nick LaRocca** (1889–1961), the band recorded its first 78 rpm record in 1917. They played "Livery Stable Blues" on one side and "Dixie Jazz Band One-Step" on the other (*JCCD1* Track 7). It garnered phenomenally high sales, international fame, and numerous imitators. Even during the 1990s, musicians were forming Dixieland jazz bands in the style of this group. Their "Dixie Jazz Band One-Step" was the first jazz record ever issued.[1]

Oliver's Creole Jazz Band

Joe Oliver's **Creole Jazz Band** was an all-star New Orleans group which, at various times, had most of the best black New Orleans jazz musicians in Chicago. Trumpeter **Joe Oliver** (1885–1938) had worked with several New Orleans bands, then moved to Chicago in 1918, worked with several more bands, and finally formed one of his own. Several recordings made under Oliver's leadership in 1923 are often cited as the first recording of black New Orleans combo jazz. Aside from accompaniments for singers, however, a band led by New Orleans-born trombonist Kid Ory had been the first black jazz combo to have its playing issued on record.[2] This chapter devotes considerable space to the styles of three musicians in Oliver's band: trumpeter Louis Armstrong, clarinetist Johnny Dodds, and drummer Warren "Baby" Dodds. (Listen to their "Dippermouth Blues" in *SCCJ* and "Alligator Hop" on *CCD1* Track 2.)

The Chicago School

Chicago was the center for a very active jazz scene during the 1920s. Musicians there can be described in terms of three main categories. One was the transplanted New Orleans black musicians. Another contained their white New Orleans counterparts,

TABLE 5.2   The New Orleans and Chicago Jazz Styles: Representative Musicians

NEW ORLEANS		CHICAGO
Joe "King" Oliver	Zutty Singleton	Muggsy Spanier
Bunk Johnson	Johnny St. Cyr	Jimmy McPartland (Austin High School)
Freddie Keppard	Lonnie Johnson	Frank Teschemacher (Austin High School)
Buddy Bolden	Omer Simeon	Dave Tough
Louis Armstrong	Jelly Roll Morton	Bud Freeman (Austin High School)
Sidney Bechet	Honore Dutrey	Joe Sullivan
Jimmie Noone	Albert Nicholas	Mezz Mezzrow
Kid Ory	Barney Bigard	Eddie Condon
Baby Dodds	George Brunies	Gene Krupa
Johnny Dodds	Leon Rappolo	

among whom were the New Orleans Rhythm Kings (Friar's Society Orchestra).[3] These two groups of musicians, in turn, were influencing a third group of younger white musicians, many of whom were Chicago natives. This young white community developed what was called *The Chicago Style,* or *The Chicago School.* Its music was modeled on the New Orleans style, but sounded more hurried. Several of these musicians (Jimmy McPartland, Frank Teschemacher, and Bud Freeman) had attended the same Chicago high school, Austin High. They subsequently earned the name of *The Austin High Gang,* though their "gang" included Dave Tough, who attended Wayne High. In addition to the Austin High Gang, the white Chicago scene included other notables (see Table 5.2).

Eventually, the Chicago musicians and the transplanted New Orleans musicians mixed with New York musicians. By the late 1920s, a strong New York scene had also developed. Key performers in the early combo jazz of New York included trumpeter Red Nichols, trombonist Miff Mole, and violinist Joe Venuti. Most of the original Chicagoans had moved to New York by the 1930s.

Early jazz has been identified by many labels which lack standard use. Certain labels have definite meanings for some jazz scholars and musicians, though they are not uniformly applied by everyone. Chicago jazz and New Orleans jazz are two of these terms. Ragtime, gut bucket, barrelhouse, Dixieland, classic jazz, and traditional jazz are others. These terms tend to be applied to solo piano styles as well as combo jazz, to include both black and white musicians, and to refer to music produced by old New Orleans and Chicago veterans as well as revivalist groups. As though this is not already confusing enough, note that the terms "ragtime" and "jazz" have frequently been used to encompass all popular music of the period, not only the jazz-related styles. The problem has worsened because novelist F. Scott Fitzgerald dubbed the 1920s "The Jazz Age." Other writers adopted the term and used it in a way that indiscriminately confused what we today call "jazz" with almost all the syncopated music that was popular in that decade.

Composed by Jelly Roll Morton; recorded on June 10, 1927, for Victor by Jelly Roll Morton (piano), Johnny Dodds (clarinet), Baby Dodds (drums); available on JCCD1 and the *Prentice Hall Jazz Collection*; reissued on Jelly Roll Morton, *Birth of the Hot: The Classic Chicago "Red Hot Peppers" Sessions* (RCA Bluebird: 66641, 1926–27, c1993), and *Jelly Roll Morton: 1926–1930* (JSP: 903, 5CD set, 1926–30, c1991).

This recording is one of the most swinging performances to come out of early jazz. If you let yourself get swept up in the excitement, Morton is so powerful a performer that his music will jump right out of the recording at you. The first minute and a half feature only Jelly Roll Morton's piano playing, yet in his forceful style you can almost hear a full band. As you listen, imagine how the same notes would sound if they were performed by an early jazz band. The left hand usually plays in the stride style, often alternating between bass notes, as though imitating a tuba or string bass, and mid-range chords, as though imitating a banjo or guitar. Melodic passages by Morton's left hand sound like trombone and tuba playing in octaves. Music from the right hand suggests trumpet melodies and clarinet ornamentation. Such an ornate style demonstrates Morton's excellent technical ability on the piano as well as his inclination towards an orchestral approach to playing.

Both the form of this composition and the style of piano playing suggest the influence of ragtime, but the swinging rhythms and improvisational sophistication extend well beyond that tradition and clearly enter the world of jazz. Other aspects of this selection are also worth pointing out. One is the frequent use of stop-time breaks. Their occurrence lends interest and drama to the performance. Musicians tend to take the construction of their solo lines in stop-time breaks quite seriously. They are acutely aware that they are more exposed during the stop-times than when accompanied by other instruments. So they tax their imaginations accordingly and try to come up with something especially interesting. Also, pay attention to Morton's changes in volume. Instead of retaining the same level, he occasionally surprises us. Though common in classical music, this practice has not been common in jazz. Morton's use of it is another indication of the broad scope in his creativity. One more thing to keep in mind is that Morton never stays with any pattern for long. He is constantly in motion, often changing the groove within a single strain. On your second or third pass, it might be easiest to listen to this piece in small chunks and not try to digest the entire piece as a whole. Try following just one part at a time to cope with music that is so packed with activity.

Terms to learn from *Demo* CD: stride style, stop-time solo break, voicing in octaves, clarinet, wire brushes on snare drum, snare drum, syncopation.

ELAPSED
TIME

0'00" **Introduction**

  4 Measures
    Begins with a figure played in octaves, followed by a highly syncopated passage, with many anticipations, as in funk music and Scott Joplin rags.

0'05" **First Strain** (A-A; 8 measures each)

  16 Measures
    Piano plays in stride style. The melody is complicated and quite syncopated. Its accompaniment frequently changes feeling and direction.

0'23" **Repeat of First Strain** (A-A)

  16 Measures
    The original melody is ornamented and modified substantially, creating a contrast to the opening presentation.

0'41" **Second Strain** (2 sections)

  16 Measures
    Left hand plays lines resembling what a trombonist might play in a band.

0'47"   Left hand stops playing, giving right hand a "stop-time" solo-break in which to improvise in the style of a jazz trumpeter.

0'58" **Repeat of Second Strain**

  16 Measures
    This section features three more stop-time solo-breaks by pianist's right hand. Some of Morton's phrases in them sound like those of jazz clarinetists.

LISTENING GUIDE *continued on next page*

1'15"	**First Strain** (A-A)
	16 *Measures*
	The left hand plays a very low-pitched part, with loud off-beats, while right hand returns to playing material from the first strain in a brassy manner.
1'32"	**Introduction to Trio Section**
	4 *Measures*
	Very fast line voiced in octaves, without accompaniment.
1'37"	**Trio Section—First Chorus: Clarinet Solo Improvisation**
	14 *Measures*
	Drummer plays timekeeping rhythm with drum stick on a cymbal, achieving a swing feeling. If you listen carefully, you will be able to hear the bass drum emphasize beats one and three, while the cymbal places an accent on beats two and four. Mere chording by piano here is a big contrast from intense activity before.
1'52"	2-*Measure Stop-time*
1'54"	8 *Measures*
	Piano continues sustained chords. Drummer plays louder and more varied patterns on cymbal.
2'02"	8 *Measures*
	Stride style piano accompaniment resumes. Some syncopated strikes on closed, semi-muffled cymbal are inserted. Notice the excellent sense of pacing here. They turn up the energy.
2'05"	Drummer plays more varied patterns, strikes more instruments.
2'09"	Piano begins stride style and introduces an entirely new rhythm that swings emphatically.
2'11"	**Second Chorus: Clarinet Solo Continued**
	14 *Measures*
	Piano plays off-beat accents with both hands, eliminating the stride feeling. Drummer is striking snare drum with wire brushes emphasizing beats TWO and FOUR. (This is termed a "back-beat.")
2'26"	2 *Measures*
	Stop-time solo-break is filled by piano starting on the upbeat, repeatedly playing one high pitch very quickly in the rhythm of swung eighth notes.
2'28"	8 *Measures*
	Off-beat accents by piano continue under clarinet solo. No bass notes. Drummer's back-beat becomes stronger.
2'34"	8 *Measures*
2'37"	From here on out there are two entirely different, equally important, improvised melodic lines coexisting, one by clarinet, the other by piano.
2'45"	**Third Chorus: Clarinet Solo Continued**
	14 *Measures*
	Drummer changes the piece's feeling by playing a parade rhythm with drum stick striking the snare drum, now achieving a darker, thumpier sound because the snares are disconnected. Piano is playing a low-pitched counter-line, not in conventional stride style.
3'00"	2 *Measures*
	Stop-time break is begun by drummer striking cymbal and immediately grabbing it to stop ringing.
3'02"	14 *Measures*
	Piano plays stride style and counter-line. Clarinet continues solo.
3'11"	4 *Measures (Final Strain)*
	These measures are "tagged" onto the end for one last bout of excitement. Drummer is accenting beats ONE and THREE on the snare drum.
3'21"	To end the piece, drummer executes a "choke" technique in which he strikes the cymbal with his drum stick and immediately grabs it to prevent ringing.

PIANO

We know that jazz piano styles were evolving in places other than New Orleans prior to 1920. In fact, many outstanding jazz pianists of the 1920s were from the East Coast. Many had played unaccompanied. Early jazz piano styles evolved from ragtime. Playing ragtime did not always necessitate reading or memorizing written music. Once the style had been absorbed, skilled pianists appeared who could improvise original rags as well as embellish prewritten ones. One jazz piano style with roots in ragtime is known as *stride style*. Stride piano playing uses percussive, striding, left-hand figures in which low bass notes alternate with mid-range chords, while the right hand plays melodies and embellishments in a very energetic fashion.[4]

Demo CD *Track 38;* *"You've Got to Be Modernistic,"* JCCD1 *Track 13*

Jelly Roll Morton

Jelly Roll Morton (1890–1941) was a pianist, composer-arranger, and bandleader from New Orleans. He was one of the first jazz pianists as well as the first important jazz composer. Morton was capable of performing in both the ragtime style and the jazz style. He perfected rhythmic techniques that altered the character of eighth-note lines so that they swung. Pianist-historian James Dapogny has pointed out that Morton used long-short, long-short patterns in playing eighth notes and that Morton alternated intensities of eighth notes so that they gave the impression of strong-weak, strong-weak (see Appendix B for explanation). By doing this and reducing adornment, Morton played with a lighter and more swinging feeling than was typical of ragtime.

Demo CD *Track 34;* *"Wolverine Blues,"* JCCD1 *Track 8*

Morton's piano style was quite involved. He often played two or three lines at a time, much in the manner of a band. It was as though trumpet parts, clarinet parts, and trombone parts were being heard coming from a piano! Morton put a variety of themes and much activity into a single piece. Sometimes he would use solo breaks in the same manner as horns in a combo. Morton mixed ragtime with less formal, more blues-oriented New Orleans styles. (For example, listen to "Maple Leaf Rag" in *SCCJ*, and see Appendix G.)

The best-known of Morton's several bands were a series of recording groups in Chicago called the Red Hot Peppers.[5] Morton employed many of the same New Orleans-born musicians shared by other black Chicago groups. However, under Morton's leadership, the resulting sounds were unusually well-organized, though they retained the spirit of music made by less tightly run bands. The imagination of Morton's compositions and arrangements on these recordings is still respected by jazz composers and scholars. (Listen to his "Black Bottom Stomp" in *SCCJ*.)

In summary, Jelly Roll Morton is historically notable because:

1. He was the first important jazz composer, and several of his pieces became well-known in rearranged form played by other bands—"Wolverine Blues," "Milenburg Joys," "Wild Man Blues," "King Porter Stomp."

2. He introduced arranging practices in his small-group performances that came to be imitated during early stages in the history of big bands.

3. He was one of the first jazz musicians to blend composition with improvisation in an elaborate and balanced way that still conveyed the kind of excitement that had typified collectively improvised jazz. In this way, Morton anticipated similar contributions by Duke Ellington, Charlie Mingus, and Sun Ra.

4. He recorded piano solos that were well-organized, forcefully executed musical statements with horn-like lines in them.

5. He helped bridge the gap between ragtime piano style and jazz piano style by loosening ragtime's rhythmic feeling and decreasing its embellishments.

Jelly Roll Morton and his Red Hot Peppers, one of the first groups to masterfully combine improvisation and well-developed compositions without losing the spirit of New Orleans jazz. *Left to right:* Andrew Hilaire (drums), Kid Ory (trombone), George Mitchell (trumpet), John Lindsay (bass), Morton (piano), Johnny St. Cyr (banjo), Omer Simeon (clarinet). Pictured here in 1926.

(Photo courtesy of Duncan Schiedt)

Earl Hines

Earl Hines (1903–1983) was an early jazz pianist who significantly influenced piano playing styles of the 1930s and 1940s. Born in Pittsburgh, Hines moved to Chicago in 1924. He brought with him an assortment of different jazz techniques, all combined in the form of one catchy style. His playing began its enormous influence during the late 1920s when he recorded with Louis Armstrong and made a series of important records of his own. This impact extended during the 1930s by way of radio broadcasts and tours with the big band he led at the Grand Terrace Ballroom in Chicago from 1928 to 1939. Musicians as far away as Kansas and Texas heard his broadcasts. The Hines style affected Art Tatum, Count Basie, Teddy Wilson, and Nat Cole. Hines had an influence on modern jazz because these players, in turn, influenced the development of modern styles. They influenced Bud Powell, for example, the single most imitated pianist in modern jazz of the 1950s.

"West End Blues," JCCD1 *Track 10*

Much of the piano music made by Hines can be called "brassy." This is partly because of the great physical force Hines employed to strike the piano keys. In fact, the sheer force of his left-hand playing broke the large, strong, bass strings on a few pianos. (Most people cannot break those strings even by smashing a fist down on the piano's bass keys.) Even when Hines played in a flowery way, a roughness remained in his sound. Rarely was anything sustained, and nearly everything had a punching quality. These properties combined with his method of phrasing to lend a brassy quality to the sound of the piano. Because his right-hand lines sometimes sound like jazz trumpet playing, **the Hines approach earned the title of trumpet-style or horn-like.** His piano lines even seem to breathe at the moments a trumpeter would breathe. Additionally they contained phrases and rhythms preferred by trumpeters rather than pianists. This manner stems partly from Hines having originally begun his musical training with the goal of becoming a trumpeter instead of a pianist. And it stems from what Hines did to overcome the piano's inability to be heard over loud band instruments. We must

Demo CD Track 41;
"West End Blues,"
JCCD1 Track 10

remember that he was playing long before electronic amplification came to the aid of jazz pianists. To manage the task of cutting through, he played very hard, phrased like a trumpeter, and doubled his right-hand melody lines in octaves.

The Hines style is the one most commonly associated with the term "trumpet-style," despite Jelly Roll Morton's having previously improvised piano passages in the manner of band instruments. This approach is historically significant because, by playing more as a horn and less in the standard piano styles, Hines paved the way for modern jazz pianists who solo with essentially the same conception that is used by jazz trumpeters and saxophonists. It is less flowery and more direct. It is less classically pianistic and more swinging. Additionally it is important to realize that the Hines approach is more flexible than the ragtime and stride approaches. Because of this, Hines had the capacity for conveying a broader assortment of musical feelings.

Earl Hines is known for a sturdy sense of tempo that persisted relentlessly despite the many interruptions in melodic flow that he made. This sense of tempo, plus his insistently percussive attack and varied syncopations, made Hines one of the most rhythmically compelling jazz pianists. (Listen to Hines on Armstrong's recording of "Weather Bird" in *SCCJ*.)

Hines was prone to introducing new and often jarring ideas into his solos in mid-flight, departing on tangents, the source of which was understood only by him. Instead of maintaining a smooth flow and consistent texture from the beginning of a piece to its end, he filled his work with surprises. In the middle of a piece, he would frequently stop a pattern, cease left-hand accompaniment, employing both hands to seemingly leap all over the keyboard before resuming any repeating pattern. On any one of his unaccompanied piano solos, he pulled a multitude of techniques into play, sometimes all in a single piece:[6]

Demo CD Tracks
37–42

1. stride style
2. walking tenths (the two outside fingers of the left hand moving in scale-wise fashion, simultaneously sounding tones of about a ten-step interval apart)
3. horn-like lines
4. flowery embellishments
5. octave voicing
6. tremolo
7. solo breaks for the right hand
8. brief double-time figures
9. off-balance left-hand rhythms that are highly syncopated, seeming to come out of nowhere

Later, these techniques prominently appeared in the playing of several generations of jazz pianists. Some historians believe that Hines was the single most pervasive influence on pianists of the swing era in the 1930s, and a few consider him to be the most influential of all jazz pianists. He did not come up with most of these techniques himself, but he combined them in a way that was absorbed by others.

Fats Waller

New York-born **Fats Waller** (1904–1943) was one of the best known stride pianists.[7] Waller played with excellent technique and a bouncing swing feeling which he used to create countless lighthearted and joyful performances. Count Basie, Art Tatum, and Dave Brubeck have all cited Waller as an influence on their styles. Waller wrote hundreds of tunes, the most familiar of which are "Ain't Misbehavin'," "Honeysuckle Rose," "Squeeze Me," and "Jitterbug Waltz." During the 1970s, an entire Broadway revue was devoted to music associated with Waller. This immensely successful show was called *Ain't Misbehavin'*, and it revived interest in Waller's work.

"Handful of Keys,"
JCCD1 Track 12 and
"I Ain't Got Nobody"
in SCCJ

Recorded in 1929 for Victor; available on *JCCD1*; reissued on *Fats Waller Piano Solos: Turn on the Heat*. RCA Bluebird: 2482, 2CD set, c1991.

Of his many recordings that delighted listeners with their cheerful and swinging qualities, pianist Fats Waller is said to have been happiest with this 1929 performance of "Handful of Keys." Waller supposedly improvised this entire piece at the beginning of one of his band's recording sessions. There are at least two good reasons for us to believe this. First, we know that he was capable of such achievements. He was reputed to walk into a publisher's office whenever he needed cash and sit down at their piano and spontaneously compose a new tune to sell. Second, the formula for this piece is so simple that it would not have proven difficult to produce spontaneously. Equally reasonable, however, is that he had thought about some lines in the piece or at least considered the piece's overall construction before he sat down at the recording studio's piano. Of all the sections in his piece, his B-section (the bridge) is the one most likely to have been improvised, as his lines for it in the second chorus and in subsequent recordings are totally different than for the first chorus. Another section quite likely to have been spontaneous is his final romp, beginning at 2′11″. It taps devices that were common to stride pianists of the time. Therefore, it could have been improvised from those devices. His ending could have been spontaneous as well.

The performance contains: (1) an eight-measure introduction, (2) two choruses of a main melody that occupies thirty-two measures in A-A-B-A form, (3) a four-measure interlude that changes the key, (4) a thirty-two measure "Trio" strain in A-B-C-D form with its own melody, (5) two choruses of the main theme in the original key, and (6) a tag. The A-section consists of a two-measure phrase that climbs the piano keys three times before a different phrase concludes the section. The bridge of the tune follows the chord progression that the bridge of George Gershwin's "I Got Rhythm" follows, though the possibility of borrowing from Gershwin is unlikely because the "Girl Crazy" show that introduced it did not play on Broadway until the year after Waller recorded "Handful of Keys."

In listening to this recording, we may at first be most inclined to hear the melodic aspects of the piano sound. With his right hand playing higher pitches, Waller managed a prettier tone quality than almost every other pianist, and these higher pitches were executed so crisply and sweetly that we might not want to bother attending to anything else. But in addition to listening for the high pitches played by Waller's right hand, it is also useful to notice the persistent *boom-chk, boom-chk* technique achieved by Waller's left-handed playing of low pitches to accompany the high pitch creations of his right hand. This combination of single bass note alternating with chord is the technique for the left hand that was used by most pianists of his era. In our description, the *"boom"* designates the bass note played on the first and third of each four beats. The *"chk"* designates the chord played on the second and fourth beats. With careful listening, you may come to appreciate the buoyant quality that Waller extracted from the piano when he struck bass keys for his bass notes. His touch enabled him to almost emulate a tuba or string bass.

Waller was one of the foremost stride pianists. The left-hand work is termed "stride" because it moves as though walking down the street in a striding fashion. (Listen to Track 38 on *Demo CD*.) You might wish to compare Waller's "Handful of Keys" (*JCCD* Track 12) with James P. Johnson's "You've Got to Be Modernistic" (on *JCCD1* Track 13). Johnson was ten years older and an influence on Waller, though Waller had a somewhat lighter touch with more spring than Johnson's. Both men were formidable composers who not only wrote entire Broadway shows, but also penned pop tunes that are still performed today.

Though there are virtues to hear in every phrase of music on "Handful of Keys," pay particular attention to the power and swing feeling evoked by rhythmic figures in Waller's romp, beginning at 2′11″. They anticipate those assigned to horns in big bands of the 1930s, and their effect is one of the reasons for the style to be dubbed the "swing" era. Also notice how cleverly Waller manipulates rhythmic emphasis in that romp and again in the ending at 2′39″ so that both the romp and the ending have unexpected stresses. This also occurs in the rhythmic devices that Louis Armstrong had so masterfully used on his 1927 scat vocal in "Hotter Than That" (*JCCD1* Track 11). Just as Armstrong catches listeners off guard if they are trying to keep time during the singer's intentionally delayed positionings, Waller's ending rhythms also potentially throw off anyone trying to keep track of the pulse. Both Waller and Armstrong were commanding in their capacity to toy with rhythms and evoke tremendous swing feeling in the listener. They set the pace for generations of jazz musicians to come. Subsequent improvisers were judged according to how well they had mastered these capacities.

LISTENING GUIDE *continued on next page*

ELAPSED TIME	MUSICAL EVENTS

Introduction

0'00"   eight-measure introduction

First Chorus

0'08"   **A**   main "Handful of Keys" melody

0'16"   **A**

0'23"   **B**   Bridge is most likely entirely improvised.

0'31"   **A**

Second Chorus

0'39"   **A-A**   Waller performs the melody an octave higher.

0'53"   **B**   Waller plays different melodic material than he did in the first bridge.

1'01"   **A**

Interlude

1'08"   Four-measure section announces "Trio" section in new key.

Trio Section (new melody in A-B-C-D form)

1'12"   **A**

1'19"   **B**

1'25"   last two measures: energetic break, descending into bass pitches

1'27"   **C**

1'34"   **D**

1'41"   single chord abruptly shifts back to the original key

Third Chorus

1'42"   **A**   "Handful of Keys" main melody returns, but its phrases are played in successively higher octaves.

1'49"   **A**

1'56"   **B**

2'02"   last two measures: break

2'04"   **A**   Section is improvised.

2'07"   Left-hand bass part becomes walking octaves, and segues into the next chorus without interruption.

Fourth Chorus

2'11"   **A**   Improvised romp, going up and down the keyboard with right hand, accompanied by return to um-chck stride style for left hand.

2'19"   **A**

2'26"   **B**

2'28"   break: ascending arpeggio (chord notes sounded one at a time) in evenly paced fashion.

2'32"   break: ascending arpeggio (chord notes sounded one at a time) in evenly paced fashion.

2'34"   **A**   first four measures: The repeated rhythm of a heavy-handed chord in treble range is staggered in relation to the bass pulse, as though evenly divided into three occurrences for every two pulses of the tune's tempo.

Ending (begins after sixth measure of A-section, ultimately adding four measures)

2'39"   precarious rhythmic gesture: one bass-range rhythm played three times but at different positions in relation to the beat

2'41"   Tempo slows slightly.

2'43"   a gentle arpeggio, the top note of which is sounded three times, as though to echo

Boogie Woogie

In addition to ragtime and stride styles, early jazz pianists developed **boogie woogie.** A prime characteristic of boogie woogie is the subdivision of each beat in the left-hand figures so that, in a measure of four beats, there are actually eight pulses ("eight to the bar"). These left-hand patterns surfaced around 1912 in southern pianists. If you hear a record of boogie woogie, you will have no trouble recognizing it because the style has been revived so often it will be familiar to you. Pianist Pinetop Smith actually entitled one of his tunes "Boogie Woogie," and his own rendition of it was a hit record in 1929. An adaptation of that piece became an even bigger hit record in 1938 and again in 1943 for trombonist Tommy Dorsey's big band. The leading boogie woogie pianists include Pete Johnson, Albert Ammons, Cow Cow Davenport, and Meade Lux Lewis (listen to Lewis's "Honky Tonk Train Blues" in *SCCJ*). Popular pianist Jerry Lee Lewis developed much of his style from this concept. Note that some ways the word "boogie" was used during the 1970s and 1980s do not fit the meaning described here.

| Demo CD *Track 38*

James P. Johnson

James P. Johnson (1894–1955) was born in New Jersey and is part of an East Coast jazz piano tradition that was developing at about the same time as combo jazz was developing in New Orleans. He was the most respected and influential of pianists who smoothed the transition from ragtime to jazz. One of the first jazz musicians to broadcast on the radio, Johnson was already a prominent figure by the time jazz began to be recorded. In 1914 he wrote "Carolina Shout," and then, when he recorded a version of it in 1921, the style behind his reputation was documented for posterity (*SCCJ*). Though stride style was played by other pre-1920s pianists also, Johnson is usually referred to as "the father of stride piano" because his own brand of stride style did the most to spread this approach. According to Johnson's biographers, Dick Wellstood and Willa Rouder, Johnson dispensed with the stiff rhythms, the broken-chord melodies and march-like bass of ragtime, while contributing a fluidity, a harmonic sophistication, and an attention to chord voicings. He perfected an orchestral approach to jazz piano playing, as though he were a one-man band. Many musicians feel that he was never surpassed in this style. At a time when informal competitions among solo pianists were common in New York, Johnson is said to have won more contests than anyone else. His speed, precision, dexterity, and imagination amazed musicians. The force and swing of his pianistic feats are legendary. Most jazz pianists who emerged during the 1920s, such as Art Tatum and Duke Ellington, said that Johnson influenced them.

James P. Johnson, father of stride piano, pictured here in 1921 at age 27. (Photo courtesy of Frank Driggs)

| Demo CD *Track 38*

"You've Got to Be Modernistic." JCCD1 *Track 13*

James P. Johnson is known to jazz musicians primarily as an innovative stride pianist, but much of his living was made from work as composer-conductor-pianist for stage shows, and accompanist for singers. Johnson wrote 230 popular tunes, and 19 symphonic works, as well as scoring 11 musicals for the stage. In fact, the famous piece "The Charleston" was written by Johnson for a stage show called *Runnin' Wild*, that was popular in 1923. So in appreciating Johnson's status in American music, we need to remember that only one aspect of his career was central to jazz history. Since

Composed and performed by pianist James P. Johnson, recorded for Brunswick on January 21, 1930; reissued on *Snowy Morning Blues* (Decca Jazz: 604, 1930, 1944, c1991)

James P. Johnson was among the two or three most significant pianists in the first 30 years of jazz. This recording documents one of his meatiest and most spirited performances. The virtuoso technique, staggering strength, and richness displayed on this recording help us understand why an entire generation of stride-style pianists were so impressed.

Pay particular attention to the stride-bass style played by Johnson's left hand almost relentlessly in this performance. The tremendous momentum of the piece is partly due to the locomotive-like power of Johnson's left-hand work and partly due to his percussive forcefulness in playing the highly syncopated right-hand parts.

Johnson worked out in advance most of what is heard here, though he varied it somewhat from performance to performance, as was the practice for pianists at that time. The choruses of the trio section contain the most improvisation, and Johnson's renditions of the first and second strains contain the least.

ELAPSED

TIME

0'00" **Introduction**

  4 Measures

0'04" **First Strain** (technically termed "first strain")

  16 Measures (A-A'-A-B, four measures in each section)

0'20" **Repeat of First Strain,** with some modifications

  16 Measures (A-A'-A-B, four measures in each section)

0'34" **Second Strain**

  16 Measures (A-A-B-A, four measures in each section)

  The striding left-hand figures are sporadic.

  Notice the syncopation and tricky interaction of the right and left hands in the B-section.

0'48" **Repeat of Second Strain,** with modifications

  16 Measures (A-A-B-A, four measures in each section)

  To appreciate how rhythmically complicated the B-section is, notice how much easier it is to count "1234 2234 3234 . . . " when you are listening to the other sections.

1'05" **First Strain**

  16 measures

  The melody is played an octave higher than before.

  The striding left-hand part resumes.

1'19" **Introduction to Trio Section**

  4 measures

  This new group of sections is termed a "trio" because it is like the third section of a march, and such sections used to be written in three-part harmony.

  In each 16-measure chorus of this trio, Johnson selects a melodic idea and varies it. Some of the choruses center around syncopated riffs in the manner that became common for swing era band arrangements, a device that is central to the pieces in the African American Retentions Sequence (*JCCD1* Tracks 3–6). And, like its effect there, the riff style here also evokes a lilting, buoyant feeling. This is some of the first piano music to "swing" in the jazz sense of the term.

1'23" **The "Trio" Section**

  First Chorus of Trio

  Johnson repeats a single riff six times.

1'40"   *Second Chorus of Trio*

  Johnson toys with a figure that involves firmly striking two adjacent piano keys in the high register of the piano and letting the resulting dissonance ring. These piano keys

LISTENING GUIDE *continued on next page*

represent the "major third" and "minor third" steps of the scale, which when crushed together approximate a "blue pitch" (*Demo CD* Track 58).

1'53"	*Third Chorus*	Johnson's melody for this chorus is played in the bass range.
2'09"	*Fourth Chorus*	This chorus is the most rag-like of all Johnson's choruses.
2'24"	*Fifth Chorus*	The melody of this chorus is like the first strain.
2'40"	*Sixth Chorus*	Johnson bases the first eight measures on one riff, the second eight measures on another.
2'54"	*Seventh Chorus*	Johnson plays his right-hand chords more frequently, thereby giving the illusion that the tempo has increased.

so much of his time was occupied writing nonjazz works, he was not very visible in the jazz scene for some years. His jazz stature was eclipsed during the 1930s by the attention given to other players. For this reason, he has not been given his proper due, even though he continued to record jazz during the 1940s.[8]

LOUIS ARMSTRONG

Trumpeter **Louis Armstrong** (1901–1971) is often called the "father of jazz." In fact, musicians often refer to him as "Pops." No list of jazz greats omits him, and most start with him. Born in New Orleans, he left in 1922 to join Joe Oliver's New Orleans style band in Chicago. The band's best known piece, "Dippermouth Blues," takes its title from another Armstrong nickname, a reference to his mouth being as large as a dipper. A third nickname, Satchmo, is a variation on the same idea: Satchel Mouth.

Although some of Armstrong's 1940s and 1950s recordings are outstanding, his most significant are the innovative series he made in 1927 and 1928 billed as "Louis Armstrong and His Hot Five" (or "Hot Seven").[9] Some of them included his colleagues from New Orleans, trombonist Kid Ory and clarinetist Johnny Dodds. Armstrong's earliest appearances on record had displayed him involved primarily with collective improvisation, as in his 1924 playing with Clarence Williams on "Cake Walkin' Babies from Home" (in *SCCJ*). But on his Hot Five and Hot Seven recordings of 1925–1928, Armstrong's dramatic solo style was showcased more than his collective improvisation skills. The music that he made in those recordings became a model for the swing era that followed.

Louis Armstrong appeared in about 50 movies and sang in most of his post-1930 performances. For instance, his vocal rendition of the theme from the Broadway musical *Hello, Dolly* was #1 for one week on the popularity charts. On February 15, 1964, he displaced the phenomenally popular singing group called The Beatles. With the success of the 1988 revival of his "What a Wonderful World" (in the movie *Good Morning Vietnam*), Armstrong demonstrated the longest run of having singles rate on the national popularity charts. He even outdistanced singers Bing Crosby and Frank Sinatra. (Crosby and Armstrong both had hits during the 1920s.) Understandably then, the post-1930s public knows Armstrong more as an entertainer than as an innovative jazz improviser. Even though they have heard his name, most people are not aware of Armstrong's monumental contributions to the history of jazz.

"West End Blues" featuring Louis Armstrong and Earl Hines

Composed by Joe "King" Oliver; recorded for Okeh on June 6, 1928, in Chicago by Louis Armstrong (trumpet and vocal), Jimmy Strong (clarinet), Fred Robinson (trombone), Earl Hines (piano), Mancy Cara (banjo), and Zutty Singleton (drums); available on SCCJ; reissued on Armstrong, *The Complete Hot Five and Hot Seven Recordings,* Vol. 3 (Columbia/Legacy: 87011, 1927–28, c2003).

Terms to know from the *Demo CD* before using this listening guide: ride rhythm, legato, staccato, pitch smear, tremolo, octave voicing, stride style, double-time, 12-bar blues, chorus, vibrato, banjo, trumpet, trombone, and clarinet. Instruments to watch on *DVD:* trumpet on Track 60, clarinet on Track 69, trombone on Track 66, and banjo on Track 43.

ELAPSED TIME

0'00" **Introduction**

The opening phrases in this piece are among the most famous in jazz history. Note the drama as Armstrong reaches up to his highest note, the one he sustains. Then listen to the manner in which he gradually descends to finish with a note that makes you eager to hear what follows. Notice his warm, brassy tone and his sure-footed manner. This introduction is a masterpiece that you might want to hear several times before listening to the rest of the performance.

The idea of a bravura solo style, particularly an unaccompanied solo passage like this, was common in light classical music that was popular in America around 1900. Virtuoso cornet soloists were frequently featured in band concerts at that time. In addition, the trumpet sounds of Mexican bands that visited New Orleans had impressed musicians there. When Louis Armstrong devised this stirring opening, he was drawing, either consciously or unconsciously, from that tradition in light classical music, and he was establishing a tradition in jazz.

0'13" Full band plays a chord.

0'16" **First Chorus** (a 12-bar blues played slowly)

Melody Played by Armstrong on Trumpet
Notice Armstrong's firm, deliberate manner and quick vibrato.
Accompaniment includes:
soft, sustained trombone notes (often preceded by a smear of pitch that begins well below the ultimate note);
sustained tones of clarinet, sometimes paralleling the motion of the trumpet line (listen for the clarinet's edgy timbre and fast vibrato);
trombone and clarinet notes together indicating the chords changing underneath the trumpet;
piano chords sounded in unison along with banjo chords played staccato on each beat ("chomp chomp chomp chomp . . .").

0'50" **Second Chorus**

Trombone Solo
The trombonist uses the high register and many smears of pitch.
Accompaniment includes:
staccato chording from banjo;
tremolo chords from piano;
slow ride rhythm played by drummer on a hand-held "Bock-A-Da-Bock" apparatus that brings together two cymbals that are each about three inches wide, played by drummer cupping the apparatus in his hand as in playing spoons.*

1'25" **Third Chorus**

Improvised Duet between Clarinet and Armstrong's Vocal
This chorus employs a call-and-response format, with the vocal supplying the responses. It is an early example of "scat" singing. Piano and banjo are chording in a staccato

*The Bock-A-Da-Bock cymbal apparatus is pictured as "cymbal tongs" on page 50 of *The Percussionist's Dictionary* by Joseph Adato and George Judy (Belwin Mills, 1984; Warner Bros.: SB 1040, 2000), available from *sheetmusicplus.com.*

LISTENING GUIDE *continued on next page*

manner on each beat. The duet's last phrase is done in harmony. No percussion instruments are used here or in the next chorus.

2'00"   **Fourth Chorus**

Unaccompanied Piano Improvisation by Earl Hines

First Four Measures
Pianist's left hand is contributing legato chording in stride style while right hand improvises flowery figures.

2'10"   *Second Four Measures*
Style of playing by right hand switches to brash character and pounds out a double-time figure voiced in octaves. This is the famous "trumpet-style" piano playing of Earl Hines.

2'20"   *Third Four Measures*
Style returns to flowery character.

2'32"   **Fifth Chorus**

Trumpet Solo

First Four Measures
Sustained high note from trumpet for 16 beats. Accompaniment includes staccato chords from piano on each beat, and sustained trombone notes, and sustained clarinet notes.

2'45"   *Second Four Measures*
Trumpet line features double-timing.

2'55"   *Third Four Measures*
Horns stop playing for 12 beats while piano plays a descending sequence of chords, striking each in bell-like fashion, linking them with a glissando. Piano sustains a chord. Armstrong returns with a long, drawn-out bluesy figure played in a markedly slowed pace. It is accompanied by long tones harmonized by trombone, clarinet, and piano to form three different chords that conclude the piece.

Armstrong was the most widely imitated jazz improviser prior to the appearance of modern saxophonist Charlie Parker in the 1940s. Armstrong's style is particularly easy to detect in three of the most prominent trumpeters of the 1930s and 1940s: Oran "Hot Lips" Page, Bunny Berigan, and Buck Clayton. His influence extended not only to trumpeters, but to saxophonists, pianists, guitarists, and trombonists. For instance, Johnny Hodges, the most influential alto saxophonist of the 1930s, said that Armstrong influenced his sax style. Players within the swing era almost universally cite Armstrong's influence. Segments of his tunes and improvisations continued to be found in the work of such post-swing era innovators as Charlie Parker and Lee Konitz.

Louis Armstrong's Historic Contributions

Let's examine a few aspects of Armstrong's work that musicians appreciated so much:

1. Armstrong showed that the New Orleans technique of collective improvisation need not be the only approach to jazz horn work. Intelligently developed solos could be improvised in a stirring manner, and the musical effectiveness of such solos need not depend much on ensemble interaction. In other words, **Armstrong was one of the first great soloists in jazz history,** and, partly because of him, post-Armstrong styles usually stressed solo improvisation instead of group improvisation.

2. Armstrong was one of the first jazz musicians to refine a rhythmic conception that
   a. abandoned the stiffness of ragtime,
   b. employed swing eighth-note patterns,
   c. gracefully syncopated selected rhythmic figures, sometimes staggering the placement of an entire phrase, as though he were playing behind the beat, a technique called "rhythmic displacement." This conveyed a more relaxed feeling than ragtime, and it exhibited more variety in the ways that notes seemed to tug at opposite sides of the beat.

   These rhythmic elements combined to produce one of the first jazz styles that could elicit in listeners what we today call "jazz swing feeling." None of these elements was entirely new with Armstrong. However, they were more clearly evident in his work as a finished product than in the playing of either his predecessors or other trumpeters of the 1920s.

3. Despite the numerous giants who have followed Armstrong in jazz history, few have approximated his skill and creativity as musical architects. Few had his degree of control over the general form of a solo. He calmly forged sensible lines that had both the flow of spontaneity and the stamp of finality. His improvisations are well-paced, succinct statements. The organization of Armstrong's phrases suggests that he was thinking ahead, yet the phrases manage to sound spontaneous, rather than calculated.

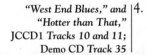

"West End Blues," and "Hotter than That," JCCD1 Tracks 10 and 11; Demo CD Track 35

4. He brought a superb sense of drama to jazz solo conception. His pacing was careful, allowing a solo to build tension. His double-time solo breaks were constructed to achieve maximum excitement, and his high-note endings ensured a properly timed peak of intensity and resolution of tension.

5. During a period when most improvisers were satisfied simply to embellish or paraphrase a tune's melody—and Armstrong himself was a master at both—Armstrong frequently broke away from the melody, and improvised original, melody-like lines that were compatible with the tune's chord progressions. This became the predominant approach for jazz improvisation thereafter.

6. Armstrong's command of the trumpet was arguably greater than that of any preceding jazz trumpeter who recorded. It became a model to which others aspired. He had an enormous, brassy tone, and remarkable range. Altogether with his rhythmic and dramatic sense, he conveyed a certainty and surging power. Even during the final decades of his career, Armstrong maintained a tone quality that was unusual for its weight, breadth, and richness.

7. Armstrong popularized the musical vocabulary of New Orleans trumpet style and then extended it.

8. Armstrong's tremendously fertile melodic imagination provided jazz with a repertory of phrases and ways of going about constructing improvisations. In other words, he extended the vocabulary for the jazz soloist.

These next two contributions are less central to what made his reputation among jazz instrumentalists, but they remain significant in the broadest sense of jazz history.

9. The Armstrong singing style influenced many popular singers, including Louis Prima, Billie Holiday, and Bing Crosby. In this way, he affected American music beyond the boundaries of jazz. Armstrong's influence was so pervasive that Leslie Gourse titled a book about American jazz singers *Louis's Children*.

Louis Armstrong, the most influential of all jazz musicians, and the most influential trumpeter in pre-modern jazz. Pictured here at age 26, in 1927, the year several of his classic Hot Five and Hot Seven recordings were made.

(Photo courtesy of Frank Driggs)

10. Armstrong popularized scat singing, a vocal technique in which lyrics are not used. The voice improvises in the manner of a jazz trumpeter or saxophonist. (Examples can be heard in "Hotter Than That," *JCCD1* Track 11.) Recent examples of the technique can be found in the work of George Benson, Al Jarreau, and Bobby McFerrin.

In the early years of jazz, the cornet was much more widely used than the trumpet. The trumpet's and cornet's tones and ranges are quite similar, and many listeners cannot tell the two instruments apart. The tone color of the cornet is said to be mellow, and that of the trumpet is said to be more brilliant. Their appearance is also a confusing factor, but one distinguishing feature is the apparent length. The tubing of the cornet, although equal in length to that of the trumpet, is organized so that it looks shorter. Some old jazz cornets are especially compact and stubby.

The prime difference between trumpet and cornet, a difference that is difficult to see, is that the inside of the cornet's tubing is cone-like, whereas the trumpet's is more cylinder-like. The technical term for the inside diameter is "bore." So, it is said that cornets have a primarily conical bore and trumpets have a primarily cylindrical bore. Their mouthpieces are also slightly different, although the instruments are played in almost the same way.

Except for Nat Adderley and Thad Jones, most modern players have used trumpet instead of cornet. Before 1927 nearly all jazz trumpeters used the cornet. The 1930s to early 1940s was a period of transition between the two instruments: every band had a so-called trumpet section, but in at least two famous bands, Duke Ellington's and Fletcher Henderson's, the trumpet section sometimes contained more cornets than trumpets. This book ignores the problem and labels most cornetists as trumpeters for the following reasons: (a) most listeners cannot detect the difference in sound; (b) it is often impossible to determine from recording data whether a player was using trumpet or cornet on a particular session; (c) the only well-known player who used cornet exclusively throughout his career was Bix Beiderbecke; and (d) trumpet tone colors in jazz vary across a range that actually encompasses the pure tones of both trumpet and cornet.

trumpet

cornet

(Courtesy C. G. Conn Company)

BIX BEIDERBECKE

Bix Beiderbecke (1903–1931) was a very important white trumpeter and composer from Iowa. His recordings are significant in early jazz, but he fits neatly into neither New Orleans nor Chicago style. He and Armstrong developed about the same time and became the leading trumpeters for the late 1920s and early 1930s. Beiderbecke's style gave young trumpeters an alternative to the model that Armstrong provided.

Composed by Lil Hardin; recorded in 1927 for Okeh by Louis Armstrong (trumpet and vocal), Johnny Dodds (clarinet), Kid Ory (trombone), Lil Hardin (piano), Johnny St. Cyr (banjo), and Lonnie Johnson (guitar). Reissued on *The Complete Hot Fives and Hot Seven Recordings*, Vol. 3. Columbia/Legacy: 87011, c2003, available on *SCCJ*.

Terms to learn from *Demo CD*: trumpet, trombone, clarinet, banjo, blue note, legato, staccato, vibrato, swing eighth notes, and syncopation. Examples to view on the *DVD*: trumpet on Track 60, trombone on Track 66, clarinet on Track 69, banjo on Track 43, solo break on Track 53, and swing eighth notes on Track 40.

"Hotter Than That" was made by a group of musicians who did not perform with this same personnel outside the recording studio. When guitarist Lonnie Johnson was not participating, the group was billed as "The Hot Five." Their recordings are routinely considered to be among the most important in jazz history. Books and scholarly theses have touted their music's virtues. Jazz fans and scholars have designated the quality of Armstrong's improvisations on their recordings as "classic." If you enjoy this selection, you will probably also enjoy their "Potato Head Blues," "Savoy Blues," "Struttin' with Some Barbecue," and "Tight Like This."

Tune titles in jazz usually do next to nothing to help listeners determine the character of the music, but "Hotter Than That" is an exception. The trumpet playing and band work here is not merely hot. It is on fire! Notice how hard-hitting the trumpet part is during the first 30 seconds. Pay attention to how authoritatively Armstrong jumps into the scat singing at 1'19". If you let yourself get swept up in this music, you can't miss how much life emerges from the playing.

This recording should aid readers who have been wondering what "swing feeling" means. It is the feeling evoked by the rhythmic properties of the music on "Hotter Than That," especially from 0'18" to 0'43", 1'19" to 1'36", and 2'35" to 2'50". Keep in mind that the combination of syncopations and swing eighth notes in Armstrong's lines is not found in all styles that have been called "jazz." For instance, it is lacking in the earliest jazz by musicians other than Armstrong and Fats Waller. It is missing in the clarinet and trombone solos at 1'01" and 2'18". It is also missing in recent jazz styles, for example, most avant-garde of the 1960s and 1970s.

Here are a few structural aspects that might give you deeper appreciation of this selection. In writing "Hotter Than That," composer Lil Hardin borrowed the chord progression from the final strain of the 1918 piece by the Original Dixieland Jazz Band called "Tiger Rag." Saxophonist Don Redman is reputed to have arranged her work for this session. Part of the performance's drama is achieved by having the band stop for the final eight beats of selected B-sections and C-sections to let a soloist continue improvising. The tempo is maintained and the passage of chords remains in effect, but we don't hear explicit statement of the beat or any chords from piano or banjo. Such a device is called a "break," and we get to hear clarinet, vocal, and trumpet featured alone at such moments.

Another structural aspect to keep in mind is how Armstrong brings to completion almost every solo idea. His overall command of the solo's form distinguished him from other jazz giants who were equally creative and instrumentally virtuosic but ended up with almost haphazard, stream-of-conscious organization in many of their improvisations.

At 1'39" we get to witness a high point in the rhythmic brilliance of Armstrong's creativity. This is one of the most celebrated passages in all of jazz, and not just because it provides a good example of scat singing by its leading practitioner. At this part of his solo, Armstrong places scatted tones at moments displaced from the beat of his accompanists. This causes an effect of his rhythm tugging at his accompanists's rhythm so much that we might lose our place if we try to account for the beat by listening to the solo line. Armstrong went way out on a limb here but knew precisely what he was doing at every moment. Ultimately, things don't fall apart, but his displacements certainly give us a precarious moment in the meantime. Close listening reveals that Armstrong is staggering the placement of his notes so that there are three notes of equal duration for every four from his accompanists. They are positioned atop the underlying passage of beats such that we might actually construe his part as a waltz and theirs as a march. Technically known as "polymetric," this device superimposes two different meters in the same time span. ("Poly" means "many." "Meter" refers to the arrangement of accents organized over the course of an entire piece. See the "Elements of Music" appendix for a step-by-step explanation of meter.)

LISTENING GUIDE continued on next page

0'00"   **Introduction (from C-section of the A-B-A-C song form)**

        Collectively improvised with trumpet playing lead, clarinet playing obbligato, and trombone playing mostly chord notes, accompanied by piano, guitar, and banjo rapping out the chords, beat by beat.

0'09"   **First Chorus (A-B-A-C, eight measures in each section) Trumpet Solo**

        A-Section

0'18"   **B-Section**

0'25"   final two measures: trumpet break, beginning with a rip

0'27"   **A-Section**

0'35"   expressive vibrato on trumpet

0'36"   **C-Section**

0'43"   final two measures: clarinet break

        Second Chorus (A-B-A-C, eight measures in each section) Clarinet Solo

0'45"   **A-Section**

0'54"   **B-Section**

1'01"   final two measures: clarinet break

1'02"   broadly bent blue note

1'03"   **A-Section**

1'12"   **C-Section**

1'19"   final two measures: vocal break by Louis Armstrong

        Third Chorus (A-B-A-C, eight measures in each section) Vocal Scat Solo

        A-Section

1'21"   accompanied by guitar counter-lines and banjo timekeeping rhythm

        B-Section

1'30"   vocal slides and bends

1'36"   final two measures: vocal break

        A-Section

1'39"   Rhythmic displacements by Armstrong's notes tug against the pulse of the accompanists.

1'48"   **C-Section**

1'54"   final two measures: vocal break

        Extension (16 measures; separate from the chorus form that precedes it)

1'56"   Voice and guitar take turns soloing for two measures each.

        Notice the interactive similarities between voice and guitar in their lines and in bending pitches of notes.

2'13"   **Four-Measure Transition** (Low-register piano notes set up next section.)

2'17"   **Fourth Chorus (A-B-A-C, eight measures in each section)**

        A-Section

        Trombone solo

2'26"   **B-Section**

2'33"   final two measures: trumpet break

2'34"   **A-Section**

2'35"   collective improvisation by clarinet and trombone, with trumpet repeating high note

2'43"   expressive vibrato on trumpet

LISTENING GUIDE *continued on next page*

C-Section

2'44"	stop-time with trumpet solo
2'48"	Stop-time ends.
2'51"	Guitar and trumpet trade twos.
2'54" **Ending**	
	The final guitar chord, sounded one note at a time (an *arpeggio*), leaves us expecting another chord that would resolve the unanswered feeling it conveys.

Beiderbecke first recorded in 1924 with a small group called the Wolverine Orchestra. Beginning in 1927 he became better known as a featured soloist with a much larger group—the famous Paul Whiteman Orchestra. Often considered the first great white jazz improviser, Beiderbecke influenced many trumpeters, the best known of whom were Jimmy McPartland, Red Nichols, and Bobby Hackett.

Beiderbecke was almost as original and creative as Armstrong, but he had less command over his instrument and a bit cooler sound. Beiderbecke's tone was softer, lighter weight, and less brassy than Armstrong's. His rhythmic approach was less aggressive. Like most early jazz players, he did not have pronounced jazz swing feeling when he began performing, but later he developed a swing feeling which approached that of Armstrong. Beiderbecke's attitude differs considerably from Armstrong's. He was less dramatic and more subtle. In contrast to Armstrong's assured, outgoing style, Beiderbecke was quieter and considerably more restrained. He played more in the instrument's middle register than did Armstrong, who liked high notes. Beiderbecke also paid more attention to stringing together unusual note choices and acknowledging every passing chord in the progression—something he knew well because he was also a good pianist. In this way, he anticipated trumpeter-guitarist Bobby Hackett, who also made masterful use of chord notes in his improvisations, acknowledging almost every passing chord. This approach brought acclaim to Hackett in his Beiderbecke-like solo on Glenn Miller's famous 1942 recording "String of Pearls."[10] (For comparison with Armstrong, see Table 5.3.)

Beiderbecke was also a composer who blended ragtime and jazz with the French Impressionist style of Maurice Ravel and Claude Debussy. His "Flashes," "In the Dark," and "Candlelights" are not well known, but his "In a Mist" has been orchestrated by numerous jazz arrangers. Beiderbecke's own 1927 piano recording of it is especially effective.[11] The piece is distinguished by its use of the whole-tone scale, a sound that was favored by Debussy (see piano keyboard illustration on page 176).

Beiderbecke and Trumbauer

Beiderbecke joined saxophonist **Frankie Trumbauer** (1901–1956) for several landmark recording sessions. Their 1927 recordings of "Singin' the Blues" and "A Good Man Is Hard to Find" represent two of the most relaxed, melodic, and tender performances in early jazz (*JCCD1* Track 9).[12] Trumbauer's instrument was a C-melody saxophone, an instrument that is a size between the alto and tenor saxophones. It is capable of a pale, light-weight tone. Trumbauer was a very precise and melodic soloist. He conveyed very relaxed feeling and employed a vibrato that was uncommonly slow for early jazz. Tenor saxophonist Lester Young, a significant figure in the beginnings of

TABLE 5.3 Comparing Louis Armstrong with Bix Beiderbecke

	ARMSTRONG	BEIDERBECKE
command of trumpet	virtuoso	solid
tone quality	full	bell-like
	hot	warm
	brassy	dry
range	wide	moderate
improvisatory character	outgoing	reflective
rhythmic conception	swinging	closer to ragtime
influences	Chris Kelly	Nick LaRocca
	Buddy Petit	Emmett Hardy
	Joe "King" Oliver	ragtime
birthplace	New Orleans	Davenport, Iowa

modern jazz, has said that he modeled his own light, cool tenor saxophone sound after Trumbauer's playing of the C-melody saxophone. Like Trumbauer, Young also sounded very relaxed and melodic and used a slower vibrato than his contemporaries.

"Taxi War Dance" and "Lester Leaps In" JCCD1 Tracks 24–25

The Trumbauer-Beiderbecke "Singin' the Blues" (*JCCD1* Track 9) performance is one of the most heralded recordings in jazz history. Many players have memorized the improvisations on it, and the Fletcher Henderson big band twice recorded the piece with a harmonized transcription of Trumbauer's solo. Jazz historians routinely cite Beiderbecke's solo for its advanced use of the tune's harmonies. The notes Beiderbecke chose for his solo go beyond the notes offered by the tune's accompanying chords and reflect a higher level of musical thinking than was common with most other improvisers of the 1920s.

CLARINET

Clarinet was more common than saxophone in early jazz, a situation that was reversed in modern jazz. Clarinet usually played countermelodies around the trumpet part. Clarinet solos were not usually as dramatic as the trumpet solos. Eventually, however, some clarinetists got away from a conception based on embellishment. By the late 1930s some early players and many swing era players were playing dramatic, well-paced solo lines.

DVD Track 69

Johnny Dodds

Johnny Dodds (1892–1940) was one of the leading New Orleans clarinetists who moved to Chicago. Dodds used an edgy tone and fast vibrato. With great confidence, he constructed fluid counterlines that managed an almost relentless activity for recordings by Joe Oliver's band in 1923. He had an aggressive solo style that featured swooping pitch bends that sometimes dwell on a single blue note. Many listeners call the effect of his playing "raw." (A jazz historian once said that some of Dodds's work could "curl your hair!") Listen to his work in the recordings of "Dippermouth Blues" by Oliver's band, "Struttin' with Some Barbecue" by Louis Armstrong's band (in *SCCJ*), and "Wolverine Blues" (*JCCD1* Track 8).

"Singin' the Blues" by Bix Beiderbecke and Frankie Trumbauer

Recorded February 4, 1927, for Okeh by Bix Beiderbecke (cornet), Frankie Trumbauer (C-Melody saxophone, a size in between alto and tenor), Jimmy Dorsey (clarinet), Bill Rank (trombone), Paul Mertz (piano), Chauncey Morehouse (drums); reissued on *SCCJ*; *Bix Beiderbecke, Vol. 1, Singin' the Blues* (Columbia: 45450, 1927–28, c1990); *The Complete Okeh and Brunswick Recordings of Bix Beiderbecke, Frankie Trumbauer and Jack Teagarden* (Mosaic: MD7-211, 7CD set, 1924–36, c2001); *Bix & Tram* (JSP: 913, 4CD set, 1924–34, c2002).

This selection was included for several reasons. (1) It is probably the most revered of all the historic recordings of cornetist Bix Beiderbecke. (2) It contains improvisations by C-Melody saxophonist Frankie Trumbauer that had enormous effect on tenor saxophonist Lester Young. So, indirectly, this work by Trumbauer helped set the pace for much of modern jazz saxophone style because Young's approach became a pivotal model. (3) It remains a model of relaxed eloquence that was possibly the first "cool jazz," long before the 1950s style of that name, because (a) its execution is restrained and understated, (b) improvisations are melodic, and (c) instrument tone colors are pale, not bright. (It is possibly the most delicate music recorded by early jazz musicians.) (4) The recording gives us an excellent example of guitarist Eddie Lang, especially during soloists's pauses and sometimes as counter-lines to the soloists. NOTE: To best appreciate the following description, check the "Elements of Music" appendix, index, glossary, and the *Demo CD* for definitions of these terms: stop-time, arpeggio (chord notes sounded one at a time), high-hat cymbals, chord progression, swing eighth notes, triplet, clarinet, cornet, and A-B-A-C song form.

**ELAPSED
TIME**

4-Measure Introduction

0'00"		4-bar ensemble line harmonized for cornet, sax, and clarinet, is answered by crisply played high-hat cymbals in open position.

First Chorus

0'07"	**A**	Saxophonist Trumbauer glides up to the first melody note very sensuously and begins paraphrasing the tune's original melody, accompanied by piano (very faint) and guitarist Eddie Lang, who is alternately strumming and playing single-note-at-a-time lines that constitute snatches of countermelody.
0'21"	**B**	High note begins next phrase.
0'31"		Stop-time solo break for Trumbauer: melodically very unusual, answered by a cymbal crash that ties up the B-section.
0'35"	**A**	Sudden pitch rise decorates the beginning note of the phrase.
0'42"		Trumbauer devises a fancy run of eighth-note triplets.
0'45"		Guitarist Eddie Lang replies with his own descending line of eighth-note triplets to fill Trumbauer's pause.
0'49"	**C**	Sax plays descending line of swing eighth notes, answered by guitar.
0'59"		Stop-time solo break for Trumbauer, again composed of eighth-note triplets, tied up by a cymbal crash.

Second Chorus

1'03"	**A**	Solo improvisation by cornetist Bix Beiderbecke eases in gently, letting each tone ring. It is concise and is in no hurry. Like Trumbauer's, his lines gracefully acknowledge the harmonies of each underlying chord as it changes to the next.
1'18"	**B**	Bluesy note in cornet line reflects the minor key in this section of song.
1'28"		Beiderbecke's stop-time solo break is more full of notes than his previous statements. Cymbal crash closes this section.
1'32"	**A**	Beiderbecke injects a rip, which is uncharacteristically assertive for this understated solo.
1'37"		Beiderbecke selects notes that both outline the flow of changing chords and make a sensible melodic line at the same time.
1'46"	**C**	Cornet majestically states his melody.

LISTENING GUIDE continued on next page

1'48"		Eddie Lang produces an ascending guitar arpeggio underneath the cornet line.
1'53"		Beiderbecke reiterates a blue note.
1'58"		Sounds of struck high-hat in partially open position announce new chorus.
Third Chorus		
2'00"	**A**	The ensemble collectively improvises, with Dixieland-style trombone lines joining them, ever so slightly verging on boisterous (by contrast with the otherwise restrained manner). Sax and cornet equally share foreground.
2'14"	**B**	Clarinet solo improvisation by Jimmy Dorsey.
2'26"		Clarinet plays a solo break. B-section is wrapped up by cymbal crash.
2'30"	**A**	Cornet takes the lead.
2'44"	**C**	Sax and cornet join together for this phrase of the melody.
2'46"		Solo break features an ascending guitar arpeggio (chord notes played sequentially).
2'51"		Cornet plays a rip.
2'52"		Cymbal is struck on beats two and four ("back-beat").
2'59"		Succinct cymbal crash sums it up.

Jimmie Noone

Jimmie Noone (1895–1944) was a more polished player than Johnny Dodds and possessed a greater command of the clarinet. Some consider Noone to be the best New Orleans clarinetist. He had a dark, warm, round tone. He often played jumping staccato lines which had a lot of flash and verve. Noone was a favorite of Benny Goodman, a leading white Chicago clarinetist who went on to become the best known clarinetist in the twentieth century. (Noone made an excellent series of recordings in 1928 with pianist Earl Hines. Their "Four or Five Times" is in the revised *SCCJ*.)

Sidney Bechet

New Orleans clarinetist and soprano saxophonist **Sidney Bechet** (1897–1959) was one of the most highly regarded musicians in early jazz. (See Figure 5.1 for a comparison of clarinet and soprano sax.) He was one of the first great soloists. In addition to Armstrong, he was one of the first improvisers to display jazz swing feeling. Like Armstrong, he double-timed and created dramatic solos. Bechet had a big, warm tone with a wide, rapid vibrato. He was a very energetic, hard-driving improviser who played with broad imagination and authority. Along with Louis Armstrong, Bechet was among the earliest improvisers to devise a stirringly dramatic way of constructing solos. He and Armstrong cultivated these approaches after they had mastered the requirements of collective, nonsolo improvisation which are essential to the New Orleans tradition. (Listen to the New Orleans-style collective improvisation in their playing on "Cake Walkin' Babies from Home" in *SCCJ*.) In this respect, they introduced a new way for jazz hornmen to be viewed in combo format. Both men eventually became regarded primarily as soloists instead of ensemble players. This helped make jazz into an improvising soloist's art. For at least the next four decades of jazz,

Figure 5.1 Clarinet and soprano sax. To compare the sounds of these instruments, listen to *Demo CD* Tracks 69–70.

(Photo courtesy of Selmer/C. G. Conn Company)

Sidney Bechet, the most famous clarinetist-saxophonist to emerge from New Orleans.

(Photo courtesy of William Ransom Hogan Jazz Archive, Tulane University)

collective improvisation skills remained almost exclusively the domain of rhythm section musicians, not hornmen.

Bechet exerted his impact on solo conception by mastering the timing of central notes and carefully using extended inflections of the note's pitch. (See pages 17 and 50 and *Demo CD* Track 50 for details.) Though capable of complicated, supercharged solo improvisations, Bechet's most popular solos are quite simple. The solos discussed by most journalists are slow-tempo performances that exemplify meticulous placement of a few carefully chosen notes. (Listen to "Summertime" and "Blue Horizon" in *SCCJ*.) The pitches of these notes are bent in manners that have been perceived as being highly sensual. "Blues drenched" is how some writers describe the sounds. The timing of these expressive devices demonstrates the command of restraint necessary for making an emotionally effective climax. This is especially evident in the ornaments Bechet employs to lead up to a central note. The scoop or smear of pitches Bechet uses to introduce a note is essential to the success of his improvisation. The long, swooping lead-in, that carries at its topmost note the precise moment for maximum dramatic effect, became standard in the vocabulary of jazz saxophonists. It was used extensively by swing era saxophonist Johnny Hodges, a Bechet disciple, and modern saxophonist John Coltrane, who followed in Hodges's footsteps.[13]

Many of Bechet's solos simply display the reworking of elementary blues phrases. The musical concepts of "bluesy" and "funky" are defined by Bechet's playing. He summarizes the instrumental equivalent of the blues singer. And, in this way, Bechet summarizes what many listeners have come to regard as the essential feeling of New Orleans style: an earthy, warm, and full sound that has searing intensity. (Listen to Bechet's "Blue Horizon" in *SCCJ*.)

TROMBONE

In ensemble improvisation, trombonists invented low harmony parts. They filled in gaps with devices similar to those of tuba and trombone in brass band music. With clarinet and trumpet filling out the middle and upper registers, trombone contributed to the combo sound in the lower range. When soloing, early trombonists tended toward a jazz trumpet conception to which they added the trombone's unique capacity for smears and slides. Rarely, however, did they play lines as intricate as those of early jazz trumpeters.

| DVD *Track 66*

Kid Ory

Kid Ory (1886–1973) was one of the first notable jazz trombonists from New Orleans. (See photo on page 69.) His husky tone and assertive presence were an important part of several early jazz combos. He had a hard, cutting tone, and a percussive attack. His work had a boisterous air about it. Ory was also a composer and group leader. His "Muskat Ramble" (later spelled "Muskrat Ramble") became a jazz standard. (Listen to Ory on Louis Armstrong's "Struttin' with Some Barbecue" in *SCCJ*.)

Jack Teagarden

Jack Teagarden (1905–1964) was from Texas, and he ultimately became one of the most loved and best known of all jazz trombonists. He paid close attention to producing and maintaining a smooth, full tone which was prettier than that of most other premodern trombonists.[14] His work projected a thoughtful, relaxed quality, even though some of his favorite phrases were technically demanding. Teagarden's unique feeling and well-formed phrases were an inspiration to the trombonists of modern jazz. His style was possibly as important to jazz trombone history as Armstrong's was to jazz trumpet history. Teagarden's career was long and productive, running from the

1920s until his death in 1964. (Listen to his solos on the Red Nichols version of "Dinah" in *SCCJ-R*.)

RHYTHM SECTION

The front line of most early jazz combos included trumpet, clarinet, trombone, and occasionally, saxophone. The rhythm section was made up of several instruments which might include guitar, banjo, tuba, bass saxophone, string bass, piano, and drums. No bands had all these instruments playing at the same time, but most drew some combination from that collection. It was not unusual for early jazz combos to be without string bass, and many early jazz recordings were made without drums. Some groups substituted tuba for string bass, and in many groups the bassists alternated brass bass with string bass. Eventually many tuba players learned to play string bass, and by the late 1930s, most had abandoned the tuba. Some groups used bass saxophone (see Figures 5.2 and 5.3). Groups often included both guitar and banjo, though some had only one of these. Usually one player alternated between the two instruments. Piano was absent from some recordings and replaced banjo and guitar on others, though usually both piano and banjo or guitar were used.

Role of Banjo, Guitar, and Bass

The banjo and guitar were often strummed on each beat. (See page 46 for illustrations.) The tuba, bass sax, or string bass frequently played on only the first and third of every four beats. This is called "two-beat style" because they played on only two beats out of every four. Prior to 1927, string bass was often bowed instead of plucked. (See page 24 for illustration of string bass.) Walking bass and two-beat style consist of longer tones when bowed than the staccato sound ordinarily produced when the bass strings are plucked.[15]

Role of Piano

Sometimes the pianist played chords in unison with the guitar or banjo, sometimes embellishments instead. In many groups, the pianist created countermelodies while the front-line instruments were playing melodies or countermelodies of their own.

Figure 5.2 Baritone saxophone—bass saxophone.
(Courtesy C. G. Conn Company)

Figure 5.3 Tuba.
(Courtesy C. G. Conn Company)

Stride style was another approach (*Demo CD* Track 38). Comping, as illustrated on *Demo CD* Track 20, was only sporadically heard during this era.

Role of Drums

Early jazz drummers are poorly heard on records because early studio equipment was not well-suited to recording drums. At that time, records were made by playing into acoustic recording horns. (See page 61.) The small end of the horn was connected to a cutting needle which made grooves in a cylinder or a disc. Any loud sound, especially a blow to the bass drum, could literally knock the needle off the cutting surface. Many recordings during this period consequently represent working bands minus their drummers. Many of the recordings that do employ drummers either omit most drum equipment entirely or muffle it so much that drum sounds are almost inaudible. We are often left with little more than the clickety clicking sound that is made by drum sticks striking a small wood block that has been hollowed out to increase resonance (heard on *Demo CD* Track 10). This was one of the only sounds drummers were ordinarily allowed to produce during the recording sessions in which engineers were apprehensive about the mechanical effects of loud sounds. However, you can detect a number of different rhythm instruments in "Dixie Jazz Band One-Step" (*JCCD1* Track 7).[16]

The drumming style described above represents only one sample in a range of sounds commonly generated by the earliest jazz drummers, though it was particularly convenient in adapting to the restrictions of early recording situations. Light, staccato sounds were also produced by striking a cowbell or the shell of the bass drum instead of the drum head that usually received the blow. These sounds were also employed in some early record dates, but, at that time, aggressive use of the snare drum and bass drum was generally limited to band engagements. A large cymbal or gong was sometimes used to signal a dramatic height in the music. Some jazz combo drummers of the 1920s also had orchestra and theater band experience, and so they brought along some of their orchestral approach when devising their combo performances. When playing on the light-sounding instruments, however, many of the earliest drummers chose patterns from military drumming and ragtime drumming, not necessarily from the tradition of orchestral drumming in which the percussionist only embellishes or reinforces other instrumental activity. The 1917–1923 drumming heard in recordings used more military than orchestral concepts. (If you have a keen enough ear, you might be able to detect these military patterns played on snare drum by Tony Sbarbaro with the Original Dixieland Jazz Band in their 1917 "Dixie Jazz Band One-Step," *JCCD1*, Track 7.)

Although we do not know exactly how he sounded, we do know what kind of instruments the early jazz drummer played. He did not have a high-hat. He had a floor cymbal apparatus which enabled him to strike a cymbal with a foot pedal, but it did not allow him to achieve the "chick" sound possible with the high-hat. He also had a bass drum, almost marching band size, two to three times as large as that which became popular during the mid-1960s (See pages 43 and 58). A snare drum mounted on a stand and a cymbal suspended above the set were also at his disposal. Wood block and cowbell were attached to the bass drum.

There are significant similarities and differences between the roles assumed by the earliest jazz drummers and those assumed by drummers in later styles. For example, on some of the earliest recordings, horn lines often existed without drum accompaniment. That these lines could exist and often did exist without drum accompaniment is especially important when combined with the observation that, on some of the pieces in which drum lines were present, drum lines constituted an additional instrument line rather than the timekeeping or "swing machine" function that drums provided for some later styles. The earliest jazz drummers could also perform in timekeeping style and often did. However, the point here is an additional one: **the earliest jazz drummers often devised lines of activity bearing rhythmic and melodic contours that were distinctly different from the contours of lines being contributed by their fellow musicians.** The practice of playing an independent line of activity was suppressed in swing, the primary jazz style of the 1930s. It enjoyed a resurgence, however, in bop, the primary modern jazz style of the 1940s. In modern jazz, this independent line of activity has sometimes been termed "chatter," and it provides a layer of boiling sounds that increases the excitement of the combo performance. The use of this activity continued throughout the 1950s and 1960s, increasing in density and importance. It has been an accepted practice for all modern drummers of the 1970s and 1980s. The rhythms used by the modern drummers were not those of ragtime, but the spirit in which they were played is analogous to the conception shown by the earliest jazz drummers.

Another important comparison can be made between early jazz drumming and later styles. The earliest drummers sometimes changed loudness, rhythm, and/or instrument for each successive soloist. Many of their accompaniment patterns, however, usually remained patterns rather than deriving spontaneously from rhythmic ideas heard in the improvised solo lines they accompanied, as later occurred in modern drumming. Spontaneous interaction between soloist and accompanist was limited.[17]

"Baby" Dodds

New Orleans drummer **Warren "Baby" Dodds** (1898–1959), brother of clarinetist Johnny Dodds, has been credited with pioneering the use of the ride rhythm. He played it on the snare drum. Later in jazz history, ride rhythms were played on the high-hat. By the 1950s and 1960s, they had become the primary timekeeping rhythms, and drummers played them on the ride cymbal.

Demo CD Tracks 3, 11, 12, and 13; "Wolverine Blues," JCCD1 Track 8

"Zutty" Singleton

Arthur "Zutty" Singleton (1898–1975), another leading New Orleans drummer, was among the first to use wire brushes to strike his drums. Brushes did not totally replace sticks, but they offered a lighter, softer sound, as well as the capacity to produce sustained sounds if dragged across and around a drum head or cymbal. Zutty also pioneered the practice of striking the bass drum on every beat. Many drummers had struck the bass drum primarily on the first and third or every four beats. Singleton can be heard playing brushes on Louis Armstrong's 1928 recordings of "St. James Infirmary" and "Tight Like This." He can be heard playing a suspended cymbal on "Skip the Gutter." And, on "No, Papa, No," Singleton can be heard briefly playing ride rhythms on a cymbal, thereby predating, by about a decade, the sound that was to characterize modern jazz timekeeping style.[18] Drummers George Wettling and Sid Catlett were influenced by Singleton. Catlett played a transitional role in jazz by helping jazz drum conceptions move from early jazz to modern jazz.

Guitar: Eddie Lang and Lonnie Johnson

During the 1920s, most guitarists confined themselves to timekeeping, or, they used simple, chorded solos when they played exposed parts. Guitar was generally ignored as a jazz solo voice until the late 1930s, partly because of the limited loudness that guitarists could generate before the electric amplification of the instrument became common. But two significant guitar soloists did record: Philadelphia-born **Eddie Lang** (1902–1933) and New Orleans-born **Lonnie Johnson** (1899–1970). Lang's work can be heard in recordings by violinist Joe Venuti, and in recordings made by the Beiderbecke-Trumbauer team, such as "Singin' the Blues" (*JCCD1* Track 9). Good examples of Johnson's music exist in combo recordings with Louis Armstrong, such as "Hotter Than That" (*JCCD1* Track 11), and a few moments with Duke Ellington, such as the 1928 Okeh version of "The Mooche."

The guitar styles that were developed by Johnson and Lang contrast markedly with each other. Johnson was a bluesier player than Lang. A favorite means for creating the earthy flavor in his work was to let a tone ring while he glided up to desired pitch. Both men were well organized in their solos, but, in his execution, Lang projects an almost classical conception. (It is notable that he was first trained as a classical violinist.) His technique was excellent, and his lines were executed more cleanly than Johnson's. Listen to the counterlines that Lang improvises delicately under the horn lines in "Singin' the Blues." Their construction and execution is almost like that of classical chamber music. Although both players are historically significant, Lang may have been the more influential of the two.

VOCAL BLUES

The "blues" refers to several different kinds of music. The first is a folk music developed in America by African slaves and their descendants. Because it was not written and it was developing before the invention of the recording machine in 1877, we really don't know how all its roots and developmental stages sounded. Researchers believe it originated from other vocal idioms such as (1) **field hollers,** that slaves devised from highly varied pitches and rhythms for the purpose of communicating among themselves while working in fields; (2) **ballads,** which come partly from European traditions for songs that tell stories; and (3) **music devised for dances,** such as the ring shout. Performing the blues involves some of the same techniques used by singers and by musicians who play stringed instruments in Senegal and Gambia, the northern parts of West Africa. For example, the earliest recorded blues have enormous variety in the ways notes are sung. In particular, what might sound like moans and wails, may indicate merely the vocabulary of drops and scoops of pitch in vocal music of the parent culture. (See page 49.) Or, what may sound to us like odd starting and stopping points in the phrases probably reflects the rich variation of rhythms common to the music that influenced the blues. Creatively toying with the rhythms and pitches in the melody notes was commonplace. The effect of these manipulations became known as "bluesy" or "soulful." Twentieth century recordings of Son House, Tommy Johnson, Charley Patton, and Robert Johnson provide us with an indication of how the nineteenth century precursors sounded.[19]

In the beginning, blues was a form of unaccompanied solo singing. As it evolved, singers began to accompany themselves on the guitar or banjo. The earliest accompaniments did not necessarily use chords or chord progressions. Accompaniments often had only one note at a time or two notes played together. Eventually singers began to use chords. At first they used only whatever chords they already knew. They didn't necessarily learn a set of harmonies that would, in turn, dictate the notes they were allowed to use in the melody, as jazz musicians later did. Usually only a few chords were employed. There was much repetition in the accompaniment and in the lyrics. As the blues developed, the pattern of words and the rhythms of words in the lyrics began to become more and more standardized. By about 1910, a rhyme scheme had been adopted that had its own rhythm. Underneath that rhyme scheme, a given progression of accompaniment chords also became standardized. It was similar to one in church hymns. This pattern of chords, in turn, set the pace for the twentieth-century tradition of blues performances that had no singing. Instrumental blues, as it has been called, evolved as its own idiom.

page 462; "Reckless Blues," CCD1 Track 3

Demo CD *Track 19*

Bessie Smith, Empress of the Blues.

(Photo courtesy of Frank Driggs)

(Listen to the trumpet, trombone, and piano solos on "West End Blues," *JCCD1* Track 10.)

Bessie Smith

"St. Louis Blues" and "Lost Your Head Blues" on SCCJ; "Reckless Blues," CCD1 Track 3

Bessie Smith (1894–1937) was the most famous early blues singer. She had enormous talent and influenced generations of singers, both inside and outside the field of jazz. Though most significant for her blues contributions, she also sang other forms of pop tunes and was part of the vaudeville entertainment scene at large. She recorded with some of the best jazz musicians, including Louis Armstrong, James P. Johnson, and Benny Goodman. Smith outsold all other African American recording artists in the 1920s.

Known as "The Empress of the Blues," Smith had a voice so powerful that it could be heard over the sound of a band, even without using a microphone. It had a weighty quality that added to the unusual intensity of her effect. She had excellent intonation and breath support. Her manner was very aggressive and hard hitting. She played with the pitch and size of her sound to extract maximum bluesiness.

Smith's songs were quite simple, and most were similar. The content was earthy and soul stirring. Her lyrics frequently recalled love affairs gone sour and feelings of self-pity and revenge accompanying such disappointments. In a straightforward manner her huge voice delivered these sentiments with seriousness and insistence.[20]

When trumpeters, clarinetists, saxophonists, and trombonists began playing jazz, they sometimes imitated the scoops and drops of pitch that blues singers used. They also decorated their songs with rhythmic displacements and tone qualities that had been demonstrated by blues singers. These nuances of rhythm, inflections of pitch, and varied timbres allowed instrumentalists to spice up bland melodies by making their rhythms less even and regular and the tone qualities and pitches of melody notes more flexible. Occasionally instrumentalists also picked tunes that had been first introduced by blues singers.

Many blues singers, not just Bessie Smith, hired jazz musicians to accompany them. At the beginning of the twenty-first century, jazz musicians were still finding employment in blues bands, and many jazz bands routinely featured a blues singer. So you see that the blues tradition contributed to jazz in at least four respects: (1) providing a model for novel sounds and displaced rhythms, (2) offering a standard set of accompaniment harmonies, (3) furnishing part of the jazz repertory, and (4) giving work to instrumentalists.

After jazz and blues had both become recognizable forms, blues continued to change over the years, parallel to, but usually separate from the course of development that jazz followed. Its progress occasionally overlapped with jazz, however. Eventually blues became a major part of popular music in America and provided one

Ma Rainey, a well-known blues singer, and the jazz musicians she employed as accompanists.
(Photo courtesy of Frank Driggs)

of the roots for rock and roll. Jazz, on the other hand, became more complicated, less popular, and some of it was considered art music, instead of popular music.

POPULAR APPEAL

The earliest jazz had a wide appeal, especially to youthful audiences and particularly to social dancers. This roughly parallels the kind of popularity enjoyed by rock during the 1950s and 1960s. But it contrasts dramatically with public response to modern jazz of later eras. Whereas modern jazz recordings rarely penetrate the pop charts, the Original Dixieland Jazz Band had several records hover near the top of the popularity charts, and jazz giants such as Louis Armstrong, Jelly Roll Morton, and Bix Beiderbecke were known to a wide public.

Like much rock and roll of the 1950s, New Orleans and Chicago styles of the 1920s are often perceived as happy music. Traditionally they have been used as entertainment to set a mood of cheer and frivolity. Though scholars and musicians often take the music quite seriously, the public associates the sound with images of exciting parties in the "Roaring Twenties." Unlike the solemn view often ascribed to modern styles, the earliest styles are usually perceived as lighthearted and fun, though many of the early classics possess masterful construction and great depth of emotion.

New Orleans and Chicago styles did not just live and die with the 1920s. Their popularity has had its ups and downs since the decade ended, but the music has persisted because demand for it has remained. For instance, there was a revival of interest in New Orleans combo jazz during the 1940s, and several players who had left music returned to careers in performing. The music at New Orleans's Preservation Hall, since 1962, has been so popular that they have always had to have several bands on hand so that one could be on tour and at least one could be in residence. For many years it has been common to find a few good Dixieland bands in every major U.S. city. In addition, many regions of America sport yearly festivals of traditional jazz.

CHAPTER SUMMARY

1. The first forms of jazz resulted from blending improvisational approaches to ragtime, blues, spirituals, marches, and popular tunes.
2. The first jazz bands used the instruments of brass bands: trumpet, clarinet, trombone, tuba, drums, and (occasionally) saxophone.
3. The earliest jazz was not recorded. We can only infer how it sounded on the basis of recordings made by New Orleans players after they had moved to Chicago.
4. The first jazz group to record was the Original Dixieland Jazz Band in 1917.
5. Chicago was the jazz center of the world during the 1920s, composed of
    a. all-star black groups such as Oliver's Creole Jazz Band which had moved from New Orleans,
    b. white bands from New Orleans such as the New Orleans Rhythm Kings, and
    c. Chicago-born imitators of the New Orleans Rhythm Kings such as the Austin High Gang.
6. One of the most historically significant New Orleans natives to first record in Chicago was pianist-composer-bandleader Jelly Roll Morton.
7. Morton was the first great jazz composer. Several of his tunes became standards: "Wolverine Blues," "King Porter Stomp," and "Milenburg Joys."

8. Morton devised a piano style that featured horn-like lines and long-short, strong-weak eighth-note patterns that swung more than ragtime.

9. Morton blended New Orleans improvisational approaches with elaborately arranged, written passages.

10. The single player who stands above all others in jazz history is New Orleans-born trumpeter Louis Armstrong.

11. Armstrong possessed a larger tone, wider range, and better command of the trumpet than most early players.

12. Armstrong's improvisations were especially well constructed.

13. Armstrong was one of the first combo players to effectively demonstrate solo improvisation instead of retaining the New Orleans tradition of collective improvisation.

14. Armstrong is possibly the most influential of all trumpeters, having been imitated by saxophonists, trombonists, and pianists as well as by trumpeters.

15. Next to Armstrong, Bix Beiderbecke was the most influential brass player of the 1920s, and he was harmonically more advanced than Armstrong.

16. In addition to a cool, thoughtful style, Beiderbecke was a composer in the tradition of French Impressionists Maurice Ravel and Claude Debussy.

17. Soprano saxophonist-clarinetist Sidney Bechet helped move jazz horn conception from collective improvisation techniques to a dramatic solo style.

18. Bechet influenced Johnny Hodges and John Coltrane, especially in the expressive timing of ornamentations which precede important notes.

19. Earl Hines helped take jazz piano conception from a traditionally pianistic orientation to a horn-like conception.

20. Hines influenced numerous other piano greats, including Teddy Wilson, Art Tatum, and Nat Cole.

21. The stride piano tradition of James P. Johnson was continued by Fats Waller, who, in turn, became the principal influence on Count Basie.

22. Vocal blues originated before jazz, then influenced jazz by offering novel sounds and new repertory.

23. Blues singers often hired jazz musicians for their bands.

24. Bessie Smith was the most famous blues singer from the 1920s.

TOP INSTRUMENTALISTS IN EARLY JAZZ	
Trumpet	Louis Armstrong and Bix Beiderbecke
Clarinet	Johnny Dodds, Sidney Bechet, and Jimmie Noone
Trombone	Kid Ory and Jack Teagarden
Drums	Zutty Singleton and Baby Dodds
Guitar	Eddie Lang and Lonnie Johnson
Piano	Jelly Roll Morton, Earl Hines, James P. Johnson, and Fats Waller

1. Original Dixieland Jazz Band, *The 75th Anniversary* (RCA Bluebird: 61098 [Victor], 1917–21, c1992). For more about this band and this period of jazz history, see Martin Williams, *Jazz Masters of New Orleans* (Macmillan, 1970; DaCapo, 1979); Nat Shapiro and Nat Hentoff, *Hear Me Talkin' to Ya* (Rinehart, 1955; Dover, 1966); Mezz Mezzrow, *Really the Blues* (Random House, 1946; Citadel, 1990); Gunther Schuller, *Early Jazz* (Oxford, 1968); and Max Harrison, Charles Fox, and Eric Thacker, *The Essential Jazz Records,* vol. 1: *Ragtime to Swing* (Mansell, 1984; Continuum, 2000).

2. *King Oliver's Creole Jazz Band: The Complete Set* (Retrieval: 79007, 2CD set, 1923–24, c1996); *Louis Armstrong and King Oliver* (Milestone: 47017, 1923–24, c1992); or *King Oliver's Jazz Band* (Smithsonian: 2001, 2LP set, 1923, c1975). Kid Ory's recordings from 1922 are on *Breaking Out of New Orleans* (JSP: 921, 4CD set, 1922–29, c2004); or *Steppin' on the Gas: Rags to Jazz, 1913–1927* (New World: 269, LP, 1913–27, c1977). For more about Oliver, see Laurie Wright, *King Oliver* (Storyville, 1987).

3. *The New Orleans Rhythm Kings* (Milestone: 47020, 1922–23, c1992).

4. Stride style left-hand consists of playing a bass note on the first and third beats and a mid-range chord on the second and fourth beats of each measure. Listen to dissected example on the *Demo CD* Track 38. Together, the two hands produced music that you might imagine as a small orchestra with a driving rhythm section. This style is very demanding for the pianist. Listen to James P. Johnson's "You've Got to Be Modernistic" on *JCCD1*.

5. For more about Morton, see Alan Lomax, *Mister Jelly Lord* (University of California Press, 1973); and Bill Russell, *"Oh, Mr. Jelly": A Jelly Roll Morton Scrapbook* (Jazz Media, 1999); Howard Reich and William Gaines, *Jelly's Blues: The Life, Music, and Redemption of Jelly Roll Morton* (DaCapo, 2003); and Philip Pastras, *Dead Man Blues: Jelly Roll Morton Way Out West* (Univ. of California Press, 2003). Also listen to and read *Jelly Roll Morton: The Complete Library of Congress Recordings by Alan Lomax* (Rounder: 1888, 8CD + 1 book set, 1938, c2005). Listen to Jelly Roll Morton, *Birth of the Hot: The Classic Chicago "Red Hot Peppers" Sessions* (RCA Bluebird: 66641, 1926–27, c1993). His "Mamanita" and "The Pearls" are on *Jelly Roll Morton 1923/24* (Milestone: 47018, 1923–24, c1992).

6. Louis Armstrong, *The Complete Hot Five and Hot Seven Recordings,* Vol. 3 (Columbia/Legacy: 87011, 1927–28, c2003); and *The Earl Hines Collection: Piano Solos, 1928–1940* (Collector's Classics: COCD-11, 1928–40, c1993). "Blues in Thirds," "Chimes in Blues," and "Fifty-Seven Varieties" are also on *Jazz Piano* (Smithsonian: 7002, 4CD set, 1924–78, c1989). See Stanley Dance, *The World of Earl Hines* (Scribner's, 1977; DaCapo, 1983); Gunther Schuller, *The Swing Era* (Oxford, 1989), 263–291; and Richard Hadlock, *Jazz Masters of the Twenties* (Macmillan, 1965; DaCapo, 1988).

7. Listen to *Turn on the Heat: The Fats Waller Piano Solos* (RCA Bluebird: 2482-2-RB, 2CD set, 1927-41, c1991) or Waller, *Complete Victor Piano Solos* (Definitive: 11297, 2CD set, 1927–41, c2006). See also Paul S. Machlin, *Stride: The Music of Fats Waller* (Twayne, 1985); and Maurice Waller and Anthony Calabrese, *Fats Waller* (Schirmer, 1977).

8. See Scott E. Brown and Robert Hilbert, *James P. Johnson: A Case of Mistaken Identity* (Scarecrow, 1986).

9. Listen to "Struttin' with Some Barbecue" and "Hotter Than That" on *SCCJ*, and see the analysis of the solo on "Hotter Than That" in Scott Reeves, *Creative Improvisation*, 4th ed. (Prentice-Hall, 2006). Gunther Schuller provides transcriptions and analyses for several of Armstrong's best solos of the 1920s in Schuller, *Early Jazz*. More from this period can be heard on: Armstrong, *The Complete Hot Five and Hot Seven Recordings* (Columbia/Legacy: 63527, 4CD set, 1925–28, c2000); or as separate CDs: vol. 1 (Columbia/Legacy: 86999, 1925–26, c2003), vol. 2 (Columbia/Legacy: 87010, 1926–27, c2003), and Vol. 3 (Columbia/

Legacy: 87011, 1927–28, c2003). Gunther Schuller provides transcriptions and analyses for several Armstrong solos of the 1930s and 1940s in Schuller, *The Swing Era*, 158–197. For more about Armstrong's life, see Max Jones and John Chilton, *Louis* (Little, Brown, 1971; DaCapo, 1988); Joshua Berrett, ed., *The Louis Armstrong Companion* (Schirmer, 1999); Gary Giddins, *Satchmo* (Doubleday, 1988; DaCapo, 1998); Armstrong's autobiography: *Satchmo: My Life in New Orleans* (Prentice-Hall, 1954: DaCapo, 1986); and Thomas Brothers, ed., *Louis Armstrong, in His Own Words: Selecting Writings* (Oxford, 1999).

10. See Glenn Miller, *The Centennial Collection* (RCA Bluebird: 59104, 1939–43, c2004); or *The Essential Glenn Miller* (RCA Bluebird: 69241, 2CD set, 1939–44, c2005).

11. Bix Beiderbecke, Vol. 1: *Singin' the Blues* (Columbia: 45450, 1927–28, c1990).

12. *Bix Beiderbecke,* Vol. 1: *Singin' the Blues* (Columbia); and *Bix Beiderbecke,* Vol. 2: *At the Jazz Band Ball* (Columbia: 46175, 1927–28, c1990). "Riverboat Shuffle" (1927) with Frankie Trumbauer is on *JCCD1*. See the biography, Richard M. Sudhalter, P.R. Evans, and W. D. Myatt, *Bix: Man and Legend* (Arlington House, 1974).

13. Hodges preferred to preface an important note with a gradual smearing of pitches, whereas Coltrane usually selected a rapid, scale-like sequence to sweep up to that central tone. (Listen to Coltrane play soprano sax and note his attention to such prefaces to his high notes on "The Promise" on *JCCD2*. Listen to the exquisite timing and very sensual results in the Johnny Hodges rendition of "Prelude to a Kiss" on *JCCD1*.) Hodges's pre-1940 playing also displayed some of the double-timing and ebullience of Bechet. For an example of Hodges's double-timing, listen to his solo on Duke Ellington's 1940 recording of "In a Mellotone" in *SCCJ-R*. For close comparison of the two soprano sax styles, play Bechet's "Really the Blues" (1938), then Hodges's "Jeep's Blues" (1938); and Bechet's "When It's Sleepy Time Down South" (1941), then Hodges's "Empty Ballroom Blues" (1938). The Hodges numbers are on Duke Ellington, *The Duke's Men: Small Groups,* Vol. 2 (Columbia/Legacy: C2K 48835, 2CD set, 1938–39, c1993); the Bechet numbers are on *The Legendary Sidney Bechet* (RCA Bluebird: 6590-2-RB, 1932–41, c1988). Hodges later slowed down and smoothed out considerably, but retained the smoothness of tone and soulful inflections of pitch learned from Bechet. During the 1960s, the soprano sax was revived by modern saxophonist John Coltrane, who called one of his compositions "Blues to Bechet." Then during the 1980s, the instrument reached its widest audience in the hands of saxophonist Kenny G, whose records sold millions of copies. See also John Chilton, *Sidney Bechet* (Oxford, 1987; DaCapo, 1996).

14. Jack Teagarden, *King of the Blues Trombone* (Collector's Choice: 279, 2CD set, 1928–40, c2002). For a biography, see Jay D. Smith and Leonard F. Guttridge, *Jack Teagarden: The Story of a Jazz Maverick* (Cassell, 1960; DaCapo, 1976).

15. *SCCJ* provides examples for these techniques. A two-beat style tuba part can be heard in portions of "Potato Head Blues" (1927) by Louis Armstrong. Walking bass alternating with two-beat style can be heard on "Black Bottom Stomp" and "Dead Man Blues" (both 1926) recorded by Jelly Roll Morton, available on *SCCJ*. A bass saxophone can be heard playing in this rhythm role on Frankie Trumbauer and Bix Beiderbecke's "A Good Man Is Hard to Find" (1927) on *Bix Beiderbecke,* Vol. 2: *At the Jazz Band Ball* (Columbia). See Figure 5.2 for a bass saxophone illustration. For more about early bass, see George M. Foster, *Pops Foster: The Autobiography of a New Orleans Jazzman* (University of California Press, 1971).

16. Listen to Warren "Baby" Dodds play wood block with Oliver's Creole Jazz Band on "Dippermouth Blues" (1923) on *SCCJ*, and listen to Tony Sbarbaro play it on the Original Dixieland Jazz Band's "Margie" (1920) or "Home Again Blues" (1921) (see footnote 1). See Appendix G for information on how to get an illustrated history of premodern drumming.

For more about these techniques, see Larry Gara, *The Baby Dodds Story* (Contemporary, 1959; LSU, 1992), and listen to *Baby Dodds Talking and Drum Solos [Footnotes to Jazz, Vol. 1]* (Folkways: 2290, 1946), available on CD by special order from Smithsonian/Folkways; phone: 888-365-5929; web: *www.folkways.si.edu*.

17. All these examples can be found on Armstrong, *The Complete Hot Five and Hot Seven Recordings*, Vol. 3 (Columbia/Legacy); or *Louis Armstrong & Earl Hines 1928* (Smithsonian: 2002, 2LP set, c1981).

18. Listen to the playing of Baby Dodds on "Dippermouth Blues" on *SCCJ* and that of Zutty Singleton with Louis Armstrong on "West End Blues" on *JCCD1* or *SCCJ*. In those examples, Dodds plays wood block and Singleton plays a pair of small, hand-held cymbals. (Wood block is demonstrated on *Demo CD* Track 10.) It would also be helpful to sample recordings that are not contained on *SCCJ*. For instance, Singleton can be heard on other Armstrong recordings of 1928: "My Monday Date" and "Sugar Foot Strut" (see footnote 17). Dodds is best heard on the recordings that Oliver's Creole Jazz Band made for the Gennett firm, not those made for Okeh. Oliver's recordings for Gennett are available on *Louis Armstrong and King Oliver* (Milestone). The 1923 "I'm Going to Wear You off My Mind" has particularly distinct wood block playing, in which Dodds's accompaniment rhythms show considerable variety, seeming to constitute a response to the rhythms of the solo lines. This might, however, have been worked out ahead and not be purely impro-

vised for this particular recording. Tony Sbarbaro can be heard on the 1917 recording of "Dixie Jazz Band One-Step" by the Original Dixieland Jazz Band on *JCCD1*. After a passage of snare drum, bass drum, and cymbals, he plays wood block and cowbell. This combination can also be heard in the 1918 recording of "Clarinet Marmalade." Note that most all of Sbarbaro's instruments can be heard in these recordings, despite what has been said about drummers not having entire drum sets in the studio. The ODJB recordings for Victor were reissued on *The 75th Anniversary* (RCA Bluebird).

19. *The Roots of the Blues* (New World: 80252, 1959, c1981) has field recordings and compares African and African American sources for blues singing style. New World Records can be found in many libraries and ordered from 701 Seventh Ave., NY, NY 10036; phone: 212-302-0460; web: *www.newworldrecords.org*. *Legends of the Blues*, Vol. 1 (Columbia: 46215, 1925–65, c1990) has Bessie Smith, Robert Johnson, Leadbelly, Lonnie Johnson, and others. *Roots of Robert Johnson* (Yazoo: 1073, c1990) has Charley Patton, Son House, and others.

20. "Reckless Blues" is on the *CCD1*, *Track 3*. For further listening: Bessie Smith, *Essential Bessie Smith* (Columbia/Legacy: 64922, 2CD set, 1923–33, c1997); *The Complete Recordings*, Vol. 3 (Frog/UK: DGF42, 1924–35, c2001); or *The Complete Recordings*, Vol. 2 (Columbia/ Legacy: C2K 47471, 2CD set, 1924–25, c1991). For a biography, see Chris Albertson, *Bessie*, rev. ed. (Yale University, 2003).

During the 1930s a new style of jazz emerged. It ultimately became the most popular kind of jazz in the twentieth century. This style began gradually during the late 1920s and continued into the 1940s. Over this period, jazz began to swing more because musicians adopted swing eighth-note patterns (page 450; Demo CD Track 44) and a looser, less stiff rhythmic feeling. **Most jazz from the 1930s and early 1940s is called "swing music," and this time in history is now known as "the swing era." Much of its music was played by bands of ten or more musicians, and so it is also called "the big band era."** Partly because of its rhythmic properties, swing-style jazz attracted millions of dancers. It also produced several excellent big bands. A few soloists with these bands went on to influence the development of modern jazz.

Benny Goodman band, 1936
(Photo courtesy of Duncan Schiedt)

TABLE 6.1 A Few Swing Style Musicians

COMPOSING-ARRANGING

Fletcher Henderson
Eddie Durham
Benny Carter
Sy Oliver
Don Redman
Duke Ellington
Billy Strayhorn
Eddie Sauter
Will Hudson
Budd Johnson
Edgar Sampson
Jimmy Mundy
Deane Kincaide

DRUMS
Jo Jones
Sid Catlett
Chick Webb
Gene Krupa
Sonny Greer
Cozy Cole
Louis Bellson
Buddy Rich
Dave Tough
Jimmy Crawford
Ben Thigpen

TROMBONE
Lawrence Brown
Dicky Wells
Trummy Young
Jimmy Harrison
Benny Morton
Vic Dickenson
Joe "Tricky Sam"
    Nanton
Bill Harris
J.C. Higginbotham
Jack Jenney
Tommy Dorsey

BANDLEADERS

Duke Ellington
Count Basie
Bennie Moten
Benny Carter
Chick Webb
Andy Kirk
Jay McShann
Cab Calloway
Benny Goodman
Jimmy Dorsey
Glenn Miller
Charlie Barnet
Boyd Raeburn
Woody Herman
Stan Kenton
Gene Krupa
Artie Shaw
Fletcher Henderson
Lionel Hampton
Bunny Berigan
Harry James
Earl Hines
Billy Eckstine
Jimmie Lunceford
Luis Russell
Claude Thornhill

TRUMPET
Roy Eldridge
Cootie Williams
Bunny Berigan
Harry James
Buck Clayton
Charlie Shavers
Frankie Newton
Henry Red Allen
Oran "Hot Lips" Page
Harry "Sweets" Edison
Rex Stewart
Harold "Shorty" Baker
Jonah Jones
Taft Jordan
Jabbo Smith
Herman Autrey

CLARINET
Artie Shaw
Benny Goodman
Barney Bigard
Woody Herman
Buster Bailey
Jimmy Hamilton

GUITAR
Django Reinhardt
Charlie Christian
Eddie Durham
Oscar Moore
Irving Ashby
Al Casey

PIANO
Art Tatum
Teddy Wilson
Billy Kyle
Mary Lou Williams
Milt Buckner
Count Basie
Duke Ellington
Nat Cole
Erroll Garner
Clyde Hart
Johnny Guarnieri
Jay McShann
Mel Powell
Jess Stacy

BASS
John Kirby
Walter Page
Jimmy Blanton
Israel Crosby
Wellman Braud
Milt Hinton
Slam Stewart

VIBRAPHONE
Red Norvo
Lionel Hampton
Adrian Rollini
Tyree Glenn

SAXOPHONE
Chu Berry
Coleman Hawkins
Johnny Hodges
Benny Carter
Willie Smith
Herschel Evans
Dick Wilson
Ben Webster
Lester Young
Georgie Auld
Don Byas
Russell Procope
Illinois Jacquet
Hilton Jefferson
Tab Smith
Flip Phillips
Pete Brown
Buster Smith
Tex Beneke
Jerry Jerome
Boomie Richman
Vido Musso
Ernie Caceres
Earl Bostic
Joe Thomas
Budd Johnson
Jimmy Dorsey

1. The preferred instrumentation for swing was **big band** rather than combo, and greater use of written arrangements therefore occurred during the swing era.
2. **Saxophones** were more common in swing.
3. **Bass viol** (string bass) appeared more often in swing.
4. **High-hat** cymbals were used more.
5. Collective improvisation was rare in swing.
6. Overall **rhythmic feeling was smoother.**
7. Swing musicians usually showed a **higher level of instrumental proficiency** in terms of speed, agility, tone control, and playing in tune.

BIG BAND INSTRUMENTATION

Big bands were made up of ten or more musicians whose instruments were grouped into three categories called **sections:** rhythm, brass, and saxophone. The rhythm section was usually composed of piano, guitar, bass viol, and drums. The brass section was, in turn, divided into trumpet section and trombone section. The saxophone section was separate from "the brass section" even though saxophones are also made of brass. Saxophones are technically classified with the "woodwind" instrument family because they originated from instruments traditionally made of wood (clarinet, flute, and oboe). They are also played in the manner of traditional wooden instruments. Incidentally, the sax section was often called the "reed section" because most saxophonists also played clarinet, and both sax and clarinet have cane reeds attached to their mouthpieces. This label was retained in later decades, even when saxophonists began alternating flute, a non-reed instrument.

The alto and tenor saxophones were the most frequently used saxophones in the big bands. By the late 1930s, most bands were also using the baritone saxophone. The soprano and bass saxophones were not common. (See Figure 6.1; *DVD* Tracks 70–73; *Demo CD* Tracks 72–73; "Cottontail," *JCCD1* Track 20 [tenor solo at 0′29″, baritone sax solo at 1′48″, and all saxes together at 2′03″], "Harlem Airshaft," Track 21 at 0′56″, and baritone solo on "Four Brothers," Track 28 at 0′53″.)

The sax section contained from three to five musicians. By the late 1940s, two altos, two tenors, and a baritone had become the standard make-up. The leader of the sax section, an alto saxophonist, sat in the middle. The baritone saxophonist sat on one end, the tenor saxophonist on the other. Saxophonists did not usually play only one instrument. Some, for instance, were required to alternate clarinet with alto and baritone saxophones.

| DVD *Tracks 69–73*

The trumpet section varied from two to five musicians. Three was the standard number during the late 1930s and early 1940s. The lead trumpeter usually sat in the middle. The trombone section ranged from one to five musicians, two to three being standard. The lead trombonist was in the center. (See *Demo CD* Tracks 59 and 78; *DVD* Tracks 60 and 66; to hear the brass section together, listen to "Cottontail," *JCCD1* Track 20 at 1′32″.)

BIG BAND ARRANGEMENTS

With the growth of big bands came an increase in the use of written arrangements. These had not been as necessary with small combos. As bands became bigger, it was

Figure 6.1 Alto (on left), tenor (middle), and baritone saxophone (right). Listen to *Demo CD* Tracks 72–74 to compare the sounds of these instruments.

(Courtesy C. G. Conn Company)

more difficult to improvise a respectable performance, though some bands did succeed in playing without written arrangements. Eventually, however, musicians had to learn to read and write arrangements to have a sufficient repertory on hand. A newcomer had much less difficulty adapting to a band that used written arrangements rather than memorized routines.

The compositional devices employed in most of the arrangements were simple. Melodies were played by the entire band in unison or in harmony. Then jazz improvisation followed, accompanied both by the rhythm section and by figures scored for other members of the group. (Sax improvisation is accompanied by rhythm section and brass figures at 0'44" in "Cottontail.") The melodies and accompanying figures were taken up in turn by one section of the band and then another. Saxes might state the A-section, brass state the bridge, and so forth. In addition to pop tune melodies, arrangements often contained variations on those themes. Some of the variations were as good as improvised solos (as at 2'03" in "Cottontail"). These were offered as passages for one section of the band to play while another accompanied them or remained silent. Sometimes portions within the passages were passed back and forth. This sounded as though one section of the band posed a question and another section answered it. This technique is called *call and response*, question and answer, or responsorial style. (It can be heard on "Cottontail," *JCCD1* Track 20 at 2'34"; and on "One O'Clock Jump," Track 5, as the recording ends.)

Short, simple, phrases called *riffs* were used by some big bands as essential elements of their style. At times, different riffs were assigned to various sections of the band and played against each other. Such *antiphonal* (an-TIFF-on-ull) activities could swing a band buoyantly and give jazz improvisation a good send-off. Sometimes entire arrangements were based on such riffs. (Listen to "One O' Clock Jump," *JCCD1* Track 5, and "Lester Leaps In," Track 25 at 2'09".)

THE RHYTHM SECTION

The rhythm section was usually composed of piano, guitar, bass viol, and drums. The propulsive rhythmic quality in most swing era recordings is partly due to the sound of the guitarist percussively strumming a chord on each beat. This is known as *rhythm guitar style*. This role of **rhythm guitarist** remained an essential part of Count Basie's band until guitarist Freddie Green died in 1987, but it had disappeared from most other big bands during the late 1940s. Although the banjo had been present in early-style bands, it dropped out of sight during the 1930s. Tuba had preceded string bass in some bands, but had been abandoned by the mid-1930s. Before the guitar and string bass became firmly established, guitarists had often been required to alternate guitar and banjo, while bassists alternated tuba (also called brass bass) and string bass (also called bass viol or bass fiddle).

Demo CD *Track 88;*
DVD *Track 44*

The **pianist** in the rhythm section occasionally played melody instead of just chords and embellishments. Comping was not the common accompaniment style during the swing era, though Count Basie did use it. Pianists of the swing era used stride style or played a chord on every beat or every other beat. They did not necessarily improvise new rhythms to flexibly fit those of the solo line, as did their successors in modern jazz.

BASS

Bassists were usually assigned timekeeping duties. The sound of the bassist was heard on the first and third of every four beats, *two-beat style*, or on every beat, *walking style*. Bassists during the swing era remained in the background, auditorily as well as visually. Bass features were very rare until the 1950s and remained relatively infrequent thereafter. In the next chapter, we will mention how Duke Ellington's bassist **Jimmy Blanton** originated melodically conceived pizzicato bass solos. But bassists in this era were usually felt more than they were heard. Some dancers and attentive listeners detected a difference in a band's rhythmic feeling when there was a weak bassist or no bassist at all. However, those same listeners rarely knew the cause for the difference.

Demo CD *Track 23;*
DVD *Track 23*

When musicians discuss this period, three bassists besides Jimmy Blanton are also mentioned: **Walter Page** (1900–1957), **Slam Stewart** (1914–1987), and **Milt Hinton** (1910–2003). (For more about Page, see the Count Basie chapter.) Hinton made his reputation playing with Cab Calloway's big band during the 1930s, but he continued to be in demand for a variety of jazz settings through the 1990s. Known for his sure sense of tempo and huge tone, Hinton acquired a nickname of "The Judge" because once he set the tempo for a piece, he was remarkably firm and authoritative in maintaining it.[1] Slam Stewart was a good timekeeper and a responsive accompanist, especially for the melodic flights of pianist Art Tatum, whom he often accompanied. Stewart is best known, however, as an inventive soloist. He is notable for a solo technique in which he bowed his bass while humming the same notes. The combination of voice and bass produced a rough-textured and original tone color. He humorously slid from note to note in his solos, but always managed to make a lot of melodic sense. Historically, Stewart's solo playing moved jazz bass a step away from the role of mere timekeeper.

DRUMS

The majority of drummers who played with big bands during this period tended to limit themselves to making the beat obvious for dancers and lending swing feeling to the band. These priorities were higher than doing as the earliest jazz drummers had done and creating a separate line of rhythmic activity that coexisted with the melodic rhythms of the horns. With the exception of striking cymbals and gongs for dramatically timed effects, many of the big band drummers played lengthy passages without doing much more than stating each beat on the bass drum and reinforcing this with a simple timekeeping pattern played on the snare drum with wire brushes or on a closed high-hat with sticks. Sometimes the second and fourth beats of each measure were emphasized by striking the snare drum with sticks. (This rhythm is called a "back beat.") Deviations from these patterns usually constituted simple embellishments of the beat or busy patterns that were quickly played when the horns were pausing between ensemble phrases. Swing drummers tended not to play new and provocative rhythms that ran counter to the horn lines. Listeners had to wait until modern jazz developed during the 1940s before they could hear drummers again offering a parallel line of activity instead of just keeping time. Listeners also had to wait to hear a substantial amount of interaction between improvising soloist and accompanying drummer. For the most part, swing drumming was quite conservative and not very light or swinging. It was not until the late 1930s that a lighter and more graceful sound was heard from big band drummers. And, even then, it was only heard in the few bands that were lucky enough to boast such drummers as Jo Jones and Dave Tough.

Jazz drumming authority Denny Brown has pointed out that the nature of the 1930s big band style restricted the jazz drummer's activity. It was decreased from the amount of rhythmic freedom that combo drummers had. The riff-based format used by big bands discouraged swing drummers from playing complex rhythmic patterns because such complexity might conflict with the melodic rhythms of the written horn parts. Brown contends that the 1930s swing era originated the idea that a jazz drummer should only be felt, not heard. Exceptions to this rule are notable, however, and **Gene Krupa's** popularity during this period might stem partly from his violating the norm. Brown suggests that Krupa's playing forecast aspects of modern drumming by being heard and by including patterns that responded to horn lines as well as building excitement. Some of Krupa's accompaniments are like solos. In that respect they are a continuation of the methods of the earliest jazz drummers and a contrast to the typical approach of swing drummers.[2]

Demo CD *Track 2*

During the late 1930s, a contrast to the Krupa style was offered by Count Basie's drummer **Jo Jones.** In place of Krupa's loud and insistent pounding of the bass drum on each beat, Jones often omitted bass drum playing altogether. In contrast to striking his high-hat while it was closed, Jones continued a ride rhythm on it while it was continuously opening and closing. He let the cymbals ring, thereby making a sound pattern that was less abrupt, more sustained. This technique, together with an unusually close coordination with the bassist, projected a more flowing feeling than other rhythm sections produced during the swing era. Jones also gave each beat more equal treatment than his contemporaries had done. The feeling Jones conveyed, and the precision with which he played, evolved into the modern jazz drummer's tendency to play timekeeping rhythms on a suspended cymbal that is now known as the *ride cymbal*. It is also notable that Jones steered clear of cowbell and wood block, which make sounds that today help us identify the corny aspects of premodern jazz drumming. (See Chapter 3, *Demo CD* Track 3; *DVD* Tracks 7–13; "Taxi War Dance" and "Lester Leaps In," *JCCD1* Tracks 24 and 25.)

BANDLEADERS

Some of the best swing bands were led by Fletcher Henderson, Count Basie, Duke Ellington, Jimmie Lunceford, and Benny Goodman.[3] Following this discussion are entire chapters devoted to Ellington and his musicians and Basie and his musicians. The Henderson and Ellington bands bridged the gap between the styles of early jazz and the swing approach. Each had begun in the early 1920s and grown larger and more sophisticated by the late 1930s.

TABLE 6.2 Musicians Prominent in the Fletcher Henderson Bands

TRUMPET
Louis Armstrong
Rex Stewart
Roy Eldridge
Tommy Ladnier
Cootie Williams
Joe Smith
Bobby Stark
Henry "Red" Allen
Emmett Berry

DRUMS
Sid Catlett
Kaiser Marshall

TROMBONE
Jimmy Harrison
Charlie Green
Dicky Wells
J. C. Higginbotham
Benny Morton

BASS AND TUBA
John Kirby
June Cole
Ralph Escudero
Israel Crosby

SAXOPHONE AND CLARINET
Coleman Hawkins
Chu Berry
Don Redman
Benny Carter
Ben Webster
Russell Procope
Hilton Jefferson
Buster Bailey

Many great early jazz and swing era improvisers worked with **Fletcher Henderson** (1897–1952) between the early 1920s and late 1930s (see Table 6.2). Henderson's was an all-star band. His style represented one major stream of big band jazz; Ellington's represented another. In his arrangements, Henderson pitted saxes against brass. He also perfected techniques of block voicing, in which the melody is the top voice of a series of chords, and each note in a chord is assigned to a different instrument or combination of instruments. It produced a thicker sound than if the line were not harmonized. Ellington used block voicing too, but he added an assortment of other special techniques that made his sound unique (discussed in next chapter). Part of Henderson's arranging reputation resulted from the use of his work by the phenomenally popular band of Benny Goodman.[4] (Listen to Henderson's band play Henderson's arrangement of "Wrappin' It Up," later recorded by Goodman, and Don Redman's arrangement of "The Stampede" [both on SCCJ]. Redman was equally important.)

Jimmie Lunceford (1902–1947) led an excellent big band that was noted for its quality of swing feeling and well-disciplined musicianship. The consistency and balance of sound projected by each section of the band was matched only by their smooth, even swing feeling. Lunceford's band had exciting solo improvisers, and it could generate musical moments of "white heat" (the title of a lively feature number).[5] Its place in jazz history was earned for this special touch and the effect it had on dancers as well as fellow musicians.

During the 1930s and 1940s, **Benny Goodman** (1909–1986) led the most well-known big band that was jazz-oriented. His big band had a very hard-driving effect and showcased its leader's swinging, technically impressive clarinet playing. He influenced almost every jazz musician who played clarinet after him. (Listen to Goodman's clarinet solos on Red Nichols's band version of "Dinah" in the SCCJ-R.) His name was so high so often on the popularity charts that he ranks above all but five other artists making recordings between 1890 and 1954. This means that Goodman was one of the most popular figures in the music industry as a whole, not just in jazz. Today he ranks with Louis Armstrong and Dave Brubeck as one of the best known musicians in all of jazz history. In addition to his impact as a clarinetist, he may be responsible for influencing the course of jazz by the exposure he provided for other outstanding improvisers. His small combos were especially effective for bringing wide recognition to such swing era stand-outs as pianist Teddy Wilson, guitarist Charlie Christian, and vibraphonist Lionel Hampton.[6] (Listen to Goodman's groups with Christian on "Seven Come Eleven," *JCCD1* Track 15, and "I Found a New Baby" in *SCCJ*.[7])

TROMBONE

DVD *Track 66* | Many of the leading trombonists in early jazz were also prominent trombonists in the swing era. Their styles became more refined, and they were found more often in big bands than in Dixieland-style combos. Jack Teagarden and Tommy Dorsey were among this group. (See preceding chapter for coverage of **Jack Teagarden**.) **Tommy Dorsey** (1905–1956) led a tremendously popular series of dance bands during the 1930s, '40s, and '50s, as well as co-leading others with his saxophonist brother, Jimmy Dorsey.[8] He is best known among musicians because he developed a method of playing trombone which produced an extremely smooth, clear tone. His mastery of the instrument, his consistently polished manner, and his high-register work, became the model for a string of highly skilled trombonists who had glossy tones and meticulous technique. **Lawrence Brown** was another standout of the era, though we treat his style in the Ellington chapter because he was known primarily to Ellington fans. The swing era spilled into the decade of the 1940s and produced an important trombonist who did not already have a reputation in early jazz. **Bill Harris** (1916–1973) was probably the most original and influential of the brass soloists featured in the Woody Herman big band of the 1940s. Harris is a transitional figure in the development of modern jazz trombone style, emerging before J. J. Johnson. He had a broad, thick tone and quick vibrato which remained for the duration of each tone. Harris played with pronounced authority and employed good high range, by 1940s standards. Harris's well-constructed solos made use of staccato and punching figures in addition to slides and smears.[9]

TRUMPET

Trumpeter **Roy Eldridge** (1911–1989) was one of the most advanced improvisers of the swing era. (Listen to his work with Benny Carter on "I Can't Believe That You're in Love with Me" in *SCCJ*.) He is often considered a link between swing and modern jazz. Eldridge had a fiery, aggressive style and unprecedented mastery over the trumpet. His imaginative choice of notes and sax-like lines bridged the gap between the style of Louis Armstrong and the modern approach pioneered by Dizzy Gillespie. Eldridge also creatively varied the size, texture, and vibrato of his tone. Sometimes it was clear and warm, at other times brittle and edgy. His high-register playing had a sweeping scope. In that register, he gave his entrances a rhythmic feeling which suggested modern jazz inflections to come.[10]

Roy Eldridge demonstrated that long, sinewy lines were possible on the trumpet. These, though easy to execute on saxophone, do not lend themselves to the mechanics of the trumpet. Eldridge's influence caused modern trumpeters to cultivate greater instrumental facility and to improvise in more intricate and unpredictable ways than their early jazz counterparts. His conception also extended the average phrase length used by improvising trumpeters. Eldridge's influence extended into the 1950s

Roy Eldridge, the most daring trumpeter of the 1930s. Eldridge often improvised in the manner of a saxophonist by using long, swooping, scale-like lines. He also liked to dart into the high register and make his sound explode like fireworks.

(Photo courtesy of Frank Driggs)

because trumpeter Dizzy Gillespie built his own influential modern style upon the foundation of Eldridge's bristling high-register work, unorthodox choice of notes, and saxophone style of phrasing. (Listen to Eldridge's solos on "After You've Gone," *JCCD1* Track 16, and "Rockin' Chair" in *SCCJ*.[11])

SAXOPHONE

The man generally considered to be the first important jazz tenor saxophonist is **Coleman Hawkins** (1904–1969). Prior to his arrival on the jazz scene in the 1920s, the saxophone was considered little more than a novelty. Hawkins's supercharged playing on it brought recognition to the horn. His command of the instrument and his deep, husky tone became a model for other saxophonists. As a result, tenor sax became one of the most popular instruments in jazz. In fact, it symbolizes jazz for many people.

"How Deep Is the Ocean?" and "Voodte," JCCD1 Tracks 17 and 18

More than most other premodern saxophonists, Hawkins demonstrated great interest in chord progressions. He loved to play over complex chord progressions, such as those in his famous rendition of "Body and Soul."[12] Often he seemed less interested in devising new melodies than in investigating the chord progressions that could be added to a tune's original accompaniment. Because of his attitude, some listeners consider Hawkins to be more of a harmonic improviser than a melodic improviser.[13]

"Body and Soul," CCD1 Track 11

Hawkins was a featured soloist with the Fletcher Henderson band from 1923 to 1934. He worked mostly with small groups thereafter. Though primarily associated with the swing era, he was also a respected figure at modern jazz sessions of the 1940s. His playing lacked the smoothness and fluid swing that typified modern jazz soloists, but his skill with difficult chord progressions helped him adjust to newer styles. Hawkins was one of the most intense and consistent saxophone soloists in jazz history. (Listen to his 1943 recording of "The Man I Love" in *SCCJ*.) A surging energy continued to flow unabated from his horn for decades. His influence was not limited to his swing era contemporaries. Such modern tenor saxophonists as Sonny Rollins and John Coltrane were also influenced by him. Hawkins, Coltrane, and Lester Young (discussed later) were the most influential tenor saxophonists in jazz history.

Don Byas (1912–1972) was more advanced than most swing tenor saxophonists and could hold his own with many modern players of the late 1940s. (Listen to his "I Got Rhythm" in *SCCJ*.) Byas had fire, enviable command of the saxophone, harmonic sophistication, and melodic daring. He loved to double-time and run through every note in each chord. More significant was his tendency to add new chords to a tune, and to use both the original and new chords in his improvisations. He had derived this method from pianist Art Tatum. The richness of his lines easily matches that of later saxophonists. Though he had much of the huskiness in tone possessed by Hawkins, Byas swung more easily than Hawkins, perhaps because the ideas that Byas devised were less varied in their rhythms. The style of Byas was widely appreciated by fellow saxophonists, and it became the primary model for two distinguished modern players: Lucky Thompson and Benny Golson.

Benny Carter (1907–2003) and Johnny Hodges were the most influential alto saxophonists of the swing era. Hodges will be discussed in the next chapter, but we will briefly examine Carter here. (Listen to Carter's "I Can't Believe That You're in Love with Me" in *SCCJ*.) The first elements of Carter's playing that usually strike listeners are the precision of his execution and the glow of his tone

Coleman Hawkins, the first important tenor saxophonist to play jazz. Often referred to as "father of tenor saxophone," he had a robust style and showed sophisticated harmonic development in his solo improvisations. Shown here at age 45 in 1947.

(Photo courtesy of Duncan Schiedt)

"How Deep Is the Ocean?" recorded on December 8, 1943, for Signature by Coleman Hawkins (tenor sax), Al Casey (guitar), Ellis Larkins (piano), Oscar Pettiford (bass), and Shelly Manne (drums); On "Voodte" add Bill Coleman (trumpet) and Andy Fitzgerald (sax and clarinet); reissued on *Classic Tenors* (Signature/CBS: 38446, c1989).

These selections present two sides in the artistry of the great tenor saxophonist Coleman Hawkins: ballad style and swinging style. "How Deep Is the Ocean?" shows his artistry with ballad playing; "Voodte" is taken at a faster tempo and is more swinging. The tune was written by Irving Berlin and follows a 32-bar A-B-A-C form. The recording includes a piano introduction, an accompaniment by piano, guitar, bass, and drums, joined near the end by sustained tones from trumpet and saxophone that were present at the same recording session. Made about four years after his slow "Body and Soul" recording, this performance may have been an attempt to repeat the popular success of that earlier number. Like his work in that 1939 hit, his playing here is quite busy, even though the tempo is slow. His improvised lines are complicated, with many twists and turns. In this respect, Hawkins anticipated the modern jazz style known as bop.

The Hawkins tone quality on the "Body and Soul" recording was full-bodied, but on "How Deep Is the Ocean?" it is not only full but also husky. Though occasionally he reached peaks of intensity with a roughening of his tone on "Body and Soul," there are even more moments on this recording when Hawkins coarsens his tone to a rousing effect. As in his "Body and Soul" performance, the saxophonist is acknowledging each and every chord in the accompaniment, filling every moment.

Our sample of the "Voodte" recording is excerpted from a longer performance, and it starts with the beginning of the passage that contains the saxophone solo. The excerpt ends with a statement of the theme that Hawkins wrote to give his recording band a framework for improvisation and a swinging mood. It fills a 32-bar A-A-B-A form whose chord changes resemble those of "I Got Rhythm," though the first few chords in the bridge are not from that tune. This theme is composed of brief phrases that frequently repeat, thus illustrating a compositional approach in jazz that is termed "riff style." Merely a springboard for the solo improvisations, the "Voodte" theme is not the main focus of the performance.

"Voodte" shows the hard-swinging Hawkins approach to medium-tempo playing. Whereas his tone on "How Deep Is the Ocean?" is husky, it bristles on "Voodte." Execution of this solo is extremely forceful and decisive. Though his solo on the ballad has several peaks of intensity, his solo on this swing number is continuously bursting with life. This sample displays Hawkins generating phrase after phrase from his horn, with rarely a pause.

quality. His sound is rich and luxurious. His solos flow with grace and lightness. There is a striking neatness and order with which Carter plays his eighth notes. They are very even and well-measured. Carter devised intelligently conceived solos that are oriented in an obvious way to the changing harmonies of his accompaniment. He was also a good trumpeter, clarinetist, and a top-notch arranger.[14]

PIANO

"Tiger Rag," CCD1 Track 6; SCCJ: "Willow Weep for Me" and "Too Marvelous for Words"

Art Tatum (1909–1956) is among the most widely admired pianists in jazz history. Even when compared with all the very fast, imaginative pianists who have emerged since the 1940s, Tatum still stands above with his impressive technical facility and unceasing energy. His style combined a variety of techniques. In his improvisations and the ways he decorated pop tunes, Tatum was unpredictable. He indulged his

Recorded in 1941 for Okeh; reissued on *Roy Eldridge with the Gene Krupa Orchestra: Uptown* (Columbia: 45448, 1940–49, c1990).

This selection by drummer Gene Krupa's big band of 1941 contains the most spectacular example of the Roy Eldridge trumpet style on record. Eldridge played higher and faster than any other swing trumpeter of the 1930s and was matched only by his own disciple Dizzy Gillespie, who became a co-founder of the modern jazz style called "bebop" in the 1940s. To put Eldridge's innovations in perspective, we need to realize that most early trumpeters and many swing trumpeters specialized in dramatic renditions of a piece's original melody. They focused much of their creativity on paraphrase and ornamentation. Approaches traditionally associated with solo improvisations by jazz trumpeters emphasized melodic construction and using arpeggios (chord notes played sequentially) more than scales as building blocks. Though drawing upon such traditions initially, Eldridge ultimately invented a new concept by also imitating the saxophone improvisations of Benny Carter and Coleman Hawkins. This led to intricate, scale-like passages that, though easy to execute on sax, were difficult on trumpet. The result was densely packed strings of tones that darted all over the pitch range. Unlike Bix Beiderbecke, Eldridge usually was not concise or restrained. Nor did he show Louis Armstrong's concern with timing and lyricism. Eldridge's emphasis on improvisatory speed and intricacy became a significant orientation for most modern trumpeters of the 1940s, '50s, and '60s, through Eldridge's disciple Dizzy Gillespie and Gillespie's disciple Fats Navarro.

Unlike many equally virtuosic jazz performances of later eras that are dead serious from start to finish, this dazzling display of trumpeting conveys a sense of whimsy. It is as though we are watching a race, in which the band is showing off how fast Eldridge can play, and continuously cheering their hero on. In fact, the beginning of this recording contains a comedy routine in which the trumpeter makes fun by quoting from two themes that are distinctly un-hip, "Yankee Doodle" and "Stars and Stripes Forever." For each quote he is met with shouts from his bandmates of "No . . . No," as though to say "Please don't start that! We've heard that patriotic stuff too much already!" "That is too corny to use, Roy!" Once he has launched his solo improvisations, however, Eldridge is plenty serious about demonstrating a comprehensive mastery of jazz improvisation and an unparalleled command of the trumpet. In other words, though the selection is meant to be showy for the sake of entertainment and light-hearted in its excitement building, it also represents substantial art. So we are getting an important slice in the history of jazz styles, though in the context of entertainment intended primarily for stage shows. In fact, most other versions of this same showpiece for Eldridge included a vocal rendition of the piece's melody because lyrics provide broader audience appeal than solely instrumental versions provide.

Several dramatic devices are used in this performance. Consult the *Demo CD* for explanation and demonstration of solo break, double-time, staccato, and high-hat cymbals. The piece is composed of five different 8-bar sections (roughly conceivable as A-B-A-C-A'). Measures 13–16 and 37–40 lend themselves to being stopped to form solo breaks.

ELAPSED
TIME

	Introduction
0'00"	Gene Krupa is striking high-hat cymbals with a drum stick.
0'03"	Eldridge quotes "Yankee Doodle."
	His bandmates yell "No . . . No."
0'08"	Eldridge quotes "Stars and Stripes Forever."
	His bandmates yell "No . . . No."
0'13"	Eldridge plays a 4-note ascending figure.
	He repeats it four times.
0'15"	Eldridge transposes his figure three scale steps higher.
	Meanwhile, his fellow trumpeters harmonize and repeat it with him four times.
0'18"	Eldridge and more of his fellow trumpeters transpose his figure higher again and repeat it four more times.

LISTENING GUIDE continued on next page

0'21"	Eldridge and fellow trumpeters transpose his figure higher again and repeat it four more times.
0'24"	A solo break allows Eldridge to go higher than the highest pitch of the transposed figure and whip up excitement to a frenzy with a densely packed stream of notes that lead into his paraphrase of the melody.

First Chorus

0'27"	Eldridge toys with the original melody to "After You've Gone."
	The band accompanies unobtrusively with sustained chords.
0'35"	A solo break allows Eldridge to improvise a quadruple-time solo line in bars 13–16.
0'51"	A break occupies bars 37–40 of the song form and features the saxes and Eldridge playing a complex figure that today is associated with modern trumpeter Dizzy Gillespie's favorite phrases.

Second Chorus

0'54"	Sam Musiker clarinet solo improvisation accompanied by brass.
1'18"	Gene Krupa drum break begins the final 4-bars of the song form, answered by staccato remarks from Eldridge.

Third Chorus

1'20"	Band resumes playing. Eldridge is producing long, scale-like phrases ascending to very high pitches. Saxes pump underneath.
1'28"	Bars 13–16 provide solo break in which Eldridge ascends to impressive heights and descends in a slippery fashion.
1'44"	Bars 36–40 provide solo break into which Eldridge dives and ultimately emits a barking sound before swallowing his notes in the lower register, then coming out romping for another lap of racing with the band.

Fourth Chorus

1'47"	Rapidly ascending line, culminating in very high pitch.
1'55"	Bars 13–16 provide solo break featuring high-pitched staccato tones.
2'10"	Bars 33–35 provide break, in which same fast tempo continues within Bob Curtis's solo piano improvisation using fully developed lines that are continuous with the pace set by Eldridge's lines.
2'11"	Eldridge replies to the piano with staccato answer in the altissimo register.
2'13"	Piano improvises another solo remark in bars 36–37.
2'14"	Eldridge replies with more altissimo staccato remarks.

Ending

2'15"	By changing the rhythms in his phrasing, Eldridge gradually slows the tempo to set up a dramatic finale.
2'20"	A band chord answers Eldridge's statement.
2'23"	In turn, Eldridge responds with a bluesy answer.
2'25"	The band chords another call. Eldridge responds.
2'29"	The band and Eldridge play the final two chords together with Eldridge providing the highest notes.
2'32"	Who won the race?

impulses and pursued musical tangents, frequently interrupting the direction of his own lines. He often employed stride-style left hand as well as horn-like lines. Tatum's playing was quite flowery, with long, fast runs which sometimes overlapped each other. He was a master at spontaneously adding and changing chords during his performance of pop tunes. This is termed *chord substitution.* Sometimes Tatum was found to be changing keys several times within a phrase and still managing to gracefully resolve the harmonic motion. (He had an enviable capacity for neatly getting out of precarious positions within the adventure of his improvisations.) Modern jazz musicians adopted both his chord substitutions and his methods of changing keys in mid-solo.

| Demo CD *Track 40*

Art Tatum, the most widely admired piano virtuoso in jazz history.

(Photo courtesy of Frank Driggs)

Rhythmically Tatum was also very inventive. His left-hand rhythms were full of surprises. He is also known for changing the piece's rhythmic feeling in mid-solo, sometimes leaving the intent listener dangling on an unresolved pattern while Tatum pursued another tangent. His right-hand playing sometimes seemed to throw showers of notes upon the listener. The rhythms in these showers were often odd combinations, not merely strings of eighth notes and sixteenth notes. But despite their complexity, Tatum's runs have been memorized by hundreds of pianists, and they have been used to decorate solos in performances by jazz pianists and popular pianists alike.

Art Tatum's impact on jazz history was enormous. His astounding mastery of the keyboard became a pinnacle for which other jazz pianists aspired. His practice of changing keys within a single phrase and adding chords were absorbed by tenor saxophonist Don Byas and modern saxophonist Charlie Parker. Tatum also influenced two highly innovative pianists who played pivotal roles during the early days of modern jazz: Bud Powell and Lennie Tristano (discussed in upcoming chapters). Both Powell and Tristano, in turn, went on to influence numerous pianists of the 1950s who further extended Tatum's impact.[15]

Art Tatum, Earl Hines, and **Teddy Wilson** (1912–1986) were the most outstanding pianists in the swing era. (Listen to Wilson's work with Benny Goodman on "Body and Soul" in *SCCJ.*) Like Tatum and Hines, Wilson also contributed to the development of modern jazz.[16] **Wilson lightened the sound of jazz piano playing and removed some of the weightiness that was found in piano styles of early jazz and swing. He replaced it with a fleet smoothness and streamlined quality.** Listeners are particularly impressed by the grace and evenness with which Wilson improvised even the fastest passages. It was as though equal attention were focused on every note, no matter how brief. His work could be dazzling.[17]

Like Tatum, Wilson is often mistaken for the type of pianist who usually plays in cocktail lounges and is therefore referred to as a "cocktail pianist." This is partly due to the pleasantness of his style. Both Tatum and Wilson influenced many cocktail pianists but do not themselves fall into this category. Melodic ideas, variety, swing, and refinement distinguish Wilson and Tatum from the multitudes of less-gifted pianists who have incorporated aspects of their styles.

Techniques of Earl Hines were especially evident in the early 1940s work of **Nat Cole** (1917–1965) and Erroll Garner. Cole was one of the first pianists to incorporate spare, hornlike lines in his playing. His lines exhibit a lightness that was not typical of the heavy-handed and flowery styles of premodern jazz. Cole also perfected a style of accompanying in which chords are played as brief,

Leading swing pianist Teddy Wilson. The sensitivity, grace, and intelligence of his improvisations were unmatched in the 1930s.

(Photo courtesy of Frank Driggs)

syncopated bursts. This eventually became known as *comping*. In 1939, Cole formed a trio composed of piano, guitar, and bass.[18] Most of his hit records of 1943 to 1949 were made with that group. The trio featured pleasant chord voicings that had a modern ring to them. The musicians closely coordinated their parts so that much of the music's rhythm was played in unison by piano and guitar, with bass lines that tightly corresponded. Highly syncopated introductions and endings were devised, and cheerful little interludes often joined the various sections of each composition. Most of each piece was worked out in advance, but there was usually room for well-paced solos whose construction was logical and easy to follow. The overall effect was light and subtle, with a snappy kind of swing feeling.

Nat Cole had a more pervasive influence than most people realize. Modern pianists Oscar Peterson, Bill Evans, and Horace Silver have all cited him as an influence on their own musical thinking. Peterson has said that Cole was the main source of his own jazz piano style and that he tried to create as tightly knit a trio technique as Cole's. For several years, Peterson led a successful piano-guitar-bass trio that played in a style that was similar to Cole's. Evans has said that he was impressed by the way Cole could take a melodic idea and develop it over the course of an improvisation. (Similar remarks have since been made about Evans himself.) Cole's piano style received less and less attention after he became one of the most popular singers in recording history. His piano playing is often overlooked because of that.

Erroll Garner (1923–1977) is a unique figure in jazz piano history because he does not fit neatly into either the swing era or the bop era and because he originated a relatively unorthodox style. (Listen to "Fantasy on Frankie and Johnny" in *SCCJ*.) He attained recognition at a time when swing had already peaked and modern jazz had already been launched. Garner had a simple, swinging style that was easy to follow. His piano trio interpretations of popular songs, including his own composition "Misty," made him one of the best known of all jazz musicians to record during the 1950s. His greatest popularity occurred during the 1950s, even though his style was rooted in the swing era of the 1930s. And though Garner played in a swing style, he recorded with saxophonist Charlie Parker, who was the most significant figure in the creation of modern jazz. Garner influenced several important modern pianists, including George Shearing and Ahmad Jamal.[19]

The origins of Garner's approach are far-flung. The sound of Earl Hines is suggested by Garner's octave-voiced right-hand lines and his pounding approach. Garner's melodic sense, however, is much simpler than Hines's, and he showed nowhere near the quantity of rhythmic surprises that typified Hines. It is notable that Garner's style evolved over the years, but he never relaxed his eighth-note conception to the streamlined feeling that was employed by modern pianists or by such advanced swing pianists as Teddy Wilson and Nat Cole. Several aspects of Garner's approach have assumed trademark quality for his name. One is that his left hand played a chord on each beat as a rhythm guitarist might, but each chord was played ever so slightly after the beat rather than directly on it. Another is a skillful use of loudness changes. (This is a trait that Ahmad Jamal might have learned from Garner.) A third prime aspect of Garner's style is a flowery manner that seems to almost drip with its extensive use of tremolo and grace notes.

Some of Garner's playing is richly orchestral, and it is harmonically like the French Impressionistic music of Claude Debussy and Maurice Ravel. Garner often voiced his melodies chordally instead of letting melody notes sound by themselves. This has led jazz historian Harvey Pekar to suggest that Garner's historical impact may have been to get pianists to think more in terms of chordal playing. Pekar says that, through a concern with chordal playing and impressionism, Garner may have begun a stream of styles which ran from Ahmad Jamal to Red Garland, and from

Garland to Bill Evans and McCoy Tyner. Pekar also notes that Garner's regular statement of the beat with his left hand influenced—possibly through Jamal—Red Garland. Garner, however, played on each beat, whereas Garland punctuated just every other beat.

Pianists have proven to be the most versatile musicians throughout music's history. Pianists who were also jazz musicians proved particularly versatile during the twentieth century. **Mary Lou Williams** (1910–1981) exemplifies this tradition. She distinguished herself as a boogie-woogie player, a swing player in the style of Count Basie, a modern jazz stylist by the mid-1940s, and she even dueted with "free jazz" pioneer Cecil Taylor in 1977. No matter what style she played, her technique was stunning, and her improvisations were intelligently conceived. Williams penned arrangements for big bands led by Benny Goodman, Dizzy Gillespie, Woody Herman, and Duke Ellington. From 1929 to 1941, her arrangements set the pace for the band Andy Kirk and His Twelve Clouds of Joy, with which she was also the top soloist. She also wrote more than 250 original compositions. Her "Zodiac Suite" particularly impressed her contemporaries. (Though it contains some jazz passages, much of the suite was derived from her study of twentieth century classical composers.) Her immense output as composer and arranger and the flair that she brought to her rendering of every new piano style is staggering.

"Walkin' and Swingin'," JCCD1 *Track 14*

Mary Lou Williams, pianist-composer-arranger who kept up with changing styles and continued effectively in the modern era.

(Courtesy of Frank Driggs)

Partly because of her multitude of talents and genre switches, it has been difficult to identify a particular stamp of personal style in Mary Lou Williams's work. By the 1940s, she had begun what became the norm for jazz musicians in the 1980s and 1990s, mastering the styles of different players in different eras and never sticking to any one of them. Williams continuously changed, assimilating more and more approaches. At various times, for instance, she sounded like Count Basie, Duke Ellington, Teddy Wilson, Art Tatum, Erroll Garner, Thelonious Monk, George Shearing, and Lennie Tristano. Williams went from ragtime and boogie-woogie to bop and beyond. She was still evolving in 1971. Documenting her influence on other musicians is also difficult. Phrases of her tunes can be found in compositions credited to others, but she cannot be identified as the major source for the style of any other jazz pianist, or even a crucial part of any other pianist's concept. For instance, though several important musicians said they admired her work, and a number of luminaries in the bop era were members of a study group that met at her home in the 1940s, no one has mentioned the particulars of her actual influence on their style. In fact, the most likely candidates, Thelonious Monk and Bud Powell, influenced her at least as much as she influenced them.[20]

Milt Buckner (1915–1977) influenced pianists of the 1940s through his use of block chording, or the so-called *locked-hands style*. This is a method of voicing a chord and making the top note of it the melody note.[21] Buckner created piano solos that were like the four-, five-, and six-part horn voicings in band arrangements of the 1930s and 1940s. It was as though each finger played the part that a saxophone would ordinarily play. This contrasts to a style in which one hand plays a single melodic line while the other occasionally plays chords. In locked-hands style, the pianist uses both hands as though they were locked together, all fingers striking the piano keyboard at the same time. During the late 1940s and early 1950s, Lennie Tristano, George Shearing, Ahmad Jamal, Oscar Peterson, and others used this technique. Red Garland and Bill Evans used it in the late 1950s. During the 1960s, many pianists, including McCoy Tyner, made extensive use of block chording. Each pianist's particular approach to block chording became a signature for his style. (Listen to Dave Brubeck on "Blue Rondo a la Turk," *JCCD2* Track 4 at 4'43" and Bill Evans on "Solar," *JCCD3* Track 3 at 7'17".)

LISTENING GUIDE

"Walkin' and Swingin'" by Andy Kirk and His Twelve Clouds of Joy, featuring Mary Lou Williams

Composed by Mary Lou Williams; recorded 1936 in NYC for Decca with three trumpets, one trombone, two alto saxophones, one tenor saxophone, piano (Williams), guitar, bass, and drums; reissued on *Andy Kirk & Mary Lou Williams: Mary's Idea* (Decca Jazz: 622, c1993).

Terms and sounds to learn from *Demo CD and DVD*: tenor saxophone (also heard at 1'51" on "Walkin' and Swingin'"), alto saxophone, trombone (also heard at 2'32" and 2'36" on "Walkin' and Swingin'"). Terms to learn from the "Elements of Music" appendix: measure (bar), A-A-B-A form, mutes, syncopation.

Andy Kirk's 12-piece band was based in Kansas City during the 1930s, though they also played elsewhere, including extended engagements in New York and Pennsylvania. "Walkin' and Swingin'" is a composition and arrangement that pianist Mary Lou Williams prepared for it. The piece became a particular favorite of musicians who appreciate Williams's creativity. Its most outstanding feature is a line that Williams composed for trumpet and three saxophones to play on the second chorus, beginning at about 0'46". The construction of this line hints at some of the melodic intricacies and syncopations that were used in the first modern jazz style, known as "bop," short for "bebop" (see Chapter 9). It is notable that Kirk shared Kansas City with several other excellent big bands, including a few that launched modern jazz: Count Basie's, which featured Lester Young, and Jay McShann's, which featured Charlie Parker. (For more about Young and Basie, see Chapter 8, and listen to "Taxi War Dance" and "Lester Leaps In" on *JCCD1* Tracks 24 and 25.) Like Lester Young and Charlie Parker, Mary Lou Williams was one of Kansas City's contributions to the roots of modern jazz.

Williams's piano remarks during this performance sound similar to those associated with Basie. This similarity could be a result of Williams imitating Basie and/or studying the same models that Basie had studied, such as Fats Waller ("Handful of Keys," *JCCD1* Track 12) and Earl Hines ("West End Blues," *JCCD1* Track 10). She certainly had plenty of opportunity to hear Basie up close while she and Basie were both based in Kansas City.

This recording also gives us a taste of tenor saxophonist Dick Wilson's playing at 1'51". Wilson was one of the top Coleman Hawkins disciples on the 1930s jazz scene. Pay attention to his deep, dark tone, and his authoritative bearing. Listen to how logically he constructs his improvised lines.

The Kansas City style for big band arrangements is characterized by brief phrases called riffs. These repeat and become essential elements of the music. A few examples occur at 2'37" and 2'47".

The piece follows a 32-bar A-A-B-A construction, whose chord changes are similar to those of "I Got Rhythm," though the bridge is not. With no introduction at the beginning and no extra measures at the ending, the performance consists of four complete choruses of that A-A-B-A construction and a two-measure (8 quick beats) interlude between the end of the first chorus and the beginning of the second. In preparing this piece, Williams employed several arranging practices that were standard for big bands of the swing era: (1) assigning the theme to the saxophones and the punctuations to the brass instruments, as in the A-sections of the first chorus; (2) inventing an intricate, jazz improvisation-like line, as constitutes the second chorus that begins at 0'46"; (3) delegating the improvised solo sections according to the song form, as she plays her own piano solo on the A-sections of the third chorus, beginning at 1'32", and she gives the bridge to Dick Wilson for his tenor saxophone solo, beginning at 1'50"; (4) call and response format (sequenced like a question and answer), as she gives the trumpets a brief riff as a question, at about 2'37", and assigns the trombone an answer; then she gives the brass instruments a call and the saxophones a response, beginning at about 2'47".

Though bass and drums play throughout the piece, their presence may be felt more than heard. You might detect them best at about 2'32" during moments when horns pause.

This arrangement departs in a significant way from standard practices of the era. In selecting instruments to play the theme of the second chorus, Williams assigned one trumpet to play with three saxophones. In other words, she drew instruments from different sections of the band: the brass section and the saxophone section. Known as "cross-section voicing," this technique was unusual for arrangers of her time, though Duke Ellington was a notable exception.

LISTENING GUIDE *continued on next page*

ELAPSED TIME	MUSICAL EVENTS	
	First Chorus	
0'00"	A	Saxophones play theme as brasses punctuate.
0'11"	A	Saxophones play theme as brasses punctuate.
0'22"	B	Brasses lead, sometimes mixed with saxes. Saxes respond.
0'33"	A	Saxophones play theme as brasses punctuate.
	Two-Bar Interlude	
0'44"		Brass and saxophones play a harmonized figure.
	Second Chorus (same chords, different melody)	
0'46"	A	One trumpet and three saxophones play boppish line.
0'57"	A	
1'10"	B	(note the valley-like contour of the moving pitches)
1'19"	A	
	Third Chorus	
1'30"	A	piano solo improvisation by Mary Lou Williams
1'41"	A	piano solo improvisation by Mary Lou Williams
1'51"	B	Dick Wilson tenor saxophone solo improvisation, accompanied by plunger-muted trumpets playing a syncopated countermelody
2'03"	A	piano solo improvisation by Mary Lou Williams
2'10"		final two measures: break for horns to play
	Fourth Chorus	
2'13"	A	Brass play highly syncopated riff, against a different saxophone riff, but one trumpet plays with saxophone part, and one trumpet plays with trombone part.
2'21"	A	Brass play highly syncopated line answered by saxes.
2'32"	B	Trumpets call and trombone responds, saxes playing underneath (drums and bass detectable as underpinning).
2'45"	A	Brass riff calls for saxes's answer.

To briefly review jazz piano history up to this time, remember that **James P. Johnson,** Willie "The Lion" Smith, and other early pianists **had contributed the stride style. Earl Hines was a pioneer in playing horn-like lines.** Meade Lux Lewis, Pinetop Smith, Cow Cow Davenport, and others **introduced boogie-woogie. Tatum had explored reharmonization.** And now **Milt Buckner had added locked-hands style** to the list of alternatives that were available for pianists to select.

GUITAR

During the swing era, guitar was beginning to be viewed as more than a timekeeping member of the rhythm section. Prior to the emergence of Django Reinhardt, most jazz guitarists had played brief, chorded solos which were technically quite modest by comparison with piano and horn solos. That changed with the

Composed by Benny Goodman and Charlie Christian; recorded on November 22, 1939, for Columbia by Benny Goodman (clarinet), Charlie Christian (electric guitar), Lionel Hampton (vibraphone), Fletcher Henderson (piano), Artie Bernstein (bass), Nick Fatool (drums); reissued on *Prentice Hall Jazz Collection*; Charlie Christian, *Genius of the Electric Guitar* (Columbia: 65564, 4CD set, 1939–41, c2002), and on Christian, *The Original Guitar Hero* (Columbia/Legacy: 86834, 1939–41, c2002).

Terms to learn from DVD and *Demo CD*: ride rhythm, walking bass, snare drum, high-hat cymbals, clarinet, vibraphone/vibraharp. Study the "Elements of Music" appendix for eighth notes, syncopation, A-A-B-A, and the functions and effects of bridges in song form.

The primary purpose of having this piece on the CD set is to sample the playing of guitarist Charlie Christian. In the first half of jazz history, Christian was the most important guitar soloist. An added feature in this particular recording is the work of vibraphonist Lionel Hampton, an enormous source of energy and enthusiasm on the jazz scene from the 1920s to 2002. The music of these two giants comes to us in the context of a combo recording led by clarinetist Benny Goodman. So it also allows a brief taste of his style, too. Goodman was better known for his popular big band, and you are urged to obtain his big band recordings from the 1930s and '40s to sample solos by him that are more exciting. While the theme is simple, and its rhythms are representative of the swing style, the solos by Christian and Hampton are relatively complex for this era. They hint at techniques that would later be explored by modern musicians in the bop era.

ELAPSED TIME

Introduction

0'00"		4 *Measures*
		Drummer uses drum sticks to play ride rhythm on opening and closing high-hat cymbals, with occasional interjections on snare drum.
0'05"		8 *Measures*
		Bass and piano enter with rhythmic figure that repeats throughout the A-section. No progression of chords.

Melody—First Chorus

0'12"	**A**	Clarinet, vibraphone, and guitar enter with melody composed of repeating riffs. Piano and bass accompany by repeatedly playing the opening bass line. Drummer maintains ride rhythms.
0'21"	**A**	Repeat of first A-section
0'28"	**B**	Clarinet improvisation. Vibraphone sustains chords over a walking bass line. Unlike A-section, the chords change regularly.
0'37"	**A**	Repeat of first A-section

Charlie Christian's Guitar Solo—Second Chorus

0'45"	**A**	Guitarist Charlie Christian opens his solo by repeating just one note, in a syncopated way. Then he begins playing short, moving lines. The solo sounds bluesy. Bass plays same opening figure to accompany the solo.
0'54"	**A**	Vibraphone adds a repeating riff behind guitar solo.
1'02"	**B**	Solo becomes more active and complex. Bass walks, and vibraphone plays sustained chords. Drummer varies his rhythms on high-hat cymbals.
1'11"	**A**	Continuation of solo. Bass returns to repeating the opening figure.

Lionel Hampton's Vibraphone Solo—Third Chorus

1'19"	**A**	Lionel Hampton's vibraphone solo is almost continuous eighth notes. Clarinet and guitar harmonize a figure in the background. Bass walks throughout entire solo.
1'28"	**A**	Continuation of solo

LISTENING GUIDE continued on next page

1'36"	B	Densely ordered solo, almost no rests. Clarinet softly plays a counterline. Guitar is not playing.
1'44"	A	Continuation of solo, almost all eighth notes.
1'47"		Hampton repeatedly plays in a syncopated way a special note that clashes with the harmony.

Benny Goodman's Clarinet Solo—Fourth Chorus

1'52"	A	Guitar is strumming chords in close coordination with walking bass as accompaniment. Drummer occasionally interjects "bombs" on the snare drum. Accompaniment in this chorus is less cluttered because there are no vibraphone or piano chords.
2'01"	A	Continuation of solo
2'09"	B	Continuation of solo
2'17"	A	Continuation of solo

Melody—Fourth Chorus

2'25"	A	As earlier.
2'34"	A	Continuation of melody
2'40"		Final 8 beats of A-section: the clarinet, vibraphone, and guitar break into short improvisations before ending the piece.

NOTE: The band ended the piece prematurely, not including the bridge and final A-section, probably because the performance was running too close to the 3-minute time limit for 78 rpm discs of that era.

appearance of Charlie Christian and Django Reinhardt. **Charlie Christian** (1916–1942) mastered what was then the almost unexplored world of electric guitar. His long, swinging, single-note-at-a-time lines gave solo guitar the stature of a jazz horn.[22] Some of his phrasing had the fluid swing and freshness of his model, tenor saxophonist Lester Young (see Chapter 8). Christian is cited as an influence by almost all modern jazz guitarists who matured before the jazz-rock era. His style provided the foundation for that of Wes Montgomery, who was the single most influential jazz guitarist of the 1960s. This extended Christian's impact long past the 1940s and well into the 1990s. George Benson, for instance, was one of many contemporary players to be influenced by Montgomery and later became a significant influence himself.

"Seven Come Eleven," JCCD1 *Track 15 and* SCCJ: *"Blues Sequence from Breakfast Feud"*

Django Reinhardt (1910–1953) was a Belgian Gypsy guitarist who was based in France, played mostly within Europe, and visited America only once. However, his recordings were available in America, and he was held in high esteem by American guitarists, especially during the swing era. Reinhardt had a technical command of his guitar that rivalled the speed attained by players of less difficult instruments. Reinhardt's playing was ornate and flamboyant, with a prominent vibrato.[23] He combined the spirited flavor of Gypsy music with the equally spirited sound of jazz. (Listen to his 1934 version of "Dinah" in *SCCJ-R.*) His lines could have the intelligence of a master composer or be merely a sequence of flourishes.

SINGERS

Billie Holiday (1915–1959) is the most influential singer associated with jazz since the early 1930s. Many vocalists began their careers imitating her. Some devoted albums to tunes they first heard Holiday sing. Nicknamed "Lady Day," she is also the

CHARLIE CHRISTIAN COMPARED WITH DJANGO REINHARDT

1. Christian's pace within solos was usually steady, whereas Reinhardt's was uneven and marked by sporadic flashiness.
2. Christian's lines were hornlike, whereas Reinhardt's were more pianistic.
3. Most of Christian's recordings were made with amplified hollow-body guitar, whereas most of Reinhardt's were made on unamplified hollow-body guitar.
4. Christian's tone was usually round and soft, whereas Reinhardt's possessed a bite and was often metallic sounding.
5. Christian drew more from blues tradition, whereas Reinhardt drew from Gypsy music and the French Impressionist composers Maurice Ravel and Claude Debussy.
6. Christian used long patterns of swing eighth notes, whereas Reinhardt used somewhat jumpier sequences, with interruptions for drawn-out pitch bends.
7. Christian preferred eighth-note lines, whereas Reinhardt often leaned more toward triplet and sixteenth-note lines.
8. Christian used very little vibrato, whereas Reinhardt employed vibrato as a key element in his approach.[24]

singer most frequently cited by jazz musicians when asked what music they would take to a desert island. This is quite an endorsement because most jazz musicians prefer instrumental music and rarely name a vocal recording among their favorites.

Holiday did not possess the power of Bessie Smith, the deep, rich voice of Sarah Vaughan, or the speed and range of Ella Fitzgerald. Yet why is she so revered? First, she was original and fresh. Second, the depth and sincerity of emotion that she communicated are unparalleled. She made lyrics come alive. Holiday conveyed the song's meaning as though speaking directly to you. The agony she portrayed in sad songs could tear your heart out. Her renditions of "Gloomy Sunday," "Strange Fruit," and a tune she herself co-authored, "God Bless the Child," had intense effects on listeners.[25, 26] On the other hand, some of her late 1930s recordings convey a carefree spirit of joy unmatched by her contemporaries.[27] No matter the mood, her tender, knowing delivery grabbed you right away.

A third reason for Holiday's stature is jazz flavor. Though she was not really a blues singer—her repertory was mostly pop and show tunes—Holiday often formed her tones as a jazz hornman, with a whine that had blues flavor. Like jazz instrumentalists, she did not always give songs a straight reading, even though she had excellent diction. Instead, she varied her delivery creatively. One of the ways Holiday transformed songs was by manipulating their rhythms. Her method of intentionally delaying the arrival of certain words and phrases is almost indistinguishable from rhythmic displacements used by trumpeter Louis Armstrong, one of her main influences. This caused an engaging syncopation and swing feeling. The combination of her bluesy inflections, jazzy accents, and improvising gave jazz flavor to her music.[28]

Holiday toured and recorded with many of the top jazz musicians of the time, including Artie Shaw, Benny Goodman, and Count Basie. Her 1938 recording sessions with Teddy Wilson, Lester Young, and members of the Basie band produced some of the most poignant and swinging recordings of the era.[29] Her 1937 recording of "Carelessly" reached the #1 position on the popularity charts, and she had 35 other recordings reach the top 20 by 1945. She was prolific during the 1940s and 1950s as well. During the 1930s, she had a range of about an octave and a half, and a light, clear

"Back in Your Own Backyard," CCD1 Track 10 and SCCJ: *"She's Funny That Way"*

Billie Holiday, the most influential singer in jazz after the early 1930s.
(Photo courtesy of Frank Driggs)

voice quality which she could make sound warm. After the 1930s, Holiday's range became more limited, and her tone got rawer. (Listen to her 1952 "These Foolish Things" in *SCCJ*.) Some listeners like her work of the 1930s the most. Others find her late recordings of the 1950s to be even more emotionally compelling.[30] Not only did her life story inspire a popular movie (*Lady Sings the Blues,* 1972), but her recordings continue to sell today, 50 years after her death.[31]

Ella Fitzgerald (1918–1996) is considered by many to be the most outstanding non-operatic singer of the twentieth century. She had near-flawless technique. Listeners were impressed by her grace and lilt. Mastery of swing eighth notes and perfect timing of syncopations gave her singing the rhythmic effect achieved by the best swing era hornmen. Delivered with such bounce and lightness, her phrases actually swung more than those of some modern trumpeters and saxophonists.

First achieving prominence in the mid-1930s, Fitzgerald had a #1 hit in her 1938 rendition of "A-Tisket-a-Tasket" with the Chick Webb Band.[32] With this group she

Ella Fitzgerald, considered by many listeners to be the most outstanding non-operatic singer in the twentieth century and a leading popularizer of scat singing.

(Photo courtesy of Frank Driggs)

recorded, toured and, for several years after Webb died, served as leader. By 1955, 34 of her other records had risen to popularity positions within the top 20. Albums of her concert appearances climbed to high positions on the popularity charts during the 1960s and again in the 1980s.[33]

Ella Fitzgerald's tone was pure and supple. Her command spanned the unusually wide range of three and a half octaves. Singing in tune proves difficult for many singers, but not for Fitzgerald. Her pitch was accurate, no matter the register or tempo of the material. Her articulation was exquisite. A remarkable agility conveyed an effortless feeling. She gave every note a lift. Her overall manner achieved great presence and warmth.[34] Her combination of spirit and ease imparted a bright touch even to ballads, as though she were never really sad. A youthful quality always pervaded her work, even when she was in her seventies. Not inclined to the melodramatic attitude of so many other singers, Fitzgerald's effect is often called "cheerful," "exuberant," or "ebullient." Many consider her creative peak to be the 1950s and 1960s, yet she was still giving remarkable performances during the 1970s and 1980s.

Though she did not invent it, Fitzgerald was scat singing's best known practitioner. Among the modern scat singers who followed, almost all cite her work as their first inspiration. On some recordings she functions as a horn, using nonsense syllables exclusively, no lyrics.[35] Fitzgerald was quite melodic in her scats. This was due in part to (1) basing portions of her passages on set routines rather than completely fresh improvisations in every performance and (2) improvising more around the melody of the original tune than from the chords of its accompaniment.[36]

"Perdido," JCCD1 *Track 19;* "Flying *Home,"* CCD1 *Track 14*

Despite her scat singing's historic visibility, that work represents only a small fraction of her output. Fitzgerald gets high marks from listeners who like a singer to stick to the melody as written. Some of the greatest pop tune composers were eager to have her perform their songs because her readings were so true to their original intent. So, in addition to her exalted position in jazz, she also had a large following among pop music listeners and is reputed to have sold over 40 million records.[37]

POPULAR APPEAL

Before we can answer the question of whether jazz itself was popular during the swing era, we first need to decide which definition of jazz to use. (Review Chapter 2 for ways to define jazz.) If music can be called "jazz" solely by its association with the jazz tradition, the swing era was a great period for jazz. And if music can be called "jazz" whenever it swings, this era clearly marks a peak for jazz. But if we employ a strict definition and require jazz to be improvised, the matter becomes sticky. In examining the extent of appeal generated by swing style jazz, we need to comment briefly on the style and size of bands, and to make some distinctions between big bands that emphasized improvisation and big bands that did not.

Though big bands were prevalent during the swing era, big band style does not necessarily mean swing style. There were also jazz-oriented big bands before and after the swing era. Many of these sounded very different from swing bands. Big band style doesn't necessarily mean jazz style, either. In the 1930s and 1940s, ten to sixteen musicians was the standard size of bands for many types of popular music. After that, the standard size decreased to about three to eight musicians.

Also during the swing era, journalists and musicians distinguished between bands that emphasized jazz improvisation and those that did not. For example, the very popular Glenn Miller big band was a swinging band. It had a handful of hit records that contained brief jazz improvisations. But the Miller band emphasized pretty arrangements and vocals more than improvised jazz solos. Therefore, despite its swinging qualities, the band was sometimes classified as a *sweet band* (as in the popularity polls conducted by *Down Beat* magazine in 1940 and 1941). This distinguished it from the *hot band* or *swing band* classification. Bands such as Count Basie's and Duke Ellington's fell into these categories because they had more solo improvisations.

With these distinctions in mind, note that this textbook discusses only the most jazz-oriented bands and soloists from the 1930s and 1940s big band scene. During the swing era, there were many big bands, though most were not primarily concerned with jazz improvisation. Some of the jazz improvisations that historians have heralded were well known by the public, but most were not. In other words, swing fans were far from unanimous in their awareness and appreciation of jazz improvisation. For jazz groups of later eras, improvisation was the primary focus of each performance. But for most big bands of the swing era, even the jazz-oriented ones, improvisation was not necessarily a first priority.

Melody and chords composed by Juan Tizol. Lyrics improvised by Ella Fitzgerald; recorded September 18, 1949, at Carnegie Hall, New York, for Norman Granz; by Ella Fitzgerald (voice), Hank Jones (piano), Ray Brown (bass), Buddy Rich (drums), Charlie Parker (alto sax), Roy Eldridge (trumpet), Tommy Turk (trombone), Flip Phillips (tenor sax); available on *Jazz Classics CD1*; reissued on CD as Parker, *Charlie Parker—Jazz at the Philharmonic 1949* (Verve 314 519 803, c1993).

This is possibly the most exciting of all the hundreds of recordings Ella Fitzgerald made. It also demonstrates how jazz singers can improvise and, more importantly, how the most famous of all jazz singers not only acted as a horn but also made up new words while she was singing.

This recording features a concert performance by Ella Fitzgerald. The context for this recording warrants telling a little history. From 1944 to 1967, concert impresario Norman Granz ran public jam sessions. Since his musicians played in auditoriums where philharmonic symphony orchestras usually performed, Granz billed his tour rosters as Jazz at the Philharmonic. Some of the greatest figures in jazz history comprised these sessions. For example, the concert tour recording excerpted here included such giants as Charlie Parker, Lester Young, and Roy Eldridge. Note that because the band's jam on this piece is much too long to fit on our CD, we have faded in after Tommy Turk's trombone solo that preceded Fitzgerald's vocal segment, and we have faded out before Flip Phillips's tenor saxophone solo that follows it.

Like that of the instrumental soloists on the program, Fitzgerald's part is also improvised. The jam is based on the chord changes to "Perdido," a tune with a 32-bar A-A-B-A construction. Our excerpt contains the two choruses that feature Fitzgerald's singing. Granz presented her as another soloist within the string of horn solos. A high trumpet note (4′02″ of the jam, 0′00″ of our excerpt) signals the first beat of Fitzgerald's solo chorus. Since her voice was initially not picked up by the recording microphone, we all but miss her first phrase. When her voice finally comes into range (4′06″ of the jam, 0′03″ of our excerpt), we hear her singing melody and lyrics that she made up herself, possibly at that very moment. Her pitches do not constitute the original "Perdido" melody, and her words are presumably spontaneous, too. The character of her words suggests how informal and light-hearted the creative process was in that situation. For example, her second phrase is "Everybody's showin' how much they like Perdido." Another equally casual line occupies the second A-section (at about 4′13″ in the jam, 0′10″ of our excerpt): "He started playin' . . . everybody starts sayin' . . . they would be payin' to hear him blow Perdido." Then for the bridge (at 4′23″ of the jam, 0′20″ in our excerpt), she sings, "Blow, blow, Phillips, blow" and "Go, go, Phillips, go," referring to tenor saxophonist Flip Phillips, the soloist slated to follow her. Another reason it seems likely that she made up all these words is because she begins to scat sing on the last A-section in her first chorus of the tune's A-A-B-A form (4′34″ of the jam, 0′31″ in our excerpt). We might reason that if she came to the jam with lyrics of her own, they would run the entire length of the song form, not just end suddenly after the bridge. So maybe she began improvising scat singing when she could not think up any more words. We know that Fitzgerald had sufficient creativity and bearing to rise to such occasions. She famously invented and performed new lyrics spontaneously when she forgot some words in the middle of singing "Mack the Knife" at a 1960 concert in Berlin. It is captured in one of her most compelling albums: *Ella in Berlin*.

When you hear this recording, notice Fitzgerald's remarkable warmth and presence. Note the exuberance for which she was justly celebrated. Also listen for her supple delivery and crisp articulation. Pay close attention to the swing feeling that Fitzgerald conveys. Keep in mind that in all of jazz history, Fitzgerald came closer than any other singer to achieving the rhythmic effect of the most swinging jazz instrumentalists. When she scatted, she might as well have been a jazz trumpeter improvising a solo.

There are some additional sounds the origins for which you might not understand the first time you hear it. Listeners at jazz concerts often become as aroused as the performers, and they vocally show their delight. The audience got very excited by the music at this jam session, and they expressed it by cheering on the soloists. Sometimes they shouted just at the mere appearance of their favorite soloists. One could speculate that when Fitzgerald's lyrics musically asked for Phillips to "blow," Phillips may have appeared on stage with his saxophone, indicating that yes, indeed he would blow. So perhaps it was Phillips's gesture which evoked the shouts we hear on the recording, during the bridge of Fitzgerald's first chorus (at about 4′23″ in the jam, 0′20″ in our excerpt) and the first two A-sections of her second chorus (at about 4′44″ in the jam, 0′41″ in our excerpt, and 4′55″ in the jam, 0′52″ in our excerpt).

Fitzgerald does follow the 32-bar A-A-B-A form of "Perdido," and the excerpted lyrics below are provided primarily to help you notice the beginnings of each section. Note, however, that tracking Fitzgerald's progress through the song form is not absolutely necessary for an appreciation of her artistry. So these indicators may be useful only if you want such information.

LISTENING GUIDE continued on next page

ELAPSED TIME FOR EXCERPT	ELAPSED TIME FOR ORIGINAL		MUSICAL EVENTS
			First Chorus
	4'02"	A	high-pitched trumpet note
0'00"			inaudible voice on first phrase
0'03"	4'06"		second phrase: "now everybody's showin'"
0'09"	4'12"	A	"he started playin'"
0'20"	4'23"	B	"so blow"
0'23"	4'26"		crowd shouting for Flip Phillips to blow
0'31"	4'33"	A	scat singing
			Second Chorus
0'41"	4'44"	A	scat singing a phrase from a band version, accompanied by louder and louder shouting from crowd
0'51"	4'54"	A	horns riffing, Fitzgerald incorporating horn riff in her first phrase
1'02"	5'06"	B	scat singing, accompanied by Parker quadruple-timing almost inaudibly
1'12"	5'16"	A	scat singing, accompanied by horns riffing
1'22"	5'26"		High-pitched trumpet note announces next chorus.

A few other points should be considered before the era is described as a successful period for jazz:

1. A significant portion of swing era hits contained vocals, and many of those that did not have singing were at least based on songs that listeners had previously learned by way of a vocal rendition. This alerts us to consider that *jazz improvisation might not have provided the primary appeal of the pieces. The popularity of those pieces might just reflect the same appeal that songs have had throughout history.*

2. Most of the swing era hits that were jazz-oriented contained only a few solo improvisations, often only one.

3. The amount of improvisation in most swing era hits was small, sometimes only 16 measures, and rarely more than a 32-bar chorus.

4. The construction of improvised solos in most hits was melodically conservative.

The big band sound, the context for the improvisations, and the tunes being improvised upon were certainly popular during the swing era. And some listeners no doubt focused primarily on the improvised solos themselves. But *for a large portion of the public, the improvisations were incidental, perhaps inconsequential, segments of the performances.* Jazz historians, being jazz fans themselves, like to believe that the adulation of the swing big bands was directed mostly at jazz qualities of the music. Most fans, however, were more entranced by the overall effect of big band music and its rhythm than by the inspiration and skill with which solo improvisers devised their lines. Traditionally in most kinds of music only a small segment of the audience has been attracted by nuances of form and innovations of method. There may have been no greater love for the qualities of jazz improvisation during the swing era than in other eras, though more improvisers were in the public eye during the swing era.

Certain jazz musicians were as well known to the general public during the swing era as rock stars are today. For instance, Benny Goodman, Count Basie, and Duke Ellington were household words during the 1930s and 1940s. The public knew them as leaders of dance bands more than as jazz musicians. Still, they were better known than the jazz giants of later eras. Even some of their soloists were well known and not just by jazz buffs. The big bands, famous and not so famous, employed hundreds of jazz musicians. This made it easier at that time for musicians to find work as performers. Unfortunately, however, most of the jobs with big bands did not include extensive opportunities to improvise because these groups worked largely from written arrangements. Opportunities to improvise were generous in smaller combos, yet steady employment in jazz combos was difficult to find.

Like rock combos since the 1950s, *one of the most important functions for swing bands of the 1930s and 1940s was to provide dance music*. Jazz functioned as dance music more during the swing era than it did thereafter. Another similarity with popular rock combos is that swing era big bands usually used elaborate costumes, showy staging, and most of them routinely featured several singers. The visual appeal of the performance, including the personality and looks of the singers, was a primary attraction for a sizable portion of the audience. Only occasionally during the swing era were jazz musicians given paid opportunities to perform just for listening, as later became customary. In summary, the popular success of jazz bands during the swing era was partly a result of their appeal to the eyes and feet of fans instead of to the ears alone.

CHAPTER SUMMARY

1. Swing differs from early jazz in
   a. more use of written arrangements
   b. less emphasis on ragtime-like compositions
   c. less collective improvisation and more solo improvisation
   d. less use of tuba and more use of string bass
   e. more swing feeling, achieved by increased use of swing eighth-note patterns
   f. increased use of high-hat cymbals
   g. replacement of banjo with guitar
   h. big band rather than small-group instrumentation
   i. saxophone becoming the predominant instrument
2. Important big bands were led by Fletcher Henderson, Duke Ellington, Count Basie, Benny Goodman, and Jimmie Lunceford.
3. The most influential saxophonists were Coleman Hawkins, Lester Young, Benny Carter, and Johnny Hodges.
4. The most influential pianists were Art Tatum and Teddy Wilson.
5. Tatum possessed phenomenal speed and was known for spontaneously changing keys and chords in pop tune accompaniments.
6. Wilson was known for his grace and his streamlining of jazz piano style.
7. Nat Cole influenced modern jazz piano style by reducing left-hand activity and making right-hand lines more horn-like.
8. Pianist Milt Buckner perfected the technique of harmonizing melody lines in a block-chord "locked-hands" fashion.
9. Roy Eldridge paved the way for modern jazz trumpeter Dizzy Gillespie by improvising fiery, saxophone-like lines on trumpet.

10. Django Reinhardt and Charlie Christian were the most prominent guitarists of the swing era.

11. Billie Holiday and Ella Fitzgerald were the most prominent singers to be associated with jazz in the swing era.

Top Big Bands	Fletcher Henderson
	Benny Goodman
	Jimmie Lunceford
	Duke Ellington
	Count Basie
Top Saxophonists	Coleman Hawkins
	Lester Young
	Johnny Hodges
	Benny Carter
Top Pianists	Art Tatum
	Teddy Wilson
	Errol Garner
	Nat Cole
Top Guitarists	Charlie Christian
	Django Reinhardt

NOTES

1. See the autobiography: Milt Hinton and David Berger, *Bass Line* (Temple, 1988). Listen to Hinton's features with Cab Calloway's big band: "Ebony Silhouette" (1941) on *Jammin' for the Jackpot* (New World: 217, LP, 1929–41, c1977) and "Pluckin' the Bass" on *Cab Calloway and His Orchestra: 1939–40* (Classics: 595, 1939–40, c1991). Notice his accompaniment work on Lionel Hampton's band version of "When Lights Are Low" on *SCCJ*.

2. See Appendix G to get Denny Brown's history of premodern drumming.

3. All the big bands mentioned in this chapter can be heard on *Big Band Jazz: From the Beginnings to the Fifties* (Smithsonian: 2202, 4CD set, 1924–56, c1983; contents listed in *Instructor's Resource Manual for Jazz Styles*), and some are also on *Big Band Renaissance* (Smithsonian: RD108, 5CD set, 1941–89, c1995). Henderson is well represented on *Fletcher Henderson, A Study in Frustration* (Columbia/Legacy: C3K 57596, 3CD set, 1923–38, c1994). Most important bands and musicians from this era can also be heard on *SCCJ*, and the Basie and Ellington bands are represented on *JCCD1*. All the pianists in this chapter, except Milt Buckner, can be heard on *Jazz Piano* (Smithsonian: 7002, 4CD set, 1924–78, c1989).

4. Henderson's arrangements can be heard on Goodman's recordings of "King Porter Stomp," "Wrappin' It Up," "Blue Skies," "Down South Camp Meeting," "Sometimes I'm Happy," "Japanese Sandman," and "When Buddah Smiles." For more about Fletcher Henderson and other important bands of the era, see Gunther Schuller, *The Swing Era* (Oxford, 1989); Stanley Dance, *The World of Swing* (Scribner's, 1975; Da Capo, 2001); George T. Simon, *The Big Bands*, 4th ed. (Schirmer,

1981); Frank Driggs and Chuck Haddix, *Kansas City Jazz: From Ragtime to Bebop—A History* (Oxford Univ. Press, 2005); Nathan W. Pearson, *Goin' to Kansas City* (University of Illinois, 1987); and Nat Shapiro and Nat Hentoff, *The Jazz Makers* (Grove, 1957; Da Capo, 1979).

5. *Jimmie Lunceford and His Orchestra, 1930–1934* (Classics: 501, c1990); listen to "Lunceford Special" on *SCCJ* or "Organ Grinder Swing" on *SCCJ-R*; or on Jimmy Lunceford, *For Dancers Only* (Decca Jazz: 645, 1935–37, c1994). A sampling ("Stratosphere," "Uptown Blues," and "Organ Grinder Swing") is available on *Big Band Jazz* (Smithsonian).

6. Benny Goodman, *Sing, Sing, Sing* (RCA Bluebird: 5630-2-RB, 1935–1938, c1987), big band; and *The Complete RCA Victor Small Group Recordings* (Victor Jazz: 68764, 3CD set, 1935–1939, c1997); or *The Legendary Small Groups* (RCA Bluebird: 63994, 1935–1938, c2002).

7. Several of the players Goodman spotlighted also led their own swing bands at one time or another: 1) trumpeter Bunny Berigan (1908–1942); 2) trumpeter Harry James (1916–1983) continued to lead big bands for decades after the end of the swing era; 3) trumpeter Cootie Williams (see chapter 7 for discussion); 4) vibraphonist Lionel Hampton (1909–2002); see page 178 for illustrations of the vibraphone (listen to his "When Lights Are Low" on *SCCJ*); 5) drummer Gene Krupa (1909–1973): his drum solos helped emancipate jazz drummers from their restricted role of being merely timekeepers (listen to his "Rockin' Chair" on *SCCJ*).

For more about Goodman, see Bruce Crowther, *Benny Goodman* (Apollo, 1987); D. Russell Connor, *Benny Goodman: Listen to His Legacy* (Scarecrow, 1988); James Lincoln Collier, *Benny Goodman and the Swing*

Era (Oxford, 1989); Ross Firestone, *Swing, Swing, Swing* (Norton, 1993); and Schuller, *The Swing Era*, 3–45.

8. Tommy Dorsey, *Yes Indeed!* (RCA Bluebird: 9987-2-RB, 1939–45, c1990); *The Best of Tommy Dorsey* (RCA Bluebird: 51087, 1935–45, c1992).

9. Harris solos on "Bijou," "Northwest Passage," "Apple Honey," and "Woodchopper's Ball" on Woody Herman, *Blowin' Up a Storm* (Columbia: C2K 65646, 2 CD set, 1945–47, c2001).

10. Listen to his blazing solo on the 1941 "After You've Gone" with Gene Krupa's band. Also listen to "Sittin' In" with Chu Berry recorded for Commodore in 1938 on the CGCD1. For a transcription and analysis of his solo on "I Can't Believe That You're in Love with Me" (on *SCCJ*), see Schuller, *The Swing Era*, 458–460. For more about Eldridge, see John Chilton, *Roy Eldridge, the Little Giant* (Continuum, 2002).

11. To detect the Eldridge character in Gillespie's earliest playing, listen to Eldridge's solo on the Gene Krupa band recording of "After You've Gone," *JCCD1* Track 24, then listen to Gillespie's playing on the Cab Calloway recording of "Pickin' the Cabbage" on *Cab Calloway and His Orchestra 1939–1940* (Classics 595).

12. Coleman Hawkins, *The Centennial Collection* (RCA Bluebird: 60086, 1929–57, c2004); and *Classic Tenors* (Signature/CBS: 38446, 1943, c1989).

13. For technical analysis of Hawkins, see Schuller, *The Swing Era*, 426–50. For a transcription and analysis of his solo on "Body and Soul," see Stuart Isacoff, *Solos for Jazz Tenor Sax* (Carl Fischer, 1985); order from: Carl Fischer Music, 65 Bleeker St., NYC, NY 10012; phone: 800-762-2328; web: *www.carlfischer.com*. See also biographies: John Chilton, *The Song of the Hawk* (Univ. of Michigan, 1990); and Burnett James, *Coleman Hawkins* (Hippocrene, 1984).

14. Benny Carter, *Cosmopolite: The Oscar Peterson Verve Sessions* (Verve: 314 521 673, 1952, 1954, c1994). See also Morroe Berger, Edward Berger, and James Patrick, *Benny Carter: A Life in American Music*, 2nd ed. (Scarecrow, 2002).

15. Art Tatum, *Piano Starts Here* (Columbia/Legacy: 64690, 1933, 1949, c1995) and *The Complete Capitol Recordings of Art Tatum* (Capitol: 21325, 2CD set, 1949, c1997). For a transcription and analysis of Tatum's "The Man I Love," see John Rodby, *Solos for Jazz Piano* (Carl Fischer, 1989). For Joseph Howard's three-volume analysis of Tatum's style, see the "Sources for Solo Transcriptions" appendix. See also John Mehegan, *Jazz Improvisation*, vol. 3 (Watson-Guptill, 1964); and Schuller, *The Swing Era*, 476–502. See also James Lester, *Too Marvelous for Words: The Life and Genius of Art Tatum* (Oxford, 1994).

16. When Wilson chose to create horn-like lines, he refined the best of Earl Hines. Wilson's work on the 1936 "Blues in C-Sharp Minor" provides an excellent demonstration of his precisely executed, intelligently conceived horn-like lines. This can be heard on *The Notable Art of Teddy Wilson* (ASV Living Era: 5450, 1933–46, c2002); or Roy Eldridge, *Little Jazz* (Columbia: 45275, 1935–40, c1989). For an analysis of his style, see Mehegan, *Jazz Improvisation*, vol. 3. For a comparison with Tatum's style, see Schuller, *The Swing Era*, 502–513.

17. Teddy Wilson, *Piano Solos* (Affinity/Charly: CDAFS 1016 [Brunswick], 1934–1937, c1991).

18. Nat King Cole, *Hit That Jive, Jack* (Decca Jazz: 662, 1936, 1940–41, c1990); "The Man I Love" (1944) and "Blues in My Shower" (1947) on *Jazz Piano* (Smithsonian); and *Best of the Nat Cole Trio: Instrumental Classics* (Capitol Jazz: 98288, 1944–49, c1992). For transcriptions and analyses, see Schuller, *The Swing Era*, 816–825.

19. For a transcription and analysis of Garner's solo on "I'll Remember April," see John Rodby, *Solos for Jazz Piano* (Carl Fischer, 1989). For

more about Garner's life, see James M. Doran, *Erroll Garner: The Most Happy Piano* (Scarecrow, 1985).

20. Andy Kirk, *Andy Kirk & The 12 Clouds of Joy with Mary Lou Williams* (ASV Living Era: 5108 [Decca], 1929–1940, c1993); Mary Lou Williams, *Mary Lou Williams 1927–1940* (Classics: 630, 1927–1940, c1992); *Mary Lou Williams 1944* (Classics: 814, 1944, c1995); *Mary Lou Williams 1944–1945* (Classics: 1021, 1944–1945, c1998), which includes the "Zodiac Suite"; and *Nitelife* (Chiaruscuro: 103, 2CD set, 1971, c1998). For biographies, see Linda Dahl, *Morning Glory: A Biography of Mary Lou Williams* (Pantheon, 1999); and Tammy L. Kernodle, *Soul on Soul: The Life and Music of Mary Lou Williams* (Northeastern Univ., 2004).

21. Buckner is heard on "Royal Family" on Lionel Hampton, *Swingsation* (Decca Jazz: 9922, 1942–47, c1998).

22. Charlie Christian, *The Genius of the Electric Guitar* (Columbia/Legacy: 65564, 4CD set, 1939–41, c2002); or *The Original Guitar Hero* (Columbia/Legacy: 86834, 1939–41, c2002).

23. Django Reinhardt, *Souvenirs* (London: 820 591, 1935–39, c1988); *The Classic Early Recordings* (JSP: 901, 5CD set, 1934–39, c2000); and *Peche a la Mouche: The Great Blue Star Sessions* (Verve: 835 418, 2CD set, 1947, 1953, c1991). For a biography, see Charles Delaunay, *Django Reinhardt* (Cassell, 1961; Da Capo, 1982).

24. For transcriptions and analyses of Christian and Reinhardt solos, see Fred Sokolow, *Solos for Jazz Guitar* (Carl Fischer, 1988). For a biography, see Peter Broadbent, *Charlie Christian: Solo Flight*, 2nd ed. (Ashley Mark, 2003). For more Reinhardt transcriptions, see *Django Reinhardt* (Amsco, 1978).

25. "Gloomy Sunday" and "God Bless the Child" are on *The Billie Holiday Collection 4* (Columbia/Legacy: 87070, 1939–44, c2003); Holiday liked this rendition of "Gloomy Sunday."

26. "Strange Fruit" is on *The Complete Commodore Recordings* (Commodore: CMD2-401, 2CD set, 1939, 1944, c1997). This compilation also contains a selection Holiday listed as being among her own favorite recordings: "Fine and Mellow." See her lyrics for it on page 462. Watch her perform it on *The Sound of Jazz* television show (available on DVD page 478).

27. Holiday's most upbeat material is on *The Billie Holiday Collection 3* (Columbia/Legacy: 87069, 1937–39, c2003).

28. "Lover Man" (Holiday, *The Complete Decca Recordings*, Decca Jazz: GRD2-601, 2CD set, 1944–50, c1991) brings together all these elements and constitutes the definitive Holiday recording for some fans. This compilation also contains "Good Morning Heartache" and a rendition of "God Bless the Child" recorded later than the one cited in footnote 25.

29. The most delightful of the recordings with Basie's musicians, particularly Lester Young and Buck Clayton, are on *The Billie Holiday Collection 3* (Columbia/Legacy); or *Billie Holiday + Lester Young: A Musical Romance* (Columbia/Legacy: 86635, 1937–38, 1958, c2002).

30. *Lady in Satin* (Columbia/Legacy: 65144, 1959, c1997) is a favorite album among listeners who like late-period Billie Holiday.

31. For biographies, see Billie Holiday with William Dufty, *Lady Sings the Blues* (Penguin, 1956, 1992); John Chilton, *Billie's Blues* (Quartet, 1975; Da Capo, 1989); Stuart Nicholson, *Billie Holiday* (Northeastern University Press, 1995); and *The Billie Holiday Companion: Seven Decades of Commentary* (Schirmer, 1997).

32. "A-Tisket-A-Tasket" is on *The Best of Ella Fitzgerald* (Decca Jazz: 659, 1935–55, c1996).

33. *The Complete Ella in Berlin: Mack the Knife* (Verve: 314 519 564, 1960, c1993). The Berlin concert was particularly exciting, and it

contains moments many fans remember well. During her performance of "Mack the Knife," Fitzgerald forgot some of the words but proceeded to invent several swinging choruses of new ones, all without missing a beat or losing any momentum.

34. Many Fitzgerald fans are impressed with the warmth and presence conveyed by her renditions of "Spring Can Really Hang You Up the Most" and "Cry Me a River" on *Clap Hands, Here Comes Charlie!* (Verve: 422 835 646, 1961, c1989).

35. "Flying Home" on the *CCD1*; Parker, *Jazz at the Philharmonic 1949* (Verve: 314 519 803, 1949, c1993), has Fitzgerald singing entirely without words, recreating horn parts from a band version.

36. "Perdido" and "How High the Moon" on Parker, *Jazz at the Philharmonic 1949* (Verve) show Fitzgerald making up new lyrics and improvising fresh scat lines. On her improvisation in "How High the Moon," she quotes a number of other tunes. Incidentally, her exciting 1960 version of this tune has a number of set routines interwoven among tune quotes; see *The Complete Ella in Berlin: Mack the Knife* (Verve).

37. Among Fitzgerald's most popular albums are *Ella Fitzgerald Sings the Cole Porter Songbook* (Verve: 314 537 257, 2CD set, 1956, c1997); *Ella Fitzgerald Sings the George & Ira Gershwin Songbooks* (Verve: 314 539 759, 3CD set, 1958–59, c1998); and *Ella Fitzgerald Sings the Rodgers & Hart Songbook* (Verve: 314 537-258, 2CD set, 1956, c1997). For a biography, see Stuart Nicholson, *Ella Fitzgerald* (Macmillan, 1993; Da Capo, 1995).

DUKE ELLINGTON

Duke Ellington (1899–1974) was **the most creative and prolific composer-arranger in jazz history, and he led the most stable and longest-lived big band.** Many musicians and historians feel that his band was the best of all jazz groups and the most interesting of swing bands. Ellington wrote more than two thousand compositions as well as many arrangements and rearrangements for them, beginning before 1920 and continuing until his death in 1974. His compositional fertility depended partly upon contributions by the musicians in his bands. Ellington chose musicians who had substantial and distinctive styles; together they made up an all-star unit that ran from the early 1920s to the early 1970s. Some of his men remained for 20 to 30 years at a stretch. Ellington often incorporated their ideas into his melodies. Many of their improvisations were so good that they also became permanent parts of the band's arrangements, as though composed. Ellington appreciated the musical personalities in his band so much that he wrote each part for a particular player. He imaginatively mixed and matched their work with his own. The collaborative result was a breadth and depth of repertory superior to every other jazz band. Recording more than any other, Ellington's band and its leader's compositions can be heard in hundreds of 78 rpm recordings, long-play albums, and compact discs.

Duke Ellington's 1942 band.
(Photo courtesy of Frank Driggs)

PIANIST

During the first three decades of his career, Ellington performed often in the stride-style tradition of pianist James P. Johnson. Thereafter, he usually performed in his own original style which, though still quite percussive, was more economical than the stride style. (Listen to "Cottontail," *JCCD1* Track 20 at 1'56".) His playing sparkled and popped with unerring swing feeling, and Ellington became distinguished for unusual harmonies and voicings. (Listen to his improvised accompaniments on "Transbluency" on *JCCD1* Track 22.) As an accompanist, Ellington was highly praised by his sidemen. They particularly liked the way his accompaniments were spare and complementary. His comping was full of spirit, and his timing and taste were near perfect.

COMPOSER

Ellington wrote many tunes, often in collaboration with his sidemen. Some of these became popular songs when lyrics were added, and a few were hits when recorded by singers apart from the Ellington band. Among his best-known songs are "I'm Beginning to See the Light," "Solitude," "Mood Indigo," and "Don't Get Around Much Anymore."[1] Nearly all jazz musicians have played at least one Ellington tune during their careers. More musicians have devoted entire albums to his music than to any other jazz composer's. During the 1980s, an entire Broadway revue, "Sophisticated Ladies," was devoted to Ellington's music.

"Transbluency," JCCD1 *Track 22*

Ellington also wrote hundreds of three-minute instrumentals, a few of which we will study in this chapter. (These instrumentals averaged three minutes because that was the standard length for one side of a 78 rpm record.) **Some of his short instrumentals paint musical portraits of famous personalities** such as the great stride pianist Willie "The Lion" Smith ("Portrait of the Lion") and the comedian Bert Williams ("Portrait of Bert Williams"). **Others paint musical pictures of places** such as "Warm Valley" and "Harlem Airshaft," or sensations such as the combination of blue and translucency, "Transblucency."

Ellington also wrote many longer pieces, and **he is widely acclaimed for having taken jazz into the format of "extended works,"** as these longer pieces are termed. (His "Creole Rhapsody" is in *SCCJ,* and his "Diminuendo in Blue and Crescendo in Blue" is in the *SCCJ-R.*) His most respected long work is "Black, Brown, and Beige," a 50-minute tone parallel to the history of the American Negro.[2] Some of his longest works were film scores; a favorite of musicians and critics is his music for *Anatomy of a Murder,* the Otto Preminger movie starring Jimmy Stewart.

ARRANGING STYLE

One of Ellington's greatest skills as an arranger was that of **capitalizing on the uniquely personal sounds of individual players.** Most arrangers occasionally showcase particular musicians, and in doing so they write parts that are well suited to the performer's talents as well as accompaniments that complement those talents. Ellington did this, too, but he also went much further. When writing for a group of instruments, he did not write parts anonymously assigned to the instruments (lead trumpeter, second trumpeter, third trumpeter, etc.), as most arrangers do. Ellington instead **wrote parts suited to the peculiar sounds and capabilities of each player in his band** (Cat Anderson, Cootie Williams, Rex Stewart, etc.). Each one of Ellington's musicians had a highly individual sound. So, even when they were not playing solos, their own unique way of sounding each pitch was considered before giving them a particular part to play. For example, if a chord were scored for three trumpets, Ellington remembered the particular tone quality that each of his trumpeters ordinarily produced for each note in that chord. He then distributed the parts of the chord among the musicians to create the overall color he wanted for that chord. In addition, sometimes he would have one trumpeter use a mute, another player without mute, and a third player sound his note with an odd tone quality that was unique to his own playing style. Ellington scored this way for saxes and trombones, too. This is one reason that when other musicians perform Ellington's arrangements the music never sounds like Ellington's band.

Another notable skill employed by Ellington is what we call **voicing across sections of the band.** This technique departs from the way most arrangers, including Ellington, routinely write passages that pit the sound of one section of the band, such as the saxes, against another section of the band, such as the brasses ("Harlem Airshaft," *JCCD1* Track 20 at 2'43"). By contrast, Ellington often wrote passages to be played by combinations of instruments drawn from *different* sections of the band. The most famous example can be heard in his 1930 recording of "Mood Indigo."[3] There he combined clarinet with muted trumpet and muted trombone, thus voicing instruments from three different sections of the band: trumpet section, trombone section, and reed section. In his 1940 recording of "Concerto for Cootie" (in *SCCJ*), he required the bassist to play notes in unison with the horns. This was unusual because bass was a member of the rhythm section, assigned primarily to timekeeping roles, and it rarely played melody parts. (Track 27 on the *Demo CD* illustrates melody lines played in pizzicato bass style.) On "Transblucency," Ellington combined clarinet (from the reed section) with trombone (from the brass section) and a woman's voice.

"Transblucency,"
JCCD1 Track 22

Another unique method employed by Ellington was placing a **wordless vocal** in an arrangement. Sometimes called *instrumentalized voice*, this became identified with Ellington, and he was applauded for its use in his 1927 recording of "Creole Love Call"[4] and his 1946 recording of "Transblucency."[5]

Other unique sounds that became associated with Ellington originated with his jobs. For instance, he often played for floor shows at New York night clubs, which needed exotic "jungle sounds." Partly to satisfy the club's demand for exotic sounds and partly because of his own admiration for New Orleans jazz, he scored for the **growl style** associated with trumpeter Bubber Miley and trombonist Joe "Tricky Sam" Nanton. For the same reasons, he liked to use clarinets in a wailing manner. He employed unusual voicings for his clarinets, and his musicians played them very intensely. The effect was stirring. Years after he finished his work at these floor shows, Ellington continued to employ these exotic sounds, and they contributed to his group's reputation as a "hot band."

*Growl style is on
Demo CD Track 81;
"Cottontail," JCCD1
Track 20 at 0'15"; and
SCCJ: "East St. Louis
Toodle-o"*

Duke Ellington's 1938 band.

(Photo courtesy of Cleveland Press Collection/Cleveland State University Archives)

BILLY STRAYHORN

From 1939 until 1967 Ellington worked closely with pianist-composer-arranger **Billy Strayhorn** (1915–1967). The two men collaborated on countless pieces, and Strayhorn was able to match and complement Ellington's style so well that most listeners, and even the band members themselves, rarely knew which of them contributed the larger portion of any particular arrangement. (Strayhorn conceded that sometimes upon later listening even he could not recognize what aspects of a piece were his and what were Ellington's.) However, there are several pieces in the Ellington repertory that are usually credited just to Strayhorn. The most famous is "Take the 'A' Train," which replaced "East St. Louis Toodle-o" as the band's theme. It is a masterpiece of composition and arrangement, and its original recording by the Ellington band is a classic. Jazz composers and arrangers consider Strayhorn to be one of the greats because his orchestration techniques were so fresh and effective. In keeping with techniques pioneered by French composer Maurice Ravel, Strayhorn selected unusual intervals for his melodies that sounded pleasant and distinctive in the context of modern harmonies. Musicians are especially fond of Strayhorn's ballads, for example "Lush Life," which he wrote while still in high school, "Chelsea Bridge," which originated in a piece by Ravel, and "Something to Live For," which was Ella Fitzgerald's favorite tune to sing. "Blood Count" and "Star Crossed Lovers" are a few of the lush ballads that Strayhorn wrote to be played in the very sensual style of alto saxophonist Johnny Hodges, the Ellington band's featured soloist.

CLARINET

Demo CD *Track 69*;
DVD *Track 69*;
"Harlem Airshaft,"
JCCD1 *Track 21*

Clarinetists **Barney Bigard** (1906–1981) and his successor Jimmy Hamilton provided pivotal voices in the Ellington sound. Both men doubled on tenor saxophone in the band, but their best-known contributions were their solo improvisations on clarinet. Bigard was from New Orleans, and he brought the expressive, soulful approach of his hometown music to Ellington's sophisticated conception of big band style. His long, legato lines swooped and darted through the band sound. Bigard played with the band from 1928 to 1942. Some of his best improvisations are found in Ellington's 1940 recording of "Harlem Airshaft." You might also enjoy studying his improvisation on "Clarinet Lament," a 1936 performance that Ellington built around Bigard.[6]

JCCD1 *Track 22*
at 1'14"

Jimmy Hamilton (1917–1994) is an original improviser with a style less intense than Bigard's. His sound is well manicured and lighter than that of most swing era clarinetists. Hamilton's conception is precise and articulate, with a cool, floating quality that suggests modern jazz. He was with the band from 1943 to 1968, and Ellington featured him extensively during the 1950s.[7]

TRUMPET

Appendix B; DVD
Track 64; Demo CD
Track 67; *"Cottontail,"*
JCCD1 *Track 20*
at 0'15"

Bubber Miley (1903–1932) and **Cootie Williams** (1910–1985) were known for their *growl style of trumpet playing and the unorthodox use of rubber plunger mutes*. Miley was one of Ellington's leading soloists from 1924 to 1929. His style furnished a playful voice for such classic Ellington recordings as the 1927 "Creole Love Call" and "East St. Louis Toodle-o."[8]

Like Bubber Miley, Cootie Williams was also influenced by the bluesy New Orleans style. From that tradition, Williams cultivated ways to spontaneously alter the size, shape, and quality of instrument sounds and achieve a vast range of musical effects. Williams was Miley's successor in the Ellington band, and he served as Ellington's main trumpet soloist. He played with the band from 1929 to 1940, rejoining in 1962 and remaining until Ellington's death in 1974. Ellington composed his 1936 "Echoes

Recorded May 4, 1940, for Victor by Duke Ellington big band (five saxes, three trumpets, three trombones, piano, guitar, bass, and drums); available on *SCCJ-R*; reissued on Ellington, *Never No Lament: The Blanton-Webster Band* (RCA Bluebird: 50857, 3CD set, 1940–42, c2003).*

"Cottontail" is Ben Webster's new tune using the progression of accompaniment chords from George Gershwin's "I Got Rhythm." Ellington wrote the arrangement. The "melody in harmony" that Webster and Ellington wrote for the sax section to play as the fifth chorus has some of the melodic and rhythmic character of a modern jazz improvisation. It remains one of the band's most famous passages. Its popularity with musicians rivals that of Webster's often-quoted solo on this recording. When it is performed, this "saxophone soli," as it is termed, has all the saxophonists standing up together.

ELAPSED TIME

First Chorus

0'00"	**A**	Melody stated by alto sax, baritone sax, muted trumpet, and trombone.
0'07"	**A**	Melody repeated with trombone and trumpet figures punctuating over guitar, bass, and drums accompaniment.
0'15"	**B**	Saxes ask musical questions, muted trumpet (Cootie Williams) answers them.

4-Measures Interlude

0'25"		This consists of a brief conversation between the sax section and brass section with rhythm accompaniment.

Second Chorus

0'29"	**A-A**	Improvised tenor sax solo (Ben Webster) with rhythm accompaniment.
0'44"	**B**	Tenor sax talks for a while with the brass section.
0'53"	**A**	Brass depart, leaving tenor to continue improvising with rhythm section accompaniment.

Third Chorus

1'00"	**A-A**	Tenor continues improvisation accompanied by rhythm section.
1'16"	**B**	Brass return to talk more with tenor sax.
1'25"	**A**	Brass depart and tenor finishes his improvisation accompanied by rhythm section.

Fourth Chorus

1'32"	**A-A**	Brass play alone, accompanied by rhythm section.
1'48"	**B**	Improvised baritone sax solo (Harry Carney) accompanied by rhythm section.
1'56"	**A**	Improvised piano solo accompanied by rhythm guitar, bass, and drums.

Fifth Chorus

2'03"	**A-A-B-A**	Sax section plays the whole chorus accompanied by rhythm section.

Sixth Chorus

2'34"	**A-A**	Brass section shouts questions, and sax section answers, accompanied by rhythm section.
2'51"	**B**	Brass section joins saxes with rhythm section steaming forward.
2'58"	**A**	Alto sax, baritone sax, muted trumpet, and trombone play the melody to its end with rhythm section accompaniment.

*The score and parts for "Cottontail" are available from *www.jalc.org.*

"Harlem Airshaft,"
JCCD1 *Track 21*

of Harlem" and his 1940 "Concerto for Cootie" to feature Williams. (Listen to *SCCJ*: "Concerto for Cootie" and "In a Mellotone.")

Some of Cootie Williams's most inventive playing was captured in Ellington's 1940 recording of "Harlem Airshaft." His work on this number demonstrates his unique mastery of wide-ranging techniques for colorfully altering pitch and tone quality. (See pages 47 and 49 for explanation and illustrations of tone quality and pitch manipulation techniques, and *Demo CD* Tracks 50–53 for examples of the doit, smear, drop, and scoop.) Williams is very calculating in the way he reaches notes, but his sound projects a great naturalness rather than cold calculation. His solos on this piece combine a diversity of techniques reminiscent of the searing sensuality and peaks of raw excitement in blues singing. Another asset is his keen sense of rhythm. Sometimes his notes are so well timed and percussively executed that the listener might assume Williams to be a drummer. In these respects, Miley and Williams helped Ellington create a more New Orleans-like sound than was common to other New York bands of the same era. Incidentally, it is no coincidence that Ellington's "jungle style" was developed during the 1920s when New Orleans-born clarinetists Sidney Bechet and Barney Bigard and bassist Wellman Braud all played with the band.

Ellington had distinctive trumpet soloists besides Miley and Williams. But the only one to achieve much fame outside the Ellington band was **Clark Terry** (b. 1920), a leading brass soloist in the band from 1951 to 1959. One of the first Ellington sidemen to show the influence of modern jazz, Terry invented a unique style that bridged the gap between the swing era approaches and the new bop style of Dizzy Gillespie. He displayed seemingly effortless command over his horn, no matter how fast or intricate a figure he chose to improvise. He had a talkative, swinging style that is easy to recognize. It spontaneously unfolded catchy melodic lines and conveyed an enthusiasm that seemed to bubble through every note (see footnote 7 in this chapter).

DVD Track 65;
Demo CD Track 60

Clark Terry also helped popularize the fluegelhorn, a kind of oversized cornet that is played in much the same manner as cornet and trumpet. Most players stress the instrument's naturally soft, dark tone quality, but Terry achieves a brassy edge, combined with a distinct fullness that is round and vibrant. No other brass player sounds like Clark Terry. (A large portion of his solos on Ellington records feature his fluegelhorn, not his trumpet.)

Figure 7.1 Listen for the fluegelhorn on *Demo CD* Track 60, where you will have the opportunity to compare its sound with that of the trumpet.

Cornet

Trumpet

Fluegelhorn

Trombone

SAXOPHONE

Johnny Hodges (1907–1970) was the best known of Ellington's sidemen. He often played position of lead alto, the saxophonist whose parts contain the melody notes instead of the harmony notes. This player leads the other saxophonists in timing and interpretation of written sax parts. His solos and his style in leading the sax section were a vital part of the Ellington sound from 1928 until 1970 (with an absence from 1951 to 1955). Nearly every Ellington album features Hodges, and he was such a consistent player that almost all these recordings contain representative examples. Hodges produced such an unusually deep, lush tone that his recorded alto sax has sometimes been mistaken for tenor saxophone. He is particularly known for a remarkable way of gliding from note to note so gradually and smoothly that it sounds almost as if his instrument were equipped with a slide, like a trombone. This technique is called *portamento*, but jazz musicians generally refer to it as *smearing*. Hodges used it to great effect in playing ballads. Ellington wrote numerous pieces to take full advantage of this well-known Hodges approach.[9]

"Prelude to a Kiss,"
JCCD1 *Track 23*

An exquisite sense of timing was crucial to the Hodges style. Hodges was a master of subtlety with his inflections of pitch, and his syncopations were especially well timed. Pre-1942 Hodges often displayed flashy double-timing like Sidney Bechet, his primary influence. But after the mid-1940s, Hodges tended to lay back very deliberately, no

---

TABLE 7.1   A Few of the Musicians Most Significant to Ellington

CLARINET AND SAXOPHONES	TRUMPET	TROMBONE
Willie Smith	Louis Metcalf	Joe "Tricky Sam" Nanton
Rudy Jackson	Bubber Miley	Lawrence Brown
Barney Bigard	Arthur Whetsol	Juan Tizol
Jimmy Hamilton	Cootie Williams	Britt Woodman
Russell Procope	Rex Stewart	Quentin "Butter" Jackson
Otto Hardwicke	Taft Jordan	Tyree Glenn
Johnny Hodges	Ray Nance	Buster Cooper
Harry Carney	Willie Cook	
Ben Webster	Cat Anderson	
Al Sears	Clark Terry	
Paul Gonsalves	"Shorty" Baker	
Harold Ashby	Johnny Coles	
	Money Johnson	**BASS**
		Aaron Bell
		Billy Taylor
DRUMS	**PIANO**	Wellman Braud
		Jimmy Blanton
Sonny Greer		Oscar Pettiford
Louis Bellson	Duke Ellington	Jimmy Woode
Sam Woodyard	Billy Strayhorn	Ernie Shepard
Rufus Jones		Wendell Marshall

TABLE 7.2	A Few of the Many Saxophonists Influenced by Johnny Hodges	
Tab Smith	Willie Smith	Woody Herman
Louis Jordan	Ben Webster	Eddie Vinson
Earl Bostic	Bobby Plater	John Coltrane
Johnny Bothwell	Charlie Barnet	Jan Garbarek

matter what the tempo. Hodges is possibly the **most influential jazz alto saxophonist to come out of the swing era** (see Table 7.2), and he is one of few jazz saxophonists to ever have hit records. He is particularly known for a romantic approach to ballad playing that has pervaded American music so much that hundreds of saxophonists are imitating it without even knowing who Johnny Hodges was. (His work on "Prelude to a Kiss" typifies that side of his talents.[10])

Aside from Hodges, Benny Carter was the most widely respected jazz alto saxophonist of the swing era. Perhaps we can learn more about both styles by comparing them. Both players had rich, full-bodied tones, but they had different rhythmic styles. Carter tended to divide the beat precisely and evenly into legato eighth notes. Hodges had a more natural rhythmic feel. The placement of notes in relation to the beat was far less obvious in Hodges's playing. Though Carter and Hodges both imparted a luxurious feel to their playing, Carter was more obvious in his constructions, Hodges more subtle. Hodges had a strikingly original way of placing accents. His accenting set him apart from most swing and early jazz players. Despite its originality, he made it sound easy and natural. Both Hodges and Carter swung easily, but Carter had more of a classical feeling to his rhythmic conception. (Get *SCCJ* and compare Carter on "I Can't Believe That You're in Love with Me" with Hodges on "In a Mellotone.")

Harry Carney (1910–1974) is usually considered the father of jazz baritone saxophone playing, which almost puts him in a class with Coleman Hawkins, the father of the jazz tenor saxophone, a soloist who influenced Carney. No other baritone saxophonist has been able to match the size and strength of Carney's mammoth, rich sound. (The differences in sound among alto, tenor, and baritone saxophones are illustrated on the *Demo CD*, Tracks 72–74). Carney's ensemble playing in Ellington's sax section often vied with that of Hodges himself. It provided a very solid foundation, often as important as that of the band's bassist. Inspired by Carney's playing, Ellington occasionally wrote in a way that gave baritone sax the lead. Carney also played clarinet and bass clarinet, each of which, in his hands, became a strong, thick-toned voice in the Ellington ensemble. Although primarily an ensemble player, Carney occasionally received feature numbers, including "Serious Serenade," "Frustration," and "Chromatic Love Affair."

Ellington's most outstanding soloists on the tenor saxophone were **Ben Webster** (1909–1973) and Paul Gonsalves. Webster played with the band from 1940 to 1943, then again in 1948 and 1949. Before Webster began full-time in 1940, Ellington had no major tenor sax soloist. But thereafter, he always featured someone in that position, and it was Gonsalves from 1951 to 1974. Though some of Webster's style was inspired by Coleman Hawkins and Johnny Hodges, Webster should not be viewed as derivative. He established his own distinctive approach. His improvisations were frequently so tuneful that the listener might assume they were not improvised, but prepared for the written arrangement. In fact, the sense of completeness in Webster's phrases has so greatly affected musicians that Webster phrases are sometimes quoted by other improvisers. His most famous phrases are in "Cottontail."

JCCD1 Track 20 at 1'48″

"Cottontail," JCCD1 Track 20 at 0'29″

Webster provided a model for how to play ballads. One trademark was delaying, ever so slightly, the delivery of crucial notes in a phrase—sometimes giving the listener a sense of suspense that was resolved when those crucial notes were finally sounded. His playing gives the listener an overall impression of being laid back. Together with his richly textured, breathy tone, and slow, marked vibrato, Webster used his delayed deliveries to create a very sensual effect. Some of his work in this vein resembles the way a crooner delivers the tones of a love song. Consistent with his sense of drama, Webster was known for changing the character of the music within a single solo by transforming his sound from smooth and soothing to hoarse and rasping. Like other Ellington soloists, Webster seemed capable of making his manipulations of tone and timing at least as important as the choice of notes themselves. Sometimes Webster made listeners hear the rush of air in his breath, not just the saxophone tone that it ordinarily energized. Partly because of the carefully marked vibrato that accompanied it, listening to that rush of air by itself could be an intimately moving experience. In fact, Webster's style is often described as romantic.[11] Apart from Coleman Hawkins and Lester Young, Ben Webster was the most influential tenor saxophonist of the swing era, and he influenced saxophonists in eras as far-flung as the 1940s and the 1970s.[12]

Paul Gonsalves (1920–1974) was Ellington's main soloist during the 1950s, '60s, and '70s. He began as a disciple of Ben Webster but also showed hints of the Don Byas approach. Despite these roots, Gonsalves's style was unique, particularly in a very unusual and fluid conception for medium- and up-tempo playing. He had a soft, diffuse tone without edge, but despite the softness of his tone, his playing had an intense urgency to it. Moreover, Gonsalves's choice of notes was so unusual that it is amazing he could deliver them as fluently as he did. And his solos invariably had substance. Though he was relatively unknown to all but Ellington band fans, Gonsalves ranks among the originators in the history of jazz tenor styles. His solos lent Ellington's music an excitement and a modern character without detracting from the warmth and sincerity that had traditionally been such prime traits of the Ellington sound. Gonsalves played with Ellington from 1951 until his death in 1974.[13]

TROMBONE

Trombonist **Joe "Tricky Sam" Nanton** (1904–1946) was **master of the growl style.** From 1926 until 1946, Nanton gave Ellington a provocative sound to use in arrangements. His most common mute was the rubber suction cup from a plumber's plunger, which he used to open and close the bell of the trombone. An additional mute, alternately termed a *pixie mute* or a *buzz mute,* was secured inside the trombone to lend a buzz to the horn's tone. With his plunger and his unorthodox blowing, Nanton came very close to pronouncing words with his trombone ("ya . . . ya").[14]

"Harlem Airshaft," JCCD1 *Track 21* at 0'35"; *page 469.*

Lawrence Brown (1907–1988) was one of the first trombonists of the swing era to play with a very smooth, large, consistent sound. His tone added a great deal of body to the sound of Ellington's trombone section. As a soloist, Brown could also play quite aggressively. Ellington wrote "Blue Cellophane" and "Golden Cress" as features for Brown. (Listen to his muted work on "Transblucency," JCCD1 Track 22, for which Brown himself composed a theme.)

DRUMS

There have been only a few drummers in the long history of the Ellington band: Sonny Greer (1919–1951), Louis Bellson (early 1950s), Sam Woodyard (mid-1955–1966), and Rufus Jones (1968–1973). Others played briefly with the band but remained

Recorded July 22, 1940, for Victor by Duke Ellington big band; reissued on Ellington, *Never No Lament: The Blanton-Webster Band* (RCA Bluebird: 50857, 3CD set, 1940–42, c2003).*

Terms to know from tracks on *Demo CD:* walking bass (23), rhythm guitar (88), wire brushes (12), snare drum (5), plunger mute (81), trombone (78), trumpet (59), clarinet (69), pitch bends (50–53), blue notes (54–58), A-A-B-A form (33).

"Harlem Airshaft" is a monumental achievement in jazz history by what most historians consider Duke Ellington's greatest band. The piece combines the gritty, soulful nature of New Orleans combo jazz with the sophisticated big band writing associated with 1930s New York. The harmonies assigned to the saxophones are slick, East Coat renderings. The earthy clarinet improvisations that are swooping and swirling around the band sound are supplied by Barney Bigard, who is a Creole from New Orleans. Trumpet improvisations are provided by Mobile, Alabama, native Cootie Williams. You might detect the influence of New Orleans natives Louis Armstrong and Joe Oliver in Williams's searing style. Notice his manipulations of tone quality and his sliding into and out of the main pitches, as at 1'16" and 1'30". Pay attention to Williams's percussive attacks for selected notes, as at 1'00" and 2'33".

Ellington delivers the unusual sound of three to five different layers of activity at almost every moment in "Harlem Airshaft." Despite the inherent potential for conflict, the saxophone parts never clash with the trumpet and trombone parts. Instead, they bounce off and complement each other. In addition, there is occasionally an improvised clarinet line weaving around several composed lines. For instance, note the relationship at 2'36" between Bigard's improvised figures on clarinet and the composed ones being played by the band. It all fits together despite the spontaneity. All the while, a very propulsive force is coming from the rhythm section combination of rhythm guitar, string bass, and drums. The action is heightened at 2'51" when three different lines are running at the same time over the hard swinging rhythm section. It seems as though the music may break into chaos but it doesn't.

There is so much going on that you should not hesitate frequently to use the pause switch on your CD player to digest it. You will often need to replay passages to catch what you missed. In some passages, such as 0'54" to 0'59", there is something new and important occurring every second.

ELAPSED TIME

Introduction

| 0'00" | 4 *Measures* |
| | Brass instruments call in harmonized, sustained tones, and the saxes respond with a melodic figure. Rhythm guitar, walking bass, and wire brushes on snare drum play timekeeping. |

| 0'05" | 4 *Measures* |
| | Saxes play the lead in harmony. |

| 0'10" | 4 *Measures* |
| | Trombones play the lead, answered by baritone saxophone. Trombones play harmonized punching figures. |

First Chorus (32-bar A-A-B-A)

0'15"	**A**	Saxes play simple melody in unison while muted trumpets repeat a background figure in harmony.
0'25"	**A**	Saxes play simple melody in unison while muted trumpets repeat a background figure in harmony.
0'35"	**B**	Saxes call in harmony and Joe "Tricky Sam" Nanton replies by blowing his trombone into a plunger mute.
0'45"	**A**	Saxes play simple melody in unison while muted trumpets repeat a background figure in harmony. Sonny Greer ends the figure by striking a cymbal, then quickly grabbing it to prevent ringing.

*The score and parts for "Harlem Airshaft" are available from *www.jalc.org.*

LISTENING GUIDE *continued on next page*

Second Chorus (32-bar A-A-B-A)

0'56"   **A**   *First 4 Measures*
Rhythm section stops playing.

Saxes play a harmonized part with sustained tones.

0'57"   drum roll underneath final sax tones

0'59"   Drummer plays syncopated figures for trumpet solo.

Second 4 Measures
1'00"   Cootie Williams opens his trumpet improvisation by percussively stating the same note repeatedly in an off-the-beat fashion. He uses the high register and shakes one of his tones as it ends. Saxes play syncopated, harmonized line underneath trumpet solo.

1'06"   **A**   Saxes play simple melody in unison while muted trumpets repeat a background figure in harmony. Repeated high notes are heard from trumpet, each figure ending on a shaken tone.

1'16"   **B**   Saxophones are repeating a climbing figure underneath the trumpet solo.

1'25"   **A**   Saxes play simple melody in unison while muted trumpets repeat a background figure in harmony.

1'31"   Williams roughens his tone and slowly slides down from his last high note's pitch.

Third Chorus

1'35"   **A**   Trombones play a harmonized melody in foreground as clarinetist Barney Bigard improvises around it, and saxes play another series of interjections underneath.

1'45"   **A**   Trombones play a harmonized melody in foreground as clarinetist Barney Bigard improvises around it, and saxes play another series of interjections underneath.

1'55"   **B**   Trumpets join trombones to repeat a sustained tone while clarinet improvisation continues, and saxes make periodic interjections underneath.

2'03"   Clarinet ends this section with a shake.

2'05"   **A**   Saxes play simple melody in unison while muted trumpets repeat a background figure in harmony. Notice Bigard's blue notes.

Fourth Chorus (32-bar A-A-B-A)

Band starts softly, gradually getting louder and louder.

2'14"   **A**   Horns softly play a syncopated, low-register melody while clarinet solo spills into the first three measures of this chorus.

Rhythm guitar and walking bass are easier to hear now.

2'19"   Cootie Williams begins a muted trumpet solo.

2'23"   **A**   Trumpet solo continues.

2'33"   Williams percussively states the final four notes of his solo directly on the beat.

2'34"   **B**   Band plays a composed call.

2'36"   Clarinet improvises a reply. The brass sound becomes clearer. Note the relationship between Bigard's improvised figures and the composed ones being played by the rest of the band. It all fits together despite the spontaneity.

2'43"   **A**   Brass call, and the saxes answer repeatedly, and clarinet improvises throughout.

2'51"   Saxophones repeat a new riff of their own.

Clarinet enters high register.

Ending has brass sustaining a chord and baritone sax sounding a low note.

relatively unknown. Ellington's drummers have performed a relatively unobtrusive role in creating the band's sound. Although all were swinging drummers, none were as historically significant as Jo Jones with Count Basie, Max Roach with Charlie Parker, Elvin Jones with John Coltrane, or Tony Williams with Miles Davis. All Ellington drummers were primarily timekeepers. There are four eras of this role in the band, reflecting Ellington's incorporating the strengths of four different drummers.

"Cottontail," JCCD1
Track 20

The classic tradition of **Sonny Greer** (1903–1982) lasted for more than half of the band's 50-year history. Ellington's first drummer, Greer used drumming techniques in the manner of early jazz drummers. He kept time on the snare drum with sticks and brushes, often switching instruments for a new chorus or to accompany a new soloist. (Listen to how hard he swings on "Cottontail.") During the 1940s, he sometimes moved his timekeeping rhythms to high-hat. And, in a few isolated instances near the end of his tenure with the band, he played ride rhythms on the ride cymbal. Though simple in style and technique, Greer was dramatic in presentation. His equipment included timpani, gongs, vibraphone, and wood blocks. Listen to his work in "Echoes of Harlem," for which he devised exceptionally adept accompaniments.

Demo CD *Tracks 10*
and 97

A new era began in 1951 when Greer left and **Louis Bellson** (b. 1924) joined Ellington. In his two-year stay, Bellson changed the technique and technology of Ellington drummers. Like a bop drummer, Bellson kept time primarily with his ride cymbal, using his left hand to play musical punctuations on his snare drum. Blessed with enviable technique, he was a precise and tasteful accompanist.

DVD *Tracks 4*
and 5; p. 26

Bellson also added a second bass drum and small tom-tom to his drum kit. Ellington took advantage of Bellson's capabilities by giving him solos. The recording of Bellson's solo on his own composition "Skin Deep" in *Hi-Fi Ellington Uptown* furnished a means for demonstrating sound quality in high-fidelity equipment that was just then becoming popular.[15] The piece became a crowd-pleasing part of Ellington's repertory. Bellson's showmanship revitalized the band's appeal when all big bands were experiencing a declining audience size and Ellington was particularly low due to the temporary loss of Lawrence Brown and Johnny Hodges. After Bellson left, his successors on the drum throne were required to perform the often-requested "Skin Deep." They also employed the modern timekeeping techniques that Bellson used.

Replacing Bellson was **Sam Woodyard** (1925–1988), Ellington's drummer of 11 years. Woodyard supplied a special spark to the band. His style was hard-swinging and unrelenting. Woodyard's approach was not complicated or flashy. He established a groove. Then, by playing so hard and so passionately, he musically challenged the band members to swing equally hard. The records Ellington made with Woodyard have an insistence in their swing feeling that is unmatched by his records from any other period (see footnote 7 in this chapter). For many Ellington fans and a number of Ellington's musicians themselves, Woodyard was the all-time favorite drummer for the band.

The Bellson-Woodyard contributions to Ellington's style were expanded by **Rufus Jones** (1936–1990) between 1966 and 1973. In addition to fulfilling the traditional duties for his position, Jones was notable for also devising original rhythms to fit music that Ellington composed on his world tours during this era.[16] In generating African, Latin American, and oriental flavors for Ellington's suites, Jones played rhythms that were new to the Ellington sound.

BASS

Over his long career of bandleading, Ellington had several outstanding bassists. (Note Oscar Pettiford's work on "Transblucency," *JCCD1* Track 22.) The greatest standout among them was **Jimmy Blanton** (1918–1942), who played with the band from 1939

Composed by Duke Ellington; arranged by Billy Strayhorn; recorded in 1957 for Columbia by Duke Ellington big band (five saxes, three trombones, four trumpets, piano, bass, and drums), featuring Duke Ellington (piano) and Johnny Hodges (alto saxophone); reissued on Ellington, *Ellington Indigos* (Columbia 4444, 1957, c1989).*

Johnny Hodges was the most influential alto saxophonist before Charlie Parker. He deepened the tone quality associated with the alto sax, and he made the romantic ballad solo an art for which he was never surpassed. "Prelude to a Kiss" epitomizes the type of feature number that Duke Ellington occasionally composed to display the Hodges ballad style.

There is nothing perfunctory about the manner in which Hodges renders a melody. Frequently Hodges strives for drama by gradually sliding up to the pitch of a crucial high note, with great deliberation, as though anticipating its flavor. Then he lingers on that note, making it very full, adding vibrato to keep it alive as long as possible. (See page 49 for graphic illustrations of smear and vibrato.) For Hodges, almost every note is long and drawn out, not hurried. He treats each one with reverence and lets it sing.

Not only is the pitch of selected notes freely bent by Hodges, but the rhythm is, too. He hardly ever played the rhythms of notes in his solos as they appeared on written sheet music. In deciding when to play each melody note, the saxophonist did not let himself be confined at all by regular passage of beats or any expectation to retain even durations of notes in a melody line. (Some listeners refer to such a free method as "natural," as opposed to squarely metric.) In the rare instances in which a note was to be played on the beat, Hodges waited until the last possible moment before starting it. To appreciate his artistry, keep in mind that to succeed as Hodges did with his rhythmic displacements, the saxophonist had to continuously maintain an extraordinarily accurate sense of where each beat fell. For every displacement, he knew exactly how far he was stretching the arrival point. He timed his syncopations with flawless precision. The combined effect of his lush tone, creative pitch bends, and rhythmic displacements was extremely sensual. Ellington termed the results of this Hodges manner "excruciating ecstasy."

This arrangement of "Prelude to a Kiss" capitalizes on the special methods of Hodges because it is taken so slowly and because the composition itself moves gradually in small gradations. This is perfect for a musician who has made a study of not rushing. In fact, Hodges does not let loose until about 3'16" (in the second bridge). When he does let loose, the tension accumulated from the extreme slowness of his A-section rendition is released with his double-timing. (Note that the arrangement jumps into a second bridge without repeating the A-section.)

ELAPSED TIME

Introduction

0'00"   Unaccompanied piano solo by Ellington sets the mood of the piece and anticipates the entrance of Hodges.

A-section

0'27"   Hodges enters, gracing his first main pitch with a brief preparatory note, then playing most of the melody notes slightly after the beat.

Accompaniment includes trombones playing slow-moving chords and string bass playing first and third beats of most measures and occasional fills.

0'47"   Hodges uses a prominent smear before landing on the pitch of a main melody note.

Second A-section

1'09"   Hodges uses a long, slow smear to preface the first note in the melody. Sax solo is accompanied initially by sustained chords from saxes and clarinet, then soon joined by trombones, then just by trombones.

1'18"   Low-pitched trombones enter in harmony.

1'28"   Hodges uses a pitch smear as dramatic lead-in to decorate an important melody note.

*The score and parts are available from *www.jalc.org*.

LISTENING GUIDE *continued on next page*

Bridge

1'48"	Downbeat is played by clarinet and saxes. Then Hodges enters, taking his time to give fullness to every tone and maximum sensuality.
2'00"	Trombones play slow-moving chords.
2'03"	Ellington inserts brief decorations on piano.
2'08"	Ellington inserts brief decorations on piano.
2'10"	Hodges plays straight quarter notes, harmonized by clarinet.
2'18"	Hodges reaches down deep and plays resoundingly a scoop of pitch on a note selected to set up a crucial note in the melody line.
2'24"	Tension is increased by adding instruments, louder playing, and chords moving a beat at a time, up the scale, with Hodges in the foreground.

A-section

2'30"	similar to first A-section

Bridge

3'10"	Entire proceedings become livelier. Sax section firmly sounds a chord and Hodges responds by improvising more freely, with less paraphrase and more melodic invention.
3'18"	Hodges engages in double-timing and using more ornaments.
3'23"	Hodges emphatically states the same note seven times, before reaching the important high note it prefaces, then he executes a gradual fall-off from the high note's pitch to the next note in his line.
3'30"	Hodges smears into a main high note and sustains it lovingly with all its fullness.
3'38"	Intensity peaks as Hodges plays very forcefully and brass get louder underneath him and inch toward the downbeat of the final A-section.
3'40"	The highest excitement is reached with all sections of the band, particularly trumpets, playing loudly, and pitch of their lines rising.

Final A-section

3'48"	Tension is resolved as loudness ends and Hodges returns to the original melody, prefaced by a long, ascending pitch smear. He is accompanied by slow-moving chords from saxes and trombones.
4'20"	Timekeeping stops to prepare for dramatic ending.
4'23"	Hodges improvises an ending line of his own.
4'30"	Band sustains a chord while Hodges improvises an afterthought over it.
4'31"	Low note on baritone sax solidifies the finality of the arrangement, and Ellington lets a low piano note ring after the other sounds fade.

to 1941. With his impressive instrumental proficiency and musical imagination, Blanton shattered traditional conceptions of jazz bass playing. **His cleanly executed solos showed that, in the hands of a virtuoso, the string bass can contribute more to a band than timekeeping.** Though Blanton's sound was also a powerful component of Ellington's intensely swinging rhythm section, Blanton is best known for the ways Ellington capitalized on his talents for solo improvisation. (His walking swings hard in "Harlem Airshaft" and "Cottontail," *JCCD1* Tracks 21 and 20, respectively.) **Ellington spotlighted Blanton in melodic roles, and he arranged parts for Blanton's bass that were like horn parts.** In the 1940 "Jack the Bear," Blanton played solo melodies, and he played in unison with ensemble horn lines. During the same year, he also played in unison with horns in "Concerto for Cootie," and he soloed on "Sepia Panorama."[17] Blanton profoundly shaped the next 20 years of jazz bass styles. For instance, the idea of voicing pizzicato bass with horns was later used in arrangements by Thad Jones. It became common in modern jazz of the 1970s and 1980s, especially in jazz-rock fusion bands. Few musicians who use the technique today realize that Ellington had been using it as early as 1940.[18]

DIVERSITY OF ELLINGTON'S MUSIC

Diversity and breadth characterized Ellington's music. The pieces in Ellington's repertory were filled with variety, and the lack of repetition within each piece is striking. When compared with the arrangements used by most swing bands, Ellington's possessed a larger number of different themes and rhythmic figures. Accompanying figures also reflected a greater assortment than was customary. (Listen to "Harlem Airshaft," and note the interweaving parts and numerous layers of activity.) In addition, Ellington's repertory was also diverse. It was so varied that we can summarize it as a number of separate books:[19]

1. An impressionistic book with arrangements that place more emphasis on orchestral colors and shading than on swinging. Examples from his pre-LP work include "On a Turquoise Cloud" and "Transblucency" (*JCCD1* Track 22)." From his LP work, examples include portions of *Anatomy of a Murder* and *Paris Blues*.

2. A book of romantic ballads. Examples from his pre-LP work include "Daydream," "Prelude to a Kiss," and "Sophisticated Lady." Examples from his LP work include the albums *At the Bal Masque* and *Ellington Indigos*. (Listen to "Prelude to a Kiss," *JCCD1* Track 23)

3. An exotic book. Examples from his pre-LP work include "Caravan," "Flaming Sword," and "Bakiff." Examples from his LP work include entire albums such as *Latin American Suite* and *Togo Brava Suite*.

4. A concert book in which each piece is a long work with much less improvisation than was usually found in his music. Examples in his pre-LP work include "Reminiscing in Tempo," "Black, Brown, and Beige," and "Deep South Suite." Examples in his LP work include *Such Sweet Thunder*, *Suite Thursday*, and *A Drum Is a Woman*.

5. A book of concertos in which each piece frames the style of one Ellington sideman. Examples from his pre-LP period include "Clarinet Lament" (Barney Bigard), "Echoes of Harlem" (Cootie Williams), and "Boy Meets Horn" (Rex Stewart). Examples from his LP work include "Cop-Out" (Paul Gonsalves) and "Lonesome Lullaby" (Ray Nance).

6. A book of music for sacred concerts, a context that brought Ellington to present new shows and use choirs, new vocal soloists, organ, and dancers. It inspired writing for different moods, such as that of prayer. It also inspired extensive lyrics (*Duke Ellington's Concert of Sacred Music* and *Second Sacred Concert*).

7. A book of swinging instrumentals, each with jazz solos, catchy ensemble themes, and punching accompaniment figures. These are evident throughout Ellington's career: "Rockin' in Rhythm" from the 1930s, "Main Stem" and "Cottontail" (*JCCD1* Track 20) from the 1940s, "Launching Pad" from the 1950s.

Johnny Hodges, Duke Ellington's star soloist, the most widely imitated alto saxophonist of the swing era. Even modern giants such as John Coltrane were influenced by his style. (Photo by Lee Tanner)

Composed by Lawrence Brown and Duke Ellington; recorded July 9, 1946, for Victor, reissued on Ellington, *The Best of the Complete RCA Victor Recordings, 1944–1946* (RCA Victor: 63462, 3CD set, 1944–46, c2000).

Terms to learn from *Demo CD*: walking bass, embellished walking (decorative two), clarinet, cup-muted trombone, 12-bar blues.

This recording is included to provide a fuller picture of Ellington's talents than what is conveyed by "Cottontail" and "Harlem Airshaft." "Transblucency" exemplifies Ellington's practice of painting musical pictures, in this case the combined impression of translucency and the color blue. The composition was developed from "Blue Light," an earlier Ellington band number containing a 12-bar blues theme composed by Lawrence Brown, the trombonist who performed it. This piece displays Ellington's imagination for unique blends of tone colors. Here he combines instrumentalized voice (wordless vocal) with instruments drawn from different sections of the band (voicing across sections). The result is a facet of Ellington's repertory that is not hard-driving or wild. It is pretty and might remind you of opera more than jazz.

This performance allows us to explore controversies about how jazz is defined. To call this a "jazz" recording stretches the conventional definition in two ways. First, it demonstrates Ellington's practice of constructing pieces in which the only improvisation of consequence lies in the accompaniment. Second, the piece is unusual because swing feeling is elicited here only by accompaniment rhythms, and only quite subtly.

Unlike most of Ellington's pieces, "Transblucency" does not use his entire band. Though he assigns the melody to his saxes in the fifth chorus, Ellington otherwise dispenses with everyone except clarinetist Jimmy Hamilton, trombonist Lawrence Brown, and bassist Oscar Pettiford. In a few choruses, the voice of Kay Davis is added as an instrument. Piano chording can sometimes be heard faintly in the background.

ELAPSED TIME

Introduction

0'00"   Piano flourishes by Ellington. At the end of the piano phrases, the bass ever so slightly anticipates the down beat of the first chorus by playing a string of triplets.

First Chorus

0'05"   Slow, 12-bar blues. The melody line is harmonized, clarinet on the lowest notes, cup-muted trombone on the middle notes, and voice on the highest notes. Piano occasionally fills in the pauses between phrases and provides counteractivity underneath sustained tones. Pizzicato bass tones provide timekeeping. Note the triplets played just before the first and third beats of selected measures. This bass style is called "decorative-two" because, of the four beats in the measure, it emphasizes only two, sometimes decorated by preceding notes. Bass is joined by piano in some of the decorations here.

Second Chorus

0'39"   Muted trombone plays the melody, accompanied by bass playing in a decorative-two style. Notice the absence of piano.

Fifth Measure
0'51"   Trombone is joined by voice and clarinet in harmony, and then the three instruments continue together. Bass accompaniment alternates between decorative-two and walking style.

1'12"   *Twelfth Measure*
1'14"   A piano flourish introduces the next chorus.

1'16"   ### Third Chorus

Clarinet and voice duet, accompanied by walking bass and piano chording. The harmony created by the two sounds, clarinet and voice, occasionally seems to create a third sound. Ellington has assigned pitches so cleverly that their combination has generated additional pitches, technically termed "heterodynes."

LISTENING GUIDE continued on next page

Final 2 Measures

1'47"   As the melody instruments end their phrase, Ellington improvises a melodic little phrase which he plays twice.

Fourth Chorus

1'54"   Sax section softly plays the flowing melody in unison while voice provides a countermelody. Piano chording accompanies softly on each beat.

2'30"   Piano re-enters percussively, as though splashing bright colors on the subdued portrait.

2'35"   **Ending**

2'38"   Vocal, trombone, and clarinet join piano.

2'47"   A marching of piano chords, then a high-register piano chord is emphatically sounded. Its ringing concludes the piece, accompanied by a very soft, arco bass note.

The vastness of Duke Ellington's contributions becomes all the more evident when you have explored a few hundred selections and then realize that Ellington also composed several operas, a couple of ballets, and about ten musical shows. We should also remember that the style of the Ellington band never really fell into any fixed category—early jazz, swing, or modern. It was always unique. Various editions of the band did portray a somewhat different character because of changes in personnel and repertory, but Ellington created a jazz classification that was practically his own. And, not only did the band present a very colorful and richly diverse repertory, it maintained creative energy for more than four decades.

ELLINGTON'S INFLUENCE

The influence of Ellington's music was also vast. Other big bands were influenced by his writing style as early as the 1930s.[20] There was an echo of Ellington in the work of several outstanding arrangers of the 1950s and 1960s.[21] Revivals of Ellington's work were frequent during the 1980s and 1990s. Avant-garde bands and composers of this period also drew upon Ellington for inspiration.[22] Ellington's piano style influenced a number of players, including the highly individualistic modernists Thelonious Monk and Cecil Taylor.

CHAPTER SUMMARY

1. Duke Ellington is among the most significant of all figures in jazz history.[23]

2. As a pianist, Ellington derived his approach from the stride style of James P. Johnson, though he also devised an original style with which he set the pace and mood for his pieces and ornamented the solos of his musicians.

3. Ellington was outstanding as a bandleader, maintaining a large ensemble from the early 1920s until his death in 1974, with many musicians remaining for more than 20 years at a stretch.

4. Ellington composed more than two thousand pieces, frequently in collaboration with his musicians.

5. A few of Ellington's pieces became popular songs, such as "Satin Doll," "Mood Indigo," and "I'm Beginning to See the Light."

6. Some of Ellington's pieces represent pioneering efforts in jazz for exceeding the brief time limit that was standard. Among his "extended works" is "Black, Brown, and Beige," a tone parallel to the history of the American Negro.

7. As an arranger, Ellington was distinctive for

    a. using a diversity of themes within a single piece

    b. voicing across sections

    c. using wordless vocals

    d. writing parts particularly for the unique capabilities of each musician

    e. mixing improvised parts with written parts

8. From 1939 to 1941, Ellington showcased bassist Jimmy Blanton, who revolutionized traditional concepts of the bassist's role by playing melody lines by himself and with the horn sections of the band.

9. Ellington's most famous saxophonists were Johnny Hodges and Ben Webster.

10. Ellington featured brass players who were masters of the growl style: trumpeter Cootie Williams and trombonist Joe "Tricky Sam" Nanton.

11. During the 1950s, Ellington featured saxophonist Paul Gonsalves and trumpeter Clark Terry.

NOTES

1. Not all of Ellington's pieces represent exclusively his own ideas. Often Ellington incorporated or developed a phrase or countermelody he had heard improvised by one of his musicians. Many works were written by Ellington's musicians or in collaboration with them; for instance, with Bubber Miley: "East St. Louis Toodle-o" and "Black and Tan Fantasy"; with Johnny Hodges: "I'm Beginning to See the Light" and "Don't Get Around Much Anymore"; with Ben Webster: "Cottontail"; with Otto Hardwicke and Lawrence Brown: "Sophisticated Lady." Trombonist Juan Tizol wrote "Caravan," "Bakiff," "Conga Brava," and "Perdido," a melody often mistakenly credited to Ellington. Barney Bigard adapted ideas of New Orleans clarinetist Lorenzo Tio and ended up contributing one strain for Ellington's "Mood Indigo."

2. Duke Ellington, *The Complete RCA Victor Mid-Forties Recordings* (RCA Victor: 63394, 3CD set, 1944–46, c1999).

3. *The Best of Early Ellington* (Decca Jazz: 660, 1926–31, c1996); and *The OKeh Ellington* (Columbia: C2K 46177, 2CD set, 1927–30, c1991). For technical analyses of Ellington's work, see Gunther Schuller, *Early Jazz* (Oxford, 1968), 318–357; and Schuller, *The Swing Era* (Oxford, 1989), 46–157.

4. *Early Ellington* (RCA Bluebird: 6852-2, 1927–34, c1989).

5. *The Best of the Complete RCA Victor Recordings, 1944–1946* (RCA Victor: 63462, 1944–46, c2000).

6. Get the *JCCD1*, and listen to Bigard's work while you study this chapter's listening guide for "Harlem Airshaft." Musicians may also wish to study the written parts and score transcribed by David Berger and available through *jalc.org*. Berger has also made available the score and parts for "Clarinet Lament." See also the autobiography, Barney Bigard, *With Louis and the Duke* (Oxford, 1986).

7. *Ellington at Newport: The Complete Concert* (Columbia/Legacy: C2K 64932, 2CD set, 1956, c1999); and *Festival Session* (Columbia/Legacy: 87044, 1959, c2004). See *Instructor's Resource Manual* for more examples.

8. Miley co-authored both. Listen to "East St. Louis Toodle-o" in *SCCJ*. Its title (sometimes spelled "todalo") is pronounced "toad-el-low," to indicate a kind of dance that imitates the low, tired, dragging walk that the term originally referred to; it is not a farewell expression.

9. Listen to Hodges play "Passion Flower" on *Jive at Five* (New World: 274, LP, 1927–46, c1976); or Johnny Hodges, *Passion Flower* (Victor Jazz: 66616, 1940–46, c1995).

10. Hodges not only influenced premodern players, he also had an impact on such modern saxophonists as Eddie Vinson, John Coltrane, and Eric Dolphy. Listen to Coltrane's recording of "Theme for Ernie," on John Coltrane, *Soultrane* (Fantasy: OJC-021, 1958, c1987), in which his ballad style recalls the fullness of sound and timing of ornaments that Hodges refined. Even as recently as the 1970s and 1980s, there was a continuation of the Hodges influence: for example, saxophonist Jan Garbarek cited Hodges as a source for his own style.

11. After studying "Cottontail" on *JCCD1*, a good place to continue listening to Webster is Ellington, *Never No Lament: The Blanton-Webster Band* (RCA Bluebird: 50857, 3CD set, 1940–42, c2003). To sample the rasping side of his musical character, listen to "Raincheck," "Mainstem," and "Blue Serge." For the crooning side, listen to "All Too Soon" and his obbligato behind the muted brass in the second chorus of "I Don't Know What Kind of Blues I've Got."

12. Webster influenced Charlie Ventura, Flip Phillips, Paul Gonsalves, Eddie "Lockjaw" Davis, Archie Shepp, Lew Tabackin, Bennie Wallace, and Scott Hamilton, to name a few.

13. Listen to "Take the 'A' Train" on *Ellington Uptown* (Columbia/Legacy: 87066, 1951–52, c2004) and the Gonsalves solos on *Ellington at Newport; Duke Ellington and His Orchestra Live at Newport 1958* (Columbia/Legacy: C2K 53584, 2CD set, 1958, c1994); *The Cosmic Scene* (Mosaic: MCD-1001 (Columbia), 1958, c2006); and *Festival Session* (Columbia/Legacy). Also see footnote 7 in this chapter.

14. Listen to Nanton's work on *SCCJ* on "Blue Serge" and "Harlem Airshaft" (also on *JCCD1*). For explanation of his methods, see Al Grey and Mike Grey, *Plunger Techniques* (Second Floor Music, 1987), available from Second Floor Music, 130 West 28th Street, NYC, NY 10001.

15. *Ellington Uptown* (Columbia/Legacy).

16. *Far East Suite* (RCA Bluebird: 66551, 1966, c1995); *Latin American Suite* (Fantasy: OJC-469, 1968, c1990); *Afro-Eurasian Eclipse* (Fantasy: OJC-645, 1971, c1975); and *The Ellington Suites* (Fantasy: OJC-446, 1959, 1971–72, c1990), which has "The Queen's Suite" and the "Goutelas" and "UWIS" suites.

17. These are on *Never No Lament: The Blanton-Webster Band* (RCA Bluebird).

18. Listen to Blanton's work on "Concerto for Cootie" on *SCCJ* and on "Pitter Panther Patter" on Duke Ellington, *Solos, Duets and Trios* (RCA Bluebird: 2178-2-RB, 1932–67, c1990); Ellington, *Never No Lament* (RCA Bluebird); or *Jive at Five* (New World).

19. See *Instructor's Resource Manual* for a list of albums containing each example.

20. Charlie Barnet's and Woody Herman's bands imitated the Ellington band, and other bandleaders had hits when they recorded Ellington pieces.

21. Gil Evans, Charles Mingus, George Russell, Clare Fischer, Sun Ra, Lalo Schifrin, Thad Jones, Toshiko Akiyoshi, to name a few.

22. James Newton, Anthony Davis, the World Saxophone Quartet, and others.

23. For more about Ellington's life and music, see his autobiography, *Music Is My Mistress* (Doubleday, 1973; Da Capo, 1976); Barry Ulanov, *Duke Ellington* (Creative Age, 1946; Da Capo, 1975); Stanley Dance, *The World of Duke Ellington* (Scribner's, 1970; Da Capo, 1980); Mercer Ellington, *Duke Ellington in Person* (Houghton-Mifflin, 1978); Mark Tucker, *Ellington: The Early Years* (University of Illinois, 1991); Tucker, ed., *The Duke Ellington Reader* (Oxford, 1993); John Edward Hasse, *Beyond Category: The Life and Genius of Duke Ellington* (Simon & Schuster, 1993; Da Capo, 1995); Eddie Lambert, *Duke Ellington: A Listener's Guide* (Scarecrow, 1999); and Stuart Nicholson, *Reminiscing in Tempo: A Portrait of Duke Ellington* (Northeastern, 1999).

For more about Billy Strayhorn, see David Hadju, *Lush Life: A Biography of Billy Strayhorn* (Farrar Straus Giroux, 1996); and Walter van de Leur, *Something to Live For: The Music of Billy Strayhorn* (Oxford, 2002).

Count Basie (1904–1984) led one of the most swinging big bands in jazz history. When compared with all others from the swing era, Basie's never seemed out of breath nor the least bit frantic. Basie led a big band almost continuously from 1937 until his death. Every edition of the band had at least two players who made important contributions to jazz history. Some editions had four or five.

BASIE THE PIANIST

Basie was originally a stride-style pianist, first inspired by Fats Waller*. Basie's manner was unique among jazz pianists. It was very light and extremely precise. His choice of notes was near perfect, and his impeccable sense of timing was equivalent to a good drummer's. In fact, Basie originally began his musical career as a drummer, not a pianist. Succinct and compact statements are hallmarks of Basie's style. When he soloed, he artfully used silence to pace his lines. The sound of his piano playing usually set the mood and tempo for each piece. Then, sometimes, the entire selection went by without the audience hearing more from Basie than a few "plink plink" interjections.

*For stride-style, listen to Demo CD *Track 38*; for Fats Waller listen to *"Handful of Keys,"* JCCD1 *Track 12*

Count Basie's 1938 band.
(Photo courtesy of Frank Driggs)

Basie's Rhythm Section During the Late 1930s to Early 1940s

"Taxi War Dance,"
JCCD1 *Track 24*

Basie led the first rhythm section in jazz history that consistently swung in a smooth, relaxed way. That famous rhythm section consisted of Basie himself (piano), Freddie Green (rhythm guitar), Walter Page (string bass), and Jo Jones (drums). Before reading about their virtues, review the *Demo CD* to familiarize yourself with the sounds of *walking bass, bass drum, high-hat cymbals, wire brushes,* and *ride rhythms.* Then listen to *Demo CD* Track 88 to familiarize yourself with *rhythm guitar.* The virtues of the Basie rhythm section are evident in their "Taxi War Dance." Listen to it while you read the following outline.

Among the special qualities of the Basie rhythm section were:

1. An excellent sense of tempo.
2. The ability to keep time and swing consistently without using a hard-driving, pressured approach.
3. Quiet, relaxed playing, which conveyed a feeling of ease.
4. Placing a fairly even amount of stress on each beat instead of pushing every other beat.
5. Emphasis on buoyancy rather than intensity.
6. Close coordination of bass, rhythm guitar, and drums.

Bassist **Walter Page** (1900–1957) contributed:

1. A supple walking bass sound. (He is considered one of the first masters of the walking style.)
2. A strong, articulated sound with life in it, not the dead thud common to many premodern bassists.
3. Playing each beat evenly.
4. Balancing his sound to mesh smoothly with piano, bass, and guitar.

Guitarist **Freddie Green** (1911–1987) was noted for:

1. His crisp strokes on unamplified guitar that sounded his rhythm chords with unerring steadiness and propulsive swing feeling.
2. His close coordination with bass and drums.

The style of drummer **Jo Jones** (1911–1985) was distinguished for:

1. Precise playing without any stiffness. Jones offered a loose, assured manner.
2. Quieter bass drum playing than was common in the swing era. Jones sometimes omitted bass drum entirely, sometimes using it only for off beat accents.
3. Quiet use of wire brushes on high-hat.
4. Ride rhythms played on high-hat continuously as the apparatus was opening and closing. Jones let his cymbals ring prominently between strokes, thereby creating a sustained sound that smoothed the timekeeping pattern instead of leaving each stroke as an abrupt sound. Jones also maintained this conception when using sticks to play ride rhythms on a separate suspended cymbal (also known as a "top cymbal").

The Basie rhythm section was noted for achieving a balance among the sounds of its members. The four parts were so smoothly integrated that one listener was inspired to compare the effect to riding on ball bearings. If you listen carefully to recordings of the band, you will notice that it is unusual for one member to dominate. Guitar, bass, and drums are all carefully controlled to avoid disturbing the evenness and balance of sound.

Tenor saxophonist Lester Young (soloist) and drummer Jo Jones (accompanist). Both men contributed to the smoothly swinging music of Count Basie's band in the 1930s.
(Photo courtesy of Robert Asen— Metronome Collection)

In Basie's chordal interjections, jazz piano had the lightness, bounce, syncopation, and flexibility of what became known as *comping*. Though he did not invent it, Basie is so thoroughly associated with comping that he might as well have. His comping was very sharp and lively. Basie comped so well and with such relaxed swing feeling that he provided the most-used model for it. To further understand comping, listen to "Lester Leaps In," focusing solely on the piano accompaniment. To elevate Basie's comping to its proper place in history, note that even by the mid-1940s many excellent jazz pianists had not learned to comp, though Basie had been doing it for over ten years. They continued in the predominant styles of the 1920s and 1930s, accompanying by (1) stride style, (2) playing a chord on each beat in the manner of a rhythm guitarist, or (3) playing flowery countermelodies and embellishments. But by the end of the 1940s, the evolution of jazz had been permanently nudged along by Basie's example, and comping had become central to modern jazz.

Demo CD Track 20; "Lester Leaps In," JCCD1 Track 25

ARRANGEMENTS

During the 1920s and 1930s there was a thriving jazz scene in Kansas City, Missouri.[1] A number of significant jazz musicians, including Basie, worked there. Though associated with "Kansas City style jazz," few were born there (see Table 8.1). Their music was not as glossy or elaborate as that of their New York counterparts; it was lighter and more relaxed. This accounts, at least in part, for its exceptional swing feeling.

Kansas City style was not based on the interweaving lines of the collectively improvised New Orleans style. Arrangements were based instead on short musical phrases called *riffs* that are repeated again and again. Riffs serve two functions. Sometimes they are theme statements, and sometimes they are backgrounds for improvised solos. A few of these riffs were written down, but many were created spontaneously during a performance ("off the top of someone's head"), learned by ear, and kept in the heads of the players. Arrangements of this kind are called *head arrangements*, and they are basic to the Kansas City *riff band style*. (Listen to a combo example of the riff style in "Lester Leaps In" [*JCCD1* Track 25] following the Listening Guide on page 158. For a best-selling example of this by a big band, listen to the final strains of "One O'Clock Jump" [*JCCD1* Track 5].[2])

TABLE 8.1 Musicians of the 1930s Kansas City Scene (birthplaces in parentheses)

Count Basie (New Jersey) pianist-bandleader

Gus Johnson (Texas) drummer

Walter Page (Missouri) bassist-bandleader

Lester Young (Mississippi) saxophonist

Buck Clayton (Kansas) trumpeter

Andy Kirk (Kentucky) bandleader-saxophonist

Herschel Evans (Texas) saxophonist

Eddie Durham (Texas) guitarist-arranger-trombonist

Buster Smith (Texas) saxophonist

Bennie Moten (Missouri) pianist-bandleader

Mary Lou Williams (Georgia) pianist-composer-arranger

Buddy Tate (Texas) saxophonist

Pete Johnson (Missouri) pianist

Charlie Parker (Kansas) saxophonist-composer

Jay McShann (Oklahoma) pianist-bandleader

Budd Johnson (Texas) saxophonist-composer

Hot Lips Page (Texas) trumpeter

Jo Jones (Illinois) drummer

Jesse Stone (Kansas) pianist-arranger-bandleader

George Lee (Missouri) saxophonist-pianist-bandleader

Harlan Leonard (Missouri) saxophonist-bandleader

LESTER YOUNG

Many of the best jazz trumpeters and saxophonists of the 1930s and 1940s played with Count Basie at one time or another. Basie's most notable soloist during this period was tenor saxophonist **Lester Young** (1909–1959). This musician was so good that he was nicknamed "Pres" (or "Prez"), an abbreviation for "president of tenor saxophone players." Young played lines which were fresher and more smoothly swinging than those of any previous improvisers. His light tone, slow vibrato, and buoyant phrases served as a model for modern jazz saxophonists and an entire subcategory of modern jazz that was called "cool jazz." Not only did he influence other saxophonists, but he also influenced guitarist Charlie Christian and trumpeter Miles Davis. Some musicians liked his work so much they copied and performed his solos note for note in their own improvisations (see Table 8.4).

To explore Lester Young's improvisatory style, let's compare it with Coleman Hawkins's. (See Table 8.3.) **Young offered a clear alternative to the heavy tone, fast vibrato, and complicated style of Coleman Hawkins.** Often, where Hawkins seemed to be chugging, Young seemed to be floating. Hawkins made improvisation sound like hard work. Young made it seem easy, like talking. Whereas Hawkins accented hard and often directly on main beats, Young was more subtle. Furthermore, Young tended to accent off beats and lightly stress portions of beats that made his lines swing gracefully. Young's playing was not as intricate as Hawkins's, but his melodic ideas were at

Recorded March 19, 1939, for Okeh by Count Basie big band; available on SCCJ; reissued on Basie, *America's #1 Band* (Columbia/Legacy: C4K 87110, 4 CD set, 1936–51, c2003).

This piece has no theme. The performance consists of improvisations and riffs over the chord progression of "Willow Weep for Me."

**ELAPSED
TIME**

0'00"   **Introduction (8 measures)**

Four Measures
Basie plays boogie-woogie figure on piano with his left hand.

Jo Jones plays ride rhythms on high-hat cymbals.

0'04"   *Four Measures*
Trumpets punctuate in unison with piano.

Trombones are "walking."

0'09"   **First Chorus (32-bar A-A-B-A) Lester Young Tenor Sax Solo**

A   Saxophone quotes the first phrase of "Ol' Man River" to begin improvisation. Timekeeping is by piano comping, guitar strumming each beat, bass walking, drummer playing ride rhythms on opening and closing high-hat.

0'17"   **A**   Boogie-woogie piano figure returns.

0'22"   Boogie-woogie figure is replaced by comping.

0'27"   **B**   Saxophone solo continues.

0'37"   **A**   Saxophone solo continues.

0'45"   **Two–Measure Introduction to the Second Chorus**

Trumpets punctuate in unison with piano.

Boogie-woogie figure returns. No walking trombones.

0'46"   **Second Chorus (32-bar A-A-B-A) Dicky Wells Trombone Solo**

A   Trombone improvises a solo, creating his own new melody.

0'51"   It sounds like Wells is poking fun.

0'54"   Wells plays one idea four times, each at a different position in relation to the beat.

0'57"   **A**   Solo continues with rhythm section accompaniment, again returning to a small combo performance.

1'05"   **B**   Solo notes outline the descending chords.

1'14"   **A**   continuation of trombone solo

1'21"   Final two measures: Trombone solo sustains one tone, and Basie plays up and down the scale on piano.

1'23"   **Third Chorus (32-bar A-A-B-A) Call and Response Passage**

A   *First Four Measures*
Trombones call and trumpets respond.

1'27"   *Second Four Measures*
Buddy Tate improvises a tenor saxophone solo. He can be distinguished from Lester Young by having a coarser tone that is darker and has faster vibrato. Tate's execution is less poised, less graceful, and has less swinging rhythmic feeling.

LISTENING GUIDE continued on next page

1'32"	**A**	Trombones call and trumpets respond.
1'36"		Buddy Tate improvises a tenor saxophone solo.
1'41"	**B**	Piano solo by Basie, using light touch in upper register.
1'49"	**A**	*First Four Measures*
		Trombones call and trumpets respond.
1'55"		*Second Four Measures*
		Tate solos with a rapid pattern repeated.

1'58" Fourth Chorus (32-bar A-A-B-A) Call and Response Passage

	A	*First Four Measures*
		Trombones call and trumpets respond with a syncopated figure that alternates muted with unmuted sound.
2'04"		*Second Four Measures*
		Lester Young improvises a tenor saxophone solo.
2'09"	**A**	*First Four Measures*
		Trombones call and trumpets respond with a syncopated figure that alternates muted with unmuted sound.
2'13"		Young enters his solo space early.
2'14"		*Second Four Measures*
		Lester Young improvises a tenor saxophone solo.
2'18"	**B**	Count Basie piano solo in the upper register, light and staccato.
2'27"	**A**	*First Four Measures*
		Trombones call, and the trumpets respond with syncopated figure that alternates muted with unmuted sound.
2'32"		*Second Four Measures*
		Lester Young improvises sax solo, rapidly alternating tone quality.

2'36" Ending (Two-Measure Unaccompanied Solo Sections)

		Two Measures
		Count Basie improvises a solo break.
2'39"		*Two Measures*
		Lester Young improvises a solo break.
2'41"		*Two Measures*
		walking bass alone
2'44"		*Two Measures*
		sticks on snare drum alone
2'46"		*Two Measures*
		Horns play a tie-it-up figure.
2'48"		High-hat cymbals "chick" shut.

A written transcription of Young's solo is available in *You Got to Be Original, Man!: The Music of Lester Young* by Frank Büchmann-Møller (Greenwood, 1990).

TABLE 8.2 A Few of the Many Musicians Who Have Been Important to Basie

TRUMPET	SAXOPHONE	COMPOSER-ARRANGER
Carl Smith	Don Byas	Eddie Durham
Hot Lips Page	Lester Young	Andy Gibson
Buck Clayton	Herschel Evans	Dicky Wells
Harry "Sweets" Edison	Jack Washington	Buck Clayton
Shad Collins	Tab Smith	Buster Harding
Emmett Berry	Earle Warren	Don Redman
Clark Terry	Buddy Tate	Jimmy Mundy
Thad Jones	Wardell Gray	Don Kirkpatrick
Joe Newman	Lucky Thompson	Ernie Wilkins
Al Aarons	Illinois Jacquet	Thad Jones
Sonny Cohn	Serge Chaloff	Frank Foster
Snooky Young	Paul Gonsalves	Frank Wess
Wendell Culley	Eddie "Lockjaw" Davis	Neal Hefti
	Frank Foster	Quincy Jones
DRUMS	Eric Dixon	Benny Carter
Jo Jones	Jimmy Forrest	Billy Byers
Shadow Wilson	Billy Mitchell	Chico O'Farrill
Sonny Payne	Frank Wess	Sammy Nestico
Gus Johnson	Marshall Royal	Al Grey
Louis Bellson	Charlie Fowlkes	
Harold Jones	Bobby Plater	
Butch Miles	Paul Quinichette	**TROMBONE**
Rufus Jones		Dicky Wells
		Benny Morton
		Vic Dickenson
		Al Grey
GUITAR	**BASS**	Henry Coker
Freddie Green	Walter Page	Curtis Fuller
	Eddie Jones	Benny Powell
	Buddy Catlett	

least as advanced. He just made them sound easier. (Listen to Young play what he came to consider one of his own best solos: "Taxi War Dance," *JCCD1* Track 24.[3])

Young's approach contrasted with Hawkins's preference for running through the set of notes contained in each chord (musicians call this "arpeggiating"). Instead of playing every note in every chord, as Hawkins often did, Young was more cool and concise. In fact, **Young sometimes purposely ignored the notes in the chords or chose others which, when combined with the chord tones, altered the effect of both the tone and the chord.** (Musicians refer to such notes as "color tones" because they have the capacity to alter the "color" of the sound, much as voicing alters the "color" of a chord.) And even when he played a solo using many notes, the result was not as densely packed as a typical Hawkins solo.[4]

TABLE 8.3   Comparison of Coleman Hawkins with Lester Young

	COLEMAN HAWKINS	LESTER YOUNG
Tone Quality	warm	cool
	dark-colored	light-colored
	heavy-weight	light-weight
	full-bodied	hollow
Rate of Vibrato	medium to fast	slow
Swing Feeling	early jazz style	more relaxed and graceful than Hawkins
Intricacy of Solos	much	less than Hawkins
Tunefulness of Improvisations	little	much
Came to Prominence with	Fletcher Henderson (1923–1934)	Count Basie (1936–1944)
Influenced	Herschel Evans	Charlie Parker
	Chu Berry	Wardell Gray
	Dick Wilson	Stan Getz
	Ben Webster	Lee Konitz
		Sonny Stitt
		Woody Herman band's "Four Brothers" sound and West Coast Style players (see Table 8.4)

Young concerned himself with only a core of melodic material. He didn't incorporate afterthoughts into his phrases, as Hawkins was prone to do. He practiced deliberate restraint. He could pace a solo so well that it seemed an integral part of the written arrangement. His gift for improvising new, easily singable melodies is unsurpassed in jazz history. There is an overriding sense of continuity in Young's improvisations that is very satisfying. Young possessed a musical storytelling talent which surfaced in nearly every improvisation.[5]

The advanced level of Young's conception was evident in his easy swing and in his placement of phrases that seemed unhindered by turnarounds and bridges. (Listen to *Demo CD* Tracks 16–19 for illustrations of chord progression organization, and see Appendix B for further explanation.) Young often transcended the phrasing style of many premodern players who had organized lines around the two- and four-bar sequences of chord progressions. The internal logic of his lines took precedence over strict adherence to the underlying harmonies and the way they were blocked out. He improvised long lines that had a fresh, expansive feeling which was unlike the crowded feeling that we often get from improvisations of other soloists.

Young's playing was strongest during the late 1930s. His first recordings were probably the best of his entire career. When he left Basie in 1940, his tone began to darken, his vibrato quickened, and the crispness of his execution decreased. He

TABLE 8.4   A Few of the Many Saxophonists
Influenced by Lester Young

Charlie Parker	Gene Ammons	Illinois Jacquet
Brew Moore	Sonny Stitt	Arnett Cobb
Paul Quinichette	Stan Getz	Morris Lane
Dave Pell	Herbie Steward	Wild Bill Moore
Bob Cooper	Richie Kamuca	Paul Williams
Bill Perkins	Al Cohn	Jack McVea
Wardell Gray	Jerry Jerome	Weasel Parker
Allen Eager	Don Lanphere	John Hardee
Zoot Sims	Jimmy Giuffre	Big Jay McNeely
Lee Konitz	Buddy Collette	Tom Archia
Warne Marsh	John Coltrane	Red Prysock
Dexter Gordon	Hank Mobley	Willis "Gator" Jackson

changed his style. His playing seemed to lose energy steadily until his death in 1959. Yet Young's work remained intelligent and swinging all those later years. In fact, his loyalty to storytelling-type improvisations increased. But after 1940, he seemed unable to jump into his solos with the animation and freshness of his early work.

KANSAS CITY FIVE; JONES-SMITH, INC.

Several of the most significant recordings in jazz history were made by small combinations of Basie band members. Variously called the Kansas City Five, Six, or Seven, depending on how many musicians were used, these combos often included the Basie rhythm section plus Lester Young, Buck Clayton, and Dicky Wells. Their 1939 recordings, such as "Dickie's Dream" and "Lester Leaps In," are combo classics. One set omitted Basie, added Eddie Durham on guitar, and featured some of the all-time best playing of Lester Young and trumpeter Buck Clayton ("Good Mornin' Blues," "Pagin' the Devil," "I Want a Little Girl").[6] Another of these combos included drummer Jo Jones and trumpeter Carl Smith and was given the group name Jones-Smith, Inc. The recordings they made in 1936, including "Shoe Shine Boy" and "Lady Be Good," are masterpieces.[7]

"Lester Leaps In," JCCD1 *Track 25*

"Lady Be Good," CCD1 *Track 7*

BASIE AFTER THE 1940S

After the 1940s, Basie retained many elements of his rhythm section style. His own piano style remained constant, and guitarist Freddie Green was still with him, playing in the same style he originated. Basie's post-1940s drummers kept time more on the ride cymbal than on the high-hat, and they played far more fills than Jo Jones had. However, his drummers were not performing in contemporary styles after the 1940s. They kept to what worked best for the Basie big band approach.

For 30 years, the Basie band had the unusual distinction of being almost the only big band that swung while playing softly. Some of the music written for the band during the 1950s and 1960s capitalized on the band's skill with dynamic contrasts: loud

Recorded September 5, 1939, for Okeh by Lester Young (tenor sax), Buck Clayton (cup-muted trumpet), Dicky Wells (trombone), Count Basie (piano), Freddie Green (guitar), Walter Page (bass), Jo Jones (drums); available on *SCCJ*; reissued on Basie, *America's #1 Band* (Columbia/Legacy: C4K 87110, 4CD set, 1936–51, c2003).

This piece consists of riffs and improvisations over the chord progression to "I Got Rhythm." A transcription and analysis of Young's solo is available in Scott Reeves, *Creative Jazz Improvisation*, 4th ed. (Prentice-Hall, 2006).

ELAPSED TIME		
0'00"	**4–Measure Piano Introduction**	
0'03"	**First Chorus (32-bar A-A-B-A) Riff Band Theme Statement**	
	A-A	Muted trumpet, trombone, and tenor saxophone play a four-measure melodic figure four times with rhythm section accompaniment.
0'19"	B	Count Basie piano solo, very lean, just indicating the moments during which chords change. He allows plenty of space for us to hear bass and drums.
0'27"	A	The three horns state original theme (that same riff) two more times.
0'35"	**Second Chorus (32-bar A-A-B-A) Lester Young Tenor Saxophone Solo**	
	A-A-B-A	Lester Young tenor sax solo accompanied by drummer Jo Jones playing ride rhythm on opening and closing high-hat, Basie's piano comping, and Page's walking bass.
1'06"	**Third Chorus (32-bar A-A-B-A)**	
	A	Young and Basie improvise counterpoint around each other.
1'14"	A	Rhythm section creates stop-time solo breaks for Young during first six measures. Rhythm section resumes normal timekeeping patterns for last two measures while Young keeps on improvising.
1'22"	B	Young continues solo with rhythm section accompaniment.
1'30"	A	Rhythm section creates more stop-times for Young.
1'37"	**Fourth Chorus (32-bar A-A-B-A) Basie and Young Trading Fours**	
	A	Basie solos the first four measures, Young does the second four.
1'41"	A	Basie solos the first four measures, Young does the second four.
1'55"	B	Basie solos the first four measures, Young does the second four.
2'01"	A	Basie solos the first four measures, Young does the second four.
2'09"	**Fifth Chorus (32-bar A-A-B-A) Call and Response Passage**	
	(This chorus uses another typical riff band device.)	
	A	*First Four Measures* Ensemble calls, "Bop bop bop–bop baah!"
2'12"		*Second Four Measures* Young responds with improvisation.
2'17"	A	*First Four Measures* Ensemble calls, "Bop bop bop–bop baah!"

LISTENING GUIDE *continued on next page*

2'21"		*Second Four Measures*
		Basie responds with improvisation.
2'25"	**B**	Basie continues his improvisation.
2'33"	**A**	*First Four Measures*
		Ensemble calls, "Bop bop bop–bop baah!"
2'36"		*Second Four Measures*
		Young responds with improvisation.

2'40"   Sixth Chorus (32-bar A-A-B-A) Call and Response Passage

	A	*First Four Measures*
		Ensemble calls, "Bop bop bop–bop baah!"
2'44"		*Second Four Measures*
		Basie responds with improvisation.
2'49"	**A**	*First Four Measures*
		Ensemble calls, "Bop bop bop–bop baah!"
		Second Four Measures
2'53"		Basie responds with improvisation.
2'56"	**B**	Basie continues his improvisation.
3'04"	**A**	Ensemble calls, "Bop bop bop–bop baah!" Then the band members collectively improvise a closing by simultaneously playing different lines in Dixieland style.

passages which instantaneously get soft; soft passages interrupted momentarily by very loud chords; passages which rise and fall in volume so gradually that one wonders how it is possible. The band maintained precision and balance at a variety of loudness levels, all without losing the unrelenting drive that is expected of jazz performances. Moreover, the band did this without sounding mechanical. In fact, it projected a warm and supple feeling.

Count Basie's band always placed more emphasis on simplicity and swing feeling than on complexity and colorful sounds. Simple, catchy riffs were the rule, even during the 1950s and 1960s when sophisticated composers and arrangers were writing for the band. Basie had previously run the band much as an oversized combo, with more emphasis on swinging solo improvisations than fancy arrangements. That approach contrasted with the highly polished, well-arranged style of Jimmie Lunceford and the elaborate embroidery of written music and improvisation that occurred in Duke Ellington's band. However, Basie's emphasis on the oversized combo format decreased somewhat during the 1950s and more so thereafter. On the other hand, the group achieved a very high level of polish, and it became known as a swinging showcase for glossy ensemble sound like Lunceford's band of 20 years earlier. (See *Instructor's Resource Manual* for a discography of this period.)[8]

CHAPTER SUMMARY

1. Count Basie was a Fats Waller-derived stride pianist with a light, precise touch, and impeccable sense of tempo.

2. Count Basie's accompaniment style constituted one of the first examples of comping.

3. Count Basie was one of the few pianists to make silence almost as important as the notes he played.

4. The 1937–1940 Basie rhythm section set the pace for modern methods of timekeeping and accompanying.

5. Basie's band played in the Kansas City style, using riffs, simple figures which were played repeatedly atop pop tune and 12-bar blues accompaniments.

6. Tenor saxophonist Lester Young offered a light-toned alternative to the deep, heavy sound of Coleman Hawkins.

7. Young was very melodic and fresh in his improvisations. He became the major model for hundreds of modern jazz saxophonists, as well as an entire subcategory of modern jazz called "cool jazz."

8. Basie always stressed simplicity and swing instead of complex arrangements, and he retained the same unhurried feeling throughout his bandleading career.

NOTES

1. For more about Kansas City style, see Frank Driggs and Chuck Haddix, *Kansas City Jazz: From Ragtime to Bebop—A History* (Oxford Univ. Press, 2005); Nathan W. Pearson, *Goin' to Kansas City* (University of Illinois Press, 1987); Gunther Schuller, *Early Jazz* (Oxford, 1968), 279–317; and Schuller, *The Swing Era* (Oxford, 1989), 222–262.

2. Many riff-based pieces that band members at first identified only by numbers were eventually given names and composer credits. Count Basie's "One O'Clock Jump" and "Jumpin' at the Woodside" are best-selling examples, available in the anthology: *Big Band Jazz: From the Beginnings to the Fifties* (Smithsonian: 2202, 4 CD set, 1924–56, c1983). Listen to this style on "Moten Swing," as recorded by the Bennie Moten band in 1932 and available on *SCCJ*. The piece is a 32-measure A-A-B-A form that is based on the chord progression to a song called "You're Driving Me Crazy." This recording will also give you a peek into Kansas City jazz history because Count Basie had been a member of both Moten's band and the Blue Devils, led by bassist Walter Page. These two groups eventually fused to become Basie's first Kansas City band.

3. In the opening to "Taxi War Dance" (on *JCCD1*), Young plays notes that purposely clash with the notes of Basie's boogie-woogie figure; then the harmonic conflict resolves when Basie comes out of the boogie-woogie figure. Another clever Young solo is his improvisation on Basie's "Jive at Five" (1939), available on *Jive at Five* (New World: 274, LP, 1927–46, c1976); or Count Basie, *The Complete Decca Recordings* (Decca

Jazz: GRD3-611, 3CD set, 1937–1939, c1992). This particular solo is especially intriguing because it foreshadows the fluffy tone and melodic approach Stan Getz was to display eight years later.

4. For a transcription and analysis of Young's solo on "Lester Leaps In" from Basie, *America's #1 Band* (Columbia/Legacy: C4K 87110, 4 CD set, 1936–51, c2003), see Scott Reeves, *Creative Jazz Improvisation*, 4th ed. (Prentice-Hall, 2006). The solo is nearly all eighth notes, but the sequences are clear despite the number of notes and surprises they contain. They are free of the many twists and turns that typify Hawkins's improvisations. For transcriptions of solos and comments about 251 Lester Young recording sessions, see Frank Büchmann-Møller, *You Got to Be Original, Man! The Music of Lester Young* (Greenwood, 1990).

5. His clarinet solos on the 1938 "I Want a Little Girl" and "Pagin' the Devil" illustrate his "storytelling" talent quite well. They are available on Lester Young, *"The Kansas City" Sessions* (Commodore Jazz: 402, 1938, 1944, c1997). Also outstanding in this regard is his tenor sax solo on "Pound Cake" (1939), available on Basie, *America's #1 Band* (Columbia/Legacy).

6. Available on Lester Young, *"The Kansas City" Sessions* (Commodore Jazz).

7. Available on Basie, *America's #1 Band* (Columbia/Legacy). "Lady Be Good" is also on the *CCD1*. For a transcription and analysis of Young's solo on "Lady Be Good," see Schuller, *The Swing Era*, 230–235.

8. To listen to more Basie performances, see *Big Band Jazz* (Smithsonian); *Big Band Renaissance* (Smithsonian: 108, 5 CD set, c1995); Basie, *The Complete Decca Recordings* (Decca Jazz); and Basie, *America's #1 Band* (Columbia/Legacy).

To read more about the Basie band and its musicians, see *Good Morning Blues: The Autobiography of Count Basie as Told to Albert Murray* (Random House, 1985; DaCapo, 2000); Stanley Dance, *The World of Count Basie* (Scribner's, 1980; DaCapo, 1985); Lewis Porter, *Lester Young* (Twayne, 1985); Porter, ed., *The Lester Young Reader* (Smithsonian, 1991); Dave Gelly, *Lester Young* (Hippocrene, 1984); Buck Clayton, *Buck Clayton's Jazz World* (Oxford, 1986); Dicky Wells, *Night People*, rev. ed. (Smithsonian, 1991); Frank Büchmann-Møller, *You Just Fight for Your Life: The Story of Lester Young* (Praeger, 1990); Luc Delannoy, *Pres: The Story of Lester Young* (Univ. of Arkansas, 1993); and Chris Sheridan, *Count Basie: A Bio-Discography* (Greenwood, 1986).

Tenor Saxophonist Lester Young
(Photo courtesy of Frank Driggs)

During the 1940s, a number of adventuresome musicians showed the effects of studying the advanced swing era styles of saxophonists Coleman Hawkins and Lester Young, pianists Art Tatum and Nat Cole, trumpeter Roy Eldridge, guitarist Charlie Christian, and the Count Basie rhythm section. "Early jazz" and other pre-1940 styles are today referred to as the "classic period." The new styles that emerged after 1940 were classified as modern jazz. These first "modern" musicians were alto saxophonist Charlie Parker, pianist Thelonious Monk, and trumpeter Dizzy Gillespie. Their music was called bebop, or just "bop." By the middle 1940s, bop had inspired a legion of other creative musicians including trumpeter Miles Davis and pianist Bud Powell. By the late 1940s, Parker and Gillespie had also influenced the music in several big bands, including Woody Herman's. This chapter will discuss the solo and combo styles of these musicians and the big bands of Herman and Gillespie.

Modern jazz did not burst upon the jazz scene suddenly. It developed gradually through the work of swing era musicians. Parker and Gillespie themselves began their careers by creating swing-style improvisations. Then they expanded on swing styles and gradually incorporated new techniques; their work eventually became a different style, but its swing era roots remained evident. Rather than being a reaction *against* swing styles, modern jazz developed smoothly *from* swing styles.

Charlie Mingus, Roy Haynes, Thelonious Monk, Charlie Parker
(Photo by Bob Parent, courtesy of Don Parent)

Bebop was considerably less popular than swing, and it failed to attract dancers. However, it did contribute impressive soloists who continued to gain disciples for the rest of the century. The first bop soloists contributed a new vocabulary of musical phrases and distinctive methods of matching improvisation to chord progressions. This became the most substantial system of jazz for the next 40 years. Even today, musicians frequently evaluate new players according to their ability to play bop. Mastery of this style was considered the foundation for competence as a jazz improviser.

Bop improvisations were composed mostly of eighth-note and sixteenth-note figures that seemed jumpy, full of twists and turns. The contours of the melodic lines were jagged; there were often abrupt changes of direction and large intervals between the notes. The rhythms in those lines were quick and unpredictable, with more syncopation than any music previously common in Europe or America. (Listen to the melody line of Gillespie and Parker's "Shaw Nuff," *JCCD1* Track 26.)

Bop players took a cue from Lester Young and often began phrases in the middle of eight-bar sections, continuing them through the turnarounds, past the traditional barriers of the eighth bar (twelfth bar in the blues). Bop performers more often overcame the tendency of premodern improvisers to stop phrases at or before *turnarounds*. (See page 467 for a nontechnical explanation of turnarounds or page 491 for examples.) They planned ahead further and mastered the improvisation of extended lines that reflected a tune's underlying chord progression less and less.

BOP HARMONY

By contrast with the earliest jazz musicians, bop musicians did more than embellish a song. As a starting point for their improvisations, they retained only the chord progressions that had accompanied a song.[1] Then they often enriched a progression by adding

---

BOP CONTRASTED WITH SWING

Bop differed from swing in a number of performance aspects:

1. Preferred instrumentation for bop was the small combo instead of big band.
2. Less emphasis was placed on arrangements in bop.
3. Average tempo was faster in bop.
4. Clarinet was rare in bop.
5. Display of instrumental virtuosity was a higher priority for bop players.
6. Rhythm guitar was rare.

Bop differed from swing in a number of stylistic respects:

1. Bop improvisation was more complex because it contained
   a. more themes per solo,
   b. less similarity among themes,
   c. more excursions outside the tune's original key, and
   d. a greater scope of rhythmic development.
2. Melodies were more complex in bop.
3. Harmonies were more complex in bop.
4. Bop tunes and chord progressions projected a more unresolved quality.
5. Accompaniment rhythms were more varied in bop.
6. Comping was more prevalent than stride style and simple, on-the-beat chording.
7. Drummers played their timekeeping rhythms primarily on suspended cymbal, rather than snare drum, high-hat, or bass drum.
8. Surprise was more highly valued in bop.
9. Bop was a more agitated style than swing was.

TABLE 9.1   A Few of the Many Bop Style Musicians

TRUMPET
Dizzy Gillespie
Fats Navarro
Howard McGhee
Miles Davis
Kenny Dorham
Red Rodney
Benny Harris
Sonny Berman
Freddie Webster
Conte Candoli
Clark Terry
Idrees Sulieman
Benny Bailey

TROMBONE
J.J. Johnson
Kai Winding
Bennie Green
Frank Rosolino

BASS
Oscar Pettiford
Ray Brown
Tommy Potter
Curly Russell
Nelson Boyd
Al McKibbon
Gene Ramey
Red Callender
Teddy Kotick
Chubby Jackson
Eddie Safranski

SAXOPHONE
Charlie Parker
Dexter Gordon
Lucky Thompson
Stan Getz
Wardell Gray
Allen Eager
Herbie Steward
Brew Moore
Gene Ammons
Sonny Stitt
Flip Phillips
James Moody
Charlie Ventura
Zoot Sims
Al Cohn
Ernie Henry
Leo Parker
Sonny Criss
Serge Chaloff
Don Lanphere
Charlie Rouse
Sonny Rollins
Phil Urso
Boots Mussulli

VIBRAPHONE
Milt Jackson
Teddy Charles
Terry Gibbs

DRUMS
Kenny Clarke
Max Roach
Joe Harris
Tiny Kahn
Don Lamond
Roy Haynes
Osie Johnson
Denzil Best

PIANO
Bud Powell
Thelonious Monk
Al Haig
Dodo Marmarosa
Joe Albany
Walter Bishop, Jr.
Duke Jordan
George Shearing
Oscar Peterson
Billy Taylor
Hank Jones
Argonne Thornton
  (Sadik Hakim)
Hampton Hawes
John Lewis
Tadd Dameron
Ahmad Jamal

GUITAR
Arv Garrison
Tal Farlow
Bill DeArango
Jimmy Raney
Johnny Collins
Barry Galbraith
Chuck Wayne
Barney Kessel
Billy Bauer
Johnny Smith

COMPOSER-ARRANGER
Gil Fuller
George Russell
Neal Hefti
Dizzy Gillespie
Charlie Parker
Thelonious Monk
Tadd Dameron
John Lewis
Shorty Rogers
Ralph Burns
Gil Evans
Gerry Mulligan

new chords. (See third example on page 491 under "12-Bar Blues Progressions.") When jazz musicians add chords or change chords in a given progression, they call it *substitution* or reharmonization because new chords are substituted in place of the old ones. Art Tatum had previously added and replaced chords underneath existing melodies. In fact, his reharmonization of "Tea for Two" is well known among jazz musicians. Coleman Hawkins had loved to improvise on complicated chord progressions and invent solo lines whose construction implied that chords had been added. His recording of "Body and Soul" demonstrates this. In these ways, Tatum and Hawkins had set the stage for the wide use of these techniques in bop style. Some bop lines implied chords that were not originally in a tune's accompaniment; these lines were sometimes played

Charlie Parker (alto sax) and Miles Davis (trumpet), two of the most influential men in modern jazz. Parker devised the bop approach, and Davis went on to develop cool, modal, and jazz-rock approaches. Pictured here in 1947 when Parker was 27 and Davis was 21.

(Photo by William P. Gottlieb)

against a tune's original harmonies to achieve purposely clashing effects. In other cases, the pianist and bassist instantaneously changed chords and chord progressions to fit the new harmonic directions implied by an improvised line.

Bop players also altered existing chords. They often based their lines more on the alterations than on the fundamental tones. So, by comparison with their predecessors, bop musicians not only used more chords, they used richer chords and created lines that drew from the enrichments. The most common alteration was the *flatted fifth* (also known as the lowered fifth or raised eleventh). It soon became identified as much with modern jazz as the lowered third and lowered seventh were identified with premodern jazz. Today all three intervals are basic to the character of jazz. Dizzy Gillespie's 1945 arrangement of "Shaw Nuff" (*JCCD1* Track 26) ends on a flatted fifth (see page 456).

Because bop musicians liked to improvise on difficult chord progressions, they sometimes wrote original progressions themselves. But a more common practice was to improvise on popular song progressions that were challenging. "All the Things You Are" served this purpose. "Cherokee" also became a favorite because the progressions in its bridge are unusual.[2]

CHARLIE PARKER

The musician who contributed most to the development of bop was alto saxophonist **Charlie Parker** (1920–1955), nicknamed "Bird." Jazz musicians and historians feel that he is the most important saxophonist in jazz history. Many musicologists consider Parker one of the most brilliant musical figures in the twentieth century. Going beyond the advances made by Lester Young, Coleman Hawkins, and Art Tatum, he built an entire system that was conveyed in his improvisations and compositions. The system embodied:

1. new ways of selecting notes to be compatible with the accompaniment chords;
2. new ways of accenting notes so that the phrases have a highly syncopated character;
3. methods for adding chords to existing chord progressions and implying additional chords by the selection of notes for the improvised lines.

Parker astonished other musicians with his tremendous fertility of melodic imagination, unprecedented mastery of the saxophone, and the dizzying pace with which he was able to improvise.[3] Parker's solos were densely packed with ideas. During his improvisations, his mind seemed to be bubbling over with little melodies and paraphrases of melodies. It was as though he had so much energy and enthusiasm that he could barely contain himself. This led to interspersing his solos with double-time and quadruple-time figures. Even in ballad renditions, he tended to ornament slow lines with double-time figures. (For a demonstration of double-timing, listen to *Demo CD* Track 35. For Parker himself double-timing, listen to the introduction to "Just Friends" on *JCCD1* Track 30.) In other words, he played fast, and he played a lot of notes. It is no coincidence that soon after Parker's mid-1940s recordings appeared, there was an increase in the average tempo, an increase in double-timing, and an increase in the average amount of melodic ideas in the improvisations of other modern jazz musicians. Though this trend had already begun during the swing era, it was also partly a function of the new example set by Parker.

Parker's timbre departed from standard swing era models. In place of the lush, sweet tone preferred by Johnny Hodges and Benny Carter, Parker used the dry, biting tone preferred by Kansas City saxophonist Buster Smith, an early model for Parker. Though Parker's tone had considerable fullness, it possessed a lighter color than the tone of Hodges. In place of the pronounced vibrato of Hodges and Carter, Parker used the slower, narrower vibrato preferred by Smith, and Parker was less prone to dwell on a few choice notes than Hodges. By comparison with Hodges, Parker sounded more hurried. As opposed to an easygoing romantic, Parker sounded like a modern composer improvising at lightning speed.[4]

Parker's Sources

Parker's improvisations were inspired by many sources. An adequate analysis of his techniques is beyond the nontechnical scope of this book, but we should note that Parker's improvisatory techniques echo the methods that are routinely employed by classical composers.[5] Though we will not be able to recognize examples of the techniques if we do not know them, we might notice other sources for his improvisations because they draw upon familiar material. Parker interspersed his lines with phrases from highly varied sources. He drew from materials as far-flung as the solos of Louis Armstrong and Lester Young and the melodies of blues singers and early jazz hornmen. He selected phrases from pop tunes and traditional melodies, themes from opera and classical music.[6]

Parker's Tunes

Parker wrote a sizable body of tunes, and their character set the flavor for bop as much as his improvisations did. Though not melody-like in the pop tune sense, they were catchy lines in a jazz vein. Most were accompanied by chord progressions borrowed from popular songs. Many used accompaniments of the twelve-bar blues chord progression. Their phrases were memorized and analyzed by hundreds of jazz soloists. His "Now's the Time," "Billie's Bounce," and "Confirmation" were played at jam sessions for decades after he introduced them. This was the musical language of bop.

Parker's Impact

Parker's impact on jazz was immense. Bop trumpeter Dizzy Gillespie cites Parker as a primary influence on his own style, and bop pianist Bud Powell modeled some of his lines on those of Parker. Methods of improvisation devised by Parker were adopted by numerous saxophonists during the 1940s and 1950s (see Table 9.2). Parker's tunes

Composed by Lewis and Klenner; recorded November 30, 1949, for Norman Granz by Charlie Parker (alto sax), Stan Freeman (piano), Ray Brown (bass), Buddy Rich (drums), three violins, viola, cello, harp, and oboe; available on JCCD1; reissued on Parker, *Confirmation: Best of the Verve Years* (Verve: 527 815, c1995).

Improvisers have used popular songs as the basis for their performances throughout jazz history, and this recording of "Just Friends" provides another example. Such pieces appeal to improvising musicians not only for their melody lines but also for the possibilities that their accompanying chords offer in guiding improvised lines. Though initially introduced by a singer and appealing to audiences partly because of the song's lyrics, these tunes sometimes become historically more important for what jazz instrumentalists do with them, as happened to this rendition by Charlie Parker. Many instrumentalists are also drawn to accompaniments like those supplied to singers, such as the orchestration here that includes three violins, viola, cello, harp, and oboe. In fact, the soloist on this recording was so happy with this ensemble that he took a similar group on the road with him and toured with the repertory of the album which first included "Just Friends."

The form of the original melody to "Just Friends" is 32-bar A-B-A-B′ (pronounced "aay, bee, aay, bee prime"). Before beginning a series of repetitions following that form, the piece opens with an introduction consisting of harp glissando (rapid string of tones rising in pitch) and tremolos (quick, continuous reiterations of a given tone) from the violins and viola. Then the cello takes the lead from 0′03″ to 0′09″. This activity builds anticipation for the arrival of the saxophone solo. Unlike the string parts that comprise the first portion of the introduction, the second part, beginning at 0′12″, consists of Parker freely improvising atop a fresh set of chord progressions. The saxophonist obviously relishes the chance because he bursts forth quadruple-timing a spontaneous series of his own phrases before he is required to state the "Just Friends" melody itself. Parker's rendering of the song is supremely inspired, and his improvised parenthetical remarks convey the boundless enthusiasm for which his playing was celebrated. He improvises through the first half of the song's chord progression. The strings take the lead at 0′47″ and play the third eight measures of the 32-bar song form. Parker returns full-force at 1′00″ with a paraphrase of the melody's final line.

After a 16-beat interlude, led by the oboe from 1′16″ to 1′22″, the key has changed so that the harmonies are now positioned a scale-step higher. This gives the mood of the piece a little lift. Parker plunges into this new setting and improvises an entire 32-bar chorus that is packed with ideas of his own and not dependent on the "Just Friends" melody. The next chorus begins at 2′21″ with pianist Stan Freeman improvising a lively solo for its first half. Parker returns at 2′50″ to play the second half, at first by briefly referencing the "Just Friends" melody, then by improvising his own melodies. Then at 3′17″, a new part of the arrangement arrives. This is technically termed "a Coda." This is a musician's term designating an extra part that is added to comprise an ending and is not within the A-B-A-B′ form. To provide a dramatic ending for the performance, this section is tacked onto repetitions of the "Just Friends" form. It presents the saxophonist with six measures of original chord changes to devour. Using these new chords, Parker ends the piece practically bubbling over with new ideas. His playing here conveys a sense of abandon, as though he would continue generating idea after idea if the recording session had not already come to a close.

To put the significance of this recording in perspective, note that the music rushes by so quickly that an improviser has only fleeting chances to spontaneously craft something that is not only original but also coherent and swinging. Most improvisers are not pleased with their own recordings because of that and because of their high standards for creativity and execution. Happily, however, this "Just Friends" recording is an exception. Parker said that it did please him. So we are sampling jazz by one of the most important forces in twentieth century music, and its high quality is confirmed by its creator.

ELAPSED

TIME	MUSICAL EVENTS
	Introduction (8 measures)
0′00″	harp glissando, violin and viola tremolo
0′02″	Cello plays the lead to 0′09″.
0′11″	Harp returns. Strings play a phrase.
0′12″	Sax improvises final four measures of introduction, quadruple-timing atop a tremolo by the strings.

LISTENING GUIDE continued on next page

First Chorus

A-Section

0'19"   Alto sax plays melody, accompanied by walking bass, ride rhythms on ride cymbal, and piano chords.

0'26"   second phrase of "Just Friends"

0'28"   Soft piano chords; strings play moving lines to fill pauses in sax lines and underneath sustained tones of melody.

B-Section

0'32"   Sax plays original melody's opening phrase.

0'36"   Sax improvises quadruple-time figures.

A-Section

0'47"   Strings state melody, slurring the notes together.

B-Section

1'00"   Alto sax states B-section of "Just Friends."

Interlude (4 measures = 16 beats)

1'15"   Oboe takes the lead, and the key of the piece modulates up from A♭ to B♭.

Alto Saxophone Solo Improvisation (A-B-A-B)

1'22"   Full chorus of original figures improvised on sax.

2'19"   **Interlude by Strings (2 measures = 8 beats)**

Stan Freeman Piano Improvisation (A-B)

2'21"   piano solo accompanied by bassist Ray Brown and drummer Buddy Rich

2'35"   piano quadruple-timing

Sax returns (A-B)

2'49"   Parker paraphrases melody, then departs entirely from it and improvises his own fresh melodies for the rest of the performance.

Coda (6 measures = 24 beats)

3'17"   Sax improvises quadruple-time figures.

TABLE 9.2   A Few of the Many Saxophonists Influenced by Charlie Parker

Phil Woods	Lou Donaldson	Sonny Rollins
Charlie Mariano	Davey Schildkraut	Ornette Coleman
Sahib Shihab	Sonny Stitt	Albert Ayler
Ernie Henry	James Moody	Wardell Gray
Sonny Criss	Jackie McLean	Dexter Gordon
Charlie McPherson	Cannonball Adderley	Art Pepper
Frank Strozier	Eric Dolphy	Bud Shank
Jimmy Heath	John Coltrane	Joe Farrell

"Things to Come" by Dizzy Gillespie Big Band

Composed by Dizzy Gillespie and Gil Fuller; recorded July 9, 1946, for Musicraft by the Dizzy Gillespie big band (five saxes, three trombones, five trumpets, vibraphone, piano, bass, and drums), featuring Gillespie (trumpet), Milt Jackson (vibraphone), John Brown (alto sax), John Lewis (piano), Ray Brown (bass), and Kenny Clarke (drums). Reissued on Gillespie, *Odyssey, 1945–1952* (Savoy Jazz: 17109 [Musicraft], c2002), and *Groovin' High* (Savoy: 0152 [Musicraft] 1945–1946, c1992).

This is the most spectacular example of big band bop on record. The music is so intricate and the pace is so fast that even musicians themselves have a hard time believing their ears the first time they hear it. Small bands customarily played intricate lines at quick tempos, a reputation of bop. But big bands were traditionally less flexible because coordinating 16 musicians is much harder than coordinating five.

"Things to Come" was developed by Gil Fuller from a combo piece of Gillespie's called "Bebop." Aside from the energetic solo improvisations of trumpeter Gillespie and alto saxophonist John Brown, we hear a vibraphone solo from Milt Jackson, who became the featured soloist with the well-known Modern Jazz Quartet. We also hear a considerable amount of inventive drumming from Kenny Clarke, one of the original pioneers of bop.

ELAPSED
TIME

0'00"   **Introduction**

Complex line played together by the trumpets with drummer underscoring some of their rhythms.

A phrase by the saxes. An exclamation by the brass instruments. Brief drum solo. No timekeeping rhythms yet from drums or bass. Other complex lines from brasses jut out at us.

Main Theme (A-A-B-A)

0'08"   *First A-section*
Saxes state the melody while trumpets and trombones punctuate it, and bass and drums play timekeeping rhythms.

0'14"   *Second A-section*
Saxes state the melody while trumpets and trombones punctuate it, and bass and drums play timekeeping rhythms.

0'20"   *Bridge*
Trumpets carry a melody while saxes accompany them.

0'26"   *Final A-section*
Saxes state the melody while trumpets and trombones punctuate it, and bass and drums play timekeeping rhythms.

0'32"   **Interlude**

Previous timekeeping rhythms stop in bass and drums. Drummer plays tom-toms under trumpets. Difficult brass lines.

0'34"   Saxes play a phrase three times.

0'37"   Trumpets play another line on top of third sax phrase.

0'40"   Gillespie begins solo improvisation without accompaniment.

Dizzy Gillespie Trumpet Improvisation (A-A-B-A)

0'42"   *First A-section*
Band joins Gillespie at beginning of A-A-B-A form.

Timekeeping rhythms resume in bass and drums.

Sax figures accompany Gillespie. Brasses occasionally add an exclamation.

LISTENING GUIDE continued on next page

0'48"	*Second A-section*
0'53"	*Bridge*
0'59"	*Final A-section*

Milt Jackson Vibraphone Improvisation (A-A-B-A)

Accompaniment: piano comping, bass walking, and drummer playing timekeeping rhythms.

1'05"	*First A-section*
1'11"	*Second A-section*
1'16"	*Bridge*
1'22"	*Final A-section*

Second Chorus of Vibraphone Solo (A-A-B-A)

1'28"	*First A-section*
	Accompaniment: piano, bass, and drums, plus countermelodies from other instruments, trumpets call in unison, and trombones echo them in harmony.
1'33"	*Second A-section*
	Accompaniment is by piano, bass, and drums, plus countermelodies from other instruments, trumpets call in unison, and trombones answer in harmony.
1'39"	*Bridge*
	Saxes sustain chords.
1'44"	*Final A-section*
	Accompaniment is by piano, bass, and drums, plus countermelodies from other instruments, trumpets call in unison, and trombones echo in harmony.
1'50"	**Interlude**
1'54"	solo break for alto sax

John Brown Alto Sax Improvisation

1'56"	*First A-section*
	Brass punctuations accompany sax solo.
2'01"	*Second A-section*
	Brass punctuations accompany sax solo.

Full Band

2'07"	*Bridge*
	Trumpets state theme and saxes answer, then accompany them.
2'12"	*Final A-section*
	Saxes play the melody with trumpet reinforcements, accompanied by occasional brass punctuations.
2'18"	**Ending**
	Complex trumpet and sax phrases dart about.
2'26"	Timekeeping stops. Saxes sustain a chord.
2'29"	Dizzy Gillespie plays the key note, then plays it an octave higher, followed by a flat fifth interval.
2'32"	Timekeeping stops. Saxes sustain a chord.
2'34"	Trombone plays the key note, then plays it an octave higher, followed by a flat fifth interval.
2'37"	Saxes fall together in pitch and then slide up together.
2'40"	Brasses play loud chord.
2'42"	Gillespie slides up in pitch to play a note high over the others.

and phrases were even heard in the earliest recordings of Ornette Coleman and Albert Ayler, leaders of the avant-garde in the 1960s. Jazz clubs were named for Parker—Birdland in New York and Birdhouse in Chicago. Parker's melodic inventiveness is so stunning that bop singer Eddie Jefferson performed Parker's "Billie's Bounce" and "Parker's Mood" with lyrics that had been written for the melodies and the improvisations. During the 1970s, a group called Supersax began using five saxes and rhythm section to play harmonized transcriptions of Parker solos. Supersax was able to treat his solos as compositions because catchy ideas are so abundant in Parker's improvisations.

DIZZY GILLESPIE

Dizzy Gillespie (1917–1993) was the first and most important bop trumpeter. Like Louis Armstrong and Roy Eldridge before him, Gillespie was his era's virtuoso instrumentalist. He was particularly noted for unprecedented agility and command of his instrument's highest register. But unlike Armstrong's and Eldridge's, Gillespie's proficiency was unmatched thereafter. Note, however, that only part of Gillespie's impact stemmed from his awe-inspiring command of the trumpet. Great instrumental proficiency was necessary for bop improvisation on all instruments. Gillespie's stirring musical ideas were responsible for much of his influence. By the time he first recorded with Parker, he had absorbed the saxophone-style lines of Roy Eldridge's approach (heard on "After You've Gone," *JCCD1* Track 16), and Gillespie had devised his own brand of bop that bristled with excitement.

Dizzy Gillespie's harmonic skills were startling, and he flaunted them. His phrases were full of surprises and playful changes of direction. He could daringly go in and out of keys within a single phrase, always managing to resolve the unexpected at the next chord. He often zoomed up to the trumpet's high register during the middle of a phrase and still managed to connect the melodic ideas logically. Sometimes he interspersed quotes from nonjazz pieces, such as Bizet's opera "Carmen" or the pop tune "We're in the Money." He often used the quote as a point of departure for developing his own phrases. Gillespie built tension by going higher and higher with syncopated notes played staccato, and then resolved the tension by coming down with legato lines. Moreover, Gillespie's lines made sense even when he played rapid cascades of notes.

Like Eldridge, Gillespie occasionally would toy with a single note, playing it again and again, each time in a different way, creating different rhythmic patterns and using changes in loudness and tone color to achieve variety in his sound. One of Gillespie's methods is especially reminiscent of Eldridge. He could make the trumpet tone brittle and then crack it resoundingly in a burst of high notes. Also, like Eldridge, he could channel all his terrific energy into a ballad, using his exceptional skill with harmony and his fertile imagination to mold a unique, personal creation.[7]

Gillespie's Impact

Gillespie exerted sweeping influence on modern jazz. His pet phrases became stock clichés for two generations of jazz trumpeters; these phrases can also be heard in the playing of pianists, guitarists, saxophonists, and trombonists. During the 1940s, he influenced numerous trumpeters.[8] Some of these players originally derived their styles from premodern sources, but they incorporated some of Gillespie's devices upon hearing him. Though only a year or two older than several of them, Gillespie influenced them as a classic model rather than a mere contemporary. Though Gillespie did not

1. A model of unparalleled trumpet mastery
2. A body of original compositions
3. A string of high quality combos and big bands featuring numerous jazz stars-to-be
4. The use of Afro-Cuban music in jazz
5. A new vocabulary of phrases and ways of matching solo notes to accompanying chords

drastically alter his trumpet style after 1947, he continued to perform regularly and remained active until his death in 1993.

Gillespie also made lasting contributions to modern jazz as a composer.[9] His "Groovin' High" and "A Night in Tunisia" became jazz standards that are still played. After being recorded with lyrics, they gained wider audiences in the 1980s. Afro-Cuban music was one of Gillespie's special interests, and he explored it in his big band numbers "Manteca," "Cubano Be," and "Cubano Bop." These pieces are among the earliest appearances of Latin American music in modern jazz.[10]

After co-leading a combo with Charlie Parker and leading a few small bands of his own, Gillespie began a series of bop big bands[11] that kept going through most of the late 1940s. He formed others sporadically thereafter. His combos and big bands saw a flow of powerful players, many of whom—Milt Jackson and John Coltrane, for example—went on to lead significant groups of their own.

THELONIOUS MONK

The emphasis of bop was on improvisation, but there were a few outstanding bop composers. **Thelonious Monk** (1917–1982) was a pianist and composer whose melodies were unorthodox and whose chord progressions severely challenged improvisers. Monk's compositions influenced the flavor of much modern jazz, and his jazz piano style influenced a number of pianists (see Table 9.3). Several musicians have devoted entire albums to his music, and a few touring bands have constructed their repertories primarily from his compositions. Monk's "Straight, No Chaser," "Well, You Needn't," and "'Round Midnight" became jazz standards.

Monk's tunes have a logic and symmetry all their own. Unlike the tunes of many composers, his are so perfectly structured and concise that they cannot withstand tampering. Monk was expert at placing accents in irregular order—his "Rhythm-n-ing"

Dizzy Gillespie invented the first modern approach to jazz trumpet playing, and he pioneered bop compositional style. He is seen here in 1964 at age 44, playing a specially constructed trumpet whose bell aims up even when its player's face is aiming horizontally or slanting down.

(Photo by Lee Tanner)

TABLE 9.3	**A Few of the Many Pianists Influenced by Thelonious Monk**	
Randy Weston	Andrew Hill	Karl Berger
Herbie Nichols	Bud Powell	Chick Corea
Cecil Taylor	Misja Mengelberg	Dollar Brand
Mal Waldron	Anthony Davis	Geri Allen

Thelonious Monk, the first bebop composer and pianist. Monk's tunes became standard repertory for generations of jazz musicians who liked his unorthodox rhythms and harmonies. Shown here in 1947 at age 30.

(Photo by William P. Gottlieb)

is exceedingly difficult to play properly because of its odd accents. He was especially skilled in ending phrases on the least expected notes, yet making the piece sound as though those phrase endings had been expected all along—his "Off Minor," for instance. Monk employed simple compositional devices with very original results. His "Straight, No Chaser" involves basically only one idea played again and again, each time in a different part of the measure and with a different ending. The shifting accents reflect a craftsmanship that can produce depth in simplicity. The melody is an ingenious invention set atop the 12-bar blues chord progression.[12]

Monk's Piano Style

As a pianist, Monk was a curious mixture. His use of stride piano techniques suggests Fats Waller. Some of his horn-like lines are reminiscent of Earl Hines. In some voicings, Monk's playing suggests Ellington's, though Monk conveys more blunt starkness. Monk's style also resembles Ellington's in the percussive way both men strike the piano keys, the dark and rough tone quality they extract from the piano, and the way that both men sometimes allow notes to ring long after the keys are struck. Monk also likes the lower register, another Ellington similarity.

Monk's comping was not like conventional bop comping style. Nor was it like the light and bouncing approach that evolved from Count Basie's methods. It resembled more of a declamation than the springy chording provided by most modern pianists. It assumed more the character of a bop drummer's snare drumming than a guitarist's chording. Monk's comping seemed to be setting up spaces framed by resounding punches. Note also that Monk often stopped comping for long passages, leaving the soloist to improvise with only bass and drums accompaniment.

Monk was one of the most original of all jazz improvisers. In fact, his inventions sound so different from other styles that some listeners feel it is misleading to classify his style as swing or bop. They would rather see his music in a category of its own. His lines often display jagged contours, and the construction for some of his improvisations is quite playful. For example, he loved to insert a whole-tone scale abruptly into his line (see Figure 9.1 and listen to the ending of "Misterioso," *JCCD1* Track 29). In

Composed by Thelonious Monk; recorded on July 2, 1948, for Blue Note by Thelonious Monk (piano), Milt Jackson (vibraphone), John Simmons (bass), Shadow Wilson (drums); available on the *Prentice Hall Jazz Collection*; reissued on *SCCJ-R* and *The Best of Thelonious Monk: The Blue Note Years* (Blue Note: 95636, 1947–52, c1991).

Terms to learn from *Demo CD*, Chapter 3, and "Elements of Music" appendix: blue notes, 12-bar blues, half-time, vibraphone, whole-tone scale (see Figure 9.1).

Though Thelonious Monk played with bop musicians, his style of improvisation and composition contrasts starkly with theirs. His solo on "Misterioso" is representative of his quirky, eccentric style. Instead of bop's intricate, densely packed lines, he opts for sparse, angular, unpredictable melodies. He often ends a phrase on a note that sounds "wrong," and some even occur at the "wrong" time, though it is precisely what Monk intended. These pitches and timings are part of his playful attempts to jar the listener. Monk's improvisational style is so different from other players of his era that it is hard to classify as bop. His music truly occupies a category of its own.

"Misterioso" is in a 12-bar blues form, but there are no "blue" notes in its melody. The theme is neither as singable as swing melodies nor as active as bop tunes. The rhythm of the melody is also unique because of its simplicity. One note is played on every pulse. If you count 1234 2234 3234 4234, the melody changes pitches every time you say a number, and the arrangement of pitches forms a rocking motion. The low-high pairs of notes are separated by six scale steps, and the bottom note moves along in scale-wise fashion as though walking. Therefore, the pattern is technically termed "walking sixths." There are no moments of silence, just continuous playing until the final note of the theme. Bass and vibraphone imitate the teeter-totter motion of the piano here.

ELAPSED TIME

0'00"   **Introduction** (8 measures)

Monk introduces the up-down motion of the melody by playing a series of pitches on the piano with his right hand.

0'03"   The tenth note is sustained.

0'06"   He plays the preceding figure again to set up the theme.

0'11"   **Melody** (12 measures)

Vibraphone and bass harmonize the melody played by the piano. Drums play simple figures that support the rhythm of the melody rather than using a jazz swing feeling.

0'45"   **Milt Jackson's Vibraphone Solo** (1 chorus—12 measures)

The tempo here is half-timed from the melody statement. Walking bass and drummer striking ride cymbal on each beat, as well as the vibraphone solo, are characteristic examples of blues playing. However, Monk's comping is quite special. Instead of syncopated chording as accompaniment, he articulates only six individual pitches, played sporadically in the lower and middle registers of the piano, to indicate the main chord changes.

1'23"   **Thelonious Monk's Piano Solo** (2 choruses—24 measures)

Listen to how unexpected and awkward Monk's note choices can sound. Some pitches feel bluesy, but others sound like mistakes. Observe, also, the irregular rhythms throughout his soloing. You may get the impression that Monk is playing a game with the listener, always trying to fool you about what he will or will not play next.

2'40"   **Melody** (12 measures)

For the closing theme statement, the vibraphone and bass play notes almost identical to the opening passage. Instead of playing along with them, as he did earlier, Monk picks out

LISTENING GUIDE continued on next page

quirky notes to emphasize, at times poking, like a child, with just one finger on each hand. He chooses individual notes and chords that clash with the melody.

3'02"   Toward the end of the piece, Monk joins the others playing the melody.

3'15"   To conclude the piece, Monk runs down his favorite scale, called the whole-tone scale. (See Figure 9.1.)

Figure 9.1 Piano keyboard illustration of a whole-tone sequence of the kind that Thelonious Monk was likely to insert in his improvisations.

whole-tone scale

his harmonies, Monk is particularly known for combinations of tones that clash resoundingly with each other. It has been playfully said that Monk could make an in-tune piano sound out of tune. Combined with an uneven rhythmic style, these harmonic characteristics made his music quite jarring.

Monk's music conveys a sense of unsettling deliberation. He uses notes so sparingly that silence is almost as important as sound. (Listen to his "Bags' Groove" solo on *SCCJ*.) The agonizing care he devotes to choosing each individual note and rhythm precludes the long, horn-like improvisations generated by most other pianists. His music is not smooth. His piano improvisations convey a sense that he is struggling to decide on every note, and then reaches that decision just barely in time to play it. Nothing is produced casually or routinely. Each phrase is played very emphatically, and with much consideration for its maximum rhythmic effect. Monk's approach is very intense and percussive. He sometimes strikes a note or chord several times in a row, as though knocking on a door. In fact, his rhythms are so pronounced and jaunty that his music does not evoke the easy rise and fall of tensions associated with most jazz lines. In the perceptions of many listeners, Monk's music swings, but for others there is insufficient relaxation and grace to allow more than a rudimentary hint of swing feeling.[13]

TADD DAMERON

Pianist **Tadd Dameron** (1917–1965) was one of the foremost composers in bop. His work covered a broad range—from the bop melody "Hot House," to his simple, but catchy line "Good Bait," to a pretty song that he scored for wordless vocal in the manner of Duke Ellington ("Casbah"). His "Hot House" and "Lady Bird" became standards among jazz instrumentalists.[14]

Much of Dameron's most distinctive work appeared in the form of arrangements for medium-sized bands. Dameron was good at getting a big band sound from a smaller group of instruments. His arrangements had voicings with the thick textures and the rhythmic style of bop piano. Using the strong, clear-toned lead of a trumpeter like Fats Navarro, Dameron would then assign melody notes in a block-chord fashion to alto sax, tenor sax, trombone, and baritone sax. The range of the voicing might encompass three octaves.[15]

JOHN LEWIS

Several of the most imaginative writers in bop were associated with the Dizzy Gillespie big band. One was **John Lewis** (1920–2001), who contributed "Two Bass Hit" and "Toccata for Trumpet and Orchestra." He also wrote hundreds of other pieces in a variety of contexts, ranging from ballet music to film scores, with instrumentations ranging from jazz combos to symphony orchestras. (Listen to his "Django" in *SCCJ*.) A special interest for Lewis was combining classical music with jazz. This idiom is called **Third Stream music.**[16] It usually consists of mixing the instrumentation and forms of classical music with jazz improvisation and jazz swing feeling. The term was coined by Gunther Schuller, a composer whose "Concertino for Jazz Quartet and Orchestra" was written for the Modern Jazz Quartet, Lewis's group.[17]

Modern Jazz Quartet and Milt Jackson

In 1952, John Lewis and three other musicians from Dizzy Gillespie's bands formed The Milt Jackson Quartet. After several personnel changes, it became the **Modern Jazz Quartet**—vibraphonist **Milt Jackson** (1923–1999), pianist Lewis, bassist Percy Heath, and drummer Connie Kay. Together they produced a delicate sound so polished and dignified that listeners likened it to classical chamber music.[18] A substantial part

The Modern Jazz Quartet: pianist John Lewis, vibraphonist Milt Jackson, bassist Percy Heath, and drummer Kenny Clarke. Formed from members of Dizzy Gillespie's big band, this group became associated with "cool jazz" because it played soft jazz that was polished and restrained.

(Photo by Bob Parent, courtesy of Don Parent)

Rotor Motor

Player's view

Audience view

Foot pedal for sustaining

Figure 9.2 Vibraphone. To most people, the vibraphone (also called the vibraharp or vibes) looks like a marimba or a big xylophone with tubes hanging under its keys. The vibraphone is played similarly to the marimba and xylophone, but it is constructed differently. Its keys are metal; those of the xylophone and marimba are wooden. The vibraphone's resonating tubes are like those of the marimba, but each tube contains a disc that twirls by means of an electric motor. The twirling discs enable the sound of ringing keys to project and sustain. The discs give the vibraphone sound a wavering character, an even pulsation called a tremolo. The sound reaches our ears in alternating pulses (wuh . . . wuh . . . wuh . . .). Tremolo is not to be confused with vibrato. Tremolo is an alternation of loudness, whereas vibrato is an alternation of pitch. Some vibraphones allow the player to control the rate of tremolo by means of a dial attached to the rotor motor. All vibraphones allow the player to start and stop sustaining the sound by means of a foot pedal.

of this character was due to the style of their vibraphonist. Despite the mechanical and percussive nature of the vibraphone, Jackson managed to extract a warm, gentle sound and project remarkable presence. This was done partly by Jackson's bluesy, melodic phrasing. Much of the effect was achieved by his careful regulation of the vibraphone's tremolo speed and his fondness for a particularly slow rate of tremolo (see Figure 9.2). He often adjusted the tremolo rate while playing, just as saxophonists adjust vibrato and blowing pressure for expressive purposes. Jackson's graceful, relaxed style meshed with Lewis's light touch on the piano and his gift for understated melody. The group created a cool kind of bop and became one of the best known bands in modern jazz. Jackson, Lewis, Heath, and Kay played together regularly until the fall of 1974 and then regrouped occasionally thereafter for tours and recordings.[19]

BASS

Few bop bassists could approximate the tone quality, agility, or imagination of Duke Ellington's Jimmy Blanton, though most walked effectively underneath the piano and horn parts.[20] Three bop bassists in particular, though, did learn Blanton's ideas and used them for developing their own styles—**Oscar Pettiford** (1922–1960),

Charles Mingus (1922–1979), and **Ray Brown** (1926–2002). (For examples of horn-like bass lines, listen to *Demo CD* Track 27.) Pettiford was present at many of the earliest bop sessions, having co-led an important band with Dizzy Gillespie in 1943.[21] The earliest recorded Mingus solos are especially significant because they are among the first on record to go beyond Blanton and incorporate bop melodic concept.[22] And it is not just their historical position and style that is notable, but also their quality. Mingus extracted a large, percussive sound from his bass, and his solos exude strength and sureness. The Mingus improvisations were developed in a compositionally sensible way that was forceful and emphasized every note. Moreover, he continued to evolve new styles for the bass and went on to become one of the top avant-garde composer-bandleaders in the 1950s and 1960s. Ray Brown was widely known because he received consistent and extensive exposure in tours and recordings with the very popular Oscar Peterson trios of 1951 to 1966. Long viewed as the most swinging modern bassist, he is widely regarded for his big tone, unrelenting drive, and melodic solos.[23]

DRUMS

Jo Jones and Sid Catlett are the swing drummers whom bop drummers cite most frequently as influences. Jones eliminated bass drum playing in some contexts and recorded some of the earliest examples of flexible interaction between soloist and drummer. (Listen to Jones on "Lester Leaps In" on *JCCD1* Track 25 and on Benny Goodman's "I've Found a New Baby" on *SCCJ*.) Catlett kept time with a more swinging feeling than was common to drummers in the 1930s. He was one of the few drummers who was able to play equally well with bands from both the swing and bop eras. (Listen to Catlett on Dizzy Gillespie's "Shaw Nuff" on *JCCD1* Track 26.)

Kenny Clarke and Max Roach

The advances made by Jones, Catlett, and others became crystallized in the playing of bop drummers **Kenny Clarke** (1914–1985) and **Max Roach** (1924–2007). Their styles advanced from swing approaches in at least three respects. First, they **increased the frequency and spontaneity of kicks and prods,** those sounds that deviate from timekeeping rhythms. (When these extra sounds were extracted from the bass drum, they were called "bombs.") Bop drummers were not merely timekeepers. The kicks and prods were developed for spontaneously accenting and coloring solo lines of horns and piano. These sounds served at least two important purposes: (a) communication between the drummer and the solo improvisers they were accompanying; (b) "chatter," the assortment of pops and crashes that provide an energetic layer of activity that increased the excitement of the band sound. (You can hear this in Roy Haynes's accompaniment to Chick Corea on "Steps" on *JCCD3* Track 4.)

A second advancement was made when **Kenny Clarke and Max Roach took a cue from Jo Jones and altered the manner of timekeeping on the bass drum by playing more gently, "feathering" the bass drum instead of pounding it.** This was a practice that became standard for at least one generation of jazz drummers beyond its originators. However, it is difficult to detect in recordings because not all the drummer's instruments were equally well recorded.

A third advancement occurred in the choice of percussion instrument used for timekeeping. In swing style, drummers reinforced the tempo by striking the bass drum and by playing a timekeeping rhythm on snare drum or high-hat. In the bop era, Kenny Clarke and Max Roach extended ways in which Jo Jones and Dave Tough had already been getting away from these devices. During the late 1930s, Jones had

Max Roach, the top drummer in bop, known for increasing spontaneous musical communication with the soloists he accompanied. Roach popularized the "chattering" in bop style drumming. Having been one of the most-recorded sidemen of the 1940s, Roach became a prominent bandleader in the 1950s and remained active in the 1990s as drummer, bandleader, and composer.

(Photo by Lee Tanner)

occasionally played ride rhythms on a single cymbal, as in Count Basie's 1937 recording of "One O'Clock Jump," and Dave Tough had already been playing ride rhythms on a large cymbal that was not part of his high-hat apparatus. Kenny Clarke is generally credited with influencing the widespread adoption of **playing timekeeping rhythms on a cymbal suspended over the drum set.** (Listen to the *Demo CD* for demonstrations and see page 497 for notations of the rhythms.)

Bop differed not only in the instruments on which timekeeping rhythms were played, but also in the way the rhythms were executed. Modern drummers continued the sustained cymbal sound popularized by Jo Jones. However, they did this on neither the opening and closing high-hat nor a single cymbal of the high-hat apparatus. They kept time on a large, thick, heavy cymbal that allowed them to extract a "ping" which would sustain until the next "ping." In other words, Jo Jones had smoothed out the manner for playing timekeeping rhythms, and bop drummers extended this to achieve an even more continuous (legato) sound. Bop drummers also emphasized snapping the high-hat shut sharply on the second and fourth beats of each measure.[24]

DVD *Tracks 8–10*; Demo CD *Track 3*

DVD *Track 7*; Demo CD *Track 2*

PIANO

Concepts of rhythm section playing did not advance as rapidly as those of solo playing. In fact, some pre-1947 Gillespie and Parker recordings contain bop-style melodies and improvisations that are accompanied by swing-style pianists, bassists, and drummers. However, bop pianists eventually mastered **comping**, a technique of spontaneous chording that flexibly interacts with the improvised solo lines. This accompaniment technique had been demonstrated by Count Basie as early as the mid-1930s. (Comping is demonstrated on the *Demo CD* Track 20; Basie's own comping can be heard on "Lester Leaps In," *JCCD1* Track 25.) Swing piano styles began to take advantage of the widening use of string bass. Pianists placed less emphasis on the left hand for supplying chorded or single-note bass lines. By the time bop was well underway, pianists had almost entirely abandoned the left hand's bass functions that were so common in stride, boogie-woogie, and swing piano; a new left-hand style evolved that was to characterize jazz piano for several decades.

Bud Powell

Bud Powell (1924–1966) is the most imitated of all bop pianists. Powell crafted his approach from Art Tatum's, with other borrowings from the styles of Billy Kyle, Thelonious Monk, and Nat Cole. Atop these foundations, Powell incorporated the style and phrases of Charlie Parker and Dizzy Gillespie. The result was one of the first modern jazz piano styles.[25]

Powell de-emphasized the activity of the left hand. In that way, he departed from the stride tradition and the "chomp, chomp, chomp, chomp" style of chording used by many swing pianists. This served to lighten the way pianists had begun playing, even more than the streamlining that had already been introduced by Teddy Wilson and Nat Cole. In place of the striding left-hand figures, **Powell's left hand inserted brief, sporadically placed two- and three-note chords that reduced his statement of harmony to the barest minimum.** Sometimes the chords sustained for a few beats. Sometimes there was no sound from the left hand at all. This comping style became the standard means that modern pianists used to suggest the chords underlying their own solo lines. This development was almost as significant within the history of solo piano conception as the emergence of comping had been for rhythm section pianists who were accompanying horn solos. In other words, **the breakthrough that Count Basie had made in lightening the manner in which a pianist supplied chords and support for an improvising soloist was paralleled by the way Powell lightened the manner in which a pianist accompanied his own solo lines.**

In his prime, Bud Powell had the speed and dexterity to create piano solos that almost matched the high-powered inventions of Parker and Gillespie. He mastered the erratically syncopated rhythms of bop and charged through his solos with terrific force. He employed the horn-like lines of Earl Hines and Nat Cole plus the florid ideas of Art Tatum. **Powell was the model for hundreds of pianists during the 1940s and 1950s, as James P. Johnson had been during the 1920s and Earl Hines had been after Johnson.**

Al Haig

Though Powell lived until 1966, he was only sporadically active throughout most of his career. Of the other excellent players, another favorite of bandleaders was pianist **Al Haig** (1922–1982). Traveling with some of the top groups, including Parker's and Stan Getz's, Haig was a very sought-after pianist and made numerous recordings. His flowing solos and tasteful comping made him a top figure on the bop scene. Haig never seemed at a loss for ideas. His touch was light and clean. In some ways he resembled Teddy Wilson. Haig could play hard, driving pieces or slow, pretty ballads. On occasion he could be quite flowery, but usually he was a very direct, swinging player.

"Shaw 'Nuff," JCCD1
Track 26

George Shearing

Two bop pianists who found much larger audiences than Haig or Powell were **George Shearing** (b. 1919) and Oscar Peterson. Shearing became known primarily for the group sound he perfected: soft, polished ensemble statements voiced for piano, guitar, vibraphone, bass, and drums, whereas Peterson's reputation was established in a trio format with bass and guitar or drums. Shearing has probably the cleanest, lightest piano sound in bop. His music sounds so refined that it has been called "polite bop." In addition to playing single-note lines and octave-voiced lines, he helped popularize the locked-hands style heard in Milt Buckner's playing of the mid-1940s, though Shearing's voicings differ from Buckner's. Shearing brought a very sophisticated harmonic conception to jazz piano. In his combo, Shearing often arranged his pieces so that each note of the melody was harmonized by his right hand on the piano, and played in unison with the vibraphone while the guitar played it one octave below with Shearing's left hand sounding the same note on the piano. Bass and drums underscored critical figures and kept time. Individual solos followed, framed by ensemble fills and endings, all well rehearsed and precisely performed. Everything swung and was well controlled.[26]

Oscar Peterson

Oscar Peterson (b. 1925) is one of the most widely envied pianists in jazz history. His extraordinary pianistic facility and endurance enable him to take tempos so fast that bassists and drummers can barely keep up with him. Peterson's ballad style is full and orchestral. He sweeps the entire keyboard with a command that amazes other pianists. Peterson has a distinctive style originating from the approaches of Nat Cole, Bud Powell, and Art Tatum. He also has incorporated the funky, gospel-flavored figures popularized by Horace Silver. Peterson has probably generated more swing feeling than any other jazz pianist from the bop era, and his concert and club date recordings are filled with sizzling renditions of pop tunes and jazz standards. He has been one of the most popular pianists in jazz, and his trios, particularly those with bassist Ray Brown, attained the status of a jazz institution. Many pianists count Peterson among their first influences. Peterson has remained a formidable force on the modern jazz scene since the late 1940s. His surging power and vitality never have seemed the least bit diminished.[27]

CLARINET

The clarinet has not been an important instrument in modern jazz. One of the most popular instruments during the swing era, it became one of the least popular during the bop era. Only a handful of clarinetists attempted to play bop on the instrument, and none of them gained appreciable recognition.[28]

GUITAR

Guitar disappeared as a member of the rhythm section during the bop era, but it returned as a solo instrument. Though bop was first pioneered as a style on saxophone and trumpet, it was soon assimilated by players of other instruments. Guitarists were among the last to learn bop style, and they did not improvise with the originality of Parker and Gillespie. Jimmy Raney and Tal Farlow were the most outstanding bop guitarists, and they were more visible during the late 1940s and early 1950s than during the developmental period of the mid-1940s.[29]

TRUMPET

Dizzy Gillespie was the leading trumpeter at the beginning of the bop era. But by the late 1940s, Miles Davis and Fats Navarro were so good at the new style that they also had imitators. When Charlie Parker and Gillespie separated, **Miles Davis** became Parker's new trumpeter. Davis and Parker recorded together from 1945 to 1948, and

Composed by Dizzy Gillespie and Charlie Parker; recorded May 11, 1945, for Guild by Dizzy Gillespie (trumpet), Charlie Parker (alto sax), Al Haig (piano), Curly Russell (bass), and Sid Catlett (drums); available on *SCCJ*; and reissued on Charlie Parker, *The Complete Savoy & Dial Master Takes* (Savoy Jazz: 17149, 3CD: set, 1944–48, c2002).

Terms to learn from the *Demo* CD: alto sax, trumpet, ride rhythm, high-hat, bass drum, solo break, A-A-B-A song form, comping, walking bass, staccato, and syncopation.

This is one of the earliest bop recordings. It presents Charlie Parker and Dizzy Gillespie in top form. Their work is guided by the chord progression of "I Got Rhythm" in a 32-bar A-A-B-A format. This is similar to the progression of chords used in the accompaniment for the television theme song "(Meet The) Flintstones," as well as "Cottontail" (*JCCD1*, Track 20). The organization of this particular performance will be easier to detect if you have already learned the strategy for keeping your place by counting beats, as explained on page 461 and illustrated for the "(Meet the) Flintstones" theme on the *Demo CD* Track 33.

The sound of bop is often incomprehensible to listeners the first few times they hear it. The contours of the phrases are jagged with unexpected accents and frequent changes of direction. The improvisers pack their solos with many different melodic ideas in rapid succession. Because of this, audiences often perceive the music as chaotic. But bop becomes more comprehensible as it becomes more familiar, and we can easily familiarize ourselves with it by replaying the recordings. Just as a foreign language becomes less forbidding as we begin to recognize its words, bop becomes more comprehensible as we begin to recognize its standard accompaniment devices and we begin to partition the solo improvisations according to those markers. After listening only a few times to a piece, we can begin to recognize phrases and follow the contours of the solos.

Here are some clues for detecting patterns in this performance of "Shaw Nuff." Keep in mind that the tempo is very fast. You will need to count "1234 1234" rapidly if you wish to follow the form of the piece by keeping track of beats. If you get lost, don't despair. Just wait and restart your counting when you hear a new soloist begin. Following the form of jazz pieces is much like watching a merry-go-round because we can jump on when the same part comes around again. Sandwiched between an introduction and an ending, the main melody for "Shaw Nuff" and all its solo improvisations follow the same 32-bar A-A-B-A form. With the beginning and ending melody statements and three solo choruses, that form occurs five consecutive times, four opportunities to catch up if we get lost. And you needn't wait for the same position in the chorus to come round again if you lose your place. Just listen for the beginning of a bridge; it sounds different from repetitions of the A-section. In addition, your familiarity with the "I Got Rhythm" chord progression will guide you.

You might want to begin getting a feeling for the tempo while you listen to the introduction. However, that section is the most rhythmically complicated of the piece, so you might find it easier to determine tempo from the middle sections of the performance.

The final eight-measure section of the introduction has the horns playing in unison. The horn line emphasizes off-beats, and it contains sudden starts and stops. It is a typically syncopated bop line. In the sixth measure of this section, the horns play the first note of the scale for the piece. Then they play it again an octave higher. Finally, they end their phrase by dwelling on a note that is the famous "flatted fifth" step of that scale. (For keyboard illustration of this interval, see page 456.) This interval became identified with bop, and it is also used to end the piece. Incidentally, Gillespie has said that they played flat fifths "just to be weird." This is consistent with the playful nature of Gillespie's style; and their flat fifth has a teasing effect here because of the abrupt way it is inserted and because the horns never resolve the tension it generates. After that note, everyone but the pianist stops playing. This provides a break in which the pianist improvises a line of eighth notes that fill the remaining eight beats (two measures) of the introduction. When all the musicians resume, we hear the main melody of the piece played in unison by the trumpet and saxophone.

ELAPSED TIME

0'0" **Introduction** (24 measures long)

First Eight Measures
A two-measure pattern played four times by piano, bass, and drums.

LISTENING GUIDE continued on next page

0'07"		*Second Eight Measures*

A four-measure phrase played twice in harmony by trumpet and alto saxophone. The end of the second playing differs from the first.

Accompaniment includes sustained piano chords played on the down beat of each measure. Bass is playing a note on every beat with a relentless driving quality. Drummer is playing ride rhythms on opening and closing high-hat.

0'13"		*Third Eight Measures*

Horns play a line in unison that contains several interruptions, emphasizes off-beats, and is accompanied only by drums (no piano or bass).

0'18"　　Solo Break: pianist plays alone as a transition to the first chorus.

0'19"　**First Chorus** (A-A-B-A)

A　　Melody is played in unison and octaves by trumpet and sax, accompanied by piano comping, walking bass, and drummer playing ride rhythms with high-hat snapping shut sharply every other beat.

0'26"　**A**

0'33"　**B**

0'40"　**A**

0'46"　**Second Chorus** (A-A-B-A)

Charlie Parker Alto Saxophone Improvisation*

Parker constructs his line mostly out of eighth notes, in smoothly rising and falling contours. Comping is sparse.

0'53"　*Second A-section*

1'00"　　*Bridge*

Parker tosses ascending and descending phrases. Piano chords are begun on down beats and are sustained for eight beats. Parker's transition into the last A-section is seamless.

1'07"　*Last A-section*

Piano chording goes back to staccato style and uses more varied rhythms than in the bridge.

1'14"　**Third Chorus**

Dizzy Gillespie Trumpet Improvisation

A-A　Gillespie begins dramatically by slurring up to a high note and decorating it with a fall-off. This exuberance is a trademark of his style. That opening figure is all the more striking because he leaves nine beats of silence after it. Then he plays a stream of eighth notes until the last measure of the first A-section. Like Parker, he also rests briefly during the eighth bar of each section. In the second A-section, Gillespie unfolds another long line composed mostly of eighth notes, and then he rests in the eighth measure. The piano chords accompanying him change every two to four beats, and they are played mostly in a staccato manner.

1'27"　*Bridge*

Gillespie begins by playing three high notes very loudly and firmly. Each piano chord lasts eight beats, and Haig strikes them on the first beat of the measure and lets them ring. Then he returns to supplying a more staccato and syncopated chording after the seventh measure of the bridge. Gillespie fills the final four measures of the bridge with a long string of eighth notes.

1'33"　**A**　Gillespie bases the first 12 beats of his line entirely on triplets, that is, three notes on each beat. After that, he returns to playing long strings of eighth notes.

1'40"　**Fourth Chorus** (A-A-B-A)

Al Haig Piano Improvisation

---

*A written transcription of the Charlie Parker improvisation from this recording is in *Creative Jazz Improvisation*, 4th edition, by Scott Reeves (Prentice-Hall, 2006).

LISTENING GUIDE *continued on next page*

Haig depends mostly on eighth notes to construct his improvisation with his right hand. He accompanies himself with chords played by his left hand. Notice how the rhythms in his lines are similar to Parker's. Accompaniment includes walking bass and ride rhythms on cymbals. The drummer drops "bombs" in the fourth, eighth, tenth, and thirteenth measures. Bombs are more frequent in the bridge.

2'07"   **Fifth Chorus** (A-A-B-A)

Same as **First Chorus** (Melody)

Accompaniment includes more bass drum "bombs" than in first chorus.

2'34"   **Ending**

Same 24-measure form as the **Introduction.** This differs slightly from the way the introduction ends because after the "call" from the horns playing a sustained flat fifth, the "response" from the piano is not a string of eighth notes, but a quick whole-tone scale. (See Figure 9.1 on page 176 for instructions on playing a whole-tone scale. Then play the numbered piano keys in reverse order to approximate the final sound of this recording.)

sporadically after that time.[30] In these recordings, Davis displayed elements of both Gillespie's and Parker's styles, though he used a lighter, softer tone and played less in the high register than Gillespie. (See page 264 for more.) Even as early as 1945, Davis was important as an original and gifted improviser. Evidence of this is found in his combo recordings with Parker and the impact they had on the styles of trumpeters Shorty Rogers, Chet Baker, and Jack Sheldon. (See next chapter for more about these Davis disciples.)

Fats Navarro (1923–1950) was the trumpeter most often mentioned as a match for Gillespie. The wide range, speed, and instrumental proficiency of Gillespie were almost equalled by Navarro. In addition to that, Navarro had a fuller, brassier tone that he used more smoothly than Gillespie. His tone was a bit clearer and more even; Navarro was not as prone to alter its size or color. However, Navarro did not have the rhythmic imagination and daring of Gillespie. As a consequence, his work was more even and had fewer surprises. Another significant difference was that Navarro used vibrato more than Gillespie or Davis, and this element became an essential aspect in the style of Navarro's influential disciple Clifford Brown. The Navarro style was spread more directly to far more trumpeters by way of Brown.[31] So the third generation Brown disciples who are prominent today are actually fourth generation Navarro disciples.

TROMBONE

J.J. Johnson

Bop style was so instrumentally demanding that it is surprising the style could be played on so difficult an instrument as the slide trombone. But there were several trombonists in the earliest days of bop, and a number of outstanding masters had emerged by the 1950s (see next chapter for details). **J.J. Johnson** (1924–2001) is the musician most prominently identified with playing bop on the trombone, though he rarely improvised

J. J. Johnson, the first bop trombonist.

(Photo by Chuck Stewart)

lines as complicated as Parker's or Gillespie's. Johnson's lines were often simple and tune-like; many of his solos are quite singable. Incidentally, this gift for melody was not restricted to jazz improvisation. Johnson was very active as a composer. His jazz albums from the 1950s and 1960s are filled with originals he penned, and he spent most of the 1970s writing and arranging music for movies and television instead of playing jazz.

J.J. Johnson departed from several traditions of jazz trombone playing by having an unprecedented command over the instrument and by

1. using very little vibrato;
2. producing a smooth, consistent sound rather than the guttural tone quality that many premodern trombonists favored. Johnson attacked each note cleanly and maintained consistent size and quality throughout its duration;
3. avoiding the dependence on wide, drawn-out slurs and rips that typified many early players. When Johnson used inflections at all, they were clipped, and they ornamented his main tones in a well-manicured way;
4. playing with a rhythmic regularity and evenness that lent his music a bounce and a smooth swing feeling, especially evident in his eighth-note lines.

Many earlier players had given their trombones a highly extraverted role in jazz by using a choppy melodic style, rough tone, and extensive pitch inflections. Johnson, on the other hand, brought subtlety to the instrument's role and increased its politeness. Consistent with this stance, Johnson's choice of mute was not the rubber plunger favored by growl-style players. It was a cup mute that made his already dark, subdued sound even more gentle and clean. Johnson narrowed the emotional range of the jazz trombone while taking on the quick pace and increased complexity of bop. In other words, he streamlined jazz trombone conception.[32]

Demo CD *Track 79;* *page 469*

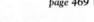

TENOR SAXOPHONE

Bop tenor saxophonists drew their styles from two primary sources: Lester Young and Charlie Parker, and several secondary sources including Coleman Hawkins, Don Byas, and others. Some preferred to play the phrases of Lester Young almost unmodified, while others merely adopted the phrases of alto saxophonist Charlie Parker and played them on tenor sax. The most original players mixed several sources with their own ideas.[33]

Dexter Gordon

Dexter Gordon (1923–1990) was the first tenor saxophonist to be recognized as a bop player. His was one of the least stereotyped bop tenor styles. Though some of his melodic ideas recalled Lester Young, Gordon's tone was deep, dark, and full, not light or hollow like Young's. He used the entire range of the tenor but had a special love for its low register. Although his style was quite aggressive, his work conveyed great ease. There was a sense of authority and majesty about his work. Perhaps the most melodic of all bop tenors, he was known for his well-paced solo improvisations that are logical, soulful, and muscular. He used a large variety of melodic devices to create his lines. His phrase lengths and rhythms were varied, and he combined bop clichés with his own inventions. Gordon loved to quote from pop tunes and bugle calls. More than any other bop tenor, Gordon was known for developing his solos by making firm statements and following through on them. This tendency increased in his playing during the 1960s and 1970s. In his later years, he offered phrase after phrase of complete musical ideas, well rounded and meaty. Gordon was a favorite player for many tenor saxophonists who were later called *hard bop*. Gordon had a strong

Dexter Gordon, the first bop tenor saxophonist.

(Photo by Bill Smith)

recording career from the 1940s into the 1980s, and his playing displayed depth and swing for over four decades.[34]

"Index," CCD1 *Track 15*; SCCJ: "Bikini"

Sonny Stitt

For flowing, powerfully swinging solos, few modern saxophonists could compete with **Sonny Stitt** (1924–1982). His instrumental speed and precision awed other players. His notes were played with a lilt and crispness, the evenness of which was unmatched. Stitt's playing had a consistently logical construction and rarely lacked continuity. During the late 1940s and early 1950s, Stitt was second only to Charlie Parker as the leading bop alto saxophonist, and his recordings with Bud Powell placed him in the highest rank of bop tenor saxophonists.[35] Stitt was not as much of an originator as Dexter Gordon, but he influenced and inspired many modern saxophonists with his own style.[36] **Stitt inspired many players partly because he had enviable command of the saxophone and played with great ease and an unusually high level of precision and consistency. He also systematized a set of patterns that characterized bop approaches to improvisation. These patterns became formula for countless players in the mainstream of modern jazz.** It was much easier to learn these patterns than to learn the less predictable and rhythmically more complex inventions of Parker. In essence, Stitt formalized a mixture of Parker, Lester Young, and his own ideas into a homogeneous method that satisfactorily handled the entire range of tempos and common bop chord progressions.

Stan Getz

Stan Getz (1927–1991) was one of the most distinctive tenor saxophonists to emerge during the 1940s. Unlike most bop tenors, he did not rely heavily on Lester Young's ideas, and he used few of Parker's and Gillespie's pet phrases. He developed an original melodic and rhythmic vocabulary instead. His phrasing and accenting were less varied and syncopated than Parker's or Gillespie's. At times, pre-twentieth century classical music seems to have influenced him more than bop.[37] Getz played in a style rhythmically more like Lester Young's than Parker's. Getz did not usually sound as relaxed as Dexter Gordon, but he was just as melodic as Gordon. His improvisations were less like bop melodies than like melodies in classical music. Some were quite pretty. That aspect of his style fit well with his light, fluffy tone and graceful approach to the sax. Some historians believe his roots in swing era style are more evident than his bop roots. Many listeners categorize the Getz style as *cool jazz*, not bop. (See the next chapter for more about cool jazz.)

Getz was one of the few bop musicians to become popular with the general public. One of the prettiest pieces the Woody Herman big band recorded was "Summer Sequence" by Ralph Burns. It was rearranged several times during the late 1940s. One segment often lifted out was "Early Autumn," a feature for Getz.[38] Other Getz hits also took the form of slow, pretty pieces. His 1952 "Moonlight in Vermont" with guitarist Johnny Smith was quite popular. His 1962 "Desafinado" with guitarist Charlie Byrd was a major event in the popularization of *bossa nova*, a cross between Brazilian music and jazz. His 1964 recording of "Girl from Ipanema," with its vocal by Astrud Gilberto, became one of the best-selling records in jazz history.[39] During the 1980s, Getz was playing as well as in the 1940s, with remarkable verve and imagination. Moreover, he was hiring accompanists who reflected styles several generations removed from bop. (Listen to Getz on "Four Brothers," *JCCD1* Track 28, and "No Figs," *JCCD2* Track 1.)

Stan Getz, one of the original "Four Brothers," the most distinctive of the "cool style" tenor saxophonists, and a pioneer of bossa nova. Pictured here in 1967 at age 40.

(Photo by Lee Tanner)

BIG BANDS

Woody Herman

A number of big bands were influenced by bop during the 1940s. Though most played primarily in swing-era styles, a few had substantial libraries of bop-style arrangements.[40] The best was led by Dizzy Gillespie, whom we have already discussed. A swing style clarinetist-saxophonist named **Woody Herman** (1913–1987) led one of the best known bop-influenced big bands, a favorite among musicians. Toward the end of the 1940s, Herman employed a number of outstanding modern soloists and composer-arrangers (see footnote 38 in this chapter). His most historically significant personnel featured four saxophonists who all had roots in the style of Lester Young and were then assimilating bop styles—baritone saxophonist Serge Chaloff and tenor saxophonists Stan Getz, Zoot Sims, and Herbie Steward. (Listen to Chaloff and Getz on "No Figs" on *JCCD2* Track 1). Though often considered part of "cool jazz" that was identified somewhat later, they were at an early peak of their creativity during the late 1940s, when bop was in full bloom. This particular Herman band has historically been termed "The Four Brothers Band" because it featured these four saxophonists and they often played a piece written for them by Jimmy Giuffre called "Four Brothers."

"Four Brothers," JCCD1 *Track 28.*

The Four Brothers Band was only one of many high points in Woody Herman's career. In 1939, his band recorded "Woodchopper's Ball," a riff-based, 12-measure blues that became a big hit. Herman also had a number of other hit records during the swing era, many as a vocalist. Then he not only survived the decline of big bands but spent the rest of his life leading a steady stream of excellent bands that often featured distinctive modern players whose styles were far removed from the swing styles—there were John Coltrane disciples among his saxophonists of the 1970s and 1980s. Throughout their history, his bands steered clear of ambitious and exotic orchestral conceptions. They always retained a looseness that was identified with Herman's band style. Herman liked his music to be swinging and direct. In fact, he edited out any passages in his men's pieces that he considered elaborate or unswinging. Herman deserves credit for his staying power as well as his allegiance to a simple and unpretentious big-band style. Known for diversity and adaptability, Herman's "herds" (as they have been affectionately called) were long a mainstay of the jazz scene.

SINGERS

The best known singer to emerge from the bop era was **Sarah Vaughan** (1924–1990). Recording with the top instrumentalists, including Dizzy Gillespie, Tadd Dameron, and Clifford Brown, she achieved a position of respect among musicians that sustained throughout her long career. Like Ella Fitzgerald, she also had a large following outside of the jazz audience. "Nature Boy" and "It's Magic" were hits for her in 1948; then her "Broken Hearted Melody" became a million-seller in 1959.

"Body and Soul," JCCD1 *Track 31;* SCCJ: *"My Funny Valentine"*

Vaughan's tone quality was darker and more richly textured than Billie Holiday's and Ella Fitzgerald's. As the years passed, her pitch range deepened into tenor and almost baritone range.

Vaughan's voice control is a source of envy among singers. She showed none of the abruptness or lost tone quality and pitch control that typify most pop singers when they shift registers. She could glide through several octaves seamlessly. Like opera singers, she favored a quick and prominent vibrato, and she milked every note for its last vibration. Also as in opera, she emphasized the maximum drama that could be extracted from each phrase.

Vaughan, a professional pianist with a working knowledge of modern harmony, was an accomplished scat singer. But like other jazz singers, she rarely performed scat

Composed and arranged by Jimmy Giuffre; *recorded December 27, 1947, for Columbia by the Woody Herman big band (five trumpets, three trombones, four saxophones, rhythm guitar, piano, bass, and drums); reissued on *Big Band Jazz* (Smithsonian: 2202, 4CD set, c1983) and *Herman, Blowin' Up a Storm* (Columbia: C2K 65646, 1945–47, c2001).

"Four Brothers" remained one of the most frequently requested numbers in Woody Herman's repertory since its first recording was released. Swing style and bop style are both evident in this arrangement. Lester Young's approach had helped spawn the evolution from swing to bop, and it is echoed here in the saxophone improvisations as well as the composed melody lines. Most of the improvised solos here differ sufficiently from swing style to be regarded as bop. Listeners also perceive this music as bop-flavored because some of the written syncopations were chosen from the favorite rhythms of Dizzy Gillespie and Charlie Parker.

There is no introduction. The performance begins directly on the first A-section of a 32-bar A-A-B-A form. The pace is rapid, so if you wish to keep your place by counting beats, be prepared to count "1234 2234 . . ." quickly. To identify the beats, you might synchronize your counting with the notes of the walking bass line or the ride cymbal.

ELAPSED

TIME

First Chorus (32 measures)

0'00"		A	Three tenors and one baritone saxophone (the "four brothers") state the theme in harmony. Their line is almost all eighth notes. Accompaniment comes from rhythm guitar, piano, bass, and drums. Brass figures punctuate the pauses when the saxophonists take a breath.
0'08"		A	Same as first A-section, except for the ending that prefaces the bridge.
0'17"		B	New theme played by same saxophonists. Brass punctuations fill the pauses.
0'26"		A	Same as first A-section

Second Chorus

0'35"		A-A	Improvised solo by tenor saxophonist Zoot Sims.
			Piano, guitar, bass, and drums accompany lightly. Brass punctuate sparingly.
0'53"		B	Improvised solo by baritone saxophonist Serge Chaloff.
1'02"		A	Chaloff continues.

Third Chorus

1'10"		A-A	Improvised tenor saxophone solo by Herbie Steward.
			Sustained saxophone harmonies provide a soft background.
1'27"		B	Improvised tenor saxophone solo by Stan Getz.
			Trombones and saxes accompany with notes that are mostly two beats long.
1'36"		A	Getz continues his solo.
			Final four measures have sustained trombone and baritone saxophone harmonies sounding softly in the background. That background indicates the progression of chords guiding the improvisation. Each chord lasts two beats.

Fourth Chorus

1'44"		A	Trumpets play a new figure in the upper register. Saxes answer them with a fresh line in unison that extends to the end of the A-section. Brass "kicks" fill the pauses. Drum fills are scattered throughout.

*The score and parts for this performance are available as item #7009276 from Hal Leonard Publishers, 7777 West Bluemound Road, Milwaukee, WI 53213 or *www.halleonard.com*.

LISTENING GUIDE *continued on next page*

1'53"	**A**	Trumpets play their figure from the preceding A-section an octave higher. Saxes answer with a new unison line that extends to the eighth measure. Trumpets play a "tie-it-up" figure in the final measures.
2'02"	**B**	Woody Herman clarinet solo. Notice his full, rich tone and his bent pitch ornaments. His choice of solo notes clearly delineates the movement of chords.
		Accompaniment includes the saxes softly playing mid-register chords on the off-beats, providing a syncopated rhythm underneath the clarinet solo. Sharply executed, staccato punctuations come from loud brass and snare drum.
2'11"	**A**	Trumpets and trombones play a loud, syncopated phrase in unison with the snare drum. Saxes answer with a phrase of mostly eighth notes that extends almost to the end of the A-section.

Fifth Chorus

2'20"	**A**	Saxes and brasses play a simple "shout" figure loudly in harmony. This adds to the excitement because it is the first time the saxes and brasses have played a figure together. Drummer fills the pauses.
2'29"	**A**	Repeat of A
2'36"	**B**	Saxes play a syncopated figure in harmony.
2'47"	**A**	Repeat of A

Ending

2'55"	*Two Measures*	Stop-time solo improvisation by Getz, answered by a "kick" from the brass and rhythm section.
2'58"	*Two Measures*	Stop-time solo improvisation by Sims, answered by a "kick" from the brass and rhythm section.
3'00"	*Two Measures*	Stop-time solo improvisation by Steward, answered by a "kick" from the brass and rhythm section.
3'02"	*Two Measures*	Stop-time solo improvisation by Chaloff, answered by two "kicks" from the brass and rhythm section.
3'04"	*Four Measures*	Stop-time with saxes playing a long, written string of eighth notes in harmony.
3'10"	*Four Measures*	Entire band plays a chord. Brasses continue sustaining it while saxes play a bluesy figure that departs from tempo. Then saxes sustain their final note to rejoin the brasses. Snare drum fills finish the piece.

improvisations. Instead, she usually chose to sing the original words. The focus of her creativity was in recasting the rhythms and embellishing the pitches. These departures exceeded mere ornamentation, but they did not take the liberties that constitute scat singing.

Straight readings of tunes were not Vaughan's routine practice. She improvised extensively with the timing of words, as though the lyrics were elastic and could be stretched to occur almost anywhere in relation to the passing beats. At the same time, she also played with the enunciation of the words and their tone's pitch and timbre. The effect is exceedingly sensual. She drew us in by toying with almost every phrase.

Sarah Vaughan, the best known singer associated with bop. Noted for recasting melodies by seamlessly changing their pitches and rhythms, she extracted the maximum drama and sensuality from each phrase.

(Photo by Popsie Randolf, courtesy of Frank Driggs)

The result was that each of her renditions became an intimate experience. Ballad performances account for her greatest achievements. The slow-paced tunes were excellent vehicles for her mastery of nuance. She luxuriated in the depth and richness of her voice and took listeners along in this celebration of sound for its own sake.

Most singers lose tone and energy as they age. Yet Vaughan's tone quality, range, and technique actually increased over the years. Her performances were impeccable during all phases of her career, with her greatest virtuosity displayed during her final 20 years.[41]

POPULAR APPEAL

With the advent of bop, the status of jazz began to resemble that of classical chamber music more than that of American popular music. It became an art music in the sense that its performance required highly sophisticated skills and it was only appreciated by a relative elite. Jazz had always required special skills because of its demand for so much spontaneous creativity, and, as far as American popular music went, it had long been in the elite. Yet bop crystallized those tendencies, removing jazz even further from the mainstream of American popular music, and turning it into a fine art music. It is important to note, however, that like all jazz styles, bop had fans who could not follow every note and chord but loved it anyway. Most jazz appeals to thousands of fans who like its sound but who lack understanding of its structure and historical

Composed by Johnny Green; recorded April 25, 1978, for Norman Granz by Sarah Vaughan (voice) and Ray Brown (bass); available on *Jazz Classics CD1*; reissued on Vaughan, *How Long Has This Been Going On?* (Pablo: 2310-821, c1987).

Terms to learn from *Demo CD*: pizzicato bass, vibrato; "Elements of Music" appendix: A-A-B-A form.

Sarah Vaughan's style, especially in the second half of her career, is to take extensive liberties with the melody lines of the songs she sings. Vaughan sings new pitches that were not in the original song. She preferred retaining a song's lyrics and changing the pitches and rhythms of the tune, instead of scat singing, though she could scat quite well. The highly imaginative result of this practice is what we hear in her 1978 rendition of "Body and Soul." With accompaniment provided only by the pizzicato string bass playing of Ray Brown, Vaughan continuously toys with the melody line. She stretches her phrases as though the tune was elastic and her breath would never run out. One indication of her adventurousness is that she does not even start her performance at the beginning of the song's A-A-B-A form. She starts at the B-section ("bridge"). Moreover, she comes on swinging, instead of adhering to the ballad mood that is traditionally applied to this composition. Only later does Vaughan render her delivery to the atmosphere of a slow ballad. Note that there is a hint of reverb added to her voice on this recording.

The meaning of the lyrics is not the main focus of Vaughan's style, at least not in this rendition of "Body and Soul." Lyrics are merely objects onto which she drapes an assortment of pitches, improvising much as a jazz trumpeter or trombonist. When Vaughan begins the ballad tempo, she takes creative license with the original tune's notes. Sometimes she repeats words and phrases. In addition, she frequently adds notes that were not in the tune at all. (In fact, she ultimately ends her performance on a note that is a half a scale step below the original tune's final note!) One instance occurs at 0'59" where she stretches out and adds "whoa o oh oh" to fill the pause before the beginning of the A-section "my days in bloom." Another example occurs at 1'11" when she indicates the movement of chords in the tune's accompaniment after "so lonely" by adding new pitches before arriving at "you." She similarly manipulates "romance" at 2'18" to carry additional pitches before ultimately sliding into "are you pretending" at 2'23". In fact, she uses so many different pitches on "romance" that the result could constitute an original phrase unto itself. In that way, she maintains momentum that would otherwise be provided by the sound of moving chords from piano or guitar.

One passage that highlights a number of different Vaughan virtues is the spontaneous sequence of afterthoughts she implements when she is about to end the performance. First, she slows the pace at about 2'58" and crafts an impromptu tag by repeating the final phrase of the song ("I give myself to you"). Notice how, in singing the "-self" syllable of "myself," she improvises a number of different pitches, slurring them together and bending the shape of the line into an entirely new mini-adventure before reaching the "to you." Then she sustains "soul" as a high note from 3'19" until 3'26", where she begins a long, terraced slide down to a low note, arriving at 3'28". Then she starts a slow vibrato at about 3'32", which continues until she ends the piece at 3'36". Two alternatives may help us appreciate the originality that she ultimately devoted to this afterthought. She could have easily made her high note the final resting place for the piece, but instead she slid away from it, venturing a considerable pitch distance down to a low note. This note, in turn, could have finished the piece not long after she landed on it. But instead of leaving it alone and ending the piece, she sustained it even more and then made it come alive by applying a very slow vibrato to it. This latter manipulation almost constitutes another adventure. These alterations exemplify how Vaughan improvised continuously and luxuriated in her sound. We might also be impressed when we realize that she required only one breath to achieve that entire final extension, from before reaching the high note at 3'19" to her last vibration of sound at 3'36". Hearing that final show of daring and virtuosity may help us understand why other singers enviously refer to Vaughan simply as "the voice," and why musicians have nicknamed her "Sassy."

The form of "Body and Soul" is A-A-B-A, but you may not detect it in this rendition because Vaughan sings so much around the beat and does not put the words where they would ordinarily go. Despite this, she does follow its form, and the excerpted lyrics below are provided primarily to help you notice the beginnings of each section. Tracking her progress through the song form, however, is not absolutely necessary for an appreciation of her artistry. These indicators may be useful only if you want such information.

LISTENING GUIDE *continued on next page*

ELAPSED TIME	MUSICAL EVENTS
	Bridge
0'00"	swinging interpretation of the song, stressing the tempo, not the meaning of the words, bassist responding with melodies of his own
	A
0'28"	"my-y-y life'll wreck, my life will wreck your beg . . . ging" Bass begins walking style.
0'44"	"gladly . . . gladly surrender . . ."
0'48"	"myself to you" Bass returns to improvising countermelodies.
0'53"	assumes the ballad tempo: "body and soul"
0'59"	Whoa . . . . . oh . . . oh . . .
	A
1'05"	ou . . . oh . . . ooh
1'06"	"my days in bloom"
1'10"	"so lonely"
1'11"	oh . . . oh . . .' oh . . . oh . . . oh . . ." indicates the movement of chords in the tune's accompaniment adding new pitches
1'14"	"you"
1'16"	"I pi . . . ine . . . for you ou ou ou ou dear
1'20"	on . . . ly"
	A
1'38"	"I spent . . ."
	Bridge
2'05"	Vaughan slides around the pitch preceding the words "I can't believe it."
2'18"	manipulates pitch on "romance" on the way to "are you pretending"
2'27"	generates four pitches for "unless" leading to "I can have . . ."
	A
2'34"	"My life . . ."
2'52"	Voice makes sudden leap to high note on "glad . . . ly."
2'58"	Voice and bass slow the pace.
3'01"	"myself to you"
	Tag (improvised ending that borrows from the song's final phrase)
3'06"	slurs into several different pitches on repeat for ". . . self"
3'19"	sings a pitch for "soul" an octave higher than original song
3'20"	sustains high note
3'26"	Vaughan begins descent down almost two octaves,
3'28"	landing on a pitch that was not the original tune's ending pitch, but a half a scale step below it.
3'32"	adds vibrato to her concluding note
3'35"	Bassist plays the key note, which is the root of the final chord, thereby tying everything together, in opposition to the unresolved feeling conveyed by Vaughan's final pitch.

significance. Fans proportionally include far more musicians than fans of pop, rock, and country music, but even musician-fans do not technically understand what every improviser does. Musicians have a greater appreciation for the underlying complexities in the music, but that appreciation must be coupled with an attraction to its sound before they will spend time and money to hear it. *Knowledge of musical techniques will increase a listener's appreciation for the music, but no understanding is necessary for a listener to enjoy jazz—modern or any other style.*

Bop was not nearly as popular as swing had been. When Charlie Parker died in 1955, he was an obscure figure compared to Benny Goodman, whose name was a household word. And yet Parker was musically a more significant force in jazz than Goodman. Several swing records sold more than a million copies, yet no bop instrumentals ever came close to that mark of popularity. There are several possible explanations for this. Many not only touch on the differences between swing and bop, but they also constitute observations that help explain the historically low popularity of jazz as a whole.

Visual Appeal

One account for why bop was less popular than swing is that bop players presented a more serious appearance, one perhaps less inviting to all but the most devoted jazz fans. **Bop did not have as much visual appeal as swing.** Most swing bands carried singers; many also featured dancers and showy staging. Bop combos, on the other hand, rarely featured singers, dancers, or showy staging. To appreciate modern jazz, people had to listen instead of watch.

Singers

Another factor affecting bop popularity is that, by comparison with swing, **bop had a scarcity of singers**. The bop listener was rarely offered song lyrics or the looks and personality of the singer delivering them. More than ever before, jazz fans now had to follow melodies without words. This made jazz more abstract and less enjoyable. Singers have traditionally been more popular than instrumentalists. Perhaps people like music with lyrics more than they like purely instrumental music because when someone sings a song, it is as though the singer is talking directly to you. This occurs because lyrics are in a language common to both performer and listener. Jazz instrumentals, on the other hand, are in a "language" known to only a tiny portion of the listening public. In addition to offering familiarity in the form of words, vocals offer familiarity in the sound source itself. The human voice produces a sound far more familiar to listeners than that of any instrument. And, because of this greater familiarity, music made with the voice can be expected to achieve greater popularity than music made with instruments.

Complexity

Listeners have historically shown that they like relatively uncomplicated music. Furthermore, they like music to be fairly predictable. They especially like themes that they can sing along with, remember, and hum by themselves. **In comparison to swing, bop is neither uncomplicated nor predictable, and the written melodies in many bop performances are difficult to follow.** A sizable percentage of bop tunes are so complicated that, even if listeners became familiar with them, it is unlikely that they could sing along with them.

It is essential to note that when we say "bop is complicated and unpredictable," we are talking about accompaniment styles as well as solo styles. The point is important when explaining popularity because relatively simple accompaniments backed even the most complicated swing era improvisations. Piano, guitar, bass, and drum parts were relatively simple, and they followed fairly predictable patterns that were quite steady. On the other hand, rhythm section accompaniment in bop style was less regular and therefore less predictable. Then as the 1940s progressed, drummers began to break up their timekeeping patterns and cultivate more and more musical surprises. Therefore, the decreasing popularity that was associated with the development of jazz styles during the 1940s might be explained partly by the increasing complexity of solo improvisations and the decreasing predictability of accompaniment rhythms.

Danceability

Danceability was another problem for bop. **People chose not to dance to bop.** Bop combos sometimes played for dances, but they were invited to do this far less often than they were hired to play strictly for listening. This is curious. People could have danced to bop. It had a steady beat and great rhythmic vitality. But somehow, this was not enough. Here are a few ideas that might account for this situation:

1. Perhaps bop's faster tempos scared away some dancers.
2. Perhaps the beat was not stated simply enough. It had to be made extremely obvious, as it was in most swing band performances.
3. Perhaps arrangements provided insufficient repetition to make dancers feel comfortable.
4. Perhaps dancers wanted singable melodies in their ears before they felt like dancing.

Abstract Sounds

The next four explanations are all part of the idea that **jazz improvisation is too abstract for the average listener** to enjoy. First, most bop melodies and improvisation resembled little or nothing that the average listener had heard before. (Listen to Dizzy Gillespie's "Shaw Nuff" [*JCCD1* Track 26] and ask yourself whether it suggests any common popular music.) **The less familiar a piece sounds, the more abstract it is to the listener.** It is harder to follow when it does not resemble a familiar pattern. The harder it is to follow, the more abstract the listener perceives it to be. And, as a rule, the more abstract something is, the less popularity it receives.

Where's the Melody?

Another aspect making bop abstract is **the barely detectable relation between an improvisation and the melody that originally came with that improvisation's chord progression.** This could upset the listener who expected jazz improvisation to consist merely of variation on a familiar theme, in the manner that singers toy with melodies or popular instrumentalists "interpret" current songs. This problem could be especially acute to the listener who asks "Where is the melody?" because he has not learned that in jazz the improvisation itself is the melody. Non-thematic improvisation had been done in jazz at least as early as the 1920s by Louis Armstrong and Sidney Bechet. But it was more abundant and drastic in bop.

Relationship Between Improvised Lines and Chord Changes

Jazz scholar Harvey Pekar has suggested a third aspect of bop that makes it abstract. He observes that **it is extremely difficult for the inexperienced listener to follow the relationship between improvised lines and chord changes in a typical bop performance.** His argument implies that (a) listeners expect to hear particular relationships between notes in a solo line and the notes in the accompanying chord, and (b) listeners will notice the presence or absence of these expected relationships. As support for this argument, we find that Charlie Parker and Dizzy Gillespie are especially known for stretching the conventional ties between solo notes and accompanying notes and that Parker and Gillespie were less popular than their predecessors. In other words, the relationship between melody notes and accompaniment notes sounded unfamiliar to those who heard bop, and that lack of familiarity decreased the amount of popularity that bop had.

Packaging

A fourth element of abstractness that might account for bop's low popularity is the **relative absence of formal packaging for improvisation and the greater length and amount of solo improvisations.** To begin appreciating this, first note that the most common size for jazz groups during the swing era was the ten- to sixteen-piece big band, but the most common size for bop was the four- to six-piece combo. Also note that big bands, no matter the era, tend to use more elaborate arrangements than combos. The arrangement style that typified swing-era, big-band performances used simple riffs to frame improvisations and accompany them. They also interrupted long improvisations, providing reference points especially effective for listeners who might otherwise be overwhelmed by the newness and unpredictability offered by jazz improvisation. In the swing format, then, improvisations were made somewhat comprehensible because the listener was required to cope only briefly with the unexpected. The riffs that accompanied the improvisations were simple and familiar, and there was a return to familiar material after each improvisation. (Compare Count Basie's "One O'Clock Jump" with Dizzy Gillespie's "Shaw Nuff," *JCCD1* Tracks 5 and 26.) In the bop format, on the other hand, musicians usually preset only the introduction, the theme, and the ending. Sandwiched between the theme and the ending was uninterrupted solo after solo. In other words, improvisation was less and arrangement was more in swing-era big bands than in bop combos. When improvisation must stand by itself because accompaniment is minimal, it is more difficult to grasp than when it is frequently interrupted and framed by familiar material. Bop was accordingly less popular than swing.

Another packaging asset available in swing format is that big bands use much of the same music in live performances as in broadcasts and recordings. This is because using written arrangements allows reproducibility that a dependence upon improvisation does not allow. Remember that both the accompaniments and the solos are improvised fresh in every bop combo performance, but rehearsed arrangements provide most of the accompaniment in swing big band performances. This is relevant to popularity because the listener who had been exposed to the music ahead of time would find greater familiarity (hence, less abstractness) in a swing performance than in a bop performance of the same tune by the same musicians. The smaller amount of repetition in the bop performance would therefore present greater listening difficulty and, hence, less popularity for bop than for swing.

There is at least one problem with these explanations, however. They require that we assume jazz fans actually follow every note in the improvisations. Yet a sizable portion of swing fans probably follow only the written parts, and a sizable portion of bop fans probably grasp only the overall feeling of the music.

Commercially Successful Bop

Further support for these arguments comes when we look at those few bop combos that did achieve commercial success: the George Shearing Quintet, the Modern Jazz Quartet, and the Charlie Ventura Boptet. All three groups used formats that frequently interspersed tightly arranged, well-rehearsed ensemble statements among the improvisations. All offered a greater proportion of simpler, more singable melodies than most other bop combos used. All played many well-known songs. The Boptet had the additional asset of singers Jackie Cain and Roy Kral, and the Modern Jazz Quartet generally produced improvisations that were simpler and easier to follow than in other bop combos. Two points are being made here. First, despite the generally low popularity of bop, a few groups and a few records did become commercial successes. Second, the music within those successes has some of the same features we have outlined for explaining the popularity of swing. In addition, note that Charlie Parker's bestselling records were those he made of well-known songs with written orchestral accompaniments, and the greatest hits for Stan Getz have been recordings of singable themes such as "Moonlight in Vermont," "Desafinado," and "Girl from Ipanema." As a final consideration, combine these two observations: the Getz recording of "Girl from Ipanema" contains a vocal, and it represents the largest selling record in the Getz career.

"Just Friends," JCCD1 *Track 30*

After considering the preceding arguments, you can see that differences in **the amount of popularity enjoyed by different styles of music can be partly explained by differences in performance practices and differences between the ways each style treats basic elements of music.** In comparing the relative popularity of bop with swing, these performance practices are relevant: appearance, amount of improvisation, repetition, the amount of packaging for improvisation, and presence of words in the music. The musical elements of melody, harmony, and rhythm are also treated differently in the two styles. Bop offered higher, faster, more complex playing. Bop featured more variety of rhythms in melody lines and in accompaniments. Bop used richer chords, more chord changes, and a more elaborate relationship between the notes of the melody and the notes of the accompanying chords. Throughout jazz history, the differences between jazz and popular music have echoed the same differences that are noted here between bop and swing. Therefore, because jazz has traditionally been less popular than most other forms of American music, its low popularity is probably due, in part, to these same differences in performance practice and use of musical elements.

Modern jazz continued the jazz tradition of influencing American popular music and symphonic music, but it seemed to carve its own sturdy path for musicians and a small audience of nonmusicians. Bop became parent of a series of other modern styles that were also less popular than swing. Jazz did not regain its popularity until the 1970s when a jazz-rock fusion brought millions of new fans.

TOP NAMES IN BOP	
Trumpet:	Dizzy Gillespie and Miles Davis
Piano:	Thelonious Monk and Bud Powell
Saxophone:	Charlie Parker, Stan Getz, Dexter Gordon
Drummers:	Maz Roach and Kenny Clarke
Composers:	Tadd Dameron, John Lewis, Dizzy Gillespie, Charlie Parker

CHAPTER SUMMARY

1. Bop differed from swing by using smaller bands, richer chords, more chord changes, faster playing with more surprises, and drier, more biting tone qualities.
2. The originators of bop included alto saxophonist Charlie Parker, trumpeter Dizzy Gillespie, and pianist Thelonious Monk.

3. Parker wrote numerous tunes based on popular song and 12-bar blues chord progressions that became standard repertory for generations of jazz musicians.

4. Gillespie devised a very unorthodox trumpet style and led a string of combos and big bands.

5. Monk played piano in a very spare manner filled with unusual rhythms and harmonies and wrote tunes rendered difficult by their odd accents and chord progressions.

6. The ideas of Tatum, Parker, and Gillespie surfaced in the piano style of Bud Powell, who was widely imitated and who significantly altered jazz piano style by reducing the activity of the left hand.

7. Tenor saxophonist Dexter Gordon extended the deep, dark-toned, swing era style and mixed it with bop approaches and his own unique lyricism.

8. Tenor saxophonist Stan Getz blended Lester Young, bop, and classical music to create an original style and became the most popular player on his instrument.

9. Pianists John Lewis and Tadd Dameron were important bop composers, and Lewis continued writing for the Modern Jazz Quartet long after the bop era.

10. Modern Jazz Quartet vibraphonist Milt Jackson devised a warm, swinging style by way of a slow tremolo rate, intelligently constructed bop lines, relaxed delivery, and funky melodic figures.

11. Bop drummers differed from swing drummers by increasing the frequency and spontaneity of kicks and prods, feathering the bass drum instead of pounding it, playing timekeeping rhythms on a suspended cymbal, and snapping the high-hat shut sharply on the second and fourth beats.

12. Bop styles and their offshoots were less popular than swing styles because they used fewer popular tunes, and had fewer singers, less predictability, and more complicated solos and accompaniments.

NOTES

1. "Indiana," "What Is This Thing Called Love," "Whispering," and "How High the Moon" respectively provided chord progressions for the bop compositions "Donna Lee," "Hot House," "Groovin' High," and "Ornithology." The chord progression of George Gershwin's "I Got Rhythm" was used so much that musicians abbreviated "I Got Rhythm chord changes" to "I Got Rhythm changes," which in turn was abbreviated to "Rhythm changes" or just "Rhythm." Pieces on *SCCJ* based on Rhythm changes include "Shaw Nuff," "Crazeology" (also known as "Little Benny" or "Bud's Bubble"), and the improvisations of Don Byas and Slam Stewart on "I Got Rhythm." "Cottontail," "Lester Leaps In," and "Voodte" on *JCCD1* are also based on Rhythm changes. This chord progression is demonstrated on the *Demo CD* Track 33.

2. Listen to Charlie Parker's solo improvisations on "Ko-Ko" on Charlie Parker, *The Complete Savoy & Dial Master Takes* (Savoy Jazz: 17149, 3CD set, 1944–48, c2002) or *SCCJ*. The introduction alternates between brief bits of composed material and improvised trumpet and sax breaks, accompanied by timekeeping from brushes on snare drum. The piece has no main theme. Most of the performance is improvisation, guided by repetitions of the accompaniment harmonies to "Cherokee," an A-A-B-A form that is 64 measures long. The ending is constructed of a brief trumpet improvisation and a "tie-it-up" figure played in unison by trumpet and sax.

3. Sample Parker's extraordinary speed and inventiveness on "Ko-Ko" and "Bird Gets the Worm," both on Charlie Parker, *The Complete Savoy & Dial Master Takes* (Savoy Jazz).

4. Listen to "Embraceable You" on Parker, *The Complete Savoy & Dial Master Takes*. This is based on a 32-bar A-B-A-C song by George

Gershwin, and it became one of Parker's most acclaimed improvisations. Notice that Parker engages in much quadruple-timing while the rhythm section remains in the accompaniment style of a ballad. The improvisation is rich with complex and unpredictable ideas. Compare Parker's dense style with the Coleman Hawkins solo on "Body and Soul" (on *CCD1* or *SCCJ*). Parker and Hawkins were both interested in playing densely packed solos. They also sequenced the notes to indicate every chord that occurred as well as other chords that might fit the progression, even though their accompanists did not necessarily sound all those chords. Both men were doing more than merely double-timing. They were quadruple-timing. It is also notable that even though Parker has the Kansas City tone color and rhythmic swing feeling of Lester Young, he leans more toward Hawkins's preference for complex improvisation than Young's preference for singable melody.

5. The best sources for studying Parker's musical thinking are Thomas Owens, *Charlie Parker: Techniques of Improvisation* (University Microfilms, 1974; see Appendix F to order); and Carl Woideck, *Charlie Parker: His Music and Life* (Univ. of Michigan, 1996). Eight Parker solos are transcribed and analyzed in Stuart Isacoff, *Solos for Jazz Alto Saxophone* (Carl Fischer, 1985); available from: Carl Fischer Music, 65 Bleecker St., NYC, NY 10012; phone 800-762-2328; web: *www.carlfischer.com*. Transcriptions and analyses of Parker's solos on "Shaw Nuff" (1945) with Dizzy Gillespie (on *JCCD1*), and on Parker's own "Now's the Time" (1953; on Parker, *Confirmation: Best of the Verve Years*, Verve: 314 527 815, 2CD set, 1946–53, c1995), are in Scott Reeves, *Creative Jazz Improvisation*, 4th ed. (Prentice-Hall, 2006). Parker's solo on "Ko-Ko" is transcribed in John Mehegan, *Jazz Improvisation*, vol. 2 (Watson-Guptill, 1962). More transcriptions are in Stan Ayeroff, *Charlie Parker* (Amsco, 1979); and

Charlie Parker Omnibook (Atlantic Music, 1978); both available from: Jamey Aebersold Jazz, Inc., P.O. Box 1244, New Albany, IN 47150-1244; phone: 800-456-1388; web: *www.jazzbooks.com*.

6. Like most great originators, Parker was a sponge. He drew effectively from numerous sources. To detect the influence of Lester Young, listen to Parker's 1940 recordings with Jay McShann, collected on *Charlie Parker, Early Bird* (Stash: 542, 1940–44, c1991). Also listen to Young's solo improvisation on "Shoe Shine Boy" (1936), then to Parker's solo on "Ko-Ko" (*The Complete Savoy & Dial Master Takes*). Several phrases recur. To notice Parker's similarity to Young and to Hawkins, listen to Parker's 1943 recordings, made on tenor sax, collected on Parker, *The Complete Birth of the Bebop* (Stash: 535, 1940–46, c1991). To detect Parker's roots in Buster Smith's thinking and saxophone style, listen to Buster Smith's solo improvisations with Pete Johnson on "Baby Look at You" (1939), available on Hot Lips Page, *Jump for Joy!* (Columbia: 65631, 1939–50, c2001); and on "Cherry Red" (1939), available on Joe Turner, *Big, Bad & Blue* (Rhino: 71550, 3CD set, 1938–83, c1994); both selections are also on *Pete Johnson 1938–1939* (Classics: 656, c1996). These Smith solos not only show the slow, narrow vibrato, dry tone, biting articulation, and Kansas-style swing feeling assimilated by Parker, but they also contain actual phrases that Parker used in devising his own solos. To hear the funky lines, pitch bends, rhythmic displacements, and asymmetrical phrasing of blues singers and early jazz hornmen, listen to "Parker's Mood" on *CDD1* or Parker, *The Complete Savoy & Dial Master Takes*.

Parker could also have been inspired by Art Tatum. There are at least four ways: (1) *Including afterthoughts.* Sometimes Parker would play a central melodic idea, then immediately play other, less important ideas, as though making parenthetical remarks about it. In other words, he was not only playing his own melody phrases but also the fills that a piano accompanist would be likely to insert whenever Parker rested. In this way, Parker was decorating his own solo with filigree, before and after main phrases. This tendency is most obvious on his ballad recordings, done with strings. Listen, for example, to his rendition of "Dancing in the Dark" on *Charlie Parker with Strings: The Master Takes* (Verve: 523 984, 1949–52, c1995). Compare this with a Tatum ballad rendition such as "Aunt Hagar's Blues" on *The Complete Capitol Recordings of Art Tatum* (Capitol Jazz: 21325, 2CD set, 1949–52, c1997). (2) *Adding chord progressions (this is called "substitution") to an existing set* and play through them, sometimes during a pause in the tune, particularly at a turnaround. Sometimes this would involve running through several other keys, a practice termed "side-slipping." Examples can be found on the bridge of Parker's solo on "Shaw Nuff" (*JCCD1* Track 26 and *SCCJ*) and on the bridge of "Red Cross" on Parker, *Complete Savoy & Dial Master Takes.* Tatum's tendency in this regard is evident in his improvisations on "I Got Rhythm" and "Tea for Two" in *I Got Rhythm*, vol. 3 (Decca Jazz: 630, 1935–44, c1993). (3) *Asymmetrical phrasing and rhythmic displacement.* Often Tatum would intentionally start a phrase in an odd position relative to the underlying beats and then continue as though the phrase's rhythms were staggered across the organization of the underlying pulse. He could also change accent patterns provocatively, as though teasing the listener with a puzzle of how to locate the down beat within his phrase. This is conspicuous in "Aunt Hagar's Blues" (*Complete Capitol Recordings*). Parker similarly changes the accent patterns, making them asymmetrical, as in the fifth phrase of his "Parker's Mood" (*CCD1*). (4) *Double-timing.* Tatum's emphasis on speed and virtuosity led him to double-time frequently. Parker is particularly prone to double-timing and quadruple-timing. These practices were not common before Tatum and Parker became popular among jazz musicians. The sequence of such influence is worth considering. Parker could have studied Tatum's approaches through recordings that Tatum made in the 1930s, but Parker had first-hand exposure, too. To cite just one example, for instance, Parker once took a job as dishwasher in a restaurant where Tatum was playing, to afford himself extended opportunity to hear Tatum. Incidentally, Parker so thoroughly absorbed Tatum's approaches that, upon first hearing Parker, saxophonist Ben Webster is said to have gone home and enthusiastically told his wife "I just heard Art Tatum on

alto sax!" For more about Parker, see Robert Reisner, *Bird: The Legend of Charlie Parker* (Citadel, 1962; Da Capo, 1975).

Jazz scholar Kent Engelhardt's research makes a strong case for Kansas City guitarist Efferge Ware influencing Parker in the technique of side-slipping. Ware was a mentor to young musicians in Kansas City (see Ross Russell, *Jazz Style in Kansas City and the Southwest* [Berkeley: University of California Press, 1971]). Jay McShann and Gene Ramey stated that Parker received instruction from Ware in harmony, specifically such techniques, while both were members of the George E. Lee band. (See Reisner, *Bird: The Legend of Charlie Parker*, and Gene Ramey, "My Memories of Bird Parker," *Melody Maker* 31 [May 28, 1955].) The recordings of both musicians suggest that Ware taught Parker the technique of side-slipping. Early examples of Parker's use of side-slipping can be heard in measures 3–4 of his solo on "Honeysuckle Rose" and in measures 48–50 in his solo on "I'm Forever Blowing Bubbles" with the Jay McShann Orchestra (*Charlie Parker: Early Bird with Jay McShann and His Orchestra*, Stash: 542, 1940–44, c1991). The use of side-slipping in both examples is distinctly similar to Ware's use of side-slipping in measures 3–4 on his own solo in "Rockin' with the Rockets" (*Harlan Leonard and His Rockets, 1940*, Classics: 670, 1940, c1992). For more detail, see the following by Kent Engelhardt: "Young Charlie Parker and Side-slipping: The Efferge Ware Connection," *IAJE Jazz Research Papers* 1996: 174–185, available from IAJE, Box 724, Manhattan, Kansas 66502; phone 785-776-8744; "Musical and Cultural Factors in the Musical Development of Young Charlie Parker as Demonstrated through Transcription and Analysis of the Improvised Solos of Young Charlie Parker with the Jay McShann Orchestra." (Ph.D. dissertation, University of Pittsburgh, 2000), available from UMI as dissertation number 301 3264; phone 800-521-3042; and "Musical and Cultural Factors in the Musical Education of Young Charlie Parker: As Demonstrated Through Transcription and Analysis of Selected Early Parker Solos" (Masters thesis, University of Pittsburgh, 1999).

7. A masterpiece of this kind was his 1945 "I Can't Get Started" solo found on *SCCJ*; transcribed and analyzed in Stuart Isacoff, *Solos for Jazz Trumpet* (Carl Fischer, 1985). Dizzy Gillespie, *The Complete RCA Victor Recordings* (RCA Bluebird: 66528, 2CD set, 1937–49, c1995) contains "Night in Tunisia," "Manteca," "Woody 'n' You," "Cubano Be," "Cubano Bop," plus Gillespie's solos with bands of the late 1930s. For more about Gillespie, see the autobiography, Dizzy Gillespie, *To Be or Not to Bop* (Doubleday, 1979; Da Capo, 1985); and Alyn Shipton, *Groovin' High: The Life of Dizzy Gillespie* (Oxford, 1999).

8. Howard McGhee, Red Rodney, Benny Harris, Conte Candoli, Kenny Dorham, Fats Navarro, Miles Davis, Thad Jones, and Clark Terry are among the many trumpeters affected by Gillespie's style of the 1940s. His influence did not end in the 1940s. Chuck Mangione's earliest recorded trumpet improvisations in the 1960s contained Gillespie phrases. Trumpeter Jon Faddis appeared during the 1970s, often quoting Gillespie recordings of the 1940s, note for note. Arturo Sandoval also appeared in the 1970s, showing a mastery of the Gillespie melodic vocabulary.

9. Gillespie wrote "Birks Works," "Emanon," "Groovin' High," "Blue 'n' Boogie," "Salt Peanuts," "Woody 'n' You," "Con Alma," "A Night in Tunisia," and other tunes, as well as original compositions and arrangements for his own big bands. See next footnote.

10. These are on Gillespie, *The Complete RCA Victor Recordings* (RCA Bluebird).

11. Listen to Gillespie's big band play his "Things to Come" on *JCCD1*; *Big Band Jazz* (Smithsonian: 2202, 4CD set, c1983); *Bebop* (New World); or Gillespie, *Groovin' High* (Savoy: 0152, 1945–46, c1992).

12. "Off Minor" and "Straight, No Chaser" are on Thelonious Monk, *Genius of Modern Music*, vols. 1 and 2 (Blue Note: 32138/38139, 2CDs, 1947–52, c2001); or *The Best of Thelonious Monk: The Blue Note Years* (Blue Note: 95636, 1947–52, c1991). Monk also recorded these tunes for other companies, but the Blue Note renditions are his first versions.

Monk's "Misterioso" (found on *JCCD1* or *SCCJ*) is another masterpiece of simplicity. A continuous sequence of notes, it has no rests, no sustained tones, just legato eighth notes. These notes are not arranged in the bop manner, either. They are smooth alternations of low and high notes. Pairs of notes, in the interval of a sixth, move up and down a scale, never stopping to rest. All are set atop a 12-bar blues accompaniment. A large portion of Monk's compositions are in 32-bar A-A-B-A form—"Epistrophy" and "Round Midnight" for example. "Round Midnight" is his most frequently played ballad; although Monk's prettiest melody, it is not conventional. Some measures contain four different chords. The tune does not even start on the first beat of the chord progression; it begins on the second beat and fits four notes into the space of that single beat. A Monk solo version of "Round Midnight" is on *Jazz Piano* (Smithsonian: 7002, 4CD set, c1989), or *Thelonious Himself* (Fantasy: OJC-254, 1957, c1987). For biographies, see Leslie Gourse, *Straight, No Chaser: The Life and Genius of Thelonious Monk* (Schirmer, 1997); Thomas Fitterling, *Thelonious Monk, His Life and Music* (Berkeley Hills, 1997); and *The Thelonious Monk Reader* (Oxford, 2001).

13. Listen to Monk play "Criss Cross," "Evidence," and "I Should Care" on *SCCJ*. For greater understanding of similarities and differences among pianists discussed here, compare renditions of "Tea for Two" from Art Tatum, *I Got Rhythm*, vol. 3 (Decca Jazz: 630, 1935-44, c1993); Bud Powell, *The Genius of Bud Powell* (Verve: 827 901, 1950-51, c1988); and Monk, *Criss Cross* (Columbia/Legacy: 63537, 1963, c2003). Monk's innovative rhythmic conceptions are summarized in the way he recast the melody. For transcriptions of Monk solos, see Stuart Isacoff, *Thelonious Monk* (Consolidated Music, 1978; Amsco, 1987); available from Jamey Aebersold.

14. Listen to Dameron's 1948 "Lady Bird" on *SCCJ*. Miles Davis borrowed its chord progression for his own "Half Nelson." Saxophonist John Coltrane and Dameron recorded an entire album of Dameron tunes in 1956, including the ballads "On a Misty Night" and "Soultrane" (Tadd Dameron, *Mating Call*, Fantasy: OJC-212, 1956, c1992). In the 1980s, an all-star New York group called Dameronia was formed to perform and record Dameron's compositions and arrangements.

15. *The Complete Blue Note and Capitol Recordings of Fats Navarro and Tadd Dameron* (Blue Note: 33373, 2CD set, 1947-49, c1995). The influence of Dameron's arranging concepts turned up in later work by Benny Golson, Gigi Gryce, and Sun Ra.

16. For Third Stream music, listen to *Mirage: Avant-Garde and Third-Stream Jazz* (New World: 216, LP, 1946-61, c1977); *The Birth of the Third Stream* (Columbia/Legacy: 64929, 1956-57, c1996); and see Gunther Schuller, *Musings* (Oxford, 1986), 114-124.

17. The Third Stream concept was not new with Lewis or Schuller nor was it unique to their era. The idea of combining jazz and classical music has influenced bandleaders and composers in every era of jazz: Paul Whiteman in the 1920s; Artie Shaw in the 1930s; Duke Ellington and John Lewis, beginning in the 1940s; and Charles Mingus, Gunther Schuller, Stan Kenton, John Lewis, George Russell, Jimmy Giuffre, Miles Davis, and Gil Evans beginning in the 1950s. The Don Ellis big bands of the 1960s and 1970s also explored Third Stream techniques.

18. Modern Jazz Quartet, *Django* (Fantasy: OJC-057, 1953-54, c1987).

19. Jackson is a fluid, clear-thinking improviser with a very fertile imagination. His refinement of bop phrasing is a significant contribution that should not be viewed solely in light of jazz vibraphone literature. Listen to his work on "Django," on *SCCJ*, and study its transcription and analysis in Scott Reeves, *Creative Jazz Improvisation*, 4th ed. (Prentice-Hall, 2006). Also listen to Jackson's solos on Thelonious Monk's "Evidence" and "Criss Cross" on *SCCJ*.

20. Present on more bop recordings than any other bassist was Curly Russell (1917-1986). He was not known as a soloist but was widely regarded as an accompanist. Tommy Potter (1918-1988) and Al McKibbon (1919-2005) also appeared often in the accompanist role with many important bop groups.

21. Listen to Pettiford in a solo role with Coleman Hawkins on his 1943 "The Man I Love" (on *SCCJ*) and in an accompanying role on Duke Ellington's 1946 "Transblucency" (on *JCCD1*). Pettiford's solos and compositions have considerable exposure on Lucky Thompson, *Tricotism* (Impulse!: 135 [ABC], 1956, c1993).

22. Parker and Gillespie melodic style appears in Mingus solos on "Mingus Fingers" (1947) with Lionel Hampton's band on *Jazz in Revolution* (New World: 284, LP, c1977); or *Hamp! The Legendary Decca Recordings of Lionel Hampton* (Decca Jazz: GRD2-652, 2CD set, 1942-50, c1996). See chapter 14 for more about Mingus.

23. Brown first gained wide recognition when the Gillespie band featured him on "Two-Bass Hit" (1947), found on Gillespie, *The Complete RCA Victor Recordings* (RCA Bluebird). Brown solos on pianist Dodo Marmarosa's "Mellow Mood" (1946) on *Jazz Piano* (Smithsonian) or *Jazz in Revolution* (New World); and on "Soon" on Oscar Peterson, *The Trio* (Verve: 314 539 063, 1961, c1997).

24. Most of this discussion will mean nothing without hearing the sounds it describes. So have a drummer demonstrate all these practices in person for you, and listen to recordings of the drummers mentioned. All can be heard on *SCCJ*: Jo Jones on Count Basie's "Doggin' Around," "Taxi War Dance," and "Lester Leaps In," and Benny Goodman's "I've Found a New Baby" and "Breakfast Feud"; Sid Catlett on Dizzy Gillespie's "Shaw Nuff"; Kenny Clarke on Miles Davis's "Boplicity" and Tadd Dameron's "Lady Bird"; Max Roach on Charlie Parker's "Klactoveesedstene" and "Ko-Ko" and on Sonny Rollins's "Blue Seven" and "Pent-Up House."

25. Powell also wrote: "Tempus Fugit," "Parisian Thoroughfare," "Celia," "Dance of the Infidels," and "Hallucinations" (also known as "Budo"). Listen to Powell's "Get Happy" (1950) on the *CCD1*; "Somebody Loves Me" (1947) on *SCCJ*; "Night in Tunisia" (1951) on *SCCJ-R*; "Tempus Fugit" (1949), "Un Poco Loco" (1951), and "Polkadots and Moonbeams" (1953) on *Jazz Piano* (Smithsonian); and get *The Complete Bud Powell on Verve* (Verve: 314 521 669, 5CD set, 1949-56, c1994); and *The Complete Blue Note and Roost Recordings* (Blue Note: 30083, 4CD set, 1947-63, c1994). See a transcription and analysis of "Un Poco Loco" from the Blue Note set in John Rodby, *Solos for Jazz Piano* (Carl Fischer, 1989). More transcriptions are in Clifford Jay Safane, *Bud Powell* (Consolidated Music, 1978; Amsco, 1990); "Nice Work If You Can Get It" from *The Complete Blue Note and Roost Recordings*, in John Mehegan, *Jazz Improvisation*, vol. 2 (Watson-Guptill, 1962); and an analysis of Powell's concepts in Mehegan, *Jazz Improvisation*, vol. 3 (Watson-Guptill, 1964). For biographies, see Francis Paudras, *Dance of the Infidels* (Da Capo, 1998); and Alan Groves, *The Glass Enclosure* (Continuum, 2001).

26. An excellent sampler is *George Shearing: Jazz Masters 57* (Verve: 314 529 900, 1949-54, c1996). Note that Shearing also achieved a successful integration of Latin American elements and bop. Armando Peraza played auxiliary percussion with him from 1954 until 1964. For an interview with Shearing, see Len Lyons, *The Great Jazz Pianists* (Quill, 1983; Da Capo, 1989; 93-101). For technical discussion of Shearing's techniques, see Mehegan, *Jazz Improvisation*, vol. 3.

27. A sample of Peterson's hottest playing is on Oscar Peterson, *At the Concertgebouw* (Verve: 314 521 649, 1958, c1994). Also listen to Peterson's 1952 studio rendition of "Night and Day" on *Jazz Piano* (Smithsonian: 7002, 4CD set, c1989). See John Mehegan's transcription of Peterson's solo on "I've Got the World on a String" in *Jazz Improvisation*, vol. 2, and "Joy Spring" in *Jazz Improvisation*, vol. 4 (Watson-Guptill, 1965). See a transcription and analysis of Peterson's solo on "All the Things You Are" from *Tenderly* (Verve: 2046, LP, 1950, c1959) in John Rodby, *Jazz Solos for Piano*. For more about Peterson, see Gene Lees, *Oscar Peterson: The Will to Swing* (Prima, 1991; Cooper Square, 2000).

28. Tony Scott, Stan Hasselgard, and Buddy DeFranco played bop on the clarinet, but their efforts did not catch on. Listen to DeFranco on "No Figs" on *JCCD2*.

29. Other bop guitarists became known during the 1950s and 1960s; among them were Kenny Burrell, Wes Montgomery, Grant Green, and Pat Martino. Tal Farlow and Pat Martino remained excellent performers in the 1990s.

30. Counting alternate takes and recordings for both Savoy and Dial record companies, Davis recorded more than one hundred selections with Parker. For transcriptions and analyses of Davis's solos from this period on "Klactoveesedstene" and "Bird of Paradise," see Stuart Isacoff, *Solos for Jazz Trumpet*.

31. Listen to Navarro on Tadd Dameron's 1948 recording of "Lady Bird" on *SCCJ*. For a wider sampling, get *The Complete Blue Note and Capitol Recordings of Fats Navarro and Tadd Dameron* (Blue Note); and Fats Navarro, *Goin' to Minton's* (Savoy: 92861, 1946–47, c1999). See page 489 for information on how to get Miles Davis, Fats Navarro, and Clifford Brown solo transcriptions and analyses by David Baker.

32. Listen to *The Eminent J.J. Johnson*, vols. 1 and 2 (Blue Note: 32143/32144, 2CDs, 1953–55, c2001); and *Trombone Master* (Columbia: 44443, 1958–60, c1989). For more about Johnson, see David Baker, *J.J. Johnson: Trombone* (Shattinger, 1979); and Ira Gitler, *The Masters of Bebop: A Listener's Guide* [*Jazz Masters of the 40s*] (Da Capo, 2001), 137–48. For transcriptions of Johnson's own favorite improvisations, see John Leisenring and Hunt Butler, *J.J. Johnson Transcribed Solos: 13 Personal Favorites* (Jamey Aebersold, 2000). See also Joshua Berrett, *The Musical World of J.J. Johnson* (Institute of Jazz Studies, 1999).

33. It is possible to classify bop tenor saxophonists in several ways, including the amounts of Lester Young's and Charlie Parker's styles that are detectable. The easiest approach lies in the dimension of tone. Bop tenor saxophonists preferred either light-weight, light-colored tones or heavy-weight, dark-colored tones. Though there are gradations within these categories, it might be helpful to first describe players in terms of the two extremes, and then form your own descriptions to refine your perceptions. The light-toned players include Stan Getz, Herbie Steward, Allen Eager, Brew Moore, and several players of a somewhat later style (West Coast): Buddy Collette, Bill Perkins, Bob Cooper, Richie Kamuca, and others. The heavy-toned players include Dexter Gordon, Gene Ammons, Lucky Thompson, Wardell Gray, Sonny Stitt, and others.

34. Listen to "Index" on the *CCD1*; or Dexter Gordon, *Settin' the Pace* (Savoy: 17027, 1945–47, c1998). For a biography, see Stan Britt, *Dexter Gordon: A Musical Biography* (Da Capo, 1989); and Ira Gitler, *The Masters of Bebop: A Listener's Guide*.

35. Though he made more than one hundred albums under his own name, Stitt recorded some of his best solos with others, including Dizzy Gillespie ("The Eternal Triangle" on *Sonny Side Up*, Verve: 314 521 426, 1957, c1997); Bud Powell ("All God's Chillun" on *Sonny Stitt/Bud Powell/J.J. Johnson*, Fantasy: OJC-009, 1949–50, c1989); and Gene Ammons ("Blues Up and Down" on Gene Ammons and Sonny Stitt, *Boss Tenors*, Verve: 837 440, 1961, c1990). For transcriptions of his solos on the albums: *Stittsville* (Roost), *Soul Electricity* (Prestige), and *Dizzy Gillespie, Sonny Side Up* (Verve), see Gary Keller, *Sonny Stitt: Improvised Tenor Saxophone Solos* (CPP/Belwin, 1985); available from Aebersold.

36. Frank Foster, George Coleman, Joe Henderson, and John Coltrane are among the saxophonists who have cited Stitt as an influence. Stitt provided the main model for the mid-1950s style of Coltrane; see Chapter 13 for more about this.

37. Briefly in 1946, Getz performed in a bop style like Dexter Gordon, as on Getz's "Opus de Bop," "And the Angels Swing," "Running Water," and "Don't Worry About Me" on Stan Getz, *The Complete Savoy Recordings* (Savoy: 17121, 1946–47, c2002). Before and after that, he favored an original style. Listen to Getz on Lennie Tristano's "No Figs" on *JCCD2*. Then compare Getz with his bandmates in Woody Herman's "Four Brothers" on *JCCD1*, or Herman, *The Thundering Herds* (Columbia: 44108, 1945–47, c1988).

38. Woody Herman, *The Thundering Herds* (Columbia), and *Keeper of the Flame* (Capitol: 98453, 1948–50, c1992). See also William D. Clancy, *Woody Herman: Chronicles of the Herds* (Schirmer, 1995); Woody Herman, *Woodchopper's Ball* (Dutton, 1990; Limelight, 1994); and Gene Lees, *Leader of the Band: The Life of Woody Herman* (Oxford, 1995).

39. Getz, *Jazz Samba* (Verve: 314 521 413, 1962, c1997); and *Getz/Gilberto* (Verve: 314 521 414, 1964, c1997). Do not let the emphasis on Getz's slow, pretty pieces lead you to overlook his exciting medium- and up-tempo style: *Stan Getz at Storyville* (Roulette: 94507, 1951, c1990); *Stan Getz Quartets* (Prestige: OJC-121, 1949–50, c1991); and *Stan Getz and J.J. Johnson at the Opera House* (Verve: 831 272, 1957, c1986).

40. For bop-influenced big bands, listen to *The Bebop Revolution* (RCA Bluebird: 2177, c1990); *Jazz in Revolution* (New World); *Big Band Jazz* (Smithsonian); *Big Band Renaissance* (Smithsonian: 108, 5CD set, c1995); and *Mirage* (New World). See also Chapter 10, footnotes 10–12, and Chapter 11, footnotes 41–47.

41. *Sarah Vaughan* (Emarcy: 543 305, 1954, c1990); and *Sarah Vaughan with Michel Legrand* (Mainstream 703, 1972, c1990). For a biography, see Leslie Gourse, *Sassy: The Life of Sarah Vaughan* (Macmillan, 1993; Da Capo, 1994).

The term "cool jazz" refers to modern jazz that tends to be softer and easier to follow than the bop of Charlie Parker and Dizzy Gillespie. "Cool jazz" avoids roughness and brassiness. Many of the musicians whose work has been called "cool" were influenced by Lester Young and Count Basie. For instance, Stan Getz and Miles Davis are often called "cool," and both were inspired by Young. The Modern Jazz Quartet's subtle, chamber music-like qualities have also been called "cool." Incidentally, this term has not been widely embraced by jazz musicians. In fact, some players have been annoyed to hear it used to describe their music. It suggested that their playing conveyed a lack of passion. Despite this, "cool jazz" is a widely used designation. We borrow it to provide a place for describing the music of several significant composers and instrumentalists.

Journalists and record companies used the term "cool jazz" extensively during the 1950s. They also gave a disproportionate amount of attention to the output of white musicians based in California at that time. Therefore, many people have the mistaken impression that all West Coast jazz of the 1950s is cool jazz or vice versa. In reality, however, the label has not been limited to the work of musicians who belong to any particular race or geographic region, and the California jazz scene of the 1950s had a number of different styles in addition to cool jazz.

Gerry Mulligan, Larry Bunker, Chet Baker, Lee Konitz
(Photo by William Claxton)

Some historians distinguish cool jazz from bop, and much of the music mentioned in the second half of this chapter is indeed simpler, softer, and more obviously melodic than the improvisations of Charlie Parker and Dizzy Gillespie. What has been called "cool jazz" also displays somewhat greater emphasis on countermelodies and preset arrangements. Note, however, that **a substantial amount of music called "cool" is not distinguishable from bop.** A solution to this labeling dilemma might be to use "cool bop" to designate some of the softer, less agitated variants. Listeners do tend to perceive some of this music as subdued and understated, even if its rhythms, harmonies, and the shapes of its melody lines derive from bop.

Here is one more example of how involved the labeling can get: The music of pianist-bandleader George Shearing was discussed in the preceding chapter about bop, yet it also is considered "cool" by some and has been termed "polite bop" by others. What we might keep in mind when considering these controversies about classification is that the playing of jazz musicians who are great because of their originality may exhibit more aspects that are unique to those particular musicians than aspects held in common with other players who came to prominence during the same era. Our tendency to categorize musicians and slot all of them into one style era or another often reflects convenience more than it reflects accuracy. It remains a necessary evil in trying to introduce a large number of musicians in a brief book.

LENNIE TRISTANO AND LEE KONITZ

"No Figs," JCCD2 *Track 1; "Subconscious Lee,"* CCD1 *Track 19;* SCCJ: *"Crosscurrent"*

Lennie Tristano (1919–1978) was a pianist, composer, and bandleader who **created a modern jazz alternative to bop** during the late 1940s. At that time, it was the most substantial alternative available. Though rarely a public performer since then, he impressed his students so much that they carried on his style.

In devising a style of his own, Lennie Tristano began by learning the work of the great masters. Art Tatum and Lester Young were particularly important influences. In developing his mastery of piano playing, Tristano learned how to play Art Tatum's difficult and impressive runs. Another piano playing technique that Tristano perfected was improvising in the locked-hands style, something we first encountered when studying the swing era and Milt Buckner. The eighteenth century composer Johann Sebastian Bach was also important to him. Tristano regarded Bach so highly that he required his students to practice Bach compositions and to learn to improvise in that style. He treated the music of Lester Young with similar reverence, requiring his students to learn Young's solo improvisations by carefully listening to recordings.

Tristano's music differed from bop in many ways. The pet phrases of Charlie Parker and Dizzy Gillespie did not find their way into his improvisations, though his work was equally complex. Sometimes several chord changes occurred in a single measure. Tristano favored long phrases, and his lines were less erratic than Parker's or Gillespie's. The contours of Tristano lines were smoother and less jumpy, and his choice of notes was original. Tristano's lines often seemed composed of notes that were a step or a half-step away from the notes in the chords. They often created an unresolved feeling. Moreover, his lines were not melodic in the pop-tune sense or the bop sense, and his phrases did not swing in the customary bop manner. Instead, his impact tended to be very tight, on top of the beat, with less pronounced syncopation and rhythmic variety than Parker or Gillespie used. Tristano's improvisations were characterized by long strings of uninterrupted eighth notes, interspersed with patches of cleanly executed sixteenth notes. Some recalled Tatum's lines, without as much lightness and bounce. The result was a high-density, virtuosic piano sound, with almost no relaxation of the tension that was built up. Tristano's playing was almost severe in its intensity.

Composed and arranged by Lennie Tristano; recorded on January 10, 1950, for Columbia by The Metronome All-Stars: Buddy DeFranco (clarinet), Kai Winding (trombone), Lee Konitz (alto sax), Stan Getz (tenor sax), Serge Chaloff (baritone sax), Billy Bauer (guitar), Lennie Tristano (piano), Eddie Safranski (bass), Max Roach (drums); reissued on *The Bebop Era* (Columbia: 40972, 1942–51, c1987).

With the exception of Tristano, Konitz, and Bauer, these musicians did not usually work together. This recording combined performers who had received the highest number of votes in various categories ("best pianist," "best alto saxophonist," etc.) of a popularity poll run in 1949 by the jazz magazine *Metronome*.

"No Figs" is included as an example of cool jazz, particularly the unique modern styles of composer-pianist Lennie Tristano and his best known student, Lee Konitz. A number of different styles have been called "cool," but Tristano's was one of the first. His was also among the few modern styles not closely tied to bop. This selection was chosen because it is one of the only recordings that brings together Tristano, Konitz, and the eminent tenor saxophonist Stan Getz. We heard Getz in Woody Herman's "Four Brothers," a performance that combined the influence of Lester Young and bop. Getz has been tagged variously as "cool" or "bop," though his style is so unique that it deserves a category of its own. Coincidentally, "No Figs" also features baritone saxophonist Serge Chaloff, another one of the original "four brothers." (Like Chaloff, the remaining soloists here, clarinetist Buddy DeFranco and trombonist Kai Winding, are not ordinarily classified as "cool." Most jazz historians classify them as bop.)

The performance begins with clarinet, alto sax, tenor sax, baritone sax, and guitar, accompanied by piano comping, walking bass, and drums. Guitar is used here as a melody instrument instead of providing chordal accompaniment. The drummer is using brushes to play timekeeping rhythms on the snare drum while snapping shut his high-hat sharply on the second and fourth beats of each measure. His close coordination with walking bass provides a steady and buoyant foundation.

"No Figs" is based on the chord progression of "Indiana," with a form that can be described roughly as 32-bar A-B-A-C. (We could describe it as A-B-A-B′ because the second "B" repeats portions of the first "B," but "C" is used here for the sake of simplicity.) This performance is composed of four choruses. No soloist plays for an entire chorus, and Konitz solos only during the last eight measures of the first chorus. The opening theme statement runs through the first three eight-bar sections of "Indiana" form, designated here as A, B, and A. Then the improvisation by Konitz occupies the fourth section, C. Getz and Winding split a chorus. Then DeFranco and Chaloff split another. Tristano solos for the first half of the fourth chorus, and then the theme and ending occupy the second half.

ELAPSED
TIME

0′00″   **Theme** (A-B-A of the "Indiana" chord progression)

A butterfly-like effect is created by complicated lines of triplets and sixteenth notes played in various harmonies and unisons by clarinet, alto sax, tenor sax, baritone sax, guitar, and piano. Notice how instrument sounds appear, disappear, and reappear in different combinations, some in harmony, some in unison. After the initial flurry of notes, a simpler line emerges with longer notes, less harmony, more unisons and octaves. Then the butterfly-like effect returns, followed again by the simpler line.

0′29″   **Lee Konitz Alto Sax Improvisation** (the 8-measure C-section)

Konitz confines himself to the upper register of his instrument. Notice his soft tone and legato phrasing. He begins his solo in a very smooth manner, using mostly eighth notes. Then he bases his phrases on triplets and ends his solo with a crisp burst of sixteenth notes.

To appreciate how much jazz alto saxophone timbres vary, contrast the Konitz sound here with the Johnny Hodges sound on "Prelude to a Kiss."

0′43″   **Stan Getz Tenor Sax Improvisation** (16 measures, A-B)

Getz's improvisation exemplifies his own light and graceful approach. His solo has a lyric singing quality. This improvisation is filled with pretty melodies, though the fluidity is occasionally interrupted with bursts of notes forming phrases that mimic the Tristano-Konitz style.

LISTENING GUIDE continued on next page

Like Konitz, Getz also stays in the upper register. This makes his tone sound like Konitz's even more than would be expected from their mutual allegiance to Lester Young's light-weight, dry timbre. Notice that Getz's solo contains a larger variety of rhythms than Konitz used.

To appreciate how much tenor saxophone timbres vary, contrast the Getz sound here with Ben Webster's on "Cottontail" and John Coltrane's on "Flamenco Sketches."

1'03"   **Kai Winding Trombone Improvisation** (16 measures, A-C)

1'25"   **Buddy DeFranco Clarinet Improvisation** (16 measures, A-B)

1'47"   **Serge Chaloff Baritone Sax Improvisation** (16 measures, A-C)

2'08"   **Lennie Tristano Piano Improvisation** (16 measures, A-B)

Almost all of Tristano's solo is in quadruple time and has the same character as the introduction that he wrote for this piece. He accents the final note of each phrase ending. Most of his notes are harmonized, making his line sound as though played in locked-hands style.

2'29"   **Theme** (8 measures, A)

2'42"   **Ending** (8 measures, C)

The line is in quadruple time, first by the piano alone, then joined by saxes, guitar, and clarinet, with the low-pitched sound of the baritone sax becoming prominent at the end. No bass or drums.

Most of Tristano's output is historically significant, and two performances—"Intuition" and "Digression"—were particularly precedent-setting.[1] As part of their training process during the mid-1940s, Tristano and his musicians had practiced improvising collectively without preset melodies, tempo, meter, or chord progressions. (See Appendix B for explanations of these terms.) Then, in 1949, they allowed a sample of this to be recorded. These performances were truly free of preset form, though much of the music conveyed a feeling of steady tempo and consistent key. In other words, **Tristano and his colleagues recorded collectively improvised "free" jazz long before Ornette Coleman and Cecil Taylor were to become famous for it.**

Tristano made very few recordings during his career—the equivalent of about seven albums. His records remain collector's items because they did not sell well. Today they are quite rare. Tristano's force on the jazz scene was partly felt through the teaching that was his primary occupation from 1951 to his death in 1978. Jazz insiders are familiar with his work and accord him significant respect. Most players after the 1950s, however, perceived him as an underground figure, or they are altogether unaware of him. He influenced a number of excellent jazz musicians,[2] but like Tristano himself, most of them also remain unknown to the majority of jazz musicians and fans. Bill Evans and Cecil Taylor are well-known exceptions, and the Tristano legacy continued because Evans, in turn, influenced Herbie Hancock, Chick Corea, and Keith Jarrett.[3]

"No Figs" and "My Lady," JCCD2 Tracks 1 and 2; "Subconscious-Lee," CCD1 Track 19; SCCJ: "Crosscurrent"

Tristano's most talented students during the 1940s were alto saxophonist **Lee Konitz** (b. 1927), tenor saxophonist Warne Marsh (1927–1987), and guitarist Billy Bauer. Together with bass and drums, Tristano joined his students and made recordings that still dazzle other musicians.

In the late 1940s, the Lee Konitz saxophone style constituted a new sound in jazz. Konitz's command of the alto saxophone astonished fellow musicians.[4] In fact, players often argued about whether it was Konitz or Parker who had the most speed and

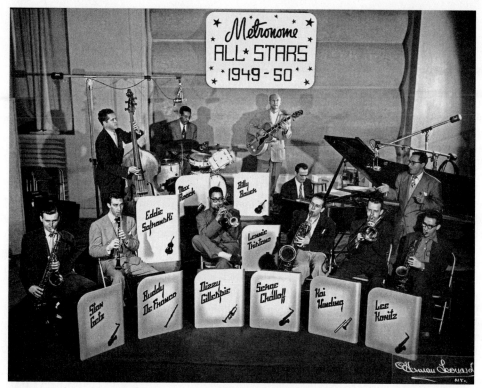

The January 10, 1950, recording session that produced "No Figs": Pete Rugolo conducts and pianist-composer Lennie Tristano plays with the all-stars. Getz, Konitz, Bauer, and Tristano are often tagged "cool jazz" style. The remaining musicians here are more closely tied to bop style. (Gillespie's solo is not heard on the *Jazz Classics* version of this performance.)

(Photo by Herman Leonard, courtesy of Bob Asen—Metronome Collection)

agility. These two saxophonists were in a class by themselves, outplaying all others. In addition, it is historically important to remember that **Konitz developed and maintained his own Tristano-inspired style at a time when most other young alto saxophonists were imitating Charlie Parker.**

The Konitz style was almost totally unrelated to Parker's.[5] Konitz played with a dry, airy tone that was soft in texture and light in weight. He employed a slow vibrato and preferred to use the alto saxophone's high register instead of its deeper tones. His sound is the alto saxophone equivalent of Lester Young's sound on tenor. This was a historic departure from the warm, syrupy lushness of alto saxophonists Benny Carter and Johnny Hodges. It also departed from the biting, bittersweet sound of Charlie Parker. Also, Konitz was not inclined to sprinkle his improvisations with quotes from pop tunes as Parker did. Konitz also differed from Parker in rhythm and articulation, rarely using staccato. His syncopations were less plentiful than Parker's. Almost all his lines were legato and not percussive at all. The overall effect of the Konitz style typified "cool jazz." (Compare the Konitz solo on "No Figs" [*JCCD2* Track 1] with solos by Parker on "Shaw Nuff" [*JCCD1* Track 26] and Hodges on "Prelude to a Kiss" [*JCCD1* Track 23].)

During the late 1940s and early 1950s, most of Konitz's solo work consisted of lines in the style of Tristano's densely packed piano improvisations. Then during the middle 1950s, especially after 1954, Konitz gradually changed his style. The most obvious difference was that he slowed his playing. He also used more ways to construct his phrases. He made more frequent use of silence and occasionally imparted a bluesy flavor to his work. His manner lost some of its snap and freshness as well as speed and agility. With his new style, Konitz occasionally performed on tenor instead of alto saxophone, and he was not as

Lee Konitz, the leading alto saxophonist in cool jazz. Konitz devised a modern jazz alternative to the style of Charlie Parker.

(Photo by Bob Parent, courtesy of Don Parent)

Composed by Bill Russo; recorded in 1952 for Capitol by the Stan Kenton big band (five trumpets, five trombones, five saxes, guitar, piano, bass, drums); available on Stan Kenton, *New Concepts in Artistry in Rhythm* (Capitol: 92865, 1952, c1989).

This selection was chosen to provide a brief introduction to the style of alto saxophonist Lee Konitz and a taste of the arranging practices that typified the Stan Kenton big band. The piece first appeared on an album that ultimately became the favorite Kenton work for many jazz musicians. The rich brass sounds that occasionally break into the foreground exemplify the Kenton style. Bill Russo was one of several very talented composers who loved twentieth-century symphonic music and emulated it in their work for Kenton's bands. Kenton promoted their work as serious concert music, even though his group was a large dance band. Note that, despite the sometimes loud, very heavy brass chords, this music is routinely considered to be cool jazz. This may be due in part to the pale, dry tone and the airy, floating quality conveyed by Konitz.

Aside from just experiencing the purity and originality of the sounds on this recording, you also may wish to tally a few distinctive features. (1) Low-pitched brass chords inch along underneath the high-pitched alto sax solo line. Aside from the notes of the string bass, these brass chords provide the clearest suggestion of harmony that ties the piece together. Most of the time, no guitar or piano chords are audible. (2) Almost entirely legato, the phrases of Konitz show no staccato articulation. (3) No swing feeling is evoked by this music, not even from the walking bass. (4) Although this music is usually classified with modern jazz, "My Lady" demonstrates no bop influence. (5) The Konitz part to "My Lady" is largely improvised. Only 12 measures, just 48 beats, of the entire piece had a written line indicated for the sax solo. The only other guidance given to Konitz was chord changes to follow while he improvised. (In most passages, the chords change every two beats, often in a scale-wise manner.) This situation was unusual, particularly in big bands. Ordinarily a pop tune provided a melody, and its chord changes provided guidance for solo improvisation after the melody itself was played. (6) The overall architecture of the piece is arch-form, first soft and light textured, then heavier and heavier, louder and louder, then gradually lighter and softer. It ends as it began, with a delicate, haunting, otherworldly beauty.

ELAPSED
TIME

0'00"	Konitz begins by improvising in high register, accompanied just by walking bass playing two notes on every beat.
0'09"	Guitar chords enter accompaniment.
0'18"	Trombones play softly in harmony, beginning on the downbeat of the main section of the song form. Konitz plays the written melody, beginning on the second beat of the song form.
0'28"	Muted trumpets enter accompaniment as sustained chords.
0'32"	Saxophones enter in harmony as sustained chords.
0'36"	Brass re-enter in harmony.
0'57"	Brass re-enter in harmony playing chords that last two beats each, moving down the scale. (Careful listening might reveal bass trombone and baritone sax in the mix.)
	Finger cymbal rings every other beat.
1'00"	No longer tied to any written line, Konitz returns to improvising over the chords that are moving underneath him, played by low-pitched trumpets and trombones.
	A finger cymbal rings on off-beats from 0'52" to 1'10".
1'13"	Very loud trumpets, trombones, and saxes play a descending scale in harmony, a typical Kenton device.
1'17"	Brass dramatically get softer.
1'37"	Trombone unison figure fills pause in sax solo.
1'42"	Konitz plays a figure in high register, and then echoes it in middle register.
1'54"	Konitz devises a figure in the middle register, then low register, and develops it in the high register. Accompaniment includes scale-wise movement of low-pitched chords by band.
2'04"	Konitz enters high register, and accompaniment gets louder and higher-pitched.

LISTENING GUIDE *continued on next page*

2'08"	Thick brass chords snake around high register loudly, with high-pitched trumpet notes on top.
2'14"	Very high-pitched trumpet note tops off the louder and louder brass passage that is inching along when Konitz gives up competing with them.
2'16"	Peak of brass excitement is relaxed with four cascades played by saxophones in harmony, a Kenton trademark. (Konitz is playing the top notes of the sax section's cascades, which is the only remaining part of the piece for him that is not improvised.)
2'20"	Konitz returns to improvising.
2'26"	Konitz double-times a complex line to 2'35" that almost swings.
2'34"	Trombones introduce new figure in their high register while sax solo briefly pauses.
2'49"	Muted trumpets enter in harmony with sustained tones over the low-pitched trombone notes.
3'07"	Konitz plays all alone.
3'14"	Sax is answered by one soft guitar chord.

fleet.[6] Among listeners who knew only his earlier work, many found this style difficult to recognize as belonging to Konitz. He toured and recorded for many years after changing his style, thereby giving jazz fans an extended exposure to this additional sound. With this alternative, Konitz became an influence on new generations of saxophonists in the 1970s and 1980s.

BIRTH OF THE COOL

In 1949 and 1950, trumpeter **Miles Davis** and arranger Gil Evans organized recording sessions of a nine-piece band known today as the Miles Davis Nonet or Birth of the Cool band.[7] The group was created by abbreviating Claude Thornhill's big band.[8]

A recording session for the 1950 "Birth of the Cool" band led by trumpeter Miles Davis. Alto saxophonist Lee Konitz and baritone saxophonist Gerry Mulligan are seated at his left. Notice the tuba in the foreground.

(Photo by Popsie Randolf, courtesy of Frank Driggs)

The nonet included Lee Konitz, who had been a member of the Thornhill band, and baritone saxophonist Gerry Mulligan, who had played and arranged for Thornhill. Like Davis, they employed light-weight tone qualities and preferred a subdued effect. Though the nonet used a standard rhythm section of piano, bass, and drums, a departure from custom was made by filling out the instrumentation with French horn and tuba. No tenor saxophone or guitar was used, though a trombone was included. (Listen to "Boplicity" in *SCCJ*.)

WEST COAST STYLE OF THE 1950s

The sound and feeling of the Birth of the Cool sessions was similar to work by several groups of predominantly white jazz musicians centered in Los Angeles during the 1950s. The influence of Konitz and Davis was evident there in saxophone and trumpet styles, respectively. Moreover, arrangers sometimes put together bands that placed tuba and French horn in melodic roles, as in the Birth of the Cool band. Though much of this West Coast jazz was indistinguishable from bop, some performances felt more like the Count Basie-Lester Young combo recordings of the 1930s than the Charlie Parker-Dizzy Gillespie collaborations of the 1940s. Some of the music was especially subdued and understated, precisely those qualities that journalists associated with Lester Young and the term "cool jazz." Frequently the music featured solo improvisations that were smoother and more obviously tune-like than bop improvisations. In addition, more emphasis was placed on composition and arrangement.

A number of other jazz styles were flourishing in California at this time, but journalists specified only this particular group of styles as "West Coast Jazz." Journalists and record companies often neglected the other styles. This accidentally conveyed the impression that cool jazz was the only style of significance in California during the 1950s. Rather than using the blanket term "West Coast Jazz," they could have done better by choosing a more specific designation such as "West Coast Cool Jazz." They also could have acknowledged that some of the playing by even the coolest of these musicians was hard swinging and hot. This textbook uses the "West Coast" term to designate only the musicians who played this particular collection of cool jazz styles because historians usually mean a West Coast brand of cool jazz when they say "West Coast Style."[9]

Many of the musicians associated with West Coast cool jazz first came to the Los Angeles area in big bands. Several such groups had disbanded there during the demise of the big band boom in the 1940s. The most notable of these were led by Stan Kenton and Woody Herman (see Table 10.2). Some of their musicians settled in California to earn livelihoods in the commercial music industry, especially in the studios that developed there to satisfy the need for background music in films. After settling, many of these players sporadically returned to those big bands for tours and recordings. Eventually the television industry also employed a considerable number of these men. Commercial music provided their livelihoods, and jazz became a part-time occupation for all but a tiny few.

Big Bands

Every style and era in jazz has been represented at least once in a large-ensemble format known as a "big band." Leaders of these bands often offer styles in addition to the one in vogue at the time of their formation. Sometimes they sample idioms that span several decades. Pianist-arranger **Stan Kenton** (1912–1979) led the best known succession of big bands in modern jazz, and he presented repertories that spanned several eras and featured numerous styles.[10] Kenton's name first became well known during the 1940s while he was leading a big band in the swing era style. The idioms of his subsequent bands were sometimes labeled "big band bop." At one time, Kenton dubbed his music "progressive jazz." And then, during the 1970s, portions of his repertory tapped jazz-rock. Despite all these labels and shifts in flavor, Kenton's contributions and the styles of his musicians are linked most closely to cool jazz. They are linked particularly with the West Coast, where he was based for many years and where so many of his musicians settled during the 1940s and 1950s (see Tables 10.1 and 10.2). Kenton acknowledged Claude Thornhill, father of the cool style for big band, as a major influence on his own approach to band writing. Kenton's featured musicians drew liberally from the cool jazz styles of Lester Young, Miles Davis, and Lee Konitz; Konitz himself played with the band for more than a year.

Kenton is one of the few jazz musicians besides Louis Armstrong, Benny Goodman, and Duke Ellington to become widely known by the American public. However, his name, unlike Ellington's or Armstrong's, represented a huge collection of different composers, arrangers, and soloists. Kenton created a composing and arranging style which owed much to Claude Thornhill, Fletcher Henderson, and Benny Carter. He is well known for the compositions and arrangements he originated himself, particularly in recordings of "Eager Beaver" and "Artistry in Rhythm," his band's theme song.[11] He also developed a piano style that was influenced partly by Earl Hines.

Kenton created a distinctive band style that is immediately recognizable. Though he did record ordinary arrangements of numerous pop tunes, and he did turn out a large body of dance music, the most impressive work he presented was nonswinging concert

TABLE 10.1　A Few West Coast Style Musicians of the 1950s

ALTO SAX
Art Pepper
Bud Shank
Herb Geller
Lennie Niehaus
Paul Desmond

BARITONE SAX
Gerry Mulligan
Bob Gordon

GUITAR
Howard Roberts
Barney Kessel
Jim Hall

PIANO
Hampton Hawes
Claude Williamson
Russ Freeman
Pete Jolly
Vince Guaraldi
Andre Previn
Dave Brubeck

BASS
Red Mitchell
Red Callender
Leroy Vinnegar
Buddy Clark
Carson Smith
Howard Rumsey
Curtis Counce
Joe Mondragon
Monty Budwig

DRUMS
Mel Lewis
Shelly Manne
Larry Bunker
Chico Hamilton

COMPOSER-ARRANGERS
Gerry Mulligan
Dave Brubeck
Shorty Rogers

Dave Pell
John Graas
Jimmy Giuffre
Bill Holman
Marty Paich
Stan Kenton

TRUMPET
Chet Baker
Conte Candoli
Jack Sheldon
Shorty Rogers
Stu Williamson
Carl Perkins

TROMBONE
Bob Brookmeyer
Frank Rosolino
Bob Enevoldsen
Milt Bernhart

TENOR SAX
Bill Perkins
Richie Kamuca
Bob Cooper
Jack Montrose
Buddy Collette
Dave Pell
Bill Holman
Jimmy Giuffre
Zoot Sims

TABLE 10.2	A Few of the West Coast Style Players Who Played with the Woody Herman and Stan Kenton Big Bands		
KENTON			**HERMAN**
Lee Konitz	Stan Levey		Bill Perkins
Art Pepper	Shelly Manne		Richie Kamuca
Bud Shank	Bob Cooper		Shorty Rogers
Lennie Niehaus	Frank Rosolino		Jimmy Giuffre
Bill Holman	Stu Williamson		Conte Candoli
Richie Kamuca	Milt Bernhart		Stan Levey
Conte Candoli	Zoot Sims		Shelly Manne
Jack Sheldon			Red Mitchell
Mel Lewis			Stu Williamson
			Zoot Sims

Note: The two bands used many of the same musicians. Most were white, were good sight readers, and played in similar styles.

music that vividly exposed rich, modern harmonies. Two and three moving parts were sometimes presented simultaneously. The weighty pieces differ from the dance-band tradition of big band jazz. A classical feeling was common in his music. In fact, the musicianship of his players was very high, with ensemble precision and tuning sometimes approaching the sterling standards of symphony orchestras. Usually performed without vibrato, his brass and saxophone parts had a dry quality that has sometimes been termed "transparent." Some pieces featured trumpet parts which were high-pitched, loud, and often block-voiced as five-note chords. These sounds were combined with

Stan Kenton's 1947 band, a platform for ambitious concert works, the most popular of modern big bands. The five trumpets, five trombones instrumentation was popularized by Kenton and adopted by college "stage bands" thereafter. (A trumpeter closest to the drummer is mostly hidden in this photo of a rehearsal with Kenton sitting at the piano.)

(Photo by William P. Gottlieb)

saxophone passages written in long strings of sixteenth notes which came up from the low range of the ensemble like fountains or descended like waterfalls.

Though Kenton's performances usually ranged from the softest to the loudest of sounds, Kenton earned a reputation for leading the loudest big band. This was partly due to the preponderance of brass instruments. It was not unusual to find five trumpets and five trombones in a Kenton band at the same time as Duke Ellington was carrying only four trumpets and three trombones. Additionally, some Kenton trombonists doubled on tuba, and one version of his band carried an entire section of mellophoniums (trumpet-French horn hybrids specially made for Kenton). The saxophone section was occasionally called upon to augment the band's massiveness by employing the unusual combination of two baritone saxophones.

Another trademark of the Kenton band sound was its glossy trombone tones. The ensemble frequently featured harmonized parts for five trombones that were performed very smoothly and lightly, no matter how loud. For more than three decades, Kenton's trombone soloists invariably preferred high-register work, and they graced the beginnings of many tones with long, climbing smears. They used a meticulously controlled vibrato which was initially slow and then quickened dramatically near the tone's end. Their approach was extraverted, but in the well-manicured way of Tommy Dorsey, rather than the rough, guttural way of earlier jazz trombonists.

To help put the Kenton band sound in perspective, a comparison with Count Basie might be helpful. Just as the feeling projected by the Basie band can be described as easygoing and swinging, the feeling projected by the Kenton band can be described as serious and intense, with an emphasis on massiveness. Much of the Kenton repertory is solemn and weighty. It is essentially twentieth-century concert music scored for trumpets, trombones, and saxophones plus rhythm section. Some of the material also required French horns, tuba, strings, and Latin American percussion instruments. The band's character was based more on elaborate arrangements than on the simplicity and swing feeling associated with Basie. Remember that the Basie band of the late 1930s functioned much as a big combo. Solo improvisation was primary, and many of the ensemble backgrounds were almost incidental to the music. Kenton's approach contrasts with Basie's because its effect was frequently similar to that of a brass choir, not a big jazz combo. The Kenton bands usually emphasized composition over improvisation. In fact, some solo improvisations were not solos in the conventional sense but embellishments of the ensemble sound. For example, the Kenton band sometimes intentionally overpowered a soloist in a loud ensemble sound, thereby turning the solo line into an ensemble line that was almost indistinct.

It was not as a pianist or composer that Kenton left his greatest mark. His major contributions to jazz history were his skill at public relations and his motivation and talent for finding and leading creative modern musicians and composers. Lying behind this contribution is the important fact that because of his band's great popularity during the 1940s—"Tampico" and "Artistry in Rhythm" were million-sellers—Kenton became financially free enough to invest in musical experiments. He channeled this freedom into hiring relatively unknown writers and commissioning ambitious compositions which had little chance of commercial success.[12] Improvisers had enjoyed these kinds of opportunities throughout jazz history, but composers had not. In addition, Kenton employed hundreds of musicians who otherwise may not have received much exposure. He must also be credited with tenacity and durability. Though he began leading bands in 1941, when the big band era was still flourishing, he continued into the 1960s and 1970s, long after big bands went out of fashion. Moreover, he was one of the founders of the college stage band movement, spawning today's enormous jazz education establishment. Jazz in schools perpetuated the big band tradition in jazz after regularly touring big bands disappeared from the jazz scene upon the deaths of Kenton, Basie, Ellington, Woody Herman, Buddy Rich, Harry James, and Don Ellis.

"A Trumpet,"
JCCD2 *Track 3*

Composed by Robert Graettinger; recorded on February 11, 1953, for Capitol by Stan Kenton band featuring Maynard Ferguson (trumpet); five saxophones, five trumpets, five trombones, guitar, bass, and drums; reissued on *City of Glass* (Capitol: 32084, c1995).

Terms to learn from *Demo* CD: staccato, syncopation, tom-tom, mallets, trombone, brass instruments. **Terms to learn from "Elements of Music" appendix**: scale, syncopation.

Robert Graettinger (1923–1957) was a modern composer who wrote concert works for Stan Kenton's big band. Though he had a jazz background, played saxophone, and had previously written for dance bands, his music here is quite serious and not intended for dancing. Graettinger's compositional methods were on a par with those of composers who wrote primarily for symphony orchestra. Kenton considered him an experimental composer and regarded him so highly that he recorded an entire album of Graettinger works that were more like modern classical music than jazz: *"City of Glass"* and *"This Modern World."* Graettinger tailored all the parts to the playing styles of the musicians in Kenton's band of that time. One of the most outstanding works in "This Modern World" was written by Graettinger for the virtuosic style of trumpeter Maynard Ferguson.

The composer took advantage of Ferguson's impressive facility with ultra-high-pitched tones. Beginning at 0'19", Graettinger has the trumpeter roaming the high register, ultimately reaching a high concert F at 0'43". Most dramatically, Ferguson sounds a double-high concert B♭ three times beginning at 2'43". The piece finally ends with sustained double-high concert B♭. An intriguing sidelight is that Graettinger based a few portions of the piece on practice routines and warm-up exercises that he had heard Ferguson use. High-pitched scales, for example, are heard going up and down, beginning at 2'21", and a repeated interval of six scale-steps apart is heard six times beginning at 2'29". Something else to keep in mind is that it is physically very difficult to play high-pitched tones softly, yet that is exactly what Graettinger requires of Ferguson after he first hits his very high note at the end of the piece, and Ferguson prevails. So, despite the piece's title of "A Trumpet," the work should really be called *"The* Trumpet" (of Maynard Ferguson).

Though most of the music that Graettinger wrote for Kenton was neither swinging nor allowing for improvisation, "A Trumpet" contains an improvised solo from 3'17" to 4'31". This is accompanied by a conventional jazz rhythm section, swinging in bop style, and following a 32-bar A-A-B-A chord progression. But that passage is almost the only music the least bit conventional in this recording. To put the rest of the piece in perspective, note that the organization of Graettinger's writing for Ferguson deviates from most feature numbers because many of the non-soloing parts in this piece are almost as important as the featured trumpet line, and parts written here for the trumpet "soloist" sometimes become enmeshed in what would otherwise constitute background, as in 0'51" to 1'01". In other words, the piece is so thick with other important lines that we cannot accurately classify it as merely a trumpet solo with band accompaniment. This aspect even characterizes the beginning of the piece when Ferguson begins his note, then sustains it while an assortment of other instruments enter, one at a time, to either sustain their own notes or travel with their own counter-lines. It is as though different color brush strokes are being applied to a canvas, and we can "hear" each one as it leaves its trail of paint behind. A similar effect occurs with brass sounds being interspersed from about 1'27" to 1'46". The composition again shows that it has its own life apart from Ferguson, from about 59" to 1'16", from 2'02" to 2'20", and from about 2'57" to 3'16".

The lines that Graettinger wrote are loaded with odd intervals that we do not usually find in jazz or American pop music. Also, the amount of independent movement by the different horns is not ordinarily present in jazz or pop music. It is more common to works by European symphonic composers such as Stravinsky, Bartók, and Hindemith. In fact, there is so much activity in this piece that the following Listening Guide cannot possibly do justice to the rich fabric of the work. So don't give up if your first few times lead you to being overwhelmed or put off by clashing sounds. That would be natural for almost any listener, considering the density of activities in this music. Pause the selection frequently and don't hesitate to rewind whenever you sense that you have missed something. You may encounter the most difficulty before 3'16". So be patient with yourself. The guide below merely alerts you to a few of the many highlights that await the attentive listener. New strands of the densely woven fibers will emerge upon repeated listening, especially if you get out of the habit of focusing solely on the highest pitched trumpet line. (For the technically inclined reader, a score is available in the doctoral thesis of Robert Morgan. See page 489 to learn how to order theses.)

LISTENING GUIDE continued on next page

Technical notes: The way the odd intervals were achieved in the lines by the saxophones at the beginning of "A Trumpet" is called a "tone row." This involves selecting pitches from the 12 tones of the chromatic scale and placing them in an odd order called a row. When adhering to this system, the composer is then writing a line in which no tone can be duplicated in the composition until all those that follow it from the original row are sounded. Graettinger reversed the order for playing that original row when selecting the pitches he assigned to the horns at 1'45".

Ferguson's warm-up scale that Graettinger incorporated into the composition at 2'21" later became termed a "bebop scale." It is basically a major scale, but it uses both the seventh step and an alteration of that seventh step (technically known as "lowered seventh"). It was heard by Ferguson and others who studied the music of Charlie Parker and Dizzy Gillespie.

ELAPSED TIME	MUSICAL EVENTS
0'00"	Ferguson sustains one tone, as trumpets and saxophones enter, one at a time, to sustain other tones.
0'11"	moving lines by saxophones; as one instrument's sound goes past another, sometimes they purposely clash, then they come apart and unclash
0'19"	Movement begins in Ferguson's high-pitched trumpet tone.
0'22"	Ferguson plays a moving line of high-pitched tones slurred together, as four saxophones sound moving lines of their own.
0'30"	Louder, more activity from brasses increases tension.
0'43"	Ferguson plays double-high concert F, followed by independently moving lines by trombones.
0'49"	Mallets striking tom-toms in background add to the building of anticipation for thicker, louder brass chords.
0'58"	Saxophone lines enter under brass lines, with Ferguson soaring above, mallets striking two different tom-toms. Steadily getting louder.
1'09"	marching of 16 chords by trumpets and trombones, mallets striking tom-toms; everything getting louder; marching of brass chords louder and louder
1'16"	Ensemble stops. Ferguson continues. Tension is released.
1'26"	Saxophones play a line of their own, ending with a see-saw figure (bottom note alternating with top note by four- then by six-scale steps) that they repeat continuously underneath staccato brass figures.
2'07"	loud brass chords
2'12"	Saxophones in harmony answer the brass remarks.
2'16"	loud brass chords
2'21"	Ferguson plays up and down his high-pitched scales.
2'29"	Ferguson plays low-register interval four times, as in a warm-up routine.
2'37"	drums enter
2'42"	Silence offers prelude to high point of piece.
2'44"	Ferguson screams his double-high C (concert B♭) three times, answered by four other trumpets in harmony, the highest pitched of which is playing tones so high that its source could be mistaken for Ferguson.
3'11"	Saxophones re-enter and trade the foreground with one line from trumpets, another line from trombones.
3'16"	"Jazz" section begins with fast walking bass, un-amplified guitar, drums, and Ferguson improvising a modern-style solo, over saxophone tones. Continuity is more obvious here and uses more familiar lines and rhythms, therefore relaxing the previous tension.

LISTENING GUIDE *continued on next page*

3'33"	Bridge of chord progression: trombones replacing saxophones under solo
3'38"	A-section of chord progression: saxophones replacing trombones
3'45"	High-pitched trumpets and trombones provide a breather for Ferguson.
3'50"	Ferguson returns.
3'53"	highly syncopated interjection by harmonized trumpets and trombones
3'57"	Ferguson resumes solo, reaching very high-pitched tones at 4'00".
4'28"	Without preset chord progressions, Ferguson continues to improvise over moving lines by saxes, syncopated punctuations by trumpets and trombones.
4'35"	Ferguson plays double-high concert B♭ (his double-high C) and sustains it while getting softer and softer to the end.

Trumpet

A number of good trumpeters have been associated with West Coast cool jazz of the 1950s and 1960s (see Table 10.1). Chet Baker and Shorty Rogers are probably the best known. Baker has the more impressive recording career as a soloist, while Rogers is better known for his writing and bandleading.

When naming "cool jazz" trumpeters, journalists usually list Miles Davis first and **Chet Baker** (1929–1988) next.[13] Unlike most white West Coast players, Baker did not gain his first wide exposure with the big bands of Stan Kenton or Woody Herman. Though he had played briefly with Charlie Parker, Baker's largest initial exposure came from his membership in the Gerry Mulligan quartet of 1952 and 1953. From there, he toured and recorded prolifically with a variety of rhythm sections until his death in 1988.

Baker is widely admired among musicians, regardless of the idiom or era being discussed. His solos swing in an easy way, and most of his playing projects a mellow mood. His tone quality is soft, not brassy. In fact, during the 1960s he stopped playing the trumpet temporarily and spent some of his career playing the mellower-sounding fluegelhorn (see photo on page 134).[14] As an improviser, Baker had a talent for being able to pick just the right few notes, and to invest isolated notes and phrases with especially affecting tone qualities. Some of Baker's best work conveys a poignant sense of striving to catch something just beyond his reach, a struggle to overcome obstacles. Often, when he finally plays that perfect note, it attains a delicate balance of fragility and triumph. A master at generating long phrases, Baker never seemed at a loss for melodic ideas, and the tuneful quality of his solos always made them sound fresh.

Shorty Rogers (1924–1994) was a trumpeter-composer-arranger based in Los Angeles during the 1950s and 1960s. He had played trumpet and written for the Woody Herman and Stan Kenton bands. With his own combos and big bands, sometimes called the Giants, he produced music that extended writing styles he had developed in his earlier compositions. His recordings of these pieces featured various combinations of the best jazz musicians living in the Los Angeles area at the time.[15] In isolated recordings, he also anticipated developments that later became better known in association with other musicians. Recordings he made with Jimmy Giuffre and vibraphonist Teddy Charles[16] are historically significant because they were among the earliest after Lennie Tristano's "Intuition" and "Digression" to display improvisation not based on prearranged chord progressions. Their 1954 work predated the Ornette Coleman recordings of 1958 and 1959 that launched an entire style centered on the "free jazz" concept. Rogers also recorded pieces in which improvisation was based on modes instead of chord changes. (For explanations of modes, see Appendices B and H.[17]) These predated the 1958 Miles Davis recording of "Milestones" and the Davis *Kind of Blue* album which launched the mode-based improvisatory styles that became common during the 1960s and 1970s. The connection with Davis is especially intriguing because Rogers derived his trumpet style primarily from the 1940s approach of Miles Davis and, like Davis, used fluegelhorn long before it became common among trumpeters.

| *pages 453 and 492*

| Demo CD *Tracks 60 and 61; page 134*

Saxophone

Many excellent saxophonists were associated with West Coast cool jazz (see Table 10.1).[18] They are known particularly for maintaining the tone quality and melodic ideas of Lester Young, though some also incorporated the advances of Charlie Parker. Most played with the big bands of Stan Kenton and Woody Herman at one time or another (see Table 10.2).

Saxophonist **Jimmy Giuffre** (b. 1921) was based on the West Coast from 1946 to 1960. Giuffre's output typifies the notion of cool jazz: He produced a soft, diffuse sound on all the instruments he played, and his lines were understated and melodic. Moreover, his mastery of silence and economy in solo construction is comparable to that of Count Basie and Miles Davis. Although he began as a saxophonist influenced by the Count Basie-Lester Young combo style of the 1930s, he went beyond Young. Additionally, he contributed strikingly original compositions and improvisations, many of which he performed on clarinet, with a special emphasis on the instrument's lowest register. Ultimately he must be ranked as one of the most daring composers and improvisers in jazz, and rhythmically he was the most creative of the West Coast musicians. The consistency, intelligence, and coherence of even his most unorthodox lines surpassed all his colleagues. His improvisations sustain a level of originality that is higher than most modern jazz as a whole, not just West Coast jazz or cool jazz. Despite the "cool" demeanor of his work, Giuffre's sounds impart a sense of intellectual intensity and adventure that lends them a character as convincing as the most outstanding bop and post-bop performances. They have little of the tentative or easygoing feeling that is conveyed by much other music made at this time on the West Coast. Unfortunately, except for recognition as composer of the "Four Brothers" piece featured by Woody Herman's band, he is almost universally overlooked by jazz fans as well as historians, and most of his best recordings went out of print, rarely to be reissued.[19]

There were several excellent alto saxophonists associated with the West Coast scene of the 1950s (see Table 10.1), many of whom were prominently featured at one time or another with the big bands of Stan Kenton. All of them used slow vibrato and produced tone qualities that were thin-textured and light in weight, displaying a dryness we ordinarily associate with Lester Young. This contrasts with the weightier, more syrupy tone qualities of Coleman Hawkins and Johnny Hodges. Though aware of Charlie Parker's approach to melodic rhythm and phrasing, they seemed to have more in common with Lee Konitz. None of them, however, demonstrated the richness of melodic inventions we find in either Parker or Konitz. The West Coast cool saxophonists were especially simple in their improvisations. It frequently sounded as though they were playing swing era solos spiced with a touch of bop flavoring.

The best known West Coast altoist was **Paul Desmond** (1924–1977). In surveys of musicians, Desmond ranks among the all-time favorites on his instrument. He is highly regarded for his good taste, melodic continuity, fertile imagination, and accurate intonation. Desmond received his widest exposure with pianist Dave

Brubeck's quartets.[20] His quartet improvisations conveyed a sense of openness and clarity. With his soft, light, pure sound, he unfolded line after logical line. Often he created an impression that his playing was effortlessly soaring above its earth-bound accompaniments.[21]

Desmond forged an instantly recognizable style that had almost nothing to do with bop—Desmond cited swing era player Pete Brown, not Charlie Parker, as his influence. And, though his tone quality closely resembled that of Lee Konitz, Desmond's style should not be considered as derivative of the Tristano-Konitz approach, either. By comparison with Konitz, he swung a bit more. Further, instead of drawing upon the complex melodic conception of Lennie Tristano as Konitz did, Desmond had his own fresh ideas, and the melodies that he improvised were less convoluted than those of the Tristano approach. Though he sometimes inserted phrases from popular songs, his improvisational material was usually free of cliché. It depended instead upon original melodic invention. He was extremely spare, playing far fewer notes per solo than probably any other modern jazz saxophonist. Many of his lines are as simple and lyrical as the best popular songs. Some of his improvisations may remind listeners of themes in the classical music of Tchaikovsky and Rachmaninoff.

Desmond's playing projects a relaxed, lighthearted mood, but the construction of his improvised lines reflects care, intelligence, and inspiration. Desmond sometimes developed musical sequences by taking a phrase and repeating it in a new key to fit the next chord in his accompaniment, each time altering it or putting it in a different place relative to the underlying beat. Some of his rhythmic displacements built tension that was finally resolved by a clever turn of phrase, as though he had escaped miraculously from a self-imposed puzzle. Other times he sounded as though he were playing duets with himself, introducing a line, then answering, paraphrasing or mimicking it.[22]

Art Pepper (1925–1982) is among the best known and most original improvisers associated with the Stan Kenton bands and West Coast jazz. He fashioned a raw, plaintive style for the alto saxophone by amalgamating the approaches of Zoot Sims and Lee Konitz. Then, at the latest stage in his career, he also absorbed the influence of post-bop saxophonist John Coltrane. His was probably the hottest style to emerge from cool jazz of the white West Coast scene. In his playing is more of a cry than ordinarily found in West Coast cool saxophonists. Another central difference is his sense of urgency and rhythmic variety. Pepper pushed hard on the beat. He favored short, staccato bursts of notes, many grouped in triplets. Sometimes he tore off a double-time figure (a stream of sixteenth notes) in a tight, crisp manner. Pepper used brief, funky phrases that were abruptly stated with searing emotion. In fact, his emotionality is prized by many fans. The emotional range of his playing runs from a joyous swing feeling, particularly evident on medium- and up-tempo pieces, to despondency; on some ballad improvisations his playing is so slow it is almost as though he purposely drags to build tension.[23]

Gerry Mulligan (1927–1996) was baritone saxophonist and a primary composer-arranger in the Miles Davis Nonet sessions of 1949 and 1950. (Listen to "Boplicity" in *SCCJ*. Mulligan contributes the first improvisation.) He also wrote for the big bands of Claude Thornhill and Stan Kenton. Mulligan used a soft, dry, light-weight tone quality whose texture has been likened to tweed cloth. By comparison with bop style, his approach was relatively uncomplicated. Rhythmically, Mulligan's improvisations were more predictable, less jarring than those of Charlie Parker and Dizzy Gillespie. His solos suggested great deliberation rather than wild exuberance. He rarely double-timed his phrases. The logic behind them was obvious, and usually they were developed quite systematically. Similarly, Mulligan's compositions were neither as complex as Lennie Tristano's nor as agitated as many bop pieces. A few are quite song-like, and they have the same gentle character projected by his improvisations. This trait, combined with his subdued tone quality, qualifies his music for the "cool" label.

In 1952, Mulligan moved to California and launched a series of piano-less quartets consisting of himself on baritone saxophone, another horn, bass, and drums. Let's take a moment to consider what it means to have a jazz group without a chording instrument. Normally, a piano provides chords to the soloists. These chords act as a sort of anchor, always reminding the horn players of where they are in the harmony that accompanies the tune. In some ways the piano chords direct the flow and texture of the music. A comping pianist complicates the sound considerably. Therefore, the absence of piano in Mulligan's groups was partly responsible for the band's simple sound texture. It also highlighted the bass, which pianos often drown out. His drummers also contributed to this effect by playing conservatively, often using wire brushes instead of sticks to strike the drums and cymbals. All of these aspects together made Mulligan's band sound "cool." While on the West Coast, he also produced material with a ten-piece band in the style of the Miles Davis Nonet. Trumpeter Chet Baker was his best-known partner in these undertakings.[24] Though Mulligan was based on the West Coast for only about three years, his music epitomizes what journalists mean by the term "West Coast cool." Mulligan maintained his piano-less format long after returning to the New York area, and, more than 30 years later, many jazz fans still considered his music "West Coast cool."

Drums

West Coast style was not known for adventuresome drumming, in either the accompaniment or solo capacity. However, one of the most novel bands to originate on the West Coast was led by drummer **Chico Hamilton** (b. 1921). Gerry Mulligan had made Hamilton the drummer in his first piano-less quartet. Then Hamilton formed a group of his own. He used an instrumentation that was even more unique: guitar, cello, bass, drums, and a hornman who played saxophones, flute, and clarinet. (Flute and cello were especially unusual to find in jazz at this time.) With tightly arranged pieces and excellent musicianship, the quintet created its own jazz style, which often resembled classical chamber music.[25] Its textures were light and pretty, and the arrangements displayed considerable variety. Sometimes several melodies sounded at the same time. This is a technique that had characterized the earliest jazz. With Hamilton's, Mulligan's, and Brubeck's groups using it, the technique had found favor again.

Chico Hamilton was one of the first modern drummers to get away from nearly always playing conventional ride rhythms as the undercurrent for a group sound. Hamilton's imagination is fertile, orchestral, and subtle. He is known for generating unusual and catchy patterns on his drums and maintaining them as consistent accompaniment figures. Instead of depending primarily on the ride cymbal and high-hat sound, Hamilton is just as likely to use a snare drum or tom-tom as the primary voice in his accompaniment pattern. Each piece features a separate rhythm pattern and percussion color. Hamilton's style is a gentle approach to creating unusual rhythmic textures instead of just defining the beat and prodding the soloists. Even when no longer based on the West Coast, Hamilton's groups continued to create a highly original brand of jazz that was full of surprises.

Guitar

Several modern guitarists were associated with the West Coast scene of the 1950s (see Table 10.1). But none have come to be more revered by jazz musicians than **Jim Hall** (b. 1930). When asked to name their favorite guitarist or their biggest influence, numerous modern guitarists mention Jim Hall. Since the mid-1960s, they mention him almost as often as they mention Wes Montgomery. Though much of his reputation has been acquired since he left the Los Angeles area for New York in 1959, many fans were first introduced to Hall through recordings he made with Chico Hamilton in 1955 and 1956 and with Jimmy Giuffre from 1956 to 1960.

Jim Hall extracts a mellow, soft tone from his guitar, and his sound is clear and pure, often bell-like in its resonance. His clean touch, gentle approach, and immaculate sense of pacing set him above almost all other jazz guitarists. There is nothing offhanded about what he offers his listeners. He begins his notes very precisely. The structure of his ideas displays a crystal clarity. He never overloads the listener with flashy acrobatics or a crowded sequence of notes. In his music, a sense of politeness coexists with a forceful continuity of purpose that suggests Hall knows exactly where he is going. He maintains high creative standards, placing great importance on playing only fresh ideas and avoiding well-worn patterns. Yet despite the pressure that this esthetic exerts, Hall's solos are free of the false starts that we would expect. Instead, we are treated to solos that bear an overall form that is often as good as any composed piece. Rather than beginning ideas and leaving them half-finished, Hall nearly always manages to complete each improvised idea, thereby personifying the meticulous composer as improviser. Because of the limitations such a strategy places on an improviser, Hall is possibly the slowest guitar soloist in jazz. This does not mean that he is not *able* to play fast, flashy lines. It means only that he chooses notes so judiciously that his pace cannot possibly be as brisk as it would be if he were performing prerehearsed patterns. Unlike many bop soloists, Hall does not ordinarily exceed the limits of his thinking and the speed of his fingers. Because he does stay within his capabilities, each note in his improvised lines is presented firmly, with a sureness of swing feeling.[26]

Piano

A number of creative jazz pianists were based on the West Coast during the 1950s (see Table 10.1). All contributed substantially to the quality of the West Coast scene, but only **Dave Brubeck** (b. 1920) achieved tremendous international fame. He performed in the San Francisco area during the 1940s and early 1950s. In the period 1955 to 1985, Brubeck ranked second in record sales among all jazz recording artists. During the 1950s and 1960s, his name became almost as synonymous with jazz as Louis Armstrong and Duke Ellington had been in the 1930s and 1940s. His fame came mostly as a bandleader and composer. Among musicians, he was universally admired as a composer, though he was not as influential as a pianist. During the 1940s he had led a series of small bands in California which employed approaches similar to the 1949–1950 Miles Davis Nonet, though they began before he ever heard the Davis recordings.[27] Then, from 1951 to 1967, he teamed with California-born alto saxophonist Paul Desmond and led a quartet which, for millions of listeners, provided an introduction to jazz. (Though associated with "West Coast" jazz, Brubeck was not a California resident during the period of his greatest acclaim. His quartet members lived in the New York area.)

The rhythmic feeling in a lot of Brubeck's playing has much in common with classical music. However, Brubeck never was a classical pianist, though after launching his jazz career he briefly studied composition with the world-renowned symphonic composer Darius Milhaud. It remains a widely held misunderstanding that Brubeck was trained primarily in the classics. Perhaps listeners believe this because of the way Brubeck's music sounds. He is one of the few modern pianists clearly to avoid standard bop melodic conception and rhythmic feeling. He is unusually inventive and depends almost exclusively on original melodic lines, not the phrases that most of his contemporaries absorbed from the music of Charlie Parker, Dizzy Gillespie, and Bud Powell. He was inspired more by Art Tatum, Fats Waller, and Cleo Brown than bop. Another reason is that much of Brubeck's invention has a distinctly classical flavor. In fact, sometimes he and Desmond improvised duets that sounded like the two-part inventions of J. S. Bach, set atop jazz bass and drums. In other words, Brubeck is a modern jazz musician who does not use the bop language, and, despite his lack of classical piano lessons, he often sounds more like Bach than bop.

"Blue Rondo a la Turk," JCCD2 Track 4

That Brubeck's work sounds classical may explain part of his popularity. By comparison with the jumpy, erratic character of bop style, his compositions and improvisations are much easier to follow. They possess a simple and tuneful quality. His creations are orderly, and they project a freshness and clarity that make the listener's job easy. In addition, most of Brubeck's pieces are pretty, and they convey a light and pleasant mood.[28]

Brubeck was rhythmically innovative. His interest in using meters unusual to jazz brought him a great deal of publicity and spawned trends among other jazz musicians. His quartet crafted a number of tunes and improvisations in odd meters such as three, five, and seven. (See Appendix B for an explanation of "meter.") His albums *Time Out*[29] and *Time Further Out*,[30] that explored those meters, were immensely popular. *Time Out* contained "Take Five," a funky and engaging theme by Paul Desmond that employed a simple accompaniment rhythm that was extensively repeated in meter of five. Brubeck was also rhythmically innovative in ways outside his adventures with odd meters. For example, he frequently improvised lines, sometimes in locked-hands style, that pitted his own separate rhythm (for example, in meter of three) against the pulse that was emanating from bass and drums (for example, in meter of two). By this strategy he was cleverly attempting to generate a provocative tension. However, the clashing rhythms were often not appreciated by those who were expecting the easy swing feeling that was ordinarily produced by other modern jazz pianists. Brubeck's mastery of odd meters led to respect among musicians, however, and it earned him a significant place in jazz history, even in the minds of musicians who were not especially influenced by his piano style.

Trombone

There are a number of highly talented trombonists associated with the Los Angeles jazz scene of the 1950s and 1960s (see Table 10.1). Among many jazz trombonists themselves, **Carl Fontana** (1928–2003) is the favorite trombonist in modern jazz. Though featured with Stan Kenton and Woody Herman, he was not consistently in

The Dave Brubeck Quartet, one of the most popular small groups in jazz history (left to right): drummer Joe Morello, bassist Gene Wright, pianist Dave Brubeck, alto saxophonist Paul Desmond. Brubeck and Desmond played together from the 1940s to the 1970s. Desmond's hit tune "Take Five" still remains popular today.

(Photo by Bob Parent, courtesy of Don Parent)

Composed by Dave Brubeck; recorded August 18, 1959, for Columbia in New York by the Dave Brubeck Quartet: Dave Brubeck (piano), Paul Desmond (alto sax), Gene Wright (bass), Joe Morello (drums); available on *Prentice Hall Jazz Collection* and Brubeck, *Time Out* (Columbia/Legacy: 65122, 1959, c1997).

This piece illustrates the cool jazz sax style of Paul Desmond and samples the West Coast-style quartet of pianist-composer Dave Brubeck. It qualifies as cool, however, only from about 2'13" to 5'33" because those sounds come in the context of what became a very creative tangent for the group: irregular meters, and because Brubeck's undertaking with this particular meter is distinctly hot. A bit of history should put this in perspective. Prior to this band's endeavors in the 1950s, most jazz was played in meter of four. In other words, you could fit the flow of music into a count of 1234 2234 3234 4234, etc. In 1959, however, Paul Desmond's composition "Take Five" was first recorded in meter of five (count 12345 12345, etc.), the present piece was played in meter of nine (count 123456789 123456789, etc.), and other pieces with odd meters were also recorded.

"Blue Rondo a la Turk" comes from Brubeck's album *Time Out*, whose title refers to the unusual time signatures (meters) that are featured on it. Because it contained such catchy themes and attractive grooves, the album became one of the best selling jazz recordings in history, and Dave Brubeck's name became almost as well known as Louis Armstrong's. "Blue Rondo a la Turk" was separately issued on a 45 rpm single on the other side of "Take Five," the most popular piece from the album. That single was distributed for jukebox play, which is notable because jazz was hardly ever heard on jukeboxes in the 1960s. The tune's title shows three influences—"blue" is a jazz term, "rondo" suggests a classical form (in which new sections alternate with old ones), and "a la Turk" refers to Turkish music. The blending of these different elements with jazz contributed to the unique sound of this composition. The form of this composition is slightly more complicated than many other jazz tunes. This shows Brubeck's attraction to some of classical music's complexities.

Brubeck first heard the two prominent rhythms used in this piece while he was traveling in Turkey. Each has nine beats in a measure, grouped differently. The opening rhythm organizes them as 2+2+2+3. Before listening to the recording, try counting like this, saying bold-faced numbers loudest (1, 3, 5, and 7):

Rhythm A: 1 (2) **3** (4) **5** (6) **7** (8 9)

The second way Brubeck divides up a measure of nine is 3 + 3 + 3. Try counting like this, with bold-faced numbers loudest (1, 4, and 7):

Rhythm B: 1 (2 3) **4** (5 6) **7** (8 9)

At the beginning of the piece, Brubeck places three groups of Rhythm A, followed by one group of Rhythm B. Try to count this at a quick tempo. Then see if you can count along with the recording and feel all the beats. Notice how the melody emphasizes the accent pattern.

Measure 1	*Measure 2*
1 (2) **3** (4) **5** (6) **7** (8 9)	**1** (2) **3** (4) **5** (6) **7** (8 9)
Measure 3	*Measure 4*
1 (2) **3** (4) **5** (6) **7** (8 9)	**1** (2 3) **4** (5 6) **7** (8 9)

A third meter used in this piece is the common 4. (Count **1**234 **2**234 **3**234 **4**234, etc.) This is used for the improvised piano and sax solos. The character of these passages marks an enormous contrast to that of the odd-metered sections. In addition to the simpler accent pattern, the beats go by at a slower pace, and the music follows a 12-bar blues form. It is a relief after the tension induced by the shifting accents of the irregular meters.

Note: To maximize your appreciation of this selection, don't try to identify all aspects at once. Make several passes, each time seeking different aspects described in the guide.

LISTENING GUIDE continued on next page

ELAPSED
TIME

0'00"	**A-section**
	This section always features three measures of Rhythm A plus one measure of Rhythm B. The piano begins playing the melody and rhythm.
0'05"	Bass and cymbal joins in. The cymbal part is quite simple.
0'11"	Alto sax begins doubling the melody. The melody here is played at a slightly higher pitch than at the beginning. The drum pattern becomes increasingly more active.
0'22"	Return to the melody in the original register, played by piano, bass, and drums.
0'34"	**B-section**
	This section, with piano on the melody, uses the same rhythmic divisions as the A-section. However, the shape of the melody is altered.
0'45"	**A-section**
	Band returns to opening material, sax playing melody, piano harmonizing it.
0'55"	**B-section**
	The B-section is varied slightly, melody played in a more chordal approach (composed of chords instead of single-note-at-a-time lines) by pianist's right hand, reinforced by cymbal, while one tone is loudly played by left hand repeatedly throughout.
1'07"	**A-section**
	Sax plays the melody, piano harmonizing it.
	Cymbal is mimicking melody rhythm.
1'18"	**C-section**
	This section, chordal in nature, still retains the rhythms of the beginning. The left hand of the pianist also plays a prominent figure at times, accenting the uneven division of pulses as the melody had before.
1'35"	**C-section Extension**
	Block chords played loudly on piano, reinforced by drums and cymbal, adding more and more intensity.
1'38"	This is the climax of the melody. Widespread chords are played in a rhythm that resembles Rhythm A. However, this short section actually combines a rhythm of 11 beats in a measure: **1** (2) **3** (4) **5** (6) **7** (8) **9** (10 11) with Rhythm B. It gives the impression of the music being stretched out, and sounds a bit slower, though you must still count at the same tempo.
1'52"	**Sax Solo: Blues Alternates with A-section** (Rondo Form)
	This section alternates sax improvisations in two measures of a 12-bar blues feeling with two measures from the A-section, sounding as if the music can't decide between blues or Turkish rhythms.
2'13"	**Paul Desmond's Alto Sax Solo Improvisation** (12-bar Blues)
	The band settles on a blues form in meter of four, and the sax solo is officially underway. Creation of an open, spacious feeling is aided by the absence of piano. Notice Paul Desmond's simple phrasing and soft tone. His rhythms are often relatively slow, and Desmond sometimes gives the music a chance to breathe by leaving space for several beats to pass after a melodic phrase.
2'37"	Second chorus of sax solo
3'01"	Third chorus of sax solo
3'26"	Fourth chorus of sax solo

LISTENING GUIDE *continued on next page*

3'52"	**Dave Brubeck's Piano Solo Improvisation** (12-bar Blues)
	Brubeck begins with single note-at-a-time, horn-like melody lines, keeping it simple, leaving lots of space.
4'16"	Second chorus: Brubeck harmonizes his lines.
4'25"	Brubeck adopts block chord style of playing his lines.
4'43"	Third chorus: Brubeck invents concise, bluesy lines played in locked-hands block chording.
5'08"	Fourth chorus: Brubeck continues with horn-like bluesy melody lines, no longer harmonized. He uses considerable silence to frame his phrases. This allows us to clearly appreciate walking bass and drummer's ride rhythms sounding on ride cymbal.
5'33"	**Alternating between Blues in 4 and A-section in 9** (Rondo Form)
	Sax improvises in meter of four on blues chords.
5'38"	Piano reiterates melody in meter of nine.
5'41"	Sax improvises in meter of four on blues chords.
5'45"	Piano reiterates melody in meter of nine.
5'48"	Sax improvises in meter of four on blues chords.
5'52"	Restatement of the melody—**A-section**
6'03"	**C-section**
	Repeated literally from before.
6'37"	The piece ends dramatically at the end of this section.

the Los Angeles area during this period, but we will discuss him here. Trombonists are awed by his outstanding improvisations and unparalleled command of the instrument. Fontana's solos have more depth and substance than the work of almost all other trombonists. Fontana comes close to improvising with the thought and fluency of a modern jazz saxophonist. Unfortunately, Fontana made so few recordings that little proof of his prowess exists for listeners who never had the opportunity to see him perform.[31] Perhaps as a result, the best-known trombonists in West Coast jazz are valve trombonist **Bob Brookmeyer** (b. 1929) and slide trombonist **Frank Rosolino** (1926–1978). Paradoxically, neither man truly qualifies as both West Coast and cool.

Brookmeyer lived in Los Angeles only sporadically, though his playing style could be called cool for several reasons. He uses a tone quality that is soft, not rough or brassy. His rhythmic conception is laid back, and his lines are light and melodic. These characteristics combine to sound altogether more like late-1930s Basie style than any bop style. He uses a combination of lip slurs and half-valve effects, and he follows through on all his ideas, never leaving the listener hanging. Most notable for Brookmeyer's relationship to cool jazz is his work as the other horn on numerous tours and recordings with Gerry Mulligan's piano-less quartets, especially after both men left Los Angeles and returned to New York. He also filled a similar role in Jimmy Giuffre's trio with guitarist Jim Hall. And, like such other West Coast notables as Gerry Mulligan, Shorty Rogers, and Chico Hamilton, Brookmeyer has made much of his living as a writer rather than as a performer.[32] Adventuresome composing for big bands made him one of the leading jazz writers of the 1980s and 1990s.

Frank Rosolino was based in Los Angeles throughout a sizable portion of his career, thereby qualifying for the "West Coast" designation. Yet, like Fontana's, his approach was a hot and fast bop style, not cool. Next to Fontana, Rosolino was often judged to possess the most speed and range of any trombonist during his era, and because of this he was one of the most influential trombonists in jazz. Like Fontana, Rosolino had also been a featured soloist with Stan Kenton.[33]

Popular Appeal

A few players in the "cool" category are the most popular musicians in modern jazz. Trumpeter Miles Davis and saxophonist Stan Getz were capable of consistently packing nightclubs and concert halls. The George Shearing Quintets and the Modern Jazz Quartet were also successful during the 1950s and 1960s. The Dave Brubeck Quartet and the Modern Jazz Quartet were among the first groups in jazz history that were sufficiently popular to tour regularly as concert artists, appearing routinely on college campuses and in recital halls previously devoted to presenting classical musicians. But such acclaim was achieved by only a few nonvocal jazz groups. For instance, Lennie Tristano, Lee Konitz, and Jimmy Giuffre remain among the least appreciated players in that same period, despite the wealth of their contributions. So to say that cool jazz had popular appeal is not entirely accurate. Only some recordings by some cool jazz musicians were popular, and only the names of a few cool jazz musicians garnered much notice beyond the usual small audience of musicians and fans.

COOL JAZZ

Roots of Cool Jazz: Count Basie, Lester Young, Miles Davis, Claude Thornhill

Traits of Cool Jazz: pale tone colors, dry sounds, understated performances, emphasis on lyricism, lack of loudness

Top Names in Cool Jazz

Saxophone: Lee Konitz, Gerry Mulligan, Paul Desmond, Jimmy Giuffre

Trumpet: Miles Davis, Chet Baker, Shorty Rogers

Piano: Lennie Tristano, Dave Brubeck

CHAPTER SUMMARY

1. "Cool jazz" is a term applied to modern styles that sound subdued because they use light, dry tone qualities, little or no vibrato, low levels of volume, and avoid high notes. Some of this music is more relaxed and melodic than bop.

2. Cool jazz of the 1950s drew upon the styles of Lester Young and Count Basie of the 1930s, Lennie Tristano and Lee Konitz of the 1940s, and the arranging practices of the Claude Thornhill band that provided the model for the Miles Davis Nonet of 1949–1950.

3. Much cool jazz is indistinguishable from bop, and a few cool players were already discussed in the bop chapter: Stan Getz, George Shearing, and the Modern Jazz Quartet.

4. Pianist-composer Stan Kenton led a string of innovative big bands, some of which were influenced by Claude Thornhill's style.

5. Kenton's repertory of the 1950s contained ambitious concert works resembling twentieth-century classical music scored for brass, saxes, and rhythm section.

6. "West Coast style" refers to cool jazz played by a predominantly white community of jazz musicians based in the Los Angeles area during the 1950s, many of whom had played with the big bands of Stan Kenton and Woody Herman.

Notes

1. Lennie Tristano, *Intuition* (Capitol: 52771, 1949, c1996); and *Lennie Tristano/The New Tristano* (Atlantic/Rhino: 71595, 1961, c1994).

2. Tristano influenced pianists Ronnie Ball, Sal Mosca, Clare Fischer, Alan Broadbent, Wally Cirillo, and Connie Crothers; saxophonists John LaPorta, Teo Macero, and Ted Brown; and trumpeters Don Ferrara and Cy Touff. For more about Tristano and Konitz, see Ira Gitler, *The Masters of Bebop: A Listener's Guide [Jazz Masters of the 40s]* (Macmillan, 1966; Da Capo, 2001), 226–261.

3. To hear the resemblance between Tristano and Evans, compare almost any Tristano piano solo with recordings that Evans made with George Russell, for example, "All About Rosie" on the anthology, *The Birth of the Third Stream* (Columbia/Legacy: 64929, 1956–57, c1996), or the solo on "Oleo" on Bill Evans, *Everybody Digs Bill Evans* (Fantasy: OJC-068, 1958, c1987). For a continuation of the Tristano legacy, listen to Hancock's solos on "Dolores" and "Gingerbread Boy" on Miles Davis, *Miles Smiles* (Columbia/Legacy: 65682, 1966, c1998), and Jarrett's solos on "Shades of Jazz" on Keith Jarrett, *Mysteries* (Impulse!: GRD4-189, 2CD set, 1975–76, c1996). For the resemblance between Tristano and Cecil Taylor, listen to Tristano, *Descent into the Maelstrom* (Inner City: 6002, LP, 1953, c1978), then to anything Taylor recorded after 1960.

4. Listen to "Marshmallow" or "Ice Cream Konitz" on Lee Konitz, *Subconscious-Lee* (Fantasy: OJC-186, 1949, c1991). Some of the best Konitz solos are on *Konitz Meets Mulligan* (Pacific Jazz: 46847, 1953, c1988). See also footnote 10 in this chapter.

5. Konitz, in turn, influenced Bud Shank, Lennie Niehaus, and Art Pepper, among others, during the 1950s; then Anthony Braxton and Bob Mover, among others, during the 1970s.

6. Konitz, *Ideal Scene* (Soul Note: 121119, 1986, c1986).

7. Miles Davis, *The Birth of the Cool* (Capitol: 30117, 1949–50, c2001); or *The Complete Birth of the Cool* (Capitol Jazz: 94550, 1948–50, c1998).

8. Miles Davis asked arranger Gil Evans to provide the smallest instrumentation that could approximate the sound of the Thornhill big band. Listen to the original band on *Best of the Big Bands: Claude Thornhill* (Columbia: 46152, 1941–47, c1990); or *The Bebop Era* (Columbia: 40972, 1942–51, c1987).

9. The term "West Coast Style" will not be used here to indicate the entire variety of jazz styles that were active on the West Coast during the 1950s, such as bebop, hard bop, Dixieland, swing, and free jazz. For a more complete picture, see Ted Gioia, *West Coast Jazz* (Oxford, 1992; Univ. of California, 1998); Robert Gordon, *Jazz West Coast* (Quartet Books, 1986); William F. Lee, *Stan Kenton: Artistry in Rhythm* (Creative Press of Los Angeles, 1980); Red Callender, *Unfinished Dream* (Quartet Books, 1985); Barry McRae, *Jazz Cataclysm* (A. S. Barnes, 1967; Da Capo, 1985); Joe Goldberg, *Jazz Masters of the Fifties* (Macmillan, 1965; Da Capo, 1980); and the notes for *Black California* (Savoy: 2215, 2LP set, 1942–1952, c1976). The absence of discussion for the fine musicians who performed in these other styles should not be taken as a rejection of their work, but only as an indication that a brief text such as this cannot do justice to all jazz styles in all regions in all periods.

10. A favorite among musicians is Stan Kenton, *New Concepts of Artistry in Rhythm* (Capitol: 92865, 1952, c1989), featuring Lee Konitz, Conte Candoli, Frank Rosolino, and Maynard Ferguson; with arrangements by Gerry Mulligan, Johnny Richards, Bill Russo, and Bill Holman. The JCCD2's "My Lady" and the CCD1's "Improvisation," both by Russo and featuring Konitz, are from this album.

11. *The Jazz Compositions of Stan Kenton* (Creative World: 1078, LP, 1956); the original recordings of these pieces are on *The Best of Stan Kenton* (Capitol: 31504, 1943–61, c1995).

12. For examples, listen to Johnny Richards's arrangements on Kenton, *Cuban Fire* (Capitol: 96260, 1956); Robert Graettinger's compositions on *The City of Glass* (Capitol 32084, 1951, c1995); Russ Garcia's "Adventures in Emotions" on *Stan Kenton Conducts the Los Angeles Neophonic Orchestra* (Capitol: 94502, 1965, c1998); *Stan Kenton: The Complete Capitol Recordings of the Holman & Russo Charts* (Mosaic: MD4-136, 4CD set, 1950–55, c1991); and Pete Rugolo's "Mirage" and William Russo's "Egdon Heath" on *Mirage: Avant-Garde and Third-Stream Jazz* (New World: 216, LP, 1947–61, c1977). See also *Big Band Renaissance* (Smithsonian: 108, 5 CD set, 1941–89, c1995). As we went to press, many Kenton records were still available by mail from: GNP Crescendo, Suite 104, 8271 Melrose Ave., Los Angeles, CA 90046; web: *www.gnpcrescendo.com*. In addition, the *Instructor's Resource Manual* for this book has a discography of Kenton albums, organized by composer-arrangers; teachers can get it by calling 800-526-0485, contacting Prentice-Hall sales representatives, or by writing College Marketing, Prentice-Hall, Inc., 1 Lake Street, Upper Saddle River, NJ 07458. Scores and parts for many of the Kenton band arrangements are available from Sierra Music Publications, P.O. Box 37, Liberty Lake, WA 99019; phone: 800-255-6551; web: *www.sierramusic.com*.

13. *Best of the Gerry Mulligan Quartet with Chet Baker* (Pacific Jazz: 95481, 1952–53, c1991).

14. Chet Baker, *Lonely Star* (Prestige: 24172, 1965, c1996).

15. Shorty Rogers, *Planet Jazz* (RCA: 21599762 [LPM 3137], 1953–54, c1998).

16. Shelly Manne, *"The Three" and "The Two"* (Fantasy: OJC-172, 1954, c1992).

17. Teddy Charles/Shorty Rogers, *Collaboration: West* (Fantasy: OJC-122, 1953, c1992).

18. Teddy Edwards, Wardell Gray, Dexter Gordon, and Harold Land are a few of the great bop players associated with California. For more about them, see Leonard Feather, *The Biographical Encyclopedia of Jazz* (Oxford, 1999); Ted Gioia, *West Coast Jazz;* and Robert Gordon, *Jazz West Coast.*

19. An outstanding undertaking for Giuffre was a trio he led with trombonist Bob Brookmeyer and Jim Hall during an 18-month period in 1958 and 1959 (*The Complete Capitol & Atlantic Recordings of Jimmy Giuffre,* Mosaic: MD6-176, 6CD set, 1954–58, c1997). Their music was light and lyrical, but also earthy and rhythmically daring. It featured close, three-way cooperation in the creation of improvised counterlines. The trio generated group improvisations that were very cohesive, original, and swinging (despite the absence of bass and drums). Another standout among Giuffre's endeavors was made after he left the West Coast for New York. On and off from 1961 to 1963, Giuffre played clarinet with pianist Paul Bley and bassist Steve Swallow. Their sound had the flavor of twentieth-century classical music, and it sometimes stemmed from improvisation that was free of preset chord progressions (*Jimmy Giuffre 3, 1961,* ECM: 849 644 [ECM 1438/39; Verve], 2CD set, 1961, c1992; and *Free Fall,* Columbia/Legacy: 65446, 1962, c1998). Subsequent work by Giuffre has preserved his tendency to lean toward experimentation.

20. Desmond penned the quartet's biggest hit, "Take Five." It sold more than a million copies in 1961 and has remained popular. See the original on Dave Brubeck, *Time Out* (Columbia/Legacy: 65122, 1959, c1997). For more about Desmond, see Doug Ramsey, *Take Five: The Public and Private Lives of Paul Desmond* (Parkside, 2005) and Gene Lees, *Meet Me at Jim & Andy's* (Oxford, 1988), 243–265.

21. Desmond was so consistently inspired that almost every Brubeck album offers representative Desmond solos. A standout is Brubeck, *Gone with the Wind* (Columbia: 40627, 1959, c1983), especially his solo on "Georgia on My Mind." Away from Brubeck, Desmond recorded some very pleasant playing, including an orchestral album in which he paraphrased well-loved popular standards as well as improvising his own new lines: Paul Desmond, *Desmond Blue* (RCA Bluebird: 63898, 1961–62, c2002). His hottest playing on record is cited in the next footnote.

22. Desmond loved to play in the alto's high range, and he was one of the first jazz altoists to use notes from the extreme high register, the *altissimo* range. Examples are on "Perdido" on Brubeck, *Jazz at Oberlin* (Fantasy: OJC-046, 1953, c1987).

23. Art Pepper, *Modern Art* (Blue Note: 46848, 1956, c1988), with Russ Freeman; and *Intensity* (Fantasy: OJC-387, 1960, c1989). See also the autobiography: Art Pepper, *Straight Life* (Schirmer, 1979; Mojo Books, 2000).

24. See footnote 13, above.

25. Chico Hamilton, *The Complete Pacific Jazz Recordings of the Chico Hamilton Quintet* (Mosaic: MD6-175, 6CD set, 1955–59, c1997), with Jim Hall and Buddy Collette; and *Gong's East* (Discovery: 70831 [Warner Bros.], 1958, c1989), with Eric Dolphy.

26. Among Hall's most famous recordings are two albums of duets with pianist Bill Evans: *Undercurrent* (Blue Note: 38228, 1962, c2002); and *Intermodulation* (Verve: 833 771, 1966, c1988). The music is pretty, with much continuity and originality. The austere and thoughtful conceptions of these two musicians are about as free from redundancy and cliché as any jazz recorded. Moreover, even without bass or drums, their music is insistent and swinging. Hall is also featured on several outstanding Paul Desmond albums. *Desmond Blue* (RCA Bluebird: 63898, 1961–62) contains some of his most relaxed and lyrical improvisations.

27. *The Dave Brubeck Octet* (Fantasy: OJC-101, 1946, 1948–49, c1991).

28. Other musicians have been attracted to Brubeck's tunes "In Your Own Sweet Way" and "The Duke." Miles Davis recorded "In Your Own Sweet Way" on *Workin'* (Fantasy: OJC-296, 1956, c1987), and "The Duke" on *Miles Ahead* (Columbia/Legacy: 65121, 1957, c1997). For more about Brubeck, see Len Lyons, *The Great Jazz Pianists* (Quill, 1983; Da Capo, 1989), 102–112; and Fred M. Hall, *It's About Time: The Dave Brubeck Story* (Univ. of Arkansas, 1996).

29. Dave Brubeck, *Time Out* (Columbia/Legacy).

30. Brubeck, *Time Further Out* (Columbia/Legacy: 64668, 1961, c1996).

31. Fontana's first album as a leader is *The Great Fontana* (Uptown: 27.28, 1985, c1988). He also plays solos on Supersax, *Salt Peanuts* (Capitol: ST-11271, LP, 1973); and Kenton, *Cuban Fire* (Capitol: 96260, 1956, c1991).

32. Brookmeyer's best work includes his recordings with Jimmy Giuffre and Jim Hall (*The Complete Capitol & Atlantic Recordings of Jimmy Giuffre,* Mosaic), and Clark Terry, *Complete Studio Recordings* (Lone Hill: 10199 [Mainstream], 1964–66, c2005). A good recording with Zoot Sims was reissued: Zoot Sims, *The Rare Dawn Sessions* (Biograph: 131, 1956, c1994). Albums he made with Gerry Mulligan occasionally come back into print and are worth looking for: e.g., Mulligan, *At Storyville* (Pacific Jazz: 94472, 1956, c1990).

33. Kenton, *New Concepts of Artistry in Rhythm* (Capitol: 92865, 1952).

The term "hard bop" was coined in the mid-1950s by jazz pianist-teacher-scholar John Mehegan. Though it certainly meant something specific to him, the term has subsequently been applied to at least four categories of jazz of the 1950s and 1960s:

1. **A gradual continuation of bop** that is often not readily distinguishable from the music of its founders. It employs musicians who achieved their greatest prominence during the 1950s. For instance, numerous recordings by Clifford Brown, Max Roach, and Sonny Rollins fit this designation. (For example, listen to J. J. Johnson's "Get Happy" *CCD1* Track 18, and "Kiss and Run," *JCCD2* Track 6.) Music by the earliest of Art Blakey's bands, particularly those with Clifford Brown, Horace Silver, and Jackie McLean also fall in this classification.[1] ("Cranky Spanky" [*JCCD2* Track 7] might represent an example of the tail end of this category.)

2. **A highly singable, bop-based music, also dubbed "funky jazz" and "soul jazz," that has melodies with bluesy, gospel-like features and has accompaniments comprised of simple, repetitive figures, some of which are Latin American.**[2,3] The music and its accompaniments in this stream were more earthy than the bop continuants of category #1. "Señor Blues" by Horace Silver (*JCCD2* Track 5) represents this category of hard bop, as do the "Jive Samba," "Dis Here," "Sack o' Woe," "Work Song," and "Mercy, Mercy, Mercy," pieces recorded by the Adderley Brothers. Note that only some of Silver's music was

Cannonball and Nat Adderley
(Photo by Herman Leonard, courtesy of Bob Asen—Metronome Collection)

funky. Most was not. (Our recognition for Silver's artistic breadth is not aided by the facts that his 1964 "Song for My Father" is funky, and it remains his biggest seller.) Silver's versatility has a counterpart in the Adderley Brothers's output. That their better known recordings were gospel-tinged has been misleading to listeners who have only limited exposure to their work.[4]

3. An extremely hard-driving later development with roots in bop that often involved **(a) composing pieces using original chord progressions instead of pop song progressions and (b) improvising lines whose construction is distinct from the repertory of Charlie Parker's and Dizzy Gillespie's favorite phrases.** This might best be exemplified by music of Art Blakey's bands in the 1960s (for example, "The Egyptian," CCD2 Track 4). The Art Farmer-Benny Golson Jazztet is another example. Some historians also place the Miles Davis bands of the late 1950s and early 1960s in this bag, omitting the *Kind of Blue* album. (This development is exemplified by improvisations and chord changes in the Davis recording "Two Bass Hit" [CCD1 Track 23] from 1958. This occurs despite the fact that the piece was initially performed by the Dizzy Gillespie big band during the bop era of the 1940s.)

4. A new approach emerging in the 1960s that, though not entirely free of bop, was based mostly on original concepts that were not part of the concurrent "free jazz" movement. This group of styles is highly diverse and never acquired a name of its own. Its saxophonists made clear departures from the approaches of Sonny Rollins and Dexter Gordon. For example, Wayne Shorter and Joe Henderson devised styles that are easily distinguished from the Rollins approach, just as pianists McCoy Tyner and Herbie Hancock came up with original styles of their own after learning the foundation provided by Bud Powell. Trumpeter Freddie Hubbard devised a new style that went far beyond Clifford Brown's and established a new approach. ("Maiden Voyage" [JCCD2 Track 8] illustrates this fourth category. In the minds of some listeners, "Masqualero" [JCCD2 Track 10] might also qualify, though most musicians do not consider it hard bop. They just call it "Mid-60s Miles Davis" style.[5])

When wrangling with these designations, keep in mind that no other bop or hard-bop saxophonist improvised lines as complex as Charlie Parker's, and no other trumpeter played as intricate and harmonically advanced lines as Dizzy Gillespie. Even the most inventive bop players fell short of the unpredictability and richness of invention we heard in the music of the pioneers. Those who came after Parker and Gillespie simplified the styles. Some of hard bop was then a matter of simplification, though some of hard bop was original. Also note that hard bop's originality was not as drastic a departure from bop as bop had been from swing.

During the 1940s, drummer Max Roach had offered an amount of "chattering" and spontaneous communication between soloist and accompanist that exceeded swing era standards. He continued this in the hard bop era of the 1950s and 1960s. Other drummers were equally intrusive or more so. Art Blakey, Philly Joe Jones, and Louis Hayes, for example, were so loud that nightclub audiences often could not hear the band's pianist, and hornmen had to straddle the microphone to be heard. Theirs

TABLE 11.1   A Few of the Many Hard Bop Style Musicians

TRUMPET
Clifford Brown
Kenny Dorham
Miles Davis
Blue Mitchell
Donald Byrd
Thad Jones
Art Farmer
Bill Hardman
Joe Gordon
Carmell Jones
Lee Morgan
Freddie Hubbard
Wilbur Harden
Tommy Turrentine
Benny Bailey
Booker Little
Nat Adderley

BARITONE SAX
Pepper Adams
Cecil Payne
Nick Brignola

ORGAN

Jimmy Smith
Jack McDuff
Richard "Groove"
    Holmes
Don Patterson
Jimmy McGriff
Shirley Scott

**COMPOSER-
ARRANGERS**
Horace Silver
Benny Golson
Gigi Gryce
Oliver Nelson
Cannonball Adderley
Nat Adderley
Wayne Shorter
Bobby Timmons
J.J. Johnson
Jackie McLean
Tom McIntosh

TENOR SAX
Sonny Rollins
John Coltrane
Jimmy Heath
Frank Foster
Clifford Jordan
Teddy Edwards
Benny Golson
Billy Mitchell
George Coleman
John Gilmore
Oliver Nelson
Stanley Turrentine
Junior Cook
Booker Ervin
Joe Henderson
Wayne Shorter
Hank Mobley
Harold Land
J. R. Monterose
Tina Brooks
Yusef Lateef

TROMBONE
J.J. Johnson
Curtis Fuller
Jimmy Knepper
Jimmy Cleveland
Frank Rehak
Tom McIntosh

ALTO SAX
Cannonball Adderley
Jackie McLean
Lou Donaldson
Gigi Gryce
Frank Strozier
Phil Woods

BASS
Paul Chambers
Sam Jones
Doug Watkins
Wilbur Ware
Bob Cranshaw
Gene Taylor
Reggie
    Workman
Percy Heath
Jymie Merritt
Butch Warren
Larry Ridley

GUITAR
Wes Montgomery
Kenny Burrell
Grant Green

DRUMS
Philly Joe Jones
Roy Brooks
Louis Hayes
Art Taylor
Roy Haynes
Roger Humphries
Elvin Jones
Lex Humphries
Max Roach
Art Blakey
Mickey Roker
Al Heath
Ben Riley
Jimmy Cobb
Frankie Dunlop
Billy Higgins

PIANO
Tommy Flanagan
Barry Harris
Cedar Walton
Duke Pearson
Bobby Timmons
Red Garland
Wynton Kelly
Joe Zawinul
Junior Mance
Kenny Drew
Horace Parlan
Les McCann
Gene Harris
Ramsey Lewis
Horace Silver
Elmo Hope
Sonny Clark

TABLE 11.2   Comparing Styles of the 1950s

	COOL	HARD BOP
tone color	light	dark
tone weight	light	heavy
tone texture	soft	raw
melodic conception	simple	complex
overall character	relaxed	hard-driving
	cool	fiery
principal influences	swing and bop	bop
sources for alto saxophone styles	Lee Konitz	Charlie Parker
sources for trumpet styles	Miles Davis	Dizzy Gillespie
		Fats Navarro
		Miles Davis
sources for tenor saxophone styles	Lester Young	Dexter Gordon
		Sonny Stitt
		Don Byas
sources for arranging practices	Claude Thornhill	Tadd Dameron
	Gil Evans	

could be a commanding presence. (Listen to Blakey's "Cranky Spanky" on *JCCD2*, and imagine how the music would have sounded in person.) Bassists ended up wrapping a microphone in a cloth and wedging it behind the bridge of their instrument to compete with the sound of the hard bop drummer. So you see that loud, highly assertive drumming was precedented in the 1940s but became a prime characteristic of hard bop in the 1950s and 1960s. It is also significant that bassists became stronger timekeepers, and many learned how to improvise pizzicato solos sporting the vocabulary of Parker and Gillespie.

Tone qualities preferred by hard bop trumpeters were rich and followed the model of Fats Navarro more than Dizzy Gillespie. Saxophonists preferred heavy, raw tones that tended to be dark, following the model of Dexter Gordon and Sonny Stitt more than Lester Young and Stan Getz. Some were raspy. Despite some exceptions, the trend was evident.

The "hard" designation may have originated partly from the sound of the rhythm section and an unrelenting drive conveyed by the band as a whole. (This music did not have the bounce that characterized much of bop.) Other characteristics are worth mentioning. For instance, despite more varied rhythms and chords in piano comping, the music generally had somewhat less of the stop and start quality that characterized much bop. Nor did it have any hint of light-heartedness or the soaring feeling of much bop. So perception that the horn's tone qualities were hard and dark and that the music was hard driving and heavy may have made the "hard bop" term seem apt.

The "bop," "hard bop," and "funky jazz" terms have been applied without much consistency. Some journalists even used the term "post-bop," thereby overlooking the fact that "post" merely means "after," and an assortment of widely differing styles of jazz have appeared after bop. During the 1990s and beginnings of the twenty-first century

TABLE 11.3	Two Cities Contributed Many Leading Hard Bop Players	
PHILADELPHIA	**DETROIT**	
Clifford Brown	Thad Jones	Yusef Lateef
Lee Morgan	Elvin Jones	Kenny Burrell
McCoy Tyner	Hank Jones	Donald Byrd
Philly Joe Jones	Barry Harris	Billy Mitchell
Jimmy Heath	Charles McPherson	Doug Watkins
Percy Heath	Roland Hanna	Pepper Adams
John Coltrane	Tommy Flanagan	Curtis Fuller
Bobby Timmons	Paul Chambers	
Benny Golson	Ron Carter	
Bill Barron	Louis Hayes	
Kenny Barron		

more confusion was created when listeners used the term "mainstream jazz" to designate these styles and their revivals. Unfortunately, that term had already been coined to designate swing era musicians who were still performing in the 1950s and 1960s. Those who used it for labeling post-bop styles were unaware of its history. Some listeners in the twenty-first century even called such styles "traditional jazz," apparently unaware that "traditional jazz" had long been the label for early jazz and Dixieland. Most musicians themselves merely referred to these styles as "bop," making no distinction between the bop of the founders and the second or third generation of bop-related styles. They focused more on the commonalities than any differences.

The sounds described in this chapter were not exclusive to any particular geographic region. Forerunners of hard bop tenor sax styles included Los Angeles-based Dexter Gordon and New York-based Sonny Stitt. Important models for trumpeters included New York-based Miles Davis and Fats Navarro. In addition, Philadelphia and Detroit (see Table 11.3) contributed many vital players, and Indianapolis contributed guitarist Wes Montgomery (see page 253), trumpeter Freddie Hubbard (discussed on pages 238–41), and trombonist Slide Hampton.

The fourth category of players can be distinguished within the overall category of hard bop. Much of their music draws upon sources outside hard bop (discussed in later chapters) and goes beyond it by devising its own stream of styles. These players made their mark in the 1960s and derived their approaches less directly from bop than did those players mentioned above. With the notable exception of saxophonist John Coltrane, who died in 1967, the most prominent among this group were still active through the 1990s and remained models for aspiring jazz musicians. The outstanding tenor saxophonists in this second wave of hard bop musicians are Joe Henderson (discussed later) and Wayne Shorter (discussed in the next chapter). The top trumpeter is Freddie Hubbard (discussed later). The pianists are McCoy Tyner (see Chapter 13), Herbie Hancock, Chick Corea, and Keith Jarrett (all discussed in Chapter 15). The drummers are Tony Williams (see next chapter) and Elvin Jones (see Chapter 13). You may recognize some of these names grouped here with the 1950s and 1960s for other styles that were developed in the 1970s. However, if we recall the versatility that is so common to jazz giants, it should not be difficult to appreciate, for example, Herbie Hancock's contributing significantly to hard bop during the early 1960s and then creating new styles in the jazz-rock fusion genres of the 1970s and 1980s.

PIANO

There were a number of excellent pianists affiliated with hard bop (see Table 11.1). Two of the most prominent were **Tommy Flanagan** (1930–2001) and Horace Silver. Flanagan was influenced primarily by Teddy Wilson, Bud Powell, Art Tatum, and Hank Jones. He had more instrumental proficiency than almost any other hard bop pianist. His touch was very clean, his lines well-conceived and effortlessly played. Yet in spite of his meticulous attention to technique, Flanagan managed to extract a warm tone from the piano. His tasteful comping, flowing solos, and polite touch provided a perfect complement to trumpeter Miles Davis, saxophonists Sonny Rollins and John Coltrane, and guitarist Wes Montgomery, whom he accompanied on many of their outstanding albums.[6] Flanagan went on to a long tenure as accompanist for singer Ella Fitzgerald and later remained active as leader of his own groups in the 1980s and 1990s.

"Señor Blues," JCCD2 Track 5

Horace Silver (b. 1928) is one of the biggest names in hard bop because of his outstanding work as a composer and bandleader. He also developed an original and substantial piano style. By the 1960s, he had replaced bop's emphasis on long, convoluted lines with his own brief, catchy phrases. Virtuosity is not essential to Silver's style. He almost never double-times. Succinctness and clarity are far higher priorities than speed and agility. His ideas unfold with a logic that is apparent even to the novice listener. Silver made considerable use of silence and employed an exacting deliberation in timing the starting and stopping points of his phrases. His improvised melodic figures are executed in a very forceful, percussive way. His solos are like his tunes—filled with simple ideas that are hummable and easy to remember. It is as though, while improvising, Silver keeps on composing at the same level of creativity and clarity that he maintains in his writing.[7]

As an accompanist, Horace Silver initially drew from bop style. By the late 1950s, however, he had perfected a new style of accompaniment. This approach used figures that sounded like prewritten setups for his soloists. This contrasted with the approach of spontaneously chording in manners that followed the shifting directions taken by the solo improvisations. In this way, the soloists in Silver's bands were supported by backgrounds similar to those in big bands, where written arrangements supply the same accompaniment figures each time the soloist improvises on that piece. The effects were twofold. There was more continuity in Silver's music than in the music produced by the comparatively informal structure of most modern groups. Yet these figures were also a restriction that limited the range of moods an improvising soloist could create. By comparison with traditional bop comping, however, Silver's accompaniment figures gave listeners something to cling to, and this may account for his greater popularity.

Horace Silver was hard bop's most prolific composer. For the Blue Note record company alone, he penned almost all the tunes on over 25 years' worth of his band's albums. Silver put together arrangements that were generally more elaborate than those of other hard bop groups. They often contained ensemble strains in the middle of a piece, as well as Latin American rhythms and hints of gospel music. Silver often voiced trumpet and tenor saxophone four or five scale steps apart. This was a particularly successful way to achieve a fullness that made the quintet sound as though it contained more than five musicians. In addition to using this technique, Silver often wrote bass figures and played them on the piano in unison with his bassist. These figures had an engaging quality that expanded the usually limited scope of bop bass

Horace Silver, the leading composer-pianist-bandleader in hard bop. Prolific and versatile, Silver composed catchy themes and arranged them for his quintets. His music swung with an appealing crispness and bounce. Many of his pieces had a funky, gospelish quality that became widely influential. "Song for My Father" was his biggest hit.

(Photo by Bob Parent, courtesy of Don Parent)

Composed by Horace Silver; recorded on February 6, 1955, for Blue Note by Hank Mobley (tenor sax), Donald Byrd (trumpet), Horace Silver (piano), Doug Watkins (bass), Louis Hayes (drums); available on the *Prentice Hall Jazz Collection,* and Horace Silver, *Six Pieces of Silver* (Blue Note: 25648, 1956, c2000).

"Señor Blues" exemplifies the category of hard bop that is funky and uses Latin American rhythms. Horace Silver's music has always helped define the hard bop genre. Unlike most bop tunes, this melody is so singable that it eventually acquired lyrics and underwent performances by singers. The instrumental version offered here was a popular recording during the 1950s and 1960s and could be found on jukeboxes in inner city taverns. Silver's solo improvisation on it is exquisitely logical and demonstrates his melodic genius. Donald Byrd's trumpet solo illustrates the Clifford Brown style that dominated young trumpeters of the late 1950s and early 1960s. The saxophone solo is by Hank Mobley, one of the most original tenors of the period and an exception to the raw, dark sound of most hard bop tenors. His sound is relatively soft, and his solos are usually quite lyrical, like this one.

A distinct aspect of this composition is the rhythm. Slower than most bop tunes, it begins with a prominent bass line, derived from Latin American influence. The bass sets the rhythmic character of the piece and establishes a catchy groove by playing a repetitive Latin American figure written by Silver. The bassist does not walk or improvise his part as in most other jazz pieces. In fact, his part is doubled by the left-hand work of pianist Silver. This combination of piano and bass creates a compelling tone quality and rhythmic vitality that can be quite engaging to listeners. Silver's right hand plays chords in a repeating rhythm unlike the highly varied and spontaneous comping of bop style accompaniment. Like Silver and his bassist, Silver's drummer plays a constant pattern throughout the piece that complements the piano/bass figure, thereby maintaining a consistent groove instead of the varied ride rhythms and high-hat closings, bombs on the snare drum, etc. that bop drummers usually employ. Silver also used these methods effectively on other pieces. The predictability and the cheerful, strutting character achieved by them probably accounts for much of their popularity.

"Señor Blues" is in compound meter. This means that each beat can be divided into three parts instead of the typical two.

To count the rhythm of this piece, repeat the syllables below:

1– and – a   2– and – a   3– and – a   4– and – a

After listening to the recording a few times, try singing along with the melody played by the trumpet. You will probably have more success with this than you would if you tried to sing a melody from a bop piece. This simple melody is made up of short, regular phrases, separated by rests, whereas bop melodies are typically more complex and less regular, resembling solos more than singable "tunes." Though a bit more complicated than the melody, the solos on this recording are lyrical, logical, and simpler than the bop improvisations of Charlie Parker and Dizzy Gillespie. Some of the faster, double-timed lines show the influence from bop, but many of the phrases are soulful and funky.

"Señor Blues" is simpler and more arranged than most bop tunes, but more aggressive and blues-oriented than cool jazz.

ELAPSED
TIME

0'00"   **Introduction**
           Bass and left hand of pianist establish feeling of the piece.

0'10"   Drums enter, as well as right hand of piano, with dark sounding chords.

0'17"   **Melody** (First Chorus—12 Measures)
           Trumpet and tenor sax play a blues-inflected, funky melody, always in harmony with each other. Rhythm section continues the feeling of the introduction.

0'48"   **Melody** (Second Chorus)
           Intensity picks up, as horns play a related melody in a higher register.

1'17"   **Donald Byrd's Trumpet Solo Improvisation** (Third and Fourth Choruses)
           Some of the lines are double-timed, while others are quite simple and bluesy. Notice that the piano continues doubling the bass line throughout the solos.

LISTENING GUIDE continued on next page

2'17" **Hank Mobley's Sax Solo Improvisation** (Fifth and Sixth Choruses)

Solo begins quite slowly, but faster double-timed figures follow.

3'16" **Ensemble Passage** (Seventh Chorus)

Bass and piano simplify figure a bit. Trumpet and sax harmonize a rhythmic passage featuring rests and many repeated notes.

3'41" **Horace Silver's Piano Solo Improvisation** (Eighth–Eleventh Choruses)

Instead of playing chords with his left hand, he continues doubling the bass line. He combines single-note, horn-like lines by his right hand, with passages of two-note chords. Several of his lines are double-timed, but he never abandons the blues feeling. Listen to the way he repeats some of his musical ideas, almost literally.

5'19" **Melody** (Twelfth and Thirteenth Choruses)

6'18" **Ending** (16 measures)

A new, written-out melody is played by the horns in harmony. The bass line continues, but this time it stays on one chord instead of moving through the blues progression. The eight-measure figure is repeated intact.

6'55" A short rest is followed by a closing bass line.

lines. It is partly for these reasons that his quintet's identity was unlike that of any other bop or hard bop group. In addition, Silver's quintet performances were consistently swinging and polished, and they featured many of the best musicians of the 1950s and 1960s (see Table 11.4). Silver remained active in the 1990s and continued to tour and record with bands of similar style and instrumentation.[8]

TRUMPET

The order of major influences on modern trumpeters begins in the 1940s with Dizzy Gillespie, then Miles Davis and Fats Navarro. However, it was the successor to these men who had the greatest impact. His name was **Clifford Brown**

TABLE 11.4 **A Few of the Many Horace Silver Sidemen**

Donald Byrd	Hank Mobley	Roy Brooks
Blue Mitchell	Bob Berg	Louis Hayes
Art Farmer	Junior Cook	Al Foster
Tom Harrell	Joe Henderson	Billy Cobham
Woody Shaw	Michael Brecker	Roger Humphries
Randy Brecker		
Carmell Jones		

(1930–1956), and he drew his style largely from Navarro, with a touch of Davis. Among musicians, Brown is probably the most widely admired trumpeter since the swing era. Brown, however, is not widely known outside the inner circles of modern jazz musicians, and he was documented on recordings from only 1952 to 1956. He did not use the peculiar note choices that typified Gillespie, nor did he convey the intimate moods that distinguished Davis. By comparison with Gillespie and Davis, he played at a high level of inspiration and execution more consistently from performance to performance. Brown used a wider, more deliberate vibrato than Gillespie or Davis, something Navarro had occasionally employed. Brown's use of a slow, even, very obvious vibrato may be responsible for its renewed use by jazz trumpeters in the 1950s and 1960s. Another distinguishing mark of Brown's style is the overall contour of his solos. Jazz historian Harvey Pekar has observed that Brown's solos are similar to those of Davis because they jump into the high register less often than Gillespie's and Navarro's, and the shape of Brown's and Davis's lines are usually smoother than Gillespie's and Navarro's. Because of this, we might regard Brown's solos as cooler than most hard bop, even though his solos are not as simple as the most concise solos of Chet Baker or Miles Davis. It is evident that Brown drew upon previous styles, but he also devised a style that was distinguishable from his sources.

Clifford Brown, the most influential hard bop trumpeter. Shown here in 1955 at the Basin Street Café in New York.

(Photo by Bob Parent, courtesy of Don Parent)

Let's consider several reasons that musicians were so impressed with Clifford Brown's playing. Most prominent was that Brown managed to suggest relaxation in his playing, even when executing intricate melodic figures. This has at least two possible causes: the perfection he achieved in making the trumpet obey his wishes, and his concern with simplifying bop instead of blazing new trails as Parker and Gillespie had. Brown also placed more emphasis on swinging than on generating surprise after surprise, as bop soloists often did. Tuneful improvisations were more common for him than for most of his contemporaries.[9] In these respects, Brown's work on trumpet parallels Sonny Stitt's work on saxophone. Brown refined a repertory of phrases and ways of moving gracefully through the chord progressions. Brown's style proved accessible to many other trumpeters because of these techniques, their fluid sensibility, and the easy swing feeling they produced. As with Stitt, Brown's contributions were also absorbed as stock vocabulary for hard bop players.

"Kiss and Run," JCCD2 *Track 6*

Clifford Brown's music projected a joyful spirit. This, together with the lilt and bounce in his lines, was contagious. He could generate long, flowing lines at furious tempos and still maintain the warmth and suppleness of his wide, glowing tone. Most other trumpeters stood in awe of Brown's dazzling speed and agility. Also, he did what is almost impossible at those frantic speeds: he kept his accurate intonation and relaxed swing feeling. His firm command of accurate articulation was unparalleled in modern jazz, and he was able to make meaty phrases come tumbling from his horn, chorus after chorus. An exuberance projected by Brown's music combined with his assured manner, pretty sound, and fertile imagination to influence an entire generation of modern trumpeters, including Donald Byrd, Bill Hardman, Louis Smith, Lee Morgan, and Carmell Jones. It inspired another group of players during the 1980s and 1990s, including Roy Hargrove, Phil Harper, Marlon Jordan, and others.

Bill Hardman on *"Cranky Spanky,"* JCCD2 *Track 7*

"Maiden Voyage," | JCCD2 Track 8 |

Miles Davis and Clifford Brown remained models for aspiring trumpeters to imitate long after they first became known among musicians. But by the 1970s, the majority of young trumpeters, including such notables as Woody Shaw and Randy Brecker, were imitating another model: **Freddie Hubbard.** Though his early playing drew from Clifford Brown, Miles Davis, and Chet Baker, Hubbard (b. 1938) had developed his own original approach by the early 1960s. His playing style departed from bop and was compatible with "free jazz" approaches of the 1960s and "jazz-rock" approaches of the 1970s.[10]

A number of characteristics can help us distinguish Hubbard from Brown and Davis. Although he incorporated some Davis methods of manipulating his tone quality and pitch, Hubbard steered clear of the way in which Davis gets away from the beat. Hubbard stuck close to the beat and liked to double-time. His sense of time is unusually precise and extremely firm. In contrast to the solemn and methodical manner of Davis, much of Hubbard's work sounds off-handed and playful. There is a looseness to his fashion that implies great creative freedom and tremendous conceptual flexibility. Instead of following through on every idea, he did not hesitate to interrupt himself if he got a new idea while he was playing an old one. His style bristles with excitement; even his ballad renditions project great verve. Like those of saxophonist John Coltrane, his improvisations exhibit a willingness to spontaneously construct and rework figures from odd combinations of notes and rhythms, not depending on stock bop phrases. In this way he was harmonically daring and impulsive. The richness and range of his imagination combined with his free manner to build a new vocabulary for jazz trumpet style.[11] (One of Hubbard's best solos can be heard on "Maiden Voyage.")

Freddie Hubbard, who developed a unique vocabulary for jazz trumpet playing that departed from paths staked out by Clifford Brown and Miles Davis and remained influential in the twenty-first century. Shown here in the 1960s when he originated his new approach.

(Courtesy of Frank Driggs)

Freddie Hubbard is almost universally envied among trumpeters for his outstanding mastery of the instrument. His tone was clear and well focused. His intonation was excellent. His articulation was crisp, and he could improvise coherently at brisk tempos and sound as though he still had plenty of strength and agility in reserve. Like Brown's, Hubbard's sense of time was very precise. Hubbard also mastered a very demanding technique called a lip trill, in which, without changing fingering or shaking the trumpet, he rapidly alternated, in legato manner, intervals of a minor third, moving the bottom note in stepwise fashion. This became a trademark of his highly virtuosic style.[12]

DRUMS

The period in jazz history that produced hard bop also produced several innovative accompaniment styles of jazz drumming. Chico Hamilton has been discussed already in the unit about "West Coast-style" cool jazz. Like Hamilton, several other innovative drummers were also important as bandleaders. Art Blakey and Max Roach are discussed here because their bands, not just their drumming, were at the forefront of hard bop. Philly Joe Jones is also discussed here because his contribution parallels that of Blakey in helping define the accompanying style in hard bop. (Elvin Jones is not discussed until the John Coltrane chapter because, though he performed innovatively during the 1950s, his innovations were most widely showcased with Coltrane in the 1960s.)

Art Blakey (1919–1991) epitomized the loosening of jazz drumming style, whereby loud, directive intrusions emerged at the forefront of the combo sound.

Composed by Herbie Hancock; recorded in 1964 for Blue Note by Freddie Hubbard (trumpet), George Coleman (tenor saxophone), Herbie Hancock (piano), Ron Carter (bass), and Tony Williams (drums); reissued on Hancock, *Maiden Voyage* (Blue Note: 95331, 1965, c1999); and *Best of Herbie Hancock: The Blue Note Years* (Blue Note: 91142, 1962–69, c1988).

This piece was included to demonstrate trumpeter Freddie Hubbard's manner, significant by itself, but also important because of its broad influence. Hubbard was the main source for the widely respected style of Woody Shaw, and it was one of the numerous styles emulated by Wynton Marsalis, the best-known "neo-traditional"/"neo-classical" trumpeter of the 1980s and 1990s. (Marsalis reveals roots in Hubbard most clearly in his solos on Art Blakey's albums of the early 1980s, such as *Album of the Year* and *Keystone 3*.) Long after the 1960s and 1970s, Hubbard remained an appealing model for young trumpeters. For instance, at the beginning of the twenty-first century, Rick Braun, the most prominent trumpeter in what radio broadcasters call "smooth jazz," derived his approach mostly from Hubbard's. And an exciting young trumpeter named Sean Jones began appearing on albums in 2003, playing in a style partly indebted to Hubbard's.

The music on this selection illustrates the fourth category of "hard bop" as mentioned at the beginning of this chapter. Hubbard's playing here does not reach back to bop, but instead shows completely fresh invention. Herbie Hancock's piano work also departs significantly from bop. The melodic content within the double-timing and quadruple-timing passages of saxophonist George Coleman's solo does, however, draw from bop methods.

This selection provides a remarkable example of Hubbard's improvisational approach. It shows his extraordinary talent as a spontaneous composer. (Hubbard's improvisations on the album from which this selection was drawn and on Herbie Hancock's *Empyrean Isles* album are among the best of his career.) Unlike many hard bop soloists who re-use standard phrases when they piece together their solos, Hubbard consistently surprises us with new ideas. Hubbard's first solo chorus on "Maiden Voyage" is so concise and well-paced in its development that its quality is on a par with any good original tune conceived intact, not merely an improvisation unfolding spontaneously at the moment of performance. This solo has been celebrated for its logic and continuity, where every phrase leads somewhere, as in the plot to a story. The trumpeter's improvisation is outstanding for the ways in which Hubbard takes a simple idea and repeats it with variations, much as a classical composer might. He proves his genius at what musicians call "motivic development," which means generating a melodic figure (a "motive"), then making something out of it by altering ("developing") it several times. For example, he generates a brief phrase, beginning at 4'06", in a clear, logical fashion. He then transposes it to a higher pitch and modifies it at 4'11". Then at 4'15" he plays it a third time in altered form at an even higher pitch.

Beginning at 2'24" Hubbard gives us a quite lyrical construction. Then he devises another new melody at 2'36" that he repeats at 2'41" and then transposes down for another variation at 2'43". Then at 2'51" he invents yet another new idea with its own unique character. At 2'59" he inserts a blues riff to get us through the 16 beats of chord #3. At 3'14" Hubbard tenses and gets more aggressive, readying us for high action in his second chorus.

Some listeners consider this second chorus as Hubbard's greatest solo passage. He begins at 3'22" with a stunning melodic invention forming a stark call in the high register that is staccato and highly syncopated, interspersed with double-time figures. The construction of this solo chorus is crafted to build tension and then hold it for a moment. Then Hubbard releases the tension at 3'28" through another set of original figures that are complicated strings of notes, in which the effect of the overall string is more important than the internal construction of the figures.

During the bridge portion of his second chorus, beginning at 3'51", Hubbard shows notable conceptual flexibility and perhaps the effects of avant-garde jazz. He produces cascades of tones that are neither swinging nor motivically organized, but instead collectively arranged to create a shimmering effect. Incidentally, the function of this device corresponds to the function that bridge sections of tunes routinely offer: providing a change of pace before returning to repetitions of the A-section. (See Appendix B and *Demo CD* Track 33 for more explanation.) Hubbard's shimmering is coordinated with impressionistic accompaniment figures from piano, bass, and drums. It may be no coincidence that Hancock mentions an ocean effect in his notes on the original album jacket.

The album from which this selection was drawn became a staple in the record collections of musicians during the 1960s and 1970s. The "Maiden Voyage" tune and its chord changes became a jazz standard that musicians were expected to know as well as musicians of the preceding era knew Dizzy Gillespie's "A Night

LISTENING GUIDE *continued on next page*

in Tunisia," Charlie Parker's "Billie's Bounce," and Jerome Kern's "All the Things You Are." Few jam sessions of the late 1960s and early 1970s omitted it.

"Maiden Voyage" contains only four chords. (See Appendix H for their technical names.) The first (X) lasts 16 beats. The second (Y) lasts 16 beats. Those first two are then repeated in the same arrangement of durations (X-Y). The third chord (Z) remains in effect for 16 beats. The fourth chord (W) remains in effect for 16 beats. The arrangement can thus be described as X-Y-X-Y-Z-W-X-Y, and the song form can be summarized as A (X-Y), A (X-Y), B (Z-W), A (X-Y). In the structural analysis below, Z-W indicates the B-section, also known as "the bridge."

As with the five-mode construction of "Flamenco Sketches" from the Miles Davis *Kind of Blue* album, analyzed on page 495, the long stretch that each chord is in effect gives us extended opportunity to detect how chords guide the invention of solo improvisation. We can begin to notice the ways soloists change their lines when the chord changes. It is especially evident here because sax and trumpet both linger on the chords occurring earliest in their solos, as if to bask in the harmonic radiance and float above the cushion of Latin-American-style rhythms coming out of the piano, bass, and drum part. The simplicity of the X-Y-X-Y-Z-W-X-Y arrangement of chords gives us a frame of reference with which we can follow Freddie Hubbard's thinking and notice how the composition's structure partly inspires the organization of ideas that the trumpeter develops over it. Hubbard wields control over the architecture of his solo by keeping in mind the architecture of the harmonies sounding under him. He gauges his inventions in terms of the moments in which the chords will change. Notice that several of his ideas occur and are completely developed within the duration of just one chord. He sometimes moves to a new idea when a new chord takes effect.

The rhythmic style of this performance exhibits a groove that is achieved without any bop style accompaniment devices such as walking bass, ride rhythms, high-hat snapping closed on every other beat, etc. Instead, it employs preset figures in piano and bass that resemble patterns common to Latin American music. Unlike Latin American music, however, the patterns do not persist unchanged throughout the performance. In fact, there is considerable variation upon them. There is also the invention of new, wide-ranging, non-timekeeping sounds, especially in the bridge portions of some solo choruses.

ELAPSED
TIME

8-Measure Introduction

0'00"		The same chord is played eight times by piano in a Latin American rhythm. While bassist is playing in unison with pianist's left-hand figure, drummer is sounding a Latin American rhythm on the ride cymbal.
0'09"		A new chord is played eight times in the same rhythm as the first chord.

Theme Statement

0'16"	X	Trumpet and tenor sax play melody in unison with lots of sustained tones.
0'25"	Y	
0'32"	X	
0'40"	Y	
0'48"	Z	Theme of A-section is played a half step higher in pitch, and sax joins piano in playing the accompanying rhythm and harmony instead of continuing unison with trumpet.
0'56"	W	
1'04"	X	
1'12"	Y	

Second Chorus: Tenor Sax Solo by George Coleman

1'20"	X	Cymbal crash announces first solo. Coleman begins with very relaxed phrases, as though hovering over the accompaniment sounds.
1'28"	Y	
1'35"	X	
1'41"		Sax begins double-timing.
1'43"	Y	Sax continues double-timing.
1'50"	Z	Sax continues by quadruple-timing
1'58"	W	Sax still quadruple-timing.

LISTENING GUIDE *continued on next page*

2'07"	X	
2'15"	Y	Bass is double-stopping (two notes at a time). Sax offers staccato figure.

Third Chorus: Trumpet Solo by Freddie Hubbard

2'21"		
2'24"		Hubbard enters with a very melodic string of phrases, employing sustained tones.
2'29"	Y	
2'38"	X	Hubbard enters with a higher-pitched idea and improvises a dreamy, perfectly crafted new melody.
2'45"	Y	
2'51"	Z	Hubbard conjures another new, highly melodic phrase.
2'59"	W	Hubbard introduces and develops a bluesy idea that carries through 3'06".
3'07"	X	Hubbard devises a lazy line of mostly soft, sustained tones that casts a gentle effect.
3'15"	Y	Hubbard becomes more active, increasing tension for high excitement to come.

Fourth Chorus: Trumpet Solo Continues

3'22"	X	Hubbard double-times a high-pitched staccato figure, and swingingly develops it into a breath-taking solo passage.
3'30"	Y	Hubbard sustains excitement. He continues his idea, stringing together phrase fragments, each of which lifts off.
3'34"		Hubbard concludes the series of rapid-fire lines with a phrase that drops, as though to say the trumpeter is through with that burst of energy, until he double-times out of it.
3'37"	X	Slurring out of his previous phrase, Hubbard invents a new idea that begins right on the start of this section. This develops into a complicated double-time creation.
3'45"	Y	Hubbard hatches another new idea, which then evolves into quadruple-timing.
3'47"		Hubbard generates a sequence of quick ascending phrases that spill into the bridge section.
3'52"	Z	Hubbard creates a shimmering effect by off-handedly scattering a string of up-and-down runs, maintaining momentum in touch with the on-going activity of harp-like arpeggios from piano, repeating bass, and coloristic cymbal sounds.
4'00"	W	Hubbard continues to off-handedly scatter a string of up-and-down runs, to 4'05".
4'06"		Hubbard introduces a new idea.
4'07"	X	
4'11"		Hubbard then transposes his new idea and plays it again.
4'15"	Y	He transposes the same idea to play a third time in altered form. Piano echoes that version of Hubbard's idea.
4'20"		Hubbard rapidly reiterates the same note, alternating timbres. He resolves the tension built by that device by making his final solo note arrive on the downbeat of the next chorus.

Fifth Chorus: Herbie Hancock Piano Solo

4'22"	X	Hancock is moving around the scale in block chords. Bass is double-stopping.
4'30"	Y	
4'35"		The piano sounds function to create colors and textures rather than melody.
4'38"	X	Floating rhythmic feeling departs from the pulse.
4'45"	Y	
4'47"		Piano sounds chords in a manner as though strumming guitar strings.
4'53"	Z	
4'56"		High-pitched tones form a tender new line that lingers as though Hancock is caressing important notes in it.
5'05"	W	Hancock hints at starting a swinging new line in double-time.
5'09"	X	Drummer double-times in response to Hancock's hint of starting a swinging new line.
5'14"		Hancock follows up on his previous hint and now briefly improvises a swinging line in double-time bop style.

LISTENING GUIDE *continued on next page*

5'16"	Y	
	Sixth Chorus: More Piano Solo	
5'23"	X	Hancock transforms the swinging line back into the dreamy manner, caressing important notes in a new melodic idea.
5'31"	Y	Hancock plays the original "Maiden Voyage" rhythm in two-handed chords underscored by cymbals, punctuated by snare drum.
5'39"	X	
5'45"	Y	
5'53"	Z	Hancock invents a new melodic phrase in high pitch range, but does not develop it.
5'59"	W	Hancock plays arpeggios and tremolos, thereby creating a shimmering effect while drummer plays triplets on cymbal; bass continues double-stopping in tune's original pattern.
6'08"	X	Resolution back to the calm chords.
6'11"		Bass returns to opening figure.
6'15"	Y	Hancock returns to block chords, as in intro. There is much decoration by cymbals.
6'23"	**Seventh Chorus: Final Theme Statement**	
7'26"		Ending vamp
7'29"		Hubbard sustains a trill until the end.

Art Blakey, hard bop drummer and bandleader. The sound of Blakey's bands helped define hard bop. They played with hard-driving, unrelenting force, always swinging with a compelling seriousness of purpose. Blakey continued to hire the top musicians for four decades, including Clifford Brown, Horace Silver, Wayne Shorter, Freddie Hubbard, and Wynton and Branford Marsalis.

(Photo by Lee Tanner)

Blakey's playing as an accompanist was so dynamic that for him to solo was almost anticlimactic. He was able to cue and underscore transitions within each piece by the figures he played and the levels of loudness he used for them. He was often found to be directing the mood and choosing the moments during which tension was to rise or fall. His former sidemen have mentioned how he made them aware of pacing their improvisations and trying to build tension and excitement gradually over the course of their solos.[13]

For over 30 years, Art Blakey led quintets and sextets that were representatives of the hard bop style. Their music was extremely intense, hard driving, and uncompromising. Their swing feeling was unrelenting and possessed a weightiness that distinguished it from those "cool jazz" styles that also swung persistently. The list of notable musicians in Blakey's bands is immense. (Table 11.5 mentions only a few.) These players often received their first wide exposure to jazz fans while they toured and recorded with him. Many of them soon became leaders of their own groups. Ordinarily, Blakey hired individualists who were relatively young but played very well and sounded distinctive. Their compositions became Blakey's repertory. The character of those compositions, in turn, became part of the band's character.

Max Roach made his reputation during the bop era and then continued to develop new bands and drumming approaches. He is best and most importantly recognized as the fountainhead of bebop and hard bop drumming styles,

Composed by Sam Dockery; recorded on December 12, 1956, by Art Blakey (drums), Bill Hardman (trumpet), Jackie McLean (alto sax), Sam Dockery (piano), Spanky DeBrest (bass); originally issued on Art Blakey, *Hard Bop* (Columbia: CL 1040, 1956, c1957); reissued on Blakey, *Hard Bop/Paris Concert* (Collectables: 5675, 1956, 1958, c1995).

This performance epitomizes what is meant by "hard bop." In fact, *Hard Bop* was actually the title of the album on which this selection was originally issued. To call this music "hard-driving" would be an understatement. It conveys a sense of seriousness and urgency that is almost overwhelming. Excitement is present from the very first beat and never lets up. These aspects indicate the attitude that was set for many Blakey groups to follow. It also gives us a terrific sample of Jackie McLean, who vied with Cannonball Adderley as the most distinctive and powerful alto saxophonist of the era. His hard-edged, extremely forceful manner delivered richly imaginative, highly melodic improvisations. (Both McLean and Adderley offered sufficiently original twists on bebop style that their playing should be easily distinguished from Charlie Parker.) The recording additionally provides an early example of trumpeter Bill Hardman, who even as recently as the 1970s remained one of the top Clifford Brown disciples.

This recording offers excellent demonstrations of Blakey's supercharged drumming, showing how his musical comments sometimes envelop soloists, and how he often seems to be goading them on to achieve more and more. Sometimes Blakey underscores the rhythms in his soloist's lines, as though a commentary on their action. This might be what is occurring at about 2'26" where Blakey follows trumpeter Hardman's melodic rhythm with a new sequence of his own that mimics Hardman's. It also might be what led to Blakey's clicking sounds that immediately follow pianist Dockery's staccato remarks at 3'34". Other times Blakey interjects his own ideas so forcefully that his soloists are obliged to incorporate his rhythms into their melodic lines or respond with complementary rhythms of their own. For instance, at 2'41" Hardman apparently crafts his line to complement Blakey's surges.

That Blakey is very conscious of song form should be no surprise because he began his career as a pianist. He thinks orchestrally when he is playing. This is obvious on "Cranky Spanky" because he uses the inherent tension-release sequences evoked by the tune's chord changes as a cue for placement of spontaneous drum and cymbal sounds that enhance the flow of his soloists's improvisations. It is as though he is conducting the band from his perch behind the drum set. For example, his trademark press rolls on snare drum often introduce and/or reinforce the onset of new choruses, where tension is usually released (particularly at 1'39", 2'03", and 3'02"). He effectively used stop-time solo breaks to launch solos by his sidemen, as at 0'32" for Jackie McLean's entrance.

Note: To familiarize yourself with distinctive features to listen for, study *Demo CD* Tracks 1–7, 20, 23, 29, and 34 for the sounds of the ride cymbal, snare drum, tom-tom, bass drum, piano comping, solo break, walking bass, and high-hat. (Blakey snaps his high-hat cymbals shut on the second and fourth of every four beats more loudly than any other drummer.) Incidentally, the twentieth chorus of "Cranky Spanky" is a walking solo for the bassist. During the 1950s, bassists were often exposed in this way to credit their work. They just kept walking as they had during their accompaniment of solos by other band members, but this time no one else soloed. Today we are more accustomed to hearing melodic bass solos, but we should also be aware of this practice.

ELAPSED
TIME

	Introduction
0'00"	unison trumpet and alto sax; no piano, bass, or drums
0'03"	drum solo break
	First Chorus
0'07"	16-bar **theme statement**, accompanied by walking bass, piano comping, high-hat cymbals closed sharply on every other beat, ride rhythms played by drum stick on ride cymbal, and Blakey contributing numerous "chattering" sounds by striking the rim of his snare drum; excitement increases
0'21"	**Second Chorus**
	Repeat of Theme
0'32"	Solo break for alto saxophonist Jackie McLean, who uses a scale-like run up to the downbeat of his first solo chorus.

LISTENING GUIDE *continued on next page*

0'34"	**Third Chorus**
	Alto Sax Solo. Notice McLean's acidic tone and insistent delivery. His improvisation is packed with brief melodies, darting from one to the next, as he skitters over what sounds like Blakey building a garage.
0'47"	**Fourth Chorus**
1'00"	**Fifth Chorus**
1'13"	**Sixth Chorus**
	McLean introduces a slightly Oriental flavor.
1'25"	**Seventh Chorus**
1'39"	**Eighth Chorus**
	Blakey's press roll announces **Solo Trumpet Improvisation.**
	Hardman begins with a paraphrase of "Dixie," subsequently developed into line after line of intricate figures that manage to keep up with the hurried pace established already.
1'51"	**Ninth Chorus**
	Tenth Chorus
2'03"	To introduce the tenth chorus, Blakey plays a roll on his tom-toms, spontaneously synchronizing with emphases on his bass drum.
	Blakey comes out of that adventure with his trademark press roll on snare drum, and is then calm for a while.
	Hardman is building his solo by repetitions of a climbing figure, rising step-wise each time.
2'15"	Blakey anticipates the eleventh chorus with syncopated clicking.
	Eleventh Chorus
2'26"	Hardman's toppling figures inspire Blakey's offset tom-tom/bass drum accents.
2'28"	**Twelfth Chorus**
2'40"	**Thirteenth Chorus**
	Hardman crafts his line to mimic Blakey's rhythmic interjections.
	Fourteenth Chorus
2'53"	Blakey brings in a new chorus with another press roll.
	Fifteenth Chorus
3'06"	**Piano solo** by Sam Dockery, whose entrance is soon re-emphasized by another Blakey press roll at 3'08".
3'10"	Blakey's high-hat cymbals snapping closed on every other beat are especially noticeable now that everything else has quieted down.
	Sixteenth Chorus
3'17"	Dockery repeats his funky crushed-chord figure, then transposes it upward and repeats it again. Its rhythm intentionally fights the timekeeping bass and drums.
3'30"	**Seventeenth Chorus**
3'35"	Blakey begins tapping the rim of his snare drum in a highly syncopated manner.
3'40"	Dockery invents a call-and-response figure for himself.
3'42"	**Eighteenth Chorus**
	Nineteenth Chorus
3'55"	Funky crushed tones are repeated again and transposed downward for more reiterations. The rhythms of Dockery's melodic adventure here intentionally conflict with the underlying beat.
4'08"	**Twentieth Chorus (Walking Bass Solo)**
	Piano stops soloing and reverts solely to comping, so we can now more clearly appreciate the fast walking bass of Spanky DeBrest, the tune's namesake. Notice the prominent "chick" sound of Blakey's high-hat.

LISTENING GUIDE *continued on next page*

Twenty-First Chorus

4'19"   **Theme statement** is presented by trumpet/sax unison, with Blakey underscoring and responding to the theme's rhythms with his own clickings on his drum rims.

Blakey is back to creating the sounds of building a garage.

Twenty-Second Chorus

4'31"   **Repeat of theme,** accompanied by more of Blakey's garage-building sounds

4'42"   solo drum break

4'44"   Unison trumpet and sax play a tie-it-up figure, resoundingly stated last time with piano and drums reinforcing it.

more so than Blakey or Philly Joe Jones. Roach is routinely cited for his clean touch and discreet accompanying, and because he does not flaunt his proficiency. He is known for intelligently developed solos that are often melodic, and a command of the drum set that never overshadows his musical sense. Few modern drummers have escaped his influence. He continued to lead hard bop-style bands during the 1990s. Roach is singled out for mention again in this chapter because he founded one of the great bands in hard bop. It was a quintet with trumpeter Clifford Brown, which toured from 1954 until Brown's death in 1956.[14] (See Chapter 9 for more about his playing.)

"Kiss and Run," JCCD2 *Track 6;* SCCJ: *"Pent-Up House"*

Philly Joe Jones (1923–1985) was among the most adventurous of rhythm section players in the 1950s. Next to Max Roach, Jones is the most widely cited influence among drummers who emerged during the 1960s. Compared with other drummers, he played more figures, and his activity was more conversation-like. His playing often

TABLE 11.5   A Few of the Many Art Blakey Sidemen

Clifford Brown	Junior Mance
Donald Byrd	Keith Jarrett
Bill Hardman	Curtis Fuller
Lee Morgan	Wynton Marsalis
Freddie Hubbard	Bobby Timmons
Woody Shaw	George Cables
Jackie McLean	Reggie Workman
Hank Mobley	Jymie Merritt
Wayne Shorter	Lou Donaldson
Benny Golson	Dave Schnitter
Johnny Griffin	Bobby Watson
Chuck Mangione	James Williams
Horace Silver	Valerie Ponomarev
Cedar Walton	Ira Sullivan

sounded as though he were reacting instantaneously to the improvisations of his fellow band members by complementing them. His fills are models of originality and assured execution that are often as melodic as the horn lines they complement. His work conveyed a constant excitement. His crisp fills on the snare drum, accents on the bass drum, and splashes on the cymbal were so well conceived that they became models of how active drummers could be without disturbing the pulse.[15]

"Two Bass Hit,"
CCD1 *Track 23*

SAXOPHONE

Cannonball Adderley (1928–1975) was one of the best improvisers to play alto saxophone after Charlie Parker died. In fact, some listeners considered Adderley to be Parker's successor, though Adderley himself felt such praise was undeserved. In a few respects, Adderley's style is like Parker's: highly fluid, supercharged, and unpredictable. However, Adderley initially derived his style not from Parker but from the swing era styles of Pete Brown and Benny Carter. Then he drew from Parker and Eddie Vinson, and his later style demonstrated advances made by John Coltrane. During his creative peak of 1957 to 1959, when he played with Miles Davis and John Coltrane, Adderley's solos were filled with little melodies. His command over the instrument vied with the virtuosity attained by Parker and Coltrane. Adderley's ability to keep up with Coltrane and sometimes surpass him was an indication of his stunning improvisational prowess.[16]

"Flamenco Sketches,"
JCCD2 *Track 9; "Two Bass*
Hit," CCD1 Track 23

The tone quality that Cannonball Adderley extracted from the alto saxophone was so deep and full that listeners sometimes mistook it for tenor saxophone. (To acquaint yourself with the differences between alto and tenor saxophone sounds, watch: *DVD* Tracks 71 and 72; and listen to *Demo CD* Tracks 72 and 73.) Listen to "Flamenco Sketches," and compare Adderley's sound with Coltrane's. Another excellent comparison of the two instruments and these two saxophonists at their peak is available in "Two Bass Hit"; some consider it to be Adderley's best solo on record.

Together with the vibrato Adderley used, the effect of his tone was warm and glowing. He bent this huge tone with blue notes and wails, thereby creating an earthy, legato style that has been called "blues drenched."[17] Contrasting with the solemn urgency of most hard bop, Adderley's playing conveys a sense of fun. He loved to double-time, and he often incorporated snippets of pop tunes into his lines.[18] A feeling of exhilaration is present when he digs into an improvisation and starts spinning out inspired lines, with their dense activity and ever-shifting directions. But Adderley was not entirely bouncy and lighthearted; he could also evoke calm and reflection. For instance, his solos on the Davis album *Kind of Blue* sound quite reflective, and they are among the most original improvisations he recorded. (One of these is in "Flamenco Sketches," *JCCD2* Track 9.[19])

On and off during the 1950s, '60s, and '70s, Cannonball Adderley co-led a series of bands with his brother, cornetist Nat Adderley. The groups enjoyed a large following and continued until Cannonball's death in 1975. Many pieces in the band's repertory constituted what journalists dubbed "funky jazz": "Jive Samba," "Work Song," "Sack o' Woe," and their biggest hit, "Mercy, Mercy, Mercy." Though most of its repertory was swinging music with little dilution of the bop style, the group was best known for its funk hits, "Mercy, Mercy, Mercy," "Walk Tall," and "Country Preacher."

There were many excellent tenor saxophonists in hard bop (see Table 11.1). Although an entire book would be required to do them justice, we will consider four stand-outs: John Coltrane, Sonny Rollins, Joe Henderson, and Wayne Shorter. John Coltrane created an original hard bop style that is well represented by recordings he made in the 1950s with the bands of Miles Davis. (Listen to him on "Flamenco Sketches," *JCCD2* Track 9.) We postpone our discussion of Coltrane to a special

Composed by Sam Coslow; recorded on March 22, 1956, for Prestige by Sonny Rollins (tenor saxophone), Clifford Brown (trumpet), Richie Powell (piano), George Morrow (bass), and Max Roach (drums); reissued on Rollins, *Sonny Rollins Plus 4* (Fantasy: OJC-243 [Prestige 7038], c1987).

Terms to learn from *Demo CD and DVD*: snare drum, tom-tom, high-hat, crash cymbal, ride cymbal, ride rhythm, comping, trumpet, tenor saxophone, bass, rhythm section, staccato.

This "Kiss and Run" recording is by one of the most celebrated bands of the modern era. Though usually billed as the Max Roach-Clifford Brown Quintet, the band was led by its saxophonist Sonny Rollins on this date because he had contracted the recording session. The drummer is Max Roach, who had been the top drummer in bop style of the late 1940s and continued his eminence during the 1950s. Notice how he provides an almost continuous commentary on the music with crackling sounds on snare drum. Note his rolls on snare drum that introduce new sections of the piece. He frequently underscores rhythms of the melody lines, too. Pay attention to the timekeeping and swing feeling he contributes by crisply snapping shut the high-hat cymbals on every other beat ("chick . . . chick") and cleanly playing ride rhythms on the ride cymbal. He was known for his speed and crisp touch.

Trumpeter Clifford Brown and tenor saxophonist Sonny Rollins, the top hornmen in hard bop. Shown here in 1956 while members of the Max Roach-Clifford Brown Quintet.

(Photo by Charles Stewart)

This rendition of "Kiss and Run" remains one of the most spectacular illustrations of Clifford Brown's virtuosity and buoyant swing feeling. These virtues are particularly evident from 0'16" to 0'26" where he flows almost effortlessly at a brisk tempo, improvising line after line of substantial melodies. Then at 3'10" he becomes quite tuneful when he generates a series of ascending arpeggios (chord notes played one at a time), followed by reduction in the density of his line by playing just one note per beat six times.

The recording also contains some of the most fluid and fertile examples of the Sonny Rollins saxophone style. In fact, this is one of the few recordings that pleased the saxophonist himself. His creative outpouring runs uninterrupted for almost three entire choruses. To be continuously generating workable new ideas for that long is an indication of the remarkable gift that Rollins shared with us. There are so many highlights in his solo that we cannot mention more than a few. One curious exploration is how he temporarily

LISTENING GUIDE *continued on next page*

plays with his solo's momentum at 1'01" by spacing out six tones and delaying their arrival times to toy with the beat. He uses a similar strategy again, beginning at 1'54", with equally tuneful results. (Rollins used this strategy more frequently in later recordings.) Not only are Brown's and Rollins's main solo portions spectacular, but the surging excitement continues long after their initial solo slots because both men return for more improvisations after the piano solo. They outdo themselves at 5'00" by exchanging four-measure improvisations, first with drums, then with each other.

Though it is not always necessary to keep your place in the song form in order to enjoy the creativity of the improvisers, you may find that a few signposts in your listening journey make the music less abstract. So here are a few structural aspects of the performance to keep in mind. The original tune itself and the improvisations that use its chord progression follow an A-A-B-A form in which the first two A-sections are eight measures long and the B-sections last 16 measures. The melody of the final A-section in each chorus, designated A' (pronounced "aay PRIME"), contains 8 additional measures, making it last a total of 16 measures.

Note that the opening and closing presentations of the main theme have the bassist and drummer not stating every beat, and the pianist not consistently comping underneath the theme. The rhythm section here plays only selected accents for the first four measures of the A-section. Combined with Max Roach's cymbal crashes, these stop-times are as dramatic as the overture to a Broadway show. Another unusual technique occurs in pianist Richie Powell's playing. He superimposes waltz meter atop the swinging bass and drums at 3'38", 6'04", and 6'38".

As in listening to complicated improvisations in other jazz recordings, you might enjoy seeking gems of singable melody that are hidden amidst the intricate lines. A few of these are already identified in the musical events guide below, as at 1'01", 1'16", 1'54", 2'04", 3'01", 3'22", and 5'49". In addition to these, try to identify others. Get ready to be patient. This is a long piece, requiring repeated hearings. There is a lot of unfamiliar territory to explore, but your persistence will pay off. Hint: Listening carefully to the drums will provide clues about the form of the piece and entry of new ideas in solos.

ELAPSED TIME

0'00"		**First Chorus**
	A	Rhythm section only plays an accent on the first beat, using cymbal crash.
		First phrase of melody stated in harmony by trumpet and tenor saxophone, opened and closed by a cymbal crash.
0'02"		Rhythm section underscores melody rhythm.
0'03"		cymbal crash
0'04"		Second phrase of melody stated alone by sax.
0'08"	A	Rhythm section only plays an accent on the first beat, using cymbal crash.
		First phrase of melody stated in harmony by trumpet and tenor saxophone.
0'11"		Second phrase of melody stated alone by sax.
0'15"		Roll on snare drum introduces B-section.
0'16"	B	Trumpet improvises.
0'29"		Roll on snare drum introduces return to A-section.
0'31"	A'	repeat of first A-section
0'38"		**Eight-Measure Extension: Sax Plays Theme**
0'43"		Cymbal crash announces final two measures of extension and trumpet break.
0'45"		**Second Chorus—Sonny Rollins Tenor Saxophone Solo**
		Solo is composed of mostly long phrases with many notes, and relatively few phrases that repeat.
	A	
0'53"	A	
1'00"	B	
1'01"		Six descending tones, spaced further apart than in previous lines, are staggered to achieve rhythmic displacement.
1'05"		Sax returns to long, densely packed bop lines.

LISTENING GUIDE *continued on next page*

1'14"	A'	
		tuneful phrase

Third Chorus—Tenor Saxophone Solo

1'28"	A	
		Cymbal crash announces beginning of new chorus.
1'36"	A	
1'42"	B	
1'54"		series of staccato notes spaced out and staggered from the beat
1'56"	A'	
2'04"		series of staccato notes, syncopated and arranged tunefully

Fourth Chorus—Clifford Brown Trumpet Solo

2'11"	A	
2'12"		two phrases, each ending with a similar idea
2'16"		short melodic idea repeated with variations
2'18"		longer phrase with many notes, pitches rising then falling
	A	
2'20"		short melodic idea repeated with variations
2'21"		long phrases with many notes
	B	
2'25"		Cymbal crash announces start of bridge.
		long, densely packed trumpet phrases
		dense "chattering" by drums
2'29"		temporary decrease in density by sounding just one note per beat, six times
2'30"		dense "chattering" by drums
2'32"		long, densely packed phrases
2'35"		dense "chattering" by drums
2'39"	A'	
2'41"		longer phrase with many notes
2'45"		a false start
2'46"		false start corrected
2'50"		intense snare-drum "chattering"

Fifth Chorus

	A	
2'53"		Cymbal crash announces new chorus; trumpet high note
3'01"	A	tune-like phrase, repeated at higher pitch, then developed more intricately
3'08"	B	
3'10"		Fast, short ascending run initiates a series of arpeggios (chord notes played one at a time, lowest to highest), then similar phrases with variations.
3'15"		temporary decrease in density by sounding just one note per beat, six times
3'21"		Roll on snare drum, then tom-tom and cymbal crash, fill the pause in trumpet solo.
3'22"	A'	short melodic phrase repeated once with variation
3'24"		lots of chattering from snare drum

Sixth Chorus—Richie Powell Piano Solo

3'36"	A	
3'38"		brief waltz-meter phrase
3'41"	A	repeats phrase

LISTENING GUIDE *continued on next page*

3'50"	**B**	
3'58"		tuneful soloing, developing idea
4'05"	**A'**	short melodic idea repeated, then varied, then evolved into new idea

Seventh Chorus

4'19"	**A**	short melodic idea repeated
4'26"	**A**	longer phrases with many notes
4'32"		Snare drum roll announces bridge.
4'33"	**B**	
4'46"	**A'**	short melodic idea repeated
4'59"		Snare drum roll announces new chorus.

Eighth Chorus—Horns Alternate Solos with Drums, Four Measures Apiece

5'00"	**A**	tenor saxophone, then drums
5'07"	**A**	trumpet, then drums
5'14"	**B**	tenor saxophone, then drums
5'21"		trumpet, then drums
5'28"	**A'**	tenor saxophone, then drums
5'35"		trumpet, then drums

Ninth Chorus—Horns Trade Fours with Each Other

5'41"	**A**	
5'49"	**A**	Tenor improvises a particularly tuneful set of phrases.
5'56"	**B**	
6'04"		Piano plays waltz rhythm in comping.
6'09"	**A'**	
6'22"		Snare drum roll and cymbal crash introduce return to final theme.

Tenth Chorus—Final Theme Statement

6'23"	**A**	sax and trumpet in harmony for first phrase, sax alone for second
6'30"	**A**	sax and trumpet in harmony for first phrase, sax alone for second
6'38"	**B**	piano solo in waltz meter over drums and bass in swing meter
6'50"		drummer rolls on tom-tom
6'52"	**A'**	sax and trumpet in harmony for first phrase, sax alone for second
7'04"		abrupt ending in fifteenth measure of A' instead of the sixteenth measure

chapter because of the size and originality of his contributions, his stature in hard bop, his large body of unique compositions, his two other new saxophone styles, and his original band style. In the present chapter, we will briefly discuss Sonny Rollins. Some feel he had his creative peak during the 1950s. He remains the favorite jazz tenor for many musicians. Then we will examine Joe Henderson, a significant saxophonist-composer-bandleader who was important in new developments during a 1960s and 1970s phase of hard bop. In the following chapter, we will evaluate Wayne Shorter, whose contribution to jazz history was threefold: he played hard bop with Art Blakey from 1959 to 1964, devised new approaches to composition and improvisation in the Miles Davis quintet of 1964 to 1969, and developed jazz-rock fusion from 1970 to 1985 with a band called Weather Report.

Sonny Rollins (b. 1930) was among the most popular tenor saxophonists of the 1950s. Though he is known today for his originality, Rollins was among the first group of musicians to adopt Charlie Parker's alto sax style for use on tenor.[20] He began recording in 1949, and his name is often mentioned along with Charlie Parker, Sonny Stitt, and John Coltrane when saxophonists themselves list their favorites.

Rollins was widely admired for the way he improvised simple melodic ideas and then developed them, producing solos that possessed integrity and continuity. His clarity of mind allowed him to transcend cliché figures, even at the high speeds which ordinarily push saxophonists to use easily fingered, well practiced patterns instead of original melodic ideas.[21]

During the 1950s, the Rollins timbre was hard, rough, and dry. It was not as deep or richly textured as Coltrane's. Some listeners called it "brittle." His vibrato was slow and very deliberate. Rollins differed from the majority of bop tenor saxophonists by using staccato phrasing instead of the almost exclusively legato style favored by them. He could manage a blunt attack, move to legato and back again to staccato. His phrases were delivered without ornamentation or any other kind of softening. The overall effect of his playing was abrupt and, though aggressive, it was not necessarily explosive or blistering. He creatively varied his articulation and the sound quality of his tone. He was so forceful and coherent rhythmically that sometimes it was as though he was using his saxophone tones to act as a drummer.

Sonny Rollins, the most eminent tenor saxophonist of the 1950s to continue the bop tradition of Charlie Parker. He subsequently developed new styles in the 1970s and 90s. Shown here at the Detroit Jazz Festival in 1991.

(Photo by John Sobczak)

Sonny Rollins is a giant in the history of improvisation. He played with a supreme confidence. He had mastered the rhythmic devices necessary to swing, and he swung whenever he wished. But he also purposely deviated from the tempo at times, as if he were inside the beat one moment and ignoring it the next. He used his remarkable sense of timing so that he could alternately stretch the durations of his notes, intentionally fall behind, and catch up whenever he wished. Rollins treated a piece as though its tempo, chord progressions, and melody were mere toys to be played with. He instantaneously redesigned them from moment to moment without reverence for their original flavor.[22] Listeners were fascinated by his unpredictability and wit.

Some listeners feel that Rollins's career reached its peak during the 1950s, that he did his most lyrical playing with Miles Davis[23] and his most swinging playing with Clifford Brown.[24] Regardless of whether you agree, there is no question that Rollins's recordings in the 1950s constitute landmarks in the history of tenor saxophone style.[25]

During the 1960s, Rollins streamlined his style[26] and explored less-conventional approaches to improvisation.[27] During the 1970s, '80s, and '90s, Rollins usually played in a way that differed significantly from his style of the 1950s and 1960s. He adopted a timbre that was broader, coarser, and more guttural. In addition, his playing had less speed and crispness of execution. Some of his lines recalled those of saxophonists associated with the popular music known as rhythm and blues. By contrast with his earlier style, his playing became simpler and funkier. Rollins retained his allegiance to lyricism, but now his roots in Charlie Parker were barely detectable. The tunes he performed were simpler, too, and their accompaniments resembled those of popular dance styles such as disco, funk, and Latin. Although Rollins occasionally returned to more bop-like playing (as with the Milestone Jazz Stars), his preferred approach during this period remained so simple and funky that it fit perfectly with the style of the Rolling Stones, the popular blues-oriented rock and roll group that used him on one of their recordings.[28] Twenty years after being the top hard bop tenor, Sonny Rollins had mastered a new style and gained a fresh audience.

Tenor saxophonist **Joe Henderson** (1937–2001) has been appreciated by fellow musicians and knowledgeable jazz fans since the early 1960s. He played uncompromising, fresh variants on hard bop, going beyond Sonny Rollins and Stan Getz, two of his inspirations. His playing strongly recalls Junior Cook (1934–1992), a saxophonist known for his recordings with the Horace Silver quintet of 1958 to 1964.[29] Like Cook, Henderson capitalized on melodic fragments in a hard, insistent way. The Cook-Henderson manner was hard-edged and raw, devoid of softness. They played as though aggressively tearing phrases off a tree of melodic ideas. Sometimes Henderson interspersed shakes, trills, and well-controlled shrieks and wails in a knife-like way. These devices supplied building blocks for his phrases, not just colorations. His agility and razor-sharp articulation were maintained at speeds that most other saxophonists only dreamt of attaining. An ability to play extremely quick figures with uncanny accuracy pervaded his improvisations. He creatively varied the speed of his vibrato, too. Henderson's improvisations were rich with invention and daring. Intense, provocative lines spilled from his horn. Some contained syncopated staccato figures, alternating with churning legato phrases. He invented swinging fragments inside a sense of tempo that was surgical in its precision. His ideas were highly syncopated in endless variations. Henderson often began his lines with brief figures that he then developed with many transformations. Lots of follow-through is evident. In his 1960s output, Henderson's improvisations frequently spoke almost as complete sentences (subject, verb, object, etc.). Henderson had a remarkable sense of continuity. Superbly gifted at inventing melodies, he usually developed each kernel of inspiration while improvising. Only occasionally did he offer the listener his unfinished thoughts while striving to get something going.[30]

Like Sonny Rollins, Henderson could swing conventionally or intentionally play free of the tempo by developing melodic figures that do not fit neatly with the beats beneath them. Henderson's playing conveyed the impression that he possessed a freedom to think very fast and clearly during the heat of improvising and play exactly what he thought, unhindered by the mechanical limitations of his instrument. He alternated swoops and flurries of notes, double-timing and quadruple-timing sporadically, but logically. Though the influence of Rollins is detectable, particularly for filtering bop-style melodic architecture, Henderson used a vocabulary pretty much his own, free of cliché. Sometimes he threw clusters of notes at us, swirling and falling in fragments that were connected loosely by his own unorthodox continuities. His was an extremely loose manner, but organic and speech-like, executed with razor-like tone and exquisite command of the instrument. Whenever he wished, Henderson could combine a wide variety of note durations. For example, he might combine eighth notes, triplets, sixteenth notes, and uneven groups before playing long strings of uninterrupted eighth notes. In this way he showed himself to be a master at staying away from playing long strings of notes that are all equal, which is so easy for improvisers to do.

Joe Henderson, who devised an original style for tenor saxophone during the 1960s that vied with John Coltrane's as the top model for the 1970s, '80s, and '90s. Shown here at the 1989 Chicago Jazz Festival.

(Photo by Nancy Ann Lee)

Henderson managed to gain considerable attention among young saxophonists at a time when the mammoth specter of John Coltrane blotted out almost all tenors other than Stan Getz and Sonny Rollins. During the 1970s, Coltrane's was the most widely imitated approach to jazz tenor, with the influence of Michael Brecker joining during the 1980s. But many players of the 1970s and 1980s incorporated selected parts of Henderson's approach. By comparison with Rollins and Coltrane, however, Henderson influenced fewer saxophonists seeking to imitate completely a single style model. Then in the 1990s, he reached his widest exposure and gained a new audience with effective marketing and a series of "concept" albums devoted to the music of better-known figures, such as Antonio Carlos Jobim, George Gershwin, Miles Davis, and Billy Strayhorn.

TROMBONE

Trombone was unusual to find in hard bop groups, but there were first-rate trombone soloists playing in some bands (see Table 11.1). Incidentally, attaching the "hard bop" designation to any trombonist of the 1950s and 1960s might not be meaningful because most trombonists who played with hard bop bands had styles that differed little from bop. **J. J. Johnson** was the most prominent trombonist of the period. He had already earned a respected place among bop instrumentalists during the late 1940s and early 1950s (see Chapter 9).[31] Johnson was the most visible of all trombonists in the 1950s and 1960s, not only because he was an excellent improviser, but also because he recorded numerous albums as a bandleader. Johnson streamlined his style during the 1960s and put together bands that made music which felt less rushed than bop. Also, several of the tunes he wrote for these bands had a funky flavor that we tend to associate with hard bop.[32] Another trombonist, **Curtis Fuller** (b. 1934), was an equally impressive improviser, yet most of his career was spent as a sideman. Consequently, he never achieved Johnson's high level of public recognition.[33] His recordings with Art Blakey and John Coltrane are outstanding.

GUITAR

There were few guitarists in the hard bop style of the 1950s, just as there had been only a few guitarists in the bop style of the 1940s. The most influential of these musicians was **Wes Montgomery** (1925–1968). Using his thumb instead of a pick, Montgomery extracted a tone from his guitar that was round and full. Some of his lines are voiced in octaves, a sound that became closely identified with him. (Listen to *Demo CD* Track 87 for examples of guitar lines in octaves and comparison of sounds extracted by pick and finger.) Influenced by bop horn styles and Charlie Christian, Montgomery played in a style that was relaxed and melodic. It projected an assured sense of swing and an unhurried, pleasant manner. His playing exudes naturalness, and most listeners perceive the overall effect to be warm and pleasant.

Montgomery systematically developed his solo improvisations in a way that began cool and built tension over several choruses to a climax. Then he would stop altogether or begin the process again. Frequently he began with lines made up of only a single note at a time, then voiced his lines in octaves, then, after a chorus of octaves, he concluded with a chorded solo. In this way, he made his sound successively thicker and more exciting in each chorus.

Montgomery's peak of creativity was the late 1950s and early 1960s. He is best known, however, for later recordings made for the Verve and A&M companies. For these popular albums, the studios provided preset orchestral accompaniments, over which Montgomery paraphrased pop tunes and improvised lightly. He played tastefully on these recordings, but his earlier work, available mostly on albums made for Riverside, is a far richer jazz vein.[34]

After Wes Montgomery, the best-known hard bop guitarist is **Kenny Burrell** (b. 1931). Sources for Burrell's style included Charlie Christian and Oscar Moore. Burrell also drew from bop-style sax and trumpet lines[35] and from the funky melodic figures identified with pianist Horace Silver. Although he is quite versatile, Burrell is particularly well known for his soulful playing on bluesy albums made with organist Jimmy Smith. Most of these albums featured relatively uncomplicated music with which he established a swinging, easygoing mood. As a result, they attained considerable popularity.[36]

BASS

The instrumental prowess of bassists steadily grew as jazz evolved. Hard bop was marked by further milestones. When young bass players of the period asked, "Who should I be listening to?" the names **Paul Chambers** (1935–1969) and **Sam Jones** (1924–1981) were added to those of Ray Brown and Charles Mingus. Chambers became widely known through the recordings he made with Miles Davis between 1955 and 1963. Sam Jones is best remembered for his work with Cannonball Adderley's groups of 1957 to 1966.[37]

DVD Tracks 20–23; Demo CD Track 21

Paul Chambers produced a huge, dark sound on his bass. The notes he chose for walking formed a continuous harmonic complement. The propulsive way he delivered his notes played a crucial rhythmic role. The phrases in his solo improvisations were bop-style and hornlike. These lines were sensible and swinging, possessing melodic and rhythmic richness. Chambers also expanded the solo potential of jazz bass playing by demonstrating a mastery over his instrument and a compositional approach to improvisation not ordinarily associated with the bass.[38]

BIG BANDS

During the late 1950s and through the 1960s, several big bands drew from the sound of hard bop. The three most prominent were led by trumpeters **Maynard Ferguson** (1928–2006), **Gerald Wilson** (b. 1918), and **Thad Jones** (1923–1986). The Jones band was co-led by drummer Mel Lewis, who took over sole leadership when Jones left in 1979. The Ferguson and Wilson bands began during the late 1950s. The Jones-Lewis band was formed in 1965. The groups led by Jones and Wilson were initially founded mostly for the musical enjoyment of freelance jazz musicians living in New York and Los Angeles, respectively. They began as rehearsal bands (also known as "kicks bands") and rarely performed away from home with their personnel intact. Most of the Jones-Lewis performances took place on Monday nights at a New York night club called the Village Vanguard. Of the three bands, only Ferguson's toured widely, sold many records, or became known much outside of relatively small markets.

Many great musicians played with these bands over the years. Ferguson's generally had the youngest and least-known musicians, whereas the earliest Jones-Lewis and Wilson groups were all-star bands. Wilson employed some of the best bop-style musicians to be found outside of New York, several of whom had become known to jazz fans long before they recorded with him. Among the musicians in the Jones-Lewis band, many already had made outstanding jazz records as bandleaders themselves. Like Jones, a few were pivotal figures from the fertile hard bop scene in Detroit (see Table 11.3).[39] Some of those same men were highly individualistic improvisers who, like Jones himself, had already made significant contributions to the explorative bands of Charles Mingus (see Chapter 14).[40]

Thad Jones is often ranked as one of the best and most original trumpeters in hard bop. His improvisations were unorthodox and daring.[41] They often contained odd intervals that were not natural to the trumpet and were as difficult as they were unique. Jones was a storehouse of imagination, and Charles Mingus, among others, ranked Jones as a musical genius. He changed his instruments, too; he was one of very few modern trumpeters to frequently perform on cornet, and he also played fluegelhorn extensively (see page 134 for illustrations).

The styles of most soloists in the earliest Jones-Lewis band can best be categorized as bop or hard bop. Much of the band's music, however, had a feeling that was lighter than the weighty, solemn intensity that is projected by most hard bop. This was partly due to the style of Jones's compositions, which were often light, playful, and full of surprises. They were filled with silences which served as ventilation. They stressed soft, staccato phrases produced by sound qualities that were well contained. They also possessed an alternation of funky unison lines with thickly voiced chordal passages. There is a pixie-like lightness and humor to Jones's melodic rhythms, and he often maintained a suspended feeling by using unconventional accompaniment patterns. He used frequently shifting densities, and occasionally deleted the rhythm section suddenly in the middle of a piece. Although the lines Jones wrote were often very difficult to play, his musicians executed them with finesse. The harmonies he constructed were rarely ordinary; they were rich without sounding muddy or affected. Jones occasionally wrote chords containing eight of the twelve notes in the chromatic scale (as in "Three In One"), a technique that is unusual among big band arrangers. (Sammy Nestico's writing for Count Basie, for example, is typically in four-note chords.) These practices contrast with the ordinary big band arrangers's penchant for massiveness and unceasing sound. Even when his melodies sound almost homespun ("Don't Get Sassy" and "Big Dipper"), they are placed in very thick chord voicings.[42] His melodies show a strong allegiance to the funky, blues tradition ("Big Dipper"), somewhat reminiscent of Horace Silver, though placed in a more elaborate setting. Jones's writing earned him great respect among jazz arrangers, and his pieces found their way into textbooks for jazz composers. He invented such a distinctive arranging style that listeners can often identify it by hearing only a single chord. The Jones arranging style was one of the most original to appear since Duke Ellington's.

The differences between the Jones-Lewis sound and that of other big bands in hard bop were also due partly to approaches employed by the band's bassist, **Richard Davis**, and its drummer, Mel Lewis. Davis contributed concepts to a big band setting that roughly paralleled what Charles Mingus and Scott LaFaro had given to combo settings: In addition to playing walking bass lines, Davis improvised accompaniments containing a great variety of fresh melodic and rhythmic figures that vigorously interacted with the solo and ensemble lines. (This approach was not new for Davis, who was already much admired for his innovative playing in avant-garde combos of the 1960s.) Compatible with the loosening and lightening done by Davis was the light, discreet drumming of **Mel Lewis** (1929–1990), whose style avoided the heavy, aggressive approaches of hard bop. A uniquely flexible accompanist, Lewis is well known for his unerring swing, versatility, and good taste.

Jazz big bands have traditionally been rooted in styles of eras earlier than the one at hand. In addition, solos have been routinely brief and frequently interrupted by screaming ensemble figures. The Jones band stood apart from these traditions. It offered plenty of uncluttered solo space to its improvisers and achieved a flexible interaction between the rhythm section and improvising soloists. During many moments in its performances, the band sounded like an up-to-date modern jazz combo. In this way it recalled Count Basie's big band of the 1930s, which often operated as an oversized combo.

Gerald Wilson was a respected composer-arranger long before he became identified with his hard bop big band. The Jimmie Lunceford and Duke Ellington bands were among the outstanding groups which had performed his work. In his band of the late 1950s and early 1960s, however, Wilson molded a unique new sound from several sources. He used outstanding hard bop soloists who played with the ferocity and bluesy mood which jazz fans had come to expect from the combos of Art Blakey, Horace Silver, and Cannonball Adderley. He used an original arranging style. It was spare, not intricate. It did not jump around, nor was it light and playful. It was hard and relentless. Each piece created and sustained a consistent mood. He emphasized depth of feeling; more often than not, that feeling was dark and serious. By comparison with all other big bands, the Wilson band achieved a groove that more closely resembled hard bop. The moods were funky and earthy, as though Wilson had created a big-band equivalent to the organ/tenor sax combos that were common at inner-city taverns during the 1950s and 1960s.[43]

Another unique characteristic of Wilson's sound was a modal flavor. Brief, wailing phrases in a minor key were repeated again and again, over a propelling rhythm. The chords changed slowly, allowing soloists to build their ideas and raise tension over a longer time than bop progressions allowed. Several of the pieces in this genre were compositions Wilson adapted after they had been introduced by Miles Davis ("Milestones," "So What," "Freddie the Freeloader"). Others were Wilson originals ("Moment of Truth," "Viva Tirado") that had the raw ferocity of hard bop as well as a certain exoticism.[44]

Before the hard bop era, **Maynard Ferguson** had already achieved a reputation as trumpeter with big bands led by Charlie Barnet, Boyd Raeburn, and Stan Kenton. His lead trumpet work with Kenton from 1950 to 1952 did much to set the character of the Kenton sound as well as to establish Ferguson's own fame. During the late 1950s, he began a series of his own big bands which prominently featured his high-register trumpet playing. Though these bands continued Kenton's emphasis on loud, flashy brass, they conveyed a different feeling: they swung. In addition, they sounded funkier. The bands had a precise, fast-moving style. Unlike Kenton, Ferguson was not especially experimental. His band belted out driving ensemble passages in a no-nonsense manner, with Ferguson often soaring overhead. Their sound was filled with raw excitement. The band seemed to thrive on fast tempos and loud playing (listen to "Three Foxes," "L-Dopa," and "Got the Spirit"). The repertory contained few slow or subdued arrangements. ("Maria," "Lazy Afternoon," and "Frame for The Blues" are the exceptions.)

"A Trumpet,"
JCCD2 *Track 3*

The Ferguson band's instrumentation also differed from that of other big bands. (See Chapter 6 for discussion of big band instrumentation traditions.) Unlike the Ellington, Basie, Wilson, and Jones bands of the same period, Ferguson's were more compact. Rather than the ordinary complement of three to five trombones, Ferguson carried only two. Instead of a sax section with two altos, two tenors, and a baritone, his had one alto, two tenors, and a baritone. Instead of the dark, full-bodied tone qualities associated with Wilson's and Ellington's saxes, Ferguson's had a bright, biting sound that was almost brassy. As the years passed, Ferguson continued to reduce the size of his band, until in the late 1960s, and again in the mid-1980s, he was all the way down to a small combo.

During the 1970s and 1980s, Ferguson's bands used electric instruments and funk-style accompaniments in the bulk of their performances. Considerable radio airplay was given to some of their pop tune arrangements, particularly their 1970 recording of "MacArthur Park"[45] and their 1972 recording of "Hey, Jude" (a tune by the Beatles, a British singing group). This was a bit of good fortune that little jazz had enjoyed since the 1940s. Ferguson's greatest popularity came with a 1976 recording of the theme song for the immensely popular movie *Rocky*. The album it appeared on, *Conquistador*, achieved gold-record status.[46] Following these best-selling pieces,

Ferguson mined the same vein by continuing to record television and movie themes, using large amounts of orchestration and small amounts of improvisation. The band also capitalized on the popularity of jazz-rock fusion by recording Herbie Hancock's hit "Chameleon" in 1974 and Joe Zawinul's hit "Birdland" in 1978. (See Chapter 16 for more about this style and these particular pieces.)

Maynard Ferguson is not ordinarily considered a historically significant hard bop trumpeter. His exceptional command of brass instruments, however, inspired many musicians of the 1960s, '70s, and '80s. This is partly because his music received such wide exposure and partly because he had an almost freakish mastery of the trumpet that extended throughout its entire range. No register was the least bit awkward for him. His facility took him to B above double-high C. Significantly, on most nights he did not simply squeal those altissimo-register notes but actually played them with good intonation and large tone.[47] Most big band high-note artists play few improvised solos, restricting their playing to trumpet section lead work in order to keep their lips set specifically for those high parts. Ferguson amazed brass players not only by playing high-register lead parts, but also by improvising solos on nearly every tune. In addition to that, his endurance was as phenomenal as his range, and he could switch to trombone or French horn right in the middle of a piece, making an immediate adjustment to it. In fact, he was a master not only of the trumpet but of all the brass instruments, and he played most of the reed instruments, too.

POPULAR APPEAL

Like bop musicians, hard bop musicians found their music to be relatively neglected by the public. Only a few managed to extract steady livelihoods from performing jazz. The historically significant bands of Clifford Brown, Art Blakey, and J.J. Johnson were unknown except to musicians and a small population of fans. During the 1950s, Sonny Rollins and John Coltrane were well known by jazz fans but almost unknown otherwise. The few jazz pieces that found their way onto jukeboxes were mostly simple, funky compositions. They were arranged with lots of very repetitive accompaniment rhythms and less improvisation than was found on most hard bop records. Some of these accounted for brief periods of success enjoyed by Cannonball Adderley and Horace Silver, especially during the 1960s and 1970s. But the highest record sales went to the organ-guitar-drums and piano-bass-drums groups of Jimmy Smith and Ramsey Lewis, respectively. These are players who musicians and critics do not ordinarily consider to be within the main stream of jazz developments, though their music helps define funky jazz, and they fit the hard bop designation more closely than they fit any other.

CHAPTER SUMMARY

1. Hard bop evolved directly from bop during the 1950s, mainly from East Coast and Midwest musicians.
2. When hard bop differs from bop, it is simpler, has more variety in accompaniment patterns, fewer pop tune chord progressions, darker, weightier tone qualities, and more emphasis on hard, unrelenting swinging.
3. Funky jazz is a subcategory of hard bop, and it is characterized by bluesy inflections of pitch and gospelish harmonies. Several pieces performed by the bands of Horace Silver and Cannonball Adderley were popular because of their funky qualities and simple, catchy melodies.
4. Drummers in hard bop were louder and more intrusive than their predecessors. Art Blakey and Philly Joe Jones further emancipated the drummer from the role of mere timekeeper.

NOTES

1. Listen to Art Blakey, *A Night At Birdland*, vols. 1 and 2 (Blue Note: 32146/32147, 2 CDs, 1954, c2001).

2. To learn what is meant by "earthy, blues-drenched, gospelish," listen to "One Day" on Track 4 of JCCD1; Avery Parrish's "After Hours" on *Jazz Piano* (Smithsonian: 7002, 4CD set, c1989); Horace Silver's "The Preacher," "Sister Sadie," "Señor Blues," or "Song for My Father"; Bobby Timmons's "Moanin' "; Nat Adderley's "Work Song," "Sack o' Woe," or "Jive Samba"; Joe Zawinul's "Mercy, Mercy, Mercy"; or Lee Morgan's "Sidewinder." If you do not have access to any of these pieces, look in the library for the *Recorded Anthology of American Music* series. From the volume called *Bebop* (New World: 271, LP, c1976), listen to the funky melody line by Horace Silver called "Stop Time."

3. Pianists Gene Harris (of The Three Sounds), Ramsey Lewis, and Les McCann, and organists Jimmy Smith, Richard "Groove" Holmes, and Jack McDuff based large parts of their styles on Silver's funky devices and became quite popular as a result. Even the original stylists Bill Evans, McCoy Tyner, and Chick Corea, whose approaches were not primarily funky, demonstrated Silver's influence by making use of his funky devices.

4. For nonfunky examples by these men, listen to Silver's "Ecaroh" on Art Blakey, *The Jazz Messengers* (Columbia/Legacy: 65265, 1956, c1991); "Moon Rays," on *SCCJ-R*; Cannonball Adderley, *Quintet in Chicago* (Mercury: 559 770, 1959, c1999); and the following Art Blakey albums: *A Night at Birdland*, vols. 1 and 2 (Blue Note); *A Night in Tunisia* (Blue Note: 64474, 1960, c2005); *Indestructible* (Blue Note: 80915, 1964, c2003); and *Buttercorn Lady* (Emarcy: 822 471, 1966, c1986).

5. Much of Davis's work is routinely classified as "cool jazz," and this label is not limited to his 1948–1950 nonet recordings. It also is applied to his early 1950s work with Sonny Rollins, Horace Silver, Milt Jackson, and others. Even his 1959 *Kind of Blue* (Columbia/Legacy) is tagged "cool jazz" by some, though it more closely fits the "hard bop" or "modal jazz" category.

6. Miles Davis, *Collector's Items* (Fantasy: OJC-071, 1956, c1987); Sonny Rollins, *Saxophone Colossus* (Fantasy: OJC-291, 1956, c1987); John Coltrane, *Giant Steps* (Rhino/Atlantic: 75203, 1959, c1998); and Wes Montgomery, *The Incredible Jazz Guitar of Wes Montgomery* (Fantasy: OJC-036, 1960, c1992). Flanagan can also be heard in two selections on *Jazz Piano* (Smithsonian), and on Rollins's "Blue Seven" on *SCCJ*.

7. For analysis of Silver's piano style, see John Mehegan, *Jazz Improvisation*, vol. 3 (Watson-Guptill, 1964).

8. Favorites among musicians are the Horace Silver albums: *Horace-Scope* (Blue Note: 37775, 1960, c2006); *Cape Verdean Blues* (Blue Note: 90839, 1965, c2004); and *In Pursuit of the 27th Man* (Blue Note: 35758, 1972, c2002).

9. See Appendix G for information on how to get Milton Stewart, *Structural Development in the Jazz Improvisational Technique of Clifford Brown* (University Microfilms, 1973). See also David Baker, *The Jazz Style of Clifford Brown: A Musical and Historical Perspective* (Studio P/R, 1982); available from Jamey Aebersold Jazz, Inc., P.O. Box 1244, New Albany, IN 47151-1244; phone: 800-456-1388; web: *www.jazzbooks.com*. Listen to "Pent-Up House" on *SCCJ*, and see the analysis in Scott Reeves, *Creative Jazz Improvisation*, 4th ed. (Prentice-Hall, 2006). For a biography, see Nick Catalano, *Clifford Brown: The Life and Art of the Legendary Jazz Trumpeter* (Oxford, 2000).

10. Also, Hubbard was probably the first great brass player to draw heavily from the approach of saxophonist John Coltrane, notably in his use of pentatonic scales, quartal harmony, and chromaticism.

11. See Stuart Isacoff, *Solos For Jazz Trumpet* (Carl Fischer, 1985), available from Carl Fischer Music, 65 Bleeker St., NYC, NY 10012; phone: 800-762-2328; web: *www.carlfischer.com*, for analyses of Hubbard's solos on "Blue Moon" and "On Green Dolphin Street." See Mike Barry and Kevin Carberry, *Artists Transcriptions: Freddie Hubbard* (Hal Leonard, 1992).

12. Though he remained active into the 1990s, Hubbard's playing on albums in the 1960s as a sideman with Herbie Hancock and Eric Dolphy represents some of his most inventive work. Listen to Herbie Hancock, *Empyrean Isles* (Blue Note: 98796, 1964, c1998); Eric Dolphy, *Out to Lunch* (Blue Note: 98793, 1964, c1999); and Oliver Nelson, *Blues and the Abstract Truth* (Impulse!: 154, 1961, c1995).

13. Listen to Blakey's work with Clifford Brown and Horace Silver from 1954, in which he is engaged in volatile rhythm section drumming years before such activity became common practice: *A Night at Birdland*, vols. 1 and 2 (Blue Note).

14. Some of the tunes they recorded remained favorites among musicians of the 1980s and 1990s: Brown's "Joy Spring" and "Daahoud." For a sample of the quintet's sound, listen to "Pent-Up House" with saxophonist Sonny Rollins on *SCCJ*; "What Is This Thing Called Love?" on *Bebop* (New World); or *Clifford Brown and Max Roach* (Emarcy/Verve: 543 306, 1954, c2000) which features saxophonist Harold Land.

15. Listen to the *Demo CD*, Tracks 11–13, to familiarize yourself with the different sounds of instruments in the drum set and the effects of sticks and brushes. Then listen to Philly Joe Jones on "Two Bass Hit" and "Billy Boy" on Miles Davis, *Milestones* (Columbia/Legacy: 85203, 1958, c2001); "Budo" on *Miles and Coltrane* (Columbia: 44052, 1955, 1958, c1988); "Tune-Up" on *Cookin'* (Fantasy: OJC-128, 1956, c1993); and "Half Nelson" on *Workin'* (Fantasy: OJC-296, 1956, c1987). "Two Bass Hit" is also on *CCD1* Track 23.

16. Cannonball Adderley's best solos from this period are found on Davis, *Milestones* (Columbia), and a recording of the Miles Davis group minus Davis: Adderley, *Quintet in Chicago* (Mercury). One of his best is on "Two Bass Hit" on CCD1.

17. For some of his funkiest playing, listen to "Them Dirty Blues" on Adderley, *Them Dirty Blues* (Capitol Jazz: 95447, 1960, c1989).

18. On Davis, *Milestones*, Adderley quotes the opening phrases of George Gershwin's "Fascinating Rhythm" in the beginning of his solo on "Milestones," and he transforms the first phrase of Vernon Duke's "I Can't Get Started" on his solo in "Two Bass Hit." "Two Bass Hit" is also on the CCD1 Track 23.

19. See Stuart Isacoff, *Solos For Jazz Alto Sax* (Carl Fischer, 1985), for analyses of Adderley's solos on "On Green Dolphin Street" (with Miles Davis) and "Sack o' Woe." See also David Baker, *The Jazz Style of Cannonball Adderley* (Studio P/R, 1980); available from Aebersold.

20. To hear the resemblance between Rollins and Parker, listen to Parker play tenor, instead of alto, on "Half Nelson" (1947) on Charlie Parker, *The Complete Savoy & Dial Master Takes* (Savoy Jazz: 17149, 3CD set, 1944–48, c2002). Then listen to Rollins with Bud Powell on *The Amazing Bud Powell*, vol. 1 (Blue Note: 32136, 1949, c2001), or with Miles Davis on *Dig* (Fantasy: OJC-005, 1951, c1987).

21. Rollins's fastest, most fluid solos are on "I Know That You Know" and "The Eternal Triangle" on Dizzy Gillespie, *Sonny Side Up* (Verve: 314 521 426, 1957, c1997), during a session in which he was prepared to keep up with the lightning-quick playing of fellow saxophonist Sonny Stitt.

22. Listen to his "Blue Seven" on SCCJ, or "You Don't Know What Love Is" on Rollins, *Saxophone Colossus* (Fantasy: OJC-291, 1956, c1987). For analyses of the Rollins solo on "Blue Seven," see Gunther Schuller, *Musings* (Oxford, 1986), 86–97; and Scott Reeves, *Creative Jazz Improvisation*, 4th ed. David Baker, *The Jazz Style of Sonny Rollins* (Studio P/R, 1980), is available from Aebersold. For a technical evaluation of Rollins's career up to 1980, see Charles Blancq, *Sonny Rollins* (Twayne, 1983). Further transcriptions and analyses are in Charley Gerard, *Sonny Rollins* (Consolidated Music, 1980; Amsco, 1988); available from Aebersold. See also Peter N. Wilson, *Sonny Rollins: The Definitive Musical Guide* (Berkeley Hills, 2001).

23. "Vierd Blues" and "No Line" on Davis, *Collector's Items* (Fantasy: OJC-071, 1956, c1987).

24. Listen to "Pent-Up House," on SCCJ, or *Sonny Rollins Plus 4* (Fantasy: OJC-243, 1956, c1987), made under Rollins's own leadership while he was a member of the Clifford Brown-Max Roach Quintet. This is among the few albums Rollins himself has said he is pleased with.

25. The all-time favorite Rollins album for many musicians is *Saxophone Colossus* (Fantasy); also impressive is *A Night at the Village Vanguard*, vols. 1 and 2 (Blue Note: 99795, 2CD set, 1957, c1999).

26. Sonny Rollins, *The Bridge* (RCA: 52472, 1962, c2003).

27. Rollins, *Our Man in Jazz* (RCA: 74321192562 [LSP 2612], 1962, c1994).

28. Rolling Stones, *Tattoo You* (Virgin: 39521, 1981, c1994).

29. Compare Cook's work on Blue Mitchell, *The Thing to Do* (Blue Note: 94319, 1964, c2004), with Henderson's work on Horace Silver, *Song for My Father* (Blue Note: 99002, 1964, c1999).

30. Listen to his work on Silver, *Cape Verdean Blues* (Blue Note); "I Have a Dream" on Herbie Hancock, *The Prisoner* (Blue Note: 25649, 1969, c2000); Joe Henderson, *Power to the People* (Milestone: 9024,

1969, c2001); and Henderson, *Double Rainbow: The Music of Antonio Carlos Jobim* (Verve: 314 527 222, 1994, c1995). For transcriptions of solos on Henderson, *Page One* (Blue Note: 98795, 1963, c1999) and *In 'n' Out* (Blue Note: 96507, 1964, c2004), see *Joe Henderson: Improvised Saxophone Solos* (Studio P/R, 1978; Columbia Pictures, c1987); available from Aebersold.

31. See Scott Reeves, *Creative Jazz Improvisation*, for an analysis of J.J. Johnson's solo on "Aquarius." See also David Baker, *J.J. Johnson: Trombone* (Shattinger, 1979), available from Aebersold.

32. J.J. Johnson, *J.J. Inc.* (Columbia/Legacy: 65296, 1960, c1997).

33. Fuller's work on these albums is representative: Coltrane, *Blue Trane* (Blue Note: 95326, 1957, c2003); Art Farmer-Benny Golson Jazztet, *Meet the Jazztet* (Chess: 91550 [Argo], 1960, c1990); and Blakey, *Indestructible* (Blue Note).

34. Listen to his "West Coast Blues" on SCCJ-R, or *The Incredible Jazz Guitar of Wes Montgomery* (Fantasy). For a transcription and analysis of Montgomery's solo on "Four on Six," see Fred Sokolow, *Solos for Jazz Guitar* (Carl Fischer, 1988).

35. *Kenny Burrell and John Coltrane* (Fantasy: OJC-300, 1957, c1987).

36. Jimmy Smith, *Midnight Special* (Blue Note: 84078, 1960, c1988).

37. Notice the buoyant, hard-driving accompaniment Sam Jones provides and listen to his pizzicato solo on "Trouble in Mind" on Adderley, *Cannonball in Europe* (Capitol Jazz: 60436, 1962, c2005).

38. Listen to how Chambers introduces the melody line to "So What" with the Miles Davis band on SCCJ. Listen to his solos on Coltrane, *Soultrane* (Fantasy: OJC-021, 1958, c1987); and *Tranein' In* (Fantasy: OJC-189, 1957, c1987).

39. *The Complete Blue Note/UA/Roulette Recordings of Thad Jones* (Mosaic MD3-172, 3CD set, 1956–59, c1997); also see footnote 42 in this chapter.

40. Charles Mingus, *Jazzical Moods* (Fantasy: OJC-1857, 1954, c1995).

41. Listen to the Thad Jones solos on *The Complete Roulette Studio Recordings of Count Basie* (Mosaic: MD10-149, 1959–1962, c1993); and on *Big Band Renaissance* (Smithsonian: 108, 5CD set, c1995).

42. *The Complete Solid State Recordings of the Thad Jones/Mel Lewis Orchestra* (Mosaic: MD5-151, 5 CD set, 1966–1969, c1994); or *Live at the Village Vanguard* (Blue Note 60438, 1967, c2005) and *Central Park North* (Blue Note: 76852, 1969, c2004).

43. Gerald Wilson, *You Better Believe It* (Pacific Jazz: 10097, LP, 1961, c1981).

44. Wilson, *Moment of Truth* (Pacific Jazz: 92928, 1962, c1989); and "Viva Tirado" on *Big Band Renaissance* (Smithsonian). All are on *The Complete Pacific Jazz Recordings of Gerald Wilson and His Orchestra* (Mosaic: MD5-198, 5CD set, 1961–69, c2000). Wilson, *New York, New Sound* (Mack Avenue: 1009, c2003) features new musicians revisiting his best 1960s compositions.

45. Maynard Ferguson, *M. F. Horn* (Columbia: 30466, LP, 1970, c1971).

46. Ferguson, *Conquistador* (Columbia/Legacy: 63557, 1976, c2003).

47. *The Complete Roulette Recordings of the Maynard Ferguson Orchestra* (Mosaic: MD10-156, 10CD set, 1958–1962, c1994); or *Big Band Renaissance* (Smithsonian). For a biography, see William F. Lee, *MF Horn: Maynard Ferguson's Life in Music* (M.F. Music U.S.A. Inc., 1997; P.O. Box 716, Ojai, CA 93024).

Miles Davis (1926–1991) was a jazz trumpeter and bandleader who played a pivotal role in the history of modern jazz because he was deeply involved in recording and promoting several styles well before they became widespread trends. His recordings have won the near universal admiration of modern jazz musicians. Over a 50-year period of productivity, Davis contributed a stylistically diverse body of music. Parts of this productivity defined jazz for three different generations of listeners. A significant slice of modern jazz history is documented in Davis-led recording sessions because he gathered the key innovators of the day for his bands. Unlike most artists, Davis never became limited to one particular band style. Among his most important contributions are:

1. Creating an original and substantial trumpet style. This was first evident in recordings that Davis made in Charlie Parker's band of the mid-1940s, and it influenced numerous trumpeters of the cool jazz and hard bop idioms (see Table 12.4).

2. Producing a large body of recordings that almost invariably contain distinctive, high-quality performances. Davis recordings served as textbooks for modern musicians in the way that recordings of Louis Armstrong and Lester Young had served his predecessors.

3. Making a significant change during the 1960s in his original trumpet style. In the 1980s, this variation was the basis for trumpet styles of Wynton Marsalis, Terence Blanchard, Wallace Roney, and others.

Cannonball Adderley, Paul Chambers, Miles Davis, John Coltrane
(Photo courtesy of Frank Driggs)

TABLE 12.1   A Few of the Top Saxophonists Who Worked with Miles Davis

Lee Konitz	Bennie Maupin	Wayne Shorter
Sonny Rollins	John Coltrane	David Liebman
Jackie McLean	Hank Mobley	Steve Grossman
Gerry Mulligan	Joe Henderson	Gary Bartz
Sonny Stitt	Sam Rivers	Cannonball Adderley
Jimmy Heath	George Coleman	Sonny Fortune

Chap. 10; SCCJ: "Boplicity"

"Flamenco Sketches," JCCD2 Track 9; "Blue in Green," CCD1 Track 24; SCCJ: "So What"

"Masqualero," JCCD2 Track 10

4. Participating in the first recording sessions that consolidated Claude Thornhill's and Gil Evans's orchestration style with the cool instrumental styles of Gerry Mulligan, Lee Konitz, and himself to become the landmark "Birth of the Cool" recordings of 1949 and 1950 (see page 209).

5. Pioneering "modal jazz" on the *Kind of Blue* album in 1959.

6. Pioneering the predominant group approaches and individual instrumental styles of the 1980s with his quintet of 1965–1968.

7. Pioneering jazz-rock fusion styles with an amalgamation of elements from "modal jazz," rock, and funk music on his *In a Silent Way* and *Bitches Brew* albums of 1969 (see Chapter 16).

Though he did not invent entire jazz idioms himself, Miles Davis organized bands of key innovators at early moments in the development of bop, cool jazz, modal jazz, and jazz-rock fusion (see Tables 12.1, 12.2, and 12.3). Moreover, he invented an original and distinctive trumpet style that fit the sound of each of his bands. Like Duke Ellington's musicians, Davis's often produced the best work of their career while in his bands. (His sidemen speak highly about his help in their own stylistic development and his judicious editing of their music.) A feeling of intelligent, well-measured musical creation pervades most Davis recordings.

TABLE 12.2   A Few of the Top Guitarists Who Worked with Miles Davis

George Benson		John Scofield
John McLaughlin		Barry Finnerty
Larry Coryell		Mike Stern

TABLE 12.3   **The Evolution of Modern Jazz Rhythm Section Styles**
Documented by Miles Davis Recordings

1950: Pianist John Lewis, bassist Al McKibbon, drummer Max Roach on *Birth of the Cool*.

1951: Pianist Walter Bishop, Jr., bassist Tommy Potter, drummer Art Blakey on "Conception," "Denial," and "Paper Moon."

1956: Pianist Tommy Flanagan, bassist Paul Chambers, drummer Art Taylor on "No Line," "Vierd Blues," and "In Your Own Sweet Way."

1955–58: Pianist Red Garland, bassist Paul Chambers, drummer Philly Joe Jones on *The New Miles Davis Quintet, Steamin', Cookin', Workin', Relaxin', 'Round About Midnight,* and *Milestones*.

1959–63: Pianist Wynton Kelly, bassist Paul Chambers, drummer Jimmy Cobb on *Someday My Prince Will Come, In Person at the Blackhawk,* and *Miles Davis at Carnegie Hall*.

1963–68: Pianist Herbie Hancock, bassist Ron Carter, drummer Tony Williams on many albums, including *My Funny Valentine, Sorcerer, Miles in the Sky,* and *Nefertiti*.

1971: Pianist Keith Jarrett, bassist Mike Henderson, drummer Jack DeJohnette, percussionist Airto Moreira on "Sivad" from *Live-Evil*.

1969–72: Groups whose rhythm sections sometimes included two or three keyboards. (Davis drew from a pool of pianists that included Joe Zawinul, Chick Corea, Keith Jarrett, Herbie Hancock, Larry Young, Harold Williams, Hermeto Pascoal, Lonnie Liston Smith, and Cedric Lawson.)

1970s: Groups whose rhythm sections sometimes included two or three guitars. (Davis drew from a pool of guitarists that included Reggie Lucas, Pete Cosey, David Creamer, Dominique Gaumont, and Cornell Dupree.)

1970s: Groups including sitar and tabla. Use of instruments native to India, such as the sitar (a stringed instrument) and tabla (drums), was as unusual in jazz rhythm sections as using two and three keyboards at once.

TRUMPET STYLE

Miles Davis created an unmistakable sound. It is so easily identifiable that we can instantly recognize it, even in the crowded mix of a rock record or the background music for a movie. Davis was a uniquely creative thinker who departed drastically from the traditions of jazz trumpet playing to give us a sound so personal that to call it "Miles Davis" seems more accurate than to call it "jazz trumpet."

The uniqueness of the Davis style can be divided into at least eight components. The first two are manners of handling the trumpet sound:[1]

1. **Alternating pitch and tone quality** at the beginnings and endings of notes. (For graphs of such pitch bending ornaments, see page 49; to hear Davis perform them, listen to "Fishermen, Strawberry, and Devil Crab" on *JCCD1* Track 2.[2])

2. **Frequent use of a Harmon mute** without its stem (as can be heard on "Flamenco Sketches," *JCCD2* Track 9; a Harmon mute is shown on page 469). His Harmon-muted solos were amplified by placing the mute directly on the stage microphone (at least until the 1970s, when he attached wireless microphones directly to his horn). This technique resulted in a wispy sound that was delicate and conveyed an intimate mood. By comparison with that of other modern trumpeters, far more of his output was muted. On many of his albums, more than half of his playing is done through the Harmon mute.[3]

3. **Using silence as an effective dramatic device.** Davis shows unusually skillful timing and dramatic construction of melodic figures. He is a master of

self-restraint. His placement of silence is at least as significant as his choice of notes, and he often lets several beats pass without playing. During the moments he is not sounding his own notes, the sound of bass, drums, and piano comes through clearly, further enhancing the mood. The effectiveness of this very lean approach also depends on the steadiness of swing feeling and overall musicality of his accompanists. Because Davis always hired the best accompanists, the silences in his own solos were filled in a highly musical, well-paced manner.[4] More than most improvisers, Davis conveyed the impression that he was editing his solos very carefully while performing them, clarifying his ideas before articulating them. In the same way that Lester Young approached improvisation with the tenor saxophone, Davis pared his thinking down to a bare core of melodic material; and like Young's solos, the best Davis improvisations seem to "tell a story."[5]

4. This component of the Davis style can be identified by comparing rhythmic conceptions. Most modern trumpeters play swinging lines, but few seem capable of **generating lines that are free from a sense of strict tempo and swing feeling,** even when they play slow tunes. In the playing of Davis's contemporaries, a very precise subdivision of each beat seems to rule the passage of notes. Davis could improvise swinging melodic figures,[6] but distinguished himself by his skill in also improvising figures that imply freedom from strict tempo and swing feeling.[7]

5. **An acute sensitivity in paraphrasing melodies.** The Davis paraphrases of popular songs were constructed in such fresh and enticing ways that the finished products are almost new melodies.[8]

6. **Mastery of economy and succinctness.** Davis was not afraid to play simply. Certainly, he did often play bop-style lines that were not simple. But often, he constructed solos of very brief, simple phrases. Many of his improvisations on slow pieces and on blues forms were comprised of no more than a few carefully chosen notes timed so well and played so expressively that the result was quite dramatic. Sometimes the entire solo was forged from such devices, as in "Solea" on *Sketches of Spain*, "Freddie the Freeloader" on *Kind of Blue*, and "Bitches Brew" on *Bitches Brew*.

7. **The cluster of traits possessed by his tone quality and preference for pitch range.** During the 1940s and 1950s, Davis played with a tone quality that was lighter, softer, and less brassy than that of most other trumpeters. He used almost no vibrato, favored the trumpet's middle register over its flashier high register, and rarely double-timed. By comparison with the styles of most other modern trumpeters, his was gentle. That trend was reversed, however, on some pieces he recorded during the 1960s in which he began to reach into the high register more often. This reversal is especially evident in his albums *Miles in Europe* and *"Four" and More*. During the 1970s he developed an even more explosive side to his style, capitalizing on the trumpet's high register, and he occasionally included long bursts of notes and splattered tones. He also incorporated electronically generated echo[9] and "wah-wah" effects into his trumpet tone. Although his later solo work seemed more outgoing, he never entirely discarded his earlier manners, and his work in the 1980s occasionally displayed all these facets.

8. **An overriding concern with sound texture in his trumpet style and the concepts of sound** that guided the playing of his bands. Certainly he had also been interested in melodic and rhythmic aspects of his music. But above all, there was a recurring creation of a glass-like smoothness of texture, extending from the bottom to the top of the band's sound. (This was evident as early as 1945 with the approach used for his solo on "Now's the Time" with Charlie Parker.) It characterized his attraction to the Claude Thornhill band sound, which drew heavily upon the concepts of French Impressionist composer Claude

Debussy. This emerged in Davis's downsized version of the Thornhill band for his *Birth of the Cool* recordings of 1949 and 1950. (Compare Thornhill's "Snow-fall" with the Davis Nonet's "Moon Dreams.") It was evident in his *Kind of Blue* and *Bitches Brew*. In these albums, his own solos were filled with sustained tones that topped off the voicings of distinctly uncluttered accompaniment chords. Consistent with his concern for sound texture, Davis is known for suggesting chord voicings to his pianists and for choosing long notes in his solos that cap the voicings in his accompaniment so well that it sounds like part of an arrangement that presets the sound quality from bottom to top. His concern with texture also dovetails into his attraction to simplicity in the construction of solos. An ever-changing line would not provide sufficient sustained tones to mesh with accompaniment chords long enough for listeners to savor the combination as a texture. The Davis concern with texture is also manifested in his retaining arranger Gil Evans as adviser even when Evans was not directly involved in large-scale recording projects. Apparently Davis felt that it was important to have available the Evans sense of sound quality and balance, even in the work of his small combos. During the jazz-rock fusion period, Davis sometimes used two and three pianists or guitarists playing at the same time, and he hired extra percussionists. Often he told them how actively to play, when to play, and when not to play. This reflected the same concern for sound texture that he had shown earlier.

THE CLASSIC MILES DAVIS QUINTET

Miles Davis made many of his historically significant recordings as a bandleader for the Prestige record company. Among musicians, the most discussed of these are *Steamin'*, *Cookin'*, *Workin'*, and *Relaxin'*. These were recorded in 1956 with tenor saxophonist John Coltrane, pianist Red Garland, bassist Paul Chambers, and drummer "Philly Joe" Jones. (For more about Chambers and Jones, see Chapter 11.)[10] The style and energy at those recording sessions were particularly evident again in *Milestones*, an album Davis made for the Columbia record company in 1958, with the same musicians plus alto saxophonist Cannonball Adderley (discussed more in Chapter 11). Though Miles Davis had long been linked with cool jazz, the band on these recordings sounds more like hard bop and later styles. The musicians played with blistering intensity. Their work had an unusual freshness and excitement that combined to make these among the most striking performances since the groundbreaking Parker-Gillespie records of ten years earlier. Many musicians and journalists consider these particular Davis albums to be as outstanding as the classic recordings by Louis Armstrong's Hot Five and Hot Seven of the 1920s and the Kansas City Six and Seven recordings of Count Basie and Lester Young of the 1930s.

These recordings marked the first time that many jazz fans heard tenor saxophonist John Coltrane. Though some journalists considered this portion of his career merely a development stage, Coltrane's style with Davis was so substantial and original at this time that he would qualify as a jazz giant even if he had never moved away from it and developed other approaches. (For details, see Chapter 13.)

The classic quintet, with the addition of Cannonball Adderley, was responsible for a landmark event in jazz history. With their recording of the "Milestones" selection in 1958, they broke away from the tradition of guiding improvisations solely by chord progressions. Most of the tunes Davis had recorded before 1958 were pop tunes or bop compositions with frequently changing chords in their accompaniment. But instead of using frequently changing chords for their improvisations on "Milestones," the musicians used two modes. (See pages 453, 465 and 492 for explanations of modes;

TABLE 12.4   A Few of the Many Trumpeters Influenced by Miles Davis

Clifford Brown	Stu Williamson	Terence Blanchard
Chet Baker	Ted Curson	Terumasa Hino
Shorty Rogers	Luis Gasca	Kenny Wheeler
Jack Sheldon	Blue Mitchell	Tim Hagans
Nat Adderley	Lester Bowie	John McNeil
Charles Moore	Tom Harrell	Herb Pomeroy
Johnny Coles	Randy Brecker	Wynton Marsalis
Eddie Henderson	Mark Isham	Wallace Roney
Jim Powell	Donald Byrd	

see page 497 for musical notation of the modes used on "Milestones.") The first mode was in effect for sixteen measures, the second mode for another sixteen measures, followed by a return to the first for the final eight measures. The improvisers using this modal format had fewer demands placed on their attention. This represented quite a contrast with the demands placed by frequently changing chords. The players correspondingly had more energy left to direct toward piecing together interesting melodies and rhythms. After the *Milestones* album (containing "Milestones") was released, the approach used on "Milestones"—the absence of changing chords—became popular among modern jazz musicians. The momentum of this trend increased upon wide acceptance of mode-based music in the Davis album *Kind of Blue*, recorded in 1959 (discussed later in this chapter). "Milestones" soon took its place in the repertory of standard jam session tunes, next to "Cherokee," "All the Things You Are," "A Night in Tunisia," and numerous pieces based on the 12-bar blues.

"Flamenco Sketches,"
JCCD2 Track 9

COLLABORATIONS WITH GIL EVANS

In 1957, Davis renewed his association with arranger **Gil Evans** (1912–1988). Together they had organized the *Birth of the Cool* sessions a decade earlier. This time they put together new works in which Davis was the only soloist with a large band. Evans conducted his own arrangements for groups of brass, woodwinds, string bass, drums, and occasionally harp. The brass section included French horn and tuba in addition to trumpets and trombones. The woodwind section included flutes and clarinets in addition to saxophones; bassoon was added for the *Sketches of Spain* album. The arrangements reflected Evans's prolific imagination and high level of workmanship. With soulful and stirring playing by Davis, these efforts were captured on *Miles Ahead*, *Porgy and Bess*, and *Sketches of Spain*. The quality of these three albums has been matched only by the greatest Duke Ellington masterpieces.

Miles Ahead was recorded in 1957, with Davis playing fluegelhorn, a previously uncommon instrument in jazz (see photo on page 134). Although Clark Terry and Shorty Rogers had played it prior to 1957, the Davis recordings provided impetus for its ensuing popularity. By the 1970s, many jazz trumpeters were doubling on fluegelhorn, and arrangers who worked for popular singers were frequently including fluegelhorn parts in their orchestrations.

The program of *Miles Ahead* includes popular tunes and jazz tunes. The pieces are connected by brief interludes that Evans composed specially to bridge the gaps between selections. The contents span moods reminiscent of the subtle, unforced swinging of the *Birth of the Cool* recordings, lush pastels in slow tempo and moments of brassy excitement. Compared to other big band writing of the 1950s and 1960s, its character was more reflective. Here Evans mastered the effective use of shading and contrast of both rhythmic and tonal dimensions. Like Duke Ellington, he freed himself of the formula writing which pitted brasses against saxes. He freely voiced across sections and assigned different parts of a melody to different instruments. Like Ellington, Evans managed to weave improvisations into the framework of a piece without sounding contrived or awkward. The sound of Davis fades gracefully into and out of the ensemble. There are brief passages in which Davis interpreted pop-tune themes, or in which he improvised on the chord progressions in the arrangements. In either case, the orchestration was perfectly conceived to match the mood and color of the Davis style.

In 1958, Davis recorded George Gershwin's opera *Porgy and Bess*. Gil Evans devised arrangements of sweeping colors and breathtaking drama. Davis reworked the familiar melodies so they acquired a new flavor. (Listen to "Fishermen, Strawberry, and Devil Crab," on *JCCD1* Track 2.)

Sketches of Spain was recorded in November 1959 and March 1960. It is nearly a classical music album because the music was almost exclusively written, except for "Solea," in which Davis developed a long modal improvisation. The best known piece on the album is from Juaquín Rodrigo's "Concierto de Aranjuez" for guitar and symphony orchestra, which was rescored by Evans for trumpet and wind orchestra, no strings.[11] "Will o' the Wisp" is from ballet music by Spanish composer Manuel de Falla. The remaining pieces are developments of Spanish folk themes: "Pan Piper," "Saeta," and "Solea." This album has proven to be exceedingly popular among non-musicians, jazz fans, and jazz musicians.

Composer-arranger Gil Evans, age 58, conducting from the piano. Evans masterminded what many consider among the best Miles Davis recording sessions: *Birth of the Cool*, *Sketches of Spain*, *Porgy and Bess*, and *Miles Ahead*. He also assisted when Davis was entering jazz-rock fusion with *Filles de Kilimanjaro*.

(Photo by Bill Smith)

Gil Evans had a long career in the field of arranging and bandleading, but he produced no other works whose quality exceeded these richly fulfilling and consistently compelling collaborations with Davis. Decades after their first release, *Sketches of Spain*, *Porgy and Bess*, and *Miles Ahead* continue to stand as monuments to combining orchestration and the jazz tradition. They remain all-time favorite albums among jazz musicians and music scholars.

Kind of Blue. In 1959, Miles Davis recorded one of the best-loved and most historically pivotal albums in modern jazz: *Kind of Blue*. On all but one selection, he used Cannonball Adderley, John Coltrane, pianist Bill Evans, bassist Paul Chambers, and drummer Jimmy Cobb. Bill Evans conceived most of the harmonies, as well as contributing one original composition ("Blue in Green," often mistakenly credited to Davis).[12] One reason the album is so important is that, instead of requiring that chords change frequently and bear preset durations, the band used formats in which the harmonies of a single chord or mode remained in effect for four or more measures (see Appendix H for explanatory musical notation). Then the group either preset the durations, as with "So What" (available in *SCCJ*, the modes of which are notated on page 496), or they left the durations up to the spontaneous discretion of the soloist (as in "Flamenco Sketches," *JCCD2* Track 9).

The final selection on *Kind of Blue* was created by an interesting improvisational technique. Instead of playing a melody and improvising on its chord changes, the sextet followed a preset sequence of five modes. Each mode served as the harmonic guide for improvisation as long as a soloist wanted to use it. Then, whenever a soloist wanted a change, he moved to the next mode. Although there were no restrictions on the duration of any mode, the soloists tended to use each mode for an even number of measures. In fact, most soloists used each mode for four measures and then moved to the next. So, despite the increased freedom allowed by this technique, the players usually chose duration patterns which typify conventional jazz improvisation.

The final selection on *Kind of Blue* is known by two different titles because many copies of the record were released with the tune titles interchanged on the second side of the album. Bill Evans's album jacket notes indicate that the piece was supposed to be called "All Blues." But after the album was released, several subsequent Davis versions of the second side's *first* selection were released under the "All Blues" title. The name that seems to have stuck for the second side's *second* selection is "Flamenco Sketches." (This appears as the final selection on the CD format.)

After *Kind of Blue* was released, many jazz musicians began using its formats instead of popular song formats. During the 1960s and 1970s, many players rejected the bop custom of using chords that changed frequently and bore preset durations. Entire performances were based on a single chord instead of a progression of different chords. Some performances contained spontaneous chord changes instead of preset changes. In summary, **the historical significance of *Kind of Blue*** was threefold: (1) it represented a set of inspired improvisations by an all-star band; (2) it was a highly palatable departure from bop-derived styles; and (3) it introduced a generation of improvisers to mode-based formats. Incidentally, it is also the most frequently cited album among recommended picks by musicians and critics.

Further historical perspective can be gained for *Kind of Blue* when we consider that at the same time it arrived, considerable attention was also being given to Ornette Coleman, a saxophonist who specialized in improvising with no preset harmonies at all. Whereas Davis was substituting long stretches of modes for rapidly changing chords, Coleman's improvisations were neither mode-based nor chord-based. Coleman spontaneously introduced a tone center and worked from that, then shifted to another and then another.

Coleman's improvisations followed only the internal logic of his melodic inventions, instead of adhering to a single key, mode, or chord progression. Unlike Davis,

Recorded April 22, 1959, for Columbia by Miles Davis (trumpet), Cannonball Adderley (alto saxophone), John Coltrane (tenor saxophone), Bill Evans (piano), Paul Chambers (bass), Jimmy Cobb (drums); available on Miles Davis, *Kind of Blue* (Columbia/Legacy: 64935, 1959, c1997). Suggestions for keeping your place while hearing "Flamenco Sketches" and following the modal construction:

1. Remember that the *first* track on the second side of the LP format of *Kind of Blue* has been labeled "Flamenco Sketches" on many copies of this album. So, if you hear a feeling of "ONE two three Four five six ONE two three Four five six" instead of a very slow "ONE two three four ONE two three four," you are listening to the wrong selection.

2. To begin synchronizing your counting with the record, notice that the piece starts with a bass note on the fourth beat of a measure that actually precedes the beginning of your counting. If you are to count accurately, you must say "FOUR" when that first note is sounding, then say "One" when the next bass note sounds. That note lasts three beats, so you must continue counting even though there is no clear statement of any beats until the pattern is repeated. In other words, to get you through the introduction and well synchronized with the tempo of the piece, you need to count "FOUR One two three FOUR One two three FOUR." When you say "FOUR One," you are acknowledging the bass notes. When you say "two three," you are acknowledging the middle of the measure, a time when the bass note is still ringing and no clear statement of beats is coming from the musicians. Eventually, you should be able to count "ONE two three four ONE two three four" with or without assistance from the musicians. This will become important later because bassist Paul Chambers sometimes plays figures that purposely delete the simple pattern outlined above and leave the listener to fill in the beats. You will have some assistance, though, beginning with John Coltrane's entrance, because drummer Jimmy Cobb starts using a wire brush to play ride rhythms on the ride cymbal. If you still have yet to figure out where the beats are by the time you are near the end of the selection, simply listen to Cobb's playing under the final Miles Davis solo. It is almost exclusively quarter notes, one note on each beat.

3. Remember that the tempo is very slow, and that you should therefore take care to not be counting twice as fast or four times as fast as the beats are passing.

4. If your mind wanders, let the sound of mode #4 refocus your attention. It has a Spanish flavor that differs noticeably from the flavors of the other modes. It has also attracted the longest improvisations from the musicians and can therefore give you the most time to get back with it. In fact, if you lose your place and all of a sudden find yourself in the middle of that mode, you can restart your counting when that flavor disappears. The disappearance of that flavor will signal the beginning of mode #5.

5. Start counting anew when a different solo voice enters. Remember that the sequence is four measures of piano and bass introduction followed by these sounds, each running five modes in sequence: muted trumpet, tenor sax, alto sax, piano, and muted trumpet.

6. Listen carefully for the bass notes that begin the measures. If a new mode is starting, this will often be signalled by the sound of a NEW bass note on the first beat of the measure.

7. To help you anticipate each new mode within a single musician's solo, keep in mind that *generally:*

   a. Miles Davis lets bassist Paul Chambers lead him to each new mode. Chambers plays the important note of the mode while Davis is silent, then Davis enters with a new melodic idea to fit the mode.

   b. Coltrane tends to increase the number of notes played per beat just before beginning a new mode. In other words, if you hear Coltrane sound like he is going faster and faster, consider the likelihood that he is requesting the next mode.

   c. Adderley suggests the upcoming mode by a peculiar choice of notes in his line. The flavor of his melody line shifts when he is about to change modes.

8. Once you know where you are, if it is the beginning of a mode, count "1234 2234 3234 4234" in order to keep your place by tallying beats as they pass. Each group of four beats ("1234") accounts for one measure. You tag the measures by saying a number to yourself at the beginning of each one. If it is the first measure for the mode, you say, "ONE two three four." If it is the second measure of a given mode, you say, "TWO two three four." If it is the third measure, you say, "THREE two three four."

LISTENING GUIDE continued on next page

Eventually, you should be able to follow the changing modes without referring to the guide. Your ears will tell you what mode is in effect at a given moment. The whole point of this exercise is to help you peek into what the jazz improviser is doing. By being able to identify the same sounds that the improviser is using as a basis for his solos, you will lessen the mystery of how solos are put together and how musicians manage to play well together without having to discuss their parts or use prewritten themes. The more you recognize in the sounds, the better prepared you are to go on to an appreciation of the compositional beauties present in the improvised lines. Listening for modes to change at the slow pace used by these performers should better equip you for listening to chords changing in conventional jazz pieces. The better you get at accurately anticipating chord changes, the more you will realize how the improviser's lines reflect his own appreciation of how the chords are progressing in a given piece. To a great extent, the progress of a melody line mirrors the progression of harmonies that lies beneath it in the accompanying chord changes. The improvised line reflects the flavor of the underlying chord, and a line improvised in "Flamenco Sketches" often bears the same character as the mode that is implied in that moment's accompaniment harmonies. Once you begin confidently following the music in this piece, it will be as though you are peering through a microscope. But instead of tiny things being made to appear large, ordinarily quick-paced improvisational processes have been slowed down for your calm examination.

ELAPSED TIME

0′00″   **Introduction**

Four measures of mode #1. The sound of this mode is indicated by bass notes and chord voicings set in a pattern previously used by Bill Evans for his "Peace Piece." What were originally left-hand parts for pianist Evans are given here to bassist Paul Chambers. The pattern has Chambers playing on only the first and the fourth beats of each measure. Pianist Evans plays chords whose harmonies flesh out the rest of the mode's flavor.

0′18″   **Miles Davis Muted Trumpet Improvisation**

(with only piano, bass, and brushes on snare drum accompaniment)

mode #1 (four measures)

0′36″   mode #2 (four measures)

0′53″   mode #3 (four measures)

1′10″   mode #4 (eight measures)

1′44″   mode #5 (four measures)

2′02″   **John Coltrane Tenor Saxophone Improvisation**

(with piano, bass, and ride cymbal accompaniment)

mode #1 (four measures)

2′19″   mode #2 (four measures)

2′35″   mode #3 (four measures)

2′52″   mode #4 (eight measures)

3′25″   mode #5 (four measures)

3′41″   mode #5

one-measure introduction to next solo by piano, bass, and ride cymbal

3′47″   **Cannonball Adderley Alto Saxophone Improvisation**

(with piano, bass, and cymbals accompaniment)

Notice that bassist Chambers plays less predictably during this solo.

mode #1 (eight measures)

4′17″   mode #2 (four measures)

4′34″   mode #3 (eight measures)

LISTENING GUIDE *continued on next page*

5′06″	mode #4 (eight measures)
	(Drummer Jimmy Cobb plays double-time and adds high-hat closings during the middle of Adderley's treatment of this mode.)
5′37″	mode #5 (four measures)
5′53″	**Bill Evans Piano Improvisation**
	(with bass and ride cymbal accompaniment)
	mode #1 (eight measures)
6′26″	mode #2 (four measures)
6′42″	mode #3 (eight measures)
7′14″	mode #4 (four measures)
7′31″	mode #5 (four measures)
7′48″	**Miles Davis Muted Trumpet Improvisation**
	(with piano, bass, and ride cymbal accompaniment)
	mode #1 (four measures)
8′05″	mode #2 (four measures)
8′20″	mode #3 (four measures)
8′37″	mode #4 (eight measures)
9′09″	mode #5 (two measures)

Note: See page 495 for musical notations and technical names of these modes. The complete score to *Kind of Blue*, with transcribed solos, is available from Hal Leonard Publications, *www.halleonard.com*. A written transcription of Coltrane's solo on this recording is available from Andrew White, 4830 South Dakota Ave. N.E., Washington, DC 20017; phone 202-526-3666.

Coleman almost never used a pianist. Improvisation using such approaches had been recorded by others before Coleman and Davis (see Lennie Tristano, Shorty Rogers, et al. in Chapter 10). But only after this work of Davis and Coleman in the late 1950s did the approach catch on with a sizable number of jazz musicians. Then, by the mid-1960s, free-form and modal approaches were mixed in the music of many bands. These related approaches became so abundant that, during the 1970s, more than half of all jazz and jazz-derived performances contained at least some modal or free-form improvisations. During that period, fewer than 20 prominent modern jazz combos played selections which fit neither modal nor free-form styles. An entire school of jazz styles embraced the practice of not presetting the harmonies for improvisation (see Chapter 14). Incidentally, the music of the so-called "new age" bands in the 1980s was also largely modal.

Many of the jazz-rock fusion bands of the 1970s and 1980s combined passages of chord progression-based improvisation with passages of mode-based improvisation. Davis himself alternated among all these formats. The impact of *Kind of Blue* was immense. The Davis innovations complemented the developments associated with Coleman to lay the foundation for ways that jazz was structured in the succeeding two decades.

THE 1959–1963 RHYTHM SECTION

The rhythm section Miles Davis used from 1959 to 1963 consisted of pianist **Wynton Kelly** (1931–1971), bassist Paul Chambers, and drummer Jimmy Cobb. Their work is documented in the albums *Miles Davis at Carnegie Hall, Friday Night at the Blackhawk, Saturday Night at the Blackhawk, Someday My Prince Will Come,* and in the selection "Freddie the Freeloader" on *Kind of Blue*. Their relaxed, even swing feeling and their lightness and bounce distinguished them from all others of the time. This was like the role played by Count Basie's rhythm section in the 1930s. Modern musicians of the era considered this Davis rhythm section to be among the most desirable accompanying units in jazz. Paul Chambers was already discussed in the hard bop chapter, but we will examine Kelly and Cobb here.

Wynton Kelly was a bop pianist who played with a lighter, less complicated feeling than Bud Powell used. He swung infectiously, and his accompaniments followed the melodic and rhythmic flights of the Davis hornmen so well that Kelly's bandmates could hardly help but swing too. Kelly was one of Davis's all-time favorite accompanists, and Cannonball Adderley also praised him highly. Kelly combined influences ranging from Powell to Horace Silver, and on *Someday My Prince Will Come,* he used the chord voicings of Bill Evans. In turn, Kelly himself was influential. Among the modern pianists who showed his influence are Herbie Hancock, Warren Bernhardt, and Keith Jarrett.

Jimmy Cobb (b. 1929) was a steady and swinging drummer. More conservative in his accompanying style than "Philly Joe" Jones, Cobb nonetheless contributed a far-reaching characteristic to modern jazz: **Cobb's ride rhythms were placed toward the front edge of the beat in a way that made them seem to pull the beat.** Though this aspect is subtle, it is quite significant because drummers before Cobb had traditionally played more toward the center of the beat. Tony Williams replaced Cobb in the Davis group, adopted Cobb's timekeeping technique, and played consistently on the leading edge of the beat. Williams had a correspondingly marked effect on the overall feeling of the Davis quintet. Then Williams, in turn, influenced other drummers who became prominent in the 1970s and 1980s.

Tony Williams, a prime force in the Miles Davis rhythm section of 1963–68.

(Photo by Charles Behnke)

THE 1963–1968 RHYTHM SECTION

In 1963, Miles Davis hired a new rhythm section composed of pianist **Herbie Hancock**, bassist **Ron Carter**, and drummer **Tony Williams**.[13] This Davis rhythm section remained intact, at least on records, from 1963 until 1968. These musicians created a new jazz idiom. Though moments in their music resembled the sounds of hard bop and free jazz, their music did not truly belong to either of those classifications. Hints of their new idiom were evident in some of their first recordings, for example, *My Funny Valentine*, of 1964. Then, by 1965, every album they produced was filled with new concepts. In addition, these concepts were packaged in performances whose quality was so finished that it belied its freshness. The innovations of this band were performed so smoothly that many listeners, especially journalists, failed to recognize its historical significance. This music disappointed so many jazz fans who expected extensive repetition of brief rhythms, recycled jazz phrases, and funky melodies that it ranked as one of the least popular phases in the Davis recording career. Yet its innovations were at least as significant as those in Davis's better known styles.

"Masqualero," JCCD2 *Track 10*

Hancock, Carter, and Williams all displayed stunning technical prowess on their instruments, creating what was probably the smoothest rhythm section sound jazz had experienced. The Hancock-Carter-Williams unit had excitement and power like the Garland-Chambers-Jones rhythm section and sensitivity and delicacy like the Bill Evans-Scott LaFaro-Paul Motian unit. (For a sample of Evans, LaFaro, and Motian, listen to "Solar," *JCCD3* Track 3.) These players had digested the work of their most impressive predecessors, combined it with in-depth knowledge and mastery of twentieth century classical music (Bartók, Hindemith, Debussy, etc.), and then built upon that foundation to create something newer and more sparkling than any other combinations. (Listen to "Masqualero" and focus your attention solely on the piano, bass, and drum parts.) This rhythm section could play persuasively in the bop manner if it wished. It could emulate the Wynton Kelly-Paul Chambers-Jimmy Cobb style. And it could work well in the quiet, reflective manner of the Evans-LaFaro-Motian unit. But it was freer, more flexible and daring than those other units, and it came up with music that sounded like no jazz ever heard before. This unit's collective originality and creativity remained unsurpassed decades after its monumental contributions to the 1967 Davis album *Sorcerer* (from which "Masqualero" is taken). Their consolidations were so startling and so well played that it took most of jazz about 20 years to catch up, as evidenced by the wave of similarly styled bands emerging in the 1980s, such as those of Wynton Marsalis and Terence Blanchard.

"Prince of Darkness," CCD2 *Track 6*

Hancock, Carter, and Williams maintained an almost magical level of rapport. They were able to play cohesively at breakneck tempos[14] or, in the context of a slow piece, they could avoid explicitly stating tempo and sound instead as though someone were conducting them through gradual accelerations and decelerations.[15] Their rapport and high level of musicianship allowed them to change rhythms, textures, and moods spontaneously at any moment of a performance, at any tempo, and on any chord progression. Their versatility and lightning quick responsiveness were extraordinary. Because of this, **the Davis group of the 1960s was one of very few jazz bands that drastically varied its levels of loudness. It was also distinguished for creating a wide variety of distinctly different accompanying rhythms and chord patterns. A clear departure from bop traditions was evident in many of their performances.**

"Masqualero," JCCD2 *Track 10, 1'33" to 5'00"*

Herbie Hancock

Pianist **Herbie Hancock** combined the best qualities of an improviser: a clear conception, fertile imagination, a highly developed sense of continuity, and excellent instrumental proficiency. He had a quick, precise touch and comped briskly. Like his colleagues in the Davis group, he was also a composer, and his improvisations revealed his keen sense of compositional balance and integrity. He was able consistently to devise coherent, well-structured solos, even for pieces that provided him with only a mode, a mood, a key, and a tempo. Hancock was able to create and perform accompaniment patterns spontaneously during group improvisations that brought the music a form, direction, and substance comparable to that of an elaborate piece which had been worked out in advance.

Hancock contributed gracefully shifting rhythms and harmonies that were more advanced than the patterns used by bop pianists or by such contemporary pianists as Bill Evans and McCoy Tyner. What he invented as underpinning for the soloists often had the character of modern symphonic music. Incidentally, Hancock's superb mastery of the piano and his creative flexibility and taste as an accompanist put him in great demand as a recording pianist. Hancock appeared on more record dates than any other jazz pianist of the 1960s. (For an outline of Hancock's career and contributions, see Chapter 15.)

Ron Carter

"Prince of Darkness,"
CCD2 *Track 6*

Bassist **Ron Carter** (b. 1937) had a slick, round tone. He walked with uncanny perfection and buoyancy. Both his tone and his sense of timing exhibited uniformly high quality. Carter played more toward the front of the beat than Paul Chambers did, thereby meshing with the timekeeping manner introduced by drummer Jimmy Cobb in the previous Davis band. He provided a sturdy yet responsive foundation for the quintet. Among musicians, Carter is often considered the most swinging accompanist after Ray Brown and Sam Jones. Yet despite his excellence as a timekeeper, Carter did not always restrict himself to walking. He incorporated other rhythmic figures, too. (Listen to his work at the beginning of "Masqualero," *JCCD2* Track 10.) He was continuously devising new ways both to underpin the group sound and to enrich the musical events that occurred around him.[16] This was no small achievement, either. Tony Williams was encircling Carter with exploding rhythmic ideas that had never been used before in jazz combos. And, at the same time, pianist Herbie Hancock was inventing new harmonies to fit these rhythms and moods, all of which had to be smoothly integrated almost at the moment they were conceived. Carter acquitted himself so well in these circumstances that Miles Davis was not the only leader who appreciated him. By the mid-1970s, Carter had been employed on more than four hundred records.

Tony Williams

Drummer **Tony Williams** (1945–1997) represented the highest level of drum technique, and he was possibly the most influential jazz drummer of the 1960s. He was very fast, and his cymbal tones were separated with crystal clarity. Williams provided a model of light, sharp sounds. His ride cymbal playing was very crisp and distinctive, and, because he used a smaller bass drum than most pre-1960s drummers, the low-register component of his drum set's sound was particularly well articulated. Williams was an extremely sophisticated rhythm section player, looser and more of a risk taker than any of his predecessors. Williams did more than kick and prod the hornmen. By the time *Filles de Kilimanjaro* was recorded in 1968, he had assumed a role so prominent that his creations often overshadowed the other sounds in the group. His was a very assertive style.[17]

Williams overflowed with imagination. He devised numerous ways to establish new moods and state the tempo. Let's mention two of them. As early as the 1964 *"Four" and More* album, he had played pieces without following the traditional custom of consistently snapping his high-hat shut on the second and fourth beats of each measure. In this way, he was keeping time only with the ride cymbal, and he was using the high-hat only for bursts of color. Then on "Freedom Jazz Dance" (in the 1966 *Miles Smiles* album) he closed his high-hat sharply on every beat, a timekeeping practice later adopted by hundreds of jazz-rock drummers. He also colored the group sound with a seemingly endless variety of cymbal splashes, snare drum fills, and imaginative rhythmic patterns distributed over all his drums and cymbals (particularly evident at the beginning and the end of "Masqualero," *JCCD2* Track 10). His work often departed from the dance band and marching band traditions of jazz drumming. Some of his methods stem from orchestral concepts in which percussion instruments perform melodic and texture-generating roles. Listening to the Davis recordings of this period will reveal why so many drummers were awed and inspired by Williams. Some musicians feel that Williams was the musician most responsible for instigating the florid constructions that came from the mid-1960s Miles Davis Quintet. It was Williams who most often provoked the other musicians into their daring flights of nontraditional playing. (To study his contributions, listen to "Masqualero" and focus solely on drums and cymbals.)[18]

THE 1964–1968 COMPOSITIONAL STYLE

Davis recorded very few conventionally constructed pieces after saxophonist-composer Wayne Shorter joined him in 1964. Most tunes Davis played during the 1950s fit conventional song forms.[19] **After 1964, Davis favored tunes that did not have bridges, complex turnarounds, or any section demarcations which could easily act as barriers to an unencumbered, free-flowing sound.** Most of his post-1964 recordings were made up of tunes which had fewer chord changes than those in pop standards by Richard Rodgers or George Gershwin, or jazz standards by Charlie Parker, Dizzy Gillespie, or Thelonious Monk.[20]

The use of space in tune construction was another trait that lent the 1965–1968 recordings their distinctive flavor. Sometimes several measures of the melody were filled with silence. Quite often, trumpet and tenor would go silent while the rhythm section continued to play and generate a mood.[21] Incidentally, these differences in compositional form led to a drastic change not only in the sound of the Miles Davis bands then, but also in other groups of that period which used them.

One other important aspect of the group's compositional style was a significant lessening in the number of rapid, jumpy eighth-note figures which typified the highly syncopated lines of bop. The Davis repertory still contained pieces with some eighth notes and syncopation, but many of the post-1964 tunes were constructed of smoothly contoured lines with frequent sustained tones. By comparison with the compositional style of bop, this new style was less densely packed. These tunes had fewer intricate figures. An airy feeling was more common than a crowded feeling. This, in turn, influenced the character of improvisations the band produced. More variety was possible because of the greater freedom implied by the openness in feeling. (To illustrate the difference between bop and this new style, compare "Shaw Nuff" [*JCCD1* Track 26] with "Masqualero" [*JCCD2* Track 10].)

Figure 12.1 Wayne Shorter's melody lines often contain strings of notes separated by the interval of a fourth. Here is part of his "Masqualero." The notes of one phrase of the melody appear on this keyboard in numbered sequence.

"Nefertiti"

The Davis Quintet performance of Shorter's "Nefertiti," on the *Nefertiti* album of 1967, illustrates both these aspects. It is 16 measures long, and it is all one section. There is a new chord in every measure, but the motion always has a slow, floating quality. Nothing abrupt or jumpy happens in either the melody or the chord changes. This melody's silences and sustained tones produce an effect unlike that of bop melodies. In addition, the entire performance consists of the melody being repeated again and again. This format was employed extensively by post-1968 Davis groups and spin-offs from those bands. Note that, with no improvised solos by anyone else, this version of "Nefertiti" is practically a feature for Tony Williams. The lazy, expansive feeling evoked by the performance suggests the impressionistic classical music of Claude Debussy ("La Mer," "Prelude to the Afternoon of a Faun") and Maurice Ravel ("Daphnis and Chloe"). The style of this "Nefertiti" performance places the burden of complexity on the rhythm section, quite the reverse of bop tendencies. So not only does the style of the melody differ from bop, the style of the accompaniment differs, too. It is a loose, highly active improvisation by piano, bass, and drums that alternates from walking bass and ride rhythms to moments with volatile drumming and very little internal repetition. Sometimes Carter is playing four times as many notes as a bassist would usually play. At other times, he is playing only a fourth as many as we would expect. Hancock does not always play conventional comping rhythms, either. This contrasts sharply with the almost unvarying sequences of walking bass, ride rhythms, and comping which typify bop accompaniment style. **The post-1964 Davis Quintet evolved away from the bop formula of quick, jumpy melodic figures on top and stable, metronomic pulse patterns on the bottom. Shorter's writing brought stable simplicity to the top, and Williams's drumming brought super-charged rhythmic complexity to the bottom. This reversal of roles later became common in jazz-rock groups, especially in the band called Weather Report.**

The three characteristics outlined above all fit with the tremendously explorative attitude of drummer Tony Williams and the effect he had upon his fellow bandmates. He spurred them to use the new freedom that came from the nontraditional song forms and to contrive a fresh sound. This resulted in their creating phrases that were unlike those in previous jazz styles, and it nudged them to devise sound masses that evolved spontaneously and freely shifted. The artistry of these musicians came together to achieve a rich product that represents a triumph in collective improvisation and delights the listeners with surprise after surprise.

In addition to their extraordinarily high instrumental proficiency, improvisatory freshness, and unique contributions to the development of jazz accompaniment style, Hancock, Shorter, Carter, and Williams managed to ensure that the variety of moods and rhythmic styles employed in the 1964–1968 Davis Quintet was vast. They recorded waltzes,[22] fast pieces,[23] slow-reflective pieces,[24] pieces in which a sequence of different rhythmic styles are created,[25] and pieces that anticipated jazz-rock fusion styles (see Chapter 16).

Wayne Shorter

Between summer of 1964 and winter of 1970, Miles Davis employed **Wayne Shorter** (b. 1933). This man proved to be one of the most outstanding tenor saxophonists in jazz of the 1960s, and possibly the most original tenor stylist to emerge after Coltrane and concurrent to Albert Ayler. Shorter was also a composer whose work provided a foundation for the new jazz idiom that was created by the Davis band of 1965–1968. Some musicians consider Shorter to be the most important jazz composer of the 1960s and 1970s. His highly original writing and playing had already been central to the Art Blakey bands of 1959–1964, and they later became central to the work of Weather Report, an innovative jazz-rock fusion band of the 1970s and 1980s.

Shorter's creativity had several sides to it. Some musicians and fans are impressed the most by the side he showed in his work with Art Blakey. They may prefer it because his improvisatory methods with Blakey represent the closest he came to hard bop and using traditional ways of devising lines, such as basing phrases on strings of eighth notes, for example. His work was fluid and extremely

Bassist Ron Carter and tenor saxophonist Wayne Shorter, photographed here while with the mid-1960s Miles Davis group.

(Photo courtesy of Bill Smith)

intense, projecting a rawness that is common to hard bop. Some listeners find this work more emotionally compelling than his other work. Despite his links with tradition, however, Shorter's playing with Blakey was largely original, its level of inspiration consistently striking.

Many musicians and fans believe that Shorter's studio recordings of 1965–1968 with Miles Davis constitute his most impressive work. Though similar in many ways to his work with Blakey, these performances highlighted an even more unconventional and exceedingly explorative side to his talents. A softness and introspective quality was exposed here that is not as evident in his work with Blakey. Though his playing in all contexts always exhibited a highly logical quality, his thinking here was more calmly logical, as though this new setting allowed him to be less hurried and more reflective. Perhaps that was why some listeners perceived this music as cool and abstract. Incidentally, the few rare recordings that are available of him playing with this band in concert and night club appearances during this period reveal him wrestling passionately with dense swaths of color and rhythm that seem to be burning through the center of the band sound, not cool at all.

Despite the highly logical stance in Shorter's music, the lines were very fresh and rarely predictable. That lack of predictability intensely attracted some listeners, though it lost others. This work could be viewed within the avant-garde category because Shorter was severely stretching the boundaries of what a jazz improviser could do without totally ignoring steady pulse and preset accompaniment harmonies. By this time, he had evolved even further away from the bop approach to melody. His lines were formed from notes of many different durations, not primarily eighth notes. And his rhythms were not necessarily those associated with jazz. In this phase of his career, he did not routinely build solos from standard bop rhythmic figures that swing in obvious ways and busily fill every moment. Some of his phrases did not swing. They intentionally floated over and past the beat instead of getting down inside it. Shorter played lines of smoother contours than those of most hard bop saxophonists. His work did not have as many abrupt starts and stops, or the bobbing up and down that typified bop. His melodic approach often recalled the concise, floating themes, interspersed with long silences, that we find in music by such nonjazz composers as Maurice Ravel, Claude Debussy, and Erik Satie.

Though some listeners think they detect the influence of Sonny Rollins or John Coltrane in Shorter's earliest playing on record (1959 and 1960), the bulk of Shorter's style is most accurately viewed as original and not derivative. Any evidence of stylistic debts to the giants who preceded him has been so thoroughly transformed in his playing that to dwell upon it is unwarranted. In his recordings with Davis, Shorter's tone quality, articulation, rhythmic conception, and melodic tendencies all differ significantly from every major saxophonist who preceded him. His playing was as free of clichés as any saxophone style yet devised. Shorter had such extraordinarily high standards for originality that he usually managed to improvise solos that were free of patterns. He tried to create something entirely new upon each opportunity to improvise, and he usually succeeded.[26]

Shorter's tone quality and manner made his playing easily distinguishable from other saxophonists. Shorter had a gray tone with a broad-textured surface and soft edges. It was a hard sound, but he could temper that hardness according to the mood of the music. Until the 1970s, his tone rarely had vibrato. Though most saxophonists depend partly on vibrato as an expressive device, Shorter cultivated so many other expressive devices that listeners tended to not miss the vibrato. He made masterful use of various attacks and releases. He could slide up into the pitch of a note or strike it head on. He could release a note by carefully tapering it or by bending its pitch up or down. The note might trail off and disappear, or it might fall and then slide up to another. Though his technique was primarily legato, he sometimes gave out stark announcements consisting of brief tones.

Recorded May 17, 1967, for Columbia by Miles Davis (trumpet), Wayne Shorter (tenor saxophone), Herbie Hancock (piano), Ron Carter (bass), and Tony Williams (drums); reissued on Davis, *Sorcerer* (Columbia/Legacy: 65680, 1967, c1993).

The melody for "Masqualero" was composed by Wayne Shorter. Like his tunes "Nefertiti" and "E.S.P.," it also features a succession of notes that are separated by the interval of a fourth (see Figure 12.1 on page 275). The second phrase of the melody has only ten notes—one pitch played three times, followed by a pitch one fourth lower that is played three times, followed by a pitch that is another fourth lower played three times, followed by a pitch that is a half step lower. Incidentally, this particular sequence of intervals contributes to the sense of mystery that much of Shorter's music evokes.

The arrangement of "Masqualero" here is almost entirely spontaneous. Unissued live recordings of this piece by the same band only remotely resemble it. Unlike the arrangements discussed in previous listening guides, there is only a hint of preset organization here, often only the tempo and a few bass notes. The piano, bass, and drum parts were being devised while they were being performed. This recording presents pianist Herbie Hancock, bassist Ron Carter, and drummer Tony Williams in a cooperative improvisation of immense scope and invention. Played with impeccable musicianship, this performance is a stunning example of master improvisers confidently working at a high level of creativity. It is essential to remember that Hancock, Carter, and Williams are not merely accompanying trumpeter Davis and saxophonist Shorter. They are working as composers collaborating in the creation of a new piece of music. They are particularly sensitive to each other's playing, and they complement one another extremely well. This performance offers more examples of spontaneous interaction than any other piece on the *Jazz Classics* CD set. The result is an extemporaneous work that takes the listener through significant changes in loudness, melody, texture, and rhythm, showing almost as much internal contrast and development as we might find in a written symphonic piece. In some respects, it even evokes the drama we expect of an opera.

The musicians were free to invent melodies and transform them throughout the performance. Some solo passages are particularly melodic, as in the sax improvisation from about 5′25″ to 5′50″. The improvisers sometimes quote or paraphrase the original melody or the improvised line of a fellow band member. Occasionally they pass it around, each player echoing another's phrase (as in Hancock mimicking Davis at about 53″ and at 1′01″ and Carter paraphrasing the melody at about 6′35″). Sometimes they play the intact sequence of notes that define the mode (as in the sax solo at about 3′43″).

Many accompaniment harmonies in this performance were chosen spontaneously during the performance itself, not planned in advance. The musicians were free to create new melodies and harmonies guided loosely by the knowledge of what notes would be compatible with those provided by the bass part and the melody that occurred at the beginning of the piece. Basically, the harmonies here only give the music a start. They do not influence the course of improvised ideas as much as chord progressions in earlier styles did. Nor do the accompaniment rhythms under the melody constrain the rhythmic aspects of the music that evolves during the performance. Though steady tempo is maintained throughout the performance, the players are free to change melody, texture, and rhythmic style from moment to moment. Unlike pre-1960s jazz, central features of this piece's organization emerge and change spontaneously.

Over the course of the performance, soloists vary the extent to which they make their phrases swing. Sometimes they lock their rhythms tightly to the underlying pulse (as in the end of the trumpet solo, at about 2′47″). The accompanists also vary in this respect. Tony Williams plays a continuous sequence of eighth notes on his ride cymbal through much of the piece, though he interrupts it sporadically to play rhythms on his snare drum and tom-toms that decorate the solo lines and change the mood of the performance. Ron Carter plays widely differing patterns on bass, never walking, though sometimes he plays the steady pattern that Wayne Shorter wrote for the piece.

Outstanding features of this performance include the remarkable freshness of the solo improvisations, the spontaneous changes in intensity (as in the steady increase from 5′30″ to 5′50″), changes in rhythmic style (it changes most dramatically at 2′37″ and 3′20″), and changes in texture. The music's texture thickens at about 1′50″ and thins at about 2′12″, then thickens again at about 2′37″ and thins at about 3′20″. Texture changes also occur at 6′30″ and 7′. It thickens considerably at 7′52″ and thins at 8′18″.

Probably the best way to begin appreciating this performance is to first make yourself comfortable in a place removed from anything you might find distracting. Use of a headset would be ideal. Close your eyes.

LISTENING GUIDE continued on next page

Empty your mind of all thoughts and feelings except the intention to let the music take you wherever it can. Pretend that you are on an unhurried journey with trustworthy guides who promise to show you many new vistas. Then just listen. Don't be concerned with trying to identify all the sounds the first time you listen. Pursue those details in repeated listenings with this guide. The virtues of this performance are not only the beauty of the sounds themselves but also the success with which the players have improvised shifting lines and textures, as though their parts were strains of movement in a ballet with three or more dancers always in motion.

The form for most of this performance of "Masqualero" is A-B-A, sections of which are eight, six, and eight measures long, respectively. Though following repetitions of that form for most of the performance, the band makes a few departures from that organization. These are noted in the descriptions of the Wayne Shorter and Herbie Hancock solos.

OPTIONAL TECHNICAL INFORMATION: Musicians describe the harmonic basis of improvisations in this piece as "playing off a pedal point" and using a "modal flavor" or "modal color." This means that one note (usually in the bass register), "the pedal," dominates throughout that section, and atop it are played strings of notes that draw from one particular mode, though the musicians do not adhere exclusively to those notes.* Periodically a single chord abruptly occurs that differs significantly in flavor from the collection of chords that have maintained a given mode for a long passage. Musicians call the use of this chord "a cadence point," a moment of resolving tension and preparing for another stretch of music. Such a chord is used here to allow a few beats of separation between sections, particularly at the end of each B-section.

ELAPSED
TIME

0'00" **Introduction** (8 measures)

Instruments: piano, bass, and drums

The proceedings begin loosely and then tighten as the horns' entrance approaches. Williams is playing complicated rhythms on the ride cymbal and rolls on his tom-toms. High-hat cymbals are vibrating against each other. Carter is playing pizzicato eighth notes and pauses, mostly irregular figures. Hancock is firmly sounding a string of chords that ascend like steps, each one ringing and separated from the next by a brief pause.

Rhythmic activity in the bass and drums is so complex that the downbeat may be hard to detect. Hancock makes the rhythm clearer. His piano chords are grouped in threes; the first chord of each group is played on the down beat.

First Statement of the Theme (A-B-A)

0'14" *A-section* (8 measures)

The opening statement can be interpreted as a dialog between the horns and the piano. The composed melody starts with a two-bar phrase and alternates with two measures of silence. Hancock uses the silence to respond to the previous melodic statement. Trumpet and sax play three notes slurred together in harmony. Hancock responds with two quick chords, then three chords that mirror the horns's opening notes.

0'22" Trumpet and sax play notes of the second phrase in octaves and unisons. The melody moves by the interval of a fourth.

Horns pause again for seven beats while the piano fills in with a brief melodic phrase of harp-like tones which complements the second hornlike phrase.

0'29" *B-section* (6 measures)

Horns return in harmony.

A brief trumpet phrase is answered by sax.

*For details, study the phrygian mode (see Appendix H) of this book, and see chapter 6 in Scott Reeves, *Creative Jazz Improvisation*, 4th ed. (Prentice-Hall, 2006). Some of Shorter's improvisation from this performance is transcribed and analyzed by Reeves. Shorter's complete solo is transcribed in *The New Best of Wayne Shorter* (Hal Leonard 672491, 1995, from *www.halleonard.com*).

LISTENING GUIDE *continued on next page*

0'36″ — Trumpet plays harmony notes beneath sax.

This statement of the B-section concludes with horns, piano, and bass uniting on two chords, punctuated by drums. These two chords (termed a "cadence point") will be heard during the solos and can be used by the listener as indications for the form. Sax trails off at the end of this section.

0'39″ — *A-section* (8 measures)

Trumpet plays the first phrase alone. Hancock's chords, higher in pitch and more sharply articulated than before, lend more tension to this second statement of the A-section.

0'47″ — Sax joins trumpet to play the second phrase of the melody, but an octave higher than before.

Hancock plays a sequence of chords slurred together, echoing the rhythm of the previous two-measure melody.

First Chorus of the Miles Davis Trumpet Solo (A-B-A)

0'54″ — *A-section* (8 measures)

Davis opens with a slow, three-note climb that is mimicked by Hancock on piano. (This follows the dialog format used in the melody statements.) Then Davis comes down from the high register with a more involved figure, and is pursued by a piano figure imitating the last few notes in that phrase.

1'08″ — *B-section* (6 measures)

Piano accompanies Davis with a slowly ascending, step-wise string of notes.

1'15″ — A transition occurs between 1'15″ and 1'20″. This is the "cadence point" (interruption in the harmony that has been sustaining underneath the first four measures of the B-section). Williams underscores the change in harmony with his drumming before the group begins the last A-section.

1'19″ — *A-section* (8 measures)

Activity lessens temporarily.

Bass is neither walking nor playing a single repeating figure. It is playing fragmented patterns of eighth notes that do not emphasize the first beat of each measure. This lends the music a suspended feeling.

Second Solo Chorus for Miles Davis (A-B-A)

1'33″ — *A-section* (8 measures)

Hancock alternates between a pair of chords and a contrasting rhythmic pattern.

Williams has begun a pattern of steady eighth notes played by drum sticks striking the ride cymbal.

1'48″ — *B-section* (6 measures)

Exploding sounds from drums; temporary departure from steady rhythms on ride cymbal. Energy has increased accordingly, and Hancock's two chords which conclude the B-section struggle to be heard through the busy texture. This lasts until about 2'15″.

1'58″ — *A-section* (8 measures)

Williams plays a slow roll on the tom-tom followed by the arrival of a high note on the trumpet.

Third Chorus of Miles Davis Solo (A-B-A)

2'12″ — *A-section* (8 measures)

Activity softens, the mood calms, as though to prepare for another barrage. Williams returns to steady eighth notes on ride cymbal.

LISTENING GUIDE *continued on next page*

2'27" *B-section* (6 measures)

Davis glosses a single tone over and over before ending his phrase.

Tom-tom roll and high-register trumpet phrase begin a new adventure.

2'37" *A-section* (8 measures)

Piano plays a repeating chorded figure in a staccato manner, which starts on the downbeat of the measure ("bump . . bump-bump . . . . . bump . . bump-bump . . ."). This rhythm persists through the next A-section, blurring the ending of this chorus and the beginning of the next (to about 3'05"). Cymbals become louder, crashing amidst the timekeeping rhythms. These alterations in piano and percussion patterns dramatically change the music's character.

Fourth Chorus of Miles Davis Solo (A-B)

2'51" *A-section* (8 measures)

Trumpet goes into the high register, squealing doit-like. Davis emphasizes the beats very prominently.

3'06" *B-section* (6 measures)

Carter is playing fragmented figures of eighth notes in the upper register of his bass, serving as a transition between the end of the trumpet solo and the beginning of the saxophone solo. Drums and cymbals get softer, evoking a mood of anticipation.

Discrepancy in following the composition's form: The band drops the final A-section.

3'16" *A-section* (8 measures) **New Chorus Starts** (A-B-A)

This section is shared by Davis fading out using the original melody line and Shorter entering during the fourth measure. The music conjures a mysterious mood.

3'22" **Wayne Shorter Saxophone Solo**

Shorter paraphrases the tune's melody, stretching each note until it is almost behind the beat.

Shorter begins with rhythms that do not swing in a particularly obvious manner. The rhythm section is propelling the piece, and Shorter's lines are oozing over it. Notice the remarkable continuity in the construction of Shorter's improvisation.

3'31" *B-section* (6 measures)

Carter is sliding pitches on his bass and playing eighth note figures interspersed by silences. He also repeats and extensively develops a single idea, interesting by itself, apart from its accompaniment value.

3'39" Just prior to the beginning of the last A-section Shorter plays a long, mournful, high note on his tenor sax. (Shorter has said that the ultimate skill is achieved when a player can make a listener cry by playing just one note.)

3'42" *A-section* (8 measures)

Carter is accompanying with a bass figure that is three beats long, setting up a pattern of accents that contrasts with the piece's underlying four-beat pulse. He continues this into the next chorus.

Second Chorus of Wayne Shorter Saxophone Solo (A-B-A)

3'56" *A-section* (8 measures)

4'03" Sax is playing syncopated tones starkly separated from each other.

4'10" *B-section* (6 measures)

Shorter pauses at the end of this section.

4'21" *A-section* (8 measures)

Shorter returns with a low-pitched sustained tone. His line then slowly climbs out of the low register, seeming to float past the beats instead of closely aligning with them.

LISTENING GUIDE *continued on next page*

Third Chorus of Wayne Shorter Saxophone Solo (A-B-A)

4'35"   *A-section* (8 measures)

Shorter creates a long melodic line that slides outside the harmonies of the accompaniment. Drums and cymbals are momentarily silent.

4'49"   *B-section* (6 measures)

Sax line climbs into the higher register, each note a half step higher in pitch. Carter accompanies with a pizzicato tremolo on bass.

5'00"   *A-section* (8 measures)

Fourth Chorus of Wayne Shorter Saxophone Solo (A-B-A+2-A)

5'15"   *A-section* (8 measures)

Piano ceases for the entire chorus. Notice the tension evoked by its absence.

5'28"   *B-section* (6 measures)

Drumming is highly active, louder, and more dense.

5'39"   *A-section* (8 measures plus an extra two measures)

Shorter creates a new, more animated mood, collaborating only with bass and drums, mostly tom-toms. He selects high pitched sax tones and seems to be having a musical conversation with drums. Shorter invents ascending phrases that logically build upon each other, each separated by silence, each higher in tension until he reaches the climax note. This peak occurs later than the eighth measure. So Hancock waits two extra measures before he returns to complement the resolution of the tension and restart repetitions of the composition's 8-6-8 measure form.

5'56"   Departure from composition's form: An extra A-section (eight measures)

Piano resumes. Hancock plays the downbeat for the first of every group of eight beats.

Once again Shorter uses his device of constructing phrases which build upon each other. This time the phrases descend, and excitement descends accordingly.

The sounds of drums and cymbals soften in anticipation of the upcoming piano solo.

6'11"   **Herbie Hancock Piano Solo (A-A-B-A-A)**

This solo has very few bop characteristics. It often sounds more like the impressionistic piano music of twentieth century composers Claude Debussy and Maurice Ravel.

Departure from composition's form: The band plays no B-section here.

A-section (8 measures)

6'25"   Departure from composition's form: The band plays an extra A-section (eight measures)

Cascades of legato notes in harmony making a waterfall-like sound. It is accompanied by a roll played by drum sticks on the high-hat cymbal and very little bass activity. This creates the illusion that timekeeping has been suspended. Notice how this has dramatically changed the character of the music.

6'39"   *B-section* (6 measures)

Hancock sounds the same piano note again and again, then a new one again and again. Each one is higher pitched than the last, giving direction to the solo line.

Bass is echoing the melody.

6'50"   *A-section* (8 measures)

7'03"   Departure from composition's form: An extra A-section (eight measures)

Second Chorus of Herbie Hancock Piano Solo (A-B-A)

7'17"   *A-section* (8 measures)

Harp-like piano tones ringing, separated by silences; accompanied by steady eighth notes on ride cymbal.

7'31"   *B-section* (6 measures)

Bass is echoing the melody.

LISTENING GUIDE *continued on next page*

7'42"   *Last A-section* (8 measures)

Hancock plays chords on the piano in a staccato rhythmic way, re-establishing swing feeling and preparing for return of the horns. Bass repeats same note again and again (termed a "pedal tone").

7'56"   **Final Melody Statement** (A-B)

A-section (8 measures)

Trumpet and tenor sax return in harmony.

They are answered by piano.

Second phrase is played in octaves by trumpet and tenor sax. Piano answers by playing notes in pairs (intervals of a fourth) ascending the keyboard.

8'10"   *B-section* (6 measures)

Trumpet and saxophone exchange the phrases of the B-section, after which the saxophone trails off.

Ending (A-B)

8'21"   *A-section* (6 measures)

No horns

8'35"   *B-section* (6 measures)

Piano, bass, and drums use the accompaniment for the B-section to tack on a conclusion.

Piano chords are played percussively with clashing voicings.

Williams is scattering strokes around his drum set.

8'42"   The piece concludes with a roll on the tom-tom with the piano sustaining the same chord that had been used to end previous B-sections (the "cadence chord").

Wayne Shorter brought an outstanding gift for melody to his solos. Listening to him improvise is like looking over the shoulder of a composer as he invents and develops themes. Not only did he invent theme after new theme, often using unusual intervals as he improvised, but he also tried to make something significant out of each kernel of melody that he invented. Shorter was a very intelligent improviser who brought a strong sense of continuity to his lines. (Listen to his solo on "Masqualero" at 3'22".) Almost every one of Shorter's solo choruses was a coherent and concise melodic statement. Moreover, he played them in a manner which was somehow graceful and ferocious at the same time. Some listeners find a bittersweet quality in his music.

"Masqualero," JCCD2 *Track 10*

Beginning in 1969, Shorter's style on studio recordings became extremely sparse. He rarely again played as fluidly or lyrically as in his 1965–1968 collaborations with Davis. This was also the time he began playing soprano saxophone. Both these changes are evident on two Davis albums, *In a Silent Way* and *Bitches Brew*, made at a time when Davis was moving into jazz-rock. Shorter continued to play both soprano and tenor saxophones with Weather Report, the jazz-rock fusion band he joined a year after leaving Davis. Shorter changed his style drastically when he joined Weather Report. Instead of long, melodic phrases, he often played short bursts of notes alternating with long silences and sustained tones. This new style meshed well with the sound of a group which depended upon unusual percussion sounds, conversational bass figures, and crackling keyboard ideas. Often Shorter let many beats pass without playing at all. Then, after playing only a note or two, he became silent again. His was a very difficult role. Instead of creating melodic improvisations, he participated in a collective effort to create undulating textures. The delicate balance achieved in the collective improvisations of Weather Report's early years is due in part to Shorter's tasteful and very disciplined sense of musical discretion. **He artfully made the difficult transition from jazz soloist in the conventional sense to ensemble improviser in the new context created by Weather Report.** (Listen to Shorter in "Surucucu," *JCCD3* Track 6, taken from a 1972 concert performance available in Weather Report's *I Sing the Body Electric*.[27])

Wayne Shorter's Composing

Wayne Shorter was one of the key composers of the 1960s and 1970s. He wrote extensively for albums of his own and contributed substantially to the repertories of three historically significant groups: Art Blakey's Jazz Messengers (1959–1964), the Miles Davis Quintet (1964–1969), and Weather Report (1971–1985). Though the details are beyond the nontechnical scope of this book, **Shorter's historical significance is partly determined by the unusual ways that he makes chords move within his compositions.** Some of his tunes place chords in sequences which had never been common to jazz. His compositions are the subject of much study by musicians and scholars, and Shorter is one of the most respected of all post-bop jazz composers. His tunes are performed and recorded by hundreds of other musicians. Many feel that his writing is an even more important contribution to jazz than his saxophone playing.

Shorter was notable for supplying Weather Report with a style for one branch of its repertory: pieces that conveyed a pastoral feeling by dreamy melodies containing many silences and sustained tones, performed at a relatively slow tempo. They often resulted in a sense of suspension.[28] An historic aspect in the performance of some of these pieces is the **reversal of character traditionally assumed by jazz melody and accompaniment, respectively.**[29] The melodies here are floating and simple, whereas the accompaniments are hard driving and complex, as in the Davis Quintet recording of Shorter's "Nefertiti."

Another aspect of Weather Report's music linked to the 1967 studio recording of "Nefertiti" is the **extensive repetition of melodic lines within a single rendition while continuous variation of accompaniment figures occurs.** This was not Shorter's idea; it stemmed from the manner in which the music was organized by Miles Davis and Tony Williams at the original "Nefertiti" recording session. However, Shorter's composition provided the impetus for this approach, and both Shorter and Weather Report's leader Joe Zawinul capitalized upon the approach in constructing pieces for the band.[30]

The facets described here only scratch the surface of Shorter's compositional contributions. For example, he also wrote a number of engaging themes that are waltzes. And he wrote pieces for Weather Report that possess a funky, dance-like sound.[31] To begin exploring the world of Shorter's music, keep in mind that Shorter's work for Miles Davis and Weather Report is easy to find because it is on Columbia records that were sufficiently popular to stay in print. However, do not let the convenience of this Columbia documentation allow you to overlook the richness contained in the many albums he made as bandleader for Blue Note records[32] and those made with Art Blakey for Blue Note, Riverside, and other companies. Many of the compositions that have attracted the attention of musicians and scholars lie in the Blue Note material.

CHAPTER SUMMARY

1. Miles Davis was an innovative trumpeter and bandleader.

2. He hired key innovators of the day at three different phases of jazz history and led them to outstanding recordings that remain landmarks of those styles—cool jazz, modal jazz, and jazz-rock fusion.

3. The Davis trumpet style is unmistakable for its tone quality, expressive variations in pitch, and judicious timing of phrases. He is not afraid to play simply, and some of his most dramatic solos are constructed of very few notes.

4. Davis displayed a concern for smooth sound texture that was evident in his trumpet sound as well as his attraction to Claude Thornhill's band sound, and a particular interest in meshing with the chord voicings of his accompanists.

5. With the help of pianist Bill Evans on the *Kind of Blue* album, Davis popularized mode-based formats in modern jazz.

6. With arranger Gil Evans, Davis recorded three famous albums: *Miles Ahead, Sketches of Spain,* and *Porgy and Bess.*

7. Tenor saxophonist Wayne Shorter contributed a fresh solo style to jazz.

8. Shorter's solos and compositions significantly affected the character of the Art Blakey band, the Miles Davis group, and Weather Report.

9. Shorter was influential in his compositional use of (a) the interval of a fourth; (b) sustained tones and silences in melody lines; (c) melodic construction that suggests a dreamy, floating quality; and (d) chord sequences previously unusual in jazz.

10. The Davis rhythm section of 1964–1968 had pianist Herbie Hancock, bassist Ron Carter, and drummer Tony Williams.

11. The Hancock-Carter-Williams unit was among the most skilled, gifted, and exploratory rhythm sections in jazz history.

NOTES

1. Though original in most respects, Davis did model his sound and some of his improvisatory concept after Freddie Webster's. From Webster and from saxophonist Lester Young, he derived the attitude that the solo improviser should try to invent a countermelody that is as majestic and song-like as the original and which sounds as though it were somehow sailing above the original. Davis also shared Webster's affection for the low register, a clear, wide tone, long notes, and an overall gentleness in manner. This is evident most in his performance of slow tunes around 1945, then beginning again in 1954, particularly with his recording of "The Man I Love." This is a piece Webster had previously recorded (in May of 1945) in a similar manner. To hear this, listen to Webster's tone quality, articulation, and overall manner on "You're Not the Kind" (1946) on Sarah Vaughan, *Young Sassy* (Proper: 27, 4CD set, 1944–50, c2001); or *Bebop* (New World: 271, LP, 1946–56, c1976), and compare Webster's playing with the Miles Davis solo on "Now's the Time" (1945) from Charlie Parker, *The Complete Savoy & Dial Master Takes* (Savoy Jazz: 17149, 3CD set, 1944–48, c2002). Davis has also cited Clark Terry and Dizzy Gillespie as inspiration for his own style. Parker's and Gillespie's influence is most evident on Davis's up-tempo improvisations from the mid-1940s.

For a transcription and analysis of the Davis solo on "So What" from *Kind of Blue* (Columbia/Legacy), see Scott Reeves, *Creative Jazz Improvisation,* 4th ed. (Prentice-Hall, 2006). All his solos on *Kind of Blue* are available in *Kind of Blue* [Transcribed Scores] (Hal Leonard: 672460, 2000);

www.halleonard.com. Other Davis solos are transcribed in Stuart Isacoff, *Miles Davis* (Amsco, 1978, 1988); available from: Jamey Aebersold Jazz, Inc., P.O. Box 1244, New Albany, IN 47150-1244; phone: 800-456-1388; web: *www.jazzbooks.com.*

For more about Miles Davis, his groups, and sidemen, see Jack Chambers, *Milestones: The Music & Times of Miles Davis* (Da Capo, 1998); Ian Carr, *Miles Davis: The Definitive Biography* (Thunder's Mouth, 1999); Miles Davis with Quincy Troupe, *Miles: The Autobiography* (Simon & Schuster, 1989); Bill Kirchener, *The Miles Davis Reader* (Smithsonian, 1997); Gary Carner, *The Miles Davis Companion: Four Decades of Commentary* (Schirmer, 1996); Paul Tingen, *Miles Beyond: The Electric Explorations of Miles Davis 1967–1991* (Billboard, 2001); and John Szwed, *So What: The Life of Miles Davis* (Simon & Schuster, 2002).

2. All Columbia albums cited in this chapter are listed with full information in the *Instructor's Resource Manual.*

3. Listen to the slowest pieces on *Seven Steps to Heaven* (Columbia/Legacy) and *Kind of Blue,* or "Summertime" on *SCCJ* or *Porgy and Bess* (Columbia/Legacy).

4. An excellent example of this is the "Freddie the Freeloader" solo on *Kind of Blue.*

5. For examples, listen to his solos on Charlie Parker's recording "Now's the Time" (cited in footnote 1 above); his own recordings of "The Man

I Love" on *Miles Davis & the Modern Jazz Giants* (Fantasy: OJC-347, 1954, c1989), "Bag's Groove" on *Bag's Groove* (Fantasy: OJC-245, 1954, c1987), "Eighty-One" (1965) on *E.S.P.* (Columbia/Legacy), "Sivad" (1971) on *Live-Evil* (Columbia/Legacy), or "So What" (1959) on *Kind of Blue* or *SCCJ*.

6. Listen to "Freddie the Freeloader" on *Kind of Blue*, and "Sid's Ahead" on *Milestones* (Columbia/Legacy).

7. Examples include the final selection of *Kind of Blue*, "Fishermen, Strawberry, and Devil Crab" on *Porgy and Bess*, or the first few measures of "My Funny Valentine" and "Stella By Starlight" on *My Funny Valentine* (Columbia/Legacy). For a transcription and analysis of the 1964 "My Funny Valentine" solo, see Stuart Isacoff, *Solos for Jazz Trumpet* (Carl Fischer, 1985); available from: Carl Fischer Music, 65 Bleecker St., NYC, NY 10012; phone: 800-762-2328; web: *www.carlfischer.com*.

8. As in his 1956 recording of "It Never Entered My Mind" on *Workin'* (Fantasy: OJC-296, 1956, c1987), his 1963 recording of "I Fall in Love Too Easily" on *Seven Steps to Heaven* (Columbia/Legacy), or his 1964 "My Funny Valentine" and "Stella By Starlight" on *My Funny Valentine*.

9. Electronically created echo is heard on *Bitches Brew* (Columbia/Legacy) and side one of *Tribute to Jack Johnson* (Columbia/Legacy). Davis used electronic wah-wah on *Live-Evil*.

10. *Cookin'* (Fantasy: OJC-128, 1956, c1993); *Relaxin'* (Fantasy: OJC-190, 1956, c1992); *Workin'* (Fantasy); and *Steamin'* (Fantasy: OJC-391, 1956, c1989).

11. This is the same classical piece that inspired Chick Corea's "Spain," which in turn was made popular in a vocal rendition by Al Jarreau.

12. Listen to Bill Evans's composition, "Peace Piece," on Evans, *Everybody Digs Bill Evans* (Fantasy: OJC-068, 1958, c1987), recorded four months before *Kind of Blue*. See also Ashley Kahn, *Kind of Blue* (Da Capo, 2000).

13. By the summer of 1964, this rhythm section had made half of a studio album, *Seven Steps to Heaven*, and three concert albums: *Miles in Europe* (Columbia), *My Funny Valentine*, and *"Four" and More* (Columbia/Legacy).

14. "Walkin'" on *"Four" and More*.

15. "My Funny Valentine" on *My Funny Valentine*, "Madness" on *Nefertiti* (Columbia/Legacy), and "Masqualero" on the *JCCD2*, or Davis, *Sorcerer* (Columbia/Legacy).

16. Listen to Carter's playing on "Pee Wee" and "Masqualero" (*Sorcerer* or *JCCD2*), "Freedom Jazz Dance" (*Miles Smiles*), and "Riot," "Fall," and "Nefertiti" (all on *Nefertiti*).

17. Compare Kenny Clarke's performance on the records Miles Davis made during the early 1950s with Tony Williams's playing on *Filles de Kilimanjaro* (Columbia/Legacy) or *Miles Smiles*. You will hear a drastic difference between the two.

18. Though it took a long time to become common in jazz, the influence of the 1963–1968 Davis rhythm section style was evident later in recordings by Joe Henderson: *The Milestone Years* (Milestone: 4413, 8CD set, 1967–75, c1994) which includes *The Kicker* (Fantasy: OJC-465, 1967, c1990); *Tetragon* (Fantasy: OJC-844, 1967–68, c1995); *Power to the People* (Milestone: 9024, 1969, c2001); *If You're Not Part of the Solution, You're Part of the Problem* (Milestone: 9028, LP, 1970, c1973); and *In Pursuit of Blackness* (Milestone: 47080, 1971, c1998). See also Joe Farrell, *Joe Farrell Quartet* (CTI: 40694 [6003], 1970, c1986). The rhythm section style of *Miles in Europe* and *"Four" and More* was later heard in records by Freddie Hubbard, Jackie McLean (*Right Now*, Blue Note: 90844, 1965, c2004), and others. The Davis Quintet

approaches on *Miles Smiles, Miles in the Sky*, and *Nefertiti* influenced the Art Lande group of the 1970s: *Rubisa Patrol* (ECM: 1081, 1976); and the Wynton Marsalis/Branford Marsalis quintet of the 1980s: *Wynton Marsalis* (Columbia: 37574, c1982); *Think of One* (Columbia: 38641, c1983); and *Black Codes (From the Underground)* (Columbia: 40009, 1985, c1985).

19. After the departure of Bill Evans and prior to the arrival of Wayne Shorter, Davis had not explored much new territory in the area of song forms. This is revealed by the repertory on *Someday My Prince Will Come* (1961), *In Person Friday & Saturday Nights at the Blackhawk* (1961), *Seven Steps to Heaven* (1963), *Miles in Europe* (1963), and *"Four" and More* (1964), and *My Funny Valentine* (1964) (all on Columbia).

20. A large number of post-1964 compositions are all A instead of A-A-B-A, A-B-A-B, or A-B-A-C. On *E.S.P.* is Shorter's "Iris," a 16-bar waltz: all A. On *Sorcerer* is Shorter's "Prince of Darkness," 16 bars long with very few prearranged harmonies. On *E.S.P.* is his "E.S.P.," 16 bars long: all A, with important and frequent chord changes. It is played twice, as 12 bars + 4-bar turnaround, then 12 bars + 4-bar conclusion. The 4-bar sections differ, but the 12-bar sections are identical.

21. *Miles Smiles* includes Shorter's "Dolores," 38 bars long, divided into phrases of 2, 2 1/2, 3, and 3 1/2 measures. These phrases are separated by spaces in which the horns do not play. Only the rhythm section is heard. They are continuing and developing patterns they had played underneath the horns.

22. Davis's "Circle" and Shorter's "Footprints" (both on *Miles Smiles*), Hancock's "Little One" and Carter's "Mood" (both on *E.S.P.*), and Williams's "Pee Wee" (*Sorcerer*).

23. Jimmy Heath's "Gingerbread Boy," Shorter's "Dolores" and "Orbits" (all on *Miles Smiles*), Williams's "Hand Jive" (*Nefertiti*), Hancock's "The Sorcerer" (*Sorcerer*), Carter's "R.J." and Shorter's "E.S.P." (both on *E.S.P.*).

24. Shorter's "Fall" (*Nefertiti*), and "Masqualero" and "Vonetta" (both on *Sorcerer*).

25. Davis's "Country Son" (*Miles in the Sky*) and the Davis-Carter "Eighty-One" (*E.S.P.*).

26. He could handle hard, raw playing, and yet his ballad work was tender. Among his most inspired and well-formed improvisations are those he contributed to Miles Davis's *E.S.P.* (1965) and *Sorcerer* (1967). Listen to his solo on "Eighty-One" from *E.S.P.* Note the middle section that is so melodic that it could be taken out of context and used as a tune. In spite of its very deliberate construction, it carries searing emotion. Listen to his improvisation on "Pee Wee" on Davis, *Sorcerer*. It is haunting in its other-worldly beauty. Listen to his solo on "Limbo" (*Sorcerer*) in which he manages a very unusual construction that hangs together with tuneful integrity despite extremely turbulent drumming all around it and the absence of piano accompaniment. Transcriptions of his solos on "Eighty-One" (*E.S.P.*) and "Masqualero" (*Sorcerer* and *JCCD2*) are in *The New Best of Wayne Shorter, Artist Transcriptions: Saxophone* (Hal Leonard).

Shorter's saxophone style influenced a number of players who became prominent during the 1980s, including Branford Marsalis, Donald Harrison, Bill Kirchner, Tim Ries, and Bob Belden. Shorter's influence has also been acknowledged by David Liebman and Michael Brecker, two saxophonists who began receiving wide acclaim during the 1970s.

27. Also listen to his work on "Umbrellas" and "Seventh Arrow" on their first album, *Weather Report* (Columbia: 48824, 1971, c1992).

28. Listen to "Three Clowns" on Weather Report, *Black Market* (Columbia/Legacy: 65169, 1976, c2002), and "Harlequin" on *Heavy Weather* (Columbia/Legacy: 65108, 1977, c1997).

29. Such melodies as "Manolete" and "Non-Stop Home," on Weather Report, *Sweetnighter* (Columbia/Legacy: 64976, 1977, c1996), possess clarity and simplicity, whereas the accompaniment is turbulent. (You might recall that, at least as early as the bop era, horn lines had traditionally been more complex than their accompaniments.) Weather Report's practice continued the manner in which the Miles Davis Quintet had performed Shorter's "Nefertiti" on Davis, *Nefertiti* (1967). The serene, floating quality of "Nefertiti" had also been present in co-leader Joe Zawinul's writing. This was evident at least as early as the 1969 Miles Davis recording of Zawinul's "In a Silent Way" and the 1970 Zawinul recording of "Dr. Honoris Causa" (*Zawinul*, Atlantic: 1579, 1970, c1990). Zawinul had been attracted by the flavor of the Miles Davis "Nefertiti" performance, and Shorter and Zawinul extended this compositional flavor when they teamed up to co-lead Weather Report.

30. Listen to "Boogie Woogie Waltz," "Manolete," and "Non-Stop Home" on Weather Report, *Sweetnighter*.

31. Listen to "Port of Entry" on Weather Report, *Night Passage* (Columbia: 36793, c1980), and "Mysterious Traveler" on *Mysterious Traveler* (Columbia/Legacy: 65112, 1974, c2002).

32. Wayne Shorter, *Night Dreamer* (Blue Note: 64467, 1964, c2005); and *Speak No Evil* (Blue Note: 99001, 1964, c1999). Sheet music for Shorter compositions is in *The World's Greatest Fakebook* (Sher, 1983); *The New Real Book* (Sher, 1988); and *Wayne Shorter Jazz Classics* (Jamey Aebersold, 1985); all available from Aebersold. See also Michelle Mercer, *Footprints: The Life and Music of Wayne Shorter* (Penguin, 2004).

In the final 40 years of the twentieth century, few musicians or composers affected jazz as much as saxophonist-composer-bandleader John Coltrane (1926–1967). This man's compositions and improvisational concepts were used not only by hundreds of saxophonists but also by pianists, trumpeters, and guitarists. Coltrane's quartet style was not only a major force during the few years the band toured, but it has continued to be influential. The immense force of Coltrane's music has inspired poetry, sculpture, and modern dance. Even a church was founded in Coltrane's name.

COLTRANE'S PRE-1960 STYLES

Relatively unknown in the 1940s and early 1950s, Coltrane performed in those years on tenor saxophone with a muscular style that drew upon the approaches of Lester Young, Dexter Gordon, and Sonny Stitt.[1] He could also be heard milking high notes in a very emotional way. This wailing into the high register, or "cry," became a Coltrane signature in the 1960s. Musicians who remember hearing him play during the 1940s say that his style was already distinctive even then, and that it had an extraordinary urgency. On the few recordings in which he made brief appearances as a sideman between 1951 and 1954, his playing reveals a very serious, highly intense craftsman.

The 1962 John Coltrane Quartet: McCoy Tyner, John Coltrane, Jimmy Garrison, Elvin Jones
(Photo by Duncan Schiedt)

Technique

Coltrane had developed a very individual style by 1955, when he first recorded with Miles Davis and started becoming known to a larger audience. By then, his roots in Sonny Stitt were evident, along with his own fresh ideas.[2] His approach was unusually vigorous. His tone was rough-textured and biting, huge and dark. Coltrane gave it a massive core and a searing intensity. It was full and penetrating in every register, from the lowest notes to the highest. He played with remarkable speed and agility. His command of the saxophone was possibly as great as any other saxophonist in jazz history. His mastery of multiphonics (controlled shrieks) also expanded the repertory of techniques to which other saxophonists aspired.[3] Coltrane's domination of the tenor saxophone inspired hundreds of other saxophonists to strive for exceedingly high levels of instrumental proficiency. Like Charlie Parker before him, Coltrane caused young players to cultivate a taste for rapid, densely packed solo improvisations.

Sonny Rollins Comparison

Coltrane's playing was not captured on record very often before he joined Miles Davis. Yet his leading contemporary, tenor saxophonist Sonny Rollins, had already made a mark in the world of jazz tenor with numerous recordings. By the time Coltrane began to record more and gain recognition of his own, Rollins was already a prominent figure, though he was four years younger than Coltrane. This may partly explain the widespread misunderstanding that Rollins came first, and explain why when Coltrane became prominent—using a style drawn in part from the same sources Rollins used—some listeners thought Coltrane was influenced by Rollins. However, the two styles can be distinguished in several respects. Coltrane's tone was larger, coarser, darker, and weightier than Rollins's. By comparison with Rollins, Coltrane played with a more searing quality, improvised in less of a stop-and-go manner, and made less use of silence. Coltrane also drew much less from Charlie Parker's style.[4] Also, Coltrane projected a less light-hearted and playful feeling than Rollins. Coltrane was less tuneful in his improvisations, and he used staccato less than Rollins.

Infatuation with Chord Changes

Coltrane's pre-1960s playing showed an infatuation with chord changes. He loved to add chords to a tune's existing chord progression. For instance, Coltrane took "Tune-Up," Eddie Vinson's 16-measure composition, and almost doubled the original number of chords. Then he added a somewhat different melody and called it "Countdown."[5] What is most significant here is not just that he added chords to an existing progression—others had often done this before—but the challenging manner in which he chose new chords and the way he improvised solos over them. His system involved stacking distantly related chords on top of each other. Then, when he improvised solos, Coltrane devoured the chord changes, trying to acknowledge every note in every chord and every scale that might be compatible with it. This was a historically significant contribution to the evolution of jazz styles. Journalist Ira Gitler described Coltrane's furiously paced streams of notes as "sheets of sound."

A peak for Coltrane's infatuation with frequently changing chords and rapid playing was the title track on his *Giant Steps* album, recorded in 1959. As in "Countdown," the chords seldom last more than two fleeting beats, and each chord stakes out new territory. Coltrane originally wrote "Giant Steps" as an exercise to gain mastery over improvising through chord progressions in which unexpected intervals separate the roots of successive chords, and few notes are held in common from one chord to another. In other words, the chords move so frequently and leap such "giant steps" that the improviser is given almost no chance to develop an idea on a given chord or to take an idea and stretch it across common tones of successive chords. The chords in "Giant Steps" change at the same pace as the melody notes. Coltrane's quick tempo and the piece's unusual construction place exceptional demands on the improviser. The piece met Coltrane's practice needs, and eventually it became a popular test piece for improvisers. It entered the ranks of other pieces possessing difficult chord changes, such as "All the Things You Are" and "Con Alma."

Ballad Style

Many listeners are familiar only with the hard-driving style that Coltrane preferred when improvising on medium-tempo and up-tempo pieces. However, Coltrane was also one of jazz history's outstanding players of slow, pretty melodies. When playing such pieces, Coltrane seemed to harness most of the energy he customarily released in his dense, multinoted passages and channel it into a few deep, full-bodied tones that seemed to glow. He blew through and past long tones and flawlessly slid from one interval to another, treating each with solemn respect. Like his early idol, alto saxophonist Johnny Hodges, he played ballads by maintaining an unusual depth and fullness of tone and an exquisite sense of timing for ornaments. For instance, Coltrane's frequent use of scale-wise lead-ins to dramatically timed high notes resembled the long, drawn-out smears that marked the Hodges approach. Some musicians feel that by listening to Hodges, Coltrane learned how to make the saxophone sing. (This is shown by his solo in "Flamenco Sketches," *JCCD2* Track 9.) [6]

Pedal Points

Coltrane popularized a number of different compositional devices in modern jazz. The pedal point is one of the best known. For example, on the *Giant Steps* album, his composition "Naima" has a single note, the *pedal point*, repeating continuously underneath the melody for the first eight measures. Then a new pedal point accompanies the second eight measures. This device achieves a drone-like effect that sustains despite shifts in the tune's harmony. It builds suspense because the listener expects a chord to change, a progression to resolve. Repeated bass notes in the pattern of pedal points became strongly identified with Coltrane's sound, especially during the 1960s. They were commonly part of the accompaniment to improvisations in pieces with Spanish and Indian flavor, a character that came to be called "modal."

1960s FORMATS

Though Coltrane never improvised pieces without planning the harmonies to be used, he did explore approaches which depended less on the preset movement of harmonies than bop did. These approaches can be labeled in two ways. Neither provides an accurate description, but both labels found a permanent place in the vocabulary of musicians and journalists. One is "free." The other is "modal."

Modal

The mode-based pieces and long improvisations of John Coltrane and his 1965–1967 associate, tenor saxophonist Pharoah Sanders, had a profound impact on jazz. This format was a new direction in Coltrane's career because such a harmonic basis for improvisation is as undemanding as the chord progression for "Giant Steps" is demanding. During the late 1950s, Miles Davis recorded mode-based pieces that proved highly influential.[7] However, the pieces by Coltrane and his disciples were even more influential. Before we discuss the details of these recordings, let's examine some tricky terminology.[8] A mode is a scale containing a predetermined selection of notes. Because his music was only loosely based on certain modes, Coltrane's 1960s playing was not always modal in the strictest sense of the word, only in the loose sense used by jazz musicians and journalists. In his "modal" work, Coltrane adhered to the overall harmonic orientation of certain modes, but he also employed notes outside the mode. Moreover, because much of Coltrane's and Sanders's work is merely based on repeating patterns of only two chords, it may be unnecessarily complicating the situation by calling it "modal." Instead, we could just specify the two chords.

One of Coltrane's most famous "modal" performances can be heard on his 1960 album *My Favorite Things*.[9] The title track is based on a well-known melody from Rodgers and Hammerstein's Broadway show *The Sound of Music*. This proved one of Coltrane's best-selling recordings, undoubtedly due in part to the great familiarity of the tune. The performance's popularity stems also from several musical components which collectively make it easy to listen to: the minor key, the simplicity in the accompaniment harmonies, its waltz meter, and the extensive repetition of short patterns (these final two components lend a hypnotic, swaying feeling). During this period many other jazz musicians liked this particular record, so they attempted to make music that evoked soothing, meditative moods by similar methods.

The strategies used to construct Coltrane's performance of "My Favorite Things" are important because they were widely imitated. Pianist McCoy Tyner uses the tune's chord progression as a guide for accompanying Coltrane's rendition of the melody. Then improvisations are accompanied by a two-chord repeated pattern of indefinite length in the key of E minor (Dorian mode), later shifted to the key of E major (Ionian mode). For constructing his soprano saxophone improvisation, Coltrane draws liberally from a single scale that is compatible with Tyner's accompaniment.[10] Such a basis for improvisation signalled a striking departure in Coltrane's style because it is so simple by comparison with the chord progression for "Giant Steps." This new approach became very popular with improvising musicians. In fact, between the late 1960s and the mid-1970s, few prominent modern jazz combos played much else. Note, however, that despite the prominence of Coltrane's "modal" style and his "free jazz," his 1960s output continued to contain pop songs and 12-bar blues pieces.[11]

Free Jazz

Coltrane was interested in the music of Ornette Coleman, the most prominent figure in "free jazz." This approach evolved away from adhering to preset progressions of chords; it also sometimes dispensed with distinctions between soloist and accompanist. (See Chapter 14.) In 1960, Coltrane recorded an album called *The Avant-Garde* with Coleman's group, minus Coleman. On the album, he performed three Coleman compositions. In 1965, Coltrane recorded an album called *Ascension*, in which he used an approach like Coleman's approach to the 1960 album *Free Jazz* (excerpted in *SCCJ*). *Ascension* employed collective improvisation with high-energy, high-density playing that departed from bop conventions of jazz phrasing and rhythmic feeling. As in *Free Jazz*, *Ascension* contained moments in which all the musicians improvised different lines at the same time. Coltrane took a cue from fellow saxophonist Albert Ayler and began improvising turbulent streams of notes, interspersed with saxophone sounds that resembled jangling cries and screams. (Ayler is discussed in the next chapter.[12]) This approach capitalized on the high register of the saxophone and mined the instrument's capacity for shrill, rasping sounds that often contained several different tones at once. These sequences of notes did not possess the melodic contours of conventional jazz improvisations. They did not evoke the easy rise and fall of tension and the swing feeling of earlier styles. Instead, they focused on development of mood and texture, replacing the earlier priorities of tunefulness and swing feeling.[13]

Improvisation on *Ascension* was neither totally collective nor totally free of pre-arrangement, nor was it atonal, which is a lack of loyalty to any given key or mode, all pitches being equally likely to occur. (For explanation of scales, tone center, and atonality, see page 454.) Careful listening will reveal a few changes of chord (or tone center) because Coltrane preset four scales for the musicians. The changes do not occur often, but they do occur. So it is not totally free of form. Collectively improvised sections are balanced in duration and texture. Brief, loosely stated ensemble passages separate the solos, which in turn receive rhythm section accompaniment. In this respect the music is also like conventional jazz. Coltrane used four other saxophonists, two trumpeters, and rhythm section. He preset the order for the solos so that no two similar instruments played back to back. This allowed a trumpet solo to follow a sax solo, for instance, rather than following another trumpet solo. Journalists have called this recording "free jazz," yet Coltrane's use of preset scales and the separation of soloist and accompanist roles renders the "free jazz" label invalid.

During the 1960s and 1970s, a number of other modern jazz musicians tried collective improvisation, with high-energy, high-density playing that contained no bop phrasing or swing feeling. Similar styles appeared sporadically during the 1970s and 1980s. Some of the impetus for this could be attributed to Coltrane because he was the most prominent bandleader to engage in this style. Note, however, that Coltrane recorded large-ensemble collective improvisation only once. He otherwise limited his use of this technique to quartet and quintet formats.

Slonimsky's and Gilmore's Influence

For a brief period during the early 1960s, much of Coltrane's work was less dense and intricate than it had been. Some of his work was quite simple and obvious in its development. He had taken a cue from the style of fellow tenor saxophonist John Gilmore, who sometimes developed solos by repeating the same rhythm with different pitches, changing the notes without changing the rhythm, sometimes placing the same rhythm at different spots in the measure, or occasionally inverting a phrase, as though peering at it from several different angles and sharing each view with the listener.[14] Coltrane also developed his solo improvisations in the logical manner he had learned from Nicolas Slonimsky's *Thesaurus of Scales and Melodic Patterns*. The book demonstrates how to vary note choices in many ways and still remain related to a fundamental chord or scale.[15] The effect of considering Gilmore and Slonimsky was to slow down and clarify Coltrane's improvisations, and devise a nonbop vocabulary.

Very soon Coltrane was back to producing high-density improvisations with very convoluted lines. But this time the twisting and turning did not reflect complex chord progressions as in his late-1950s "sheets of sound" period. Instead, these new patterns only *sounded* as complex. They were a speeded-up variant of the Gilmore and Slonimsky methods, and they were set atop relatively unchanging accompaniment harmonies. Those patterns and the formulas that Coltrane refined became common vocabulary for an entire generation of improvisers. During the 1990s, more than 30 years after he introduced them, these patterns were still considered fundamental building blocks for jazz improvisations, not just among saxophonists, but also among trumpeters, guitarists, and pianists.

THE CLASSIC QUARTET

Coltrane was a member of the Miles Davis groups on and off for almost six years, making his earliest Davis recording in 1955, his last in 1961. During this period, Coltrane also recorded with a few other leaders. Though he also made recordings on which he led the session, he did not lead a group of his own with a consistent personnel and a sound that was uniquely identifiable until 1960, when he was no longer touring with Davis. After several different combinations of musicians, he finally settled on pianist McCoy Tyner, bassist Steve Davis, and drummer Elvin Jones. He used a number of different bassists during the 1960s, but after Steve Davis played with him on several albums in 1960 and 1961, Coltrane used Jimmy Garrison the most. Garrison was with Coltrane on most of the remaining recordings, and stayed with the saxophonist even after Tyner left in 1965 and Jones left in 1966. **The Coltrane quartet was one of the most important groups in jazz history, and some historians consider it to have been the most influential of all jazz combos.**[16]

"The Promise," JCCD2 Track 11; "Your Lady," CCD2 Track 3

Elvin Jones

Some listeners consider **Elvin Jones** (1927–2004) the most overwhelming drummer in jazz history. He has established a position on the drums that equals the power and innovation established by Charlie Parker and John Coltrane on the saxophone. Like Parker and Coltrane, Jones is a remarkably consistent performer. He seems to play every tune as though it is his last chance. An almost superhuman energy and endurance are associated with him, and his imagination seems to match his energy.

"The Promise," JCCD2 Track 11; "Your Lady," CCD2 Track 3

Jones avoids the relative simplicity and repetition of most pre-1960 drummers. He rarely plays the obvious. In fact, in his most adventuresome work, he even avoids directly stating the first beat of each measure. His conception of the beat is a wider unit in time than had been usual with previous drummers. His timekeeping is steady but loose, filled with rhythmic subtleties. He roams through his drums and cymbals, distributing portions of triplets. He phrases in threes instead of twos and fours. He often begins his triplex division of time at the middle or end of a beat, and continues to juxtapose a staggered waltz feeling across the duration of several measures (see pages 440, 449). During all that time, he still maintains a basic meter of four and swings infectiously.

With Coltrane's group, Jones was able to play many rhythms at once and have the entire sound swell and heave like an ocean under Coltrane's playing. Jones was one of the first drummers to play polyrhythmically and still swing hard in a loose, flowing way. Earlier drummers who attempted to use polyrhythms had sounded stiff and self-consciously calculating (for definition and explanation of polyrhythm, see page 445).

While listening to Elvin Jones, you might get the impression that he is juggling. Things seem forever in the air, never sharply defined in exact, predictable proportions. But the different rhythms played simultaneously were not just randomly different; they were constructed to complement each other. And, in a broad sense, they fit together. It might not be obvious unless you listen carefully to four- and eight-measure sequences in their entirety. Some of his figures purposely omit a stroke or two but let you feel the missing stroke in the overall pattern. He distributes the parts of his triplets so that perhaps the first third is silent and the next two are sounded on snare drum. Or perhaps the middle member is omitted. Sometimes the first two members of a triplet will sound on the snare drum and the third on the high hat or the bass drum. It might be because of his complexity and lack of predictability that few drummers ever managed to sound like him.

Jones wove his parts around those of his bandmates in as important a way as any front-line hornman at a Dixieland

Elvin Jones, Coltrane's drummer from 1960 to 1966. Jones demonstrated how it was possible to play polyrhythmically and still swing hard in a broadly paced manner. He almost verged on free-style, yet his oceans of sound, heaving and swelling, still carried the pulse and guaranteed a sure momentum underneath Coltrane's improvisations.

(Photo by Lee Tanner)

jam session.[17] The whole character of the Coltrane quartet reflected his highly interactive style. Jones played with the surging power and imagination of two or three drummers combined, and his force was absorbed quite musically into the quartet concept. In fact, the style of Elvin Jones was possibly the most indispensable part of that ensemble concept.

After leaving Coltrane, Jones formed a sequence of high-quality groups which, during the late 1960s and throughout the 1970s, offered some of the rare jazz neither significantly influenced by rock or electric instruments nor predominantly modal in orientation. He usually employed two tenor saxophonists and a bassist, but no piano. He employed some of the best saxophonists playing at that time, and most of his tenor men were influenced by Coltrane.[18] The music in some of his groups almost achieved the solemn urgency that had been created by the Coltrane quartet.

McCoy Tyner

Coltrane's pianist from 1960 to the end of 1965 was **McCoy Tyner** (b. 1938). Creating an original approach from the linear style of Bud Powell, the block chording of Red Garland, and the voicings of Bill Evans and Horace Silver, he achieved a fresh approach to jazz piano. He already had been a distinctive and aggressive stylist in the Art Farmer-Benny Golson Jazztet, but went on to carve a very personal style. His was one of the most easily recognizable styles in all of jazz, and he was a prime force in jazz piano of the 1960s and 1970s. He was almost as influential as Evans and at least as influential as Herbie Hancock.

Pianist McCoy Tyner in performance in the 1990s.
(Photo by C. Andrew Hovan)

Tyner's extensive use of chords voiced in fourths was widely adopted (see Figure 13.1). His extremely percussive, ringing style of comping became a model for pianists of the late 1960s and the 1970s, especially those playing in Coltrane-inspired groups. His fast solo lines also inspired numerous pianists, though few could match his imagination. The five-note (pentatonic) patterns he perfected as basis for his lines soon became stock solo vocabulary for numerous pianists (see Table 13.1). His originality and influence were so extensive that he even affected well-established pianists.

TABLE 13.1	A Few of the Many Pianists Influenced by McCoy Tyner	
Chick Corea	Lonnie Liston Smith	Michael Cochran
Alice McLeod Coltrane	Onaje Allan Gumbs	Joanne Brackeen
Kenny Gill	Harold Mabern	John Hicks
Bobo Stinson	Ronnie Mathews	Hal Galper
Joe Bonner	Stanley Cowell	Gil Goldstein
Bill Henderson	Hilton Ruiz	Henry Butler

Left hand
(fifth)

Right hand
(fourths)

Figure 13.1 Piano keyboard illustration of fifths in left hand and fourths in right hand

McCoy Tyner's playing furnished a center for the Coltrane quartet sound. It was as though he established a pivot for the seesawing of sounds that were being generated around him. His stability in this capacity was partly due to his frequent use of a loud, held note (technically called a pedal point) or a loud, held interval (usually a fifth) played with extreme force by his left hand. His right hand sounded chords in a manner that achieved a bell-like ring. His selection of notes for the chords lent them a very open quality derived from using intervals of a fourth. (See Figure 13.1, and try it out for yourself on the piano. If you strike the keys with tremendous force, you might approximate the sound of McCoy Tyner.) These clear, open-voiced chords represented more stability than was occurring in the saxophone and drum sounds around them. In most groups of this period, the bass part was the simplest and steadiest. But in the Coltrane quartet, Tyner's piano part vied with the bass part in its steadiness. (See page 492 for a technical explanation of these harmonies, and listen to Tyner play them on "The Promise," *JCCD2* Track 11.)

Jimmy Garrison

Jimmy Garrison (1934–1976) was an imaginative bass player who held his own within the fiercely active Coltrane quartet. He had a large, deep, rough tone quality and remarkable stamina. McCoy Tyner praised his timekeeping skill. In addition to walking, Garrison invented rhythms which countered and complemented those of Tyner and Jones. Of all the bassists Coltrane used, Garrison seemed the perfect fit because he intuitively understood the unorthodox directions that Coltrane and Jones were taking.

Occasionally, Garrison took to strumming his bass almost as though it were a guitar. His use of double stops (two strings sounding together) and his strumming have been widely imitated. He was not the first to use such techniques, but his particular handling of them might have been the stimulus behind their popularity with jazz bassists of the 1960s and 1970s. Some of Garrison's double-stopping may have had its source in Coltrane's interest in drones and in music employing two tones sustained together, five scale-steps apart. In the modal music of their native cultures, bagpipes, sitars, and tambura achieve exactly that effect. Coltrane's use of two bassists on "Olé" (on his *Olé Coltrane* album) and "India" (on his *Impressions* album) also might derive from that interest.

The Sweep

One of the most significant advances made by the 1960s Coltrane quartet was a pioneering move toward a sweeping, broadly paced organization of parts, a change in feeling that was partly due to **a departure from:**

1. explicit statement of the markers for each measure;

2. accompaniment style in which chords changed frequently;

3. dependence on simple ride rhythms and walking bass patterns; and

4. bouncing solo lines of eighth-note sequences with few sustained tones.

This new, widely imitated approach produced music that seemed to breathe more deeply and build excitement more broadly and solemnly than earlier jazz styles. Phrases spanned larger units than the four- and eight-measure progressions typical of most jazz improvisation. There was more creation of a suspended feeling, which, each time it resolved, proved dramatic in effect. Much of the new feeling was directly caused by **the particular collection of techniques** that the group refined:

"The Promise," JCCD2 *Track 11*

1. Sustained and repeating sustained tones in the bass part (pianist's left hand, bassist's plucking), which are technically termed *pedal points.*

2. Drum patterns whose basic unit occupied several measures instead of just a few beats.

3. Sustaining piano chords (sounding them loudly and letting them ring).

4. Using a single mode (or a two-chord pattern) for a long time, instead of using numerous changes in harmony.

5. Long saxophone glissandos that were carefully timed and spanned a large portion of the saxophone's pitch range:

   a. sometimes used to preface a dramatically placed high note.

   b. sometimes evoking a rhapsodic effect.

   c. sometimes snaking in and around a central idea. (These are evident in Coltrane's solos on "The Promise" on *JCCD2* Track 11 and on "Your Lady" on *CCD2* Track 3.) The rhythmic construction of these glissandos departed from swing feeling and approximated an orchestral concept in which the melody lines are not so rigidly tied to the beat.

6. Use of sustained tones in saxophone solos (allowing listeners a point of focus and relief from having to follow ever-changing melodic contours).

7. Long-term continuity of mood, as though the composition and lengthy improvisations were conceived almost in their entirety instead of being merely a sequence of tune and solos that strung together swinging phrases in jam session manner.

TABLE 13.2 A Few of the Many Saxophonists Influenced by Coltrane

Pharoah Sanders	Pat LaBarbera	Frank Foster
Charles Lloyd	Bob Berg	Joe Henderson
Joe Farrell	Sonny Fortune	David Young
Wayne Shorter	Jan Garbarek	Harold Land
Gato Barbieri	Michael Brecker	Frank Tiberi
John Klemmer	Andrew White	Gregory Herbert
Nathan Davis	James Spalding	Bennie Maupin
Lew Tabackin	Ernie Krivda	Carlos Garnett
Robin Kenyatta	Joe Lovano	Steve Marcus
Steve Grossman	Charles B. Owens	Teddy Edwards
Billy Harper	Bob Mintzer	Steve Lederer
David Liebman	Manny Boyd	Rich Perry
John Surman	Bill Evans	Cannonball Adderley

COLTRANE'S IMPACT

John Coltrane exerted a striking effect on his listeners. People who hated his music fought in print with those who were impressed by it. Some felt jazz history ended with Coltrane, whereas today many feel it just started with him. Not long after Coltrane formed his own group, there were so many saxophonists imitating him that jazz journalists began complaining about a general lack of originality as vehemently as they had responded to the wave of Charlie Parker disciples who arose during the 1950s. Coltrane was the subject of numerous scholarly analyses, and the 1980s saw an increased flow of publications which evaluated Coltrane's work from a technical standpoint.[19] Saxophonist Andrew White was so inspired by Coltrane's music that he transcribed more than seven hundred recorded Coltrane solos, note for note. (See Appendix G for information on how to get the White transcriptions, including those for "The Promise" and "Flamenco Sketches.")

Each of Coltrane's style periods caused many musicians to try the techniques that Coltrane had popularized. First it was densely packed lines and difficult chord progressions. Coltrane's manner of replacing the chord changes from standard tunes was widely adopted. Musicians began making their own chords move in the manner demonstrated by Coltrane in his "Giant Steps" and "Countdown" progressions. Then it was modal style and pedal points. After that, it was simultaneous collective improvisation and the creation of frantic turbulence that emphasized textures more than development of melodic improvised lines. Sometimes it appeared as though a large community of musicians had decided that Coltrane was their guide, and they would postpone generating their own ideas until they could see what he would do next. Even musicians already known for considerable originality felt the impact of Coltrane's work.[20]

Soprano Saxophone

"The Promise," JCCD2 *Track 11; "Your Lady,"* CCD2 *Track 3*

About the time he formed his own groups (1960–1961), Coltrane began playing soprano saxophone in addition to tenor. Soprano saxophone had been used on

John Coltrane playing soprano saxophone, the instrument he helped popularize during the 1960s.
(Photo by Bill Smith)

Composed by John Coltrane; recorded on October 8, 1963, for Impulse! at Birdland, in New York City, by John Coltrane (soprano sax), McCoy Tyner (piano), Jimmy Garrison (bass), and Elvin Jones (drums); reissued on Coltrane, *Live at Birdland* (Impulse!: 198, 1963, c1996).

This performance offers a succinct and representative sample for the middle period of the classic Coltrane quartet. This recording conveys how the group sounded in a typical setting because it was recorded live during a performance at Birdland, a New York nightclub. This selection clearly demonstrates the unique accompanying style of this innovative rhythm section, using its polyrhythmic approach, solemn and broadly paced kind of swing feeling, Tyner's pedal points, and Jones's complex layers of sound. (Jones's triplet patterns are conspicuous throughout the performance.) The form of the composition is typical of many Coltrane pieces from this period because it has long stretches in which only two chords alternate (musicians call them "G minor" and "C seven"). This pattern became a preferred form during the 1960s, '70s, and '80s. This particular performance is also outstanding for its distinctly melodic, five-chorus piano solo by McCoy Tyner. It catalogs many of the much-imitated methods that Tyner developed. This selection also contains a Coltrane soprano sax solo in the style that became widely imitated during the 1970s and 1980s. It features his climbing, scale-like runs, his expressive bends of pitch, and dramatically timed peaks of tension. Coltrane often prefaced high notes with a very deliberate climb, and ultimately sounded as though he were squeezing the high notes out of his horn. As in the Johnny Hodges approach, the way Coltrane prefaced each important high note was almost as essential as the note itself. This is central to an impassioned effect we term "the cry." Coltrane's solo also shows his characteristic approach to working over brief figures from many different angles. This performance was also chosen because it provides many illustrations of "the sweep."

Listen for the flowing drum patterns that run throughout the accompaniment, especially the prominent use of tom-toms. The patterns used here differ considerably from the timekeeping patterns we heard in previous selections on *JCCD1* and *JCCD2*. This is the style that Elvin Jones invented.

The piece is performed in a medium tempo. There is no introduction. The performance begins with Coltrane playing the melody and the rhythm section accompanying him. Bass and drums play more densely as the performance unfolds, and the peak of intensity occurs in Coltrane's last two solo choruses. Things wind down gradually from there, though the final melody statement is so liberally ornamented it sounds like Coltrane is unwilling to restrain his creative juices and return to the theme for an ending.

The first time you listen to this, just sit back and let the sounds wash over you. The music has a sure momentum that will carry you along with it. The next several times you listen, you may begin to notice that there is a rocking back and forth motion achieved by the combination of walking bass, drummer's timekeeping patterns, and the piano accompaniment's use of two chords alternating with each other. When McCoy Tyner accompanies himself in his solo, we can hear him playing the first chord two or three times in succession then the second chord once, sometimes twice. Then he repeats the cycle. This persists for long stretches and helps the band get into a groove. However, you will also notice that the groove is periodically interrupted by a bridge. You may begin to recognize its occurrence by the sound of a new chord (musicians call it "F seven"). It is often signalled by a loud, held bass note on piano that contrasts with the steady rocking motion that we have come to expect. The new bridge chord is in effect for eight beats, and then it begins alternating with another chord (musicians call it "D seven") that is also in effect for eight beats every time it comes along. The bridge lasts for eight measures, about 12 seconds. The drumming is more complicated and less predictable during these interruptions, though timekeeping is still maintained. Because the bridge departs from the repeating patterns, it serves to build tension that is ultimately resolved by a return to the repeating pattern. And if you lose your place, it can signal you.

Accompaniment chords for all solo choruses follow a slightly different sequence of durations than under the melody statements. The form is 16-16-8(Bridge)-8, in which the accompaniment chords are the same for the first 16, second 16, and the final 8 measures.

Technical Note: For the accompaniment to the melody, the A-section has eight measures of a G minor chord alternating with a C seven chord (four beats each), then at 12 seconds into the piece, two measures of F seven, two measures of D seven, two of F seven again, two more of D seven. That 16-measure sequence repeats. Then beginning at 47 seconds into the piece, there are eight more measures of G minor alternating with C seven.

LISTENING GUIDE continued on next page

**ELAPSED
TIME**

0'00" **First Chorus** (A-B-A-B-C)

Melody Statement by Coltrane on Soprano Saxophone

Each section lasts eight measures, and the C-section is accompanied by the same chords as the A-section.

Accompanying the sax, the piano plays resounding bass notes and sustained mid-range chords. They see-saw with a bass note on the first beat and a chord on the third beat of each measure.

0'12" B (8 measures)

0'23" A (8 measures)

0'34" B (8 measures)

0'46" C (8 measures)

0'57" **Second Chorus** (A-A-B-A, 8 measures in each section)

Piano Solo Improvisation by McCoy Tyner

This is an exceedingly melodic improvisation based on brief phrases that often seem to answer each other. Tyner plays each note very forcefully.

1'10" *Second A-section*

Piano, bass, and drums firmly establish what musicians call a "groove." This is a strong sense of swing feeling that makes you feel good. It is steady and unrushed, but not lazy. It is always going forward, as though strutting.

The solid walking bass provides a firm frame of reference for the passage of beats. The drumming is simpler here than underneath the melody statement.

1'16" Tyner is quadruple-timing the rate of notes in the line played with his right hand while he comps at a normal rate with his left hand.

1'23" *Bridge*

Drumming becomes more complex.

1'34" *Last A-section*

Tyner improvises a funky melodic idea, played in harmony by his right hand while he comps in a lower register with his left hand.

1'47" **Third Chorus** (A-A-B-A)

1'51" Tyner is quadruple-timing his melody line.

2'00" *Second A-section*

Tyner improvises a funky, harmonized line.

2'12" *Bridge*

2'25" *Last A-section*

Tyner improvises a funky, harmonized line.

2'37" **Fourth Chorus** (A-A-B-A)

Tyner improvises a simple line in the high register that develops readily by continuously transforming a single idea.

2'50" *Second A-section*

A cymbal crash begins this section.

3'02" *Bridge*

Tyner uses locked hands-block chording to play an idea that includes an answer within the logic of his overall statement. Drumming activity increases.

3'14" *Last A-section*

Tyner develops a funky, harmonized line from his first idea. Drumming returns to more conventional rhythms.

LISTENING GUIDE *continued on next page*

3'27"	**Fifth Chorus** (A-A-B-A)
3'33"	Tyner begins by quadruple-timing.
3'40"	*Second A-section*
3'44"	Tyner trills.
3'52"	*Bridge*
	Tyner begins with a funky, repeated idea that is harmonized.
4'00"	Tyner ends this statement with quadruple-timing.
4'05"	*Last A-section*
	A cymbal crash begins this section.
	Tyner improvises a clear, simple melody line from another idea.
4'17"	**Sixth Chorus** (A-A-B-A)
	Tyner uses a pattern of offering resonant bass notes as a call and a block-chorded line as a response. Drumming is more active.
4'30"	*Second A-section*
	A cymbal crash begins this section.
4'41"	A brief drum roll announces the beginning of the bridge.
4'43"	*Bridge*
	Cymbal crashes and tumultuous drumming occur throughout. Snare drum and tom-toms are prominent.
	Bass drum sounds are conspicuous two measures before the last A-section.
4'55"	*Last A-section*
	Drumming is coordinated with the drama of the piano solo.
5'07"	**Seventh Chorus** (A-A-B-A)
	Coltrane Soprano Saxophone Solo
	Notice how Coltrane rises into the pitch of his first note.
	Drumming activity increases.
5'15"	Coltrane uses a scale-wise run to preface an important high note.
5'20"	*Second A-section*
5'26"	Coltrane is quadruple-timing to 5'45". His playing is hot immediately, displaying the urgency for which he is distinguished.
5'33"	*Bridge*
	Coltrane is quadruple-timing. Drum sounds are churning underneath the sax sound. Loud, held bass tones are emanating from the piano.
5'46"	*Last A-section*
	The sax part is very forceful, and the cymbal crashes are timed as responses to Coltrane's high notes.
5'57"	**Eighth Chorus** (A-A-B-A)
	Sax is quadruple-timing until 6'08".
6'10"	*Second A-section*
	Coltrane plays the same note again and again, coming at it from different angles.
6'23"	*Bridge*
	Coltrane prefaces his high note very emotionally, then plays as though he is squeezing it out of his horn.
6'31"	Coltrane often reiterates a note, each time coming at it from a different angle.
6'36"	*Last A-section*
	Coltrane quotes and paraphrases the original melody.

LISTENING GUIDE *continued on next page*

6'48"   **Ninth Chorus** (A-B-A-B-C)

    Final Theme Statement

     Oceans of percussion support Coltrane's melody line.

7'02"   *Bridge*

     Coltrane is liberally ornamenting his original melody line. Many of his main melody notes are reiterated emphatically.

7'13"   *Second A-section*

     Coltrane makes more reiterations of selected notes in restating the melody.

     Piano creates a rocking motion by repeating a pattern having a bass note on the first beat, a chord on the third beat.

7'26"   *Second Bridge*

7'38"   *C-section*

7'49"   a long roll on cymbal

8'00"   Tension is resolved when the piano chord sustains, cymbals ring, and the bass improvises a finish.

Note: A written transcription of Coltrane's solo is available from Andrew's Music, 4830 South Dakota Ave. N.E., Washington, DC 20017; phone 202-526-3666.

recordings by Sidney Bechet, Johnny Hodges, Charlie Barnet, and Steve Lacy, but it had not caught on as a standard jazz instrument. A few years after Coltrane first recorded on it, however, the soprano saxophone had become quite popular with jazz saxophonists. By 1970, most tenor saxophonists were performing on it. Even players who were not necessarily followers of Coltrane began soprano. Such well-established jazzmen as alto saxophonist Cannonball Adderley and tenor saxophonist Sonny Rollins began recording with soprano sax. Some players adopted it almost to the exclusion of their tenors.[21] Coltrane's popularization of the instrument coincided with a practical problem that saxophonists encountered: trying to be heard over the loud rhythm sections of the 1970s. The range and tone quality of the soprano saxophone helped saxophonists cut through the sound created by the increasing numbers of drums and amplified instruments prevalent in groups of the 1970s. The attraction to soprano saxophone can be attributed partly to the attraction of players to Coltrane, partly to the practical advantages of its sound, and partly to the search for fresh sounds that has always characterized jazz musicians.

CHAPTER SUMMARY

1. John Coltrane was an innovative saxophonist, composer, and bandleader who had enormous impact on modern jazz, particularly in the 1960s.

2. He devised several original styles of saxophone playing, first inspired partly by Lester Young, Dexter Gordon, and Sonny Stitt during the 1940s, and then partly by Ornette Coleman, John Gilmore, and Albert Ayler during the 1960s.

3. Coltrane's first new style was evident in recordings he made in the Miles Davis bands of the 1950s.

4. Coltrane played such energetic, densely packed solos that his late-1950s playing was described as "sheets of sound," though he was also a remarkably restrained player of lush ballads.

5. As a composer Coltrane was known for devising progressions of chords which change frequently and in ways that severely challenge improvisers, as in his "Giant Steps."

6. Coltrane's compositions and arrangements popularized pedal points and drone notes in jazz accompaniments, as in his "Naima."

7. Coltrane's "classic quartet" used pianist McCoy Tyner, bassist Jimmy Garrison, and drummer Elvin Jones from 1961 to 1965.

8. The quartet popularized "modal" styles of improvisation in which accompaniment harmonies do not change frequently.

9. The quartet refined methods of achieving a sweeping, broadly paced organization of parts which was more dramatic and orchestral than previous improvisational styles in jazz.

10. Coltrane's albums *Ascension* and *Meditations* were influential models in "free" jazz approaches where all musicians often improvised different lines at the same time in a high-energy, turbulent manner.

11. Elvin Jones was one of the first drummers to play very polyrhythmically and still swing hard.

12. McCoy Tyner popularized voicing chords in fourths and constructing lines from five-note patterns.

13. Coltrane popularized the soprano saxophone in modern jazz.

NOTES

1. Listen to Coltrane's 1951 solo on "We Love to Boogie" on Dizzy Gillespie, *School Days* (Savoy Jazz: 17256, 1947, 1951–52, c2003); and compare it to Lester Young's solo on Basie's 1939 "Pound Cake" (Count Basie, *America's #1 Band*, Columbia/Legacy: C4K 87110, 4CD set, 1936–51, c2003), and Young's 1945 recording of "D. B. Blues" on Lester Young, *The Complete Aladdin Sessions* (Blue Note: 32787, 2CD set, 1942–48, c1995). Then compare the "We Love to Boogie" solo with Dexter Gordon's work from 1947 on Gordon, *Settin' the Pace* (Savoy: 17027, 1945–47, c1998). To hear the similarities with Stitt, listen to Coltrane's work on "Oleo" from Miles Davis, *Relaxin'* (Fantasy: OJC-190, 1956, c1992), with Stitt's work on "The Eternal Triangle" on Dizzy Gillespie, *Sonny Side Up* (Verve: 314 521 426, 1957, c1997). For more about Coltrane's career, see Lewis Porter, *John Coltrane: His Life and Music* (University of Michigan, 1998); J. C. Thomas, *Chasin' the Trane* (Doubleday, 1975; Da Capo, 1976); C. O. Simpkins, *Coltrane: A Biography* (Herndon House, 1975; Black Classic Press, 1989); and Ashley Kahn, *A Love Supreme: The Story of John Coltrane's Signature Album* (Viking, 2002).

2. Listen to *The New Miles Davis Quintet* (Fantasy: OJC-006, 1955, c1982); then Miles Davis, *Steamin'* (Fantasy: OJC-391, 1956, c1989); *Cookin'* (Fantasy: OJC-128, 1956, c1993); *Workin'* (Fantasy: OJC-296, 1956, c1987); and *Relaxin'* (Fantasy).

3. Wind instruments such as saxophone and clarinet can be coaxed to produce two or more sounds at the same time. Some of these multiphonics, to give them their technical name, sound like chords. In his "Harmonique" on John Coltrane, *Coltrane Jazz* (Rhino/Atlantic: 79891, 1959, c2000), Coltrane used this method to harmonize a melody note. During the mid-1960s he frequently used multiphonics for controlled screeches that helped create peaks of musical excitement. An isolated example is his solo on "Chasin' the Trane" (1961) on Coltrane, *Live at the Village Vanguard: The Master Takes* (Impulse!: 251, 1961, c1998); there are many instances on Coltrane, *Meditations* (Impulse!: 199, 1965, c1996); *Expression* (Impulse!: 131, 1967, c1993); and *Live in Seattle* (Impulse!: GRD2-146, 2CD set, 1965, c1994).

4. To hear the Parker roots in the Rollins style, listen to Parker play tenor sax on "Half Nelson" (1947) on Charlie Parker, *The Complete Savoy & Dial Master Takes* (Savoy Jazz: 17149, 3CD set, 1944–48, c2002).

5. "Countdown" is on Coltrane, *Giant Steps* (Rhino/Atlantic: 75203, 1959, c1998). The written music for this piece is available, with recorded rhythm section accompaniment, on Jamey Aebersold, *John Coltrane: For All Musicians, A New Approach to Jazz Improvisation*, vol. 28 (Aebersold, 1983); available from: Jamey Aebersold Jazz, Inc., P.O. Box 1244, New Albany, IN 47150-1244; phone: 800-456-1388; web: *www.jazzbooks.com*. Scott Reeves, *Creative Jazz Improvisation*, 4th ed. (Prentice-Hall, 2006) discusses Coltrane's chord progression style with a transcription of the solo on "Giant Steps." More transcribed solos and analyses of this Coltrane period appear in Stuart Isacoff, *Solos for Jazz Tenor Saxophone* (Carl Fischer, 1985); available from: Carl Fischer Music, 65 Bleecker St., NYC, NY 10012; phone: 800-762-2328; web: *www.carlfischer.com*.

6. Almost every album that Coltrane made for the Prestige label contains at least one ballad. *Mating Call* (Fantasy: OJC-212, 1956, c1992), under Tadd Dameron's leadership, has several lush ballads. Coltrane, *Soultrane* (Fantasy: OJC-021, 1958, c1987) features "Theme for Ernie" and "I Want to Talk about You." Slow tunes were also the format for some of Coltrane's best compositions. Listen to "Naima" from *Giant Steps*, "After the Rain" from *Dear Old Stockholm* (Impulse!: 120, 1963, c1993), "Wise One" and "Lonnie's Lament" from *Crescent* (Impulse!: 200, 1964, c1996), "Dear Lord" from *Transition* (Impulse!: 124, 1965, c1993), and "Ogunde" from *Expression* (Impulse!: 131, 1967, c1993). SCCJ has Coltrane's "Alabama."

7. "Milestones" on Davis, *Milestones* (Columbia/Legacy: 85203, 1958, c2001); and "So What" on *Kind of Blue* (Columbia/Legacy: 64935, 1959, c1997), also on SCCJ.

8. If you are not familiar with the concepts of scale, mode, chord progression, or song form, you may find it helpful to study pages 451–459 before going further in this chapter. Musician readers may also wish to examine pages 490–494.

9. Coltrane, *My Favorite Things* (Rhino/Atlantic: 75204, 1960, c1998).

10. Coltrane recorded several other improvisations that were based mostly on long stretches of repeating, two-chord patterns. In 1961 he recorded "Olé" on *Olé Coltrane* (Rhino/Atlantic: 1373, 1961, c2000), and "Impressions" on *Live at the Village Vanguard: The Master Takes* (Impulse!). In 1962 he recorded *Coltrane* (Impulse!: 215, 1962, c1997) including "Tungi," "Miles Mode," and "Out of This World," all of which featured long passages of improvisation based on a single mode or a two-chord repeating figure.

11. For example, he recorded an entire album of blues tunes: *Coltrane Plays the Blues* (Rhino/Atlantic: 79966, 1960, c2000). In 1964 he recorded *Crescent* (Impulse!), including "Bessie's Blues," and *A Love Supreme* (Impulse!: 155, 1964, c1995), with another 12-bar blues titled "Pursuance." In concert performances he frequently included standard tunes, such as "Bye, Bye, Blackbird" and "Inch Worm."

12. Compare Coltrane's playing in the beginning of his solo on "Expression" on *Expression* (Impulse!), or in the middle of "Mars" on *Interstellar Space* (Impulse!: 314 543 415, 1967, c2000), with Ayler's playing in the middle of "Ghosts" on Albert Ayler, *Spiritual Unity* (ESP 1002, 1964) and JCCD3.

13. Coltrane, *The Avant-Garde* (Rhino/Atlantic: 79892, 1960, c2000); and *Ascension* (Impulse!: 314 543 413, 1965, c2000). For other examples, listen to *Meditations* (Impulse!), and *Live in Seattle* (Impulse!).

14. The technically inclined reader may notice the mutual use of isorhythms that is demonstrated by Gilmore on his solo in "Jet Flight" on Sun Ra, *The Futuristic Sounds of Sun Ra* (Savoy: 0213, 1960–61, c1993); and by Coltrane in the middle of his solo on the November 5, 1961 recording of "Impressions" on Coltrane, *Live at the Village Vanguard: The Master Takes* (Impulse!). The formula for Coltrane's and Gilmore's above-cited solos may be roughly likened to alternating word order and loudness in repetitions of a brief sentence ("Let's go get the truck.") in this way: "Let's go get truck the." "Let's go get THE truck." "Let's go GET the truck." "Let's go get truck THE." Then, perhaps changing to "Let's go get the CAR." "The CAR get." "Get the CAR." And so forth. If this analogy does not make sense to you, listen again to the musical passages cited in footnote 13 above, and note the ways both saxophonists develop solos by systematically reworking very brief, three-to five-note, melodic fragments.

15. The formula for the chord progression to Coltrane's "Giant Steps" composition was suggested in the preface to Nicolas Slonimsky, *Thesaurus of Scales and Melodic Patterns* (Scribner, 1947; Collier Macmillan, 1986, vi), in which a sequence of pitches that were three scale steps apart appeared. This "thirds cycle" also occurred in the bridge of the Rodgers and Hart pop song "Have You Met Miss Jones?"

16. Its effect was particularly notable in records by Pharoah Sanders, the Bobby Hutcherson-Harold Land groups, and those of David Liebman, McCoy Tyner, Charles Lloyd (1966–69), John Handy (mid-1960s only), and Gato Barbieri.

17. Listen to Elvin Jones with Coltrane on "Sun Ship" (*Sun Ship*, Impulse!: 167, 1965, c1995) and "Your Lady" (*Live at Birdland*, Impulse!: 198, 1963, c1996).

18. Joe Farrell, George Coleman, Frank Foster, Steve Grossman, David Liebman, and others.

19. Publications containing transcriptions and analyses of Coltrane's work include: *The Music of John Coltrane* (Hal Leonard, 1991); Don Sickler, *John Coltrane: Improvised Saxophone Solos* (CPP/Belwin, 1986); David Baker, *The Jazz Style of John Coltrane* (Studio P/R, 1980); David Dempsey, *John Coltrane Plays Giant Steps* (Hal Leonard, 1996); Stuart Isacoff, *Solos for Jazz Tenor Sax*; Scott Reeves, *Creative Jazz Improvisation*; Barry Kernfeld, "The Two Coltranes," *Annual Review of Jazz Studies 2* (1983): 7–66; and Lewis Porter, "John Coltrane's 'A Love Supreme': Jazz Improvisation as Composition," *Journal of the American Musicological Society* 38 (Fall 1985): 593–621. The first six publications are available from Jamey Aebersold (see note 5). The last two can be found in many college music libraries and large public libraries. If you cannot find them, ask a reference librarian for assistance. For interviews with Coltrane about his methods, see Carl Woideck, ed. *The John Coltrane Companion: Five Decades of Commentary* (Schirmer, 1998), 83–156.

Transcriptions for most of the Coltrane solos discussed in this book, including the solos on "Flamenco Sketches" and "The Promise," heard on JCCD2, are available separately from Andrew White, 4830 South Dakota Ave. N.E., Washington, DC 20017; phone 202-526-3666. White has published over 700 Coltrane solo transcriptions.

20. Chick Corea credits Coltrane for inspiring the compositions "Litha" and "Straight Up and Down." He also cites Coltrane's *Meditations* and *Ascension* for influencing his own free-form approach used on Chick Corea, *The Complete "Is" Sessions* (Blue Note: 40532, 2CD set, 1969, c2002). "A Love Supreme" was recorded by jazz-rock stars John McLaughlin and Carlos Santana. "Giant Steps" has been standard repertory for jazz musicians since the 1970s.

Coltrane had a marked influence on saxophonists during the 1960s (see Table 13.2). Along with Ornette Coleman, Coltrane became the primary model for new saxophonists to study, and several older players also incorporated his techniques in mid-career. Such established players as Frank Foster, Harold Land, Teddy Edwards, and Cannonball Adderley all demonstrated the acquisition of Coltrane techniques. Adderley absorbed some of the Coltrane approach while playing in the Miles Davis band with him during the late 1950s. (There are a few particularly Coltrane-like moments in Adderley's solo on "Fun" on Cannonball Adderley, *Mercy, Mercy, Mercy*, Capitol: 29915, 1966, c1995.) Coltrane's influence even showed up in Woody Herman's big band, an unlikely context because its saxophone section had been identified with the sound of Stan Getz and cool jazz. Many of Herman's players of the 1970s and 1980s have used Coltrane's methods, and the band recorded Coltrane's compositions "Naima" and "Giant Steps."

In tallying Coltrane's disciples, note that Coltrane was rarely the only influence these players had. Woody Herman's 1970s saxophonists, for example, drew from a variety of sources, and the most outstanding players who were affected by Coltrane have shown marked individuality as well as the influence of other sources. Joe Farrell, for example, also cited Charlie Parker as a primary influence. Michael Brecker cites Coltrane as a main influence but also cites King Curtis, Junior Walker, Wayne Shorter, and David Liebman.

21. On their post-1968 Miles Davis recordings, Coltrane disciples Steve Grossman and Dave Liebman played more soprano than tenor. Saxophonist Joe Farrell, another player who absorbed portions of the

Coltrane style, recorded an entire album, *Moon Germs* (CTI: 61630 (6023), 1972, c2002), on soprano; and Wayne Shorter used only soprano on *Super Nova* (Blue Note: 84332, 1969, c1988). In fact, Shorter rarely played his tenor in the 1980s or 1990s, devoting himself to a distinctive manner of improvisation that he devised particularly for the soprano. Among soprano saxophonists, Liebman is the most accomplished. For many years he performed only on that instrument, though he was an impressive tenor saxophonist as well. He possesses phenomenal speed and agility, possibly more than any other saxo-

phonist. Liebman devised his own improvisational methods, and though he cites Shorter and Lennie Tristano as inspirations in addition to Coltrane, perceptive listeners can instantly recognize Liebman and distinguish him from less original Coltrane disciples. Aside from the series of albums he recorded with pianist Richie Beirach under the group name Lookout Farm, Liebman's most outstanding album may be the trio recording with bassist Frank Tusa and drummer Bob Moses: Liebman, *Open Sky* (PM: PMR-001, 2LP set, 1972, c1973); Liebman, *Drum Ode* (ECM: 1046, 1974) is also excellent.

John Coltrane

(Photo by Bob Parent, courtesy Don Parent))

The music of individuals who are ahead of their peers in developing the newest, freshest creations can be referred to as "avant-garde." Although this term has been applied in recent writing about numerous jazz styles that were prominent during the 1960s and 1970s, as though "avant-garde" was an actual style of its own, all of the chapters of this book could justifiably contain the term "avant-garde" in their titles because they are concerned with the music of innovators. For instance, some early jazz by Louis Armstrong, bop by Charlie Parker, and cool jazz by Lennie Tristano was ahead of its time and could justifiably be called "avant-garde." So although this chapter is the only one called "avant-garde," it should not be assumed that this term applies only to the music of the 1960s and 1970s that is discussed in it. New kinds of jazz in the 1960s and 1970s were often merely *called* "avant-garde," "the new thing," or "out music," instead of earning original names such as Dixieland or bop. This classification was very loose, and it (a) led some outsiders to assume not only that the different musicians of this period had more in common than they actually did, but also that (b) this was the only period in which "avant-garde" jazz was created.

Don Cherry and Ornette Coleman, 1987
(Lebrecht Music and Arts Photo Library)

This chapter touches a diversity of very unusual musicians, composers, and band-leaders. It discusses several significant modern styles and musicians whose contributions are particularly difficult to classify. It ranges in time frame from bandleaders Sun Ra and Charles Mingus, who were already active in the 1940s, to composer Anthony Braxton, who did not become widely noticed until the 1970s. Not only does the chapter touch bandleaders and composers, but it also touches radically innovative saxophonists such as Albert Ayler and Eric Dolphy. Moreover, the chapter treats specialty bands that achieved distinction for their creativity and uniqueness, such as the Art Ensemble of Chicago and the World Saxophone Quartet.

When acknowledging the use of the "avant-garde" label, don't overlook Chapter 13 for more explanation of John Coltrane's contributions. His playing was avant-garde in the 1950s and the 1960s. Note also that there were other fine avant-garde musicians and composers who were active in jazz during this period but are not mentioned here because we lack the space to do them justice. Entire books could be devoted to the innovations of Paul Bley, George Russell, and Don Ellis, for example.

"FREE" JAZZ

One of the approaches employed by about half the musicians in this chapter is "free jazz." The most common jazz meaning for "free" is improvisation that is not tied to any progression of chords that was agreed upon before the performance. Sometimes it also applies to music that is not tied to steady tempo. The classification is most closely associated with **Ornette Coleman** and **Cecil Taylor**. A model for much of this music is a 1960 Coleman album called *Free Jazz*[1] which contains simultaneous collective improvisation by two bands attempting to remain free of preset key, melody, chord progressions, and meter. (The excerpt from this album that is found in *SCCJ* displays some, but not all, of what is later described here.[2])

Using the term "free jazz" to designate the music of Ornette Coleman can be misleading because very little of the music on the *Free Jazz* album is entirely free of tempo, key, or traditional distinctions between soloists and accompanists. Moreover, there is some preset melody, organization of themes, or other structure in a substantial portion of his other albums. The word "free" is enclosed by quotation marks for the chapter title because it is not entirely accurate in labeling the music of Coleman, Taylor, or their followers.

Even though only *some* "avant-garde jazz" of the 1960s and 1970s was free-form, the term "avant-garde" has been used *interchangeably* with "free jazz" in commentaries by a few journalists and historians. This chapter's title is phrased *1960s and 1970s Avant-Garde and "Free" Jazz* so that you will not overlook the distinction that was missed by those journalists and historians. Because some avant-garde jazz of the era constituted free jazz and some did not, the **"and"** should signal us to discriminate the characteristics. For example, of the musicians treated in this chapter, bandleader Sun Ra presented free-form passages only in a small portion of his music. Though interested in the music of Ornette Coleman, bandleader Charles Mingus never recorded extended passages that departed entirely from chord progressions. Another illustration is Eric Dolphy. His improvisations were so unconventional that they sounded free-form to many listeners despite being tied to movement of preset harmonies and steady tempo.

Most free jazz groups omitted piano because historically the jazz pianist had assumed a role of providing chord progressions, and restrictions created by preset chord progressions were exactly what these musicians were trying to free themselves from. Another possible reason for the scarcity of pianists in free jazz is that few pianists were comfortable improvising without the suggestion of chords or key. It was as though, having been the harmonic gatekeepers for so long, they were not comfortable trying to function when such gates as chord progressions and song forms were removed. (For explanations of these traditions, see Chapter 3 and the *Demo CD*.)

The next three characteristics of free jazz are incidental to freedom from preset chord progressions. They are included here because they happen to be identified more with free players than with bop or cool players. First, **many free players earned a reputation for more extensive manipulations of pitch and tone quality than had been common since early jazz.** Ultra-high-register (altissimo) playing was common, as were shrieks, squawks, wails, gurgles, and squeals. Rough, hoarse tone qualities were also common. Second, **the improvisation of textures sometimes assumed greater importance than the development of melodies. The "free jazz" label was often applied to music of high energy and dense textures that maintained turbulent activity for lengthy periods.** Some free players became so firmly identified with "energy playing" that the "free jazz" label was often attached to high-energy, non-electronic music of *any* kind, not just the kind in which preset keys and song forms were absent. Third, **the free players' conception of melody displayed a loosening of bop practices.** In the playing of some avant-garde musicians, free jazz signalled an end to long, convoluted streams of eighth-note figures that reflected the movement of favorite chord progressions in conventional bop patterns. Phrasing was often more fragmented. Sustained tones were alternated with screeches and moans. There was an unfinished quality in many performances.

Another trend was also more common in free jazz than in bop—**the adoption of non-European musical approaches which neither rely extensively on chord progressions nor use much harmony. This includes some types of music from Africa, Indonesia, China, the Middle East, and India.** This interest led to an amalgamation of jazz with music of non-European cultures, sometimes termed **Third World music**, or just **World Music**. It manifested itself in the use of non-Western instruments and the cultivation of non-Western approaches to playing European instruments. This development might have occurred with free players because free jazz's rejection of piano and preset harmony was musically not too distant from these non-European forms of music that also omitted chord progressions or chord instruments. It resulted in a form of music that is simpler than bop. In this way, it considerably extended the range of sounds used by jazz musicians. The persistence of these elements in free music marks one of the first such lasting blends since the periodic infatuations jazz had shown with Latin American music.

ORNETTE COLEMAN

One of the most influential forces in jazz since the 1950s is **Ornette Coleman** (b. 1930). Some consider him as historically significant as Charlie Parker.[3] Coleman is primarily an alto saxophonist, though he also plays trumpet and violin. On his 1958–1959 recordings, he displayed a soft, pure tone, and he moved from note to note in legato fashion, as if smoothly sliding along small subdivisions of pitch. His tone had neither the edge of Charlie Parker's nor the body of Cannonball Adderley's. Coleman began his notes more bluntly and used a slow vibrato. In later years, he made his tone somewhat brighter and gave it an edge. Though he seems able to play almost everything he attempts, he lacks the ultra-high-level command of his instrument that is possessed by Parker, Adderley, and Lee Konitz. (Compare Coleman's sound in "Civilization Day" [JCCD2 Track 12] with Parker's in "Just Friends" [JCCD1 Track 30], Adderley's in "Flamenco Sketches" [JCCD2 Track 9], and Konitz's in "My Lady" [JCCD2 Track 2].)

Coleman is one of the freshest, most prolific post-bop composers; by the mid-1970s he had already written every tune on more than 20 albums. In 2007 he was recognized for his compositions and improvisations by winning the Pulitzer Prize. His style is quite original, and he has an exceptional gift for melody. Some of his tunes are quite catchy. Like those of Thelonious Monk, some of Coleman's tunes sound simple, despite their unusual rhythmic and harmonic qualities. The playfulness of Coleman's tunes is also reminiscent of Monk's work.[4]

"Civilization Day," **JCCD2** *Track 12*

Although often called free jazz, Coleman's music actually has quite a bit of self-imposed structure. Constant tempo is usually employed. Written and memorized tunes are usually used during some portion of his performances. Moreover, there is nothing haphazard about the freedoms with which he and his sidemen play. They are limited by their own decision to listen to each other carefully, and they plan their music while they improvise. Coleman's brand of free jazz also casts instruments in conventional solo and accompaniment roles. In his trio, Coleman usually seems to be soloing while his bassist and drummer accompany. Though there is interaction, give-and-take, and mutual stimulation, there is little doubt that Coleman is the soloist. (Listen to "Dee Dee" on *CCD2* Track 5.)

For a trio performance to be truly free of role conventions, the three instruments would have to be undifferentiated in their roles: the absence of a solo voice would be as common as the presence of a solo voice; the drums would be accompanied by sax and bass just as often as the sax was accompanied by drums and bass. Actually, if "free" means freedom from conventional roles or song forms, there would not be any solos at all, since solos and accompaniments fulfill roles that are as conventional as constant tempo, meter, key, and chord progressions. True musical freedom can indicate the ability of a musician to play whatever is in the musician's head, regardless of its adherence to musical conventions. The problem is that this is not humanly possible. Musicians are not capable of being so "free." Musical conditioning—and the very process of learning to play an instrument—prevent so great an independence. Therefore, this extreme definition of musical freedom is not too helpful in describing free jazz, and it is clearly not a description of Ornette Coleman's music.

In short, Coleman's music is free only in some respects: It is free of preset chord progressions and their chorus lengths. Some, though not most, of his work is also free of meter and constant tempo. The music does not lack a sense of key, it is not atonal, and it is certainly not random. (See pages 451–454 for discussion of scales, modality, tonality, and atonality.) Coleman freely changes keys, but he usually stays in each one

Ornette Coleman, alto saxophonist and the leading figure in "free" jazz. Shown in 1972 at age 42 with bassist Charlie Haden and drummer Eddie Blackwell.

(Photo by Bill Smith)

"Civilization Day" by Ornette Coleman, Don Cherry, Charlie Haden, and Billy Higgins

Composed by Ornette Coleman; recorded for Blue Note on September 9, 1971, by Ornette Coleman (alto sax), Don Cherry (pocket trumpet), Charlie Haden (bass), Billy Higgins (drums); available on the *Prentice Hall Jazz Collection*; reissued on Coleman, *The Complete Science Fiction Sessions* (Columbia/Legacy: C2K 63569, 2CD set, 1971–72, c2000).

This selection highlights the influential style of Ornette Coleman, the most eminent of the avant-garde "free jazz" musicians. It also features his best known sidemen. His long-time bassist Charlie Haden has become widely loved by musicians since first appearing with Coleman and also has gone on to be part of numerous significant projects of his own, including his Liberation Music Orchestra and The Quartet West. Drummer Billy Higgins has consistently been a favorite of modern musicians. A prime feature of this "Civilization Day" recording is its taste of Don Cherry, the most original trumpeter to appear after Miles Davis. He is an impressively fertile source of new ideas, compounded into each improvisation. Including Cherry on this compilation CD is topical, too, because much media attention during the late 1990s was focused on trumpeter Dave Douglas, whose primary inspirations were Cherry and Miles Davis. Incidentally, Cherry also influenced the mid-1960s style of Davis.

This explosive and intense recording begins with a melody largely made up of rhythms and phrasings not so different from bop. Though some free jazz performances attempt to avoid any bop influences, Ornette Coleman viewed his early work as a logical extension of this music. "Civilization Day," recorded in 1971, shares several similarities to the recordings of Charlie Parker and Dizzy Gillespie made in the 1940s. For example, the melody, which begins and ends the recording, is played by alto sax and trumpet. But this piece is quite unlike bop in many ways. The horn players on the theme statement, Ornette Coleman and Don Cherry, play with non-refined tones, in a sloppy unison with one another, as the drummer and bassist start and stop irregularly. Though a swing feeling in the drums combines with a walking bass line to accompany the solos much of the time, as they would in bop, the soloists play unpredictably, producing unusual sounds and shocking lines. A few of Cherry's lines are simple enough to sing (as at 0'33", 0'39", 0'42", 1'50", and 2'14"), doctored with extra vibrato, but most are fast, frenetic sequences of almost continuous eighth notes. Coleman's solo is filled with extraordinary vigor from the beginning. He often reaches for high notes, and then falls aggressively from them. Unfettered intensity lasts throughout. Notice that there is no piano player. The piece has no chord changes at all, avoiding the type of harmonic guidelines typical of most other types of jazz.

ELAPSED TIME

0'00"	**Theme**
	Trumpet and alto sax, more or less in unison. Bass and drums play sporadically.
0'15"	**Collective Improvisation**
	Trumpet and sax improvise freely without bass and drums, seeming to argue and outplay one another.
0'27"	**Don Cherry's Trumpet Solo**
	Cherry begins with a line of almost continuous eighth notes. Walking bass, ride rhythms on ride cymbal, and chatter on snare drum return to accompany him. Haden plays each note twice in succession within his walking lines.
0'33"	Cherry interrupts continuous eighth notes to make declarative statement of melody.
0'39"	melody statement
0'42"	melodic improvisation
0'46"	melodic improvisation
0'49"	Cherry begins long sequence of continuous eighth notes.
1'50"	melodic improvisation to 1'59"
2'14"	another new melody
2'18"	another new melody

LISTENING GUIDE *continued on next page*

2'54"	**Ornette Coleman's Alto Sax Solo**
	Solo begins with no drums, just bass. Coleman jumps into his solo full force and pursues it with enormous intensity. The improvisation is jammed with hundreds of ideas. Some are little melodies. Some are squeals, wails, and bleats. All come gushing out of his horn at very rapid pace.
3'08"	Drummer Higgins enters with ride rhythms on ride cymbal. Notice how Higgins becomes more and more active with increasingly prominent remarks on snare drum.
4'07"	Coleman inserts a simple melodic idea, running to 4'15".
4'35"	Higgins makes a pronounced sequence of cymbal crashes coordinated with snare drum, complementing Coleman inventing new riffs that bounce off them.
	Billy Higgins's drum solo
5'18"	maintains intense, hurried feeling
5'48"	**Theme**

long enough for us to hear that he is, indeed, in a particular key.[5] Also, his key changes are logical and obvious; they reflect the melodic integrity of his improvised lines.

Coleman attempts a difficult task when he rejects the use of preset chord changes. Without the rise and fall of musical tension indicated by chord changes, his music still has the rise and fall of tension generated by his bassist and drummer; but that is all he has to support and inspire his creations musically. Outside of that, every measure is taxing his imagination, calling upon him to fill it with an interesting and meaningful line. But because none of those measures are supplying any organizational ideas in the form of chord changes, Coleman's improvising cannot fall back on the underlying musical motion of chord changes or on the supportive sound of a pianist's comping. By foregoing preset chord changes, and their associated chorus lengths, turnarounds, and bridges, he has brought us an especially abstract—and challenging—form of musical experience.

Despite the freedom of his improvisational approach, Coleman's improvised lines often resemble chord progression-based lines. For Coleman, melody is primary and harmony secondary. Sometimes it may sound as though he is inventing chord progressions as he improvises lines, but this is only because the harmonic logic of those lines resembles that of chord progression-based lines we have heard elsewhere. The construction of his lines is ruled by his musical past in the same way that our perception as listeners is ruled by our past listening experiences. Coleman plays freely, but in his lines we can hear organization like that in more conventional improvisation. Some of this comes from the very melodic nature of much of his work. (In fact, Coleman has been called the supreme melodist.) The feeling of a definite key (tone center) is present in each portion of his solos, though he changes keys at will.[6] Also, part of the chord-progression feeling in Coleman's music stems from the approach taken by his bassists, especially Charlie Haden. Though Coleman's bassists follow the harmonic directions indicated by his improvisations, at times they also take the lead themselves. Coleman's line may suggest a chord progression which the bassist will complete, or vice versa. Coleman and his bassist remain alert to chord progressions that are suggested in each other's lines.

Modern jazz has been influenced by Ornette Coleman's tunes because they are so original and by his unique saxophone style because it is so emotional and melodic (see Table 14.1). But Coleman has had just as much impact through his decision to discard

TABLE 14.1	A Few of the Many Musicians Influenced by Ornette Coleman	
John Tchicai	Roscoe Mitchell	James "Blood" Ulmer
Marion Brown	Jan Garbarek	Ronald Shannon Jackson
Dewey Redman	Anthony Ortega	Jamaaladeen Tacuma
Jimmy Lyons	Albert Ayler	Charlie Haden
Sonny Simmons	John Coltrane	Pat Metheny
Prince Lasha	John Carter	Joseph Jarman
Henry Threadgill	Charles Brackeen	Paul Bley
Carlos Ward	Keith Jarrett	Saheb Sarbib
Archie Shepp	Bobby Bradford	
Oliver Lake	Don Cherry	

chord changes and his belief that an improviser can let the melody go its own way and not be directed by preset progressions of chords.

Coleman's *Free Jazz* album of 1960 paralleled Miles Davis's *Kind of Blue* in its impact on improvisational approaches. *Kind of Blue* popularized modal approaches; *Free Jazz* contributed to more frequent use of free-form approaches. Coleman used two pianoless quartets on the album. The first included his regular quartet: trumpeter Don Cherry, bassist Charlie Haden, and drummer Eddie Blackwell. The second was made up of alto saxophonist-bass clarinetist Eric Dolphy, trumpeter Freddie Hubbard, bassist Scott LaFaro, and drummer Billy Higgins. (These names are important because all these men are giants in post-bop jazz.) The eight musicians played together, sometimes improvising all at once, never using any preset arrangement of themes, chord changes, or chorus lengths. Tone centers were evident, though they were not agreed upon in advance.

Despite the album title, the music on *Free Jazz* is not entirely free. There are prearranged ensemble passages, solos with rhythm section accompaniment, and a bass duet. Some of the solos, especially Freddie Hubbard's, sound as though they were based on a preset chord progression, though the progression is suggested only by the resemblance of his improvised line to other progression-based lines. Brief themes recur in the improvisation and are passed back and forth among group members. Rarely are all eight players improvising at the same time. Both bassists and both drummers play throughout most of it, but usually a single horn surfaces while the others stay out. Occasionally, all the horns return to embellish the prominent voice.

Other jazz groups had recorded collectively improvised free pieces at about the same time or before Coleman's first recordings. (See Chapter 10 for Tristano, Giuffre, Rogers, et al.) But these were isolated efforts, and the approach did not catch on in the main stream of jazz styles. After Coleman's *Free Jazz*, however, a number of other musicians also recorded in a similar format; some of them are discussed in this chapter.

DON CHERRY

Don Cherry (1936–1995) was a trumpeter, composer, bandleader, and a leading figure in free jazz. A regular member of Ornette Coleman's groups in the late 1950s and early 1960s, he played on all of Coleman's important early recordings, including *Something Else*,[7] *Change of the Century*,[8] and *Free Jazz*. Though strongly influenced by

Coleman, Cherry also cited bop trumpeters Fats Navarro and Clifford Brown as influences. Consistent with this bop connection, Cherry recorded improvisations which closely follow preset chord progressions and contain phrasing and note choices that derive from bop methods.[9] In other words, Cherry was not exclusively a free jazz player. However, like Coleman's, most of Cherry's recorded improvisation goes its own way spontaneously instead of relying on a preset progression of accompanying chords. Cherry's improvisations are strikingly original, filled with lines and melodic fragments which draw little from standard jazz cliché. Cherry did not ordinarily use chord instruments in his bands, and he devoted a considerable portion of his career to playing types of Oriental, Turkish, and Indian music that also omit chording instruments and chord-progression-based compositional forms.

"Civilization Day,"
JCCD2 Track 12

Cherry was quite flexible as an improviser, capable of constructing logical solo lines as well as spontaneously constructing parts for collective improvisation.[10] In this way, he was a throwback to the earliest improvisers, for whom sensitivity and instantaneous flexibility were essential to making good collective music. He could improvise lines which swing and stick close to the beat. He could also play against meter, as though ignoring the beat and resisting swing. In this way, what Cherry does rhythmically is analogous to what he does harmonically. (Musicians call conventional playing "inside" and the other approach "outside.") Because many modern players are comfortable with only one of the two approaches, it is notable that Cherry was adept at both.

After the mid-1960s, Cherry spent considerable time in Europe and devoted much of his recording to music which is not closely related to the jazz tradition. This body of music is frequently dubbed "World Music." Cherry's interests led him to compose and perform extensively in groups using such instruments as the tamboura, sitar, finger cymbals, conch horn, African finger piano, and gong. Cherry learned to play flute, bamboo flute, and assorted percussion instruments at this time. This music makes much use of drones and extensively repeated accompaniment figures. Some pieces are based entirely on chants in which the same few notes are played over and over again. For the jazz listener, there is often little in this music to distinguish it from its nonjazz sources.[11]

CECIL TAYLOR

Cecil Taylor (b. 1929) is a pianist, composer, and bandleader who developed a unique and specialized style of modern jazz during the late 1950s and early 1960s. His style is not merely different, innovative, or unconventional; rather, it is **a major alternative to the main stream of modern jazz styles.** (Listen to *SCCJ*: "Enter Evening," but note that it is among the most tame of all Taylor's recordings. The vast majority of his recorded music sounds wild and extremely turbulent.)

Taylor does not play with modern jazz swing feeling, and he frequently emphasizes musical textures rather than musical lines. Although quite syncopated, his rhythms tend to be played slightly ahead of or on top of the beat, and they lack the lilt and buoyancy of conventional jazz rhythmic style. As jazz scholar Harvey Pekar has noted, Taylor does not try to swing: his music is too tense to swing.

The manner in which Taylor goes about making music differs from most jazz traditions. Taylor's notes often seem to be generated in layered groups, designed to create textures of sound and sound shapes instead of singable phrases that lope along. The textures are rich in internal movement; they seem to shimmer and explode. In fact, much of Taylor's music is composed of quick, tightly packed, staccato figures. They are played in a manner that is very percussive, with few moments of serenity. Some observers have commented that Taylor seems to "attack" the piano keyboard, and they are astounded because he has the skill to strike odd

Pianist Cecil Taylor, the musician who created a striking alternative to all other modern jazz styles. His music emphasized dramatically changing textures instead of hummable melodies. His ideas exploded in note clusters, shimmered and popped instead of swinging. Pictured here in 1990 at age 61.

(Photo by Grace Bell)

sequences of piano keys with tremendous force at a dizzying pace and not miss any. What almost universally impresses listeners is that most of his performances seem to draw on a continuous source of high energy and maintain a feverish intensity for long periods.

Taylor began playing without preset chord progressions or constant tempo, and frequently without a bassist, during the 1960s. His earliest recordings, however, show that he once based his improvisations on familiar tunes and chord changes.[12] He often played free of the harmonic restrictions imposed by a preset progression of chords, though he did pre-plan what he called "unit structures." These were specific phrases and overall concepts about the architecture that the piece should assume. His preparation for performance does involve extensive rehearsal, and he does provide his musicians with musical figures to play. However, he does not always dictate the exact synchronization of parts, their timing, or tempo. In addition, he requires his musicians to improvise some passages without the guidance of preset themes, chord progressions, or chorus lengths. They are freely improvised. In other words, Taylor's music is not entirely free-form, but it is free of the preset forms that most jazz musicians use.

Some of Cecil Taylor's group performances begin with a theme loosely stated by horns and accompanied by his piano improvising in a florid, orchestral fashion. Then a collective improvisation begins in which nearly everyone participates. The emphasis is on creating textures. The style is not melodic in the pop-tune sense, the swing-era sense, or the bop sense. Some textures change gradually, others abruptly. Occasionally, a pre-organized ensemble portion erupts. Usually, the group creates a whirlpool of sound and maintains a frantic pace.[13]

Brief portions of some Taylor improvisations are genuinely atonal. This is unusual in jazz, and in Taylor's work as well, because even the most adventuresome free-form improvisations are usually organized around tone centers, keys, modes, or shifting tone centers.[14] More than any other jazz style, Taylor's resembles the music of mid-twentieth-century composers Karlheinz Stockhausen, Olivier Messiaen, and Luciano Berio. His improvisations have a hint of Thelonious Monk or Duke Ellington, but generally they sound more orchestral than jazz-like.

ALBERT AYLER

Tenor saxophonist **Albert Ayler** (1936–1970) was one of the most original improvisers to emerge after Charlie Parker and Ornette Coleman. His style remains one of the most unusual in jazz history. He perfected an approach that was instrumentally very demanding. Ayler's lines ran the entire range of the tenor saxophone and through at least an additional octave beyond the conventional "highest note." He played throughout that range with swooping, swirling legato figures, and a light, slippery tone. His sound sometimes resembled the tone of a C-melody saxophone. Ayler made moans and wails an essential part of his musical vocabulary. Much of his music was strikingly voice-like. His vibrato was sometimes slow, at other times moderately fast, but always very natural, and delivered in a driven sort of way. In his extended high register, Ayler played with the ease that good players exhibit only in the conventional midrange of the tenor saxophone. His playing often sounded like rapid, legato violin playing. These elements created an otherworldly quality. There was never anything mechanical or academic about Ayler's playing. Whether listeners enjoyed it or not, Ayler's music provided an intensely emotional experience for them.

Ayler's rhythmic conception was not like bop rhythmic conceptions. In fact, it was unlike any swinging jazz style. Like his melodic approach, his rhythmic approach had more in common with classical and folk music than with jazz. (See Chapter 2 for more about different types of swing feeling.) Ayler swung in a manner which only approximated conventional jazz swing feeling. Much of his work did not swing at all. The lack of swing feeling was often caused by a continuously high level of tension, in place of the alternation of tension and relaxation that typifies bop.

Like Ornette Coleman, Ayler followed preset harmonic and rhythmic structures only loosely, and he preferred bands with no chording instrument. Ayler's bassists were some of the same gifted musicians employed by Coleman and Bill Evans. His drummers were of the "free" school, concerned little with simple timekeeping, very interested in group interaction and the creation of varied sounds and textures.[15] Like

Albert Ayler, the leading tenor saxophonist in free jazz. His style was so innovative and compelling that it inspired John Coltrane during the 1960s and numerous avant-garde saxophonists thereafter.

(Photo by Bill Smith)

Composed by Albert Ayler, recorded for ESP on July 10, 1964, by Albert Ayler (tenor saxophone), Gary Peacock (bass), and Sunny Murray (drums); available on *Spiritual Unity* (ESP DISK 1002).

This performance of "Ghosts: First Variation" contains passages illustrating "free jazz," from about 0'56" to 4'12". The term indicates improvised jazz that exhibits little or no adherence to steady tempo, chord progression, or standard traditions of jazz instrument playing techniques. And if the improvisation constitutes variations on the opening theme, the connection between the theme and the variations is not obvious. To call all the music on this track entirely "free" would be misleading, however, because Ayler quite clearly plays a complete melody at the beginning and end, within a steady tempo, and he occasionally refers to it during his improvisations. Though there is no chording instrument such as piano or guitar, the mere absence of chord sounds does not necessarily mean that there is no progression of harmonies at work in the minds of the musicians. Even the melody itself can serve as a frame of reference to guide improvisations. Moreover, despite the lack of explicit timekeeping sounds from bass and drums, some listeners derive a broadly paced kind of loose, rocking motion from bassist Gary Peacock's solo. Therefore, the solos are neither entirely free nor entirely non-free.

If you are interested in more than just the esthetic experience of this music, there are at least two questions you might ask yourself while listening to the improvised sax and bass solos in this selection: Can you detect any hint of a pulse, non-periodic or otherwise? Can you detect any reference to the opening theme, its spirit, or any of its harmonies? This performance is significant conceptually because the musicians are inspired by the opening theme but not following it rigidly to guide their improvisations. In other words, they are drawing freely from its content but not borrowing its form. They may be "developing" what they heard in the main theme, giving us their impressions of it, but not adhering to its progression of accompaniment chords.

An all-time favorite among saxophonists, this example of tenor saxophonist Albert Ayler became a textbook for free-style sax improvisation. Particularly between 1'24" and 2'12", Ayler's improvisation is free of the types of note groupings that jazz listeners have come to expect. Standard conventions of melody are not relevant in these passages. Flurries of rapidly paced notes are swirling in the air. Evidence of singable melody is not to be sought here. The overall effect of the resulting texture seems to be the point of this music. The techniques responsible for the turbulence heard here became models of high-energy improvising for John Coltrane, Pharoah Sanders, and generations of others. And, if Ayler is following a predetermined progression of chords or playing variations on the original melody, it is not obvious. The music here might as well be considered free.

Another central aspect of Ayler's creativity is the manner in which he seamlessly alters the sound of his saxophone from one tone quality to another. On this recording he employs a diverse spectrum of sounds, and he quite flexibly slips and slides through the pitch range with them. Vying for prominence within some of his sounds are two or more different tones. (Such combination tones are technically known as "multiphonics," derived from multi = many, and phonics = sounds.) The precarious wobbling between the various components in a given tone evokes a provocative, otherworldly effect. At times it is as though Ayler's saxophone is creaking.

An intriguing distinction between this particular performance and most other jazz is that, with respect to making the beat obvious, Peacock is mostly responding to Ayler rather than following the conventional jazz approach in which bassists assertively lead the timekeeping by laying down at least the first and third of every four beats, if not each and every one of them. Within much of the opening and closing theme statements, where steady tempo is maintained, Peacock usually devises figures that rise up out of the main beats that are implied by important notes in Ayler's melody, rather than laying down the beats himself or playing them in unison with Ayler. In other words, Peacock's notes come after the beat instead of arriving on the beat. Very rarely does Peacock even briefly play "one" (state the down beat) or play successive beats at all. Even when he does state downbeats, he states the sound slightly after the beat, instead of maintaining the modern jazz tradition of stating it right on or slightly before the main beats: as at 0'11", 0'23" to 0'25", 0'29" to 0'32"; then at 4'29" to 4'30" and 4'32" to 4'35" and 4'38" to 4'43", 4'47" to 4'48" and 4'49" to 4'50". Note that the presence of Gary Peacock on this recording is a treat because he was one of a small number of extraordinarily facile and imaginative bassists of the era, Scott LaFaro and Richard Davis being the better known in this category. They followed the lead of Charles Mingus in conceiving that it was acceptable occasionally to handle the bass as though it were a flamenco guitar, so free and capable were their minds and fingers.

LISTENING GUIDE *continued on next page*

This selection provides a glimpse of Sunny Murray's innovative approach to jazz drumming. Murray was possibly the most important "free jazz" drummer. Murray perfected the non-explicit approach and was frequently employed by pianist Cecil Taylor for generating textures and coloration more than swing feeling. This extends the orchestral concept of percussion instead of the traditions of marching and dancing that had previously pervaded jazz drumming. NOTE: To appreciate the extent of originality demonstrated by this music, we must tally jazz traditions that are not evident: ride rhythms, walking bass, high-hat snapping shut crisply every other beat, swing eighth notes in the melody line, and danceable pulse. The amount of innovation here might well be inversely related to its listenability. So give it a few hearings before attempting to identify all the highlights that are mentioned below. This music proves difficult for many listeners. But repeated attempts will pay dividends in appreciation. It is very sincere music, and a taste for it can be acquired. Be patient with yourself, and come back to it a few weeks later. You might be surprised by how much more you detect upon each rehearing.

ELAPSED
TIME

Introduction

0'00" Unaccompanied tenor sax offers a low-note call followed by a response of two mid-range staccato notes.

8-Measure Introductory Theme

0'02" Low register, coarse-toned, legato line eases into the middle register.

0'09" Using voice-like split tones, occasionally resembling animal cries, sax repeats introductory phrase and eases into statement of main theme.

First Chorus

A-section (16 beats)

0'11" **Theme Statement** is executed in the high register by sax, with a twangy manner that is very soulful due to much pitch flexibility.

Sax is accompanied by Peacock plucking his bass strings, so high-pitched and light in timbre that they resemble cello or guitar more than bass sound. Murray offers an ever-changing undercurrent of drum and cymbal sounds; almost continuous ringing and irregular patter on several different cymbals and snare drum struck with wire brushes.

0'15" resounding low note by bass on the downbeat, followed by an arpeggio

0'16" another resounding bass note run up to the downbeat of his first solo chorus

0'17" **A'-section** (16 beats)

0'22" **B-section** (16 beats)
Bass offers fragment of a walking pattern.

0'27" **B'-section** (16 beats)

0'33" **A-section** (16 beats)
Bass offers broken walking pattern.

0'39" **A'-section** (16 beats)

0'44" **B-section** (16 beats)
Sax refers to original melody but wildly varies it, as bass interjects.

Drummer creates more dense texture by using wire brushes on snare drum.

0'51" **B'-section** (16 beats)
Sax line departs from melody, goes off on far-flung tangents.

Density of drumming increases.

0'56" paraphrase of introductory theme (as in 0'02")

1'01" Bass almost provides textures instead of resounding tones.

Bass creates a flourish almost in the style of flamenco guitar.

1'04" **A-section**

1'07" Sax wails in otherworldly manner via slippery movement from one pitch to another. Quick vibrato intensifies this effect.

LISTENING GUIDE *continued on next page*

1'15"		Sax quotes A-section's concluding melodic figure, and then departs completely from any further references to the original melody.
1'20"		Bass offers complex, unpredictable counter-lines, which combines with drumming to enhance the swirling activities.
1'24"		Sax eases into frenzied flurries of notes.
		A rolling momentum is detectable, without explicit statement of beats; bass figures convey this inexorable inching along.
2'03"		Bass seems to be anchoring the proceedings in a feeling based on three pulses.
2'12"		Multiphonic honk temporarily interrupts Ayler's steady flurries of notes.
2'18"		Melodic fragment emerges amidst the flurries. It paraphrases original melody.
2'27"		Ayler ascends to the altissimo register, more split tones.
2'28"		rapid, repeating, high-pitched pizzicato bass
2'31"		New phrase sounds almost like another instrument intervening.
2'33"		oft repeated shake
2'39"		chain-saw-like sounds, with sporadic occurrences of very high pitch
2'50"	**Bass Solo**	
		made primarily of fragmented phrases, mostly high-pitched, rapidly executed, sometimes sounding like distorted echoes of the original melody
3'29"		double-stopping
3'40"		deep tones briefly inserted
4'02"		Resounding tones again are inserted.
4'12"	Ayler returns.	
		Ayler paraphrases his original introductory low-pitched line in a guttural, legato manner, as at 0'02".
4'22"	**Theme Statement A-section**	
4'32"	**B-section**	
		Tempo is more obvious now, especially as bass plays on every beat.
		Murray is tapping irregularly, keeping cymbals shimmering as music fades away.
4'37"	**B'-section**	
4'44"	**A-section**	
4'47"	**A'-section**	
4'52"	**A-section**	
4'57"	**A'-section**	
5'05"		Ayler gently offers rocking between mid-register and high pitches.
5'10"		Bass sustains low pitch as a conclusion, which is the root note of the tune's key. This provides a sense of resolution or closure since the listener feels that the tune has returned "home."

Coleman, Ayler also used a Charlie Parker tune on one of his first recordings.[16] Like Coleman, Ayler also followed its harmonies only loosely. In other words, he acknowledged bop but did not actually play in the bop style.[17]

Ayler triggered a major style change for John Coltrane in the mid-1960s, and he had a sustained impact on numerous other saxophonists considered avant-garde during the 1970s and 1980s.[18] The close adherence to tempo that was central to bop and bop's offshoots largely disappeared in players who were affected by Ayler. His rhythmic elasticity was absorbed into the styles of many avant-garde players. A number of players drew from the combined influences of Ayler, Coleman, and Coltrane. These new players perpetuated the timbres and erratic contours associated with free jazz, even when performing pieces that followed preset chord changes and tempo.

CHARLES MINGUS

Charles Mingus (1922–1979) is historically significant as:

1. one of the first virtuoso bass soloists to appear after Jimmy Blanton,
2. a bandleader who employed unorthodox techniques and all-star personnel; and
3. a prolific composer-arranger who
    a. created unique blends of premodern and modern jazz traditions, ranging from Jelly Roll Morton and Duke Ellington to bop;
    b. drew from such diverse sources as Negro gospel music, Mexican folk music, and twentieth-century European concert music; and
    c. wrote distinctive melodies.

His music was always avant-garde, and that is one reason Mingus is treated in this chapter. But unlike Cecil Taylor, Ornette Coleman, and Albert Ayler, Mingus was not primarily a free jazz player. Most of his music was highly structured.

Mingus did not become widely known until the late 1950s, though he had been making highly creative recordings as a bandleader since the mid-1940s. By the late 1950s, when his work began to be issued by major record companies, he had already recorded as bassist with such modern giants as Miles Davis, Charlie Parker, and Dizzy Gillespie (for discussion of his stature as a bassist, see page 179). Historically significant as a bassist, Mingus is at least as significant as a composer and bandleader. Like Ellington's, his name represents an entire idiom which, though rooted in other idioms, is uniquely his own.

Charles Mingus, bassist-bandleader-composer, second only to Duke Ellington in achieving colorful integration of composition and improvisation. He drew from symphonic music and folk songs, modern jazz and avant-garde chamber music. His solo style inspired hundreds of jazz bassists, and his combo innovations influenced generations of nontraditional bandleaders. Pictured here in 1951 at age 29.

(Photo by Bob Parent, courtesy of Don Parent)

Mingus wrote more than 150 pieces, many of which have been rearranged and recorded several times. He explored styles as diverse as:

1. program music ("Pithecanthropus Erectus," the story of man[19])
2. funky, bluesy, gospel-oriented music, with shouting and hand clapping ("Better Git It in Your Soul"[20])
3. Third Stream music ("Revelations"[21])
4. bop (with Charlie Parker, Dizzy Gillespie, Bud Powell, and Max Roach[22])
5. almost free jazz (portions of "What Love"[23])
6. music for film (*Shadows*)

Mingus employed diverse instrumentations, including the following:

1. his own solo piano[24]
2. jazz quintets of trumpet, tenor saxophone, piano, bass, and drums[25]
3. pianoless quartet[26]
4. five trumpets, four trombones, tuba, cello, oboe, flute, six saxophones, piano, bass, and three drummers[27]
5. two trumpets, trombone, French horn, flute, bassoon, two saxophones, harp, piano, guitar, vibraphone, two basses, and drums (see footnote 21, in this chapter)

Throughout his career, Mingus displayed the influence of Ellington. The methods of Ellington are obvious as early as Mingus's 1946 recording of "Bedspread," made as a 78 rpm single for the Four Star firm. Even the style of improvisations in it shows a similarity to the Ellington approaches. Mingus has composed and recorded pieces dedicated to Ellington, such as "Duke's Choice" and "An Open Letter to Duke." Ellington-like use of plunger-muted brass playing has appeared in Mingus works. The Johnny Hodges alto saxophone style has, at the request of Mingus, been incorporated into the playing of such otherwise non-Hodges-styled saxophonists as Charlie Mariano, Jackie McLean, and John Handy. Mingus has also recorded several Ellington compositions.

Mingus is far better known for his combo recordings than for his big band material. The Mingus combo approaches are distinguished because they seldom resemble the jam session format adopted in most modern jazz concerts and recording sessions. Mingus relies heavily on the alternation of composed and improvised passages and on preset accompaniments instead of being restricted to only a unison theme statement, followed by a string of improvised solos with improvised accompaniments, and another theme statement. These sustain the listener's interest by frequently interspersing familiar material so that the listener is not required to concentrate for long periods on continuously changing improvisations. Also to Mingus's credit is that, despite the amount of planning in his performances, a looseness prevails, and a feeling of naturalness is conveyed by his music. In many performances, Mingus rejected conventional bop accompaniment patterns in favor of preset statements which broke the flow of music by introducing stops and changes of style in mid-performance. Portions of some solos were accompanied by nothing more than hand clapping and shouting. Drumming might use a waltz pattern one moment and a conventional jazz pattern the next moment. Some passages contain many stop-time solo breaks. The tempo might be slow one moment and doubled the next. In fact, Mingus is one of the few bandleaders in jazz history to explore the gradual speeding and slowing of tempo. And, like the finished products of Jelly Roll Morton and Duke Ellington, the Mingus material rarely sounded anonymous. It could not be mistaken for an ordinary recording session run in a more conventional fashion.[28]

Composed by Charles Mingus; recorded on May 5, 1959, by John Handy (tenor sax), Shafi Hadi (alto sax), and Booker Ervin (tenor sax), Jimmy Knepper (trombone), Horace Parlan (piano), Charles Mingus (bass), Danny Richmond (drums); reissued on Mingus, *Mingus Ah Um* (Columbia/Legacy: 65512, 1959, c1993).

This selection is taken from one of Mingus's best-known albums, *Mingus Ah Um*. As in other pieces on that album, this piece displays the leader's talent for blending his musicians' ideas with his own compositional ideas. The result is music that is kaleidoscopic in its range of colorful sounds, rhythms, and textures, yet coherent at the same time. Much of the improvisation seems scattered when taken by itself, but it is somehow unified with the overall piece. Rather than the hard-driving character of bop, this piece conveys an elastic momentum that has a cushiony feeling. It does not swing in the usual jazz sense, but it nevertheless pulls the listener along in a teasing kind of way. Rather than the abandon of free jazz, this selection has considerable sense of structure, but the improvised sax solos veer away from conventional models and verge on the avant-garde. The ways the accompaniment keeps changing also make the approach highly unconventional. Extremely sensual, the effect of this music seems smoldering. The first sax solo, for instance, alternates between playful and searing.

This piece is interesting and innovative on a number of levels. It is an excellent example of Mingus's small group arranging. Note the unusual instrumentation: three saxophones, trombone, piano, bass, and drums. Though the composition is in a typical song form, A-A'-B-A', "Fables of Faubus" is not 32 bars long. It is 71 bars long. Each section can further be broken down into distinct parts, containing a wide array of musical material, continually alternating between several stylistic feelings. As a composer/bandleader, Mingus distinguishes himself here in a number of ways; for example, he (a) devises moments where several melodies are running at the same time without getting in each other's way, (b) presents different melodic ideas in succession that contrast with each other yet make sense in the overall proceedings, and (c) intersperses irregular accompaniment rhythms that would ordinarily throw off the soloists and the listeners but don't. As a bassist, Mingus shows his versatility when he (a) creates a solid accompaniment for the rest of the band, (b) switches between faster and slower lines, and (c) improvises a melodic solo.

Terms to know from *Demo CD* before following this listening guide: legato, staccato, scoop, smear, fall-off, walking bass, trombone, alto saxophone, tenor saxophone, snare drum, double-time; from the "Elements of Music" appendix: triplets, A-A-B-A form. See pitch bends illustration on page 49.

ELAPSED
TIME

0'00"   **Introduction** (8 measures)

Two tenor saxophones play legato line in unison, while some notes are doubled by trombone. Drums and piano rest.

Melody

0'16"   **A-section**
Part 1 (8 measures)
The alto sax joins in, playing a contrasting line (the main theme) that alternates a variety of staccato and sustained tones. Trombone adds a related line. Drums and piano join in.

0'32"   Part 2 (11 measures)
Trombone plays a melody in unison with the three saxes. Swing feeling occurs momentarily because walking bass enters and drummer plays ride rhythms on ride cymbal, snaps high-hat shut crisply every other beat. Snare drum underscores melody rhythms, sometimes adds "chatter."

0'54"   **A'-section**
Part 1 (8 bars)
same as earlier

1'11"   Part 2 (10 measures)
Begins as earlier, but trombone has melody with alto sax.

1'23"   deliberate hits articulated by several instruments

LISTENING GUIDE continued on next page

1'30"	**B-section**
	Part 1 (8 measures)
	Tenor sax performs the melody in its high register. Trombonist adds a countermelody in his. Alto sax plays a third part that resembles a moan. The feeling is similar to Part 1 of the A-section.
1'34"	Alto sax and trombone play sighing sounds.
1'46"	**Part 2 (4 measures)**
	Rhythm section moves to a double-time feeling. Tenor sax plays a slow-moving melody, while alto sax improvises faster figures. Trombone lines start slow, then get faster.
1'54"	**Part 3 (4 measures)**
	deliberate punctuations played by piano, bass, and drums, similar to second part of the A-section, second part
1'58"	Alto sax and trombone play sighing sounds.
2'02"	**Part 1 (8 measures) + Part 2 (10 measures)**
	Tenor saxes and trombone play the melody. Alto sax and trombone punctuate, and also play last part of the melody. Notice the bass playing pizzicato triplets that preface important down beats.
2'38"	**Tenor Sax Solo by John Handy** (A, A′)
	Notice the accompaniment styles alternating between halting, jagged rhythms and a steady, relaxed swing.
	Sax improvisation is filled with cries and melodic fragments that sound like exhortations. It is made very soulful by extreme flexibility of pitch, such as legato smearing from note to note, occasionally reaching into the alto sax range in a wailing, speech-like way. He sometimes plays as though he is draping strings of notes over the accompaniment and not sticking just to standard durations of notes or crisply articulated bop phrases. This happens especially when rhythm section is playing halting, jagged rhythms.
3'00"	double-timed bop phrases (mostly when walking bass and ride rhythms are happening)
3'14"	cries and melodic fragments that sound like exhortations
3'20"	cries and melodic fragments that sound like exhortations
3'30"	double-timed bop phrases (mostly when walking bass and ride rhythms are happening)
3'48"	**Piano Solo by Horace Parlan** (B, A′)
	The first part of the B-section begins by alternating between two bars of standard timekeeping and two bars of double-time.
	Parlan's approach to this solo is very funky, as though he is decorating the interruptions by dripping bluesy ideas over them.
4'11"	gospel-like phrases from piano, atop halting, jagged bass and drums figures
4'20"	Bass makes a snapping sound from the string bass that does not let the tone ring.
4'44"	Piano generates a melodic figure whose rhythm the bass and drums eventually join to finish the piano solo section in a declamatory way.
4'53"	**Tenor Sax Solo by Booker Ervin** (A, A′)
	Soulfully played with assorted wail-like pitch bends, this sax improvisation has much the character of the first, but it uses a different melodic vocabulary, is executed with somewhat less urgency, and takes fewer chances.
	Accompaniment alternates swing style with the halting, jagged routine used previously, and the absence of flowing ride rhythms on the cymbal.
5'53"	double-timed bop phrases from sax
6'02"	**Bass Solo by Charles Mingus** (B, A′)
	Listen to Mingus's fat sound and very deliberate manner. His thinking is well organized across the architecture of the entire improvisation. Try to detect the little melodies he comes up with. It is interspersed with blues inflections, as at 6'36", 6'39", 6'41", 6'51", and 6'54".
7'00"	Drums lay down the same kinds of rhythms used to end the piano solo.
7'05"	**Closing Melodic Statement** (B, A′)
	similar to opening statement
8'08"	Piece ends with a series of rhythmic punctuations.

Mingus's unorthodox approaches to combo performance had several significant impacts. They forced improvisers away from producing purely bop-styled solos in an uninterrupted stream. They gave improvisers a varied background which, in turn, elicited more varied solos. They gave listeners brief, reassuring chunks of music in the form of figures that became familiar because they regularly recurred during the piece. This allowed listeners to latch onto something familiar amidst the flow of freshly improvised solos. This is important because, in most bop performances, familiar material was offered only at the beginning and the end of a piece. The Mingus technique of placing recurring devices *within* the piece offered listeners something that they could not ordinarily expect from other kinds of modern jazz (though this approach later became associated with bands led by former Mingus sidemen Thad Jones and Ted Curson).

To achieve a successful integration of composed and improvised music, Mingus obtained a high degree of artistic cooperation from his musicians. As a bandleader and arranger, Mingus had a sense of what players to cast in what roles and how to pry out maximum distinctiveness in a performance. He colorfully mixed snips of improvisations with his written ensemble sounds to weave unusual textures. Then, instead of thrusting their favorite phrases unthinkingly onto his music, the players were forced to appreciate his musical wishes and give those wishes higher priority than they gave their own. Players had to interpret his demands as well as contribute original twists of their own. Performance was often indistinct from rehearsal. The music amounted to a workshop endeavor in that Mingus gave his musicians sketchily written parts, dictated parts to them by playing phrases on the piano or the bass, and described in words the conceptions which he wanted converted to music.[29]

ERIC DOLPHY

Modern jazz has known numerous virtuoso saxophonists, but **Eric Dolphy** (1928–1964) could be called virtuoso on three different instruments: flute, alto saxophone, and bass clarinet. Dolphy mastered the complete range of every instrument he played, and he capitalized on almost every sound it could produce. He even studied bird calls and mimicked them in his solos. Slides and smears connected Dolphy's notes. Sometimes his lines bounced and twittered exuberantly.

Dolphy was also a composer whose pieces were as peculiar as Thelonious Monk's. Dolphy's tunes contained odd intervals and syncopations that were even more jarring than Monk's because they came at the listener much faster. Upon first hearing them, listeners often perceive Dolphy's compositions as erratic and unpredictable. Like his solo improvisations, they are so unusual that some listeners at first assumed the notes were not related to the chord changes in the accompaniment. Listeners thought that Dolphy either did not know what he was doing or was intentionally fooling people with random note choices. His style perfectly fit the "avant-garde" and "out" characterizations. Some listeners even mistook it for free jazz. Contrary to what some thought, however, Dolphy was quite sincere and thoroughly schooled. He knew exactly what he was doing, and connected every note to chords in the accompaniment. His connections were far less obvious than in earlier jazz styles. They were not so remote, however, that his playing could qualify as truly "free" jazz.

Dolphy's first well-known recordings were made with the Chico Hamilton quintet during the 1950s. He then recorded with Charles Mingus from 1960 to 1964. Many musicians regard his collaborations with Mingus to be among the most outstanding recordings in this period of jazz history. In 1961 and 1962, Dolphy toured and recorded with fellow saxophonist John Coltrane.[30]

Dolphy's 1958–1959 work with Chico Hamilton's group was rooted in bop phrasing and swing feeling.[31] His later work, however, was characterized by explosive torrents of notes that were connected by neither conventional melodic development nor bop phrasing. He could also play with swing era lushness, sometimes on the same piece that displayed the wild and jumpy side of his style.[32]

Dolphy's impact was not as extensive as Ornette Coleman's or John Coltrane's, but there were musicians after the mid-1960s who played his tunes, composed in his style, and drew upon his improvisational methods. Saxophonists and flutists were especially impressed by Dolphy's consummate mastery of his instruments and his courage to use it to invent and perform what often seemed outrageous sounds. He opened new horizons by showing that such an unorthodox manner could work.

FREE DRUMMERS

Several highly imaginative drummers have been associated with free jazz (see Table 14.2). They developed a style which did not rely on repetitive ride rhythms, high-hat closings, and bass drum patterns. Though much of their work did imply tempo, the rhythms they invented only sporadically stated it. All four of the drummer's limbs in this "free drumming" style performed a function similar to the "chattering" done by bop drummers' left hands on snare drum. (For an explanation of bop drumming, listen to the *Demo CD*.) In other words, "chattering" came from the entire drum set. These free-style drummers were not relegating their right hands to stating a consistent timekeeping rhythm. Nor were they using their left feet to consistently snap shut their high-hat on every other beat. All four limbs were devoted to generating an undercurrent of activity that popped and crackled with ever-changing sounds. **By comparison with swing era and bop methods of rhythm section drumming, free-style produced sound patterns that were less predictable. They offered varieties of color and shading that were more extensive. This was a complete departure from the traditions of marching bands and dance bands. Free jazz drumming more closely follows an orchestral concept of percussion because it emphasizes color and shading instead of timekeeping.**[33]

"Ghosts: First Variation," JCCD3 *Track 2; "Mars,"* CCD2 *Track 7*

FREE BASSISTS

A number of fine bassists have been associated with free jazz (see Table 14.2). Most have played in more conventional settings, too. In this chapter we are singling out two of the best known, Charlie Haden and Dave Holland.

Charlie Haden (b. 1937) is the bassist most prominently associated with Ornette Coleman during the 1950s and 1960s. He also received wide exposure during the 1970s as a member of the Keith Jarrett Quartet, a band which drew considerable inspiration from Coleman's music. Though usually classed with free jazz musicians, Haden is known for playing that is firmly tied to movement of harmonies, a skill that is fundamental to nonfree styles. In fact, his work is usually bound more closely to jazz traditions than is the work of those he accompanies. One of his greatest contributions was to translate what free hornmen were doing into more conventional time feeling. This helped unify the group sound by anchoring the hornmen's creations when they were without feeling of formal meter. It also brought swing feeling to many musical ideas that probably would not have swung themselves.

"Civilization Day," JCCD2 *Track 12*

As an accompanist, Haden constructs lines that move with unerring logic, no matter how quickly directions change in the solo lines. He manages to pick up direction that momentarily occurs in solo lines and instantaneously align himself with it. This is a skill he shares with the playing of fellow bassists Dave Holland in Sam

TABLE 14.2 Some of the Many Musicians Who Have Improvised
Without Preset Chord Progressions

SAXOPHONISTS
Ornette Coleman
Eric Dolphy
Albert Ayler
Archie Shepp
Bill Smith
Henry Threadgill
Sam Rivers
David Murray
Oliver Lake
Anthony Braxton
Roscoe Mitchell
Joseph Jarman
John Coltrane
Dewey Redman
John Gilmore
Danny Davis
Marshall Allen
Pharoah Sanders
Sonny Rollins
Gato Barbieri
Marion Brown
John Tchicai
Jimmy Lyons
Ken McIntyre
Steve Lacy
Pat Patrick

BASSISTS
Charlie Haden
Dave Holland
David Lee
Malachi Favors
Fred Hopkins
Jimmy Garrison
Scott LaFaro
Charlie Mingus
Buell Neidlinger
Bob Cranshaw
Henry Grimes
David Izenzon
Gary Peacock
Richard Davis
Steve Swallow
Alan Silva

PIANISTS
Lennie Tristano
Keith Jarrett
Paul Bley
Sam Rivers
Sun Ra
Cecil Taylor

TRUMPETERS
Bobby Bradford
Freddie Hubbard
Don Cherry
Don Ayler
Lester Bowie
Bill Dixon
Dewey Johnson
Eddie Gale Stevens
Ted Curson
Leo Smith

**DRUMMERS
ASSOCIATED
WITH FREE JAZZ**
Milford Graves
Sunny Murray
Andrew Cyrille
Rashied Ali
Beaver Harris
Barry Altschul
Charles Moffett
Don Moye
Steve McCall
Dennis Charles
Ed Blackwell
Billy Higgins
Paul Motian

Rivers's groups and Malachi Favors in the Art Ensemble of Chicago. All three bassists represent the strongest connection with conventional jazz that each of their respective groups displays. They are also distinguished by a higher level of instrumental facility than their horn-playing colleagues display. Haden, Holland, and Favors use very full, warm tones. They favor a clean, firm sound rather than the rough-hewn, explosive quality used by the hornmen they accompany. In fact, Haden makes the richness of his tone an element in his vocabulary of musical devices. He attaches more importance to single tones and the ways they can be manipulated than was the fashion with most bassists during the 1960s and 1970s. He is concerned more with sound than speed, and he is not interested in improvising bass solos in the style of hornmen. Each of his notes reflects intense deliberation. Haden contrasts with most of his contemporaries in that he is not concerned with intricacy.

Dave Holland (b. 1946) is known for music he played with such chord-progression-based musicians as Miles Davis and Chick Corea as well as for his playing in free-form settings. No matter the setting, Holland always seems to choose the right notes and fit them together in a highly musical way that is complete and warm at the same time. He has a conception of broad scope, an imagination that rivals Scott LaFaro's, and a swinging manner of timekeeping. Holland's playing exudes strength and confidence. His tone glows with a unique color and the vibrato he gives to many long tones. Naturalness is a pervasive feeling in his style. He can take racing tempos and still swing and sound pretty. Ballads are a joy for his approach. In addition to being present in many ground-breaking recordings of Miles Davis and Chick Corea, Holland was also leader on an important record session that has been associated with avant-garde jazz: *Conference of the Birds* (see footnote 33 in this chapter). His work with numerous groups led by saxophonist Sam Rivers parallels the work Charlie Haden did with Ornette Coleman and Keith Jarrett; but Holland has more speed and agility than Haden and uses those abilities in ways that are not part of Haden's style. Holland can play horn-like bass solos in the bop manner as well as create action-filled textures as accompaniment in free jazz contexts.

CHICAGO AVANT-GARDE

A number of stylistically related black musicians from Chicago began gaining attention during the late 1950s and early 1960s. They finally received wide critical recognition during the late 1970s. The music of these players helped define avant-garde jazz for the 1960s and 1970s.[34] This stream of Chicagoans can be considered as three groups: **(1) the musicians associated with Sun Ra, beginning during the 1950s, (2) the Association for the Advancement of Creative Musicians (AACM), an alliance of black players spearheaded by pianist Richard Abrams in the mid-1960s, and (3) the most well publicized of all AACM members, the Art Ensemble of Chicago and saxophonist-composer Anthony Braxton, who became well known in the 1970s.**

Sun Ra

Sun Ra (1915–1993) was an immensely creative pianist, composer, arranger, and bandleader active as a professional musician since the 1930s. He formed his own big band during the 1950s. Like Duke Ellington's, many of Ra's principal sidemen stayed with him for 20 and 30 years at a stretch. He wrote and performed in a kaleidoscopic range of musical styles. Sun Ra's output is uniquely his own music, but its diversity is most expediently characterized by comparison with similar work of better-known musicians:

1. Some pieces resemble the chant music of Africa.
2. Some works suggest the mode-based work of John Coltrane in the 1960s.[35]
3. Some of Sun Ra's mid-1950s music almost sounds like a modern jazz version of Duke Ellington's music in the 1940s.[36]
4. Some of Sun Ra's work of the mid-1960s resembles contemporary classical music using electronically altered and synthesized sounds.[37]

Differences between Sun Ra's writing and that of conventional big bands can be summarized easily by saying that Sun Ra capitalized on the diversity that is possible

The Sun Ra band of 1990 (pianist Sun Ra is standing at far left).
(Photo by Nancy Ann Lee)

with big band instrumentation and overlooked by most other bandleaders. For instance, Sun Ra:

1. used many different combinations of trumpets, trombones, saxophones, piano, bass, and drums;

2. extended the range of tone colors by adding electronic instruments (he employed electric piano and synthesizers long before rock groups made their use common);

3. made imaginative use of timpani, celeste, xylophone, bass marimba, bells, and chimes;

4. used saxophonists who played instruments unusual in jazz, such as piccolo, oboe, bassoon, and bass clarinet;

5. required all his sidemen to double on percussion instruments;

6. sometimes created passages by means of simultaneous collective improvisation instead of composition;

7. gave performances in which pieces were not separated, where the entire evening was an uninterrupted sequence of unusual sounds;

8. based pieces on chants instead of chord progressions.

Sun Ra's use of synthesizers and the overall conception for many of his 1960s albums, especially *Heliocentric Worlds of Sun Ra, Vols. 1 and 2*,[38] suggest the work of twentieth-century classical composers Edgard Varèse and Krzysztof Penderecki. Central to such work is the notion that music can consist of sound by itself instead of sound in the conventional form of melody and harmony. Chunks of sound are sequenced in place of the standard ideas of melody and chord progression. When Sun Ra and his improvisers addressed themselves to this style, the result had a more natural and flowing character than similar music performed by symphony orchestra musicians.

Sun Ra was also active in the free jazz approach. Portions of his performances were collectively improvised with little apparent prearrangement (for example, *Astro Black, Magic City*, and *Heliocentric Worlds of Sun Ra, Vol. 2*). His free jazz passages differed from those of Ornette Coleman and John Coltrane because they had more evident continuity and compositional organization. It is also important to recognize that Sun Ra succeeded artistically with free-form collective improvisation in big band contexts. This is something other leaders have not attempted. Large ensembles pose great difficulty for free jazz because of the problems musicians must overcome in considering and reacting to so many other sounds that are being improvised at the same time as their own. Sun Ra's achievement is therefore quite significant.

Sun Ra is like Duke Ellington in several ways. His fascination with widely diverse textures and his unconventional arranging methods are two similarities. He also had that rare skill of being able to oversee combinations of improvisation and composition and blend them in a unified form. Like Ellington, Sun Ra brought out the best in his sidemen who, in turn, adapted their improvisatory styles to the varying moods within his compositions.

Saxophonists **Marshall Allen** (b. 1924) and John Gilmore were Sun Ra's strongest improvisers, and both remained with the band for more than 30 years. Allen, who can play all the woodwind instruments, contributed extremely imaginative oboe and piccolo solos to Sun Ra's recordings. He also improvised free-form, high-energy alto saxophone solos that capitalized on the instrument's altissimo register and departed totally from conventional organization of pitches and jazz swing feeling. In his playing, long sequences of squeals and screeches were connected with tremendous intensity and developed organically to set the mood for Sun Ra's pieces.

John Gilmore (1931–1995) is respected among knowledgeable jazz musicians, and has recorded with the noted bands of drummer Art Blakey and pianists Andrew Hill and Paul Bley. (See page 293 for Gilmore's influence on John Coltrane.) He stands out among post-bop saxophonists for a distinctive, hard-hitting style, and is known for a very raw, hard bop approach. He also devised an approach whereby individual notes are not as important as the overall contours and timbre of the sound. Like Albert Ayler, Gilmore refined a high-energy style of swirling legato figures that are not melodic or rhythmic. They are like extended screams and growls that help generate a mood and a sound mass.

Apart from John Gilmore, few of Sun Ra's sidemen have recorded with better-known bands. One exception is trombonist Julian Priester, who worked with the band of drummer Max Roach and was part of an innovative septet led by pianist Herbie Hancock during the 1970s. Incidentally, like Sun Ra's of the early 1960s, **Herbie Hancock's group of the early 1970s used synthesizer, varied percussion sounds, piccolo, and bass clarinet, and often produced music resembling that of twentieth-century composer Edgard Varèse. That Varèse-like style, as practiced by Hancock and Sun Ra, resembled background music for science fiction and space travel films, and it was popularly labeled "space music."**

Sun Ra's live performances were accompanied by singing, dancing, costumes, and unusual lighting. A Sun Ra concert was a multimedia experience. This has been unusual in modern jazz, though common in rock. Though entertaining for some of Sun Ra's listeners, it was distracting for others, and his reception suffered among some musicians and critics. Listeners fail to take Sun Ra's music seriously also because Sun Ra places a humorous emphasis on philosophy, astrology, space travel, and astronomy. Another factor behind his failure to attract a wider audience is his diversity. Though it is unfair to judge any jazz musician's work on the basis of merely one album or a few live performances, it can be particularly misleading in judging Sun Ra's career because his output has such breadth. Unfortunately, however, many listeners dismiss him after hearing only a small slice of his music. Sun Ra remains the most controversial musician in this chapter.

Sun Ra contributed major innovations in jazz composition as well as introducing synthesizers and big band free-form improvisation to jazz. Yet despite the unusual breadth, depth, and originality of his music, Sun Ra is relatively unknown. His recordings number over one hundred, but because he produced and distributed many of his best albums himself, most of his ground-breaking recordings are not known by musicians and jazz critics.

The Association for the Advancement of Creative Musicians (AACM)

The Association for the Advancement of Creative Musicians (AACM) is a Chicago-based collective of modern jazz musicians founded in the early 1960s by saxophonist Fred Anderson and pianist Muhal Richard Abrams. It organized concerts, recordings, training, and promotion for black musicians who had an affinity for jazz that was not squarely within the bop tradition. Their music was almost exclusively non-electronic and separate from jazz-rock. Some of the AACM's music resembles Sun Ra's, Ornette Coleman's, and the work of Charles Mingus in several respects. First, its **rhythmic feeling lacks the flowing, easy character of conventional jazz and is more like the unpredictable nature of modern concert music.** Second, **solos are often freely improvised and inspired more by the mood of the piece than by standard bop patterns.** Third, **the music uses a larger assortment of accompaniment rhythms than was common to bop.** And fourth, **the proceedings display a rough quality** consistent with the Mingus concept that each performance is really a public workshop rather than a finished product.

The Art Ensemble of Chicago: Roscoe Mitchell, Joseph Jarman, Lester Bowie, Malachi Favors

The Art Ensemble of Chicago emerged during the late 1960s. The group made music that did not follow a strict set of rules. They chose styles freely and refused to base their music on the expectations of a particular idiom or audience. They embraced the music of the whole world as their repertory. Though they sometimes applied conventional jazz approaches, the group performed in a broad range of styles. Many of their approaches have not been squarely within the jazz tradition. In their work they have:

1. mimicked street bands of foreign countries,
2. performed lighthearted dramatic sketches,
3. recited poetry,
4. worn costumes and stage makeup,
5. made sounds for sound's sake instead of following traditional concepts of melody and harmony,
6. improvised without following preset progressions of chords.

Some of the Art Ensemble's music is similar to that of Ornette Coleman, Don Cherry, and Albert Ayler. Their jazz solo conceptions owe much to Coleman. Their large assortment of tone qualities and pitch bends resemble the methods of Ayler. As in the bands of Ayler and Coleman, they did not use piano. Many of their recordings dispensed with the conventional jazz drum set, although all group members played percussion instruments. Timekeeping and a harmonic background were provided solely by bassist Malachi Favors, who had outstanding technique and distinctive improvisational flexibility. Without his strength and imagination, much of the group's music would be weak.

The Art Ensemble members seemed to play almost every instrument, including ones that most listeners had never seen before. They collected instruments from all over the world, and their stage setting looked like a museum. To simplify the task of identifying the players, we should note that **Lester Bowie** (1941–1999) was primarily a trumpeter, **Malachi Favors** (1937–2004) concentrated on bass, and **Joseph Jarman** (b. 1937) and **Roscoe Mitchell** (b. 1940) are primarily saxophonists. In addition to percussion instruments, Mitchell plays soprano, alto, tenor, and bass saxophones, clarinet, and flute. Jarman plays soprano, alto, tenor, and bass saxophones, clarinet, bassoon, flute, oboe, and vibraphone. After 1970, drummer **Don Moye** (b. 1946) had also been recorded with the group.

The Art Ensemble of Chicago used musical elements that had been relatively neglected in the mainstream of modern jazz styles. The group repackaged ideas that the originators of free jazz had pioneered, presenting them in a less frantic and more humorous way. A notable contribution was the group's practice of taking a brief melodic fragment and altering it over long stretches within a performance. Another feature was that the group sometimes offered unusual instruments and varied inflections of pitch and timbre just for their own sake, instead of rapidly flowing bop lines. Strict tempo was often rejected. The group's repertory of the 1970s was also distinguished by its avoidance of traditional format in which improvised solos are strung together one after another, without a storytelling quality to unify the piece. During the 1980s, however, they did record several albums that imitated traditional approaches to modern jazz.

The Art Ensemble of Chicago in 1973 (left to right): Roscoe Mitchell (tenor sax), Lester Bowie (trumpet), and Joseph Jarman. (The large shiny instrument in the foreground is a bass saxophone. The large instrument obscuring Jarman is a bass drum.) Group member Malachi Favors is not in view.

(Photo by Bill Smith)

The Art Ensemble offered simplicity and careful use of silence in place of complex chord progressions and virtuoso displays of technical prowess. In fact, the group made more use of silence and changes in loudness than most jazz-oriented groups since Jimmy Giuffre's of the 1950s and 1960s. This puts them in direct contrast with John Coltrane's high-energy, dense-textured music of the 1960s and the loud, repetitive jazz-rock of the 1970s. The Art Ensemble was one of the first groups since the Modern Jazz Quartet to become known for exploring soft and gentle sounds.[39]

Anthony Braxton

One of the most broadly talented figures to emerge during the prominence of the AACM is **Anthony Braxton** (b. 1945). If ever there was a jazz-oriented musician whose work resists categorization, it is Braxton. He performs on almost all the woodwind instruments ever invented, yet the tone color he extracts is unlike the accepted model for each. He sometimes improvises solos with conventional modern jazz accompaniment, yet his solo lines do not resemble standard modern jazz approaches of Charlie Parker or John Coltrane.

Though he is usually classed within the jazz idiom, very little of Braxton's music swings in the jazz sense. (See Chapter 2 for explanation of "swing feeling.") Though sometimes suggesting atonality, Braxton's lines resemble less the truly atonal music of Arnold Schoenberg than an odd blend of Lee Konitz and Eric Dolphy. In addition, some of his unaccompanied work draws upon Oriental methods of tone alteration, timing, and motivic development. His large-scale work for symphony orchestra, however, clearly displays the influence of his favorite non-jazz composers, Karlheinz Stockhausen, Krzysztof Penderecki, and John Cage.[40]

Braxton organizes groups whose instrumentation is unusual, such as two unaccompanied saxophones or just saxophone and trombone. Yet when employing big band instrumentation, his orchestrations dance back and forth between parade music, snatches of jazz history, and twentieth-century concert music.[41] Braxton seems to be tireless and blessed with endless imagination, but because his music goes far beyond jazz idioms, he should not be viewed only as a jazz musician.[42]

THE WORLD SAXOPHONE QUARTET

The Black Artists Group was formed in St. Louis during 1968 along organizational lines and musical views similar to those of the AACM in Chicago. Three saxophonists from this organization became prominent in the late 1970s and early 1980s: **Oliver Lake** (b. 1942), **Julius Hemphill** (1940–1995), and **Hamiet Bluiett** (b. 1940). These men recorded in numerous combinations and performed extensively on their own during that period. Their highest critical acclaim was earned when they performed in combination with Los Angeles-born saxophonist **David Murray** (b. 1955) in a group they founded in 1976 and called the World Saxophone Quartet (WSQ). Though flute and clarinets are also used, the WSQ usually has Lake and Hemphill on alto, Murray on tenor, and Hamiet Bluiett on baritone saxophone.

The WSQ drew partly from the approaches of Ornette Coleman and Albert Ayler, but placed a greater emphasis on composition. They borrowed and extended the diverse tone colors associated with free jazz players and such earlier bands as Duke Ellington's. The group was inspired by the free-form collective approaches of Coleman but achieved a greater balance of contrasts by carefully alternating

The World Saxophone Quartet of 1989 (left to right): Hamiet Bluiett (baritone saxophone), David Murray (tenor saxophone), Julius Hemphill (alto saxophone), and Oliver Lake (alto saxophone). This group extended the work of Albert Ayler, Ornette Coleman, and Eric Dolphy into the 1980s and 1990s by making new music that combined avant-garde solos, collectively improvised, and written passages. Each of these men was also an important bandleader and composer in his own right. Each introduced new ideas that contrasted significantly with the most visible movements of the period, such as the second and third generation of jazz-rock fusion and various revivals of swing, bop, and hard bop styles.

(Photo by John Sobczak)

prewritten parts, improvised solos, and simultaneous collective improvisations. They also achieved greater clarity of sound by performing without piano, guitar, bass, or drums.

The music of the WSQ is especially distinctive because much of it is delivered in a lighthearted manner. Diversity and activity seem the key guidelines. Some passages recall classical composer Igor Stravinsky's writing for woodwinds, while others suggest Ellington's saxophone writing. Like the Art Ensemble of Chicago, the WSQ is significant for offering a unique refinement of free-form methods combined with numerous traditions of jazz and nonjazz sources.[43]

POPULAR APPEAL

The styles described in this chapter continue to be the least popular. During their earliest years, groups playing these styles were not wanted by most jazz clubs, and few record companies showed interest in recording them. The passage of almost 50 years has done little to change this. Due to low demand, most of the pivotal recordings by Don Cherry, Albert Ayler, Sun Ra, and Cecil Taylor are frequently out of print, and many never sold enough copies to absorb production costs. No album by any musician discussed in this chapter ever penetrated the list of "top 200" best-selling albums in any year. Not much modern jazz is played on the radio, but the situation is especially unfortunate for free jazz. Some major cities never heard more than a few samples of free jazz during the entire decade of the 1960s. Although musicians usually blame their fate on a lack of promotion, several other styles of modern jazz have managed to sell without much promotion. This suggests that even if the avant-garde styles had been promoted, their popularity would still have been limited. The problem is that most listeners find them unswinging, harsh, and chaotic. So, ironically, this music of great innovation has received very little exposure.

CHAPTER SUMMARY

1. Free jazz improvisation does not adhere to preset progressions of chords and sometimes also dispenses with preset melody and steady timekeeping.

2. Free jazz has wider variation in pitch and tone quality than bop, and some free jazz involves lengthy collective improvisations that are loud and frenzied, in which textures are more important than melodies.

3. Prominent free saxophonists include Ornette Coleman and Albert Ayler.

4. Free jazz pianist Cecil Taylor is known for his virtuosity and his practice of improvising dense textures and turbulence.

5. Prominent bassists in free jazz include Charlie Haden and Dave Holland.

6. Trumpeter Don Cherry was Ornette Coleman's sideman in the late 1950s and early 1960s, one of the most original improvisers to appear since bop, and one of the most-dedicated to World Music.

7. Free jazz drummers perfected approaches that depart from marching band and dance band traditions by generating an ever-changing undercurrent of activity instead of standard timekeeping patterns.

8. Charles Mingus was an innovative modern bassist and a bandleader-composer who combined composition and improvisation while creatively altering accompaniment patterns.

9. Eric Dolphy was a virtuoso on flute, alto sax, and bass clarinet who devised jarring improvisations that were totally unpredictable and wrote tunes that were as odd as those of Thelonious Monk. Though perceived as free-form by some listeners, his lines were actually rooted in chord progressions and steady tempo.

10. Sun Ra and other avant-garde players from Chicago departed from bop practices of melody, chord progressions, and swing feeling, in addition to incorporating World Music.

11. Beginning in the 1950s, pianist Sun Ra's big band methods demonstrated some of the most varied voicings since Duke Ellington's.

12. Sun Ra explored collective improvisation in big band music during the 1960s and 1970s and was one of the first jazz composer-arrangers to extensively use synthesizers and electric keyboard instruments.

13. The Association for the Advancement of Creative Musicians was a Chicago-based collective founded by Richard Abrams during the 1960s.

14. The Chicagoans stressed continuity between composition and improvisation.

15. The AACM's Art Ensemble of Chicago, which gained prominence during the 1970s, consisted of trumpeter Lester Bowie, saxophonists Roscoe Mitchell and Joseph Jarman, bassist Malachi Favors, and drummer Don Moye.

16. Multi-instrumentalist Anthony Braxton is a composer and improviser of sweeping scope who does not play in bop style and whose music draws from non-Western music, the styles of Eric Dolphy and Lee Konitz, and twentieth-century symphonic music.

17. The World Saxophone Quartet was composed of David Murray, Julius Hemphill, Oliver Lake, and Hamiet Bluiett. It demonstrated a successful integration of written passages and freely improvised parts without rhythm section accompaniment.

NOTES

1. Ornette Coleman, *Free Jazz* (Rhino/Atlantic: 75208, 1964, c1998).

2. During the 1960s, aspects of these methods were also incorporated into the styles of John Coltrane, Albert Ayler, and a few of the groups they influenced. Coltrane's name has become prominently associated with free jazz despite the relatively small representation of these kinds of approaches in his recorded output and the fact that almost none of his music is free of preset musical organization.

3. There are numerous similarities between Parker and Coleman. A few suggest the influence of Parker on Coleman; others merely show that both men drew from similar sources. Though Coleman's timbre was unique, it resembled Parker's more than it resembled that of Johnny Hodges, Benny Carter, or Lee Konitz. Coleman's playing also had the soulfulness of Parker's and the explosions of slippery notes found in some Parker improvisations. Both had a gift for melody. Both used a lot of bluesy inflections of pitch and timbre. (On his first few recordings, all for Contemporary, Coleman's inflections and their timing resemble Parker's.) Like Parker, Coleman also liked to quote pop tunes briefly. For instance, themes from "If I Loved You," "Hawaiian War Chant," "Cherokee," and "Blues in the Night" have all been interjected in his improvisations at various times. Coleman also used a few bop phrases in his improvisation and recorded Parker's tune, "Klactoveesedstene" on *Paul Bley at the Hillcrest Club* (Inner City: 1007, LP, 1958, c1976).

Although I disagree with the statement, I have heard Coleman called "just another bebop alto player." It is understandable how the occasional bop phrasing, steady tempo, and bluesy melodic figures in Coleman's playing might lead a listener to call him a bebop player. But though Coleman's improvisations had some flavor of bebop, they did not follow the bebop manners of navigating through the chord changes. What is remarkable about that view is that it coexists with a completely different response to Ornette Coleman's style: many people, after all, consider him a revolutionary figure. For more about Coleman and other avant-garde musicians of the 1960s, see John Litweiler, *Ornette Coleman: A Harmolodic Life* (Morrow, 1993); David G. Such, *Avant-Garde Jazz Musicians* (University of Iowa, 1993); Todd S. Jenkins, *Free Jazz and Free Improvisation: An Encyclopedia* (Greenwood, 2004); John Gray, *Fire Music: A Bibliography of the New Jazz, 1959–1990* (Greenwood Press, 1991); A. B. Spellman, *Four Jazz Lives* (Pantheon, 1966; Univ. of Michigan, 2003); Ekkehard Jost, *Free Jazz* (Universal Edition, 1974; Da Capo, 1981), 44–65; and Gunther Schuller, *Musings* (Oxford, 1986), 76–85.

4. A number of musicians have shown interest in Coleman's compositions. Pianist Keith Jarrett has written and improvised in the style of Coleman as well as dedicating a tune to him: "Piece for Ornette." Saxophonist Roscoe Mitchell titled one of his pieces "Ornette," and bassist Charlie Haden wrote a piece called "O. C."

Though many of Coleman's pieces are simply springboards for improvisation, some have been arranged for ensembles. His "Forms and Sounds" was scored for flute, oboe, clarinet, bassoon, and French horn; his "Saints and Soldiers" and "Space Flight" were arranged for two violins, viola, and cello (*Forms and Sounds: The Music of Ornette Coleman*, RCA Bluebird: 6561-2-RB, 1968, c1987). "Skies of America," which Coleman considers one of his best works, was scored for symphony orchestra (*Skies of America*, Columbia/Legacy: 63568, 1972, c2000).

5. To be technically accurate, it must be said that Coleman works off shifting tone centers.

6. Coleman used nine different keys in improvising on "Dee Dee" on *Ornette Coleman at the Golden Circle, Vol. 1* (Blue Note: 35518, 1965, c2002) and CCD2 Track 5.

7. Coleman, *Something Else* (Fantasy: OJC-163 [Contemporary], 1958, c1988).

8. Coleman, *Change of the Century* (Atlantic: 81341, 1959, c1992).

9. Listen to "Jayne" on Coleman, *Something Else* (Fantasy: OJC-163 [Contemporary], 1958, c1988).

10. Listen to his work on Sonny Rollins, *Our Man in Jazz* (RCA: 74321192562 [LSP 2612], 1962, c1994). See also Jost, *Free Jazz*, 133–162.

11. Don Cherry, *Eternal Now* (Antilles: 7034, LP, 1973, c1974).

12. Cecil Taylor, *Jazz Advance* (Blue Note: 84462, 1955, c1991); and *Love for Sale* (Blue Note: 94107 [UA], 1959, c1998).

13. Taylor, *Nefertiti, the Beautiful One Has Come* (Revenant: 202, 2CD set, 1962, c1997); Taylor's most widely discussed examples of this are

Unit Structures (Blue Note: 84237, 1966, c1987) and Conquistador (Blue Note: 90840, 1966, c2004). For more about Taylor, see Spellman, Four Jazz Lives; Jost, Free Jazz, 66–83; Len Lyons, The Great Jazz Pianists (Quill, 1983; Da Capo, 1989), 301–311; and Schuller, Musings, 65–75.

14. Taylor, Silent Tongues (1201 Music: 9017 [Freedom], 1974, c1975).

15. Albert Ayler, Spiritual Unity (ESP 1002, 1964).

A monumental compilation of historic archival material is available in a lavishly boxed set: Albert Ayler, Holy Ghost: Rare and Unissued Recordings (Revenant: 213, 1960–70, 10CD set, c2004). Disc 1 is exceedingly valuable for listeners who are interested in the controversies surrounding the possibility that Ayler never followed chord changes when improvising. It has Ayler playing with a conventional jazz group performing jazz standards, but not following the same key or chord changes that his accompanists are using. On Disc 1 there are also several powerful performances with his Spiritual Unity band and an extraordinary, 21-minute performance by pianist Cecil Taylor with Sunny Murray, containing two intense passages in which Ayler and Taylor improvise together. On Disc 2 there are several more tracks with Ayler's Spiritual Unity band, some with the addition of trumpeter Don Cherry, featuring impassioned improvisations. Disc 6 has a version of "Ghosts" with lyrics. The final 2 CDs are composed of long, free-ranging interviews with Ayler. The package includes a 208-page book of essays and discographies, with a biography and a list of every known public performance by Ayler. It is available from www.revenantrecords.com.

16. "Billie's Bounce" on My Name Is Albert Ayler (Black Lion: 760211, 1963, c1995).

17. Ayler's style lived on in the playing of tenor saxophonist David Murray, whose first album, Low Class Conspiracy (Adelphi: 5002, LP, 1976, c1976), demonstrated that he had learned the Ayler techniques and begun to use them masterfully. Murray further honored Ayler by composing "Flowers for Albert" (Flowers for Albert, India Navigation: 1026, 2CD set, 1976, c1997). In listening for the Ayler connection in Murray's playing, note that after his first two albums, Murray's playing began to sound less and less like Ayler's.

18. Ayler's effect on Coltrane is especially evident on John Coltrane, Meditations (Impulse!: 199, 1965, c1996) and Interstellar Space (Impulse!: 314 543 415, 1967, c2000).

19. Charles Mingus, Pithecanthropus Erectus (Atlantic: 8809, 1956, c1987).

20. Mingus, Mingus Ah Um (Columbia/Legacy: 65512, 1959, c1993).

21. The Birth of the Third Stream (Columbia/Legacy: 64929, 1956–57, c1996); also on Big Band Renaissance (Smithsonian: 108, 5CD set, 1941–89, c1995).

22. The Quintet: Jazz at Massey Hall (Fantasy: OJC-044, 1953, c1989).

23. The Complete Candid Recordings of Charles Mingus (Mosaic: MD3-111, 3CD set, 1960–61, c1989) or Charles Mingus Presents Charles Mingus (Candid: 79005, 1960, c2000).

24. Mingus Plays Piano (Impulse!: 217, 1963, c1997).

25. Mingus Moves (Collectibles: 6363 [Atlantic], 1973, c2002).

26. Charles Mingus Presents Charles Mingus (Candid) with Eric Dolphy, Ted Curson, and Dannie Richmond.

27. "Half-Mast Inhibition" and "Bemoanable Lady" on Mingus, Pre-Bird (Mercury/Verve: 538 636, 1960, c1999).

28. The album Mingus Ah Um (Columbia/Legacy) illustrates the varied accompaniment devices Mingus used. The version of "Fables of Faubus" on this album (and on JCCD3) switches accompanying style several times. It goes beyond the more subtle alterations in comping, bass lines, and drum fills which occur routinely in most modern jazz combo perfor-

mances. "Bird Calls," from the same album, shows an integration of collective improvisation with more structured approaches. It is well managed, as is his "Ysabel's Table Dance" (1957) on Mingus, Tijuana Moods (RCA Bluebird: 63840, 1957, c2001). For more, see Charles Mingus: More Than a Fakebook (Jazz Workshop; Hal Leonard, 1991); Brian Priestley, Mingus: A Critical Biography (Quartet, 1983; DaCapo, 1984); and Jost, Free Jazz, 35–43.

29. In the 1960 Mingus quartet with trumpeter Ted Curson and drummer Dannie Richmond, there was an exceptional level of empathy between Mingus and Dolphy. The two have an extended dialog on "What Love" that is filled with humor and flexible interaction. The conversation between Mingus's pizzicato bass and Dolphy's bass clarinet is so human that it almost makes you think words are being exchanged; it is very coherent and skillful. See footnote 23 above.

30. Dolphy solos on "India" and "Spiritual" on Coltrane, "Live" at the Village Vanguard: The Master Takes (Impulse!: 251, 1961, c1998). Coltrane, The Complete 1961 Village Vanguard Recordings (Impulse!: IMPD4-232, 4CD set, 1961, c1997), has better Dolphy solos from these sessions. Coltrane, Olé Coltrane (Rhino/Atlantic: 79965, 1961, c2000) features Dolphy (identified as "George Lane" on the album jacket). Before his death in 1964, Dolphy also made a number of albums as a leader, such as Out to Lunch (Blue Note: 98793, 1964, c1999), but some of his best work was documented on Mingus recordings.

31. Some of his alto saxophone playing of that period sounds like Charlie Parker and Cannonball Adderley, though his main influence was fellow Californian Sonny Criss; he was also quite familiar with Johnny Hodges, as shown on Dolphy's unaccompanied alto saxophone solo, "Tenderly," on Dolphy, Far Cry (Fantasy: OJC-400, 1961, c1989); and his work on Chico Hamilton, Gongs East (Discovery: 70831 [Warner Bros.], 1958, c1989).

32. In his long duet with arco bass on the first half of "You Don't Know What Love Is" on Last Date (Fontana: 822 226, 1964, c1964), Dolphy's flute solo is so rich in tone quality, sounding as though he savored the vibrations of each note before proceeding to the next.

33. Listen to Sunny Murray's playing on "Trance" on Cecil Taylor, Nefertiti, or on Albert Ayler, Spiritual Unity (on "Ghosts: First Variation" on JCCD3); or listen to later examples of a similar style in the drumming of Barry Altschul on "Q & A" and "Interception" on Dave Holland, Conference of the Birds (ECM: 829 373 [1027], 1972, c1987); or on "Thanatos" and "Vendana" with bassist Holland on Chick Corea, A.R.C. (ECM: 833 678 [1009], 1971, c1994).

34. Much of this Chicago activity was occurring well before the first recordings of Ornette Coleman became available. We can therefore assume that much of it originated with the Chicagoans and was not derivative. However, the second wave of Chicagoans and their St. Louis relatives, the Black Artists Group, clearly derived some inspiration from Coleman and Albert Ayler. For more, see Jost, Free Jazz, 163–199; also see the interview with Sun Ra in Lyons, The Great Jazz Pianists, 83–92. In addition, see John F. Szwed, Space Is the Place: The Lives and Times of Sun Ra (Pantheon, 1997; Da Capo, 1998); and Hartmut Geerken and Bernhard Hefele, Omniverse Sun Ra (S. J. Geerken, 1994), which includes a tapeography, bibliography, filmography, photos, and original essays; available from S. J. Geerken, Wartaweil 37, D 82211 Herrsching, Germany.

35. Sun Ra, Nubians of Plutonia [combined with Angels and Demons at Play] (Evidence: 22066, 1959, c1993).

36. Sun Song (Delmark: 411, 1956, c1990) and Super-Sonic Jazz (Evidence: 22015, 1956, c1991).

37. Astro Black (Impulse!: 9255, LP, 1972, c1973) and The Magic City (Evidence: 22069, 1965, c1993).

38. The Heliocentric Worlds of Sun Ra, Vols. 1 and 2 (ESP-DISK: 1014 & 1017, 2 CDs, 1965).

39. Art Ensemble of Chicago, *A Jackson in Your House* (Fuel 2000: 302 061 146, 1969, c2001); *Americans Swinging in Paris: The Pathe Sessions* [including *People in Sorrow*] (EMI: 539667, 1969–70, c2002); *Nice Guys* (ECM: 827 876 [1126], 1978, c1987); and *Urban Bushman* (ECM: 829 394 [1211], 2CD set, 1980, c1982).

40. Anthony Braxton, *For Four Orchestras* (Arista: 8900, 3LP set, 1978, c1978). For background, see Graham Lock, *Forces in Motion* (Quartet, 1985; Da Capo, 1988), and Ronald Radano, *New Musical Figurations: Anthony Braxton's Cultural Critique* (University of Chicago, 1993).

41. Braxton, *Creative Orchestra Music* (RCA Bluebird: 6579-2-RB [Novus], 1976, c1987).

42. Other examples of Braxton's work: *Three Compositions of New Jazz* (Delmark: 415, 1968, c1991); *For Alto* (Delmark: 420, 1968, c2000), solo saxophone; and *Five Pieces 1975* (Arista: 4054, LP, 1975, c1975).

43. *SCCJ-R* contains a version of "Steppin'" from World Saxophone Quartet, *Live in Zurich* (Black Saint: 120 077, 1981, c1984). Of their many recordings, fans often prefer *Steppin' with the World Saxophone Quartet* (Black Saint: 120027, 1978, c1979) and *Revue* (Black Saint: 120056, 1980, c1982).

Ornette Coleman's band without Coleman: Don Cherry (pocket trumpet), Charlie Haden (bass), Eddie Blackwell (drums), and Dewey Redman (tenor sax). During the mid-1970s, this ensemble went by the name of "Old and New Dreams." (Photo by Bill Smith)

MILES DAVIS

BILL EVANS, HERBIE HANCOCK, CHICK COREA, AND KEITH JARRETT

The most influential jazz pianist to emerge after Bud Powell was Bill Evans. The most widely imitated pianists after Evans were McCoy Tyner, Herbie Hancock, Chick Corea, and Keith Jarrett. All four men showed the combined influence of Powell and Evans. Each of these musicians became an important composer and bandleader in his own right. These pianists attracted large popular followings and had record sales and concert receipts that exceeded the recognition of both Powell and Evans. This chapter is devoted to the piano styles of Evans, Hancock, Corea, and Jarrett and their respective group styles.

Bill Evans, 1975
(Photo by Veryl Oakland)

Bill Evans (1929–1980)[1] played with Miles Davis for about nine months during 1958 and 1959. This exposure brought him wide attention among jazz musicians and fans. He became known particularly for his work on the important Davis album *Kind of Blue*. Shortly before his involvement with *Kind of Blue*,[2] Evans had made a trio record called *Everybody Digs Bill Evans*.[3] Its "Peace Piece" provided the basis for "Flamenco Sketches" on *Kind of Blue*.

Prior to 1959, Evans displayed considerable dexterity, and his style included elements from several sources. His long, fast, smoothly contoured eighth-note lines remind us of saxophonist Lee Konitz, one of his early favorites. Because Konitz derived his style from pianist Lennie Tristano, the Evans approach indirectly derives from Tristano's influence. Evans's piano solos also borrowed elements from bop pianist Bud Powell. Occasionally, Evans also used some bluesy figures which might be traced to pianist-composer Horace Silver, a far-reaching force during the 1950s. The manner in which Evans developed his ideas across a solo improvisation also reflects his debt to Nat Cole, who had also influenced Powell and Silver. In addition, Evans cited George Shearing as having opened his ears to the beauties of tone.

The Bill Evans style is unique in the history of jazz piano. His tone and conception are delicate without being fragile. On slow pieces, he sometimes creates a harp-like effect by sounding single tones and letting them ring, as though to savor each

JCCD2 *Track 9* vibration. (Listen for this in his solo on "Flamenco Sketches.") Though he possessed considerable dexterity, his work was never flashy. Though he was physically quite strong, he usually steered clear of an aggressively percussive manner. Evans crafted his improvisations with exacting deliberation. Often he would take a phrase, or just a kernel of its character, and then develop and extend its rhythms, melodic ideas, and accompanying harmonies. Then within the same solo he would often return to that kernel, transforming it each time. And while all this was happening, he would ponder ways of resolving the tension that was building. He would be considering rhythmic ways, melodic ways, and harmonies all at the same time, long before the optimal moment for resolving the idea.

An unheard, continuous self-editing occurred while Evans improvised. Evans spared the listener his false starts and discarded ideas. Though he had a creative imagination, Evans rarely improvised solos that merely strung together ideas at the same rate they popped into his head. The results of these deliberations could be a swinging and exhilarating experience for the listener. However, they reflected less a carefree abandon than the well-honed craftsmanship of a very serious performer working in the manner of a classical composer. "Introspective" is the adjective most frequently applied to his music.

Bill Evans refined an approach to rhythm in jazz improvisation that has been called "non-obvious pulse," "floating pulse," "phrasing across the bar line," and "de-emphasizing the beat." (For an explanation of beat, meter, and rhythm, see pages 446–448.) His work was rhythmically very involved. He frequently constructed phrases without starting or stopping them on main beats. He did not necessarily accent beats that indicate the meter of the piece—the first of every four beats, in meter of four, for example. In other words, his phrases did not necessarily accent beats in ways that jazz listeners had come to expect—the manner of march and dance rhythms. Though his melodic ideas are very rhythmic, many are not obvious in terms of the beat. Evans may, for instance, stagger a melodic figure across several measures, always accenting the upbeats, never squarely accenting a downbeat. He may float past it instead. This contrasts with the rhythmic tendencies of most jazz pianists. Evans conceived his improvisations in reference to the meter and tempo of the piece. Yet listeners often could not gain a clear indication of this unless they also heard walking bass or ride rhythms as a reference. Unlike most hard bop pianists, Evans evolved away from playing strings of bouncing eighth notes that explicitly delineated each beat and formed contours that evenly rose and fell. The architecture of his lines was more complex, and tension was resolved less often. These tendencies became far more pronounced later in his career, but they were already evident in his widely acclaimed Village Vanguard sessions of June 25, 1961. (This was the last recording he made with bassist Scott LaFaro. It came to be known as the "Village Vanguard session" because it was recorded live during an appearance at that New York nightclub, and it was originally issued on an album called *Sunday at the Village Vanguard*. It is represented by "Solar."[4])

"Solar," JCCD3 *Track 3*

Despite Evans's refinement of non-obvious pulse, he did swing. In fact, many of his admirers praised his quality of swing feeling. Evans was not swinging, however, in the perceptions of listeners who were accustomed to hearing a relaxed, easily rolling line that frequently accented the first of every four beats.

Several trends in the Bill Evans style had been summarized after *Kind of Blue* when Evans made the first of four albums with bassist Scott LaFaro.[5] Before *Kind of Blue*, he had already begun ridding himself of bop clichés, devising an original style that offered an alternative to bop-based approaches. Rarely after 1959 did he play lines with disconnected or staccato tones. He favored a legato style instead. Most of Evans's lines were composed of smoothly connected notes. His left hand gained importance and was soon sustaining chords in almost every measure instead of merely punctuating right-hand lines. The melodies he improvised were frequently chorded, note for note, by the locked-hands technique. He worked out methods for voicing his chorded lines in terms of modes and tight clusters of notes. (See pages 453–454 for more about modes.) Evans drew from the harmonies of French composers Claude Debussy and Maurice Ravel. He frequently employed chords that were composed of notes that were four scale-steps apart. These quartal harmonies had provided the foundation for the Davis album *Kind of Blue*. (See page 492 for technical explanation.)

| SCCJ: *"So What"*

With its non-obvious pulse and modal organization of harmonies, the Evans style departed from bop traditions almost as drastically as had Cecil Taylor's. However, Evans was not generally recognized as an avant-garde figure, even though some of the music he recorded at the Village Vanguard session was avant-garde, and Miles Davis had sought him for help in making his own music more advanced. We can understand why few but Davis recognized Evans's advances if we recognize that the non-obvious

Bill Evans, the most influential modern pianist after Bud Powell. Evans popularized the jazz use of harmonies based on modes and adapted the chords of French composers Maurice Ravel and Claude Debussy. He also perfected methods of "floating pulse": subtle ways of phrasing so he avoided accenting the most obvious beats. Shown here in 1960, at age 31, when he was collaborating with bassist Scott LaFaro and developing radically new approaches to jazz trio playing.

(Photo by Chuck Stewart)

Composed by Chuck Wayne; recorded for Riverside on June, 25, 1961, at the Village Vanguard in New York City by Bill Evans (piano), Scott LaFaro (bass), and Paul Motian (drums); reissued on Evans, *Sunday at the Village Vanguard* (Fantasy: OJC-140, c1987); and *The Complete Village Vanguard Recordings, 1961* (Riverside: 3RCD-4443, 3CD set 1961, c2005).

This selection is drawn from one of the most pivotal albums in post-bop. It has become a "desert island choice" for many musicians. The recording brought together three unorthodox thinkers who worked tirelessly to realize their goals of formulating jazz of depth and substance that was stylistically fresh. Though not routinely mentioned as avant-garde in the sense of Ornette Coleman's and Cecil Taylor's albums, *Sunday at the Village Vanguard* certainly was avant-garde because it dispensed with important conventions, and succeeded esthetically while doing that.

Bill Evans had several different stylistic phases in his career. The JCCD set samples two of them. His piano voicings, modal thinking, and very spare solo style affected the sound of "Flamenco Sketches," on CD2, a selection taken from the Miles Davis album *Kind of Blue* of 1959. "Solar" was selected to (a) provide the clearest example of the unique approach that Evans and bassist Scott LaFaro developed for playing together and (b) illustrate LaFaro's revolutionary solo style. Unlike traditional bass playing that provides a very predictable foundation for the soloists, LaFaro does not walk. Moreover, his rhythms contain very little repetition. LaFaro's role here can be likened to an ever-changing counter-activity. Sometimes it is not clearly subordinate to Evans but instead seems to go its own way. For example, in the first few choruses (from 0'11" to 0'56"), **concurrent with Evans, LaFaro improvises melody lines of his own, in the character of the "Solar" melody.** Some listeners have construed it as an almost continuous musical conversation with Evans. In the first four choruses, two interweaving melodies are offered instead of the usual format in which piano melody is accompanied by walking bass. Both melodies come in and out of the foreground. Though LaFaro's lines are usually somewhat subordinate to Evans's, they are denser, more varied, and closer to the foreground than bass parts had traditionally been. For instance, LaFaro only occasionally plays downbeats in the first eight measures of the second from last rendition of the theme at 8'06" to 8'12". Then at 8'17" LaFaro uses his high register and a triplet feeling to paraphrase an echo of the theme and does it again at 8'31". **LaFaro's accompaniment does not resemble the ways bassists had traditionally accompanied jazz pianists.**

This performance of "Solar" also illustrates subtle ways of phrasing that came to characterize more and more Evans solos after the 1950s. Termed **"non-obvious pulse"** or **"phrasing across the bar line,"** these approaches are particularly evident in the fifth chorus (beginning at 0'56") and the seventh chorus (beginning at 1'22"). In the fifth chorus, almost all the accents in Evans's line are on the off-beat, and all three of his phrases are staggered across several measures. They are rhythmically displaced, never starting or clearly resolving on a strong beat, for example, the moments when we usually tap our feet or click our fingers. (If you are counting "1234 1234," Evans makes it difficult for you to know where "1" is.) He achieves this again, even more thoroughly, in the thirty-sixth chorus (beginning at 7'17").

Occasionally **Evans seems to stretch figures out so they sound half-time.** For example, at the end of the thirty-fourth chorus (at 7'01"), he creates a half-time effect with a triplet feeling. The rhythms that Evans uses are so subtle in their relationship to the underlying pulse that we may have difficulty verifying the passage of beats and the beginnings of choruses if we ignore the drummer's timekeeping rhythms. Even then it is challenging on this recording because drummer Paul Motian's timekeeping style itself draws upon such a diverse collection of rhythms. In other words, Evans intentionally blurs conventional landmarks in the composition so thoroughly that **this recording represents a significant departure from a jazz tradition of rhythmic obviousness.**

Evans also achieved a significant departure from jazz tradition by moving away from harmonic obviousness when he transcended the positions in his phrases relative to the chord progression where we expect pauses. This means that he did what Ornette Coleman tried to do but without entirely abandoning chorus structure or chord progressions. This was a new kind of jazz piano style. By comparison with swing style and bop style improvisers, chorus beginnings and endings are much less obvious. Both Evans and LaFaro demonstrate such a sense of continuity in their solos here that often we are not reminded at all of where one chorus ends and another begins. It is as though Evans and LaFaro conceived their lines in units that were longer than previously customary. Paul Motian also contributes to the blurring of chorus beginnings by omitting typical drum figures (known as "fills") in the final measure of each chorus that we would expect to end on the downbeat of the next chorus. To obscure the effect of the turnarounds is a considerable achievement. **So, with Evans hardly ever indicating an obvious pulse and rarely playing**

LISTENING GUIDE *continued on next page*

chords, and with drummer Paul Motian playing displaced, fragmented patterns, we have an extremely complicated two-part invention, improvised by piano and bass, that remains unified only by the collective genius of these extraordinary musicians.

"Solar" gives us a full-length example of the solo style originated by Scott LaFaro. His energy seemed unquenchable, and the attitude conveyed by his work here is sheer impetuosity. As a melodic improviser, he is richly inventive, executing fluid, horn-like lines, chorus after chorus after chorus. (He solos for 15 choruses!) But it was primarily his speed and dexterity that astounded musicians when they first encountered this solo (at 3'33"). Incidentally, prior to LaFaro, most jazz bassists had plucked their strings with just their forefinger or used two fingers at a time to pull the string with great force. LaFaro innovated by alternating several different fingers in sequence, thereby expanding the potential for speed and fluency almost as a classical guitarist. (In the photo on page 347, he is alternating first and second fingers.) This recording is a landmark in the history of jazz bass playing.

Evans uses four different ways for playing melody in this performance: He (a) plays the melody in harmony for the first two choruses, (b) improvises his solo line voiced in octaves from the third chorus (30") to the eleventh chorus (2'13"), (c) solos with single-note-at-a-time lines from the middle of the eleventh chorus (2'18") until the sixteenth chorus (3'15"), (d) voices his solo lines in locked-hands block chording at the thirty-sixth chorus (7'17") and thirty-eighth chorus (7'41").

The composition was written by guitarist Chuck Wayne, though it has always been mistakenly credited to Miles Davis. It is 12 measures long, but it does not follow the chord progression of a typical blues. In fact, the first eight measures were inspired by the chord progression of "How High the Moon." Evans does not adhere to the melody as written. In his first theme statement he edits out the line usually contained in the third and fourth measures, the line usually contained in the seventh and eighth measures, and the line musicians usually play in the twelfth measure. He sustains chords in those positions instead.

This form is not as easy to follow as 12-bar blues and 32-bar A-A-B-A forms. But it may be especially hard to keep your place on this particular recording because (a) in creating their complex rhythmic displacements, the musicians mask chorus beginnings and endings, (b) Evans blurs the movement of chords in the tune's structure, thereby removing some of the chord progression cues that we ordinarily expect, (c) Evans goes for long stretches without comping, thereby omitting chord change cues that we would otherwise use for keeping our place, and (d) the melodic continuity in the solos by Evans and LaFaro often spills across chorus endings, making it challenging to detect the beginning of a new chorus. The solution is to follow the timings provided below.

Terms to learn from the *Demo CD* before using this Listening Guide: high-hat (Track 2), ride cymbal (Track 3), snare drum (Track 5), piano comping (Track 20), walking bass (23), embellished walking (24), horn-like pizzicato bass (27), non-repetitive bass style (28), half-time (36), left-hand comping, right hand lines (37), octave-voiced piano lines (41).

Terms to learn from Chapter 3 and Appendix B: chorus, turnaround, chord changes, walking bass, comping, ride rhythm, high-hat, ride cymbal, snare drum, octave, triplet, and eighth note (particularly the explanation of syncopation by accenting the "and's" which are also know as "up-beats").

ELAPSED TIME

0'00"	**First Chorus**

Melody Statement by Evans on Piano
Evans plays the first four measures alone in octaves and the second four measures in harmony.

0'10"	LaFaro plays the melody's last four measures with Evans, accompanied by Motian's ride cymbal, accents on snare drum, and high-hat cymbals, and then devises other counter-lines.
0'15"	**Second Chorus**

Evans Restates the Melody
Evans harmonizes his piano phrases. LaFaro echoes melody in his low register, and then contrives countermelodies. Motian plays ride rhythms on ride cymbal, closes high-hat cymbals every other beat, and accents on snare drum.

0'29"	**Third Chorus**

Evans starts his solo improvisation, voicing all his lines in octaves. (His right hand melody is doubled by his left hand, separated by the interval of an octave.) He is not comping for himself. No harmony is stated until 2'18". LaFaro paraphrases the melody.

LISTENING GUIDE *continued on next page*

0'42"	**Fourth Chorus**
	Evans and LaFaro continue to improvise counter-lines to each other, LaFaro occasionally quoting the melody.
0'55"	**Fifth Chorus**
	LaFaro moves to a less melodic and more rhythmic role. Evans phrases his own improvisational ideas in rhythmic ways that do not convey the pulse of the piece in a particularly obvious manner.
1'08"	**Sixth Chorus**
	Evans continues to voice his improvisations in octaves and not comp for himself.
1'21"	**Seventh Chorus**
	Piano solo is filled with rhythmic displacements. Evans places most phrases on off-beats, shifting entire ideas later than when we would expect them to fall, stretching the tension by not landing on a first of four beats.
1'35"	**Eighth Chorus**
1'47"	**Ninth Chorus**
1'50"	Beginning in the fourth measure of this chorus, Evans constructs about 12 measures's worth of lines from quarter-note triplet figures. LaFaro continuously varies the rhythm of his timekeeping figures.
2'00"	**Tenth Chorus**
2'12"	**Eleventh Chorus**
	LaFaro plays the same low note 11 times, letting each ring.
2'18"	After the fourth measure of this chorus, Evans stops voicing his lines in octaves and begins to play one note at a time instead. He generates solo lines with his right hand and comps lightly and infrequently with his left hand. The character of his lines is more relaxed, and Evans takes more chances now. This pattern persists until the sixteenth chorus. Bass plays resounding low notes (to 2'23").
2'25"	LaFaro plays same note five times ("pedals") for 16 beats, then another note four times for another 16 beats (to 2'31").
2'25"	**Twelfth Chorus**
2'37"	**Thirteenth Chorus**
2'50"	**Fourteenth Chorus**
	Meter of three is implied here by LaFaro instead of the tune's meter of four that Evans and Motian are in.
3'01"	Obvious piano-bass communication: As Evans increases the density of his improvisation, so does LaFaro. Bass actually rises to similar pitch range. Together, they increase the intensity of the music.
3'02"	**Fifteenth Chorus**
	LaFaro's accompaniment rhythms are extremely varied.
3'15"	**Sixteenth Chorus**
	Evans paraphrases the melody, harmonizing thicker and thicker as the chorus unfolds.
3'27"	**Seventeenth Chorus**
	Evans fades out.
3'33"	**Scott LaFaro Bass Solo**
	LaFaro begins his bass solo with an ascending scale during the sixth measure of the chorus.
3'40"	**Eighteenth Chorus**
	LaFaro hints at the original melody. Fluid, horn-like lines come from the bass in a facile manner.
3'48"	Piano's comping chords are intentionally delayed in relation to the beat.

LISTENING GUIDE *continued on next page*

3'52"   **Nineteenth Chorus**

Evans stops playing piano until the thirty-second chorus. LaFaro's lines are packed with fresh ideas, composed almost entirely of eighth notes.

4'04"   **Twentieth Chorus**

LaFaro is emphatically reiterating two-note figures. Then he comes out of that motive with scale-like lines that spill seamlessly into the next chorus.

4'18"   **Twenty-First Chorus**

LaFaro's improvisation is composed of scale-like lines.

4'29"   **Twenty-Second Chorus**

LaFaro designs sporadically connected lines of almost continuous eighth notes.

4'41"   **Twenty-Third Chorus**

LaFaro's lines reach into high register then descend to low register and return again to high register.

4'52"   **Twenty-Fourth Chorus**

LaFaro alludes to the original melody.

5'04"   **Twenty-Fifth Chorus**

It temporarily sounds like LaFaro is ending his solo, but then he gets a second wind and forges ahead for six more choruses.

5'17"   **Twenty-Sixth Chorus**

5'29"   **Twenty-Seventh Chorus**

LaFaro's solo is constructed of almost continuous eighth notes.

5'42"   **Twenty-Eighth Chorus**

5'46"   LaFaro plays a five-note pattern five times that runs against the grain of the meter.

5'54"   **Twenty-Ninth Chorus**

6'05"   **Thirtieth Chorus**

6'17"   **Thirty-First Chorus**

6'30"   **Thirty-Second Chorus**

Evans returns with improvisation voiced in octaves.

6'43"   **DRUMS TRADING CHORUSES WITH PIANO**

Thirty-Third Chorus: Paul Motian Drum Solo

Paul Motian's drum solo for entire chorus. Bass continues to play.

6'54"   **Thirty-Fourth Chorus**

Evans improvises a chorus voiced in octaves.

7'01"   Evans is ending his chorus with half-note triplet displacements.

7'05"   **Thirty-Fifth Chorus**

Paul Motian's drum solo for entire chorus. For the first eight measures, LaFaro paraphrases the melody at same time.

7'17"   **Thirty-Sixth Chorus**

Evans improvises entire chorus in locked-hands block chording, sustaining each chord after using starting points that are all staggered in relation to the beat.

7'30"   **Thirty-Seventh Chorus**

Drum solo for entire chorus. LaFaro also plays during the first eight bars.

7'41"   **Thirty-Eighth Chorus**

Evans improvises entire chorus in locked-hands block chording, using much rhythmic displacement.

7'53"   **Thirty-Ninth Chorus**

Drum solo for entire chorus. Motian uses much rhythmic displacement.

LISTENING GUIDE *continued on next page*

8'05"   **Fortieth Chorus: Return to Melody**

Evans restates the melody.

Evans plays the melody harmonized and changes its rhythms at the end.

8'17"   **Forty-First Chorus: Melody Repeats**

Evans restates the melody.

Evans toys with the rhythms of harmonized melody. LaFaro echoes it in high register, playing triplets.

8'30"   **Vamp for Ending** formed over repeating sequence of two chords

Motian is crafting varied rhythms on closed high-hat, while Evans is playing harmonized line in a rocking motion composed of quarter-note triplets implying a meter of three.

8'34"   LaFaro is repeating a seven-note figure in a meter of four against the triple meter implied by Evans.

8'36"   Evans is gently sounding very high-pitched piano keys, chosen higher and higher, letting them ring, as though plucking harp strings.

8'44"   Ending Vamp to fade-out with unaccompanied bass repeating his seven-note figure.

pulse and the modal organization of harmonies were subtle, not particularly jarring differences from the ways that most jazz had sounded before Evans. We should also keep in mind that Evans mostly played tunes that listeners recognized. For instance, he often chose pretty melodies, though they were chosen partly because they provided interesting chord progressions for inspiring improvisations. His best-known composition, "Waltz for Debby," exemplifies this aspect of his taste.[6] Moreover, Evans liked waltzes, an unusual preference for a jazz musician. Among the waltzes to which he gave his tender treatment were "Someday My Prince Will Come," "Alice in Wonderland," "Tenderly," "Skating in Central Park," and "I'm All Smiles."

Rhythm Section Innovations

During 1961, **Scott LaFaro** (1936–1961) demonstrated advances that were as historically significant as those of Jimmy Blanton two decades earlier. **LaFaro demonstrated that the bass can contribute ensemble interplay that provides a feeling of grace and freedom for the underpinnings of a group sound, and he devised a fresh conception for improvising bass solos.** LaFaro is also influential for having pioneered using more than just one or two fingers to pluck the bass strings. Previously, bassists had primarily employed only one or two fingers instead of borrowing from the technique of classical guitarists as LaFaro did. LaFaro's new technique lent added speed and allowed greater intricacy and continuity in his lines. (See photo on page 347.)

"Solar," JCCD3 Track 3

The idea of pianists and bassists engaging in musical conversation had been explored by Duke Ellington and Jimmy Blanton in 1940.[7] Evans and LaFaro refined this idea, and it was most dramatically apparent in their last recording together. LaFaro sometimes walked and sometimes soloed. But more often he vigorously supplied nonrepetitive figures that pitted an extra counteractivity against the sounds of piano and drums. While Evans was playing a written melody or improvising a fresh line, LaFaro contributed a great diversity of musical ideas. He would throw in melodic figures of his own. He would mimic or answer Evans. Sometimes he would underscore the figures Evans and Motian played. In addition, LaFaro often fed ideas to Evans. **LaFaro was not merely a timekeeper capable of impressive solos. He was a melodic player as important to the Evans trio as a saxophonist or trumpeter was to the standard jazz quintet.** LaFaro set the pace for a whole school of modern jazz bassists who possessed spectacular instrumental facility like his. (Listen to Gary Peacock in Albert Ayler's "Ghosts: First Variation," *JCCD3* Track 2.) And like LaFaro, they interacted with pianists and drummers in imaginative and highly active manners.[8]

It was partly the Evans piano style that made possible LaFaro's contributions to these new concepts of jazz trio playing. One crucial aspect was its leanness. There are more limitations in a Bud Powell-style trio because the pianist fills up most of the spaces with long lines of his own. Rhythmic interaction between bassist and pianist is also restricted because the bassist must focus on explicitly stating the beats and has little chance to do much else. Evans, by contrast to Powell, did not require the bassist to explicitly state each beat. The way Evans voiced chords provided another freedom for the bassist. The notes that Evans selected for his chords allowed bassists more latitude because their own notes were less likely to duplicate or clash. Incidentally, the ways Evans voiced chords for and reharmonized popular songs became models for the playing of those songs by many other musicians. **Evans provided the perfect context for the blossoming of LaFaro's new approach to bass improvisation because he left room for the bass in the forefront of the combo sound and because Evans encouraged LaFaro to capitalize on the opportunity by taking chances and trying all sorts of nontraditional techniques.**[9] This was also the manner in which Evans collaborated with LaFaro's most gifted successors, Eddie Gomez and Marc Johnson. This style allowed them more room for creativity than they experienced with other bandleaders.[10]

Drummer **Paul Motian** (b. 1931) contributed an approach of great imagination and discretion to the Evans trio recordings of 1961. He decorated the combo sound and played accents which complemented the rhythms of LaFaro and Evans. Motian masterfully used wire brushes to obtain light, crisp sounds from his snare drum and cymbals. (For demonstration of typical techniques, listen to the *Demo CD*.) His highly original drum style employed contrasting sound textures and tone colors as elements of musical interest in themselves. In addition, his pioneering use of rhythmic displacement allowed him to interact more sensitively and inventively than most previous jazz drummers had done. His style of interactive coloring in the intimate trio context became a model for drummers playing in similar settings, and it contributed to the emancipation of the rhythm section. Incidentally, Motian furthered these innovations when he played with the Keith Jarrett quartet during the 1970s. On selected pieces with this latter group, he nearly eliminated repetitive timekeeping patterns from his playing and was somehow able to *sound* free of meter while still playing within it.

The Bill Evans trio recordings of 1961 involve a great deal more than piano accompanied by walking bass and timekeeping drums and cymbals. Instead, they are composed of three continuously shifting parts which sway together. The tempo is usually steady, but it is not always made obvious by loud and clear statement of every beat. Some listeners perceive this music as Evans, LaFaro, and Motian carrying on three-way musical conversations in tempo.[11] Their musical words and phrases are both long and short, fluid and abrupt; they are not necessarily strings of eighth notes organized in the bobbing, bouncing fashion that typifies bop, nor the long, smoothly contoured eighth-note lines that typify Lennie Tristano and Lee Konitz. In other words, the group offered considerable melodic variety and considerable rhythmic variety. Swing feeling is merely one of several different rhythmic possibilities they explored.

Scott LaFaro, the brilliant bassist who played with Bill Evans from 1959 to 1961. He set the pace for an entire generation of bassists who showed spectacular instrumental facility and mastered melodic-interactive approaches to accompaniment style. Shown here in 1960 at age 24.

(Photo by Jim Marshall)

| *Demo CD Track 28*

The most historically significant contributions of the Evans-LaFaro-Motian trio recordings of 1961 were to loosen the common practices of the bop-style rhythm section which had become standard during the 1940s and 1950s—walking bass, drummer playing ride rhythms and snapping shut high-hat cymbals on the second and fourth beats, pianist playing long strings of eighth notes. Though they occasionally played in conventional bop style, especially before the June 1961 sessions, their impact was to help emancipate the piano, bass, and drum roles.[12] The calm thoughtfulness, subtlety, and delicate interaction among Evans, LaFaro, and Motian provided an alternative to the more straight-ahead style of the Oscar Peterson trios, or the gospel-like orientation of other groups led during the same period by Ramsey Lewis, Les McCann, and Gene Harris (of the Three Sounds).

HERBIE HANCOCK

Herbie Hancock (b. 1940) played with Miles Davis from 1963 to 1969 and became the most sought-after band pianist of the 1960s. Many musicians feel that Hancock's freshest work is the playing he did with Davis. (See pages 273–283 for more.) Hancock comped in a brisk manner and used a gentle, even touch. Somehow he managed to sound light and airy, yet muscular and firm at the same time. Hancock created consistently stimulating, swinging, and polished piano improvisations. His playing nearly always has a meticulous and finished quality. His execution is firm and swinging without being violent or insistent. Both his solo work and his accompanying convey politeness and sensitivity. Hancock has shown broad scope and versatility; his style is compatible with several different streams of modern jazz. He has contributed immeasurably to hundreds of records—not only those of the Miles Davis quintet. He was so impressive during the 1960s that many excellent pianists drew from his style in the process of devising their own approaches: Kenny Kirkland, George Cables, Larry Willis, Warren Bernhardt, Jim McNeely, Marc Cohen (Copland), Joey Calderazzo, Billy Childs,

Herbie Hancock, the pianist and composer who made significant impacts in three different phases of modern jazz: hard bop, the mid-1960s Miles Davis Quintet, and the jazz-rock/jazz-funk genres of the 1970s and 1980s. Hancock was the most in-demand accompanist among modern jazz musicians of the 1960s, and then he became the main inspiration for hundreds of young pianists during the 1970s because of his top selling *Head Hunters* and *Thrust* albums. Shown here in 1983 at age 43.

(Photo by Veryl Oakland)

Kevin Hayes, Geri Allen, Marcus Roberts, Danilo Perez, Gonzalo Rubalcaba, Uri Caine, and Fred Hersh. Even Chick Corea showed Hancock's influence.

Hancock absorbed several influences while he was developing his style during the late 1950s and early 1960s. Some of his playing has the funky, bluesy figures and the rhythmic bounce that typified Horace Silver and Wynton Kelly. He was also inspired by the chord voicings and movement of harmonies perfected in the music of Clare Fischer, a prominent pianist-composer-arranger. But Bill Evans was Hancock's most significant source. The Evans use of harp-like, ringing tones surrounded by silence surfaced in Hancock's playing, as did Evans's chord voicings and mode-based thinking. Other similarities to Evans include Hancock's smooth legato lines and locked-hands style. Like Evans, he also frequently improvised passages in which accents went against the meter, and he let his ideas float free of reference to the underlying beat. In such excursions, Hancock drew from the ideas of twentieth-century classical composers Maurice Ravel, Claude Debussy, and Paul Hindemith.[13] But he did not merely imitate the music of his models. There was a tremendous sense of flexibility and openness in his improvising, resulting in a great amount of freedom and variety in his music. He extended the methods of his models and added so many original ideas that his style is instantly recognizable. (Listen to and compare the Evans work on "Solar," JCCD3 Track 3, with the Hancock work on "Masqualero," JCCD2 Track 10.)

One of Hancock's greatest contributions was to help free the pianist from the accompanying patterns that had become commonplace for hard bop pianists. In the Miles Davis quintet, where he had an almost magical rapport with his equally daring companions, Hancock mixed the impressionistic and mode-based harmonic approaches of Claude Debussy and Maurice Ravel with the polyrhythmic approaches to accompaniment devised by drummer Tony Williams. For example, his work in the *Sorcerer* album is sometimes indistinguishable from modern classical music, sprinkled with melodic fragments and suspensions. (Examples of this are at 6'11" to 7'56" in "Masqualero.") He could give the listener the impression of movement even when chords were not actually moving—at least as they might move in the 12-bar blues and the popular songs of earlier eras, in which chords were treated as though their "function" were to "resolve" to another chord.

Hancock fulfilled the trends that were already occurring in the Davis group when he joined—basing improvisations on modes instead of chord changes, using chords more for their sound quality (musicians call it a chord's "color") than for their capacity to increase and decrease tension when they change. In these new contexts, there were long passages in which chords did not change, yet the amount of activity Hancock generated made up for the absence of "functional" chord changes. In the Davis quintet, Hancock coordinated with Tony Williams and bassist Ron Carter to pinpoint a mood and go with it rather than be a slave to a progression of chords. His rapport with Carter and Williams was so remarkable that he could also change a mood abruptly and then instantaneously develop rhythms and harmonies to carry it. He also allowed his improvised melodies to dictate the harmonies, rather than the reverse, which had been the standard. This marked a significant freedom associated with the groundbreaking Hancock-Carter-Williams rhythm section. All this and more can be heard in "Masqualero."[14]

Another measure of Hancock's creativity is his productivity and originality as a composer and arranger. By the early 1970s, he had written every tune on eight of his own albums, and he had written or co-authored many tunes on seven more. His "Dolphin Dance" is one of the most revered of all modern jazz compositions. Musicians are unanimous in their praise of the clever progression of chords and pedal points that are intertwined with its delightful melody. Hancock's "Maiden Voyage" (JCCD2 Track 8) became a staple for young musicians of the 1960s and 1970s, especially because of its modal construction. (Listen to the 1964 original recording, and see page 495 for a technical analysis.) His funky, bluesy piece "Watermelon Man" became very popular, especially in Mongo Santamaria's version during the mid-1960s. The big bands of Woody Herman, Si Zentner, and Maynard Ferguson all played their own arrangements. It was performed by almost every wedding band in America whenever a funk piece was requested. By the 1980s, Hancock had captured a slice of the dance music market with numerous albums of funk music.

To survey the first 15 years of Hancock's compositional productivity on records, it may help to group his output by idiom: (1) the lush, classical music style of "Suite Revenge" on *Death Wish*,[15] background music for the Charles Bronson movie, (2) the rock-influenced *Fat Albert Rotunda*,[16] (3) the funky, hard bop approach of *Taking Off*,[17] (4) Gil Evans-like work on *The Prisoner*, (5) writing that recalls music of Sun Ra on *Sextant*[18] and *Crossings*,[19] (6) the style of the 1960s Miles Davis Quintet on *Maiden Voyage*[20] and *Empyrean Isles*,[21] and (7) the Sly Stone-influenced style of *Head Hunters*[22] and *Thrust*.[23]

Hancock did much of his creative writing after he left Miles Davis and began leading his own groups.[24] The music of Hancock's first post-Davis group capitalized on some of the advances made in the Davis groups of the 1960s. For *The Prisoner*, Hancock wrote legato passages for trumpet, trombone, and tenor saxophone, employing sustained tones which had few eighth-note figures or jumpy syncopations. In accompanying the horns, Hancock, his bassist, and drummer generated considerable activity in the manner that he had done with Carter and Williams in the Miles Davis quintet.

Hancock's second post-Davis band recorded the albums *Mwandishi*, *Sextant*, and *Crossings*. For these works, Hancock developed concepts that had been apparent on Davis albums of the late-1960s: *Nefertiti*, *In a Silent Way*, and *Bitches Brew*. There was extensive use of synthesizers and exotic percussion effects. In place of the busy, lightning-quick phrases of bop, Hancock frequently substituted legato lines of sustained tones that conveyed a languorous feeling. The emphasis was more on developing moods than conventional jazz swing feeling, complicated chord progressions, or intricate solo lines. In place of the standard tone colors of sax, trumpet, piano, bass, and conventional drum set, each of Hancock's seven group members was responsible for a larger assortment of sounds. His trumpeter doubled on fluegelhorn and percussion. His trombonist played tenor trombone, baritone trombone, and bass trombone. His saxophonist played alto flute, soprano saxophone, piccolo, bass clarinet, and percussion. Hancock often played electric piano, with echo and fuzz effects to alter its tone. Also, in addition to bass and drums, Hancock carried one musician who played nothing but synthesizer. Such a practice was unusual for the early 1970s, though it became common in the 1980s. Partly because he used synthesizer and it had been associated with science fiction films, Hancock's style on these albums was often referred to as "space music."

Despite the innovations and the high-level musicianship in Hancock's first two post-Davis bands, there was not enough demand for their music to pay its expenses. Partly for this reason and partly out of a stated desire to reach larger audiences, Hancock embarked on a string of styles that were less jazz-like and more in the genre that young audiences of the period wanted for dance and party music. For more than 20 years after he was forced to disband his *Mwandishi/Crossings/Sextant* band, Hancock enjoyed immense popular acclaim for styles that he devised, in part, from models within a popular black genre known as *funk music*. His first big hit came when he imitated the style of Sly Stone by creating the *Head Hunters* album, which sold over a million copies. (Listen to the original "Chameleon," JCCD3 Track 7, from that album.) Then, with the success of its follow-up *Thrust*, and many albums of discotheque-type dance music, Hancock was assured of selling about 200,000 copies of each new album, even when most jazz albums rarely sold more than 15,000 copies. The music had less and less jazz improvisation in it and more and more dance rhythms that were highly syncopated and repetitive. Melodies were simple and heavily rhythmic. Though much of the public routinely places it in the jazz category, Hancock himself has said that he does not consider this music to be jazz. As of this writing, his widest recognition has come from a 1983 work called "Rockit." The recording is a light-hearted construction of novel sound effects that are packaged with an engaging funk rhythm, all tightly arranged with the same sense of balance and completeness we have come to expect from Hancock. It appeared in *Future Shock*, an album selling over a million copies, which stayed on the popularity charts for more than a year.[25] As a single, "Rockit" remained in the popularity charts for nine weeks, and as a video it was one of the 15 most popular of the year.

Funk music is not all that Hancock pursued after his innovative septet disbanded. Frequently he has regrouped the original rhythm section from the 1960s Miles Davis group to record and tour with other musicians who model their playing after the Davis quintet—Wynton and Branford Marsalis, for example. Though Hancock is no longer breaking ground in that context, these bands have consistently been of the highest quality, and they have generated considerable excitement. In summary, decades after first impressing the jazz world with his own original playing and composing, Herbie Hancock has continued to make that original style available. Furthermore, he has also expanded the breadth of his activities by adding a repertory that pleases the larger pop music audience.

CHICK COREA

Chick Corea (b. 1941) followed Herbie Hancock as pianist in the 1968 Miles Davis quintet. He performed with Davis from the fall of 1968 to the summer of 1970. Corea soon joined the ranks of Hancock, Bill Evans, and McCoy Tyner as the most prominent and most imitated pianist in jazz.[26] His style originated with aspects from the jazz piano approaches of Bud Powell, Horace Silver, Bill Evans, and McCoy Tyner and the classical pieces of twentieth-century composers Paul Hindemith and Bela Bartók.[27] Like Tyner, Corea voiced chords in fourths—musicians call it *quartal harmony*—and devised lines from five-note scales—musicians call them *pentatonics*. He went beyond Tyner, however, by using other advanced voicings in addition to fourths.[28] Corea may also have absorbed ideas for using fourths from Horace Silver.[29] These voicings proved especially effective for the electric piano, an instrument that was becoming popular when Corea's career was taking off. The overtones produced by the instrument make chords voiced in the manner of bop pianists sound muddy, whereas the open quality achieved by voicing in fourths is less easily muddied by the electric instrument.

Latin American music also inspired Corea's style. Early in his career, Corea had played in several bands that featured Latin American music.[30] Even in non-Latin jazz contexts, Corea's playing bears the double-time feeling of Latin American music. He plays his notes in a manner that is very even, with each one markedly emphasized. (For explanations of double-time and staccato, listen to *Demo CD* Tracks 35 and 45.) Corea's crisp, percussive touch enhances the Latin feeling. This is also consistent with his bright, very spirited style of comping.

In 1968, Corea summarized his vocabulary of melodic, rhythmic, and harmonic strategies in *Now He Sings, Now He Sobs*, an album of original compositions and improvisations with bassist Miroslav Vitous and drummer Roy Haynes. (This album is represented by "Steps," *JCCD3* Track 4.) This album inspired hundreds of pianists, and it became a staple in the record collections of modern jazz musicians.[31] In 1981, the trio regrouped and made two more albums together.[32]

On and off between 1969 and 1972, Corea led a trio with bassist Dave Holland and drummer Barry Altschul. Free-form improvisation was featured on two of their albums, *The Song of Singing* and *A.R.C.* In some

Chick Corea, pianist-composer-bandleader. Shown here in the 1970s playing electric keyboard and wearing shirt bearing his first fusion band's name: Return to Forever.

(Photo by Warren Browne)

Composed by Chick Corea; recorded for Solid State in March, 1968, by Chick Corea (piano), Miroslav Vitous (bass), and Roy Haynes (drums); reissued on Corea, *Now He Sings, Now He Sobs* (Blue Note: 38265, 1968, c2002).

This selection is taken from the most revered Chick Corea album, *Now He Sings, Now He Sobs*. The music represents the earliest summary of Corea's compositional and improvisational vocabulary, and it offers some of the best playing on record for drummer Roy Haynes. This album is as historically significant to Corea followers as *Sunday at the Village Vanguard* is to fans of Bill Evans.

When this recording was made, drummer **Roy Haynes** (b. 1926) had already been a favorite of jazz musicians since the 1940s. Though neglected by jazz journalists and historians, he is ranked by musicians as a peer of Max Roach and "Philly Joe" Jones. He preceded Tony Williams by decades in several of the ways he emancipated the drummer from the role of mere timekeeper. Some feel that he outshines Roach and Jones and is unsurpassed as the most creative and tasteful of modern drummers. Many would make Haynes their first choice as accompanist. *Now He Sings, Now He Sobs* contains possibly his best and most well-recorded work on record, though few listeners knew he was on it because the manufacturer failed to list personnel on the album jacket. At the time the album was recorded, bassist **Miroslav Vitous** (b. 1947) was just becoming known among musicians and had yet to attain the stature he later gained as cofounder of Weather Report, the pioneering jazz-rock fusion group. Vitous possesses phenomenal technique and a fertile imagination. (Listen to "Surucucu," *JCCD3* Track 6, for examples of Vitous performing in a freer role and using arco technique.)

Now He Sings, Now He Sobs is pivotal not just because the music is so well played and swinging, but also because its style is not really bop or hard bop. The manner of choosing notes for the lines is fresh, and so is the manner of relating the lines to the chord voicings. They are not necessarily all bop-derived.[33] By comparison with Bud Powell, Corea places his left-hand jabs in a higher pitch range, constructs them out of different intervals, and does not phrase his right-hand lines in the legato manner of a jazz saxophonist. Instead, Corea plays as though every note has a little point on it. The rhythms in the compositions and the improvised lines differ considerably from bop, too. They do not bear the same patterns of accents that typify bop style. Some of this playing also has the ring of classical music, especially that of Bartók and Hindemith. Though classical music does not swing, some of its compositional strategies and flavor were embraced by Corea. The sparkling touch of Corea and the bright tone quality he extracts from the piano also remind us of classical music. Corea's higher pitch range and staccato tendencies seem to make the music dance with a snap and lightness that are not often conveyed by bop piano styles. Despite these differences, however, the music has a few bop characteristics. Most of the music keeps a steady tempo and follows chord progressions. The bassist walks, and the drummer plays ride rhythms. The pianist plays long strings of eighth notes with his right hand and syncopated jabs of comping with his left hand. Moreover, most of the music swings with an easy rise and fall of tensions.

The *JCCD3* version of "Steps" includes the introduction, two renditions of the theme in an up-tempo, 12-bar blues form, 22 choruses of piano improvisation, two more renditions of the theme, and a coda. On the original album version, a drum solo smoothly evolves from the coda and introduces a new piece, "What Was." The fade-out on the *JCCD* version does not exclude any part of the trio performance or the form of the "Steps" composition. It merely stops before the drum solo and "What Was."

ELAPSED TIME

0'00" **Introduction**

Corea's notes here, though fast and spirited, are relatively free of steady tempo, and the ideas roam loosely through the waves of sound that comprise this section. Initially the introduction may seem confusing. However, after you have listened to the entire piece several times, you may begin to recognize fragments of ideas in the introduction that recur in Corea's solo choruses. The bass is silent, but Roy Haynes accompanies the piano with light, clicking sounds made by striking the rims and shells of his drums with his sticks, and he makes faint "ching" sounds by operating his high-hat with its foot pedal.

0'43" Tempo begins

LISTENING GUIDE *continued on next page*

0'47"   **First Statement of Theme**

The beginning of the 12-bar form occurs when piano and bass sound an interval of two low-pitched notes (a fifth apart) three times in succession (bum . . . . . . bum . . bummmmmmmm . .). Then the mid-register melody line begins. The piano rhythms are underscored by very light cymbal and snare drum sounds.

If you try to use the melody to help you identify the piece's 12-bar blues form, you may become confused because the melody line does not begin until the third measure of the form.

0'57"   **Second Statement of Theme**

1'06"   **First Solo Chorus**

You should have less difficulty determining the beginning of the solo improvisation than the beginning of the theme. The solo starts on the first beat of the first measure of the form, when walking bass and ride rhythms commence. To keep your place by counting measures, remember that the tempo is fast. Then synchronize your counting with the bass: "1234 2234 3234 . . . 11 234 12 234."

Corea comps for himself by playing three-note chords in jabbing, often syncopated ways with his left hand. Frequently he lets his right hand rest, and all we hear is the sound made by his left hand.

1'15"   **Second Solo Chorus**

In this and most subsequent choruses, Corea's lines are generally played in the piano's upper register.

1'25"   **Third Solo Chorus**

Notice how Haynes continuously varies the timekeeping rhythm that he plays on the ride cymbal.

2'49"   **Twelfth Chorus**

Corea plays the first six measures with both hands locked together in block chord fashion. The seventh measure is played by his left hand alone, then he returns to his pattern of staccato three-note chords (usually voiced in fourths) in the left hand and long strings of eighth notes in the right hand.

3'46"   **Eighteenth Chorus**

Corea plays long strings of eighth notes near the center of the piano keyboard.

3'56"   **Nineteenth Chorus**

Corea does not play any eighth notes in this chorus, but instead plays syncopated $1\frac{1}{2}$- and 2-beat chords for the first six measures. Then he plays block chords directly on the beat for the remainder of the chorus. This departure from the relatively steady pattern of previous choruses inspires Roy Haynes to respond with a considerable amount of crackling sounds on the drums.

4'13"   **Twenty-First Chorus**

The last four measures are filled with chords played by both hands locked together.

4'24"   **Twenty-Second Solo Chorus**

The first six measures are filled with chords played by both hands locked together. The remaining measures are filled with low-pitched chords providing a transition to the return of the theme.

4'36"   **Theme Statement**

4'43"   **Theme Statement**

4'55"   **Coda**

settings, they were joined by saxophonist Anthony Braxton, with whom their group name became Circle.[34] This period of Corea's output reflects the influence of pianist Paul Bley, bassist Gary Peacock, and saxophonists John Coltrane, Albert Ayler, and Ornette Coleman. The music also drew from twentieth-century composers John Cage and Karlheinz Stockhausen. Corea's use of the free-form approach resulted not only in the turbulent music found on A.R.C. and *The Song of Singing,* but also in the serene pieces he freely improvised in his *Piano Improvisations Vols. I and II.*[35]

After Circle disbanded, Corea formed a new group with himself on Fender Rhodes electric piano (an instrument that produces a light, vibraphone-like tone), bassist Stanley Clarke, Airto Moreira—a Brazilian drummer who had played with Miles Davis together with Corea—and singer Flora Purim, Airto's wife. Airto had played auxiliary percussion with Davis, but he used a conventional drum set with Corea. The group's sound was light and happy, full of Latin American rhythms and Spanish themes. (Listen to "Captain Marvel" on CCD2 Track 8.) The name of the group and its first album was *Return to Forever.* Their second album was titled *Light as a Feather.*[36] These two albums became favorites among musicians, especially young players who were active during the 1970s. With this band, two of Corea's most popular tunes became known: "Spain" and "La Fiesta." Within a few years, the influence of this sound was evident in a number of jazz-rock fusion bands.

The group Chick Corea carried through the middle 1970s was strongly influenced by rock and funk music, often displaying the insistent, machine-like sound of hard rock. Corea employed rock-influenced electric guitarists—first Bill Connors, then Al Dimeola. Corea retained bassist Stanley Clarke, now playing electric bass guitar more than acoustic bass. Drummer Lenny White rounded out the group. White's style was a very full, active approach which combined aspects of the Tony Williams techniques with those of modern rock drummers, funk drummers, and Latin American percussion ensembles. Some of the group's material was orchestral, very involved, and highly imaginative. Some of it moved between rock, classical, and jazz idioms. The records made during this period sold well, and independent recording careers soon resulted for Clarke and Dimeola.[37] White and Dimeola left Corea during the summer of 1976, though the Return to Forever group name was retained for a number of Corea's subsequent projects. Thereafter, Corea appeared in a wide assortment of contexts. Al Dimeola, Stanley Clarke, and Lenny White went on to lead bands of their own, occasionally regrouping with Corea to tour and record.

Corea was a prominent composer during the 1960s and 1970s. His "Windows" and "Crystal Silence" became jazz standards. Al Jarreau's vocal rendition of Corea's "Spain" was a hit record. Like much of Horace Silver's work, many of Corea's compositions are more than merely a melody whose accompaniment chord progression provides material for solo improvisations. Some pieces have different sections, each with a distinctive rhythmic and tonal flavor. For example, "Windows," "Spain," and "Litha" are melodies and arrangements all rolled into a single package.[38] Also like Silver, Corea writes pieces that make good use of preset bass lines in the accompaniment, particularly those with a Latin American flavor.[39] In addition, many Corea compositions feature bass doubling the melody of the piano and horn parts, no matter how rapid and intricate the line. This arranging practice took advantage of the high-level instrumental proficiency of jazz bassists during the 1970s and 1980s.[40] It was widely imitated in jazz-rock groups of the 1980s and 1990s.

Corea's acoustic jazz of the 1960s and 1970s did not gain a particularly wide audience. For instance, albums such as *Now He Sings, Now He Sobs, A.R.C.,* and *The Song of Singing* were frequently out of print for years at a time. On the other hand, his jazz-rock fusion music acquired a wide following, he became known for his use of synthesizers, and the Chick Corea Elektric Band of the 1980s managed to be among the few jazz groups known to a large audience.

KEITH JARRETT

After Corea left Miles Davis in 1970, pianist **Keith Jarrett** (b. 1945) took his place and performed with Davis until the winter of 1971. Like a few other Davis sidemen, Jarrett had also played with Art Blakey. But Jarrett's widest pre-Davis exposure had come as a member of saxophonist Charles Lloyd's quartet, beginning in 1966. In recordings with Lloyd, Jarrett had proven himself a powerful improviser whose talents and stature paralleled Herbie Hancock and Chick Corea. Jarrett had as much or more command of the piano as they, but more important, he had his own distinctive approach: He was a piano original. Jarrett's playing demonstrated imagination of enormous scope, and he seemed able to draw from any musical idiom and incorporate its elements in a convincing way. In Jarrett's playing were bits of Bill Evans,[41] twentieth-century classical composers Bela Bartók, Alban Berg, and Maurice Ravel, American gospel music,[42] country music, and Ornette Coleman. Innovative modern pianist Paul Bley had the most influence on him.

Keith Jarrett, the innovative pianist who extended the Bill Evans trio style by fusing it with music of Ornette Coleman, Paul Bley, John Coates, and his own original ideas. Jarrett also devised an original approach to unaccompanied soloing that made him one of the most sought-after concert pianists of the 1970s and 80s. Shown here in 2000 at age 55.

(Photo by Patrick Hinely)

Often Jarrett's lines project a singing quality. (Sometimes you can hear Jarrett humming the lines as he plays.) These lines have the sweep of an inspired human voice or a surging saxophone improvisation. In fact, Jarrett plays soprano saxophone at some of his concerts, and he is quite accomplished on the instrument. The long, legato sax lines he creates are mirrored by his long, legato, sax-like piano lines.

Jarrett is also a prolific and original composer. He has written mounds of material for his own albums and contributed significantly to the records of Charles Lloyd and Norwegian saxophonist Jan Garbarek. Some of his albums contain extended performances with little or no improvisation; in these pieces, the line between classical music and jazz is blurred.[43]

Keith Jarrett devised a distinctive quartet sound from 1971 to 1976 with tenor saxophonist Dewey Redman, bassist Charlie Haden (both from Ornette Coleman's band), and drummer Paul Motian, formerly of the Bill Evans trio. Jarrett's group arranged a unique combination of:

1. elements from approaches of bands led by Paul Bley and Ornette Coleman[44]
2. elements of the Bill Evans style[45]
3. extension and development of rubato style
4. long, vamp-based improvisations which were funky in Jarrett's unique way
5. World Music approaches (Redman playing musette, band members using several unusual instruments such as steel drums, finger cymbals, etc.)
6. unique, non-bop timekeeping techniques used by Motian and Haden
7. group improvisations which use rubato

Beginning in the 1970s, Jarrett made many albums and concert appearances as an unaccompanied solo pianist. It is notable that Jarrett was one of the few pianists of that time who did not regularly play electric piano. It is also noteworthy that Jarrett's improvisations were more spontaneous than those of most jazz pianists because he rarely used melodies or chord progressions that were set beforehand. His playing could be funky, earthy, and gospelish,[46] or pretty and orchestrally lush.[47] Sometimes he clearly stated a tempo. Other times he implied only a momentum. Jarrett is one of the few pianists to improvise free jazz and to show the influence of Ornette Coleman's melodic style.[48] Like Coleman, he avoids staccato phrasing, works from shifting pedal points, has a way of bursting forth with slippery streams of notes, and occasionally lends his playing a twangy flavor reminiscent of country music.

As an unaccompanied solo pianist, Jarrett created one of the first jazz sounds since the Modern Jazz Quartet's whose appeal crossed the line from jazz audiences to audiences customarily more fond of symphonic music. He is one of the first solo jazz musicians to consistently pack auditoriums throughout the United States and Europe and earn a satisfactory living as an improviser. Jarrett attracted audiences comparable to those of a nonimprovising classical virtuoso. The *Köln Concert* of 1975 is his most popular album in this style, and it had sold 9.5 million copies by 1995. Among the explanations for this style's appeal are:

1. a rhapsodic style evoking a warm, sweeping mood
2. Jarrett's seemingly effortless control of the keyboard
3. vamp-based passages in which brief accompaniment figures repeat again and again and are easy to follow
4. the clarity of his thinking
5. the music's classical rather than jazz feeling[49]

Jarrett's influence on jazz pianists has been slower to take hold than Herbie Hancock's and Chick Corea's. However, there are several players worth noting who recall Jarrett's sound: Bobo Stinson, Art Lande,[50] Richard Beirach,[51] Brad Mehldau,[52] and Lyle Mays (who played on numerous albums with Pat Metheny's group during the 1970s and 1980s). Other pianists, less gifted than Lande, Beirach, and Mays, have imitated the simplest aspects of Jarrett's style, particularly the lengthy, vamp-based improvisations which seem soothing. They have become central to a popular kind of music known as "new age," which is frequently confused with jazz because it is improvised and many of its practitioners have previously played jazz. The improvisations of these latter imitators can be distinguished from those of Jarrett because the lines are far less rich with melodic ideas, and the rhythms are much simpler. Rarely do Jarrett's imitators attain the sweeping feeling that Jarrett can elicit in the listener, nor do they play with quite the smoothness and vitality that Jarrett displays.

Another format that exposed Jarrett to many listeners was his set of collaborations with bassist Gary Peacock (b. 1935) and drummer Jack DeJohnette (b. 1942). Peacock had begun receiving wide attention during the early 1960s, partly as a result of his astounding technical facility and his ground-breaking explorations with the innovative saxophonist Albert Ayler. He had also played with Jarrett's main influences, Bill Evans and Paul Bley. DeJohnette had played alongside Jarrett in the Charles Lloyd band of 1966–1968 and the Miles Davis bands of 1969 to 1971. Musicians generally rank DeJohnette as among the most musical of all jazz drummers and one of the top to emerge after Tony Williams and Elvin Jones. He has played with a wide assortment of great jazz musicians and led numerous groups of his own that produced distinctive music that was unlike any other genres of the time.

Jarrett's recordings with Peacock and DeJohnette often feature a repertory of pop tunes and jazz standards. Among their best known albums are *Standards Vol. 1*, *Standards Vol. 2*, and *Standards Live*. Musicians are also partial to their renditions of standards on the albums *Tribute* and *The Cure*. Understandably, then, this format has become known as Jarrett's "Standards Trio." They sometimes feature straight-ahead swinging in the style of trios led during the 1950s and 1960s by Wynton Kelly and Ahmad Jamal. Much of their music is also inspired by the trio music of Bill Evans from the 1950s and 1960s. The amount of substance in Jarrett's improvisations and the sensitivity and good taste of Peacock and DeJohnette were pinnacles to which other musicians aspired. In fact, pianist Brad Mehldau began garnering considerable attention in the 1990s for his own trio recordings that were inspired in part by the music of Jarrett and the Standards Trio.

Keith Jarrett (piano); recorded in 1976; issued on *Staircase*. (ECM: 1090, 1976, c1994).

"Sundial, Part 1" is one of the most compelling recordings of the free improvisatory approach that Keith Jarrett perfected for solo piano. In fact, you might find its final 90 seconds to be a breathtaking experience. The selection comes from *Staircase*, an album often cited by musicians as their favorite Jarrett solo album. This recording illustrates the aspect of his stylistically varied career that gained him the largest audience.

To fully appreciate this recording requires undivided attention. The piece is not background music. Nor is it dance music. A darkened room or closed eyes would be an ideal start. You also need to be far from all distractions in order to let your mind and emotions go everywhere that this music can take you. Forget the timed listening hints the first few times you hear this recording. To become preoccupied with form and technique would be a mistake. Jarrett lets his spontaneous ideas dictate the form. His musical feeling flows accordingly. So should yours.

In this piece, Jarrett takes us on an adventure in which he roams within certain harmonies that stay in effect for long periods. He continuously generates new melodies that adhere seamlessly. It is as though he allows himself to enter a trance where his years of studying twentieth-century classical music surface. He draws from his understanding of Paul Bley, Maurice Ravel, and Bill Evans, as well as early music such as J. S. Bach and Gregorian chant. In the inspiration of the moment, Jarrett borrows their harmonies and molds new strains of his own. For instance, his ideas at 4′08″ to 4′21″ bear resemblance to piano music by Claude Debussy and Ravel.

Unlike much of earlier jazz, Jarrett's solo piano pieces are not based on pop tunes or jazz standards. They don't even borrow their chord changes from those sources. In fact, Jarrett does not depend on any preset progressions of chords or modes at all. For instance, in the beginning of "Sundial, Part 1," Jarrett emphasizes ideas that fit just one scale (technically known as the F♯ Aeolian). Then, little by little, he shifts the sound's center of gravity by using different bass notes. Ultimately, he introduces other chords that move the piece along, but always very gradually, not disturbing the music's continuity. He gives each idea respectful attention, thereby allowing us to let it to sink in before taking us to new musical shapes and colors.

The first 40 seconds of music contains two lines moving at the same time, with silence between tones. One line is higher pitched and louder than the other. Sometimes the tones sound in response to each other. Sometimes the tones of the lower line complement those in the higher-pitched line. It is as though Jarrett is dangling high-pitched tones in the air while scattering lower-pitched tones underneath to harmonize. Unlike jazz comping, in which chords of mid-range pitches are frequently jabbed by the pianist's left hand while the right hand creates melody lines of higher pitches, we have to wait until 0′54″ before we first hear a chord from Jarrett's left hand. And even when it does occur, its existence is fleeting.

Jarrett lets his melody tones ring, almost the way they might resonate if chanted in the halls of a monastery. The effect here is quite meditative, which may partially explain the music's broad appeal. Another way that Jarrett achieves the meditative effect is by playing slowly, and not bunching notes together. He lets his melodies emerge very gently, never hurriedly.

The rhapsodic way in which they are devised and paced gives his lines a singing quality. It is no coincidence that at 6′23″ we can actually hear Jarrett singing along with these piano melodies. Perhaps he had been singing them silently all along. But now the muse within him also had to emerge from his throat.

Jarrett launches a new direction at 5′37″ with a strong two-tone bass sound that is sustained, and then rapid, high pitched figures, executed by the right hand, that culminate in a bluesy figure at 5′46″. Then he changes chords at 5′56″, and eases into a sequence of lines and chords, almost as though playing a lush Broadway song of romance that has preset chord changes, supplying a florid decoration at 6′12″. He gets really caught up in rhapsodizing and can be heard singing his piano lines at 6′23″ and especially from 6′36″ to 6′55″. Then it is as though he takes a rest from 7′11″ to 7′14″. From there he launches his most commanding segment, featuring extraordinarily ringing tones that are voiced in octaves, spaced with majestic pauses, and a range of different volumes.

At every moment he demonstrates a concerted control over the architecture of the improvisation. Jarrett is working here as a serious composer making on-the-spot decisions. We need to appreciate the extraordinary patience and foresight required of the improviser to achieve the drama of these results as the solo unfolds. Skillful recording techniques are also required to adequately represent the full richness and ringing of his piano tones. Pay particular attention to the crystalline quality of sustained high pitches

LISTENING GUIDE *continued on next page*

beginning at 7′19″ and culminating at 8′40″. For this reason, producer Manfred Eicher can be considered a collaborator. The ending of the piece is made so striking because of the special pairing of Eicher's sound engineering with Jarrett's touch, taste, and compositional attitude.

Technical Notes: Here are a few highlights for readers who want technical qualities pointed out. Though he sticks with the F♯ Aeolian through much of the piece, consider that Jarrett opens new vistas when he introduces another scale at 1′53″, then again when he switches to a major scale at 2′53″ and begins a series of major chords, as in a Bach chorale, to 3′56″. Corresponding changes in the music's effect occur when Jarrett moves to another key at 4′54″ and again at 6′04″ when he moves to a major key, and again at 7′38″. The density of the texture changes with fast right-hand movement at 5′39″.

Jarrett becomes very dramatic when he is stating a new melody in a marked manner and voicing his ideas in octaves at 3′44″ and again at 7′44″. In these moments he is drawing pitches from the scale that originally began the piece and letting them ring.

CHAPTER SUMMARY

1. Pianist Bill Evans came to attention during the late 1950s and became the most influential pianist since Bud Powell.

2. Though derived partly from the Tristano approach, Evans's style was original, especially in his voicings and his modal thinking.

3. With bassist Scott LaFaro and drummer Paul Motian, Evans devised a fresh approach to trio playing in which explicit statement of every beat was replaced by a highly flexible and varied group style, and the roles of soloist and accompanist were often blurred.

4. LaFaro's remarkable speed and imagination pushed jazz bass styles ahead as Jimmy Blanton's had 20 years earlier.

5. Evans influenced Herbie Hancock, Chick Corea, and Keith Jarrett, all of whom, in turn, led innovative bands and influenced many other pianists.

6. Hancock refined the Evans style, added the influence of Wynton Kelly, and raised accompanying techniques to a high level of imagination and variety while with Miles Davis.

7. Hancock led several groups of his own that played his many original compositions, including "Maiden Voyage" and "Watermelon Man."

8. Hancock's mid-1970s group, the Head Hunters, became a model jazz-rock-funk band and enjoyed very high record sales.

9. Chick Corea looked to Bill Evans as only one of many sources for his original piano style. Horace Silver, Thelonious Monk, Bud Powell, McCoy Tyner, and several classical composers also influenced Corea. His playing is more crisp and staccato than that of Hancock or Evans, and he favors Spanish themes and Latin American rhythms.

10. Corea popularized the use of fourths in compositions and piano voicings, and used them in ways that Evans and Tyner had not.

11. Corea's tunes were very popular. "Spain" and "Windows" became jazz standards.

12. Keith Jarrett showed the influence of Bill Evans—and that of Ornette Coleman—in developing his own piano style.

13. Jarrett was one of the most original composer-pianist-bandleaders of the 1970s, combining free jazz, funk, and a rhapsodic classical piano style that made him the most successful solo concert pianist in jazz history.

14. Jarrett's quartet of the 1970s mixed the methods and musicians associated with Ornette Coleman and Bill Evans and added country music, World Music, and funk music in original combinations.

Notes

1. For more about Bill Evans, see Peter Pettinger, *How My Heart Sings* (Yale University, 1998). For commentary about Evans, Herbie Hancock, Chick Corea, and Keith Jarrett, see Len Lyons, *The Great Jazz Pianists* (Quill, 1983; Da Capo, 1989); and the booklet that accompanies *Jazz Piano* (Smithsonian: 7002, 4CD set, 1924–78, c1989). *Jazz Piano* also presents Evans-LaFaro-Motian on "Autumn Leaves" (1959) and "Waltz for Debby" (1961 live), and a live solo recording by Evans: "I Loves You Porgy" (1968). A transcription and analysis of the Evans solo on "Nardis" (*Explorations*, Fantasy: OJC-037, 1961, c1987) is in John Rodby, *Solos for Jazz Piano* (Carl Fischer, 1989); order from: Carl Fischer Music, 65 Bleecker St., NYC, NY 10012; phone: 800-762-2328; web: *www.carlfischer.com*. A transcription of "Peri's Scope" (*Portrait in Jazz*, Fantasy: OJC-088, 1959, c1987) is in John Mehegan, *Jazz Improvisation*, vol. 4 (Watson-Guptill, 1965).

2. Recordings with Davis in 1958 include Miles Davis, *'58 Sessions* (Columbia: 46835, 1958, c1991); and most of Davis, *Miles and Coltrane* (Columbia: 44052, 1955, 1958, c1988).

3. *Everybody Digs Bill Evans* (Fantasy: OJC-068, 1958, c1987); the first Evans trio record is *New Jazz Conceptions* (Fantasy: OJC-025, 1956, c1987).

4. Because of this famous recording and his other work, Bill Evans influenced various stages in the careers of many modern jazz pianists, especially in the jazz use of chord voicings originally identified with French Impressionist composers Maurice Ravel and Claude Debussy. Listen to the second movement of Ravel's "Sonatine" to hear one source for Evans's chord voicings. To detect the influence of the Evans voicings and manner in others, listen to Herbie Hancock on "My Funny Valentine," especially the introduction (Miles Davis, *My Funny Valentine*, Columbia/Legacy: 93593, 1964, c2005), and on "Pee Wee" (Davis, *Sorcerer*, Columbia/Legacy: 65680, 1967, c1998); Chick Corea on Stan Getz, *Sweet Rain* (Verve: 815 054, 1967, c1983); Keith Jarrett on "Pretty Ballad" from Jarrett, *Somewhere Before* (Atlantic: 8808, 1968, c1981); and Jarrett on "Ellen David" from Charlie Haden, *Closeness* (Horizon: SP-710, 1976).

5. *The Complete Village Vanguard Recordings, 1961* (Riverside: 3RCD-4443, 3CD set, 1961, c2005); or the original albums: *Sunday at the Village Vanguard* (Fantasy: OJC-140, c1987); and *Waltz for Debby* (Fantasy: OJC-210, c1987).

6. On *Jazz Piano* (Smithsonian).

7. "Pitter Panther Patter" and "Mr. J. B. Blues" on Duke Ellington, *Solos, Duets and Trios* (RCA Bluebird: 2178-2-RB, 1932–67, c1990); or Ellington, *Never No Lament: The Blanton-Webster Band* (RCA Bluebird: 50857, 3CD set, 1940–42, c2003).

8. The clearest example of this style is on "Solar" on JCCD3, or Evans, *Sunday at the Village Vanguard*.

9. Listen to the Evans-LaFaro recordings and compare with work by the trios of Art Tatum, Bud Powell, Oscar Peterson, or Ramsey Lewis. Evans, Powell, and Peterson examples can be found on *Jazz Piano* (Smithsonian).

10. In some passages, Evans's bassists do not emphasize all four beats of each measure but instead concentrate only on the first and third. (Listen to "All of You" on *Sunday at the Village Vanguard*.) LaFaro's playing often seemed to decorate the first and third beats and let the second and fourth beats pass. Even though four beats are present, only two are emphasized; musicians would say the music is "in two" or "two-beat style." What LaFaro did here is called a "decorative two feel."

11. An example of this is "Solar" on JCCD3, or Evans, *Sunday at the Village Vanguard*.

12. A vivid illustration of this influence is provided by listening to the rhythm section style of pre-1963 Miles Davis records, such as *Milestones* (Columbia/Legacy: 85203, 1958, c1997) or *Miles Davis at Carnegie Hall* (Columbia/Legacy: C2K 65027, 2CD set, 1961, c1998); then listening to Bill Evans, *Sunday at the Village Vanguard* (1961), before listening to the rhythm section on any 1963–67 Davis albums, particularly "All of You" on *My Funny Valentine*, "Circle" on *Miles Smiles* (Columbia/Legacy: 65682, 1966, c1998), or "Pee Wee" on *Sorcerer* (1967). The difference between pre- and post-1963 styles reflects the influence of the 1961 Evans trio concepts.

13. The Evans influence can be heard in Hancock's playing on Davis, *My Funny Valentine*. And, at times, the Tristano-like approach that Evans used in constructing lines is also evident in Hancock's work, as on solos with Davis in "The Sorcerer" (*Sorcerer*), "Agitation" (*E.S.P.*, Columbia/Legacy: 65683, 1965, c1998), and "Orbits" (*Miles Smiles*). The flexible and intelligent interaction between Hancock, Ron Carter, and Tony Williams on "Pee Wee" (*Sorcerer*), and between Hancock, Buster Williams, and Albert Heath on "He Who Lives in Fear" on Herbie Hancock, *The Prisoner* (Blue Note: 25649, 1969, c2000) recalls the sensitive interaction in the 1961 recordings of Bill Evans, Scott LaFaro, and Paul Motian.

14. Listen to Hancock's trio rendition of his composition "The Sorcerer" on *Jazz Piano* (Smithsonian).

15. Herbie Hancock, *Death Wish* (One Way: 26659 [Columbia], 1974, c1996).

16. Hancock, *Fat Albert Rotunda*, 1969 on *Mwandishi* (Warner Bros.: 45732, 2CD set, 1969–71, c1994).

17. Hancock, *Takin' Off* (Blue Note: 37643, 1962, c1996).

18. Hancock, *Sextant* (Columbia/Legacy: 64983, 1972, c1998).

19. Hancock, *Crossings*, 1971 (on *Mwandishi*, Warner Bros.: 45732, 2CD set, 1969–71, c1994).

20. Hancock, *Maiden Voyage* (Blue Note: 95331, 1965, c1999).

21. Hancock, *Empyrean Isles* (Blue Note: 98796, 1964, c1998).

22. Hancock, *Head Hunters* (Columbia/Legacy: 65123, 1973, c1997).

23. Hancock, *Thrust* (Columbia/Legacy: 64984, 1974, c1998).

24. Hancock had led groups in recording studios before and during his years with Davis, but they were not usually working bands. Most were put together solely for the recordings.

25. Hancock, *Future Shock* (Columbia/Legacy: 65962, 1983, c1999).

26. Jan Hammer, Richard Beirach, Jeff Lorber, Kenny Kirkland, Andy LaVerne, Rachel Z, and Mulgrew Miller were among the many who exhibited Corea's influence.

27. The mid-1960s recordings that Corea made with Blue Mitchell show the influence of Bud Powell and Horace Silver. His work with Herbie Mann and Cal Tjader points up his use of Evans and Tyner as sources. (See *Instructor's Resource Manual* for discographies of Mitchell, Mann, and Tjader records featuring Corea.) Though drawing from Tyner, Corea's style differs from Tyner in several respects. For example, in Tyner's reharmonization of popular-song chord progressions, his use of fourths simplifies the movement of harmonies, whereas Corea's delineates the movement of harmonies. Though both Tyner and Corea occasionally venture outside their harmonies, Corea's "outside" lines usually return to the harmonies in a more systematic way where Tyner uses his outside playing more for its coloristic value alone. Though both improvisers use pentatonics, Tyner tends to use them more against pedal points, whereas Corea employs them as much in lines that are set atop moving chords.

Though similar in many ways to Bill Evans, Corea devotes a very large portion of his output to voicing in fourths, whereas Evans tends toward a balance of quartal and tertial harmonies. Though both Evans and Corea play notes in a very marked manner, Evans is more legato and Corea more staccato. To hear Corea's resemblance to Evans, listen to Evans on the final selection of Miles Davis, *Kind of Blue* (Columbia/Legacy: 64935, 1959, c1997), or on "Peace Piece" on *Everybody Digs Bill Evans*; then listen to the title track from *Return to Forever, Where Have I Known You Before* (Polydor: 825 206, 1974, c1985); or "Song for Lee Lee" on Chick Corea, *Piano Improvisations*, Vol. 2 (ECM: 829 190 [1020], 1971, c2000). Also listen to other Evans solos on those albums, then to Corea's solos on Stan Getz, *Sweet Rain* (Verve). Corea's compositions, "Tones for Joan's Bones" (Corea, *Inner Space*, Atlantic: 305, 1966, c1988) and "Windows" (Getz, *Sweet Rain*) reflect the Evans style of chord voicing.

28. See page 296, footnote 27, and page 492 for more about sounds created by fourths. Fourths are used extensively in the melody line of his tune "Litha" and his left-hand comping on Corea, *Now He Sings, Now He Sobs* (Blue Note: 38265, 1968, c2002). The chord voicings on *Now He Sings, Now He Sobs* are reminiscent of music by Paul Hindemith.

29. Corea demonstrated a few of Silver's devices on Blue Mitchell, *The Thing to Do* (Blue Note: 94319, 1964, c2004), which was recorded by the Horace Silver quintet with Corea in Silver's place. Even Corea's compositions on the album are in Silver's style.

30. Corea played with the bands of Willie Bobo, Cal Tjader, Herbie Mann, and Mongo Santamaria, all of which featured Latin music.

31. Corea, *Now He Sings, Now He Sobs* (Blue Note). Some musicians learned to play its music note for note, and we are indebted to a few of them for transcriptions of his piano part. Bill Dobbins prepared *Chick Corea: Now He Sings, Now He Sobs* (Advance Music, 1988), and a number of observations about Corea's style that appear in this chapter were made originally by Dobbins in personal communication with the author. Scott Reeves transcribed and analyzed Corea's solo on "Matrix" in Reeves, *Creative Jazz Improvisation*, 4th ed. (Prentice-Hall, 2006); a few of his ideas are presented in this chapter. Both these books are available from: Jamey Aebersold Jazz, Inc., P.O. Box 1244, New Albany, IN 47150-1244; phone: 800-456-1388; web: *www.jazzbooks.com*. The recording of "Matrix" is also on *Jazz Piano* (Smithsonian).

32. Corea, *Trio Music* (ECM: 159 454 [1232], 1981, c2001); and *Trio Music Live in Europe* (ECM: 827 769 [1310], 1984, c1986).

33. Even though "Matrix" and "Steps" (on JCCD3) are 12-bar blues tunes, listeners do not usually recognize them as blues because of the fresh way Corea treats their form. Portions of his solos avoid traditional ways of announcing the significant chord changes that earlier pianists would make at the fifth, ninth, and eleventh measures. For some of Corea's solo passages, the arrival points are determined exclusively by the direction of the melodic line. Sometimes he leaves out those moves;

other times he stretches the traditional time before playing them. In other words, he restructures the tension points. The ways bop pianists favored for adding chords to make more movement within the 12-measure progression are also missing. When Corea does add chords, their identity is not as pronounced, because voicing in fourths makes the origin of the chord ambiguous. Moreover, sometimes Corea phrases in ways that do not neatly fit the three four-measure phrase organization his predecessors were inclined to use when playing the blues. He starts and stops his lines in nontraditional places, but the result does not sound odd. Incidentally, it is precisely the fact that it does not sound odd, coupled with the smoothness and finished quality of his constructions, that masks the music's adventuresome construction for some listeners. Many have failed to appreciate the newness of Corea's ideas because the presentation was so smooth that it failed to jar them.

The selection on *Now He Sings, Now He Sobs* called "Now He Beats the Drum, Now He Stops" also begins with a traditional foundation: the chord progression to "How Deep Is the Ocean?" But Corea takes that set of chords, combines it with a few ideas from a Bill Evans rendition, and composes a fresh and original piece that sounds like nothing ever heard before.

34. Corea, *Song of Singing* (Blue Note: 84353, 1970); and A.R.C. (ECM: 833 678 [1009], 1971, c1994). During this time Corea also appeared on the Miles Davis albums: *In a Silent Way* (Columbia/Legacy: 86556, 1969, c2002), *Bitches Brew* (Columbia/Legacy: C2K 65774, 2CD set, 1969, c1999), *Live at Fillmore East* (Columbia/Legacy: C2K 65139, 2CD set, 1970, c1997), and *Black Beauty* (Columbia/Legacy: C2K 65138, 2CD set, 1970, c1997). *Black Beauty* is the only Davis album in which Corea solos at length, and it is well worth having since it constitutes some of the best work of his career.

35. Corea, *Piano Improvisations*, Vol. 1 (ECM: 811 979 [1014], 1971, c2000); Vol. 2 (ECM: 829 190 [1020], 1971, c2000); all selections were spontaneously conceived and performed, with the exceptions of "Song for Sally," "Song of the Wind," "Some Time Ago," "Trinkle Tinkle," and "Masqualero."

36. Corea, *Return to Forever* (ECM: 811 978 [1022], 1971, c1999); and *Return to Forever, Light as a Feather* (Verve: 557 115, 1972, c1995). See a transcription and analysis of Corea's solo on "Spain," from *Light as a Feather*, in John Rodby, *Solos for Jazz Piano*.

37. Stanley Clarke's *School Days* was a hit, as were Al Dimeola's *Elegant Gypsy* and *Casino*.

38. Listen to "Windows" and "Litha" on Stan Getz, *Sweet Rain* (Verve).

39. For example, the bass lines that accompany his "Señor Mouse" (Gary Burton, *Crystal Silence*, ECM: 831 331 [1024], 1972, c1987) are central to the composition. Without them, the melody would not convey the same flavor.

40. John Patitucci's playing of the rapid melody line to Corea's "Got a Match" from *The Chick Corea Elektric Band* (GRP: 9535, 1986, c1986) dazzled listeners in the 1980s.

41. To detect Jarrett's debt to Evans, listen to "Shades of Jazz" on Keith Jarrett, *Mysteries* (Impulse!: IMPD4-189, 4CD set, 1975–76, c1996); and "Ellen David" on Charlie Haden, *Closeness* (Horizon: SP-710, 1976). For more about Jarrett, see Ian Carr, *Keith Jarrett: The Man and His Music* (Da Capo, 1992).

42. Jarrett's style is a curious blend of influences. There is a hint of Wynton Kelly in his playing on Art Blakey, *Buttercorn Lady* (Emarcy: 822 471, 1966, c1986). Bill Evans and Ornette Coleman are obvious. Jarrett's piano style and quartet sound of the 1970s were based on the style of pianist Paul Bley and his group that included saxophonist John Gilmore, bassist Gary Peacock, and future Jarrett drummer Paul Motian. They are documented on Paul Bley, *Turning Point* (Improvising Artists: 373841, 1964); and *Turns* (Savoy: 1192, LP, 1964, c1987). Jarrett has cited Bley, *Footloose* (Savoy: 78987, 1962–63, c1995) as a favorite.

Influences converged for Jarrett in a friendship that began with pianist John Coates around 1957. Coates's favorites included Paul Bley, Ornette Coleman, black gospel music, and "early white American music." Both men eventually showed similar amalgams of these, though Coates perfected his first, and Jarrett listened to Coates. A late example is *The Piano Sound of John Coates* (Omnisound: 1004, LP, 1974, c1974).

43. Jarrett, *In the Light* (ECM: 835 011 [1033/34], 2CD set, 1973, c2000).

44. Jarrett wrote melodies in Coleman's style as well as soloing in it. Redman soloed in the Coleman style, and Haden's unique approach was central to both the Coleman and Jarrett groups.

45. Listen to Jarrett's up-tempo piano lines on "Shades of Jazz" and his slow playing, with its sustained tones and chord voicings on "Rainbow," both on Jarrett, *Mysteries* (Impulse!). Compare this with Evans, *Sunday at the Village Vanguard*, or *Everybody Digs Bill Evans*.

46. Listen to Jarrett's "In Front" on *Jazz Piano* (Smithsonian); or on Jarrett, *Facing You* (ECM: 827 132 [1017], 1971, c2000).

47. Jarrett, *Staircase* (ECM: 827 337 [1090], 2CD set, 1976, c2000); and *Radiance* (ECM: B0004314-02 [1960/61], 2CD set, 2000, c2005).

48. It helps us hear Jarrett's debt to Coleman when Jarrett omits left-hand playing and improvises lengthy, saxophone-like solos with his right hand. In fact, when accompanied only by drums and bass (especially Charlie Haden) and not playing in a two-handed pianistic style, Jarrett often sounds like Coleman transferred to the piano. For more comparisons between Coleman and Jarrett, listen to Jarrett's soprano saxophone playing on "Pocket Full of Cherry," originally on *Bop-Be*, reissued on Jarrett, *Mysteries* (Impulse!); and "Encore (a-b-c)" on Jarrett, *Eyes of the Heart* (ECM: 825 476 [1150], 1976, c1991). Jarrett's stylistic debt to Coleman is particularly evident in his solos on Jan Garbarek, *Belonging*

(ECM: 829 115 [1050], 1974, c1988). Despite all the similarities between styles, even to employing the same sidemen, at least three differences between Coleman's and Jarrett's approaches are evident: (1) Coleman is more complex than Jarrett, more varied and unpredictable in his improvised lines, and he draws upon a wider selection of moods and tempos than does Jarrett; (2) Jarrett possesses very high-level technique, and, because of the uniformity in touch this affords, he plays more smoothly than Coleman, and his music is less jarring; and (3) the notes in Jarrett's lines usually seem more loyal to the original key that a given piece is in, and Coleman shifts pedal points more often.

49. In a substantial portion of Jarrett's unaccompanied solo improvisations, the musical vocabulary is classical. Much of this work sounds like piano pieces by Maurice Ravel. (Listen to "Gaspard de la nuit: Le gibet" for one source in the work of Ravel.) This sound might provide a bridge for listeners who are not accustomed to jazz but are acquainted with symphonic music, especially the familiar works of French composers Ravel and Claude Debussy. For many such listeners, the only aspect that separates this portion of Jarrett's work from classical music is that Jarrett's is largely improvised.

50. Lande's affinity for Jarrett is particularly evident on Art Lande, *Red Lanta* (ECM: 1038, 1973).

51. Beirach's affinity for Jarrett is most noticeable on David Liebman, *Forgotten Fantasies* (A&M/Horizon: SP-709, LP, 1975, c1976). Note that his style has more resemblance to Chick Corea and Herbie Hancock and their mutual influence from Bill Evans. Beirach, however, can be identified for his own style, as well. He has, in turn, influenced other pianists.

52. Jarrett's influence on Brad Mehldau is particularly evident on "Exit Music (for a film)" in Brad Mehldau, *Art of the Trio 4: Back at the Vanguard* (Warner Bros.: 47463, 1999, c1999).

The first group of jazz styles to attain widespread popularity after the swing era was called jazz-rock fusion. This collection of approaches became a dominant stream of jazz during the 1970s, and it spawned styles that became the main popular music for an entire segment of the music market in the 1980s and 1990s. The first portion of this chapter clarifies what is included in this category. The middle portion discusses the major contributions of **Miles Davis, Larry Coryell, John McLaughlin, Joe Zawinul, Jaco Pastorius,** and **Pat Metheny.** (The fusion styles of **Herbie Hancock** and **Chick Corea** were examined in Chapter 15, and those of **Wayne Shorter** were mentioned in Chapter 12.) The final portion is postponed to Chapter 17: "1980 to the Present," with discussion of smooth jazz and acid jazz.

Herbie Hancock
(Photo by Grace Bell)

DISTINGUISHING JAZZ FROM ROCK AND FUNK

Jazz of almost any period can be distinguished from rock and funk music because rock and funk typically have:

1. shorter phrase lengths
2. less frequent chord changes
3. less complexity of melody
4. less complexity of harmony
5. less improvisation, especially in accompaniments
6. much more repetition of melodic phrases
7. more repetition of brief chord progressions
8. simpler, more repetitive drumming patterns
9. more pronounced repetition of bass figures

More is preset in rock and funk performances than in jazz performances. Not only does jazz ordinarily require solos to be improvised anew each time they occur, it also requires that the accompaniments for the solos be improvised. Even the accompaniments for the theme statements spontaneously differ from performance to performance.

Rhythmic feeling provides another means for distinguishing jazz from rock and funk music. Where jazz emphasizes flexibility and relaxation, rock stresses intensity and firmness. Rock and funk music seem to sit on each beat, whereas jazz projects a shuffling feeling. Jazz musicians describe the time sense of rock and funk musicians as "straight up and down." On the other hand, jazz attempts to put forth a lilting, bouncy feeling that seems to pull each beat along.

Instruments preferred by jazz musicians are often different from those of rock and funk musicians. Jazz musicians usually place less emphasis on electronic instruments and high amplification of acoustic instruments.

Jazz, rock, and funk music share similar roots in work songs, the blues, and gospel music, but they represent the products of two divergent lines of musical evolution (see Figure 16.1). For example, jazz employs aspects of formal European concert music and steers away from vocals; it is primarily instrumental music. Sometimes it is as intricate as twentieth-century symphonic music. Rock and funk music, on the other hand, emphasize vocals and stick largely to elementary compositional forms. Rock and funk favor the four-chord, 12-bar blues and other brief chord progressions that repeat continuously. While rock and funk became a part of the popular music mainstream, jazz acquired a status like classical chamber music because its audience was small and specialized. While it is true that blues singers from early in the twentieth century, such as Leadbelly, Robert Johnson, and Bessie Smith, are routinely cited in jazz history texts, they are usually mentioned in discussions of the origins of jazz rather than the dominant course of jazz itself. The stream of stylistic evolution that runs from Leadbelly through B. B. King to Jimi Hendrix is essentially separate from the evolution of most jazz styles. Religious music had influenced blues singers such as Bessie Smith, and it continued to influence popular music, as exemplified by such recently popular singers as Aretha Franklin and James Brown. However, it influenced jazz somewhat less.[1]

Prior to the 1950s, blues and gospel music were especially influential in popular music made by black performers who were marketed to black audiences. Ranging from Bessie Smith in the 1920s to Louis Jordan in the 1940s, these performers made music for what were called "race records." In 1949, this category acquired a new name—rhythm and blues (R & B)—and it strongly influenced another style of popular music called rock and roll (see Figure 16.1). In addition to its R & B roots, much rock also reflects the predominantly white musical streams of country music or hillbilly music.

One early form of rock was called rockabilly, and early Elvis Presley exemplifies this style. Rock also reflects western swing. This is a form that combines hillbilly music and jazz with a diversity of ethnic traditions that range from the dance music of Cajuns and Czechs to that of Mexicans, Germans, and Poles. Rock is distinctly removed from jazz, being less like jazz than R & B had been. Rock and R & B remain similar, however, because they both emphasize extremely simple melodies, extensive pitch bending, reliance upon ostinato, and strict adherence to steady tempo.

Some R & B in the 1960s contained accompaniment rhythms more complicated than those in rock. During the late 1960s, some styles which extended R & B became the source for intricately syncopated drum patterns and bass figures. Some of the musicians working for Motown recording artists[2] and for singer James Brown,[3] for example, devised accompaniment patterns which were more complicated than those used at the time by rock groups. The work of accompanists for Sly Stone[4] during the early 1970s was especially complex. By this time, many people were beginning to call this music "soul" and "funk" instead of R & B. However, this new pair of labels still served the same purpose: identifying a primarily African American form of popular music. It was the accompaniment style for this funk-soul category, more than rock, which influenced a number of jazz musicians during the 1970s (see Figure 16.1). Therefore, **the jazz-rock label itself is not entirely appropriate for the music that it identifies.** "Jazz-funk" might be a more accurate designation.[5]

Some jazz musicians remained unaffected by funk, and many funk groups continued unaffected by jazz. But much of the music produced by jazz groups during the 1970s and 1980s demonstrated a larger number of funk characteristics than had previously been used in modern jazz, and some funk groups attempted to incorporate more of the improvisation and advanced harmonies found in jazz.

FORERUNNERS OF JAZZ-ROCK

Mid-1960s forerunners of the "jazz-rock" approaches include the 1966 band called the Free Spirits[6] with guitarist Larry Coryell, the 1967 quartet of vibraphonist Gary Burton and Coryell,[7] and the Fourth Way, a 1968–1971 band with pianist Mike Nock and violinist Michael White.[8] The greatest popular acclaim did not go to these groups, however. It went to Blood, Sweat & Tears,[9] an eight-piece band featuring vocals in a James Brown and Ray Charles style with horn work similar to that of Brown and Charles. Next was the 1968 group called Chicago,[10] a seven-piece pop band featuring solo voice singing as well as four- and five-part harmony. Its horn parts were often voiced for trumpet, trombone, and saxophone, in the style of late-1960s Motown. After them was the 1970 group called Ten Wheel Drive,[11] a ten-piece band whose style was similar to that of the first two. These three groups were identified by music journalists as "jazz-rock" bands, and they were phenomenally successful with the record-buying public.

Journalists gave much attention to the horns and improvisation in Ten Wheel Drive, Chicago, and Blood, Sweat & Tears. Listeners and journalists assumed that such elements lent jazz character to the music, that it was innovative, and that it justified the "jazz" part of the "jazz-rock" label. Yet R & B bands, including those of soul singer James Brown, for example, had been using horns and improvisation since the 1950s. In other words, some elements presumed to be significant contributions by Chicago and Blood, Sweat & Tears merely reflected existing traditions within popular music (see Figure 16.1). Their horn parts were modeled after the James Brown and Motown brass style rather than jazz. And their singing style was patterned after soul singing. Admittedly, the harmonies written for their horns were more advanced than Motown's and James Brown's, but such sophistication had already been common in pop music and was not exclusive to jazz, either. Almost the only element these bands

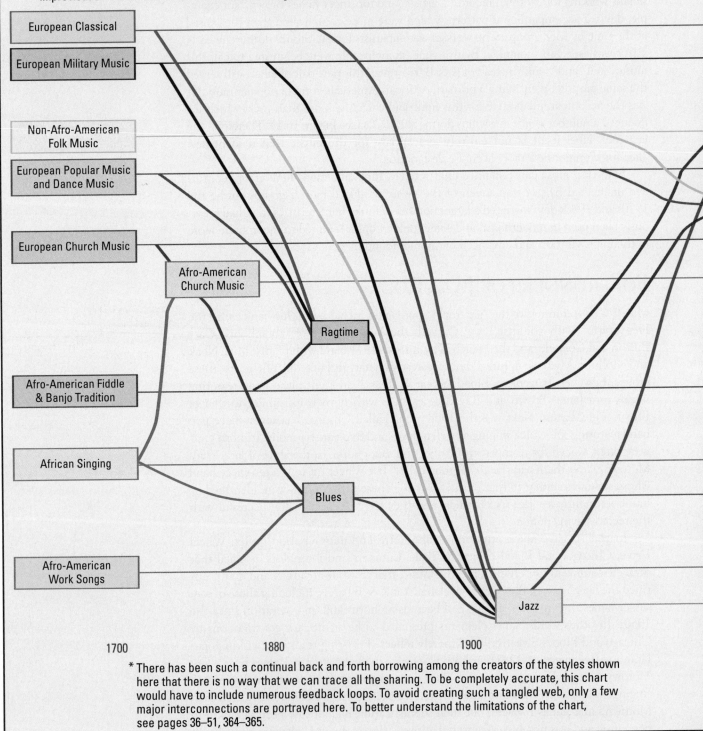

Figure 16.1 Chart of Parallel Streams Distinguishing Jazz from Rock and Jazz-Rock*

Jazz and rock share a few similar origins, but they are separate styles.

Their origins constitute musical streams that continued by themselves and remain alive today.

Chicago, BS&T, and Ten Wheel Drive are offshoots of soul music, more than offshoots of jazz.

Rhythm & Blues evolved into soul music and already had a tradition including jazz improvisation before soul music influenced Chicago, BS&T, and Ten Wheel Drive.

European Classical

European Military Music

Non-Afro-American Folk Music

European Popular Music and Dance Music

European Church Music

Afro-American Church Music

Ragtime

Afro-American Fiddle & Banjo Tradition

African Singing

Blues

Afro-American Work Songs

Jazz

1700   1880   1900

* There has been such a continual back and forth borrowing among the creators of the styles shown here that there is no way that we can trace all the sharing. To be completely accurate, this chart would have to include numerous feedback loops. To avoid creating such a tangled web, only a few major interconnections are portrayed here. To better understand the limitations of the chart, see pages 36–51, 364–365.

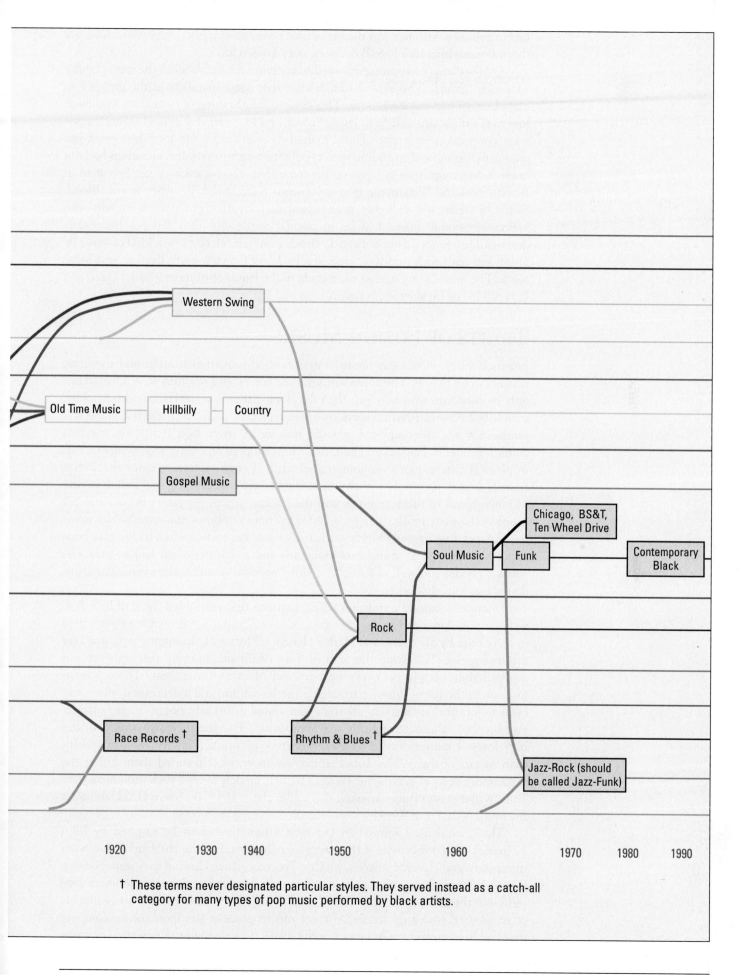

Western Swing							

Old Time Music Hillbilly Country

Gospel Music

Chicago, BS&T,
Ten Wheel Drive

Soul Music Funk Contemporary Black

Rock

Race Records † Rhythm & Blues †

Jazz-Rock (should
be called Jazz-Funk)

1920   1930   1940   1950   1960   1970   1980   1990

† These terms never designated particular styles. They served instead as a catch-all
category for many types of pop music performed by black artists.

had in common with jazz was the occasional presence of a brief, improvised solo. Yet this was something that R & B had long been known for.

Another line of reasoning was used in applying the jazz label to the most popular "jazz-rock" groups. This was the knowledge that some members of the groups had played jazz or had jazz aspirations. This colored the thinking of journalists who overlooked the traditions of R & B, James Brown, and Motown and instead assumed a primary connection with jazz. These journalists overlooked the long history of jazz musicians touring and recording with popular non-jazz groups. Jazz musicians had not made those groups into jazz groups any more than the presence of jazz hornmen in Blood, Sweat & Tears made that group into a jazz band. In other words, Blood, Sweat & Tears was a highly professional and creative group of musicians who performed several different styles of popular music; but they did not necessarily demonstrate a fusion of jazz with rock. Bands which developed a new kind of music by fusing jazz with rock and funk were led by Larry Coryell, Gary Burton, and Mike Nock. The most lasting fusions were made in the bands of trumpeter Miles Davis and in bands led by his sidemen between 1968 and 1975.[12]

TRAITS OF FUSION MUSIC

Jazz-rock fusion mixed jazz improvisation with the instrumentation and rhythmic conception of R & B. The compositions, tone colors, and rhythms were adopted not only by musicians who were just then developing their own styles, but also by older, established players. Rhythm sections began replacing piano with electric piano and synthesizer, and they replaced acoustic bass viol ("string bass") with electric bass guitar ("Fender"). Pianists and guitarists often adopted repeating accompanying riffs in place of the spontaneous comping which had been customary since the 1940s. Bassists began accumulating the syncopated and staccato figures found in the Motown bands of the late 1960s and the backup groups for James Brown and Sly Stone of the early 1970s. (See page 24 for instrument photos and page 500 for notations of rock bass figures.) Much as the early swing era bassists often had to play brass bass (tuba) as well as string bass viol, early fusion bassists often had to play bass guitar ("Fender") as well as string bass viol ("acoustic"), and many eventually abandoned bass viol altogether.

Drummers learned new timekeeping patterns that resembled those of R & B as well as Latin American styles. (See page 503 for notations of drumming figures used in recordings by Sly Stone and Herbie Hancock.) Jazz-rock drumming style was very full and active. Following the lead of Tony Williams, initially the high-hat was snapped shut sharply on every beat instead of every other beat. There was an increase in the use of drums, particularly the bass drum, and a decrease in the use of cymbals for timekeeping. The rhythms were stated insistently, not in the jazz manner that regularly alternated tension with relaxation. The jazz-rock style maintained a high level of tension for long periods. There was considerably less bounce and lilt than in jazz of the 1950s. Timekeeping was more strictly stated than during the exploratory years of jazz in the 1960s. The first models for jazz-rock drummers were Tony Williams and Billy Cobham; then, after the mid-1970s, Steve Gadd, and after the mid-1980s, Dave Weckl.

The jazz-oriented soloists in jazz-rock fusion tended to be inspired by John Coltrane's early-1960s style if they were saxophonists, Freddie Hubbard if they were trumpeters, and Herbie Hancock, McCoy Tyner, or Chick Corea if they were pianists. Bop melodic rhythms were not compatible with most jazz-rock accompaniment patterns, but the 1960s style of Coltrane's and Tyner's lines were. Pianists and guitarists often adopted repeating accompaniment riffs in place of the spontaneous comping that had been customary in jazz since the 1940s. Development of repeating patterns

TABLE 16.1   A Few of the Many Jazz-Rock Musicians and Bands

INSTRUMENTAL GROUPS AND THEIR LEADERS

Lifetime (Tony Williams)

The Head Hunters (Herbie Hancock)

Return to Forever (Chick Corea)

Mahavishnu Orchestra (John McLaughlin)

Free Spirits (Larry Coryell)

Fourth Way (Mike Nock)

Eleventh House (Larry Coryell)

Blackbyrds (Donald Byrd)

Prime Time (Ornette Coleman)

Spyro Gyra

Word of Mouth (Jaco Pastorius)

The Decoding Society (Ronald Shannon Jackson)

Caldera

Oracle

Soft Machine

Jeff Lorber Fusion

The Crusaders

Weather Report (Joe Zawinul and Wayne Shorter)

Miles Davis

Hiroshima

Steps Ahead

Yellow Jackets

Fourplay (Bob James)

Pieces of a Dream

SINGER-BASED BANDS

Blood, Sweat & Tears

Chicago

Ten Wheel Drive

Chase

TRUMPET

Randy Brecker

Tom Browne

Michael Lawrence

Lew Soloff

Miles Davis

SAXOPHONE

Michael Brecker

Wayne Shorter

David Liebman

Steve Grossman

Grover Washington

Eddie Harris

Ronnie Laws

David Sanborn

John Klemmer

Kenny G

Najee

PIANO

Herbie Hancock

Chick Corea

Joe Zawinul

Jan Hammer

Jeff Lorber

Milcho Leviev

George Duke

Bob James

Lyle Mays

GUITAR

Pat Metheny

Mike Stern

Al Dimeola

John McLaughlin

Larry Coryell

Steve Khan

Blood Ulmer

Larry Carlton

John Scofield

Bill Frisell

Alan Holdsworth

George Benson

VIOLIN

Michael White

Jerry Goodman

Jean-Luc Ponty

Michael Urbaniak

VIBRAPHONE

Gary Burton

Roy Ayers

DRUMS

Tony Williams

Billy Cobham

Steve Gadd

Lenny White

Leon Chancler

Ronald Shannon Jackson

Peter Erskine

Al Foster

David Weckl

Omar Hakim

Alphonse Mouzon

BASS GUITAR

Michael Henderson

Stanley Clarke

Jaco Pastorius

Rick Laird

Jeff Berlin

Jamaaladeen Tacuma

John Patitucci

Victor Bailey

Marcus Miller

in a funk music style usually took higher priority than comping, though the more adventuresome accompanists played spontaneously and responsively. The less jazz-oriented pianists in fusion devised their own simpler styles or imitated players who leaned more toward the rock side of the jazz-rock mix. The less jazz-oriented saxophonists used models from R & B and R & B-oriented jazz such as King Curtis, Junior Walker, Maceo Parker, Wilton Felder, and Hank Crawford. Popular models during the 1980s were Dave Sanborn and Michael Brecker (see Chapter 17). Then Grover Washington, Kenny G, and Najee were the most-imitated among young fusion saxophonists of the 1990s.

MILES DAVIS

In addition to developing many extensions of existing jazz styles, the 1964–1968 Miles Davis Quintet was one of the first established jazz groups to begin mixing the musical devices of rock and funk music with those of jazz. Rhythmic styles other than bouncy, swinging jazz patterns occur throughout their records. Drummer Tony Williams sometimes played straight, repeating eighth notes on the ride cymbal instead of playing the "ching chick-a ching" pattern. Occasionally, he also stated each beat by sharply snapping closed the high-hat, instead of closing it only on every other beat. Bassist Ron Carter sometimes complemented those drumming patterns with simple, repeating bass figures that did not fit traditional walking bass rhythms. All of this evoked a feeling that was similar to the rhythmic feeling of rock.[13] One album in particular, their 1968 *Filles de Kilimanjaro* (coming directly after *Miles in the Sky*), clearly signalled a trend away from jazz sound. It not only used electric piano and bass guitar, it also contained military-like drumming patterns that resembled the insistent playing of rock drummers more than the relaxed and lilting playing of modern jazz drummers.

The next two albums that Davis recorded became significant in directing modern jazz of the 1970s.[14] These records were *In a Silent Way* and *Bitches Brew*, both made in 1969. They contained a variety of musical approaches, but their dominant accompaniment style was a combination of jazz and funk. Their dominant melodic style was reminiscent of the floating, almost motionless feeling of Wayne Shorter's "Nefertiti"; and Shorter's tune "Sanctuary" was included on *Bitches Brew*.

Partnership with Joe Zawinul

In a Silent Way marked the beginning of Davis's important **partnership with pianist-composer Joe Zawinul,** who had been with the Cannonball Adderley quintet during the 1960s. Zawinul's ideas, compositions, arrangements, and keyboard playing helped lead the Davis band to a new style. In that way Zawinul played a role in the Davis career that was similar to those of Gil Evans in the late 1940s and late 1950s, Bill Evans on *Kind of Blue*, and Shorter from 1964 to 1969. Davis recorded Zawinul pieces of the "Nefertiti" style: "In a Silent Way" (*In a Silent Way*) and "Pharaoh's Dance" (*Bitches Brew*). Davis also used Zawinul's compositions on later albums, though Davis's name mistakenly appears as composer instead of Zawinul's on the album labels.[15]

Instrumentation

The post-1968 music of Davis differed in several respects from his 1963–1968 style. For example, **instrumentation** was altered as follows:

1. Electric piano and organ replaced conventional piano; and Davis often employed two or more electric keyboard instruments at once.
2. Electric bass guitar replaced acoustic bass viol (see page 24 for illustration).
3. Electric guitarists were more frequently employed; at one time, he had three in a single band.
4. The Davis saxophonists of this period played soprano sax more often than any other instrument. The soprano had the potential for penetrating and carrying its sound over drums and electric instruments, where a tenor might not cut through.
5. Davis usually employed two or more drummers. By the early 1970s, he had settled into the practice of using one player on conventional drum set and another on auxiliary percussion such as conga drums, shakers, rattles, gongs, whistles, and a large number of instruments native to Africa, South America, and India. Davis sometimes additionally used Indian musicians playing the sitar (a stringed instrument) and tabla (drums).

Rhythm Section Concept

The **rhythm section concept** was another way in which Davis's post-1968 groups differed from his 1963–1968 groups. The later groups featured elaborate configurations of colors and textures. His accompanists played with a very high level of activity. The beat was easily detectable, but it was surrounded by a mass of constantly changing sounds. Sometimes they were delicate and gentle. Sometimes they were turbulent. Textures often seemed to be created for their own sake rather than as accompaniments. For example, the textures on *In a Silent Way* and *Bitches Brew* were as much in the forefront as the written melodies and improvised solo lines. The textures were generated by several electric keyboard instruments (piano and organ), guitar, basses, and several drummers. Sources for the bass lines include rock formulas, a freely improvised nonwalking style, and figures borrowed from Latin American music. (See notated rock and Latin American bass figures in pages 500–501.)

Performance Format

Performance format and harmonies differed from previous jazz styles. Most post-1968 Davis music centered on a few repeated chords, a repeating bass figure, or a mode, rather than a sequence of frequently changing chords. The tunes reflected Wayne Shorter's composing style, particularly its departures from bop. Complexity was now concentrated in the rhythm section figures rather than in the melodies. This new format used medleys instead of the entire band stopping before going on to the next tune, everyone taking a turn soloing. Davis often set up a new mood and its harmonies by playing chords in a rhythmic fashion on an electric keyboard instrument. In this way he often dictated the tempo and rhythm for the next passage. Davis used this method to make transitions gracefully between moods within the medleys. Davis conducted the transitions between tunes, and his bassists led the way by changing the patterns of their repeating figures. The bass was the pivot in this music; **bass figures were as essential to the 1970s and 1980s style as complex chord changes had been to hard bop.** The albums *Live-Evil*, *Black Beauty*, and *Agharta* documented this music.

The electric jazz-funk band that ended a five-year retirement for trumpeter Miles Davis in 1981 (left to right): soprano saxophonist Bill Evans (his tenor sax is sitting to his right), bass guitarist Marcus Miller, Miles Davis (wearing hat, holding trumpet), Mino Cinelu (playing conga drum), Al Foster (playing full drum set). Guitarist Mike Stern, a regular member of this group, is not shown.

(Photo by Mark Vinci, 1982)

Despite the marked simplification in rhythm section harmonies, improvising soloists tended to retain considerable harmonic complexity. John Coltrane had perfected techniques for spontaneously superimposing sequential patterns atop relatively static accompaniments. Such patterns were devised in ways that made them sound as though they possessed the direction that one ordinarily detects in a progression of chords. The listener would hear a coherence that is normally associated with melody lines that closely mirror an underlying set of chord progressions. This time, however, that coherence did not necessarily derive from any progression of chords. This approach provided harmonic interest without depending on the movement of chords we ordinarily require to attain a similar effect. Coltrane and his pianist McCoy Tyner had developed these approaches for improvising on mode-based forms and repeating bass figures. The saxophonists and guitar soloists who worked with Miles Davis during the 1970s and 1980s used these same approaches. It is important to note that these techniques replaced the bop concepts of jazz phrasing; none of Charlie Parker's or Dizzy Gillespie's pet phrases were used. In fact, much of the lyricism that had been associated with bop was not evident in this new style. Improvisers seemed more intent on creating moods than melodies.

Personnel

After 1968, Miles Davis changed sidemen more frequently than he had in his late-1950s and his mid-1960s bands. For example, each new album during the 1968–1973 period had new personnel. Also, the musicians on tour were not always the same as those on the album. John Coltrane had been with Davis on and off for five years; Wayne Shorter had also stayed approximately five years. But after Shorter left, Davis employed more than five different saxophonists in five years.

Personnel in the Davis rhythm sections were more stable, however. After various combinations of pianists, bassists, and drummers, Davis settled for several years on drummers Al Foster (conventional set) and M'Tume Heath (conga drums and auxiliary percussion) and bass guitarist Michael Henderson. Between the 1971 departure of pianist Keith Jarrett and the mid-1980s, the Davis band often appeared without a keyboard instrument. Davis did, however, occasionally use one himself to begin pieces by setting up a mood with chords and rhythms. After 1971 he almost always carried at least one guitarist, sometimes using three at the same time.[16] Beginning in the mid-1980s, Davis again carried two keyboardists, as he had done briefly during the early 1970s. He also added a guitarist and a saxophonist.

Trumpet Style

For the new jazz-rock idiom, Davis added new dimensions to his trumpet style. As he had done on many live recordings of the 1960s, he again played fast, sweeping runs in and out of his extreme high register. He wired his instrument to an amplifier and connected electronic attachments which simulated echo (by means of a tape loop device called an Echoplex, evident on the title track from *Bitches Brew*). Sometimes he created alterations of tone color by means of the wah-wah pedal (evident on "Sivad" in *Live-Evil*). He could be quite violent and sound much like a rock guitarist, or he could play in the tender, mournful manner he had displayed on *Porgy and Bess* and *Sketches of Spain*.

Sometimes most of the band would become silent while Davis quietly played with only one other musician, but that was rare. Usually the mood was very outgoing and full of unrelenting tension. The level of musicianship was very high, and the complexity of the music set it apart from rock. It was often quite similar, however, to the loud turbulence of many rock bands of the 1960s and 1970s. Admiration for such non-jazz musicians as Jimi Hendrix and Billy Preston was evident in Davis's music.

John McLaughlin, virtuoso guitarist-composer who led the Mahavishnu Orchestra, a top fusion band of the 1970s.

(Photo by John Sobczak)

The post-1968 Davis recordings displayed a blend of the jazz tradition, funk music, and the music of India and South America. It was infused with the spirit of Coltrane, but the tone colors were those of rock.

1980s Formula

The mid- and late-1980s recordings of Davis sometimes contained unimprovised accompaniments produced for him by Robert Irving III and Marcus Miller. Davis added his trumpet sound to funk vamps that had been prepared by computerized synthesizers. His formula for much of the 1980s was to employ a Jimi Hendrix disciple on guitar and a Coltrane disciple on saxophone, both of whom could play hot solos on demand. This was placed atop thick layers of sounds produced by electronic keyboards, a drummer playing in a funk style that had been adapted for the Davis bands by Al Foster, and a bassist playing in the funk style of Marcus Miller. Davis rarely allowed his keyboardists to solo. His music of this period was highly arranged and not as freewheeling and explosively daring as in the period of *Live-Evil*, *Black Beauty*, and *Agharta*. It was energetic, however, and its sound usually remained distinguishable from most pop music of the period.

JOHN McLAUGHLIN

John McLaughlin (b. 1942) is a British guitarist who had been active in British rock bands[17] and jazz groups since the late 1950s. He first became known to American musicians during the period 1969–1971 when he began playing with Lifetime, the fusion band of drummer Tony Williams, and when he started recording with Miles Davis (see footnote 12).

McLaughlin is notable for his phenomenally high level of instrumental proficiency, and he has become one of the most prominent jazz guitarists since Wes Montgomery. Despite his being considered a jazz musician, McLaughlin used a tone which was unlike traditional jazz guitar quality. It was hard, not soft, cutting, not smooth, and metallic, not warm. In short, it had the color and texture preferred by rock guitarists, not jazz guitarists. Also, he frequently altered the size and shape of his tone by use of a wah-wah pedal and a phase shifter. (The phase shifter produces a subtle swirling of the sound.) Another point of contrast between McLaughlin and more traditional jazz guitarists is that most of his improvisations contain far less of the pronounced syncopation and the easy, relaxed, swing feeling that had previously typified jazz. Improvisations in McLaughlin performances were unlike the bouncy conception which was part of the Charlie Christian, Wes Montgomery, and Kenny Burrell styles. McLaughlin performances also lacked the gentle lyricism that characterizes improvisations by Jim Hall.

The syncopations in John McLaughlin's lines were more typical of rock than of jazz. And his solos were often composed of long strings of sixteenth notes periodically interrupted by held tones which McLaughlin expressively distorted in waveform and in pitch. The inflections he preferred were refinements of those customary in rock and in blues guitar playing. McLaughlin's rhythmic conception and his melodic conception had more in common with classical music and the 1960s improvisations of John Coltrane than with standard bop practice. In his long lines of sixteenth notes, he often chose sequences reminiscent of the patterns used by Coltrane. Both McLaughlin and Coltrane had studied the music of India and were fond of basing their solos on modes learned from this study.

During the early 1970s, McLaughlin played a custom-made electric guitar with two necks, one with six and the other with twelve strings. He also worked with the vina, a seven-string Indian instrument that has four playing strings and three accompanying strings. During the late 1970s, he played another specially built instrument inspired by the vina, with a form like an autoharp's, a scalloped fingerboard, and accompanying strings.

McLaughlin's work in Lifetime and in his own Mahavishnu Orchestra projected unusually high intensity, partly due to high amplifier settings and a stress on rapid-fire, multinoted themes with extremely busy accompaniment. The interaction and determination displayed by such Mahavishnu albums as his 1971 *Inner Mounting Flame* and his 1972 *Birds of Fire* come from a high level of cooperation and mutual inspiration between drummer Billy Cobham, electric bass guitarist Rick Laird, and electric pianist/synthesist Jan Hammer. Many listeners feel that these recordings remain benchmarks for ensemble cohesion and inspired jazz-rock improvisation. Feeling for this music was so high that *Birds of Fire* in 1973 reached the very high position of number 15 on *Billboard*'s record sales chart in the popular album category. Most jazz albums never even reach position number 200. These two Mahavishnu albums are also distinctive for their use of irregular meters—time signatures which, though common to Indian music, had previously been rare in jazz and rock.[18] Many listeners consider this to have been the greatest of all fusion bands.

Not all of McLaughlin's 1970s output consisted of high-intensity electronic music. He also recorded on hollow-body guitar in his 1970 *My Goal's Beyond*,[19] an album which McLaughlin personally lists among his favorite works. It contains one side of overdubbed, self-accompanying, solo guitar improvisations and one side with saxophone, violin, acoustic bass, and drums. There is an expansive and exhilarated feeling in the solo side, especially in McLaughlin's rendering of his original composition "Follow Your Heart." Though he left the nonelectric approach for a few years right after this album, McLaughlin returned to it when touring and recording with Shakti, an Indian music ensemble composed of violin, tabla, mrindagam, and ghatam. His fondness for the nonelectronic sound also emerged in what many fans consider to contain his best solo: "Rene's Theme," a duet with fellow guitarist Larry Coryell on Coryell's *Spaces*[20] album of 1970. This pairing with Coryell recurred during the 1980s when McLaughlin toured in duo and trio with several other guitar giants, all playing hollow-body guitar: Coryell, Al Dimeola, Christian Escoude, and Spanish flamenco guitarist Paco de Lucia.

Guitarist Larry Coryell, one of the first musicians to devise original combinations of jazz, rock, and country music. He began a series of innovative bands during the late 1960s.

(Photo by Bill Smith)

LARRY CORYELL

Guitarist **Larry Coryell** (b. 1943) is especially significant in jazz history because he was one of the first to blend the styles of country music, blues guitar, and rock with established jazz styles. He did this during the mid-1960s while playing in the bands of drummer Chico Hamilton and vibraphonist Gary Burton. Coryell's own group, the Free Spirits, was also active in 1966, well before the historic rise of rock-influenced jazz groups in 1969 and 1970 (see footnote 6). Burton had been attracted to Coryell's work with the Free Spirits and the possibilities that it suggested for jazz. The 1967 *Duster* album contains several passages in which Coryell solos in a style clearly drawn from rock (see footnote 7). Burton and his other sidemen follow Coryell's lead and manage to approximate the flavor and intensity of Coryell's work. Burton further pursued this avenue with guitarist Jerry Hahn on a 1968 album called *Country Roads and Other Places,* and then continued to employ excellent guitarists who were interested in combining country music, rock, and jazz. Along the way, Burton introduced Mick Goodrick and Pat Metheny.[21]

The Free Spirits, Foreplay (Coryell's 1969–1972 band), and the Eleventh House (a later band) were all jazz-rock groups, but Coryell was not strictly a rock guitarist. As early as his time with Chico Hamilton, Coryell had proven himself to be an unusually imaginative and technically proficient improviser of jazz lines. His playing could be distinguished from McLaughlin's because Coryell's note beginnings were more percussive; they had more "pop." In addition, he was given to greater variety in his solos than McLaughlin. The twists and turns in Coryell's lines suggested more jazz roots. All these comparisons are easy to make because McLaughlin performed on Coryell's *Spaces* album, which documents a time when both guitarists were at a peak of creativity and technical prowess.[22]

JOSEF ZAWINUL

Joe Zawinul (1932–2007) was a pianist and composer who moved from his native Vienna, Austria, to the United States in 1959. His first great impact was made with the bands of saxophonist Cannonball Adderley between 1961 and 1970, during which time he authored two of the band's most popular funk hits, "Mercy, Mercy, Mercy"[23] and "Walk Tall." His next great success came when Miles Davis used his "In a Silent Way" as the title track for a 1969 album that pioneered the fusion of jazz improvisation with electronic instruments and funk accompaniment patterns. Davis also included Zawinul's "Pharaoh's Dance" on *Bitches Brew* and used Zawinul as chief arranger for *In a Silent Way* and *Bitches Brew.*

In 1971 Zawinul founded an innovative jazz-rock fusion band called Weather Report. With this band's 1977 *Heavy Weather*[24] album, he enjoyed his greatest record sales since "Mercy, Mercy, Mercy." (The album became a certified "gold" album because it sold more than 500,000 copies.) It contained Zawinul's "Birdland," an arrangement of catchy, syncopated phrases in extended repetition. This piece was inspired by the composer's memories of hearing the Count Basie band at the New York nightclub called Birdland. It epitomizes the danceable, riff-band style favored by Basie, though translated here into jazz-rock. "Birdland" received wide exposure in discotheques and in recordings by the Maynard Ferguson big band and the vocal group Manhattan Transfer. It was later redone for a Quincy Jones album called *Back on the Block*. (Listen to the original "Birdland" on *JCCD1* Track 6. It is positioned immediately following Count Basie's "One O'Clock Jump" so that listeners can compare Zawinul's approach with the music that inspired it. The complete recording is in *CCD2* Track 11.)

Zawinul made significant contributions in the use of electronic instruments for jazz. He had used the Wurlitzer electric piano on Adderley's 1966 recording of "Mercy, Mercy, Mercy," and he subsequently employed a Fender Rhodes electric piano on tour. Singer-bandleader Ray Charles had previously carried electric piano, as had Sun Ra, but it was not common in jazz until Zawinul began using it. Miles Davis was so taken with the Fender Rhodes when he heard Zawinul playing it in Adderley's band that he required its use by three successive pianists in his own bands—Herbie Hancock, Chick Corea, and Keith Jarrett—thereby influencing subsequent work by those men with their own groups. The Rhodes became the most common keyboard instrument in jazz groups of the 1970s; even such non-fusion pianists as Bill Evans and Oscar Peterson recorded with it. Zawinul was also one of the first musicians to master the Oberheim Polyphonic[25] and the Arp and Prophet synthesizers, as well as the ring modulator.[26]

One of the leading composers of the 1970s, Zawinul demonstrated a creativity which parallels that of Charles Mingus in the 1950s and Duke Ellington in the 1940s. He generated a broader variety of melodic and accompaniment rhythms than possibly any other jazz composer of the 1970s. Zawinul wrote numerous pieces that touched highly diverse tone colors and moods. Throughout his albums with Weather Report run playful melodies with highly imaginative accompaniments.[27] His "In a Silent Way" and "Arrival in New York" are impressionistic tone poems.[28]

Zawinul encouraged the use of a wide assortment of exotic percussion instruments by his musicians. He produced unusual timbres and rhythms by playing clay drum, tambura, xylophone, steel drums, and African thumb piano. Gentle sounds are conjured by ocarina, hollow-body guitar, thumb piano, and tambura on his "Jungle Book."[29] And like Ellington, Zawinul arranged wordless vocals.[30] The breadth of timbral spectra in Weather Report's work might explain how Zawinul's music found its way onto the turntables of demonstration units in stereo equipment stores. Weather Report's creations had joined symphonic music as a vast source of varied timbres and loudnesses by which to judge the quality of sound systems.

WEATHER REPORT

When Joe Zawinul left Cannonball Adderley's quintet in 1971, he joined saxophonist Wayne Shorter and bassist Miroslav Vitous to develop new concepts in improvisatory music for a band they called Weather Report. Zawinul, Shorter, and Vitous were joined by two drummers. One played on conventional drum set, and one played exotic percussion instruments, creating sound effects for which Airto Moreira had become known in the bands of Miles Davis. It should be noted that Weather Report performed in a broad range of styles that combined jazz with nonjazz styles in original

"Surucucu" by Weather Report

Composed by Wayne Shorter; recorded January 13, 1972, in Tokyo, Japan, by Weather Report: Wayne Shorter (soprano sax), Joe Zawinul (piano), Miroslav Vitous (bass), Dom Um Romao (auxiliary percussion and vocal), and Eric Gravatt (drums); reissued on Weather Report, *I Sing the Body Electric* (Columbia: 46107, 1971–72, c1990).

Weather Report originated numerous approaches in their 15-year career. (An excerpt from their biggest hit concludes the African-American retentions sequence on *JCCD1* Track 6.) Though most famous for their funk music performed with electric instruments and their role as the premier jazz-rock fusion band, they are also historically significant for the way they loosened the roles of the rhythm section instruments and spontaneously devised collective interplay that was smoother and pleased more listeners than similar "free" jazz of the 1960s. Aside from the music on the band's first album (*Weather Report*, Columbia 48824 [30661], 1971, c1992), little of this loosely organized work is demonstrated in their studio recordings. We are therefore fortunate to have this concert recording available as documentation.

This performance draws partly upon a composed theme, Wayne Shorter's "Surucucu." But the musicians do not neatly divide their improvisations into a set number of beats that parallel the theme, nor do they use the theme to provide a chord progression that strictly prescribes the motion of harmonies for improvisation. The arrangement is spontaneous, and the theme is represented only in very fragmented form, a phrase here and there being played out of tempo by Shorter. Moreover, the sequence of sections here does not follow the traditional pattern of introduction, theme, solo choruses, theme, end.

Most of the sounds in this performance will be unfamiliar. The first sound was made by Dom Um Romao slapping his face and changing the shape of his mouth while making vocal sounds articulated by quick tongue movements. The zither-like sounds that accompany Romao's voice are produced by Joe Zawinul playing what is technically termed "prepared piano." Before the performance, he had prepared the piano strings by laying weights on top of some, wedging pieces of rubber between others, attaching clothes pins to others. Zawinul caused the piano strings to vibrate sometimes by plucking them himself and sometimes by depressing the piano keys in the conventional manner.

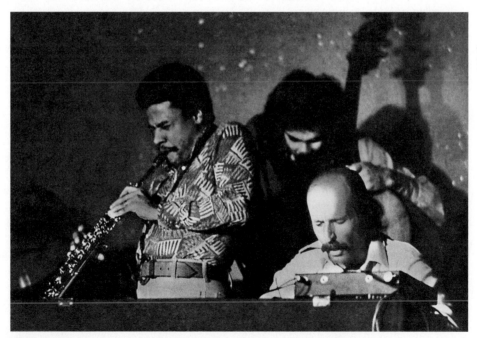

Wayne Shorter (soprano saxophone), Miroslav Vitous (bass), and Joe Zawinul (piano), founding members of Weather Report and masters of collective improvisation. Pictured here in the early 1970s.

(Photo by Bill Smith)

LISTENING GUIDE continued on next page

To appreciate how the music of Weather Report is unique, it is helpful to notice what is not heard: walking bass, ride rhythms, comping, and bop style horn solos. (Compare the "Surucucu" performance, for instance, with the playing of Chick Corea, Miroslav Vitous, and Roy Haynes on "Steps" on *JCCD3*.) It is also important to recognize that the piece hangs together and has its own momentum without depending on many of the devices that propel standard jazz performances. There are exceptions. Vitous does briefly play repeating patterns on bass, as at 1'25" into the piece, and Gravatt sometimes maintains long strings of repeated eighth notes distributed across different cymbals and drums, for example at 1'33". Their most common practice, however, is to invent variations on steady rhythmic figures rather than strict repetitions of them.

ELAPSED TIME

0'00"	voice, accompanied by prepared piano and the sounds of Romao slapping his own face
0'27"	chords on prepared piano (to 0'39")
0'34"	the tinkling of a triangle
0'45"	trills played on a wooden flute
0'53"	Percussion enters; bass sustains deep-pitched tones.
1'07"	wire brushes playing snare drum and cymbals (to 1'15")
1'10"	slide whistle
1'18"	Bass interjects sporadic comments.
1'20"	Timekeeping rhythms begin on cymbals struck with drum sticks.
1'25"	resonant, low pitched tones of highly amplified bass viol, played pizzicato in a timekeeping manner, accompanied by cymbals
1'27"	Zawinul is strumming the strings inside the piano (to 1'50").
1'33"	a single squawk from Shorter's soprano sax
	steadily repeating eighth notes on drums and cymbals
1'39"	chords played on prepared piano
1'50"	a sequence of sustained sax tones (to 2'32") (a paraphrase of the "Surucucu" melody) accompanied by acoustic piano
2'17"	Zawinul strumming the strings inside the piano
2'20"	"Surucucu" melody in ascending sax tones which are detached from each other, ending with a high, scream-like sound and fall-off at 2'30"
2'34"	Rhythm section unwinds, then resumes its pace.
2'40"	strumming inside piano (to 2'50")
2'55"	high-pitched descending arpeggios on piano
3'05"	stop-time
3'07"	Zawinul plays highly amplified Fender Rhodes electric piano and makes it sound like the distorted tone of a rock musician's electric guitar (to 3'35").
3'30"	Sax and electric piano improvise against each other, accompanied by bass and percussion (to 3'53").
3'53"	Shorter acts as though a member of the rhythm section by producing an unaccompanied, repeating figure in a fast staccato manner.
4'01"	Shorter's staccato figure accompanies Vitous, who has abandoned an accompanying role in favor of a melodic line played by bowing highly amplified upright bass.
4'04"	duet between legato sax and bass (to 4'36")
4'15"	fade out

ways, thereby "fusing" assortments of different styles. In other words, they invented some of their own styles, but only a few of them qualify as jazz-rock fusion. The **collective improvisation of musical textures and the emancipation of rhythm section instruments from conventional roles were significant aspects of Weather Report's approach.**

Miroslav Vitous was a bassist uniquely able to improvise melodies as well as the average horn player, and he had already demonstrated his ability to alternate roles when he abandoned the timekeeping role in several selections on his own album *Infinite Search.*[31] Vitous had a sophisticated melodic sense that put him in a class with such outstanding bass soloists as Paul Chambers and Scott LaFaro. He was also very capable with bowed bass. Vitous had a keen sense of what to play for the sake of creating interesting rhythmic textures and how to keep his instrument's voice in sensitive musical conversations with other group members. Vitous did not merely break up walking bass lines or play in a decorative-two feeling. **The Vitous contributions to Weather Report included fragmented melody statements, bowed sustained tones, and syncopated interjections.** He could just as easily bow melody in unison with a sax line as feed rock-style bass figures into the group texture. Vitous could play in unison with a rhythm the drummer was stating on ride cymbal or underscore a pattern being played on piano. Or, he could quickly go back and forth. Vitous had cast off the restraints of traditional bass playing and had become a textural improviser in the Weather Report context. Moreover, his work made sense, too. It was not just the flashy playing of a gifted showoff.

"Surucucu," JCCD3
Track 6

Airto Moreira overdubbed percussion parts in the recording studio for Weather Report's first album. Though he never performed with the band, his imaginative, highly original use of Latin American percussion instruments provided a model for the unique combination of sounds that Weather Report refined. Dom Um Romao, another outstanding Brazilian percussionist, was the band's regular percussionist. Within a few weeks of the band's inception, Eric Gravatt became the band's regular drummer. The band then underwent numerous personnel changes, and, by the mid-1970s, bassist Miroslav Vitous was gone, and the only founding members who remained were Shorter and Zawinul. Then after 1985, Shorter and Zawinul were leading separate groups.

Weather Report came on the scene with the standard instrumentation of saxophone, piano, bass, and drums. They also had an auxiliary percussionist, but that was not unusual; many 1950s and 1960s jazz groups had employed conga drummers or other auxiliary percussionists to add a Latin American flavor to their sound. What was unusual is that in its earliest albums, **Weather Report did not use its conventional instrumentation in conventional ways.** It was rare for bassist Miroslav Vitous to play walking lines, or for the drummer to play standard ride rhythms or snap the high-hat closed sharply on every other beat. Zawinul usually did not comp for Shorter, and the auxiliary percussionist was not restricted to the conga drum.[32]

Collective Improvisation

Weather Report explored an unusual approach to combo improvisation on their first three albums.[33] (On *JCCD3* Track 6, this approach is exemplified on "Surucucu," from Weather Report's *I Sing the Body Electric.*) **Instead of adhering to roles consistent with bop traditions, the instruments in Weather Report performed a variety of different roles.** Spurts of melody might come from any member, not just from the saxophone. Rhythmic figures and fills could come from any member, not just from a bassist or drummer.

The kinds of interaction between members were so varied that **in some pieces there was no distinction between soloist and accompanist.** One player's sound might stand out momentarily from the ensemble texture, but it soon blended into the overall texture again. In this situation, every member had to be capable of playing melodically as well as merely adding to the overall texture of the group sound in a nonmelodic fashion. Weather Report's members developed special techniques for managing such tasks. (See Chapter 3 for an explanation of standard jazz solo and accompaniment roles.)

The swing and bop convention of solo choruses was not evident on Weather Report's first album. One particular voice such as saxophone, piano, or bass did often hold the focal point for a few moments. However, it maintained much more continuity with the entire piece than did conventional jazz solos. Swing and bop style soloists had adhered to fixed chorus lengths, and they were improvising without much regard for whether mood or color was developed or continued from the preceding solo.

In Weather Report's first three albums, each member's work contributed to the prevailing mood and color rather than to a solo concept. They did not usually feature themselves. They played primarily to serve the group sound. This produced a variety of consistently maintained musical feelings and flavors. Weather Report offered a greater variety of moods and sound textures than most bop, cool, and hard bop groups. Only bands led by such versatile composers as Duke Ellington, Charles Mingus, and Sun Ra had achieved comparable breadth.[34]

Away from Improvised Textures

Weather Report did not entirely abandon collective approaches, but much of their work after their 1973 *Sweetnighter* album left collectively improvised approaches in favor of more repeated, written themes and preset rhythm section figures. Many of these rhythms were freshly devised by Zawinul, not borrowed from Latin American or funk music models. With *Sweetnighter*, Weather Report began including more compositions constructed of brief phrases repeated continually and accompanied by a more repetitive, funk-influenced rhythm section style. With this new emphasis on repetition and funk, Zawinul sought to capture a larger segment of the record-buying market. And, as exemplified by "Boogie Woogie Waltz" on *Sweetnighter*, this music departed from the style of the band's earlier innovations. Their discotheque hit "Birdland" on their 1977 *Heavy Weather* album exemplifies these methods. The new strategy led to wider popular acceptance of the band. Much of Weather Report's music during the 1980s, especially the pieces without Shorter, is essentially party music. It was conceptually less daring than the group's earliest efforts. When we consider Weather Report's music, we must distinguish between the collectively improvised and the preset, highly repetitive phases.

Historical Significance

In summary, Weather Report is significant in jazz history for a number of different reasons.

1. Their first three albums:
    a. brought simultaneous collective improvisation to a new level of refinement;
    b. offered collective improvisation that was rhythmically compelling at the same time as it was rich with wide-ranging tone colors; and
    c. demonstrated the improvisation of textures more than jazz solo lines and did this in a way palatable to much larger audiences than previous attempts had attracted.

2. Their group concept afforded a unique opportunity for emancipation of the bassist from bop roles.

3. The band evolved a form of jazz-funk that featured more improvisation than most other fusion bands used.

4. It was one of the first fusion bands to achieve popular recognition without using vocals.

5. It made more original and extensive use of exotic rhythms than previous jazz groups.

6. The band combined the talents of several jazz giants and gave them a unique platform for creative composing and improvising.

JACO PASTORIUS

In 1976, bass guitarist **Jaco Pastorius** (1951–1987) joined Weather Report. To understand the roles he assumed in the band, note the four ways Zawinul called upon his bassists to perform. First is the standard jazz technique of **walking bass** (as demonstrated by Miroslav Vitous on "Eurydice" in Weather Report's first album, CBS 30661). Second is a **nonrepetitive, interactive approach** (exemplified by Scott LaFaro's work with the 1961 Bill Evans trio in "Solar"). This was demonstrated by Miroslav Vitous in his improvisations within "Waterfall" on Weather Report's first album. This technique requires that the bassist second-guess his colleagues, discreetly omit many notes, and play only when it will do the most good. It also demands considerable imagination. Third is what is commonly called "**funk bass**" (see page 500 for notations). This is the repetition of highly syncopated bass figures, often filled with staccato notes, which are played with a contagious feeling that moves people in a way peculiar to funk music. These types of figures were common in the popular dance music of the 1970s and 1980s. This technique was not a specialty for Miroslav Vitous, though it was for his replacement, Alphonso Johnson. The fourth role of the bassist in Weather Report was to **solo.** This was, however, not a high priority for Weather Report bassists until Pastorius joined the group. Pastorius was outstanding in all four bass roles. He walked persuasively.[35] He played in the nonrepetitive, interactive style.[36] He played funk style with great naturalness.[37]

"Solar," JCCD3
Track 3

Pastorius appreciably altered the character of Weather Report's sound and the rhythmic feeling that went with it.[38] The bassist's fluid tone, his use of vibrato at the end of some notes, and his ease of playing all combined with his high energy and playful spirit to propel the band in a lighthearted way not previously part of the group's sound. In Pastorius, Zawinul found an enticing soloist with all the other qualities he had originally sought from Miroslav Vitous and Alphonso Johnson. And he discovered a versatile and original composer who contributed "Barbary Coast," "Teen Town," "Havona," "Punk Jazz," "River People," and "Three Views of a Secret" to the Weather Report repertory.

Weather Report concerts during the late 1970s always featured an unaccompanied Pastorius solo. The bassist drew upon electronic means for altering sound in ways reminiscent of guitarist Jimi Hendrix. Pastorius used playback echo to provide spontaneous accompaniments for his improvisations. He extracted chords from his instrument and capitalized on overtones to orchestrate his performance as though he had an entire band behind him. He demonstrated the same prodigious speed that had impressed listeners who heard his 1976 recording of the intricate bop melody "Donna Lee."[39]

In 1982, Pastorius left Weather Report and launched his own unique group called Word of Mouth. Using no keyboard instruments or guitars for chording, Pastorius employed trumpet and saxophone paired with steel drum and his bass to state melody lines. On this band's first album,[40] he employed the sound of harmonica as well as thick-textured ensemble writing at times reminiscent of Gil Evans and Thad Jones. Like Zawinul, Pastorius used the gentle sound of children's voices as an additional seasoning in his timbral repertory.[41] Diversity was the byword of his presentations. Pastorius explored a unique spectrum of tonal textures. He tapped orchestral music and the music of the Caribbean as well as American pop styles such as soul music.

Pastorius set the pace for a new generation of jazz bassists. He became the most imitated bassist after Jimmy Blanton, Paul Chambers, and Scott LaFaro. Many talented bassists entered the jazz scene during the 1970s and 1980s. And because electric bass guitar was the instrument most preferred in jazz and jazz-rock fusion groups of the 1970s, there was a great need for an inspiring model to imitate. Pastorius became that model, in part because he received wide exposure due to Weather Report's wide popularity. Pastorius also became a model because the speed and grace with which he played were almost hypnotizing. Practice rooms were soon humming with the sounds of bass guitarists attempting to duplicate the Pastorius rendition of "Donna Lee." However, Pastorius held the attention of new bassists not just with his speed. He impressed them also with a special tone quality composed of overtones that were not associated with funk bassists or jazz bassists. It had a high center of gravity and a slippery texture. He capitalized on overtones that allowed his instrument to project a delicacy that had not been associated with it before. The way he used it also departed from tradition. He played his rhythmic figures with a very graceful legato quality that any classical orchestra player would be proud to produce. He imparted a singing quality to his solo lines and to many of his accompanying lines as well. By the mid-1980s, numerous fusion records were being issued which made fans listen very closely before they knew the sound was not Pastorius but merely a facile Pastorius disciple. However, even if the disciples succeeded in replicating his tone and speed, their playing could be distinguished from the model by the boldness and vigor of Pastorius's ideas and the swaggering character with which he carried them out.

PAT METHENY

Pat Metheny (b. 1954) is a guitarist-composer-bandleader who became one of the biggest names in jazz of the 1970s and 1980s. His initial exposure came as a featured soloist with vibraphonist Gary Burton's group from 1974 to 1977 (see footnote 21). He then formed his own group with keyboardist Lyle Mays and continued with it through-

Pat Metheny, 2005
(Photo by C. Andrew Hovan)

Composed by Paul Jackson, Harvey Mason, Bennie Maupin, and Herbie Hancock; recorded in 1973 by Herbie Hancock (Arp Odyssey Synthesizer, Hohner D Clavinet, Arp Soloist Synthesizer, Fender Rhodes Electric Piano), Bennie Maupin (tenor saxophone), Paul Jackson (electric bass guitar), Harvey Mason (drums), Bill Summers (conga drum); available on the *Prentice Hall Jazz Collection*; reissued on Hancock, *Head Hunters* (Columbia/Legacy: 65123, 1973, c1997).

This performance is drawn from one of the highest selling albums in jazz history: Herbie Hancock's *Head Hunters*. The piece illustrates (1) one of the funk accompaniment styles that proliferated during the 1970s and became common practice thereafter, (2) several of the electronic instruments that bands of the fusion period carried, (3) the style of saxophone playing discussed in the next chapter under "soul saxes," and (4) how Hancock can make jazz over an accompaniment style that is totally unlike swing or bop.

Note: The complete original "Chameleon" runs 15 minutes and 43 seconds, and most of it is composed of a repeating riff and no solo improvisation. Therefore, we have excerpted the final six minutes because it contains the characteristic bass figure that ties the piece together, a substantial solo improvisation by Hancock, and a good sample of tenor saxophone soloing. Bennie Maupin selected a soul sax, funky approach to fulfill the pop music demands of this piece, though he was stylistically quite versatile, played many different woodwind instruments, and was widely respected for a non-pop style of improvisation. Incidentally, his lines here are more inventive and better developed than those of most soul saxes (see next chapter), who became far better known than Maupin. This excerpt begins at the beginning of Hancock's second solo and fades out during the sax improvisation at the same time that the original recording faded out.

Hancock's solo lines are improvised on Fender Rhodes electric piano, the most common keyboard instrument in jazz during the 1970s. The piano lines played by Hancock's right hand are accompanied by the funk rhythms of electric bass guitar, a conga drum, a complete drum set with heavy emphasis on snare drum and high-hat cymbals, Hancock's own synthesizer figures, and, once in a while, comping chords played by his left hand. A variety of sounds played on synthesizers weave in and out behind the solo. Flute-like synthesizer sound occurs at 0'51", 0'59", and 1'59". A violin-like synthesizer sound occurs at 0'00", 1'07", 2'14", and 3'05". These sounds were overdubbed after the initial recording. In his solo, Hancock alternates between strings of assorted melodic ideas scampering over the funk accompaniment and long pauses. Sometimes the pauses seem to be motivated by the interruptions of the synthesizer figures. Other times, they seem to be opportunities to consider new possibilities. The composition's opening bass line returns at 3'17", played by synthesizer, after which the piano solo resumes. The next time the opening line recurs, it is followed by a soulful tenor sax solo.

ELAPSED TIME

0'00"	**Herbie Hancock's Fender Rhodes Electric Piano Solo**
	Hancock improvises flowing lines in upper register.
	Dense, funk-style drumming, lots of crackling snare drum sounds, conga drum, and popping figures from bass guitar accompany Hancock's piano improvisation. Chords are briefly sustained by synthesizer making violin-like sounds.
0'34"	Clavinet offers a simple countermelody until 0'44". Hancock's solo is less predictable than its accompaniment.
0'51"	Synthesizer makes syncopated flute-like sounds.
0'59"	more flute-like interjections
1'07"	Synthesizer makes sustained violin-like sounds to 1'23".
1'12"	Hancock's improvisation is scampering over the funk accompaniment.
1'26"	Drummer is striking high-hat while it is closed and lets it ring open briefly after each stroke. Snare drum figures coexist with high-hat figures.
1'40"	Hancock plays a brief figure eight times, each with a different ending.
1'59"	more flute-like synthesizer interjections to 2'12"
2'12"	sustained violin-like synthesizer sounds to 2'21"
2'21"	Hancock's line is harmonized.

LISTENING GUIDE continued on next page

2'29"	Syncopated chords temporarily replace single note at a time lines until 2'34".
3'05"	syncopated violin-like synthesizer sounds
3'17"	Tenor sax joins piano to sound one of the main themes.
3'49"	Ensemble plays original theme.
	Hancock's solo is interrupted several times by sustained chords from a violin-like synthesizer sound, during which complementary snare drum activity is prominent.
4'38"	Sax plays with ensemble, restating the ending figure.
4'49"	return of opening bass line played by synthesizer
4'58"	Electric bass guitar repeats high-pitched figure.
5'09"	**Bennie Maupin Tenor Sax Solo**
	Maupin's solo is typical of soul sax soloists: cutting tone, short funky phrases, lots of blue notes, pitch scoops prefacing important melody notes. Accompaniment includes original bass figure on synthesizer, punching staccato figures from another synthesizer, popping figures from electric bass guitar, drum sticks striking closed high-hat, and snare drum interjections. The recording ends with a fade out.
6'46"	fade out

out the 1980s. Originally influenced by Wes Montgomery, Metheny also incorporated elements of country music and the approach of Ornette Coleman in the process of developing his own unique style. Many of his compositions and solo improvisations have a twangy, loping, country music flavor. Known for his good taste and excellent sense of balance, he plays with an inspired lyricism that makes his solos flow gracefully and naturally. There is a remarkable evenness to his playing. In fact, Metheny plays syncopated rhythms in such a smooth way that they don't sound syncopated. His lines are nearly always legato, and his facility is so good that each note is cleanly played and linked smoothly to the next. Among guitarists, Metheny is also known for popularizing a sound that depends partly on electronic means for reverberating his notes by means of studio-quality equipment that he carried with him.[42] His affinity for Ornette Coleman and for Keith Jarrett, who has roots in Coleman, make Metheny's style especially compatible with that of his pianist, Lyle Mays, a Jarrett disciple. Together, Mays and Metheny have pioneered lush combinations of electronic alterations of keyboard and guitar sounds and integrated them rhythmically into an original quartet concept.[43] Their group sound is remarkably spacious and uncluttered. The music conveys a clear sense of openness. Though some of his music from the late 1980s falls into the "new age" category, Metheny might best be viewed as a fusion player who is sufficiently versatile and creative to play well in a number of different jazz styles. In fact, he even recorded an extremely turbulent album of free jazz with Ornette Coleman.[44]

Demo CD Track 97

POPULAR APPEAL

By 1990, rock had been popular twice as long as swing in the mainstream of American music, and jazz-rock fusion itself had been popular for more than two decades. Fusion became the first jazz style since the swing era to gain popular acceptance anywhere near the level accorded swing, and it lasted at least as long as the swing era. By incorporating elements of R & B and rock into their music, several established jazz figures achieved popular success that rivaled all the peaks of recognition accorded to jazz players since the end of the swing era's wide appreciation of jazz-oriented band music.[45]

Though jazz instrumentals ordinarily sold fewer than 10,000 to 20,000 copies, jazz-rock albums of the 1970s and 1980s frequently sold more than 100,000 copies.[46]

This new success for jazz musicians did not depend so much on jazz character as on jazz-rock character. As with swing era big band recordings, those pieces presenting the least improvisation tended to enjoy the most popular acclaim. As with the hits of the swing era, jazz-rock hits were identifiable by simple, repeating riffs syncopated in a catchy way. Much of what went by the jazz-rock label consisted of little more than funky rhythm vamps, elementary chord progressions, and an improvised solo riding on top.[47] This music was so popular that, in addition to the "jazz-rock" and "jazz fusion" labels, it also acquired the label of "crossover" music because sales of the records crossed over from the jazz market into the popular market.

There are several possible explanations for the new popularity of jazz and jazz-rock in particular. First, rock had already been popular for more than 15 years by the time that Herbie Hancock's *Head Hunters* was released. (Listen to "Chameleon" on *JCCD3* Track 7 .) So perhaps when jazz **adopted the electric instruments and the accompaniment rhythms associated with rock,** and rock was so familiar already, the instruments and rhythms provided a bridge of similarity for listeners that eased them into a music that had otherwise been strange and difficult to listen to. A second possibility is that the **increased prominence of drums was more inviting to dancers.**

Third is the **relative simplicity of chord progressions** found in jazz-rock. The new music was more involved than rock had been, but it was harmonically less complex than other jazz styles. A fourth explanation involves the **extensive use of repetition**

Herbie Hancock's first fusion band: Hancock (Fender Rhodes electric piano), Buster Williams (bass guitar; his acoustic bass is lying on its side, between him and the drums), Bennie Maupin (bass clarinet), Billy Hart (drums), Eddie Henderson (fluegelhorn), and Julian Priester (trombone; only partially shown). This photo was taken in 1971, near the time the band recorded *Sextant, Mwandishi,* and *Crossings.*

(Courtesy of the Cleveland Press Collection/Cleveland State University Archives)

for a single accompaniment pattern. Technically it is known as *ostinato*, which means that a particular rhythm or brief melodic figure is repeated continuously. It was fundamental to most of the jazz-rock hits of the 1970s, and its use might explain the enormous popularity of the boogie woogie style of jazz piano playing during the 1940s. Many of the largest-selling recordings in any category of music are distinguished by their simplicity, rhythmic vitality, and extensive use of repetition. This combination of features could also account for much of jazz-rock's commercial success.

JAZZ-ROCK FUSION

Roots of Jazz-Rock Fusion

1. Accompaniment styles of pop bands led by James Brown and Sly Stone
2. Improvisational styles of John Coltrane and McCoy Tyner
3. Song forms based on brief, repeating chord progressions called vamps
4. Electric keyboard instruments and electric bass guitar
5. Auxiliary percussion instruments from Latin America and India

Top Names in Jazz-Rock Fusion

Bandleaders: Miles Davis, Joe Zawinul, John McLaughlin, Herbie Hancock

Guitarists: Larry Coryell, John McLaughlin, Pat Metheny

Drummers: Tony Williams, Billy Cobham

Saxophonists: Wayne Shorter, Michael Brecker

CHAPTER SUMMARY

1. Jazz and rock represent separate streams in African American music which have occasionally overlapped.
2. Jazz differs from rock in its smaller amount of repetition, larger amount of improvisation, greater complexity, and higher musicianship.
3. Chicago Transit Authority (Chicago), Blood, Sweat & Tears, and Ten Wheel Drive ought not to be called jazz-rock because they used little improvisation and had more roots in soul music than in rock and roll.
4. These three groups represent amalgamations of existing trends, such as the band styles of James Brown, rather than a fresh style.
5. The most original fusions of funk and jazz occurred in bands of Larry Coryell, Gary Burton, Miles Davis, and the bands launched by their sidemen.
6. The most prominent jazz-rock guitarists were John McLaughlin, Larry Coryell, and Pat Metheny.
7. Their tone color and rhythmic conception departed from jazz guitar tradition and drew more from urban blues and rock practices.
8. John McLaughlin plays with phenomenal speed and precision, and draws from the music of India and John Coltrane.
9. McLaughlin led several innovative bands containing musicians who were themselves important jazz-rock bandleaders.
10. Pianist Joe Zawinul wrote the funk hits "Mercy, Mercy, Mercy" and "Walk Tall" while with Cannonball Adderley's band.
11. Zawinul's arrangements formed the basis for the important 1969 Miles Davis jazz-rock albums *Bitches Brew* and *In a Silent Way*.

---

12. In 1971, Zawinul and Wayne Shorter founded Weather Report, an innovative fusion band which lasted until 1985.

13. Weather Report originally began with much collective improvisation.

14. Weather Report eventually adopted approaches employing extensive repetition and the feeling of soul music, culminating in Zawinul's riff-based hit "Birdland." Their later approaches influenced "smooth jazz."

15. Jaco Pastorius was the bass guitarist with Weather Report from 1976 to 1982, and his sound became an important model for bassists.

16. The post-1968 work of Miles Davis displayed a blend of the jazz tradition, funk music, and the music of India and South America.

NOTES

1. What impact African American gospel music had on modern jazz was usually felt in the simplest styles, those containing characteristics similar to the African American popular music known as rhythm and blues. These jazz styles were created by commercially successful players who, although possessing jazz skills, remained on the periphery of important jazz developments: the Earl Bostic and Eddie Vinson bands of the 1940s and 1950s; organ and saxophone combinations beginning in the late 1950s, such as those of Jimmy Smith and Stanley Turrentine; the piano trios of Les McCann, Ramsey Lewis, and the Three Sounds; the combos led by King Curtis; pianist Ray Charles and the saxophonists he employed, including Hank Crawford, David "Fathead" Newman, and James Clay.

2. Listen to the bass figures and drum patterns on "Reflections" (1967) or "Love Child" (1968) by the Supremes; or listen to "I Heard It Through the Grapevine" (1967) by Gladys Knight and The Pips, or "Cloud Nine" (1968) by the Temptations. All these are available on *Hitsville USA: The Motown Singles Collection* (Motown: 37463-6312, 4CD set, 1959–71, c1992); or see various *Greatest Hits, Ultimate, Anthology, Gold*, or *Definitive* compilations by Motown artists.

3. Listen to the rhythm section style on James Brown's 1967 "Cold Sweat," available on James Brown, *20 All Time Greatest Hits* (Polydor: 314 511 326, 1956–74, c1991); or Brown, *Star Time* (Polydor: 849 108, 4CD set, 1956–74, c1991).

4. Listen to Sly Stone's "In Time" on Sly & the Family Stone, *Fresh* (Epic: 32134, 1973, c1990); see page 503 for a transcription of the drum part.

5. The style, which during the late 1970s and early 1980s was called disco, is a blend of funk and Latin American rhythms played at the tempos most conducive for dancing (usually about 120 beats per minute, the standard march tempo). It refers mostly to an accompaniment style which has been heard under almost every kind of solo line, from the singing of Donna Summer to swing-era melodies to excerpts from Beethoven compositions. This style of music should also be removed from the umbrella category of rock.

6. Free Spirits, *Out of Sight and Sound* (Sunbeam: 5018 [ABC 593], 1966, c2006).

7. Gary Burton, *Duster* (Koch Jazz: 7846 [RCA], 1967, c1997).

8. The Fourth Way, *Sun and Moon Have Come Together* (Harvest: SKAO 423, LP, 1969, c1972).

9. Blood, Sweat & Tears, *Blood, Sweat & Tears* (Columbia/Legacy: 63986, 1968, c2000).

10. Chicago, *Chicago Transit Authority* (Rhino: 76171, 1969, c2002); and *Greatest Hits*, vol. 1 (Chicago: 3009, 1969–75, c1995).

11. Ten Wheel Drive, *The Best of Ten Wheel Drive* (Polydor: 314 527 420, 1969–71, c1995).

12. Miles Davis, *Bitches Brew* (Columbia/Legacy: C2K 65774, 2CD set, 1969–70, c1999); Weather Report (Joe Zawinul and Wayne Shorter), *Weather Report* (Columbia: 48824, 1971, c1992); Tony Williams Lifetime (with John McLaughlin and Larry Young), *Emergency!* (Polydor: 314 539 117, 1969, c1997); Mahavishnu Orchestra (John McLaughlin), *The Inner Mounting Flame* (Columbia/Legacy: 65523, 1971, c1998); and *Birds of Fire* (Columbia/Legacy: 66081, 1972, c2000); Return to Forever (Chick Corea), *Hymn to the Seventh Galaxy* (Polydor: 825 336, 1973, c1991); and Herbie Hancock, *Head Hunters* (Columbia/Legacy: 65123, 1974, c1997).

13. Listen to hints of rock in the accompanying patterns on "Eighty-One" on *E.S.P.* (Columbia/Legacy: 65683, 1965, c1998), "Freedom Jazz Dance" on *Miles Smiles* (Columbia/Legacy: 65682, 1966, c1998), "Masqualero" on *Sorcerer* (Columbia/Legacy: 65680, 1967, c1998) or the JCCD2, and "Frelon Brun," "Tout de Suite," and "Filles de Kilimanjaro" on *Filles de Kilimanjaro* (Columbia/Legacy: 86555, 1968, c2002).

14. For these sessions, Miles Davis drew from a pool of drummers—Tony Williams, Jack DeJohnette, Lenny White, Charles Alias, and Jim Riley. His pool of keyboard players included Herbie Hancock, Chick Corea, Joe Zawinul, and Larry Young. Wayne Shorter played tenor and soprano saxophones, Bennie Maupin played bass clarinet, John McLaughlin played guitar, and the bassists included Dave Holland and Harvey Brooks.

15. Most Davis recordings made after 1969 list Davis as sole composer despite the fact that usually he was performing the compositions of others. Zawinul's "Orange Lady," which is the last third of "Great Expectations" on *Big Fun*, is wrongly credited to Davis. Hermeto Pascoal's "Little Church" and "Selim" are wrongly credited to Davis on *Live-Evil*.

16. For details on the many changes of personnel and instrumentation in this period, see Jack Chambers, *Milestones: The Music and Times of Miles Davis* (Da Capo, 1998); see also Paul Tingen, *Miles Beyond: The Electric Explorations of Miles Davis, 1967–1991* (Billboard, 2001).

17. McLaughlin had collaborated in 1963 with bassist Jack Bruce and drummer Ginger Baker, both of whom later joined Eric Clapton in the rock group Cream.

18. Over the years, McLaughlin's groups also offered fine examples of jazz-rock violin playing: first Jerry Goodman; then, in 1974, Jean-Luc Ponty, whose recordings with his own bands have been among the best-selling in all of jazz-rock.

19. John McLaughlin, *My Goal's Beyond* (Knit Classics: 3010, 1970, c1999).

20. Larry Coryell, *Spaces* (Vanguard: 79345, 1970, c1989).

21. Gary Burton features Goodrick and Metheny on Burton, *Ring* (ECM: 829 191 [1051], 1974, c2001); and *Dreams So Real* (ECM: 833 329 [1027], 1975, c2001).

22. Like McLaughlin, Coryell also demonstrated considerable interest in non-rock playing during the late 1970s and early 1980s. He performed as an unaccompanied solo guitarist and played duets with guitarists Philip Catherine, Steve Khan, McLaughlin, and violinist Michael Urbaniak.

23. Cannonball Adderley, *Mercy, Mercy, Mercy* (Capitol: 29915, 1966, c1995).

24. Weather Report, *Heavy Weather* (Columbia/Legacy: 65108, 1977, c1997).

25. This is exemplified on side one of *Heavy Weather*.

26. Zawinul first recorded with ring modulator in 1971 on "Seventh Arrow" on Weather Report's first album, *Weather Report* (Columbia: 48824, 1971, c1992).

27. "Man in the Green Shirt" (*Tale Spinnin'*, Columbia/Legacy: 65110, 1975, c2002) and "The Juggler" (*Heavy Weather*).

28. Both are on Joe Zawinul, *Zawinul* (Atlantic: 1579, 1970, c1990).

29. "Jungle Book" is on Weather Report, *Mysterious Traveler* (Columbia/Legacy: 65112, 1974, c2002). During a period of jazz history when electric instruments dominated the sound of most albums, Zawinul used strains of unamplified piano on the recording of Wayne Shorter's "Blackthorn Rose" (*Mysterious Traveler*), precisely sounding each tone, paced as though to savor its every vibration. He also used it in combination with sustained organ tones in his "Five Short Stories" (*Tale Spinnin'*).

30. Zawinul used his own voice in this capacity on his "Badia" (*Tale Spinnin'*) and "Jungle Book" (*Mysterious Traveler*), and that of bassist Jaco Pastorius on "Birdland" (*Heavy Weather*), also on CCD2 Track 11 and excerpted on JCCD1 Track 6. Zawinul combined Wayne Shorter's tenor saxophone tone with the soft texture of a children's choir on "The Orphan" (8:30, Columbia: 57665, 1979, c1994).

31. Miroslav Vitous, *Infinite Search* (Collectibles: 6176 [Embryo], 1969, c2001).

32. "Eurydice," on Weather Report's first recording (*Weather Report*, Columbia: 48824, 1971, c1992), has the drummer playing ride rhythms and closing the high-hat on every second and fourth beat with a sax solo followed by a piano solo, etc. Even in such a conventionally formatted performance, there are portions that deviate from the standard bop roles. For example, drummer Alphonse Mouzon often closed his high-hat on all four beats and interjected musical comments to the point where, instead of just keeping time and coloring the sound, he is heard in the forefront of the group. Bassist Miroslav Vitous often abandoned the walking role and instead contributed embellishments to the ensemble. Pianist Zawinul did not always comp behind saxophonist Shorter, but set up delicate flourishes, played counter-melodies, and sometimes did not play at all. Airto Moreira overdubbed interjections of colorful, speech-like sounds throughout the proceedings with his cuica, an instrument in which the player gently slides his fingers along a stick which in turn alters the tension of a specially connected drumhead and causes it to vibrate.

33. *Weather Report* (Columbia: 48824, 1971, c1992); *I Sing the Body Electric* (Columbia: 46107, 1971–72, c1990); and *Sweetnighter* (Columbia/Legacy: 64976, 1973, c1996).

34. Representative examples of such collective improvisation are "Seventh Arrow" and "Umbrellas" on Weather Report's first album, *Weather Report,* and "125th Street Congress" on *Sweetnighter.* The music seems spontaneous except for the rehearsed figures that occur at the beginning, end, and occasionally within the pieces.

35. "Crazy About Jazz" on Weather Report's eleventh album, which bears the same title as their first: *Weather Report* (Columbia: 37616, 1981, c1987).

36. "Dara Factor One" (*Weather Report*, Columbia: 37616, 1981, c1987), and "Dream Clock" (*Night Passage*, Columbia: 36793, c1980).

37. Listen to the funk bass style Pastorius used in accompanying soul singers Sam and Dave on his own album (*Jaco Pastorius*, Epic/Legacy: 64977, 1976, c2000), and the dancing feeling he lent Weather Report's "Barbary Coast" (*Black Market*, Columbia/Legacy: 65169, 1976, c2002), "Palladium" (*Heavy Weather*), and "River People" (*Mr. Gone*, Columbia/Legacy: 46869, 1978, c1991).

38. Pastorius's effect on Weather Report will reveal itself if you compare the sound of the band's *Heavy Weather*, on which Pastorius is prominent, with the sound of *Sweetnighter* or *Mysterious Traveler*, which are earlier albums without him.

39. Jaco Pastorius, *Jaco Pastorius* (Epic/Legacy).

40. Pastorius, *Word of Mouth* (Warner Bros.: 3535, c1981) was sufficiently popular to penetrate the *Billboard* "Top 200" in album sales during 1981.

41. On "John and Mary," Pastorius used the same children's choir that Zawinul used on "The Orphan."

42. Among the phase shifters, Metheny used a combination of a Chorus (which takes the harmonics of the note and reinforces some and cancels others in a continuous motion) and Lexicon digital delay (which repeats the note at a delay of about 20 milliseconds—this contrasts with ordinary reverb because this is just one simple repeat, and it contrasts with concert hall reverb, which is thousands of repeats at various delays). Chorus effect acts as a detuner: takes the signal, detunes it, gives it a fatter sound, and shifts the pitch. Flanging, Chorusing, and echo are all time-delay techniques. Flanging is a very small delay, 30–40 milliseconds; Chorusing is from 40 ms to where the human ear can detect it, to 90 ms. Where the ear can discern between original signal and the delay is called an echo. In Chorusing, you increase the feedback (the number of repeats); typically, the repeats will tend to fade in intensity, the more there are. This makes it sound like many players, non-synchronized, because of the slight imperfections in timing and pitch, thereby increasing the harmonics. The device will modulate the time delay slightly. It sweeps the time back and forth, from 1 or 2 ms away from 60 ms delay to 20 ms away from 60 ms—this is called the depth of modulation. It also adjusts for speed of modulation. The device mixes the direct signal with the repeated signal. Chorusing was originally devised to synthesize the Leslie organ effect. Digital delay converts the signal to a code via sampling, whereas an analog system will color the sound and degrade it.

43. Pat Metheny, *The Pat Metheny Group* (ECM: 825 593 [1114], 1978, c2000); and *Offramp* (ECM: 817 138 [1216], 1981, c1999). Two Metheny albums sold more than 500,000 copies apiece: *Still Life (Talking)* (Geffen: 24145, c1987); and *Secret Story* (Geffen: 24468, c1992).

44. Pat Metheny/Ornette Coleman, *Song X: Twentieth Anniversary* (Nonesuch: 79918 [Geffen 24096], 1985, c2005).

45. It had been unusual for jazz instrumentals to be among the top hundred best-selling albums for any given year; yet Herbie Hancock's Sly Stone-influenced *Head Hunters* reached position 13 on the *Billboard* chart, selling over a million copies, and Miles Davis had the greatest success of his career with his rock-flavored *Bitches Brew*. The album reached position 35, selling more than 500,000 copies, far more than any of his previous albums that had reached "the Top 100."

46. Trumpeter Chuck Mangione's rock-flavored *Feels So Good* (A&M: 4658, 1977) sold about 2.2 million copies. Spyro Gyra's *Morning Dance* (Infinity: 9004, 1979) sold over a million copies. Kenny G's *Duotones* (Arista: 8496, 1986) sold over 6 million copies, as did George Benson's *Breezin'* (Warner Bros.: 2919, 1976). After the Jazz Crusaders dropped "jazz" from their name and began playing

rock-oriented material, "The Crusaders" enjoyed hit after hit; *Southern Comfort* (1974), *Images* (1978), and *Street Life* (1979) each sold over 500,000 copies.

47. This was the formula for several hits by saxophonists Grover Washington, Jr. (*Mr. Magic*, Kudu: 20, 1974) and Kenny G ("Songbird"), guitarist Earl Klugh (*Living Inside Your Love*, Liberty: 667, 1976), and the bands of Jeff Lorber (*Soft Space*, Inner City: 1058, 1978) and Spyro Gyra (*Spyro Gyra*, Amherst: 1014, 1977).

BOOKS ABOUT ROCK AND JAZZ-ROCK

Belz, Carl. *The Story of Rock*. 2nd ed. Harper and Row, 1987.

Brown, Charles T. *The Art of Rock and Roll*. 3rd ed. Prentice-Hall, 1992.

Brown, Geoff. *James Brown: Doin' It to Death, a Biography*. Omnibus, 1996.

Brown, James, with Bruce Tucker. *James Brown: The Godfather of Soul*. Macmillan, 1986; Thunder's Mouth, 2002.

Charlton, Katherine. *Rock Music Styles: A History*. 4th ed. McGraw-Hill, 2003.

Clifford, Mike, ed. *The Illustrated Encyclopedia of Black Music*. Harmony Books, 1982.

Coryell, Julie. *Jazz-Rock Fusion*. Hal Leonard, 2000.

DeCurtis, Anthony, ed. *The Rolling Stone Illustrated History of Rock and Roll*. Random House, 1992.

Gillett, Charlie. *The Sound of the City*. 2nd ed. DaCapo, 1996.

Hildebrand, Lee. *Stars of Soul and Rhythm & Blues*. Billboard, 1994.

Hitchcock, H. Wiley and Stanley Sadie, eds. *The New Grove Dictionary of American Music*. Grove, 1986.

Larkin, Colin. *The Encyclopedia of Popular Music*. 4th ed. 10 vols. Oxford Univ. Press, 2006.

Nicholson, Stuart. *Jazz-Rock: A History*. Schirmer, 1998.

Stuessy, Joe. *Rock and Roll: Its History and Stylistic Development*. 4th ed. Prentice-Hall, 2003.

Thompson, Dave. *Funk*. Backbeat, 2001.

Tingen, Paul, *Miles Beyond: The Electric Explorations of Miles Davis, 1967–1991* (Billboard, 2001).

Vincent, Rickey. *Funk: The Music, the People, and the Rhythm of the One*. St. Martin's, 1996.

Wesley, Fred. *Hit Me, Fred: Recollections of a Sideman*. Duke University, 2002.

Blues:

Cohn, Lawrence, ed. *Nothing but the Blues: The Music and the Musicians*. Abbeville, 1993.

Evans, David. *Big Road Blues*. Univ. of California, 1982; DaCapo, 1987.

Oliver, Paul. *The Story of the Blues*. Northeastern Univ., 1997.

Palmer, Robert. *Deep Blues*. Penguin, 1981.

Joel Whitburn:

Top Pop Singles 1955–2002. Record Research, 2003.

The Billboard Albums, 1956–2005. Record Research, 2006.

Bubbling under the Billboard Hot 100, 1959–2004. Record Research, 2005.

Top R&B/Hip-Hop Singles, 1942–2004. Record Research, 2004.

Pop Memories 1890–1954. Record Research, 1986.

Billboard Pop Hits, Singles & Albums, 1940–1954. Record Research, 2002.

All available from: Record Research, P.O. Box 200, Menomonee Falls, WI 53052-0200; phone: 800-827-9810; web: *www.recordresearch.com*.

Jaco Pastorius

(Photo by Tom Copi, courtesy Frank Driggs)

Several trends emerged during the 1980s and 1990s that we can identify as jazz styles. Each had adherents who were sincere players, earnestly producing music enjoyed by particular audiences. None of the improvisers, however, were the caliber of John Coltrane, Miles Davis, or Charlie Parker, and none of the composers made contributions as original or substantial as Duke Ellington or Thelonious Monk.[1]

NEW AGE

During the 1980s, a new idiom of popular music surfaced. Record stores initially did not have bins for displaying it, so clerks placed it in the jazz bins because they thought it sounded more like jazz than classical music or rock. Even after this music earned a bin of its own, much of the public continued to call it "jazz." Record store clerks sometimes described it as a mixture of jazz and classical music, or "classical jazz," and it was found in the jazz bins of many stores even at the end of the decade. Eventually it earned the name "New Age."

DJ with left hand on mixing board, right on turntable.
(Photo by Randy Norfus)

Though the music employs improvisation as one of its methods, improvisation is about all it has in common with most jazz. It does not swing. In fact, its rhythms are purposely designed to avoid creating any of the tension that jazz swing feeling requires. The methods for creating this music prevent evoking tension in other ways, too. Harmony is not jarring. Tone qualities are soft and smooth. Changes are made only in the most gradual ways. Often, the same chord or mode remains in effect for an entire performance. Sound levels are usually low and remain that way for long stretches. Changes in loudness are rarely sudden. Models for this music were provided by Tibetan chant music, Native American flute music, and work by modern classical composers Lamonte Young, Terry Riley, Philip Glass, and Steve Reich. Those composers, in turn, had been influenced by Gregorian chant music as well as the sounds of nature—wind and waves, for example—and such continuous industrial sounds as an air conditioner's steady hum. Since these four composers reduced music to a bare minimum of materials and activity, their musical approach was called "minimalism." Some of the music superficially resembled some of the unaccompanied piano improvisations of Keith Jarrett during the 1970s, as well as the solo piano pieces of French impressionist composers Claude Debussy and Maurice Ravel that had inspired some of Jarrett's work. Both products were calm and soothing. Neither projected jazz swing feeling. Much of it explored the sonorities of a single chord or brief chord progression.[2] Some of this music was dubbed "ambient music" and used as soothing background music. Some was adopted by yoga instructors to help their clients relax. Birthing rooms also employed the music for easing labor pains of women delivering babies.

The recording firms Narada and Windham Hill became particularly known for supplying these sounds. The Paul Winter Consort and its spin-off group, Oregon, made music like this. Harpist Andreas Vollenweider promoted a similar sound and gained considerable popularity for it during the 1980s. Pianist George Winston improvised long, vamp-based passages that meander and seem soothing. Winston's records sold millions of copies, his concerts packed auditoriums, and his style was dubbed "new age."[3]

SMOOTH JAZZ

During the mid-1980s, hardly any jazz of any style was available on the radio. Only a miniscule number of small-range stations were broadcasting jazz. The architects of a new format seeking greater listenership knew that selection of jazz recordings had to be based on listener surveys identifying types of jazz that would appeal to a wide audience of adults. Many of the radio stations that had broadcast New Age format during the 1980s gradually introduced music having more active and louder drumming, more intrusive bass lines, and rougher sounding saxophones. This is quieted, refined funk music that lacks the intensity of major jazz styles, such as hard bop. Improvised solos in it are stylized rather than adventuresome. Phrases in the solos are relatively simple by comparison with bop and bop-derived improvisations. This radio format began in 1986 as "The Wave," and was additionally termed "Smooth Jazz." Ultimately the format attracted the largest new adult radio audience of the 1990s. Almost every major city had a smooth jazz radio format available around the clock. By 2006 the only commercial radio stations that broadcasted any type of jazz in the United States were dedicated to smooth jazz. In most cities only a few hours per week of other jazz styles were available on the radio, and they could be found only by sampling programming across an assortment of college stations and affiliates of National Public Radio. Whereas more than one hundred smooth jazz stations were active, only a handful of stations featured other types of jazz.

Smooth jazz radio provided jazzy background music with a beat. Many listeners chose to have this music around them because they found it pleasant and just as easy to ignore as to hear. It relaxed them. It was intentionally much less challenging to listeners than other modern jazz. Musicians dubbed it "fuzak" because it is jazz-rock fusion as soft and pleasant as the highly processed music that the Muzak firm once piped into elevators and the waiting rooms of physicians and dentists. Informally, it had been termed "elevator music." Most styles of jazz have had their easy-listening variants, and this was fusion's.[4]

During the 1990s, some radio stations characterized this fare as "light jazz and soft rock." By the mid-1990s, most New Age radio formats had been replaced by "smooth jazz," sometimes called "cool jazz." Historically, these terms were unfortunate designations because the music sounded no smoother than ballads of the swing era, and it had nothing in common with cool jazz of the 1950s. Furthermore, a portion of the programming was music not derived from jazz. In fact, during the beginning of the twenty-first century, the architects of the format were including such nonjazz styles as Motown and pop singers (such as Luther Vandross) who were identified by their surveys as appealing to the same audience. So omitting the "and soft rock" designation during the late 1990s further confused new listeners who were trying to learn what sounds represented "jazz."

A few of the bands whose music was occasionally selected for broadcast on "The Wave" radio stations had jazz backgrounds: The Crusaders, Yellow Jackets, Pieces of a Dream, and Spyro Gyra, for example. (Note, however, that only some of their work fit the "smooth jazz" designation.) Several established jazz musicians also made music aimed at this market, among them: pianist Bob James,[5] guitarists Lee Ritenour, Larry Carlton, Earl Klugh,[6] and George Benson.[7] For them, it was an additional style in which to become fluent. Bob James, for instance, had previously recorded avant-garde jazz, accompanied singer Sarah Vaughan, and composed for movies and television. George Benson had toured with hard bop groups in the 1960s. Like their pop jazz predecessors of the 1940s and 1950s, such as the jump bands of Louis Jordan and Earl Bostic and the wailing rock sax of King Curtis, these musicians chose not to play the intricate and extended improvisations they were capable of. Instead, they played simpler music containing improvisations that were more obviously melodic. It was intentionally less challenging than hard bop and considerably less difficult to follow than most avant-garde and "free" jazz. This compromise was made to ensure musicians their livelihoods, and it worked as well for them as it had for their jump band predecessors because these improvisations proved more accessible to most listeners.

Though perceived by many musicians as more decorative than substantial, and though used as soothing background music by some listeners, smooth jazz soloists were revered by many who were just as intent on every vibration as listeners who followed more complex jazz. This means that at the beginning of the twenty-first century, jazz was defined for the majority of album-buying Americans by the music of saxophonists Kenny G, Dave Koz, and Boney James; guitarists George Benson, Earl Klugh, and Larry Carlton; pianists Joe Sample, Bob James, and David Benoit; and trumpeters Rick Braun and Chris Botti, to name just a few stand-outs. These musicians smoothed out a melding of Latin American, blues, hard bop, and funk music to produce a form of jazz more acceptable to listeners than pure jazz had been. During the 1990s and the beginning of the twenty-first century, this sound was often indicated by the term "contemporary jazz," as distinguished from "traditional jazz," which was the term that broadcasters and journalists used to designate hard bop and the imitators of the mid-1960s Miles Davis band, such as the Marsalis Brothers. The "contemporary jazz" term was also employed to identify wide use of electric instruments and accompaniment styles borrowed from the pop music of the day, whereas "traditional jazz" came to indicate predominantly non-electric ("acoustic") instruments and bop-style accompaniment methods. The official radio broadcasting category that included smooth jazz was **New Adult Contemporary.** In at least two respects the function of this music was equivalent to the function served by the "sweet bands" of the 1930s and 1940s, such as those of Glenn Miller and Tommy Dorsey. Both styles had jazz roots but emphasized refinement over exploration, and both therefore became palatable to wide audiences instead of just a small group of dedicated fans. Unlike other kinds of modern jazz, this sound was not relegated to small nightclubs and limited-range radio stations. It was heard frequently in airports and shopping malls, auditoriums and arenas.[8]

To further place smooth jazz in historical perspective, note that during the 1950s and 1960s, background music radio stations and the Muzak company offered instrumental pop music, much of which was derived from sounds of the swing era from a decade or two earlier. Now their counterparts during the 1980s and 1990s had become dedicated to smooth jazz, which is a style that was also modeled after some pop music of a decade or two earlier. The difference was that "a decade or two earlier" now meant some of the models the smooth jazz musicians were imitating included 1965–1968 recordings of Wes Montgomery,[9] 1972–1980 work of Grover Washington, Jr.,[10] some of the more subdued approaches within late-1970s output of Weather Report,[11] and the most refined of Motown. But unlike most of its background music antecedents, this radio format programmed selections that usually contained improvised solos. In fact, there was a considerable amount of jazz improvisation in the recordings that were broadcast by smooth jazz radio stations. *The extent of improvisation was one element that qualified smooth jazz as jazz, rather than merely a continuation of the instrumental pop tradition of background music.*

ACID JAZZ

The term "acid jazz" was coined during 1987 by English disc jockeys Gilles Peterson and Chris Bangs at a weekend-long party in England termed a "rave," where each room provided a different kind of music. One was a type of dance music originating in Detroit and Chicago called "house music." Some of it was intended to accompany the effects of taking the drugs called "ecstasy" and LSD, nicknamed "acid." So it became known as "acid house music." Announcing the availability of jazz in one of the rooms, Peterson reportedly remarked to the partiers, "Now that you've had your fill of 'acid house,' we're going to give you **acid jazz.**" Though originally offered as a joke, the term was soon applied whenever disc jockeys combined current pop dance music with excerpts from old jazz albums. Gilles Peterson and other British disc jockeys particularly liked funky hard bop recordings of the 1960s from the Blue Note and Prestige firms, sometimes by Art Blakey, Horace Silver, Lou Donaldson, Herbie Hancock, and Grant Green. Gilles Peterson's firm, in turn, founded a subsidiary called Acid Jazz, and some of the groups they hired thereby defined the genre.[12] Like the swing style of the 1930s and 1940s, acid style first functioned primarily as dance music. Some of it later came to serve just as well for "easy listening," and some acid jazz recordings found a place on broadcasts by "smooth jazz" radio stations.

At the same time, rap groups were beginning to borrow jazz sounds. They had at least two reasons. First, they needed a new way to get accompaniments cheaply. So they were excerpting the introductions, during which the pace and feeling of the original selections were established. In the early years, they borrowed accompaniment riffs from the funkiest of jazz records because the riffs helped provide a continuous pattern of repeating rhythms under their rap. Second, some rappers believed that their performance would gain a jazz flavor if any element associated with jazz were incorporated. This might consist of a brief part of a trumpet or saxophone improvisation, a few piano chords that typified jazz of the 1960s or 1970s, a walking bass pattern, or a jazz drummer's ride rhythm. Some rappers felt that just naming famous jazz musicians within the rap itself would make their product more hip. Within some acid jazz selections, even those without rap, jazz horn work is overdubbed in a way that merely decorates whatever else is happening. It is not the main focus of attention.[13] For example, sometimes horn sounds provided only minor coloration, while the drum beat remains the most prominent aspect of the sound. This reversed the roles traditionally occupied in most jazz. Drums were background, while horns were foreground. *Though using jazz solos as decoration reversed the trend for jazz, it continued a long tradition in popular music.* "Hot solos," as they were called, had been added to otherwise nonjazz pieces as early as the 1920s. They were commonly included in performances by R&B singers of the 1940s and 1950s. Rock and roll bands frequently carried a saxophonist for this purpose in the 1950s. Soul and funk bands of the 1960s and 1970s had used brief jazz improvisations.

Sampling

Much of acid jazz depends upon electronically excerpting portions of old albums. This procedure is called "sampling." Among producers, the term is used in two slightly different ways. The older meaning refers to recording samples of a given instrument's tone from each pitch range. The result remains stored in a computer to be altered according to the programmer's wishes. Entire melodies and accompaniments can be pasted together by electronically changing the pitch and rhythms of that tone. The synthesizers can even determine the ways that tones begin and end. In this way, the programmer can give them the character of a live hornman or human voice. This had been common in pop music products since at least the early 1980s.

The newer meaning for "sampling" is the one that applies more to acid jazz. Entire phrases from an old album are recorded into a computer. Then they are re-synthesized into another recording apparatus if a new album is being created. Or they are re-synthesized into playback facilities if a disc jockey is using them spontaneously at a dance party. In some of the earliest acid jazz mixtures, disc jockeys sampled more than just accompaniment phrases. They excerpted a few moments of intact music from an old jazz album.[14] The particular way the phrases were mixed was determined by the creativity of the disc jockey. Performing these procedures became a career for disc jockeys who termed themselves **mixers.** When devised during a dance party, the resulting mixtures were not usually saved. When devised in the studio, however, the mixtures often became part of CDs that the disc jockey copyrighted and marketed as new material. Often he took credit for what he called "programming."

Looping

In many acid jazz selections, the instrumental phrase that was sampled came from the accompaniment portion of an old recording. It was then repeated continuously by a process called "looping." This produced an accompaniment groove. On top of this was placed (1) an assortment of additional sounds from samples or (2) electronically synthesized sources. Often the additions included (3) a loud snare drum sound on every other beat.[15] This is known as a **back beat** if it happens on the second and fourth of every group of four beats. Sometimes the addition was (4) a closed high-hat cymbal struck twice for each beat, thereby providing a continuous pulse. (5) A strong bass drum rhythm was also added in some mixes. Usually all these elements were combined. Then a collection of (6) new raps and (7) jazz improvisations were placed on top of that foundation.[16] In summary, *acid jazz was not invented by musicians. It was invented by disc jockeys and rap artists.*

Overdubbing

The methods for creating acid jazz were not entirely new. For instance, overdubbing had been used already for several decades in pop music. But among most jazz musicians and purist fans, it was considered cheating. Though it was uncommon in jazz until the 1970s, guitarist Wes Montgomery's popular recordings of the 1960s had expanded the practice.[17] By the 1980s, most of Miles Davis's albums used at least some overdubbing.[18] Also, for more than a decade already, disc jockeys had been devising original mixtures by adding sound effects to recordings and by taking sounds from one recording and adding them to another.

Sampling was not new, either. For example, by the mid-1980s, composer-arrangers owned electronic samples of most musical instrument sounds. This conveniently allowed composers to excerpt and reprocess sounds to create complete performances without hiring musicians. *Producers had assumed the role of performers several years before the emergence of acid jazz.*

What was new with acid jazz was the extent to which disc jockeys became involved in making the music themselves, instead of only playing the work of others. Musicians were hired by disc jockeys to record fresh improvisations on top of accompaniments prepared by synthesizer, drum machine, and loops.[19] Occasionally, a disc jockey actually toured, as though a bandleader. He would plug in his playback equipment and allow one or two musicians to perform live music over the recorded sounds.

DJ Logic, one of the best known turntablists. Treated as a musician for his interactive role with strong musical sense, he appeared on albums by jazz bandleaders such as Steve Coleman, Dave Douglas, and Medeski, Martin & Wood, and he occasionally acted as a bandleader himself. Shown here in performance at the Beachland Ballroom in Cleveland, 2004.

(Photo by Jeff Forman)

Turntablists

The converse of this situation had been presented by jazz musician Herbie Hancock when he added a disc jockey to his touring band to contribute his own original sounds. Some were made by scratching records with the stylus while the system was connected to loudspeakers. This technique became so popular that its practitioners acquired the name of "turntablists," later subsumed under "DJ," not to be confused with people who merely play recordings intact for parties and radio broadcasts. The new role of DJ also mixes music by running records on two separate turntables at the same time, changing its music's meter, tempo, and pitch, and in some cases, creating new melodies from old materials to actually create new music. The modern DJ's signature is derived from what he does with his selection of materials. DJ Logic and Grandmaster Flash are among the best known. (Hancock's hit recording "Rockit" had incorporated such sounds.) Some work by turntablists contributed to the rhythm section or background sound effects. Other work took a melodic lead. By 2005, the technique had become so common in pop music that competitions were being held for turntablists, and college courses were offered in "turntable," just as they had traditionally been offered for "trumpet," "percussion," "piano," etc. In jazz bands of this period it was not unusual to see a turntablist treated as an instrumentalist. In fact, among some audiences for the newest forms of jazz, the top turntablists were better known than jazz musicians. Note that at this time in pop music there were groups composed entirely of rappers and turntablists, with no musical instruments at all.

Categories of Acid Jazz

From selection to selection, the amount of improvised jazz that could be found in "acid jazz" varied widely. The term eventually became applied to hip-hop music that was only slightly jazzy and usually did not have fresh jazz improvisation. In the mid-1990s, "Acid Jazz" appeared on the labels of some recordings that contained only rap music.

As it evolved, the "acid jazz" term came to be applied to a wide assortment of music. Some, but not all music under this umbrella can be loosely classified into three categories.

1. **Fusions devised by disc jockeys of jazz elements with various pop dance music styles** current from the mid-1980s into the 1990s, such as hip-hop,[20] techno,[21] trip hop,[22] and rap. Medleys were devised spontaneously by disc jockeys during parties in England. Some medleys and mixtures were prepared in studios and issued for sale. Some of their mixtures incorporated excerpts from the funkiest hard bop albums of the 1960s and 1970s, particularly the selections that maintained a groove and had tempos similar enough to loop into the continuous medleys. Selections featuring organ and guitar were particularly welcome.

   Though most music in this category is described above, a slice of their programming somewhat overlapped smooth jazz that contained improvisation but rarely swung in the jazz manner. Tempo and rhythmic feeling were stiffer in most acid jazz than in most smooth jazz. Statement of tempo was more elastic in smooth jazz because machine-made rhythms that typify acid jazz are perfectly constant, whereas live performers, as smooth jazz uses, do not keep absolutely perfect time when they are playing. Their rhythms are more elastic. Though many listeners do not realize when they are hearing a drum machine, real drumming has an organic quality not conveyed by electronic imitations. A drum machine supplies neither the richness and depth of tone qualities nor the spontaneous variations in rhythms of a live drummer. The most important missing feature is the subtle ebb and flow of tensions. Incidentally, smooth jazz recordings that employ drum machines more closely resemble acid jazz.

2. **Fresh music** made specifically for this audience by bands around the world, not just England and America. Their music exhibited a range of styles, some made by musicians using drum machines and loops themselves, some not much different from early 1970s jazz-rock fusion.[23]

3. **Renamed music from earlier recordings.** Several U.S. and British record companies during the mid-1990s applied the "acid jazz" designation to their old recordings and resold them. This succeeded as long as the selections were sufficiently funky and sustained a groove. Record companies reclassified several of their previous recording artists as "legends of acid jazz," for example, Ahmad Jamal, Roy Ayers, Houston Person, and Don Patterson. Some companies used the term "roots of acid jazz" to designate their old music by Wes Montgomery and Jimmy Smith. They sold it in different combinations of selections, with new album covers and new commentary. In other words, "acid jazz" served more as a marketing term than a musical style. It was so loosely applied in music stores that a customer might have to seek the "rap music" bins to find it.

Dominant Aspects of Acid Jazz

Despite the diversity of sounds that have been called "acid jazz," at least three aspects of acid jazz make all but the third category something more than a mere marketing term. **(1)** The most dominant aspect is the accompaniment rhythm and the way it feels. This is termed **"the groove."** It is important because much of this music was meant to stimulate dancing. **(2)** Another aspect is that **few chord changes** occur. Often, an entire selection revolves around two chords that continuously alternate with each other. Much of it borrows the introduction from some other funky recording, for instance, from soul music, disco, or boogaloo. Then the selection repeats that introduction continuously, with occasional variations. Based almost entirely upon an introduction, the harmonic content of most acid jazz selections is understandably limited because the function of an introduction is to set the pace, not offer harmonic development. **(3) Melodic development is less elaborate** than in any other style of jazz. In fact, many acid jazz selections have no melody at all.

In these three respects, acid jazz is more African than any other jazz style because much African folk music is focused primarily on rhythm and tone quality, not melodic or harmonic development. It is no coincidence that one category of pop music from the mid-1990s that was being incorporated into British acid jazz around 1996 was called "jungle jazz."

By the beginning of the twenty-first century, few writers or publicists were using the term "acid jazz." The methods described above were still common, however, and new bands were still appearing whose music exemplified the style. Incidentally, the final recording of Miles Davis's career can be classified as acid jazz, and it even featured a rapper Davis had sought.

THE SOUL SAXES AND "CONTEMPORARY JAZZ"

The 1980s and 1990s saw the wide acceptance of a long tradition in funky, soulful saxophone styles. Jazz that emphasized grit more than melodic or harmonic complexity became immensely popular. These saxophone playing styles emulated blues singing and gospel singing by using short, simple phrases and voice-like cries, wails, and moans. The tone qualities were not the light-weight, dry, pale timbres associated with cool jazz saxophonists Stan Getz, Lee Konitz, or Paul Desmond. Nor were they the rich, lush, smooth timbres of swing era saxophonists Johnny Hodges and Benny Carter. Instead, they were coarse, and were delivered with a hard-edged insistence. Their accompaniment sounds were rough, too, stressing granite stability, not the elasticity, variety, and surprises that typified bop-influenced approaches. They established a groove and stuck with it. Usually electric instruments supplied these back-ups—organ, guitar, electric piano were common—and drummers played patterns more common to funk and soul music than bop traditions. Their models were the accompanists for singers James Brown and Sly Stone, and Latin American music. (For an example of the style, though not done by a player commonly identified with it, listen to Bennie Maupin's solo in Herbie Hancock's "Chameleon," *JCCD3* Track 7.)

Roots for the funky, soulful traditions had been evident during the 1940s with Earl Bostic and Eddie "Cleanhead" Vinson. The most-used models became available during the 1950s and 1960s in the playing of several saxophonists from the American South, particularly Texas. Most had roots in bop, though often they simplified so much that bop character was not easily detected. (1) A prototype for this style was Fort Worth-born King Curtis (1934–1971), a tenor saxophonist on many New York recording sessions and a regular with the rock group called The Coasters, the singer Aretha Franklin, and the rock band led by Duane Eddy.[24] (2) Another was Arkansas-born Junior Walker (1931–1995), the tenor saxophonist on Motown recordings with his own band, The All-Stars.[25] (3) A number of these saxophonists had been with the band of singer Ray Charles during the 1950s and 1960s: Memphis-born Hank Crawford,[26] Dallas-born David "Fathead" Newman,[27] and Dallas-born James Clay. (4) Houston-born Wilton Felder[28] achieved considerable exposure when recording with pianist Joe Sample and the Jazz Crusaders, beginning in 1961. Interestingly, the Jazz Crusaders maintained popularity through to 1983 by changing their name to The Crusaders, decreasing jazz improvisation, and substituting funk-style accompaniment for bop-style accompaniment. (5) The style of North Carolina-born alto saxophonist Maceo Parker[29] personifies the searing tone, insistent delivery, short, clipped phrases, and gospel singing-like exclamations that became popular somewhat later through David Sanborn and his disciples. Parker was heard often with singer James Brown.

In all the sounds of these saxophonists there was a "twang" that had not been present in the traditional jazz saxes, even those coming from the American South and Southwest: Lester Young, Ben Webster, Ike Quebec, Herschel Evans, or Charlie Parker. A quicker, steadier vibrato combined with an extra emphasis on scoops of pitch beginning important notes also helps distinguish the style from most hard bop and cool sax styles. (To understand vibrato and scoops of pitch, see page 49 and *Demo CD* Tracks 46–53.) It is this characteristic, in addition to the striving for simplicity, that sets the soul saxes apart from the main stream of jazz saxophone sounds. After a period in which vibrato was slow, this soul sax style speeded it up.

Not all of the important roots for the soul saxes of the 1980s and 1990s came from the American South. (6) Pittsburgh-born Stanley Turrentine (1934–2000) had pioneered these traits during the 1960s, after first beginning his career in hard bop, then crafting an individual approach that emphasized simplicity and a very funky flavor. He devised an exceptionally melodic manner, far more concise than other hard bop styles. Quite significant in Turrentine's sound is a characteristic "twang" that was not common to hard bop but became essential to the soul saxes heard on smooth jazz radio. Turrentine preceded the (7) more influential Buffalo-born Grover Washington, Jr. (1943–2001) and may well be the stylistic grandfather of many soul saxes who are now classified as part of the "smooth jazz" idiom described next.

During the 1980s, these soul/funk influences were manifested in at least three different branches: (1) a refined **"smooth jazz"** style, (2) a rough, raw style, and (3) a more complicated, jazz-oriented style. Though the so-called "smooth" variant still had the edginess of its models's sound and retained the insistent, shouting quality that characterized its roots, this variant serenaded more than it exhorted. The style drew partly from the alto saxophone and soprano saxophone playing of Grover Washington, Jr.,[30] whose *Winelight* album sold over a million copies during the 1980s. Washington was not only an influence but also a successful example himself until his death in 2001. Washington was more widely known than his models Hank Crawford and David "Fathead" Newman (whose "Hard Times" recording significantly influenced Washington). Then Najee, Boney James, Dave Koz, Kirk Whalum, and others crafted their own versions of this approach and attained prominence during the 1990s. By 2005, James and Koz were immensely popular and influencing disciples of their own. Koz even had his own radio show.

(1) The biggest seller among the smooth variant of soul saxes was **Kenny G** (b. 1959). By the mid-1980s he had already attained top-seller status. Building upon the 1960s style of Wilton Felder and 1970s style of Grover Washington, Jr., Kenny G softened their manners and simplified their tendencies toward melodic development. He stressed ornamentation more than generating new melodic ideas. The instrument heard most on his hits is the soprano saxophone, but he also plays the other saxophones. For example, his alto and tenor playing are prominent on the *Silhouette* album, allowing us to better detect his Washington and Felder roots, respectively. The music does not swing in the manner of 1930s jazz or the bop patterns of subsequent styles, but Kenny G does improvise. Moreover, he derives his music from the jazz tradition, which is obvious in his work with the Jeff Lorber Fusion band of the 1970s.[31] No matter how they are classified by most jazz musicians or purist jazz fans, his CDs remain in the jazz racks of music stores, not in the rock, pop, or classical racks. Furthermore, his music is heard primarily on "jazz" radio, not on "classical" or "rock" radio.

To put Kenny G's success in perspective, we need to keep in mind that (a) selling 7,000 copies would be deemed a successful sales run for albums by most non-smooth jazz musicians, but (b) most failed to surpass 3,000, and (c) many excellent jazz albums

Alto saxophonist David Sanborn, shown here at the 2002 Tri-C Jazzfest, Cleveland.

(Photo by Randy Norfus)

sell in the hundreds, not the thousands. (By 2003, the average sales run for a good jazz album produced by an independent label, not by one of the big four conglomerates, was 500–800 copies.) Charlie Parker never had a gold record (500,000 copies), and John Coltrane only had one (*A Love Supreme*). By contrast, however, Kenny G's albums not only went gold, but usually multi-platinum (several million copies). His *Silhouette* sold more than four million copies, his *Duotones* album with the hit "Songbird" sold more than six million copies, and his *Breathless* sold more than 12 million copies. A pervasive part of the auditory landscape for about 20 years, his music is so common that millions of people hear it all the time, recognize that it is familiar, but don't know that it is Kenny G making the sound. With sales exceeding 50 million albums, he is the most popular saxophonist in jazz history and the top selling instrumentalist in music history as a whole, not just jazz.

(2) A second branch of the third generation of soul saxes is the rough, raw style that is extremely aggressive, almost scorching in its intensity. It is exemplified by alto saxophonist **David Sanborn** (b. 1945) and his disciples. Influenced in part by Maceo Parker and Hank Crawford, his alto sax presence was popular with a broad base of listeners for its very hot brand of funky playing. Almost untouched by bop, his style was fluent, bursting with energy, and densely packed with soulful phrases. It is distinguished by the immediate, emotional cry that characterized Hank Crawford's manner. Having toured with the Paul Butterfield Blues Band and Motown singer Stevie Wonder during the 1970s, Sanborn was already an established voice in the hard-edged, soulful blues approach by the time he achieved the widest exposure during the 1980s on television. He appeared in his own television series, titled *Night Music,* and he frequently appeared on *Late Night with David Letterman* and *Saturday Night Live*. His sound was also heard with such pop singing groups as the Rolling Stones, The Eagles, and David Bowie, among others. Sanborn was second only to Kenny G as the most widely heard saxophonist since 1986. Though hardly smooth, his playing could be heard frequently on "smooth jazz" radio. By 2002, he had sold about seven million albums world-wide. Seven of his albums sold more than 500,000 copies apiece.[32] During the 1980s and 1990s, Sanborn continued to have significant influence on young, still-developing saxophonists, such as Dave Koz.

(3) A more complicated, more jazz-oriented branch of the soul sax tree emerged in the style of **Michael Brecker** (1949–2007). Beginning in 1970, he became a major force in saxophone styles, possibly more influential among non-smooth jazz saxophonists than anyone aside from Coltrane and Joe Henderson. Brecker invented a new approach by mixing the methods of John Coltrane, Wayne Shorter, and Stanley Turrentine with his own original ideas and the King Curtis/Junior Walker funky styles. Brecker's approach had its own vocabulary and became the most imitated jazz tenor sax style of the 1970s and 1980s. He emphasized virtuosity. Impressive speed and agility are hallmarks of his style; Brecker filled almost every moment with rapid-fire, multi-noted exclamations. It was as though he was racing all the time. (Listen to "Above and Below" on *JCCD3* Track 8.) His lines were packed with his own original patterns, often played in quadruple-time, and all delivered with very hot, funky expression. He played with an intensity that never let up, even for a moment.[33]

Brecker, like King Curtis, was known primarily as a sideman, though he was also involved as co-leader in bands called Dreams, The Brecker Brothers, and Steps Ahead. Hundreds of recording sessions employed him when a hot, fluid, funky flavoring was desired. His playing is heard on more than 900 albums. His sound was on recordings by Paul Simon, James Taylor, Joni Mitchell, Richard Tee, and Steely Dan, to name just a few of the pop stars he accompanied. Not limited to the commercial funk role, Brecker also had been in demand for more straight-ahead, post-hard bop situations, as when he toured with Horace Silver and Herbie Hancock or recorded with McCoy Tyner. During the late 1980s, when he began making a new string of albums as a leader, he became better known than when he had served primarily as a sideman. By 2001, he had six albums out as a bandleader for the same company and had mounted several tours fronting his own groups.

Tenor saxophonist Michael Brecker, shown here at the 2003 International Association of Jazz Educators Convention in Toronto.
(Photo by C. Andrew Hovan)

BUT IS IT JAZZ?

When fusion arrived, many musicians and jazz fans did not consider it to be a form of jazz. Most of them eventually softened in their view, but some still consider fusion styles to be separate from the descendants of Dixieland, swing, and bop. This was not an unprecedented kind of response to a new jazz style among jazz fans. Big band swing had been classified as nonjazz by many Dixieland fans during the 1930s and 1940s. They felt that it was not true jazz, partly because it represented a dilution of jazz traits. Collective improvisation did not occupy as much of each performance as it did in early jazz, for instance. Swing big bands emphasized refinement more than spontaneity. Today, both Dixieland and swing recordings are located in the jazz bins of music stores. A similar response had occurred before fusion arrived. Many jazz fans had reacted to the avant-garde music of Ornette Coleman and Cecil Taylor by saying that it was not jazz, either. Despite the views of some musicians and purist jazz fans, however, both the avant-garde of Coleman and Taylor and the fusion of Miles Davis, Weather Report, and Kenny G continue to be found in the jazz bins of music stores, along with swing and Dixieland, and not in the classical or rock bins. This indicates that—at least to the outsiders—these styles sound more like jazz than like anything else. (Were the outsiders missing the distinctions? Or were the insiders missing the commonalities?) The next few paragraphs examine how listeners might be evaluating and classifying what they hear.

Different Definitions

Different people use different criteria for deciding whether a given performance is jazz. For those whose definition requires both improvisation and jazz swing feeling, much music by Weather Report fails to qualify because its rhythmic properties do not resemble the swing era or bop grooves, though they did achieve a groove of their own that proved infectious. The piano music of New Age stylist George Winston would not qualify because it fails to swing. Music stores, on the other hand, use much looser criteria and display both Weather Report and George Winston in their jazz bins.

Composed by Randy Brecker; recorded in 1992 by Randy Brecker (trumpet), Michael Brecker (tenor saxophone), Mike Stern (guitar), George Whitty (keyboards), James Genus (bass), Dennis Charles (drums), Bashiri Johnson (conga drum); available on *Return of the Brecker Brothers* (GRP: 9684, c1992).

Terms to learn from *Demo CD* and the "Elements of Music" appendix: staccato, tenor saxophone, chromatic scale, meter, triplets, sixteenth notes.

This recording illustrates one of the top fusion bands, including Michael Brecker, the most jazz-oriented of the soul saxes. We cannot peg the entire proceedings as fusion style, however, because the horn solos could stylistically fit over a rhythm section used by Miles Davis or John Coltrane in the mid-1960s. Moreover, the pitches and the chord changes selected for the melody lines that Randy Brecker wrote in "Above and Below" are far more sophisticated than those found in any pop music that provided roots for fusion.

On "Above and Below" we hear instruments that are not particularly common to swing or bop: electronic keyboard synthesizers, electric guitar, electric bass guitar, and auxiliary percussion. This remains a common format in fusion bands today. The ways they are played also depart significantly from swing and bop approaches. The bass part and drum part typify the more intricate varieties of jazz-rock fusion. For instance, instead of string bass ("acoustic bass") playing walking lines (a note on every beat), this piece uses electric bass guitar playing rhythms based on sixteenth notes (up to four notes on every beat) and placement of accents in odd positions among those sixteenth notes. Significant too is that occasionally the bass plays the melody, not just the accompaniment. The drummer's work also qualifies the music as fusion because it emphasizes drums more than cymbals and sixteenth-note subdivision of each beat instead of triplet subdivision. In other words, the rhythm section is not playing swing or bop style.

Fusion music frequently incorporates rhythm patterns from Latin American music. "Above and Below," for instance, employs baião, a rhythm originating in Northern Brazil with roots in Africa. We are also treated to the extra rhythm and tone colors of the conga drum.

Trumpeter Randy Brecker and his younger brother Michael were among the most prolific hornmen in jazz since the end of the 1960s. The intelligence and authority in their improvisations and the precision of execution in their performances were so dependable that hundreds of singers and bandleaders called upon them to play at their recording sessions. Randy had devised a style based in part on the approaches of Miles Davis and Freddie Hubbard. Michael had amalgamated an approach of his own, though it was initially inspired by John Coltrane and the soul sax styles of Junior Walker and King Curtis, among others. In addition to listening to this 1992 sample of the Brecker Brothers, you are encouraged to seek their work on the 1972 Horace Silver album, *In Pursuit of the 27th Man*, which is an all-time favorite of jazz musicians. The top solos are found on its "Liberated Brother" and the selection "Gregory Is Here," which is also available on CCD2 Track 9 Though they played straight-ahead jazz with Horace Silver, the Brecker Brothers had also been among the founders of jazz-rock fusion. Their 1969 band Dreams, with drummer Billy Cobham, was one of the first to fuse jazz traditions with funk music.

This recording of Randy's composition "Above and Below" is from one of the sessions in which the Brecker Brothers themselves were the bandleaders and presumably could do whatever they wished. It is one of the most fiery examples of their playing on record. Randy's solo is exceedingly well constructed and loaded with ideas. It flows and drives. Michael's solo comes on strong and demonstrates all the style traits that were so widely imitated: his favorite phrases, his technique of racing through the chord changes by double-timing and quadruple-timing, his mastery of the ultra-high pitches, his soulful manner, and his tone so hot that it sings. When you hear this recording, notice the remarkable warmth and presence. Note the exuberance for which these musicians were justly celebrated. Also listen for their supple delivery and crisp articulation.

Your first listening should be done before reading the rest of this guide, especially the timed-events portions. But you may wish at least to take mental notes on your experience. Then you can use the following guide to enhance your experience of the music on subsequent listenings. Musicians may like consulting the technical-notes portions of this guide. But non-musicians need not risk becoming distracted or intimidated by such aspects.

LISTENING GUIDE *continued on next page*

Technical Notes

Tone Qualities. Alteration of instrument sound plays a role in the effect of "Above and Below." In his first solo chorus, the trumpeter is playing through an electronic device that adds other sounds to his instrument's natural tone. Randy Brecker switches it off before 1'54". Achieved with special fingerings and blowing techniques, tenor saxophonist Michael Brecker occasionally creates multiple tones at once on his instrument. The result is called a multiphonic (multi = many; phon = sound). He ends his solo with such sounds. The intensity of the music's effect is enhanced by the rawness of these multiphonics and Brecker's use of ultra-high pitched saxophone tones and very rapid melodic figures.

Song Form. The construction of "Above and Below" is neither the usual 12-bar blues nor the 32-bar A-A-B-A pattern found frequently in swing and bop. The organization of parts in "Above and Below" draws from a collection of different sections. Some actually have an extra measure and don't fit into traditional 8-bar units. Some moments contain a section that is only two beats long, rather than the conventional length of four beats. Two different sections occur between the main melody and the main solo improvisations. They are designated as "Tag" and "Interlude." The Tag includes lines improvised on a keyboard synthesizer. In other words, the musicians never let listeners relax with one particular groove for long before startling them with another. Note that the use of the term "tag" for our listening guide here is not the usual use. Ordinarily musicians use the term to designate an ending. We use it here just to distinguish a part that recurs and differs from the part that Randy Brecker designated as "interlude" and the part we designate as "main melody."

Meter. The introduction is not based on the four-beat units used by most jazz tunes, including "Above and Below." It is based in three-beat units (waltz meter). The durations of tones in the introduction are so syncopated that most listeners would never notice that they run over a foundation of waltz meter. Another clever compositional twist is that the pitches in the introduction at 0'00" form a waltz version of the pitches in the main melody section at 0'28". The rhythms used to carry those same pitches at 0'28" are so different that listeners might not recognize that the main melody section uses almost the same sequence of pitches as the introduction.

Melody Pitches. Another outstanding feature is that the melody's pitches include all the pitches in the chromatic scale. In the first four measures, for instance, the melody does not sound any given pitch again until all the others have been sounded. In other words, every pitch gets an equal chance to be heard before it gets its turn again. This is unusual. In most tunes, certain pitches recur, and others are rarely heard if ever heard at all. See the "Elements of Music" appendix for explanation of scales, key, harmony, modes, tonal, and atonal.

Chord Changes. The way chords guide the solo improvisations is unusual, too. Chord changes in accompaniments for melodies in swing and bop pieces usually continue to cycle after the theme statement and provide accompaniment for solos. By contrast, however, the accompaniment chord changes for the main solos on "Above and Below" occur only under the solos at 1'24" and 3'29", not under the theme statements at 0'28", 0'48", 6'10", or 6'30".

ELAPSED TIME	MUSICAL EVENTS
	Introduction (8 measures in waltz time)
0'00"	melody by electric guitar and keyboard synthesizer, in a waltz meter, fast tempo, with complex rhythm and harmony
	Tag (4-measure phrase)
0'14"	Meter switches from waltz to four-beat with bass and drums accenting between the beats, underneath improvised line by synthesizer.
	Tag (4-measure phrase)
0'20"	tag repeated with improvised melody by synthesizer, ending with bass riff punching insistently with drums
	Main Melody (8 measures)
0'28"	Trumpet, tenor saxophone, guitar, and synthesizer play main melody, some notes in unison, others in harmony. Melody's pitches are unusual sequences positioned in a rhythmically complex way, accompanied by bass, drums, and conga drum in Brazilian rhythmic formula called baião.

LISTENING GUIDE *continued on next page*

Tag
0'41"   tag repeated with improvised melody by synthesizer, ending with distinctive bass riff

Main Melody (8 measures)
0'48"   Trumpet, tenor sax, synthesizer and guitar repeat the melody, underscored by rhythm section, pause filled by drum improvisation.

Tag
1'01"   Tag recurs with synthesizer improvisation.

Interlude (10 measures)
1'07"   Trumpet, sax, guitar, and synthesizer play melody as drums and bass accent off-beats.

Improvised Trumpet Solo (Randy Brecker)
1'24"   trumpet solo accompanied by tag, played four times by synthesizer, bass, and drums.

1'50"   two-measure break by ensemble and one-measure break by drums

1'54"   Solo resumes, accompanied by baião rhythm, and a repeating 16-measure chord progression from organ-like synthesizer, in which each chord lasts eight beats.

2'20"   dramatizing first phrase with a fall-off

2'24"   Second phrase is begun with a rip.

2'40"   high-pitched staccato notes

2'47"   slides up to very high note

3'11"   Trumpet solo ends.

Interlude
3'12"   Synthesizer, guitar, horns play interlude, with many drum fills.

Improvised Tenor Saxophone Solo (Michael Brecker)
3'29"   solo quadruple-timing, accompanied by tag, played four times

3'54"   solo interrupted by same three-measure break used at 1'50", ending with drum fill

3'59"   Sax solo resumes, accompanied by a repeating 16-measure chord progression in which each chord lasts eight beats of guitar sustained tones, guitar chords, and the baião rhythm from bass, drums, and conga drum.

4'24"   Sax solo continues, building in intensity with higher pitches.

4'39"   multiphonics

4'50"   Sax solo continues with even more intensity.

4'55"   extremely high pitches and phrases that use notes deliberately outside those of the accompaniment harmony

5'05"   multiphonics

5'13"   Multiphonics end the sax solo.

Interlude
5'15"   Horns play with synthesizer and guitar as drums and bass accent off-beats.

Improvised Drum Solo
5'32"   drum solo, accompanied by bass and synthesizer repeating the tag six times

Main Melody
6'10"   horns, synthesizer, and guitar

Tag
6'23"   The tag is performed twice, with improvised solo on synthesizer.

Main Melody
6'30"   Melody is repeated by horns, guitar, and synthesizer, embellished by numerous drum fills.

Tag
6'43"   synthesizer improvisation over tag, performed twice

LISTENING GUIDE *continued on next page*

Coda

6'53"	bass riff played three times by keyboard, guitar, and bass
6'57"	Horns join keyboard, guitar, and bass on bass riff.
7'00"	emphatically played chords by horns, guitar, and synthesizer
7'02"	Final note is topped by a fall-off from trumpet and guitar.

Jazzy Pop. Let us examine three other labelling dilemmas. (1) For those who find jazzness in music whenever it uses saxophones and a particular accompaniment style, music by Kenny G qualifies as jazz, even though it would not qualify by a strict definition that requires swing era or bop rhythmic properties. *Musicians might be more specific, though, and call music of Kenny G "jazzy pop."*

Rap. (2) Classification procedures are so loose that jazz journalists once contemplated including rap in the jazz category. Perhaps this was suggested by the African American origins they share. However, (a) most rap does not have melody. It is poetry recited atop a repeating funk rhythm. Though rhythmically compelling, (b) most rap does not swing in the jazz sense, and (c) not much of it is freshly improvised for each performance.

Jazzness in Acid Jazz. (3) If a personal perception of jazzness increases with the number and the obviousness of aspects that remind a person of jazz, then acid jazz performances would qualify to the extent that they featured *instruments* associated with jazz (such as Harmon-muted trumpet) and *harmonies* associated with jazz (such as the piano chords on *Kind of Blue*), even without improvisation or swing feeling. If any passages conveyed swing feeling, for instance, they would bear more jazzness.

Watered-Down Jazz. There is another motive for saying something is not jazz despite its roots in the jazz tradition: *rejection of pop jazz.* By saying that a style is not jazz, some fans imply that (1) improvisation does not occupy as much of each performance as in more serious jazz and/or that (2) improvisations in it are (a) not as elaborate or (b) not as well-crafted or (c) not as rhythmically compelling as in other styles. Or it is a way that these fans say (3) they do not like it and are therefore refusing to give it their stamp of approval by calling it "jazz." Some dislike it because of reasons #1, 2a, 2b, or 2c. Some dislike it for other reasons.

A portion of the labeling controversies continues a tradition. *There has long been reluctance among musicians and purist fans to include within the jazz category any watered-down variants of a style that derives from the jazz tradition.* This was why distinctions were made between swing bands and sweet bands during the 1940s (see page 121). Count Basie's fit the former category, and Glenn Miller's fit the latter, for instance. Some jazz fans did not even consider Glenn Miller's to be primarily a jazz band. During the 1990s, comparable distinctions could be made between saxophonists Michael Brecker and Kenny G. Some did not even consider Kenny G to be primarily a jazz improviser.

Classification Fairness. To be fair in classifying styles, we need to consider the actual characteristics of the music, not just the reactions of listeners. When one listener dislikes a style, this does not necessarily mean that another listener will also consider it bad music. We have also learned that if one listener does not consider a musical style to be jazz, this does not necessarily mean the style will not qualify as jazz for another listener. Much of the problem in determining what does and what does not qualify as "jazz" stems from fans judging new music by their feelings about it rather than by referring to musical characteristics that can distinguish styles and identify their origins. Such fans let how much they like the music cloud their judgment of how well the music's characteristics fit a given tradition. They overlook the criteria for defining jazz because they are so passionate about their own tastes.

KLEZMER JAZZ

A nationally occurring revival in Yiddish Klezmer music by musicians of varied backgrounds (not just jazz) inspired clarinetist Don Byron to spend much of the 1980s investigating the possibilities of blending it with jazz.[34] There was a burgeoning interest in Eastern European Jewish music and the variations developed upon it in twentieth-century America. Some of this interest was emerging during the 1970s, but it bloomed fully during the 1980s and 1990s. Much of this was happening in Boston at the New England Conservatory of Music. Byron and saxophonist-clarinetist Chris Speed appeared in widely varied contexts, often joined by alto saxophonist John Zorn and trumpeter Dave Douglas.

In addition to mentioning their fusing Klezmer music with jazz, we need to make note of other trends that are historically significant for Byron, Douglas, Speed, and Zorn. (1) Many of their explorations had nothing to do with jazz or Klezmer music. For instance, cartoon sound track music, movie music, and classical music are just a few of the nonjazz attractions they explored. Classification of their output is challenging because of this. Though Zorn's classical music managed to get cataloged with classical music, the other nonjazz projects of these musicians often appeared in the jazz bins of music stores primarily because the musicians had a reputation for jazz and marketers did not make appropriate distinctions. (Perhaps they did not have separate bins for such other kinds of music.) (2) Versatility and the pursuit of numerous unrelated projects characterized the activities for many of the most talented new musicians of the 1980s and 1990s, not just Byron, Zorn, Douglas, and Speed.

John Zorn, alto saxophonist-composer-bandleader. Shown here in 1990. Distinguished for his contributions to Klezmer jazz, as well as avant-garde classical music and symphonic writing, he is a virtuoso instrumentalist who brings conceptual originality to all the diverse genres he explores.

(Photo by Michael Macioce)

John Zorn (b. 1953), saxophonist, composer, bandleader, is probably the most versatile and hard working figure associated with Klezmer jazz in the 1990s.[35] Originally a rock musician, he became interested in Lee Konitz and Paul Desmond. He mastered bop styles by the end of his teen years, and he can still offer a passable imitation of Phil Woods, the Charlie Parker disciple on whom Zorn modeled his early playing. Moreover, he reveals an understanding of the Ornette Coleman Trio concept whenever he wishes. (Listen to "Dee Dee," CCD2 Track 5, for an example of the Coleman Trio concept.) Zorn's most distinctive contributions were the more than 250 works collectively termed *Masada*.[36] In these, Zorn absorbed Yiddish folk music and combined it with the methods of Ornette Coleman and Phil Woods. With his collaborators, trumpeter Dave Douglas, bassist Greg Cohen, and drummer Joey Baron, Zorn created impassioned improvisations with virtuosic execution that had a groove all their own. They swung infectiously without following bop traditions for accompaniment rhythms.

Composed by Dave Douglas; recorded December 21, 1993, by Dave Douglas (trumpet), Brad Shepik (guitar), and Jim Black (drums); available on The Tiny Bell Trio (Songlines: 1504, c1994).

Klezmer music experienced a revival of interest in the United States during the 1970s and 1980s. Clarinetist Don Byron was investigating its possibilities for jazz, and he had included trumpeter Dave Douglas in his Klezmer project *Don Byron Plays the Music of Mickey Katz*. Looking for ways to expand the vocabulary of his own music, Douglas also began listening to folk music of Macedonia, Serbia, Croatia, Bulgaria, and Hungary. Much of what Douglas wrote for his Tiny Bell Trio was inspired by such music. The elements taken from it for the "Red Emma" recording were the 9/8 meter (counted "one-two, one-two, one-two, one-two-three") and a scale having a flavor of that region's music (technically known as the "C harmonic minor scale") and some variations that Douglas put around it. Though the basic 2 + 2 + 2 + 3 meter he used is a typical Balkan dance rhythm, Douglas contends that in writing "Red Emma" he was not necessarily attempting to emulate Balkan dance music or to force any new identity on that rhythm or on his band's jazz playing. Douglas feels that the music on "Red Emma" really comes from the jazz tradition more than from any traditional East European music. He contends that, in that sense, it is very American.

Within the recording you might notice some novel sounds from the trumpet. Douglas is attracted to such sounds for their coloristic value. Some show his light-hearted approach to the piece. They fit with his playfully altering the timing of the melody's tones, their pitch range, and sound quality. His intentional drops of pitch at the ends of tones, his occasional pinched tones, and hint of a growl all serve to spice up the music. Douglas also plays a lot in the low and middle ranges of the trumpet, thereby producing other sounds with which many listeners may not be familiar. Note that neither his pitch range nor his alterations of tone quality characterize music of the Balkans. In fact, clarinet is the common wind instrument in Klezmer music, not trumpet. Rather than reflecting any Balkan influence, his toying with sound and his swoops from very low to very high pitch ranges are more indicative of the trumpeter's highly accomplished command of his instrument and his fearless attitude in improvising.

The song form of "Red Emma" consists of a two-measure section that is played four times as an introduction and is used later as a finishing portion referred to as "D-section." This pattern also provides the basis for open-ended improvisation. For example, in the trumpet solo, it is repeated sixteen times, from 1'49" to 2'34". The second section of "Red Emma" is eight measures long, designated "A-section." The pattern is followed by a middle section that is designated "B-Section." It is also eight measures long and repeated. Then a new section occurs in a major key, and it is six measures long and designated "C-section." The final section is a repeat of the original introductory two measures, now termed "D-section." It is repeated at liberty in the solos. The solos follow A-B-C-D, with D open-ended.

Note: If you are getting overly concerned with the underlying song form, you might miss the essence of the "Red Emma" musical experience. Therefore, the following guide highlights only a few events in order to cue those listeners who are curious about the arrangement and wish to distinguish the lines that were preset from the lines that were improvised. Such references are not absolutely essential for enjoying the music. You might have more fun just listening and forming your own impressions. Keep in mind, however, that all the drum parts and guitar parts are improvised throughout the performance, though they follow the structure of the song form that the trumpeter composed.

ELAPSED TIME   MUSICAL EVENTS

Main Theme Statement

0'00" Introduction

     Trumpet plays melody in low and middle pitch registers, soon joined by guitar chords, tambourine, and high-pitched drums, played lightly in meter of 9.

0'12" A-section

0'22" B-section

0'34" B-section repeats

0'44"   Guitar line sounds a transition to C-section.

LISTENING GUIDE continued on next page

0'45"	C-section
0'54"	D-section (repeat of intro)
0'57"	low-pitched trumpet notes
1'06"	conclusion of D-section
1'08"	**Improvised Trumpet Solo**
	A-section
1'10"	trumpet flourishes, accompanied by double-time feeling from drums and guitar
1'19"	B-section
	cymbal crashes
1'24"	high-pitched trumpet tones
1'40"	C-section
1'49"	D-section
1'50"	low-pitched trumpet tones
1'52"	trumpet growl
1'54"	bluesy repetitions of a two-note figure ten times
2'00"	Pitch fall-offs decorate several tones.
2'08"	pinched tones integrated into trumpet line
2'11"	string of double-time improvisations
2'19"	high-pitched tones
2'22"	Trumpet quotes original melody of introduction (D-section).
	Guitar Solo
2'34"	break for guitar to begin solo
2'36"	Trumpet plays accompanying line under guitar solo; much activity of sticks on snare drum underneath.
2'51"	Trumpet continues improvised accompaniment.
3'09"	C-section
3'18"	D-section
	high-pitched drum tones
3'25"	Guitar, trumpet, and drums converge on one rhythm.
	Drum Solo
3'29"	drum solo, accompanied lightly by trumpet
4'01"	Trumpet and guitar play final phrase of tune's D-section over end of drum solo.
	Melody
4'07"	Tempo increases as trumpet reiterates melody.
4'16"	B-section
4'33"	C-section
4'40"	Instead of adhering to original end of main melody, trumpet improvises and guitar improvises countermelody to trumpet.
4'42"	D-section
4'50"	dramatic ending by descending arpeggio in unison from guitar and trumpet
4'53"	stinger

The other musician most closely identified with Klezmer jazz is trumpeter **Dave Douglas** (b. 1963). With enviable command over the trumpet and swaggering confidence, he has performed improvisations in conventional hard bop, as with Horace Silver (1987–1990), and in mid-1960s Miles Davis style. He has also recorded sterling examples of classical trumpet playing (as on non-jazz albums by John Zorn and Uri Caine). In fact, the influence of modern classical music gives his jazz trumpet improvisations part of their unique flavor. For instance, the music on his *Parallel Worlds* album is influenced by twentieth-century classical composers Anton Webern and Igor Stravinsky. But he shows himself to be a truly fresh voice in Zorn's *Masada* jams and Douglas's own Tiny Bell Trio.[37] (Listen to "Red Emma" by Tiny Bell Trio on *JCCD3*.) There he composed new frameworks from varied traditions for Eastern-European and Middle-Eastern folk music. He combined aspects from the jazz trumpet styles of Miles Davis, Don Cherry, and Lester Bowie with his own original ideas to improvise solos within the fresh frameworks he had composed. (On *JCCD2* listen to "Masqualero" to sample the Davis style he imitated and "Civilization Day" to sample the Cherry style he imitated.) As a composer and bandleader, Douglas has proven endlessly explorative. Employing instruments rarely found in jazz such as violin and accordion, he mixed jazz improvisation with European folk traditions and came up with fresh music, again and again.

Trumpeter Dave Douglas, shown here at the 2000 Knitting Factory Jazzfest in New York.

(Photo by Michael Macioce)

LATIN JAZZ

In the 1980s and 1990s, combinations of jazz improvisation with Caribbean and South American music seemed to get more recognition than ever before. Afro-Cuban musicians landed recording contracts with major North American firms, and they were featured in newspapers, magazines, televised awards programs, and movies. Cuba contributed several exciting jazz instrumentalists to the U.S. jazz community. Jazz festivals around the United States were routinely presenting "Latin jazz" groups. The genre was even canonized in 2004 when the Lincoln Center for the Performing Arts founded a resident repertory band there for Latin jazz. Recall that this was home to the New York Philharmonic Orchestra and the Metropolitan Opera. Therefore, adding a Latin jazz band represented serious recognition of the music's value.

Latin jazz's ascendance to broad media attention in the 1980s and 1990s belies a long tradition. Cuban bands were including jazz improvisation at least as early as the 1920s, and some of them appeared in New York at that time. Cuban dance music had helped spawn ragtime during the 1800s, and the influence of Cuban musicians has been almost continuous since then. The rhumba in the 1930s and the mambo in the 1940s and 1950s saw so much popularity in North America that at East Coast balls attended by wealthy society people it was not unusual to have three different bands alternating: a swing band (perhaps in the style of Benny Goodman), a sweet band (perhaps in the style of Guy Lombardo or Wayne King), and a Latin band. Jelly Roll Morton wrote several pieces that used Latin American rhythms and recorded them during the 1920s. Duke Ellington had recorded pieces with Latin American flavor during the 1930s and 1940s. The Cuban mambo was popular in New York during the

Latin Jazz bandleader Tito Puente playing timbales. Notice the two cowbells suspended in front of the timbales. Seen here at the 1990 Detroit-Montreux Jazz Festival.

(Photo by John Sobczak)

1940s, and Latino bandleaders mixed their rhythms and percussion instruments with improvisation and harmony of concurrent modern jazz styles. By the end of that decade, bandleaders Dizzy Gillespie and Stan Kenton were carrying auxiliary percussionists on tour with them to play the portions of their repertory devoted to Latin American styles. In the 1950s and 1960s, Cal Tjader and George Shearing did the same. Saxophonist-bandleader Stan Getz enjoyed tremendous popularity when he embraced Brazilian repertory that combined North American cool jazz with samba. His 1962 and 1963 recordings lent impetus to a bossa nova craze in the United States. In fact, bossa nova repertory became standard fare for jazz musicians thereafter.

During the 1980s and 1990s, New York musicians who had learned Afro-Cuban styles gained appreciation that was no longer limited primarily to audiences composed of Latin American immigrants and knowledgeable insiders. The oldest and most important of these names had already been a major figure in jazz since the 1930s. Cuban trumpeter-composer-arranger **Mario Bauzá** (1911–1993) had played and written for several of the best jazz-oriented swing bands, not just bands that specialized in Afro-Cuban music. In fact, it was as a member of Cab Calloway's band in the 1930s that Bauzá had exerted profound influence on fellow bandmate Dizzy Gillespie, and it was as musical director of Chick Webb's band that he initiated the career of singer Ella Fitzgerald. He is considered the father of Latin jazz, originally dubbed "Cuban jazz." In 1943 he composed his "Tanga," one of the earliest Latin jazz pieces. This work was recorded by singer-bandleader Machito (Frank Grillo) and the Afro-Cubans, using Latino percussionists and North American hornmen.[38] Bauzá thereby created an early melding of Cuban rhythms with jazz harmonies, improvisation, and instrumentation. Over the years, Bauzá added more and more jazz instrumentation to Machito's band, for which he continued to compose and arrange until 1976. This became the model for the 1947 collaboration between Dizzy Gillespie and Cuban composer-conga drummer Chano Pozo that produced their Cubop composition "Manteca." It was also the model for Stan Kenton's excursions into Latin jazz. What makes Bauzá especially relevant to the present chapter is that his first widely known albums as a Latin jazz bandleader were not made until the 1980s, and the albums that some consider his best were not made until 1992 and 1993.[39]

Two of the best "Latin bands" that gained prominence in the 1980s and 1990s had also been around long before this new recognition. They were led by **Tito Puente** (1923–2000) and Eddie Palmieri. Both leaders were New York-born of parents who had Puerto Rican heritage. Prior to the 1980s, their bands had been termed "mambo bands" and "salsa bands." Now they were also being promoted as "Latin Jazz bands."

A bandleader since the 1940s, Puente played marimba, vibraphone, and percussion. Among the percussion instruments he played, the timbales received the most emphasis. This Cuban instrument consists of two short, metal drums without drumheads on the bottom and is a descendent of the timpani (kettle drum) used by Cubans to play their high-society music called *danzon*. They are positioned on a waist-high rack that also has cowbells attached, and a splash cymbal. The cowbells have their clangers removed and are played with a drum stick. The rhythms played on these percussion instruments have African origins that have been retained in Caribbean culture from the time of slavery. North American drumming rudiments were added to the repertory by Puente, and he featured timbale solos in band performances. Puente brought the timbales greater recognition, and made it his main instrument. (Timbales are pictured on page 410.)

Unlike the pulse in jazz for swing dancing, in which we have high-hat sounding on 2 and 4, and ride cymbal sounding on 1, 2, 3, and 4, there is a rhythmic pattern in Latin American music called clavé, around which each type of dance is centered. The clavé rhythm is different for each dance and essential to the feeling evoked by the dance band. For example, mambo and rhumba each has its own distinct clavé rhythm.

In the Puente bands, the leader's timbale playing is joined by one musician playing conga drum and one playing bongo drums. Sometimes the timbale player or the bongo player plays cowbell. One or two singers are also common, and they also play cowbell, clavés, maracas, and guiro (scraper). This function is essential because the rhythm they play evokes the particular feeling appropriate for each type of dance. Sometimes the hornmen also play percussion instruments when not blowing their horns. In the improvisation section, piano plays both a harmonic and a percussive role by repeating an eight-beat pattern called the *montuno*. In this way the piano links the harmonic structure to the rhythmic structure. The rhythms coming from these percussionists are packed with syncopations that represent African retentions. They provide layers of accompaniment that lend Afro-Cuban music its essence. Together these musicians create a very busy and exciting sonic texture. (To hear somewhat similar rhythms, listen to the piano and bass parts on *JCCD2* in "Señor Blues" and "Maiden Voyage.")

In most jazz performances, the bass supplies a steady pulse while syncopation results from the soloists's improvised notes tugging against it. The jazz practice of walking bass, however, is not followed in Afro-Cuban music. A more complicated pattern called the *tumbao* is played by the bassist. This pattern accents the "and" of the second beat and accents the fourth beat to produce an effect analogous to a swinging hammock. Because the bassist does not emphasize the first and third of every four beats, it is often difficult for jazz listeners to discern the organization of beats in the music. The first beat of any four is not even sounded. This means that in Afro-Cuban music the off-beat is actually used as an accompaniment.

Significant as a composer-arranger, Puente wrote arrangements in the 1950s that used big band jazz instrumentation.[40] He even had a "Latin jazz" album at that time, thereby anticipating the way his mambo bands would be tagged 30 years later. Like Bauzá, Puente blended North American jazz harmony, instrumentation, and improvisations with Cuban rhythms and percussion instruments. During the 1980s and 1990s, not only did Puente maintain a large dance band, but he also toured with a smaller band that emphasized jazz solo improvisations.[41]

A bandleader since the early 1960s, pianist **Eddie Palmieri** (b. 1936) was the all-time master at devising cross rhythms. He displaced the positions of his phrases and comping in seemingly endless new ways relative to the underlying beat and still managed to make sense and evoke dancing. As in jazz of all periods, the lines of influence ran in both directions. Latin American rhythms influenced jazz, and jazz improvisations and harmonies influenced the playing of the Latin band musicians. During the late 1970s and early 1980s for instance, Palmieri exhibited the influence of McCoy Tyner, who himself had assimilated African and Latin American rhythms during the late 1960s and early 1970s. Historically, Palmieri was as significant as a bandleader-composer as he was as a pianist. For a number of years he has carried hornmen who were already established in non-Latin Jazz.[42]

The most eminent Cuban jazz musicians to become known to North American audiences during the 1970s and 1980s were initially part of a Cuban band called Irakere.[43] The leader of Irakere was pianist **Chucho Valdés** (b. 1941). Widely respected in jazz circles for his pianistic power and virtuosity, he is also very eclectic, choosing material as stylistically far flung as Thelonious Monk and Bill Evans, as well as standard repertory from Cuban popular music. His imagination for inventing compelling rhythms impressed many musicians. Two members of the band ultimately relocated to the United States: alto saxophonist **Paquito D'Rivera** (b. 1948) and trumpeter **Arturo Sandoval** (b. 1949). They became mainstays on the North American jazz scene of the 1990s. Quite accomplished as musicians in classical music, not just jazz, both were impressive instrumentalists. Sandoval, for instance, occasionally played the intricate phrases of Dizzy Gillespie's improvisations that were situated in a stratospherically high register. A huge tone and majestic manner characterized Sandoval's work.[44] D'Rivera also had command of the altissimo register and exhibited crisp articulation. He developed his own jazz vocabulary such that his playing became instantly recognizable. The improvisations of D'Rivera conveyed a very confident, exuberant attitude, and the effect was highly animated and light-hearted. Though both could handle non-Latin musical contexts, neither Sandoval's nor D'Rivera's improvisational vocabulary was entirely bop-derived.[45] In other words, one of the main contributions of Sandoval and D'Rivera was a unique fusion of modern jazz style phrasing with Afro-Cuban style phrasing.

"Miami," JCCD3 *Track 10*

The Afro-Cuban music of Irakere and many other Latin Jazz groups showed more African characteristics than any other kind of jazz. Afro-Cuban music was far more polyrhythmic than swing or bop-style because it contained (a) more layers of accompaniment rhythm, (b) more complicated rhythms in those layers, and (c) more extensive repetition of those rhythms. In fact, it may be that what jazz fans perceive in Afro-Cuban music as accompaniment or predominately background is actually the foreground.[46]

There is an Afro-Cuban tradition of offering horn solos as an additional layer of activity to increase excitement, not as the primary focus of interest as in most modern jazz. Horn solos in Afro-Cuban music often served as decoration, providing a coloristic function. This resembled the function played by their counterparts inserted into performances by swing bands of the 1930s and 1940s and the hot sax solos inserted between vocals during rock and roll performances of the 1950s.

When comparing the importance of solos in Afro-Cuban traditional music with their importance in jazz, also consider the brevity of solos in Afro-Cuban music and the practice of not offering numerous solos in a given piece. In pure jazz, especially since the 1950s, the solos tend to be lengthy, and several musicians get to play solos in each piece. Recall too that, though the most popular swing bands and sweet bands of the 1930s and 1940s all carried capable jazz improvisers, most music featured them only briefly. The swing bands of Count Basie, Benny Goodman, Duke Ellington, and Fletcher Henderson, with their emphasis on solo improvisations, were the exceptions.

Composed by J. Marquez; recorded July 1982 by Paquito D'Rivera (alto saxophone), Jorge Dalto (piano), Jeff Fuller (bass), Ignacio Berroa (drums), and Daniel Ponce (percussion); available on *Mariel* (Columbia: 38177, c1982).

Terms to learn from the "Elements of Music" appendix and *Demo* CD: swing eighth notes, legato, staccato, comping, syncopation, alto saxophone, voicing in octaves. **Learn from *Listening to Jazz* DVD:** alto sax, comping, electric bass.

"Miami" is Afro-Cuban jazz that is characterized by certain melodic, harmonic, and rhythmic patterns. The pianist plays a *montuno*, which is an integral part of Afro-Cuban music. This is a brief, syncopated melody that is harmonized and continuously repeated. Like comping, it provides harmonic support at the same time as rhythmic support for the soloist, and it is often played with both hands. Unlike jazz comping, however, it does not react to the soloist's rhythms because it is a set pattern rather than an improvisation. The pianist stops the montuno and reverts to comping at 1′01″. He resumes montuno at 4′38″.

Bass patterns here are not walking lines. Instead, the bassist plays a highly syncopated pattern, less dense than the pianist's montuno. It is almost like a slow-motion countermelody. Often, he will not even play on the first beat of a measure. This, in turn, adds to the rhythmic complexity of the music.

Two drummers are working with D'Rivera here. One plays the drum set that we ordinarily associate with jazz. The set drummer in Afro-Cuban style does not play the typical ride rhythm on ride cymbal. He plays highly syncopated rhythmic patterns on various parts of the drum set. The other drummer plays conga drums. The conga drummer also plays highly syncopated rhythms. The result is a rich collection of rhythms.

The tone colors and pitches of the drums in Afro-Cuban music are quite varied. Careful listening will reveal higher pitches and lower pitches on the conga. One conga drum is typically bigger than the other, which lends it a lower pitch. The conga drum can produce different tone qualities and pitches depending on how the player strikes it. Which part of the hand the player uses is important. For instance, whether the player uses the inside of the palm or the heel of the palm makes a difference. Using finger tips will extract an entirely different sound than using the palm. In "Miami," elements of the percussion background are more prominent at some times than others. For instance, at 0′18″, the drummer strikes the wooden side of a drum with his sticks, producing a sharp, clicking sound. At 1′48″, the conga drummer plays a prominent polyrhythm (three notes in the time of two notes that the other musicians play).

"Miami" is constructed in a 32-measure A-A-B-A form, in which the second and third A-sections differ somewhat from the first. So we designated them as A′ (pronounced "aay-PRIME"). This second A-section is the same as the first, except that it ends with a slightly different melody and chord progression (heard at 0′17″; see below). The way it ends is in the form of a short rhythmic figure. We can listen for this not only in the melody statements, but also when it is quoted in some of the improvised solos. In fact, the saxophonist and the pianist end some of their improvisations by playing this very figure.

Cuban-born alto saxophonist Paquito D'Rivera has remarkable command of his instrument and a supercharged sense of fun. Both of these properties are demonstrated by very fast, ultra-high-pitched playing at 0′41″, 0′53″, 1′51″, 2′40″, 4′51″, and elsewhere. The tones in this extremely high range are termed "altissimo register." Playing them requires different fingerings and blowing methods than are required for the conventional range of pitches. Though the saxophonist makes it sound easy here, the technique is formidable. Similar praise is warranted for incorporation of shakes into his improvised melodies in the highest ranges of pitch, as at 0′51″.

Afro-Cuban jazz has a reputation for being hot almost all the time. D'Rivera's blistering pace and frequent forays into the altissimo register exemplify this aspect of it. The saxophonist tears into his improvisation with a torrent of quick ideas. At 0′33″, his solo intersperses fast flurries of notes with less hurried melodic ideas; some melodies are ablaze with very high-pitched tones. D'Rivera seems to revel in his virtuosity, just as a championship runner crosses the finish line grinning widely with arms raised in victory, showing joy and pride. (Flaunting one's mastery typifies Cuban musicians who possess extraordinary skill.) The Afro-Cuban style, which is inherently exciting itself, combines with the saxophonist's amazing instrumental technique and attitude to propel the playing to the level of excitement we hear in "Miami."

D'Rivera's melodic improvisational vocabulary is not drawn exclusively from the main models that U.S. jazz saxophonists traditionally imitate: Charlie Parker, Lee Konitz, and Ornette Coleman. Though he does speak the bop language, D'Rivera melds it with patterns from his own classical music training and from approaches used by horn soloists in Afro-Cuban jazz. In other words, he has his own recognizable style.

LISTENING GUIDE continued on next page

Discerning ears can tell when D'Rivera is the soloist. They will not confuse his playing with that of other particularly extraverted alto saxophone stylists such as David Sanborn or Phil Woods.

In addition to the burning saxophone sounds on "Miami," we are treated to an electrifying piano solo by Jorge Dalto that typifies the flashiness preferred in Afro-Cuban traditions, though he was originally from Argentina. Other points of interest include a quote by D'Rivera from Dizzy Gillespie's tune "Salt Peanuts" at 1'16" and by Dalto from Gillespie's improvisation on his 1945 recording of "Bebop" at 4'24". Quoting is a common practice among jazz improvisers.

Perhaps the best way to appreciate this music is first to allow yourself to get swept up in its energy and enthusiasm. "Miami" goes by so fast that you need not be concerned with catching all the highlights tallied by the listening guide. But if you wish to investigate them, don't hesitate to frequently use the pause switch and reverse button on your CD player.

ELAPSED TIME	MUSICAL EVENTS
0'00"	**Introduction—Alto Saxophone Plays Final Phrase of A-section as Intro**
	Rhythm section plays only the first beat, and saxophone plays alone for break.
0'02"	Piano, bass, and drums play rhythm of the melody with saxophone.
0'04"	**First Chorus—Melody Played by Alto Saxophone**
	A
	Rhythm section is playing rhythmic patterns common to Afro-Cuban jazz with pianist playing a montuno.
0'11"	**A'**
0'17"	Ensemble plays a short rhythmic figure.
0'18"	**B** Piano and alto saxophone play unison legato on fast melody.
0'26"	**A'**
	Second Chorus—Alto Saxophone Solo
0'33"	**A** begins sax solo with very high-pitched shake
0'40"	**A'**
0'42"	altissimo register
0'47"	**B**
0'51"	interspersed with shakes and
0'53"	intentional, high-pitched squeals
0'55"	**A'**
1'01"	**Third Chorus**
	A piano comping instead of montuno as accompaniment
1'08"	**A'**
1'13"	extremely high-pitched melodic ideas
1'16"	**B**
	quoting Dizzy Gillespie's tune "Salt Peanuts"
1'20"	shakes incorporated in melody lines
1'23"	**A'**
	ascends to very high register
1'29"	beginning of a short melody repeated with variation
	Fourth Chorus
1'30"	**A**
	short melodic idea repeated 11 times with variations, accompanied by piano comping

LISTENING GUIDE *continued on next page*

1'37"	**A'**	
1'40"		altissimo notes
1'44"	**B**	
1'51"	**A'**	
		altissimo notes

Interlude—Unaccompanied Alto Saxophone Solo Improvisation

1'58"		
2'26"		melodic figure repeated at lower and lower pitch
2'38"		altissimo playing
2'43"		one phrase played three times in different ranges
2'49"		altissimo playing
2'56"		altissimo playing
3'02"		ending phrase of "Miami" melody
3'03"		Conga drum joins the alto saxophone, and sax responds by a series of highly syncopated staccato ideas.
3'14"		Sax states the end of the main theme.

Fifth Chorus—Piano Solo Improvisation

3'17"	**A**	
		Piano soloing starts by emphasizing crushed tones to emulate blue pitch.
3'24"	**A'**	
		Piano incorporates several other crushed tones for bluesy quality.
3'31"	**B**	
3'38"	**A'**	

Sixth Chorus

3'45"	**A**	
		quadruple-timing a flashy figure six times, indicating the notes in each chord as it goes by
3'51"	**A'**	
		Piano plays funky melodic figure 12 times with variations.
3'58"	**B**	
	A'	
4'05"		one chord played rapidly four times and again four times
4'06"		higher-pitched chord played rapidly four times and again four times
4'08"		final phrase of the original theme, harmonized

Seventh Chorus

4'11"	**A**	
		Piano repeats ornate melodic figure several times in a descending pattern.
4'18"	**A'**	
		melody voiced in octaves
4'24"	**B**	
		Pianist plays Dizzy Gillespie ("BeBop") lick in octaves using both hands.
4'31"	**A'**	
4'36"		Pianist plays harmonized main theme.

Eighth Chorus—Sax and Drums Trading Eight-Measure Solo Improvisations

4'38"	**A**	
		eight measures of sax, accompanied by piano montuno

LISTENING GUIDE *continued on next page*

4'45"	A'	
		eight measures of drums and percussion
4'51"	B	
		eight measures for sax, venturing into altissimo register
4'58"	A'	
		eight measures of sticks playing cowbell and fingers playing roll on conga

Ninth Chorus—Sax and Drums Trading Four-Measure Solo Improvisations

	A	
5'05"		four measures of sax improvisation, accompanied by piano montuno
5'08"		four measures of drums and percussion
	A'	
5'12"		four measures of sax improvisation
5'15"		four measures of sticks on cowbell and fingers on conga
	B	
5'18"		Piano and sax in unison play original B-section melody.
	A'	
5'25"		Sax plays original melody, ending pitched in highest octave.

So you can see that the role of jazz solo improvisation in traditional Afro-Cuban music was not so different than in North American popular music of the 1930s, '40s, and '50s. In this regard, *the Afro-Cuban music that received so much recognition in North America during the 1980s and 1990s represents more a tradition of popular dance music than pure jazz.* This was made particularly evident in the 1997 album and 1999 film about the Cuban band called *The Buena Vista Social Club.* Keep in mind that in Cuba, just as in North America, jazz musicians were versatile. Though they may have wished to specialize in jazz, and there were Cuban bands devoted solely to jazz, musicians were more likely to find employment if they performed traditional or commercial music rather than pure jazz. So that is precisely what they did.

Another reason for limiting improvisation is that, as with swing in North America during the 1930s and 1940s, Latin jazz in Cuba has traditionally served primarily as dance music. Therefore, the main goal of the musicians was to generate a rhythmic feeling that inspired dancing; musicians term this "a groove." To sustain that feeling during a piece is essential. Too much variety would disturb it. So, unlike bop combos in which such as creative drummers Max Roach and Art Blakey continuously varied their timekeeping rhythms and improvised kicks and prods to communicate with the soloists, the Afro-Cuban bands established accompaniment rhythms and stuck with them throughout the piece, often maintaining a feverish intensity from start to finish.

HIP-HOP JAZZ

Acid jazz continued through the 1990s, but it also spawned an interesting offshoot that ran concurrently on the jazz and avant-garde pop music scenes. Drummers and bassists imitated the acid jazz sounds of the drum machines, scratching rhythms of disc jockey/"mixers," as well as the sampling and the loops thereof. With this they made live music that bore the groove previously achieved only by the mixers. They also added their own ideas. As a source of originality, they could chop up the samples, fuse them together, and phrase them across larger units of time than they had come from. Mixers had actually doubled the speed of some samples, and this served as an additional example to the drummers. Combining different elements offered endless variations. Some musicians were attracted to this source of fresh sounds because they felt it offered a richness not offered by swing rhythms. It provided the desired manic esthetic that was sufficiently spastic and hyper-complex to satisfy their tastes and inspire new concepts in solo improvisations. The approach was dubbed **drum 'n' bass.** Their work often resembled Herbie Hancock's "Rockit" and Miles Davis's *Bitches Brew* and *On the Corner*. Note that most of these groups were not in the jazz idiom. They were more clearly within avant-garde pop, variants on what was termed "techno" or "electronica." But a few were jazz groups with highly explorative improvisers such as saxophonists Chris Speed and Josh Smith.[47] It is important to keep in mind that not all bands offering this approach used it all the time. The drum 'n' bass groove was just one within an assortment of different grooves for them. Most of these musicians merely added it to their already varied palette. In fact, albums by some of these musicians presented a sample of almost every different groove that they were exploring during that phase in their evolution.

To better appreciate the historical place of the drum 'n' bass genre, note that its emergence came after several jazz musicians had focused interest on superimposing jazz improvisation atop the accompaniments for rap music, better know as "hip-hop." Saxophonists Greg Osby and Steve Coleman were among the musicians who pursued this during the 1980s, and saxophonist Branford Marsalis formed the band Buckshot Lefonque to try this during the 1990s.[48] All these musicians had careers in other styles of jazz, but they decided to experiment with this style for a while, and their interest produced a body of music with a decidedly different feeling from bop and bop-derived jazz.

To further place the drum 'n' bass genre in historical perspective, remember that the incorporation of pop music accompaniment styles into jazz reflects a long tradition. Jazz originated by musicians who were hired to play music for such dances as the quadrille and the schottische. Later they were called upon to accompany the stomp and the slow drag, for which they obliged by creating swing style and slow blues, respectively. They adapted marches and rags to satisfy the dancers, too, and ended up inventing Dixieland out of that. Then during the 1950s, Brazilian musicians liked U.S. cool jazz so much that they mixed it with samba and invented a soft, gentle version called "bossa nova" (Portuguese for "new beat"). During the 1970s the music for the dance known as "boogaloo" was tried by a number of jazz musicians, and their funkiest playing was set atop it.

Hip-hop accompaniment was merely one of many different grooves explored by alto saxophonist **Steve Coleman** (b. 1956). To peg Coleman's talent solely as "acid jazz" or "hip-hop jazz" would do his creativity a grave disservice. He did succeed, however, at crafting compelling improvisations over such grooves. His solos clearly drew from swinging jazz traditions, not pop music cliché that would be easy to do within that context. Like his model Maceo Parker, who rode atop similar vamps on recordings of singer James Brown, Coleman projected an inviting flow and punch. His improvisations also bear a conceptual similarity to those of fellow Chicagoan Anthony Braxton because his note choices are so unusual. He thinks very hard about inventing strings of notes whose relationships to one another are not at all expected by the ears of most jazz fans. Though he does not attempt atonality (absence of key feeling, bordering on randomness) as Braxton does, Coleman probably comes closer to it than any hornman other than Braxton. Coleman also cites Charlie Parker as an influence, but it is not obvious in the lines Coleman devises. In fact, his lines sound more like Ornette Coleman's than Charlie Parker's. Incidentally, despite his striking freshness,

Coleman is not exclusively avant-garde. He has also performed with more conventional bands such as those of Thad Jones-Mel Lewis and Dave Holland.

Coleman is probably as important as a bandleader, composer, and conceptual thinker as he is as an improvising saxophonist. He accumulates top-notch musicians for his Five Elements bands, and he features guest appearances by an assortment of luminaries. Coleman is open to diverse sources, and he smoothly incorporates music from other cultures he has visited, such as India, Cuba, Africa, and Brazil, as well as rap music from African-American culture. He has employed numerous accompaniment styles, ranging from swinging bop style to modified hip-hop. He has explored the opportunities afforded by ensembles of varied size and instrumentation, including instrumentalized voice, synthesizer, and even a DJ scratching records. He has composed most of the music on his albums, all of which are distinguished by their departure from convention.[49]

NEO-SWING JAZZ

During the 1990s, a renewed popularity of swing dancing revived the music of the 1930s and 1940s big bands and their imitators. Classes in almost every major city were devoted to teaching the jitterbug and Lindy hop. Many jazz musicians found employment in new swing bands playing for these dancers, even though many of them were playing styles quite unlike their preferred jazz approaches. The movie *Swing Kids* sparked some of the ensuing popularity. The public was also reminded by the touring musical revue about Louis Jordan called *Five Guys Named Moe*. Remarkable sales sometimes accompanied new albums by young musicians imitating the late 1940s/ early 1950s "jump bands" of Louis Jordan and Louis Prima, and the hottest of the 1930s swing bands, such as Cab Calloway's and Fats Waller's. They also drew upon early 1950s rockabilly. (Brian Setzer's *Dirty Boogie* sold more than two million copies. The Royal Crown Revue and the Squirrel Nut Zippers were also successful.[50]) Improvisations in these new groups tended not to be substantial in their development or originality. Excitement and danceable rhythm were the main goals. That this music had some jazz content caused many people to believe that jazz was experiencing renewed popularity. The truth was that popularity for most jazz at this time had actually hit a new low, and the jazzy music for the dance craze did not contain much fresh jazz improvisation.

NEO-CLASSICAL JAZZ

In the history of jazz, imitation has traditionally been a first step toward developing a young musician's understanding of the intricacies in serious improvisation. This usually involved deep study of at least one significant style and learning how to play like a particular master. Dizzy Gillespie, for instance, learned the complicated style of Roy Eldridge. The next step was practicing long and hard to arrive at a fresh contribution. This process was called "finding your own voice." Referring again to our example of Gillespie, recall that he used Eldridge's approach as a foundation from which to devise an even more complicated style that contained mostly Gillespie's own original ideas. Sometimes a young musician would study two or more different styles and combine them in a distinctive way. For example, Charlie Parker combined elements of Buster Smith's and Art Tatum's styles with a wide assortment of other sources such as Lester Young, blues, and classical music. Miles Davis combined elements from the styles of Freddie Webster, Dizzy Gillespie, and Charlie Parker. During the 1950s, John Coltrane drew from Sonny Stitt's style, then during the 1960s from John Gilmore's and Albert Ayler's. Keith Jarrett combined approaches of Bill Evans, Ornette Coleman, and Paul Bley.

Though the great innovators all came up with something new, the majority of jazz musicians either remained imitators, or they offered a twist to an existing style that made their own playing distinguishable from their model's style. The improvisers who came up with distinctive twists are known by insiders, but their names and those of the remaining musicians are not recognized by most jazz fans today because they have not interested historians enough to write about them or include them in compilations of historic recordings. For example, many of the best young trumpeters of the 1930s and 1940s did not go beyond Louis Armstrong or Bix Beiderbecke, and many of the 1950s did not go substantially beyond the 1940s style of Fats Navarro or the early 1950s style of Miles Davis. Similarly, numerous saxophonists of the 1940s and 1950s were content to learn the phrases of Lester Young and piece their own solos together with them. Once they learned his phrases, they continued playing in that style throughout their careers. They played well but did not receive much attention from journalists or historians because they were not original.

During the 1980s and 1990s, a trend emerged in which a number of the most talented newcomers stopped with the imitation stage, but did not stop after learning just one model. They went from style to style. The mastery of their instruments and the immense work they devoted to learning other styles was impressive. During the 1970s and 1980s, for example, it was not unusual for a young pianist to begin by learning Herbie Hancock's or Chick Corea's approach. The young pianist might record and tour in that style and subsequently learn another style, such as Thelonious Monk's or Oscar Peterson's, then tour and record in it. Some pianists of the 1980s and 1990s even went on to learn a third style. For instance, a few eventually specialized in stride-style or ragtime for a while. It was not unusual for young saxophonists to first learn one style period of John Coltrane, then tour and record in that style. Almost as often, they then moved to learning another style. Sometimes it was from an earlier era. For instance, a few learned Ben Webster's approach of the 1940s after first learning Coltrane's of the 1960s. A few began with Ornette Coleman's and then went back in history to learn an earlier style. A number of trumpeters moved back and forth between the mid-1960s styles of Miles Davis and Freddie Hubbard. In other words, the new breed of jazz musicians alternately took on the character of different historic figures, but never developed substantially new approaches of their own.

Dixieland and swing styles had been revived periodically ever since first appearing. A similar phenomenon was now evident. For example, in 2005 there were young bands playing in the styles of the 1965 bands of Miles Davis and Art Blakey. This amounts to a 40-year interval, like that which separated young musicians in the 1960s from the 1920s-style Dixieland they played. So we see that the infatuation with the past during the 1980s and 1990s was nothing new. In fact, it represents a continuation rather than a departure. The music during this period was not new. But four attitudes about it were new: The wide availability, press coverage, and lionization of the revivers accidentally conveyed the impression (1) that the revived music was actually new and (2) that the improvisations in it were almost as substantial as those of the models they imitated. Some listeners who had limited access to major recordings by previous innovators mistakenly assumed the newcomers were originators and that they were improvising as well as the jazz giants. (3) This was also coinciding with a tendency for more musicians than ever before, both young lions and old veterans, to be looking backward for sources of inspiration instead of inventing fresh approaches.[51] These trends conveyed the message that (4) an important function of young jazz musicians was "preservation." Just as the Preservation Hall Jazz Band had been maintaining the work of its New Orleans ancestors, the Lincoln Center Jazz Orchestra in New York, for example, was now attempting to preserve the work of several previous generations.

"Express Crossing," JCCD3 *Track 11*

Composed by Wynton Marsalis; recorded in 1993 by the Lincoln Center Jazz Orchestra, featuring Wynton Marsalis (trumpet) and Kent Jordan (piccolo); available on *Prentice Hall Jazz Collection*, and *Jazz: Six Syncopated Movements* (Columbia: CK 66379).

Terms to learn from Demo CD: mutes, brushes on snare drum, alto saxophone, flute, trumpet, trombone.

In writing "Express Crossing" for big band, trumpeter Wynton Marsalis paid homage to a 1933 composition by Duke Ellington entitled "Daybreak Express." Both of these works imitate the sound of trains. This music takes us all the way from the beginning sounds of a train's journey to when the train reaches its final destination. On its way, we hear full-speed and half-speed adventures. Both pieces were motivated by a sense of fun and they achieved it through unusual compositional techniques.

During the 1980s and 1990s, journalists and historians argued about the place of highly publicized young jazz musicians who were not creating new music, even though the history of jazz had always emphasized originality and innovation. Because of the clear influence of earlier jazz, "Express Crossing" fits the "neo-classical" label that these commentators placed on those musicians. Aside from the inspiration of "Daybreak Express," from 60 years earlier, other elements also qualify "Express Crossing" for that classification. The Dixieland tune "Tiger Rag," from 1918, provided the chord progression for the muted trumpet/piccolo duet from 0'48" to 1'30" and the big band passage from 3'41" to 4'40". Swing band style of the 1930s is in effect at 3'41". A quasi-bop style of the 1940s characterizes the trumpet solo at 1'31".

"Express Crossing" is comprised of many different sections, showcasing different tempos, different genres, regular and irregular meters (making it difficult to tap your foot with it), clashing harmonies, honking sounds from saxophones, growls from the trumpet, and use of a nontraditional jazz instrument (piccolo). This means that, in addition to the "neo-classical" classification, the piece additionally qualifies for the "poly-stylistic post-modern" classification that commentators invented. The derivation and meaning of the term is understandable if we recall that "poly" means "many," "post" means "after," and "modern" refers to almost anything originating since bop, as bop was deemed the first "modern" jazz style.

ELAPSED TIME	MUSICAL EVENTS
0'00"	**Section 1**
	The ensemble chords imitate a train whistle, piccolo on top.
	Snare drum played with brushes imitates a train rushing ahead.
0'11"	dialog between two saxophones
0'13"	sax honk
0'14"	Section 1 repeated, but with added sax lines
0'23"	dialog between two saxophones
0'25"	sax honk
0'26"	**Section 2**
	Several quick melody lines swirl around, as bass walks in double time.
0'39"	**Section 3**
	Tempo is slower. Piano and bass emphasize a line.
	Horns play assorted honks and whistles.
0'47"	**Section 4**
	Original fast tempo. Piccolo and saxophones race through hurried lines, while brass punctuate with irregularly spaced chords.
1'06"	Rhythm section pauses, while the brasses make a "wah-wah" effect.
1'09"	Activity increases. Brasses continue "wah-wah" effects. Piccolo and saxophones continue their runaway melody.

LISTENING GUIDE *continued on next page*

1'26"	Brasses growl.
1'28"	muted tones alternating with unmuted tones
1'31"	**Section 5—Muted Trumpet Improvisation by Wynton Marsalis**
	Accompaniment harmonies are as Section 4.
1'49"	solo break for trumpet
1'52"	sounds like a train chugging
2'11"	rhythm section break: trombone "blat" answered by trumpets and saxes.
2'14"	**Section 6** (written piccolo line alternates with unmuted trumpet improvisation)
2'16"	unmuted trumpet improvisation
2'19"	piccolo solo
2'22"	saxophone honks
2'28"	bass slapping
2'30"	saxophone honk
2'32"	wah-wah muted brass
2'38"	full ensemble interjections
2'41"	full ensemble interjections
2'57"	**Piano Transition**
	Piano rushes through a series of high pitches, then lands on a low note.
3'00"	**Section 7—Simultaneous Flute and Muted Trumpet Solo Lines**
	Marsalis plays muted trumpet line using odd pitches simultaneously with flute line using odd pitches, accompanied by drummer striking snare drum with brushes, and an alternation of abrupt brass and saxophone chords.
3'27"	abrupt stop by rhythm section, single, short, low tones by trombones alternating with saxophones
3'31"	**Section 8**
	Musical ideas combined from Section 1 with the swift piccolo line of Section 4.
3'41"	**Section 9**
	Tempo slows.
3'42"	swing-era style melody by muted trumpet and saxophones in harmony, contrasted by a group of muted trumpets
3'56"	Piano plays a high-pitched melody in octaves.
4'11"	Muted trumpet and saxophones continue their harmonized line, with punctuation by muted trombone.
4'41"	**Section 10**
	Band returns to the fast, opening material.
4'52"	**Ending**
	The train decelerates, reaching its final destination.
	syncopated punctuations by saxes and muted brasses
	piano hammering a high-pitched two-note combination sound 47 times
4'55"	piccolo alternating with muted trombones, punctuated by saxophone chords
	After a few final whistle blows, brushes on snare drum conclude the piece, slowing train to a halt.

The most famous musician to emerge during this period and adopt this new attitude was trumpeter **Wynton Marsalis** (b. 1961). Widely respected for his career as a classical trumpeter, he also crafted believable imitations of Freddie Hubbard and Miles Davis in jazz recordings with Art Blakey and Herbie Hancock during the early 1980s. (Listen to 2′21″ to 4′21″ of "Maiden Voyage" on *JCCD2* for an example of the Freddie Hubbard style that Marsalis imitated.) Then he made several albums in the mid-1960s Miles Davis style, with new compositions, solos, and accompaniment honoring the advances made by Davis, Wayne Shorter, and their innovative rhythm section of pianist Herbie Hancock, bassist Ron Carter, and drummer Tony Williams. (Listen to 0′54″ to 3′21″ of "Masqualero" on *JCCD2* for the Miles Davis style that Marsalis imitated.) For this music, he hired musicians who could play in the style of Davis accompanists, such as Kenny Kirkland, who played remarkably like Herbie Hancock. He also hired his older brother Branford Marsalis, who at the time was the best Wayne Shorter disciple. Wynton Marsalis has since focused his career on learning earlier styles, such as Louis Armstrong's and the devices of the muted style associated with pre-modern trumpeters Bubber Miley and Cootie Williams. He spent much of the 1990s recreating the music of Duke Ellington. (Listen to "Express Crossing" in *JCCD3* Track 11.) He even learned how to compose in the style of Ellington and won a Pulitzer Prize for one such piece.[52] An articulate spokesman for jazz, Marsalis has ultimately reached a large audience, achieved wide name recognition, and has become an effective educator. He cultivated respect for jazz as a serious art form in ways similar to Leonard Bernstein's educational programs during the 1950s and 1960s that spread understanding and appreciation for classical music.

Concurrent to the rise of talented young musicians who rotated among various historic styles was a proliferation of "ghost bands" that continued the music of deceased bandleaders. These groups were often led by musicians who had played with the former bandleaders whose names they now borrowed as banners for their own bands. Many musicians enjoyed successful tours by booking under slogans such as "The Count Basie Orchestra under the leadership of Grover Mitchell," "The Woody Herman Band under the leadership of Frank Tiberi," "The Mingus Dynasty," "Sphere" (Thelonious Monk's music), "The Art Blakey Legacy Band," "The Dizzy Gillespie Alumni All-Stars," etc. There was also a proliferation of repertory bands that provided opportunities analogous to theatrical companies in which actors become very good at playing different roles, putting on different plays they had mastered, perhaps a collection of William Shakespeare or George Bernard Shaw, for example. Some cities had "jazz orchestras" for this purpose, such as the Lincoln Center Jazz Orchestra and the Carnegie Hall Jazz Orchestra in New York.

Collectively, these styles were variously pegged (1) **neo-classical**, (2) **neo-traditional**, or (3) **retro**. They were the most-played (4) **classic** or (5) **mainstream** styles during the 1980s and 1990s. Musicians themselves generally refer to this music as (6) **straight-ahead** and (7) **acoustic.** The broadcasting industry confused the matter by using the term "classic jazz" to designate almost all non-avant-garde jazz styles other than smooth jazz, not just the neo-classicists, but also older musicians themselves and those who offered original twists on older styles. This included bop and bop-derived styles as well as the 1960s approaches of Miles Davis and John Coltrane. The term "mainstream" was widely interchanged with "classic," and some broadcasters, marketers, and journalists also used (8) **traditional** to designate all but smooth and avant-garde styles of jazz. These terms were unfortunate choices because (a) "classic" and "traditional" had long been the accepted descriptions for the original New Orleans and Chicago combo styles of the 1920s and the subsequent Dixieland revival, and (b) "mainstream" had been coined in the 1950s to classify swing era musicians who were still active. The "traditional" term did, however, distinguish them from "smooth jazz" because many referred to smooth jazz as "contemporary jazz," quite the opposite of traditional. The "acoustic" term succeeded in distinguishing them from the electronically processed sounds of funk and fusion bands as well as most "smooth jazz" productions, but it failed to distinguish them from the New Age music that was created without electronics and from various amalgams of jazz with World Music such as Klezmer jazz.

SINGERS

A number of jazz singers emerged during the 1980s and 1990s. Ironically, however, the one with the most adventuresome style, the one who garnered the most respect from musicians and singers, and the one who attained the greatest new recognition, had been active since the late 1940s, had already performed with Miles Davis, and toured with Sonny Rollins: **Betty Carter** (1930–1998). Initially inspired by bop instrumental styles and Sarah Vaughan's vocal style, Carter had established a reputation as a facile scat singer by the early 1950s. As her career unfolded, Carter took more and more chances in her performances. The trend toward increasing adventurousness was so strong that familiarity with her 1948–1951 recordings in the Lionel Hampton band would not help a listener identify Carter as the singer on albums she made during the 1990s. Her best-known recording was a 1960 album of duets with fellow singer-pianist Ray Charles, but it bore very little resemblance to the work she was most widely hailed for. Moreover, when she finally attained wide media exposure in the 1990s, her style had become so unconventional that new listeners found it difficult to believe that even her recordings of the 1960s were from the same vocalist.

Betty Carter, jazz singer, widely respected for creatively paraphrasing melodies so radically that they might as well be jazz hornlines. (Photo by Randy Norfus)

Betty Carter thought like a jazz instrumentalist. Instead of conjuring an overall mood or story line throughout a piece, she often asserted a brief melodic fragment forthrightly, then abandoned it to explore yet another and another. Like a painter always tinkering with the thickness and tint of paint on every inch of canvas, Carter endlessly toyed with the size and pitch of her tones, rarely striking one head-on or sustaining it. (One example of her amazingly fertile imagination is an improvisation that lasted 25 minutes: "Sounds.") She shaped her sounds with unceasing variation. This talent accounts for a major part of her artistry. She glided through pitch ranges in a slippery manner that is even more drastic than the manner of Sarah Vaughan's last style period. Her wide-ranging explorations alternately expanded and compressed the durations of melody notes, and Carter often phrased far behind the beat, adding new pitches, slurring to and from original melody notes by way of these new ones. This exceeds the amount of variation and embellishment within what had been termed "interpretation." What Carter did actually constituted re-composition. And these excursions were not merely private indulgence. More than one listener described her effect as having a compelling immediacy. Like Vaughan, Carter was irreverent about lyrics, using them more as an excuse to get her own pitch excursions going. In fact, unlike most singers in the eyes of jazz instrumentalists, Carter is perceived as a musician.[53]

POPULAR APPEAL

With the exception of a few standouts, jazz had less exposure and fewer performance outlets during the 1990s and the beginning of the twenty-first century than at any other time in its history. The number of nightclubs featuring jazz on a regular basis was smaller than ever before, and the fees paid to the musicians in them were lower. Aside from a few recordings by several immensely popular singers whose recordings somehow got placed in the jazz category along with instrumentalists, the jazz portion of U.S. recording sales was less than two percent by 2003. The number of musicians able to extract a living by performing jazz decreased, too. Those few non-smooth jazz musicians who managed to live on earnings from jazz usually depended heavily on appearances at European jazz festivals. They could not survive from performance opportunities in the United States alone. Many depended partly on fees as touring instructors at jazz clinics in schools and colleges. A number of eminent jazz musicians acquired full-time positions as college instructors and would not have been able to remain in the field of music without such jobs. Hundreds of excellent jazz players, including more than a handful of world-class musicians, served as adjunct professors in colleges and universities. In fact, most of the jazz improvising going on in America during this period occurred in high school and college bands. Despite the decrease in paid opportunities for performing jazz, more and more students chose to learn how to play it. Jazz majors proliferated in college and university music schools, and the level of musicianship among many young players was so high that a number of high school and college bands were better than some professional bands.

NEW STYLES OF THE 1980S AND 1990S

New Age, Acid Jazz, Smooth Jazz, Neo-Classical Jazz, Klezmer Jazz, Neo-Swing, Hip Hop-Jazz

Top Names in New Age	George Winston, Andreas Vollenweider, Oregon
Roots of the Soul Saxes	Maceo Parker, Junior Walker, King Curtis, Stanley Turrentine, Hank Crawford, David "Fathead" Newman
Top Soul Saxes	Dave Sanborn, Michael Brecker, Grover Washington, Jr.
Top Names in Smooth Jazz	Grover Washington, Jr., Joe Sample, Bob James, Kenny G, David Benoit, Rick Braun, Dave Koz, Boney James, George Benson
Top Name in Neo-Classical Jazz	Wynton Marsalis
Top Names in Klezmer Jazz	Don Byron, John Zorn, Dave Douglas
Top Names in Latin Jazz	Eddie Palmieri, Tito Puente, Mario Bauzá, Paquito D'Rivera, Arturo Sandoval

CHAPTER SUMMARY

1. New Age music features soft tone qualities, few changes of chord and texture, nonjarring rhythms. Pianist George Winston is its best known practitioner.
2. Smooth jazz is a quieted, refined funk music melded with Latin American accompaniment. It was the most popular jazz style after the mid-1980s. Its best

known practitioners include guitarist George Benson, pianist Bob James, and Kenny G, the most popular saxophonist in history.

3. Acid jazz was created initially by disc jockeys who excerpted accompaniment vamps from funky hard bop recordings and overlaid synthesized sounds, raps, and new jazz improvisations. It later became a style that was also produced live, not just through sampling. Turntablists became treated as musicians and bandleaders.

4. David Sanborn was the second most popular saxophonist during the 1980s and 1990s. He and Michael Brecker were the most influential models for the new crop of jazz saxophonists with a bent toward the soul sax tradition.

5. A swing dance craze during the 1990s boosted interest in 1930s band styles and "jump bands" of the late 1940s and early 1950s.

6. Backward-looking "neo-classical/neo-traditional" musicians and their repertory bands received the most media attention, though not substantial record sales. The most prominent neo-classicist was trumpeter Wynton Marsalis.

7. Fresh styles were devised by saxophonists John Zorn, trumpeter Dave Douglas, and their colleagues, which frequently incorporated Yiddish Klezmer music with Ornette Coleman and Don Cherry approaches.

8. A number of musicians combined jazz improvisation with accompaniment styles from hip-hop, acid jazz, and other pop genres, some of which were called "drum 'n' bass."

9. Latin American jazz enjoyed its greatest recognition during this period, and bands that had previously been termed "mambo" bands and "salsa" bands were promoted as "Latin jazz." The best-known veteran bandleaders were Tito Puente and Eddie Palmieri. The top new Cubans in the United States were trumpeter Arturo Sandoval and saxophonist Paquito D'Rivera.

10. Though there were fewer places to play jazz and lower fees for doing so, the number of high school and college students who chose to learn how to play jazz was higher than ever before.

NOTES

1. By comparison with such recent models as Sonny Rollins, Freddie Hubbard, Joe Henderson, Wayne Shorter, and Keith Jarrett, the new soloists did not devise improvisations with the sheer number of original phrases or the richness of melodic development that jazz listeners had come to expect from the top improvisers.

The work of some groups represented offshoots of the fusion explorations of Davis and Herbie Hancock from the 1970s. For instance, Coung Vu emulated *In A Silent Way* and *Bitches Brew*. Bill Laswell actually used unedited early-1970s tapes of Miles Davis's Columbia recordings as a basis for his own productions.

Other creative streams of music during this period included the perpetuation of methods devised by Ornette Coleman, Albert Ayler, Cecil Taylor, and John Coltrane in the hands of second- and third-generation free jazz players. Many hailed from Chicago, but pockets of free jazz also remained in Los Angeles (Bobby Bradford and Horace Tapscott, for instance) and New York jazz communities (Charles Gayle, Billy Bang, David S. Ware, Matthew Shipp, for example), and a steady stream continued to emerge from Europe (Peter Brotzmann, for example). Some of these musicians had played during the 1960s and 1970s with Cecil Taylor (Ken McIntyre and William Parker, for example) or the Chicago avant-garde (Fred Anderson and Anthony Braxton, for instance). Most of the work offered by new musicians in this period simply mined the veins that had been pioneered by those giants. Examples of contemporary free jazz include William Parker, *In Order to Survive* (Black Saint: 120159, 1993, c1995), Charles Gayle, *Consecration* (Black Saint: 120138, 1993, c1993) and *Kingdom Come* (Knitting Factory: 157, c1994), and Peter Brotzmann, *Sacred Scrape* (Rastascan: 015, 1992, c1994).

2. Jarrett's unaccompanied solo improvisations are far more varied, far more dynamic, and should not be confused with either minimalism or the popular idiom it spawned. And his jazz work, particularly that of his "Standards Trio," is not related at all to this movement.

3. George Winston, *December* (Windham Hill: 1025, 1982).

4. For instance, softer, more refined renditions of early jazz in the 1920s were produced by Paul Whiteman, of swing in the 1930s by Glenn Miller, of bop in the 1950s by the George Shearing Quintet and the Ahmad Jamal Trio, and of swing during the 1950s by the Jackie Gleason "For Lovers Only" series with trumpeters Bobby Hackett and Billy Butterfield (18 albums, including the best-selling *Music, Martinis and Memories*), and of hard bop in the 1960s by Wes Montgomery's albums *Bumpin'* (Verve: 314 539 062, 1965, c1997) and *A Day in the Life* (A&M: 75021 0816, 1967, c1989). These exemplify jazzy "background music" precedents for the smooth jazz of the 1980s and 1990s.

5. Bob James and Earl Klugh, *One on One* (Warner Bros.: 45141, 1979). James also leads Fourplay: *Fourplay* (Warner Bros.: 26656, 1991); and

Between the Sheets (Warner Bros.: 45340, 1993). Each of these three albums sold more than 500,000 copies.

6. Earl Klugh, *Low Ride* (Capitol: 46007, 1983). *Living Inside Your Love* (Capitol: 48385, 1976, c1995) and *Low Ride* (Capitol: 12253, c1983) exemplify smooth jazz.

7. George Benson, *In Flight* (Warner Bros.: 2983, 1977) sold more than one million copies. *Breezin'* (Warner Archives: 76713, 1976, c2001) set the pace for smooth jazz.

8. Among Kenny G's albums, *Breathless* (1992) sold more than 10 million copies, *Miracles* (1994) sold more than 6 million copies, and *Silhouette* (1988) sold more than 4 million copies.

9. Wes Montgomery, *Bumpin'* (Verve: 314 539 062, 1965, c1997) is a typical album that influenced smooth jazz. *A Day in the Life* (A&M: 75021 0816, 1967, c1989) sold more than 500,000 copies. For a sampler, see Montgomery, *Greatest Hits* (A&M: 31454-0519, 1967–68, c1996).

10. Grover Washington, Jr., *Winelight* (Elektra: 305, c1980) sold more than a million copies and became a model for Kenny G and music on smooth jazz radio. For a sampler, see *Grover Washington's Greatest Performances* (Motown: 374 635 307, 1972–78, c1992).

11. "Harlequin" on Weather Report, *Heavy Weather* (Columbia/Legacy) exemplifies the slice of Weather Report's output that was imitated for smooth jazz formats.

12. U.S.-issued samplers of London-based groups include: *This Is Acid Jazz*, vol. 1 (Instinct: 225, c1991); and *This Is Acid Jazz*, vol. 2 (Instinct: 244, c1992). *The Best of Acid Jazz: A Five-Year Retrospective* (Instinct: 317, c1995) represents several nations.

13. "Keep On" on *This Is Acid Jazz*, vol. 2 (Instinct) uses saxophone as decoration. "Move Y'all" on *A New Type of Jazz* (New Breed: 020, c1994) uses fragments of muted trumpet and piano as decoration for a rap.

14. US3, *Hand on the Torch* (Blue Note: 80883, c1993) was created by British disc jockeys and musicians who excerpted old jazz albums, then added raps and new instrumental jazz improvisations; it sold more than 2 million copies worldwide. *The New Groove, The Blue Note Remix Project*, vol. 1 (Blue Note: 36594, c1996) excerpted old jazz albums, then added drum machine beats and new raps.

15. "Cutting Loose" on *This Is Acid Jazz*, vol. 2 (Instinct) uses loud back beat from snare drum, steady bass drum (synthesized), and synthesized bass guitar. "Racial Facial" on *A New Type of Jazz* (New Breed) has loud back beat by synthesized snare drum, with loops, using horns as occasional decoration.

16. Guru, *Jazzmatazz*, vol. 1 (Chrysalis: 21998, c1993) began each selection with an electronically created rhythm track, then had a jazz musician record a new solo improvisation over that, and a fresh rap was then overdubbed.

17. See footnote 8.

18. Miles Davis, *doo-bop* (Warner Bros.: 26938, c1991) uses overdubbing of Davis's trumpet solo improvisations as well as a rapper.

19. "T.S.O.J." on *A New Type of Jazz* (New Breed) uses drum machine, synthesizer, and loops and has fresh jazz improvisations overdubbed.

20. One hip-hop compilation is *The Source Presents: Hip-Hop Hits*, vol. 1 (Polygram: 314 536 204, c1997).

21. One techno compilation is *Rave 'Til Dawn: Techno's Finest* (SBK: 27018, c1993).

22. One trip hop compilation is *Red Hot Trip Hop* (Street Beat: 1021, c1996).

23. Prominent touring bands are Jamiroquai, James Taylor Quartet, The Brand New Heavies, The Groove Collective, Ronny Jordan, Incognito,

the 11-piece Count Basic (not a typographical error) from Austria (represented twice on *This Is Acid Jazz*, vol. 3: *New Voices*, Instinct: 338, c1996), and the 10-piece Liquid Soul from Chicago. Some music of these last two (particularly Count Basic's "Sweet Luis" and Liquid Soul's "Ricky's Hat") differs little from typical jazz-rock band fare of the 1970s, thereby furthering the breadth of music which store clerks of the late 1990s were told to "file under acid jazz." Instrumentation differs somewhat, however, in that rapper, turntable operator (for scratching), and extra percussionists are often included.

24. King Curtis, *King of the Sax* (Fuel 2000: 61378 (Enjoy), [1962], c2004); *Have Tenor Sax Will Blow/Live at Small's Paradise* (Collectables: 6418, 1959, c2000) and *Soul Meeting* (Prestige: 24033, 1960, c1994) illustrate one of the soul saxes.

25. Jr. Walker, *Shotgun* (Motown: 314 530 245, 1965, c2001) and *The Ultimate Collection* (Motown: 314 530 828, 1962–96, c1997) illustrate one source for Michael Brecker's sax style.

26. Hank Crawford, *Mr. Blues Plays Lady Soul* (Collectables: 6244 [Atlantic], 1969, c1999) and *Soul Survivors* (Milestone: 9142, 1986, c1986) illustrate one source for the sax styles of Kenny G and Dave Sanborn.

27. *House of David: The David "Fathead" Newman Anthology* (Rhino: 71452, 2CD set, 1952–89, c1993); Ray Charles, *Blues + Jazz* (Rhino: 71607 [Atlantic], 2CD set, 1950–59, c1994); or *Fathead: Ray Charles Presents David Newman* (Collectibles: 6541 [Atlantic], 1958, c2005); all three include Newman's "Hard Times" recording of 1958.

28. Jazz Crusaders, *The Best of the Jazz Crusaders: The Pacific Jazz Years* (Blue Note: 89283, 1961–66, c1993); The Crusaders, *Southern Comfort* (MCA: 6016, 1974, c1997); and *Street Life* (Blue Thumb: 701, 1979, c1996) illustrate one source for Kenny G's sax style.

29. Maceo Parker, *Roots Revisited* (Verve: 843 751, c1990) illustrates one source for Dave Sanborn's sax style.

30. Grover Washington, Jr., *Mr. Magic* (Motown: 530 103, 1974, c1995) and *Winelight* (Elektra: 305, c1980) were very influential in smooth jazz, particularly pop saxophone styles of the 1980s and 1990s, such as Kenny G's.

31. Kenny G, *Duotones* (Arista: 8496, c1986); *Silhouette* (Arista: 8457, c1988); *Breathless* (Arista: 18646, c1992); and *The Moment* (Arista: 18935, c1996); see also Jeff Lorber, *The Definitive Collection* (Arista: 14639, c2000).

32. David Sanborn, *Straight to the Heart* (Warner Bros.: 25150, c1984); and *Upfront* (Elektra: 61272, 1991, c1992); see also Bob James, *Double Vision* (Warner Bros.: 25393, c1986).

33. Michael Brecker, *Michael Brecker* (MCA: 5980, c1986); and *Don't Try This at Home* (Impulse!: 42229, c1988). Brecker's most acclaimed solo, "Gregory Is Here," is on CCD2 or Horace Silver, *In Pursuit of the 27th Man* (Blue Note: 35758, 1972, c2002); see also Brecker Brothers, *Heavy Metal Bebop* (One Way: 31447, 1978, c1995); and Claus Ogermann, *Cityscape* (Warner Bros.: 23698, 1982, c1995).

34. This period marked the incorporation of World Music into a number of jazz styles. Music of Eastern Europe, the Middle East and India also attracted a number of jazz improvisers during the 1980s and 1990s. Though daring, using these bases for jazz was not new, however. For instance, in 1939 trumpeter Ziggy Elman had explored Yiddish approaches with the Benny Goodman band. During the 1960s and 1970s trumpeter Don Ellis recorded improvisations on Bulgarian-inspired pieces and the music of India, which has much in common with the techniques of the Balkan and Middle Eastern music that was now being studied more frequently. Ornette Coleman had worked with musicians in Morocco during the 1970s, and at about the same time Don Cherry had explored Arabic music, as well as the forms and sounds of music native to China and Indonesia. In 1964 Cannonball Adderley had recorded improvisations based on Yiddish forms when he used the Broadway show *Fiddler on*

the Roof as the basis for an album of jazz. Several albums by guitarist John McLaughlin explored similar approaches during the 1970s, and one of McLaughlin's groups called Shakti not only followed the odd meters and scale-based harmonies of this music, but it actually featured musicians from India playing them. Even during the 1990s, McLaughlin was touring with groups basing their music on approaches common to Indian music.

35. Jazz is just one of Zorn's interests. He is a musical force of immense scope and energy. One of the leading innovators in the 1990s, he tackled twentieth-century classical music so successfully that his string quartet recordings now reside in libraries around the world. His symphonic writing is known even to music scholars who specialize in the traditional big names of twentieth-century "serious" orchestral music: Bartók, Stravinsky, Berg, Stockhausen, and Varèse. He also mounted numerous projects in improvised music in which chance is systematically incorporated. (Zorn hired some of the same musicians from his jazz bands when he pursued these projects.) He also prepared interpretations of movie music and had his own rock band at this time.

36. *Masada Live in Jerusalem 1994* (Tzadik: 7322, 1994, c1999); and *Masada Live in Middelheim 1999* (Tzadik: 7326, 1999, c1999).

37. Dave Douglas, *Parallel Worlds* (Soul Note: 121226, 1993, c1993) and *Witness* (Bluebird: 63763, 2000, c2001) illustrates his eclectic compositional style. *Dave Douglas: The Tiny Bell Trio* (Songlines: 1504, 1993, c1994); *Constellations* (hatOLOGY: 542, 1995, c2000) and *Tiny Bell Trio Live in Europe* (Arabesque Jazz: 0126, 1996, c1997) illustrate his blending Eastern European music with jazz.

38. Machito and the Afro-Cubans, *Carambola: Live at Birdland* (Tumbao: 024, 1951, c1992) includes Bauzá's "Tanga"; *The Original Mambo Kings* (Verve: 314 513 876, 1948–54, c1993) includes Machito with Mario Bauzá, Charlie Parker, Howard McGhee, and Dizzy Gillespie; *Ritmo Caliente: Machito and His Afro-Cubans* (Proper Box: 48, 4CD set, 1941–51, c2002) includes Bauzá's "Tanga" as well as jazz musicians Brew Moore, Zoot Sims, Milt Jackson, Flip Phillips, Howard McGhee, and Charlie Parker.

39. Mario Bauzá, *Tanga* (Pimienta/Universal: 360628 [Messidor 15819], 1991, c2004).

40. Tito Puente, *The Complete RCA Recordings*, vol. 1 (RCA: 78911, 6CD set, 1949–60, c2000); *The Complete RCA Recordings*, vol. 2 (RCA: 88222, 6CD set, 1949–60, c2001); or *The Essential Tito Puente* (RCA/Legacy: 69243, 2CD set, 1949–62, c2005).

41. Tito Puente, *Mambo Diablo* (Concord Picante: 4283, c1985); *Royal T* (Concord Picante: 4553, c1993); *Special Delivery* (Concord Picante: 4732, c1996).

42. Eddie Palmieri, *La Perfecta* (Fania: 8170 [Alegre], 1966, c2003); *The Sun of Latin Music* (Musical Productions: 6253 [Coco], 1973, c1991); *Unfinished Masterpiece* (Musical Productions: 6259 [Coco], 1975, c1991); *Palmas* (Elektra Nonesuch: 61649, 1993, c1994); and *Vortex* (TropiJazz/ RMM: 82043, c1996).

43. Irakere, *The Best of Irakere* (Columbia/Legacy: 57719, 1978–79, c1994), with Chucho Valdés, Paquito D'Rivera, and Arturo Sandoval; *Live at Ronnie Scott's* (World Pacific: 80598, 1991, c1993), with Chucho Valdés.

44. Arturo Sandoval, *Jam Miami: A Celebration of Latin Jazz* (Concord Picante: 4899, c2000), with Sandoval, Chick Corea, Claudio Roditi, Poncho Sanchez, et. al.; *Tumbaito* (Messidor: 15974, 1986, c1992).

45. Paquito D'Rivera, *The Best of Paquito D'Rivera* (Columbia/Legacy: 85342, 1981–87, c2002); *Paquito D'Rivera/Arturo Sandoval: Reunion* (Pimienta/Universal: 245 360 610 [Messidor 15805], 1990, c2004); *Paquito D'Rivera Presents 40 Years of Cuban Jam Session* (Pimienta/Universal: 245 360 632 [Messidor 15826], 1993, c2004).

46. Jerry Gonzalez with The Fort Apache Band and Jesus Alemany and Cubanismo! were among the other top Latin jazz bands playing during the 1990s and beginning of the twenty-first century.

For more on Latin jazz, see these books: Leonardo Acosta, *Cubano Be, Cubano Bop: One Hundred Years of Jazz in Cuba* (Smithsonian, 2003); Steven Loza, *Tito Puente and the Making of Latin Music* (Univ. of Illinois, 1999); and John Storm Roberts, *The Latin Tinge: The Impact of Latin American Music on the United States*, 2nd ed. (Oxford Univ., 1999).

47. Birth (Josh Smith, Jeremy Bleich, and Joe Tomino) *Birth, The Live Disc*, and *Find* (available from *www.birthsound.com*) are albums that illustrate drum 'n' bass with avant-garde improvisations atop it. Chris Speed, *Deviantics* (Songlines: 1524, 1998, c1999) illustrates Klezmer jazz and drum 'n' bass.

48. Branford Marsalis, *Buckshot Lefonque* (Columbia: 57323, c1994) illustrates mixing rap, hip-hop, and jazz in the acid jazz manner.

49. Steve Coleman is so extraordinarily fertile as a composer and bandleader, an entire chapter is warranted to do his contributions justice. Analysis of his saxophone improvisations alone would require serious study. However, in such a painfully brief text as *Jazz Styles*, the best we can hope to offer is a recommended sampling of albums: *Motherland Pulse* (Winter & Winter: 919001 [JMT], 1985, c2001); *World Expansion* (Winter & Winter: 919010 [JMT], 1986, c2002); *Curves of Life* (RCA Victor: 31693, 1995, c1995); and *Genesis & The Opening of the Way* (RCA Victor: 52934, 1996–97, c1997).

50. Royal Crown Revue, *Mugsy's Move* (Warner Bros.: 46931, c1996); Brian Setzer, *The Dirty Boogie* (Interscope: 90183, c1998).

51. Even established innovators looked backwards for inspiration during the 1980s and 1990s. For example, Chick Corea recorded a Bud Powell album. Keith Jarrett toured and recorded with a trio playing jazz standards in the style of Wynton Kelly and the Bill Evans Trio of the 1960s. Dave Douglas recorded an album in the style of late-1960s Miles Davis Quintet: *The Infinite* (RCA: 63918, 2001, c2002).

52. See Art Blakey, *Album of the Year* (Timeless: 155, 1981, c1982) and *Keystone 3* (Concord: 4196, 1982, c1990) for examples of Wynton Marsalis's Lee Morgan/Freddie Hubbard phase. See *Wynton Marsalis* (Columbia: 37574, c1982); *Black Codes (From the Underground)* (Columbia: 40009, 1985, c1985); and *J Mood* (Columbia: 40308, 1985, c1986) to illustrate his mid-1960s Miles Davis phase. See Marsalis, *Blood on the Fields* (Columbia: 57694, 3CD set, 1995, c1997) to illustrate his Ellington phase.

Note: The solos by most of the neo-classicists imitating styles of the 1950s and 1960s did not show the clarity, inventiveness, or level of melodic development common to improvisations by such major but lesser known soloists from the 1950s and 1960s as saxophonists Wardell Gray and Hank Mobley, trumpeters Kenny Dorham, Art Farmer, Lee Morgan, Conte Candoli, Donald Byrd, or Blue Mitchell, pianists Sonny Clarke, Wynton Kelly, or Red Garland.

53. *Inside Betty Carter* (Capitol Jazz: 89702, 1964–65, c1993). The most spectacular examples of Carter's chance taking are found in recordings of public performances; *The Audience with Betty Carter* (Verve: 422 835 684, 2CD set, 1979, c1988) is possibly the best.

This chapter treats a few outstanding figures whose contributions do not neatly fit any of the classifications provided by previous chapters. Despite the fact that each of these musicians is prolific and original, none are well known beyond jazz insiders. Though all are American, much of their touring and recording has been done in Europe.

CARLA BLEY

Carla Bley (b. 1936) is a composer and bandleader who has written a wide assortment of compositions that cumulatively fit no conventional jazz category. Spearheading the cutting edge Jazz Composer's Orchestra, she was initially part of the free jazz movement. Bley has been continuously active since the 1960s and always remained avant-garde, no matter what decade she was living in. Her stature is indicated partly by the sizable number of eminent musicians who have recorded her compositions. The distinctiveness and originality of her accomplishments is so wide that we might consider Bley to have predated what commentators in the twenty-first century have awkwardly termed "poly-stylistic post-modernism." The term has been applied to characterize the careers of John Zorn, Dave Douglas, and Don Byron (see Chapter 17), and it fits the entire career of Charles Mingus (see Chapter 14).

Maria Schneider big band at the 2005 JVC Jazz Festival, New York
(Photo by Takehiko Tokiwa)

The character of Bley's pieces spans a range than runs from a lush ballad ("Fleur Carnivore"[1]) to works for big band that are loud and swinging (such as "Floater,"[2] "Birds of Paradise," and "On the Stage in Cages"[3]). Some employ unusual chord progressions (as in "Strange Arrangement"[4]). Her writing is always well edited, strikingly melodic, and never muddy. Her sources range from English music hall to Thelonious Monk ("On the Stage in Cages," "Strange Arrangement," "Batteriewoman") to tango ("Reactionary Tango") and Anglo-American church music (*The Carla Bley Big Band Goes to Church*[5]). She mixes and matches these sources in odd combinations that end up sounding perfectly natural. Standouts among her most ambitious works include her opera "Escalator Over the Hill,"[6] her suite "A Genuine Tong Funeral" (with vibraphonist Gary Burton),[7] and her writing for bassist Charlie Haden's Liberation Music Orchestra. Additionally, some of her music has nothing to do with jazz (for instance, "End of Vienna"[8]).

Bley was one of the first jazz writers whose work says, in effect, "There are no rules." It is as though she starts from point zero for each piece. If the sounds are pleasing, the piece doesn't have to be a set form. It can be just notes. It could be merely a springboard for improvisation. Her arrangements are very open, not fitting the big band tradition of densely packed, busy figures. Instead, the band usually functions as a big small group, with plenty of time for soloists to stretch out with little interruption. She considers a number of her pieces just to be frameworks for jazz musicians, with a snippet of music at the beginning and end, but huge holes in the middle for free improvisation. A prime characteristic of her work is extreme economy. Her arrangements are so spare that we might call her a minimalist, in the tradition of nonjazz composers Erik Satie and John Cage, though occasionally she might remind us of jazz composers Thelonious Monk and Duke Ellington as well.

A sense of playfulness is more prominent than any other characteristic in Bley's music. Her irreverent sense of humor is striking, and it recurs in both the construction of her pieces and her choice of tune titles (for instance, "On the Stages in Cages," "The Girl Who Cried Champagne," and "Song to Anything That Moves"). She even wrote a spoof on baseball stadium organ playing ("Baseball," *JCCD3* Track 12),[9] and a comic reworking of national anthems ("Spangled Banner Minor and Other Patriotic Songs"[10]). Sometimes we might conclude that she hardly takes anything seriously, though her craft is unquestionable. In fact, she subscribes to the idea that avant-garde saxophonist Albert Ayler's music gave her the license to be maudlin. Some of her pieces are so exaggerated in their effects that she has certainly succeeded in following his lead. Much of her work sounds like music for the theater because it is intentionally so melodramatic.[11]

It is important to note that, though seen often at the piano, Bley does not pretend to be a virtuoso and does not even consider herself a jazz improviser. Her piano solos are modest and very deliberate. They are just as tuneful as her compositions and never off-handedly facile. Often she uses the piano for outlining melodies and harmonies, not for drawing attention to herself pianistically.

Carla Bley, 1989.
(Photo by Patrick Hinely)

JOE LOVANO

Young tenor saxophonists of the 1990s and the first decade of the twenty-first century were still drawn to the styles of John Coltrane, Joe Henderson, and Michael Brecker. But the approach of **Joe Lovano** (b. 1952) had also begun finding imitators. This

Composed by Carla Bley; recorded in 1999 in Oslo, Norway, for Watt by Lew Soloff (trumpet), Wolfgang Puschnig (alto saxophone), Andy Shepard (tenor saxophone), Gary Valente (trombone), Larry Goldings (organ), Carla Bley (piano), Steve Swallow (bass), and Victor Lewis (drums); available on *4×4* (Watt/ECM: 30, 1999, c2000); reissued on *Bley, :rarum xv Selected Recordings* (ECM B 0001795, c2004).

Carla Bley's "Baseball" is inspired by the sounds that we often hear from an organist at a big city baseball game. In the music you will hear those trademark phrases, but you will also hear Bley moving their pitch up a few times. This shows how Bley can cleverly make music out of the simplest elements. Unlike much modern jazz that is serious and very intricate, Bley's music is fun and not nearly as complicated. But don't mistake the fun and simplicity for lack of originality. Bley is strikingly fresh in her creativity, and the result swings, too.

Bley creatively varies the presentation of parts in her music. In this way, she takes us on an adventure in which we are not likely to get bored. Sometimes, for instance, she changes accompaniment rhythm or meter, as when she switches from a modified New Orleans street beat to a waltz. Drummers in New Orleans parade bands invented this particular street beat, and it is also found in pop music from New Orleans, such as that of the Meters. The passage at 2′55″ is in waltz meter, which is a dramatic contrast from the rhythm of the New Orleans street beat that precedes it. During a few moments, the street beat rhythm is actually played in waltz meter. Other times it is played against waltz meter.

The melody in "Baseball" consists primarily of just two phrases: a three-note phrase and a four-note version of the same phrase. The chords in the progression that accompany it move in very small steps, not the usual pitch ranges of most tunes. Sometimes the effect of the alternating chords is mysterious. The two alternating chords lend the music a Spanish flavor, especially during the trombone solo. It is as though bullfight music meets baseball music.

The sections that organize the main portions of the piece follow an A-A-B-A structure. The bridge (B-section) consists of two two-note phrases that could be construed as a "call," followed by the four-note phrase that opened the recording's beginning. In this location, that four-note phrase could be construed as a "response." Incidentally, the A-sections are eight measures long, whereas the bridge is only six measures long. This makes the ending of the bridge feel premature and abrupt.

Despite the 8-8-6-8 construction of sections for statements of the main melody, the improvised sections of "Baseball" use an eight-measure bridge. This accommodation makes the solos easy to follow because eight-measure sections are typical of songs in A-A-B-A form, whereas six-measure sections are rare.

The piano solo paces the passage of chords so that each chord lasts twice as long as it did for the organ solo that preceded it. The trombone solo follows a somewhat different set of chord changes. Instead of A-A-B-A, the chords are arranged A-A-A′-A′-B-A-A, in which A′ (pronounced "aay PRIME") designates the transposition of the chord's pitch up a half a scale step.

ELAPSED TIME	MUSICAL EVENTS	
	Introduction (6 measures)	
0′00″		Unaccompanied organist plays "Baseball"'s first phrase three times at successively higher pitch levels.
0′06″		the "Charge" fanfare
	Theme Statement (8-8-6-8 measures)	
	First Four Measures	
0′08″	**A**	Saxes, trumpet, and organ play the melody's three-note and four-note phrase,
0′10″		then play it again in harmony.
	Second Four Measures	
0′12″		Organ and rhythm section play waltz rhythm over modified New Orleans street beat.
	First Four Measures	
0′17″	**A**	Saxes, trumpet, and organ play in unison the melody's three-note and four-note phrase, then
0′19″		they play same phrase in harmony.

LISTENING GUIDE continued on next page

Second Four Measures

0'22"   Organ and rhythm section play waltz over modified New Orleans street beat.

Bridge

0'26"   B   Trumpet and trombone play two two-note phrases.

0'28"   Saxophones respond with the original four-note phrase in harmony.

0'30"   Trumpet and trombone play two two-note phrases at a lower pitch level.

0'32"   Saxophones respond with the original four-note phrase in harmony.

First Four Measures

0'34"   A   Saxes, trumpet, and organ play in unison the melody's three-note and four-note phrases,

0'36"   then play them again in harmony.

Second Four Measures

0'38"   Organ and rhythm section play waltz over modified New Orleans street beat.

Organ Solo Improvisation (Larry Goldings)

     A-Section (8 measures)

0'42"   A   Solo logically takes brief idea and transforms it several times.

            accompanied by drummer playing modified New Orleans street beat on snare drum

     A-Section (8 measures)

0'51"   A   particularly melodic solo line

     B-Section (8 measures)

1'00"   B   Solo employs a brief melodic idea and logically transforms it several times, at lower pitches that correspond to the chord changes. Drummer switches timekeeping from snare drum to cymbal.

     A-Section (8 measures)

1'09"   A   Organ uses brief, funky lick for solo line. Drummer returns to snare drum.

            Brief phrases echo each other.

Second Chorus of Organ Solo

1'18"   A   chorded solo line; accompaniment chords move by small steps.

1'27"   A   Organ returns to unharmonized melody.

1'36"   B   One brief musical idea is transposed to lower and lower pitches, transformed over several repetitions.

1'45"   A   Densely packed flourishes comprise the foreground.

Third Solo Chorus for Organ

1'54"   A   New phrase gives solo a different character. Organ repeats brief phrase at successively lower pitches; accompanied by sustained chords from saxes and brasses.

2'03"   A   solo uses whole-tone scales (see page 176 for keyboard diagram), lines successively lower in pitch.

2'14"   B   Organ harmonizes the melody line in chord form.

2'21"   A   Funky chords comprise solo line.

Interlude 1

2'30"   A   With halting accompaniment, guttural trombone call alternates with saxophone response.

2'40"   A'   Trombone call alternates with trumpet-saxophone response, this time pitched a half a scale-step lower.

2'50"   B   Horns launch four-measure-long excerpt of waltz meter "Take Me Out to the Ballgame" ("For it's one, two, three strikes, you're out in the . . .").

LISTENING GUIDE *continued on next page*

2'54"		Original four-note phrase causes premature conclusion of interlude.

Improvised Piano Solo by Carla Bley

Throughout Bley's improvisation, note the chord changes cycling in left hand, dreamy melody in right hand, using stretched-out waltz meter atop drummer playing modified New Orleans street beat on snare drum.

2'57"	A	**16-bar section** (deceptive note choices as though secretly changing keys, wandering cleverly through unlikely chord changes)
3'19"	A	**16-bar section**
3'33"	B	**16-bar section** (particularly melodic solo ideas)
3'51"	A	**16-bar section** (organ joins accompaniment)
3'55"		new melodic idea

Interlude 2

4'10"		four-note phrase by organ
4'14"		the "Charge" fanfare by organ using discordant pitches
4'16"		drum rolls
4'26"		cymbal crash

Trombone Solo Improvisation (Gary Valente)

sound quality: *raucous tones achieved by over-blowing*

accompanying chords: *alternating pair of chords, not exactly the previous chord progression; lends a Spanish flavor*

4'29"	A	**8 bars**
4'38"	A	**8 bars**
4'47"	A'	Harmony is raised a step.
4'56"	A'	**8 bars**
5'05"	B	**8 bars (new harmonies and several changes)**
5'14"	A	**8 bars**
5'23"	A	**8 bars**

Second Chorus of Trombone Solo

5'32"	A	**8 bars**
		particularly melodic new phrase
5'41"	A	**8 bars**
5'50"	A'	harmonies move up a half a scale-step
6'00"	A'	
6'09"	B	**8 bars (new harmonies and several changes)**
6'18"	A	short figure introduced, then transformed four times
6'27"	A	new melodic idea
6'36"		**Theme Statement (8-8-6-8 measures)**
		Ending
7'11"		Horns suggest a reprise of "One, two, three strikes . . ." in waltz meter.
7'16"		Band plays one note, then leaves trombone alone to solo.
7'23"		Band plays one note, then leaves trombone alone to solo.
7'31"		Organ begins reprising "Charge" fanfare.
7'38"		Three-note phrase and four-note phrase, followed by drum figure and one loud band note featuring trombone in foreground and high-pitched trumpet.

Tenor saxophonist Joe Lovano, shown here at the 2001 Tri-C JazzFest in Cleveland.

(Photo by Jeff Forman)

saxophonist crafted possibly the most eclectic approach of the period. Lovano differs in attitude from his contemporaries who are sometimes termed "neo-classical jazz" saxophonists because they alternated between a Sonny Rollins phase, an Ornette Coleman phase, a Ben Webster phase, and a John Coltrane phase. Unlike neo-classical musicians, Lovano does not rely on a fixed vocabulary of formula patterns. By contrast, Lovano combined the Rollins, Coleman, Webster, and Coltrane sources, added that of Dewey Redman, and carried his broad palette to a rich assortment of diverse musical settings that he created for himself.[12]

Instead of tapping a particular repertory for each situation, as the method-actors among his contemporaries might, Lovano let each situation extract new strains from his own imagination. It was not as though he "adapted" to each new situation so much as he fed off the fresh stimulation it offered and then created something new. His playing gives the impression that he has an inexhaustible supply of ideas, rather than any fixed bag of tricks.

Conceptual freedom pervades the construction of Lovano's lines. When improvising, he breaks up his lines with an enormous variety of rhythms, containing references to numerous styles. He alternates between long strings of swing eighth notes and swirling legato figures of indeterminate duration. Lovano uses extremely long phrases, often containing other phrases within them. Sometimes it seems as though the contours are spiraling. Within them he double-times and triple-times sporadically. Using a soft, half-spoken tone, continuously changing its shade and color, Lovano pauses at various rest-points, getting a second wind within a single phrase. It is analogous to watching a bird fly, light on a branch, followed momentarily by a burst of flight, then only temporarily lighting on another before resuming flight. All the while, his solo line courses through the entire pitch range of his horn again and again. A generosity of spirit prevails, as if Lovano has boundless energy and is continuously offering one idea after another.

There is nothing predictable in Lovano's improvising. A sense of striving for originality remains a higher priority than polish or completeness. He is always stretching, never content to coast. Never perfunctory, his work has an earnest quality, and, though very complicated, his playing conveys remarkable naturalness.

THE PAUL MOTIAN TRIO

The most explorative side to Lovano's 1980s output was displayed in a trio that combined the saxophonist with drummer Paul Motian and guitarist Bill Frisell. With no bass and often with no explicit timekeeping patterns, the band sounded free of chords and timekeeping without actually discarding them. It was so loose and elastic that listeners never knew what was coming next. It was avant-garde jazz played by musicians who were thoroughly grounded in traditions of swinging jazz that adhered to preset chord progressions. In other words, all three men had well-established reputations in what musicians call "straight-ahead jazz," but they applied their depth of experience and originality to stretch the boundaries of the beat and each tune's harmonies. In the Motian Trio, Lovano impressed jazz fans having a taste for the abstract.

The Paul Motian Trio music stands out in regard to two important freedoms. First, the chord sequence for each piece is usually maintained throughout the improvisations, but the durations for those chords are free. How long each remains in effect depends on interactions among players. Second, Motian's drumming sports non-repetitive timekeeping rhythms that are continuously varying and rarely emphasize an obvious beat. This had been germinating while Motian was playing with Bill Evans during the 1950s and 1960s. (See page 347 for more about Motian's work with Evans.) Then it developed further when he was a member of the Keith Jarrett group of the 1970s. So, despite Motian's having been around for a long time before the 1980s when he got more attention as a bandleader, his music was truly avant-garde in the 1980s. In 2007 it was still one of the most adventuresome groups that was performing and recording.[13]

MARIA SCHNEIDER

Maria Schneider (b. 1960) is a composer and bandleader who became prominent in the 1990s. Like the other figures in this chapter, she was first appreciated and given exposure in Europe more than the United States. Several features of her writing stand out:

1. Unlike standard formats for band arrangements such as a 32-bar chorus structure that repeats continuously with variations, Schneider's formats sport much longer sections and much less repetition (for instance, "Wrygly"[14]). Most don't cycle at all. They are composed freshly throughout with their own original form, thereby fitting the "through-composed" designation.

2. Schneider's pieces can run from 8 to 20 minutes and often don't begin solo improvisation until more than three minutes into the piece (for instance, "Concert in the Garden" and "Choro Dançado"[15]). Though previously used by Duke Ellington, long stretches without improvisation are unusual in jazz writing (for instance, "Gush"[16]).

3. Schneider uses improvising soloists; but when she calls upon them, their role is almost like that of an actor in a play. The solo becomes integral to the feeling of overall development and fabric of the piece instead of a display for the player's virtuosity as in conventional big band jazz.

Maria Schneider, 2005.
(Photo by Takehiko Tokiwa)

4. Tone color is another respect in which Schneider's music departs from common practices. She favors flutes, clarinets, muted trumpets, and trombones more often than saxophones and unmuted brass. In fact, it may be accurate to describe the effect of much music by Schneider as pastel and delicate. This departs from most big band jazz with its bright tone colors.

5. Schneider emphasizes soft sounds and uses shifts in volume quite subtly. ("Gush," for example, is a long, very gradual crescendo all the way to the end.) This practice differs from such tendencies of big band jazz as prolonged loud passages and intentionally blunt pronouncements.

6. We rarely find bluesy feeling or bop character in her music.

7. By contrast with traditional big band jazz, much of Schneider's work recalls the albums that Gil Evans scored for Miles Davis, such as *Quiet Nights* and *Sketches of Spain*.[17] Her later music even carries the influence of Brazilian and flamenco music ("Choro Dançado" and "Bulería, Soleá y Rumba"[18]) that one hears on these Gil Evans recordings.

8. In addition to the presence of South American and Spanish rhythms, some of her work evokes the floating feeling achieved by pseudo-rubato passages in recordings of Bill Evans and Keith Jarrett. In other words, it is not hard driving, and the beat is not routinely made obvious. Whereas much big band jazz elicits images of swing dancers in the 1930s, Schneider's music tends to elicit images of ballet.

9. Much writing for jazz groups is inspired by self-imposed technical puzzles and technical exercises. By contrast, many of Schneider's pieces are largely autobiographical, evoking her own experiences, such as sailing ("Coming About"[19]) and flying ("Hang Gliding"[20]). This fits what at the beginning of the twentieth century became known as "Impressionism." French orchestral composers Claude Debussy and Maurice Ravel exemplify this style. Not entirely coincidental is that Schneider borrows harmonies from these same composers and the jazz arrangers who favored them.

The nine characteristics identified here cumulatively lead some listeners to feel that Maria Schneider is creating her own idiom in the jazz world.

ECM STYLE

Throughout jazz history there have been recording companies whose founders revealed their personal tastes by what they recorded. But nowhere has a particular jazz style become more associated with one firm than it has with **ECM** (abbreviation for Editions of Contemporary Music), founded in Germany by classical bassist and composer Manfred Eicher in 1969. Beginning with the release of music recorded in 1971 by pianists Keith Jarrett[21] and Chick Corea, Eicher made a name for himself among jazz fans (see Chapter 15).

"Sundial, Pt. 1,"
JCCD3 Track 5

Though they do not apply to every ECM recording artist, a few characteristics distinguish ECM productions. Clarity and perfection of sound quality are often the first aspects that strike our ears. Accompanying this sound quality is the effect of being in a reverberant room with the music. A deliberate use of sustained tones and silences soon becomes conspicuous. It is as though the quality of the music and its reproduction is enticing listeners to savor each tone as it rings, one at a time. We also notice that lush harmonies prevail. The calm pacing of the music will soon become evident. Most ECM music is not as busy as previous jazz styles. Another overriding quality is a sense of refinement. For instance, rhythms are not abrupt, and tones are not harsh. Lastly, some of the melodies and accompaniments remind us more of folk music and classical music than of swing or bop.

Note that for the purposes of this survey "ECM Style" refers only to one slice of ECM's output. ECM's artists are versatile, and most have made significant contributions in styles other than the one most closely identified here with "ECM Style." In fact, some artists recorded in one style for ECM and another style for another company, and some have had ECM record more than one of their styles. In some cases, the same album may not only contain tracks with typical "ECM Style" but also contain other tracks that use different styles. In other words, the characteristics identified here only represent generalizations about some of the music on a number of albums that best fit what listeners have loosely termed "ECM Style." The recording firm has produced more than a thousand albums, and much of what is in the ECM catalog today deviates from those generalizations. For instance, the slice of ECM's output concerned with jazz-rock fusion styles and the classical music recordings that contain no improvisation are not discussed here.

Most of Eicher's earliest recording artists were concerned with creating a new idiom that broke with jazz traditions, and a few showed stylistic debts to Bill Evans (see pages 339–46 for more on Evans). Evidence of an Evans influence was manifested in at least four ways:

1. Evans's lush chord voicings provided a beginning for devising their harmonies.

2. His techniques for avoiding bouncy phrases seem to have been helpful.

3. The pre-Evans practice of crafting phrases in compact units was not followed by ECM artists as much as by pre-Evans improvisers.

4. A marked emphasis on continuity of mood and melodic development was reflected.

Melodies on ECM albums were not devised in bop style; they were not as jumpy. Their accompaniments were not played in bop style, either. ECM artists rarely maintained jazz traditions for walking bass or standard ride rhythms. Chording accompaniment usually did not consist of comping in the jazz sense of chording in irregular syncopations. Harmonies were sometimes presented in styles of folk music guitar playing that follows a continuous pattern where chord notes are played one at a time (arpeggiated). Sometimes a repeating rhythm was used. Some accompaniment devices resembled accompaniments in classical music.

Departures from traditional chord progressions were so drastic in some of the new ECM music that "free jazz" is an accurate designation. This is true even though free-form performances recorded by ECM were unlike most free jazz of the 1960s that was known for rough sounds and chaotic textures. Portions of Chick Corea's A.R.C.[22] album were freely improvised, as was most of the music on his *Piano Improvisations Vol. 1* and *Vol. 2.*[23] Most music on Keith Jarrett's unaccompanied solo piano albums was freely improvised, and some of Jarrett's trio albums, such as *Inside Out*[24] and *Changes,*[25] were made without setting chord progressions beforehand.

Refinement was so essential to the music produced by Eicher that the ECM house style might be termed "cool jazz," though it differed significantly from music bearing that label during the 1950s. Instead of the bright tone colors associated with swing and bop, the tone colors associated with ECM were muted. They were sometimes termed "pastel." Languorous, meditative lines were frequently emphasized instead of the highly animated lines that seemed to be continuously flowing from the improvisers in hard bop and avant-garde jazz of the 1960s. Though the musicians were virtuosi, and all were capable of creating jazz swing feeling, there was often a sense of suspended motion in the ECM music instead of hard swinging. Often their pieces were tone poems in which the players attempted to convey impressions of visual sensations through sounds. For instance, an entire album by guitarist-composer Pat Metheny was called *Water Colors,*[26] and it contained tunes titled "Lakes," "Oasis," and "Icefire." The *Solstice*[27] album by guitarist-composer Ralph Towner featured compositions with titles such as "Drifting Petals," "Red and Black," and "Sand."[28]

Though electric instruments and rock-inspired accompaniments prevailed at this time in jazz history, much of Eicher's output was by non-electronic instruments, and it was not based on the dance rhythms of rock and funk music. Ralph Towner, one of ECM's main guitarists, recorded several albums using classical guitar, and he emphasized subdued textures in his music. The rhythms and harmonies of his work often specialized in gentle sounds inspired in part by light classical music and folk music of other cultures. When ECM music was made by electronic instruments, the effect was not usually as edgy as most jazz-rock fusion. For instance, though Pat Metheny, another of ECM's main guitarists, recorded mostly on electric guitar, his sound was usually more like the soft, well-manicured tone and rounded articulation of Jim Hall than the metallic quality and explosive articulation of rock guitarists. Additionally, Metheny's lines were graceful, and the tones in them were usually sustained and slurred together.[29]

Eicher attracted a number of improvisers who specialized in making sustained tones plentiful instead of using the rapid twists and turns that characterized bop style. A considerable amount of ECM music seems to be celebrating tone colors for their own sake, rather than using tones primarily for conveying a melody or rhythm. The artists achieved a glossy effect when striving for sustained tones and rich, new chords. They used floating melodies and chords that evoked a sense of mystery. This is exemplified by (a) the ringing of guitar tones by Ralph Towner and Pat Metheny (who innovated the simultaneous use of two amplifiers and a digital delay device called "Chorusing"), (b) the resonating bass tones by Eberhard Weber,[30] (c) the singing saxophone tones of Jan Garbarek,[31] and (d) the resounding piano tones of Keith Jarrett.[32]

Demo CD *Tracks 90 and 96*

"Sundial, Pt. 1," JCCD3 *Track 5*

In keeping with these ideals, Eicher paid remarkable attention to sonic detail while producing and engineering the recordings himself. For example, he sought the best pianos and best microphones for recording Jarrett. Sometimes he recorded in churches and monasteries for the special effect their acoustics offered. Eicher's musicians traveled to Germany and Norway to achieve perfection and beauty that was available only in highly specialized studios with the best equipment in the world. ECM earned a reputation for clarity and resonance of recording quality that was unprecedented in jazz. Eicher maintained a glass-like quality in each recording, and added reverberation to an extremely clear sound.

Part of the clarity in ECM music derives from the compositional forms his musicians used. In some of the pieces, chords did not change as fast as was typical in bop, though they did change, and the ways they changed were fresh. Eicher's artists attained an expansive feeling partly by avoiding the 12-bar blues and 32-bar A-A-B-A forms that had used progressions of chords in 8-beat units. They usually avoided pop tunes and bop standards. Also contributing to this effect was a less rushed feeling than what was characteristic of previous jazz styles. Pacing seemed more relaxed at ECM recording sessions. By comparison with hard bop, the tempos were slower, too. ECM music also avoided the harshness and abruptness that was often found in hard bop of the 1950s and 1960s and in many avant-garde styles of the 1960s. By contrast, a number of ECM albums were inspired by music of India, Africa, and Tibet, whose intent was to calm the listener. The attraction to the music of India led some ECM musicians to use drones and high-pitched, soft-sounding percussion instruments. The intent to calm the listener was common in ECM music. For instance, the *Officium* album[33] of 1993 by Jan Garbarek was inspired in part by Gregorian chant, and it attracted a huge audience of listeners beyond the usual jazz market, probably for its appeal to calm emotions.

Many of the sounds that crystallized the ECM style originated when Eicher paired the compositions and piano playing of American Keith Jarrett with Norwegian saxophonist **Jan Garbarek** (b. 1947) to make such albums as *Belonging, My Song,* and *Luminessence.*[34] Musicians in the 1970s often said that Garbarek's saxophone style was the most original since the emergence of Wayne Shorter and Albert Ayler. The saxophonist was partly inspired by Johnny Hodges, John Coltrane, Albert Ayler, and Ornette Coleman. Like Hodges, his timing of tones achieved maximum drama and sensuality. The construction of his phrases sounded like it was the result of great patience and deliberation, with restraint of notes. Like Ayler and Hodges, his vibrato was prominent. His long, ringing tones were stretched, as in an echo chamber. (Listen to his solo on "My Song" in Jarrett's album *My Song*.) This differed from the busy tendency of Coltrane and his disciples. Like Ayler, Garbarek often achieved a haunting quality that seemed to float over a shimmering accompaniment. Like Hodges, Garbarek could make the saxophone sing rhapsodically. This facet in Garbarek's work is found on the Charlie Haden album, *Folk Songs*,[35] where Garbarek collaborated with Brazilian guitarist-pianist Egberto Gismonti. Other milestones in this vein include *Red Lanta*[36] with Jarrett disciple Art Lande on piano, *Sol Do Meio Di*[37] with Gismonti, and *Solstice*[38] with guitarist Ralph Towner.

Emphasizing Garbarek's rhapsodic side here is not to say that his talent lacked other sides. In fact, elsewhere he emulated the frantic approach exemplified by late-period Coltrane, and he occasionally showed some Ornette Coleman touches (as in his Coleman-like solo on "The Windup"[39]).

| CCD2 *Track 10*

Guitarist Pat Metheny and vibraphonist **Gary Burton** (b. 1943) did some of their best work when recording for Manfred Eicher. In fact, Metheny was introduced to many listeners originally through his work on Burton's ECM albums (see page 382 for more on Metheny). Burton had already made conceptual breakthroughs as vibraphonist and bandleader, and he had toured and recorded with pianist George Shearing and saxophonist Stan Getz. Though he already had a distinguished recording career before appearing on ECM albums, Burton became familiar to many listeners first by his stunning music with Chick Corea on their ECM duo album *Crystal Silence*[40] (which led to tours and two award-winning follow-up albums). Thus, Burton's numerous albums for Eicher helped define the ECM sound for many listeners.[41] Having previously recorded Carla Bley's innovative suite *A Genuine Tong Funeral*[42] for RCA, Burton recorded for ECM another album of unusual pieces by Bley: *Dreams So Real*.[43] As he had on albums for RCA, Burton continued championing the fresh music of European composers Michael Gibbs and Eberhard Weber (whose *Colours of Chloe* album[44] had become a celebrated pace setter for the ECM sound; listen to Burton's *Seven Songs* and *Passengers*[45]).

Burton's vibraphone style contrasts with Lionel Hampton's swing style and Milt Jackson's bluesy bop style. Elements of distinction include absence of tremolo in the instrument's sustained tones (Burton does not use a foot pedal; see illustration on page 178), few references to funky jazz, and less reliance on swing eighth notes or the syncopations that are customarily associated with jazz. Country music is recalled in some of Burton's music, especially when playing with Metheny, who also favored a country-style twang. Aside from references to Bill Evans, Burton came up with a vocabulary of his own.

Though Chick Corea moved through a number of different styles during his career, some fans consider his best music to have been recorded by Manfred Eicher. His unaccompanied solo piano albums *Piano Improvisations Vol. 1* and *Vol. 2* provided an introduction to his talent for numerous listeners, and they remain favorites among Corea fans. They are perfect examples of a new kind of music that moved far beyond its sources in bop, Coltrane, and Bill Evans. Sounding more like classical music than jazz, this new sound drew from the jazz tradition by its dependence on improvisation and occasional hints of swing feeling. Corea's compositions on the ECM albums offered new concepts in tune construction and feeling (see pages 351–354 for more on Corea). His *A.R.C.* album on ECM with bassist Dave Holland and drummer Barry Altschul comes closer than any of Corea's other albums to matching the level of creativity and crisp sonic qualities that were achieved on his landmark *Now He Sings, Now He Sobs*.[46]

| "Steps," JCCD3
| *Track 4*

It is also important to recognize that there are well-informed observers who prefer to think of ECM as representing an artistic management approach rather than a musical style. Such observers have watched Eicher provide an open laboratory for musicians to develop new approaches to creative improvised music, with minimal concern for market forces that require recording companies to think in terms of categories such as "world music," "folk music," "classical music," or "jazz." In other words, Eicher's "formula" is—paradoxically—the negation of formula, trusting as he does in the artistry of the musicians. With the artistic freedom that Eicher grants his musicians, they can approach the recording studio as a workshop to combine, recombine, and evolve styles. Most of these artists had recorded for other firms before recording for ECM, and most had already shown innovation. That they did their best work for ECM, and developed further innovations, however, is proof of Eicher's effectiveness.

The well-informed observers who downplay the existence of an "ECM Style" emphasize the stylistic diversity of projects undertaken by ECM artists rather than any commonality that characterizes music of the ECM catalog that is described here.[47] Note, however, that the assortment of styles may have something in common that is not evident at a superficial level. Eicher's choices reflect his high-level taste and esthetic judgment, thereby indicating deep qualities that he is personally reacting to. Such qualities are held in common among works of music as wide ranging as those he has recorded of Steve Reich, Pat Metheny, and thirteenth-century composer Perotin. So despite its stylistic diversity, the ECM catalog still reflects the tastes and vision of one man. Moreover, it reflects the fact that musicians must meet very high standards for uniqueness and originality before they will be invited to record for ECM.

But Is It Jazz?

Much of what has been termed "The ECM Style" is more closely aligned with folk, world, and classical music than with jazz. Swing eighth notes and the typical syncopations of swing and bop styles are rare. Some of the music's sources in Irish, Spanish, and Middle Eastern folk music are more evident than any sources in African-American blues or gospel music. Some of the guitar music improvised by Ralph Towner could be construed as part of classical guitar literature instead of continuing the jazz tradition of Charlie Christian and Wes Montgomery. Garbarek's saxophone improvisations over choral chants on *Officium* don't swing or closely resemble previous jazz styles. Some of Keith Jarrett's unaccompanied piano improvisations are almost indistinguishable from written "classical" music by twentieth-century European composers.[48] Therefore, a few commentators prefer classifying Jarrett's piano recitals as "improvised concert music" and excluding it from the jazz category altogether.

"Sundial, Pt. 1,"
JCCD3 Track 5

So what is the answer? Is "The ECM Style" jazz or not? Music of the ECM artists is treated in this *Jazz Styles* book because it is highly dependent on improvisation, and it is made by musicians who are best known for jazz. Though informed by classical music and by World Music, **most of ECM style does stem from jazz tradition** despite lacking the funk or swing of pre-1970 styles of jazz. Just as some jazz fans initially did not include jazz-rock fusion in the "jazz" category but eventually softened in their views, perhaps similarly reluctant observers will ultimately consider the amalgamations offered by the ECM artists to be "jazz styles." On the other hand, perhaps we need new category names for classifying types of improvised music that are not really ethnic or classical music and are so remotely related to jazz that we are currently stretching the "jazz" label to accommodate them.[49]

CHAPTER SUMMARY

1. Among the American stand-outs who were initially better known in Europe than the United States during the 1970s through the 1990s were composer-bandleaders Carla Bley, Maria Schneider, Joe Lovano, and Paul Motian.

2. Bley was always avant-garde, having begun with free jazz and continued with her own strikingly original compositions that used minimalism and playful theatricality for small and medium-sized bands of unorthodox improvisers.

3. Lovano crafted an original saxophone style from the approaches of Dewey Redman, John Coltrane, Sonny Rollins, and Ornette Coleman. Never content to rely on a set collection of patterns, he was remarkably fresh every time he played, and he devised a wide assortment of contexts to inspire his creativity.

4. Drummer-composer Paul Motian led avant-garde bands without bass. He specialized in making timekeeping patterns that obscured the beat and using harmonies in ways that made the band sound free without actually being free of preset chord progressions.

5. Maria Schneider invented a style of writing for big bands that veered from the loud, blunt pronouncements of the tradition and its displays of instrumental virtuosity. Her approach emphasized long passages of written parts, low volume, light tone qualities, and impressionistic themes.

6. Record producer Manfred Eicher built a reputation for jazz recordings on his ECM label that featured the most distinctive new musicians of the period playing in acoustically perfect settings with crystalline results.

7. ECM artists became known for jazz that often sounded more like classical music and ethnic music than anything listeners had previously heard. The blends of these sources were so original that the music defied classification, and listeners ultimately called them "ECM Style."

8. Leaders in the ECM catalog included Keith Jarrett, Chick Corea, Jan Garbarek, Pat Metheny, Ralph Towner, and Gary Burton.

1. Carla Bley, *Fleur Carnivore* (Watt/ECM: 21, 1988, c1989).

2. Bley, *Social Studies* (Watt/ECM: 422 831 831 [11], 1981, c2000).

3. Bley, *Big Band Theory* (Watt/ECM: 314 519 966 [25], 1993, c2000).

4. Bley, *The Very Big Carla Bley Band* (Watt/ECM: 23, 1990, c1991).

5. Bley, *The Carla Bley Big Band . . . Goes to Church* (Watt/ECM: 314 533 682 [27], 1996, c2000).

6. Bley, *Escalator Over the Hill* (Watt/ECM: 422 839 310 [EOTH], 1968–71, c2000).

7. Gary Burton, *A Genuine Tong Funeral* (RCA Victor: 66748, 1967–68, c1999).

8. Bley, *Fancy Chamber Music* (Watt/ECM: 314 539 937 [28], 1997, c2000).

9. JCCD3 Track 12, or Bley, *4×4* (Watt/ECM: 012 159 547 [30], 1999, c2000).

10. Bley, *European Tour 1977* (Watt/ECM: 8, 1977, c1978).

11. Other Carla Bley recordings include: *Looking for America* (Watt/ECM: 31, 2002, c2003); and Carla Bley/Steve Swallow, *Duets* (Watt/ECM: 20, 1988, c1988); a good overview is Carla Bley, *Selected Recordings, :rarum xv* (Watt/ECM: B0002795-02, 1971–1999, c2004).

12. Joe Lovano, *Viva Caruso* (Blue Note: 35986, 2001, c2002); and John Scofield, *Meant to Be* (Blue Note: 95479, 1990, c1991).

13. Paul Motian, *One Time Out* (Soul Note: 121 224, 1987, c1989); *On Broadway*, vol. 1 (Winter & Winter: 919 029 [JMT], 1988, c2003); *Paul Motian in Tokyo* (Winter & Winter: 919 052 [JMT], 1991, c2004); *At the Village Vanguard* (Winter & Winter: 919 080 [JMT], 1995, c2005); *Sound of Love* (Winter & Winter: 910 008, 1995, c1997); and *I Have the Room Above Her* (ECM: B0003966-02 [1902], 2004, c2005).

14. Maria Schneider, *Evanescence* (ArtistShare: 0006 [ENJA], 1992, c2005).

15. Schneider, *Concert in the Garden* (ArtistShare: 0001, 2001–04, c2004).

16. Schneider, *Evanescence* (ArtistShare 0006).

17. Miles Davis, *Quiet Nights* (Columbia/Legacy: 65293, 1962, c1997) and *Sketches of Spain* (Columbia/Legacy: 65142, 1959–60, c1997).

18. Schneider, *Concert in the Garden*.

19. Schneider, *Coming About* (ENJA: 9069, 1995, c1996); to be reissued by ArtistShare. This and all other Schneider music is available at artistshare.com.

20. Schneider, *Allegresse* (ArtistShare: 0005 [ENJA], 2000, c2005); the most recent recording is Maria Schneider, *Days of Wine and Roses: Live at the Jazz Standard* (ArtistShare: 0017, 2000, c2005).

21. Keith Jarrett, *Staircase* (ECM: 827 337 [1090], 1976, c2000).

22. Chick Corea, *A.R.C.* (ECM: 422 833 678 [1009], 1971, c2000).

23. Corea, *Piano Improvisations*, vol. 1 (ECM: 811 979 [1014], 1971, c2000); vol. 2 (ECM: 829 190 [1020], 1971, c2000).

24. Jarrett, *Inside Out* (ECM: 440 014 005 [1780], 2000, c2001).

25. Jarrett, *Changes* (ECM: 422 817 436 [1276], 1983, c2000).

26. Pat Metheny, *Watercolors* (ECM: 422 827 409 [1097], 1977, c2000).

27. Ralph Towner, *Solstice* (ECM: 422 825 458 [1095], 1974, c2000).

28. Drummer-composer-bandleader **Jack DeJohnette** (b. 1942) created fresh music for a number of ECM albums, some of it as leader, some as sideman. His recurring appearances on ECM albums almost make him the ECM "house drummer." DeJohnette, *Oneness* (ECM: 314 537 343 [1637], 1997, c2000) is among the most explorative such works that conveys the airy feeling and calm effect associated with ECM albums by other artists. It contains tune titles such as "Free Above Sea" and "Priestesses of the Mist." His other contributions to the ECM catalog often depart from the atmospheric and exhibit rousing, swinging music, as sampled in Jack DeJohnette, *Selected Recordings, :rarum xii* (ECM 80001797, 1971–97, c2004).

29. Metheny, *Pat Metheny Group* (ECM: 422 825 593 [1114], 1978, c2000); and *Offramp* (ECM: 422 817 138 [1216], 1981, c1999).

30. On Gary Burton, *Ring* (ECM: 422 829 191 [1051], 1974, c2001).

31. On "My Song" from Jarrett, *My Song* (ECM: 422 821 406 [1115], 1977, c1999); *Luminessence* (ECM: 422 839 307 [1049], 1974, c2000; and Art Lande, *Red Lanta* (ECM: 422 839 383 [1038], 1973, c1987).

32. Keith Jarrett, *Staircase* (ECM: 827 337 [1090], 1976, c2000).

33. Jan Garbarek, *Officium* (ECM: 289 445 369 [1525], 1993, c1999).

34. Jarrett, *My Song*; and *Luminessence*; a good overview is Garbarek, *Selected Recordings, :rarum ii* (ECM: 440 014 165, 2CD set, 1974–95, c2002).

35. Charlie Haden, *Folk Songs* (ECM: 422 827 705 [1151], 1979, c2000).

36. Lande, *Red Lanta*.

37. Egberto Gismonti, *Sol Do Meio Dia* (ECM: 422 829 117 [1116], 1977, c2000).

38. Towner, *Solstice*.

39. Garbarek, *Belonging* (ECM: 422 829 115 [1050], 1974).

40. Gary Burton/Chick Corea, *Crystal Silence* (ECM: 422 831 331 [1024], 1972, c1999).

41. Burton, *Selected Recordings, :rarum iv* (ECM: 440 014 195, 1973–86, c2002).

42. Burton, *A Genuine Tong Funeral* (RCA Victor: 66748, 1967–68, c1999).

43. Burton, *Dreams So Real* (ECM: 422 833 329 [1072], 1975, c2001).

44. Eberhard Weber, *The Colours of Chloe* (ECM: 422 833 331 [1042], 1973, c2001); Gary Burton, *Ring*.

45. Burton, *Passengers* (ECM: 422 835 016 [1092], 1976, c2001).

46. Corea, *Now He Sings, Now He Sobs* (Blue Note: 38265, 1968, c2002).

47. Jarrett, *Radiance* (ECM: B0004314-02 [1960/61], 2CD set, 2000, c2005).

48. These observers contend that "ECM Style" is a simplistic overgeneralization, perhaps even a myth. They point out that there is less homogeneity to ECM recordings than to Blue Note recordings, for example. Some listeners may think first of the pastoral quality of some of the iconic ECM recording dates. Yet, for example, Jan Garbarek's work with Fateh Ali Khan on *Ragas and Sagas* certainly appealed to audiences beyond the usual jazz market, but not always because its music calmed emotions; it was perceived as ecstatic by other listeners. Marked exceptions to this discussion's generalizations of style characteristics include works by Anthony Braxton, such as his playing with Chick Corea in the band called Circle; Sam Rivers, as in his own album *Contrasts* (ECM 1162) or his playing on Dave Holland's album *Conference of the Birds* (ECM 1027); the Art Ensemble of Chicago; Terje Rypdal; Dave Holland's Quintet, as in *Prime Directive* (ECM 1698) or *Seeds of Time* (ECM 1292) and Holland's Big Band, as in *What Goes Around* (ECM 1777); and the many recordings of pop tunes and jazz standards by the Keith Jarrett Trio playing in styles inspired by the 1950s and 1960s trios of Wynton Kelly, Bill Evans, and Ahmad Jamal, as in *Standards Vol.1, Standards Live, Tribute,* and *The Cure.* The position of the well-informed observers becomes more and more tenable as the number of "exceptions" begins to approach the number of clear examples of a hypothetical "ECM Style."

49. For more about ECM, see Steve Lake and Paul Griffiths, ed., *Horizons Touched: The Music of ECM* (Granta, 2007) and John Schaefer, *New Sounds: A Listener's Guide to New Music* (Harper and Row, 1987), 189–219. For a technical analysis of the music, see Paul Rinzler, "Defining a New Style in Jazz History—The ECM Style," in Charles T. Brown, ed., *Jazz Research Papers, 1990.* (International Association of Jazz Educators, Manhattan, Kansas; *www.iaje.org*).

APPENDIX A
Brief Outline of Jazz Styles

Not strictly chronological; many styles overlap the same time periods, and most have continued long after their inception. Many innovators continued playing for decades after their style emerged.

Time	Style	Hornmen	Pianists	Composers-Arrangers	Rhythm Section Musicians
1920s	Early Jazz	Louis Armstrong Sidney Bechet Bix Beiderbecke	James P. Johnson Earl Hines	Jelly Roll Morton	Baby Dodds Zutty Singleton Pops Foster
1930s	Swing	Coleman Hawkins Roy Eldridge Johnny Hodges Benny Carter	Art Tatum Teddy Wilson	Duke Ellington Fletcher Henderson Sy Oliver	Chick Webb Dave Tough Sid Catlett Walter Page Gene Krupa
Late 1930s	Transition to Bop	Lester Young Don Byas	Nat Cole		Count Basie Rhythm Section 1937–43 Jimmy Blanton
1940s	Bop	Charlie Parker Dizzy Gillespie Dexter Gordon Stan Getz	Thelonious Monk Bud Powell Al Haig	Thelonious Monk Tadd Dameron Dizzy Gillespie	Kenny Clarke Max Roach Oscar Pettiford Roy Haynes
Late 1940s	Transition to Cool & West Coast	Lee Konitz Miles Davis	Lennie Tristano	Claude Thornhill Gil Evans	
1950s	West Coast	Gerry Mulligan Chet Baker Art Pepper	Dave Brubeck	Gerry Mulligan Shorty Rogers Jimmy Giuffre	Chico Hamilton
1950s	Hard Bop	Clifford Brown Sonny Rollins Thad Jones John Coltrane Cannonball Adderley Miles Davis	Tommy Flanagan Horace Silver Red Garland	Horace Silver Benny Golson Cannonball Adderley Jackie McLean Gigi Gryce	Art Blakey Philly Joe Jones Paul Chambers Sam Jones Wilbur Ware
Late 1950s	Transition to Modal Jazz and Free Jazz	Miles Davis John Coltrane Ornette Coleman	Bill Evans Cecil Taylor	Charles Mingus Miles Davis	

Time	Style	Hornmen	Pianists	Composers-Arrangers	Rhythm Section Musicians
Early 1960s	*Coexistence of Hard Bop, Free Jazz, and Modal Jazz*	Eric Dolphy	Bill Evans McCoy Tyner Cecil Taylor	John Coltrane Ornette Coleman Wayne Shorter Charles Mingus Don Cherry	Elvin Jones Bill Evans Trio with Scott LaFaro Cecil Taylor with Sunny Murray
Mid-1960s		Freddie Hubbard Joe Henderson Wayne Shorter Don Cherry	Herbie Hancock	Wayne Shorter John Coltrane Herbie Hancock	Miles Davis's 1963–68 Rhythm Section
Late 1960s	*Transition to Jazz-Rock*	Miles Davis	Joe Zawinul	Joe Zawinul	Tony Williams

1970s	*Coexistence of AACM, Jazz-Rock, and Modal Jazz*	AACM players
		Michael Brecker,
		  Dave Sanborn
			Keith Jarrett
			Herbie Hancock
			Chick Corea
			Joe Zawinul
				Chick Corea
				AACM
				Joe Zawinul
				John
				  McLaughlin
					Miroslav Vitous
					Airto Moreira
					Jaco Pastorius

1980s	*Coexistence of New Age, Smooth Jazz, Jazz-Rock, and Neo-Classical Jazz*	Grover Washington, Jr. Kenny G Dave Sanborn Michael Brecker Joe Henderson	Keith Jarrett Herbie Hancock Chick Corea Joe Zawinul	Pat Metheny Anthony Braxton	Jaco Pastorius Paul Motian Roy Haynes
1990s	*Coexistence of Acid Jazz, Jazz-Rock, Neo-Classical, Hip Hop Jazz, Klezmer Jazz, Neo-Swing*	John Zorn Dave Douglas Paquito D'Rivera Joe Lovano Steve Coleman Kenny G	Keith Jarrett Herbie Hancock Chick Corea Joe Zawinul Danilo Perez	John Zorn Dave Douglas Maria Schneider Carla Bley	Joey Baron Brian Blade John Patitucci Roy Haynes

APPENDIX B
Elements of Music

In describing the nature of jazz and the characteristics of different styles, several basic musical terms are quite helpful. This chapter is devoted to defining some of these terms, and I urge all readers, including those who are musically knowledgeable, to examine them carefully.

When people think of jazz, they usually think of rhythm first. But because the word rhythm is often used to describe a large variety of musical characteristics, some uses convey inaccurate or contradictory meanings. Much of the confusion can be avoided by first understanding three related terms for which rhythm is often mistaken: beat, tempo, and meter.

Beat

Music is often said to have a pulse. The unit of pulse is called a beat. When you tap your foot to music, you are usually tapping with the beat. Here is a visualization of the pulse sequences we call beats.

Tempo

Tempo refers to the speed or rate at which the beats pass. If you describe a piece of music as fast, you probably mean it has a rapid tempo, not that it occupies a short time span. When the beats continue at a regular rate, we say the tempo is constant. A clock's ticking is a good example of constant tempo. If the passage of beats is rapid, the speed is called "up tempo."

Meter

The beats in music are rarely undifferentiated. They are usually heard as being grouped. Meter describes the type of grouping. Our perception of grouping results when sequences of beats are set off from each other. This occurs in several ways. Every third or fourth beat may be louder or longer than the others. It may be distinctive because it has a different pitch or tone quality. Those differences are perceived as emphasis or accent. If we hear a sequence of beats grouped in fours, it may be due to a pattern of accents which creates this effect: ONE two three four ONE two three four. That pattern represents a meter which musicians simply call "four."

If the beats fall into the pattern, **ONE** two three, **ONE** two three, **ONE** two three, musicians say that the music "is in three" or in "waltz time."

Meters of four and three are quite common, but there are also meters of five, six, seven, and others. A meter of five might sound like **ONE** two three four five **ONE** two three four five, **ONE** two three four five, with a large accent on the first beat and no other accents. Or there may be a strong accent on the first beat and a smaller accent on the fourth: **ONE** two three FOUR five **ONE** two three FOUR five **ONE** two three FOUR five; or a smaller accent on the third beat: **ONE** two THREE four five

ONE two THREE four five **ONE** two THREE four five. A meter of six usually feels like **ONE** two three FOUR five six **ONE** two three FOUR five six.

Each group of beats is called a **measure.** When the meter is three, there are three beats in a measure; when the meter is four, there are four beats in a measure.

Rhythm

In the broadest sense, rhythm simply refers to the arrangement of sounds in time, and therefore encompasses beat, tempo, and meter. But rhythm has come to mean something more specific than these features. In fact, beat, tempo, and meter furnish the framework in which rhythm is described.

Imagine a continuous sequence of beats occurring at a constant tempo, with four beats to a measure. The steady beat which in musical notation is represented by a string of quarter notes can also be visualized as a series of boxes, representing equal amounts of time. Our meter would be called "four." Each beat is called a quarter note, and each unit of four beats constitutes a measure.

The sound within a measure can be distributed in an infinite number of ways, one of which includes "filling" the measure with silence. Rhythm is the description of how that measure or a sequence of measures is filled with sound.

Let us take a few examples, numbering the four parts of the measure one, two, three, and four, respectively. We shall create rhythms by using a single sound mixed with silence. First, divide a measure into four equal parts, filling only the first and third with sound.

We have a rhythm. It is not complex, but it does what a rhythm is supposed to do: it describes the distribution of sound over time. In fact, this is the bass drum part in numerous marches, and it is the string bass part in many slow dance pieces.

Now, instead of taking just one measure, take two measures as a unit of repetition. In other words, the rhythm is two measures long.

Finally, repeat a one-measure rhythm to fill two measures's worth of time. This might be heard as a two-measure rhythm or as two one-measure rhythms.

Rhythm is the distribution of sound over time, but rhythm also refers to the way sounds are accented. Usually, the first beat of a measure is accented. An example would be the typical OOM pah pah accompaniment for a waltz. In a measure of four, the first and third beats are often accented, as in the BOOM chick BOOM chick drum pattern used in much popular music.

Syncopation

Examining our use of accents can lend understanding to a rhythmic element called *syncopation*, a crucial aspect of jazz feeling. For example, if we expect to hear a sound on every beat but only hear it in a few odd places, the upset we feel is the result of syncopation. This upset can be very stimulating and contribute a prime component of jazz feeling.

Examine this manner of filling two measures.

Note that the sounds which occur, bordered by silence, in positions other than on the first and third beats seem to stand out. They seem to be self accenting. If we additionally stress these odd positions by making the sounds in those positions louder than the sounds in other positions, syncopation is enhanced: one TWO three four ONE two three FOUR.

The concept of syncopation partly depends on a listener's expectations. For example, if we are expecting to hear *ONE* two THREE four, but we actually hear one *TWO* three FOUR, we are experiencing syncopation. Jazz drummers often keep time by playing boom CHICK boom CHICK (one TWO three FOUR) instead of BOOM chick BOOM chick. This syncopation is part of what makes a performance sound like jazz. Another frequently used syncopation occurs when we hear one two three FOUR when we are expecting to hear ONE two three four. So you see that rhythm involves the arrangement of stresses in addition to just describing the arrangement of sound over time. We have also seen that a phenomenon called syncopation results when the sounds are arranged or stressed in unexpected ways. Of course, what is expected depends on what the listener is accustomed to hearing. Therefore the statement that syncopation consists of unexpected accent is inadequate. Perhaps a more useful definition involves the accent of beats other than the first and, in measure of four beats, also the third beat. Silence can also be syncopating. For example, if we encounter silence at a time when we are expecting to hear ONE, the feeling of syncopation results.

Eighth Notes

To understand more complex syncopations and another essential element of jazz feeling, the swing eighth note, requires an acquaintance with ways in which beats are divided into smaller units. Here is a measure in four, with four quarter notes to the measure. We can divide each quarter note in half to produce eighth notes.

There are two eighth notes for every quarter note. If we place accents on the eighth notes according to the way we previously accented the measure of quarter notes, we have *ONE* two three four FIVE six seven eight. The time span for a measure of eight eighth notes is identical to that in a measure of four quarter notes, but keeping track of eight eighth notes is cumbersome. So we express the eighth notes in terms of subdivided quarter notes, saying "and" for the second half of each quarter note (every other eighth note): one and two and three and four and. Each word, whether it is the name of a number, called a **downbeat**, or the word "and," called an **upbeat**, represents an eighth note.

Syncopation occurs when any upbeats receive more emphasis than downbeats. Accenting the "and's" is essential to rhythms frequently employed in jazz. The final two beats in a measure are often divided into eighth notes with the last one accented the most: three and four AND. Many notes that appear in written form on the first beat of a measure are played on the and of the fourth beat in the preceding measure when given a jazz interpretation. The practice of playing a note slightly before or slightly after it is supposed to be played is a syncopating device that jazz musicians apply to pop tunes in order to lend jazz feeling to a performance.

Triplets

The quarter note can also be divided into three equal parts to produce what are called eighth-note triplets.

Sixteenth Notes

Here, each quarter note is divided into four equal parts, called sixteenth notes.

Dotted Eighth-Sixteenth Note Pattern

So far we have examined equal divisions of the quarter note. But it is also possible to divide it into notes of unequal value, for instance, a long note and a short note. One such pattern consists of a dotted eighth note followed by a sixteenth note. A dot after a note means that the note receives one and a half times its usual value; therefore the dotted eighth note has the combined value of an eighth note and a sixteenth note.

Tied Triplet Figure

Another long-short pattern is based on the triplet division of the quarter note. The pattern is called a tied triplet figure. Here, the first note has the value of two-thirds of a quarter note, and the second has the value of one-third.

Jazz has one rhythmic quality that, to my knowledge, is not found in any other kind of music: jazz swing feeling. A discussion of it appears in the "What Is Jazz?" chapter, but that discussion hinges on the *swing eighth note* which is examined next.

Having heard the term "swing eighth note," you might wonder how, if an eighth note is simply half the duration of a quarter note, we can have different types of eighth note, swing eighth note being one of them. Strictly speaking, you cannot have different types. An eighth note is an eighth note. Our descriptive language is loose enough, however, that we can use the term to label notes of slightly more or less duration than the eighth note is understood to receive.

Legato and Staccato

This looseness in applying the term "eighth note" is not exclusive to jazz musicians. Non-jazz musicians often use terms such as **legato,** which means long or slurred together or connected. They use the term **staccato,** which means short, abruptly separated. A legato eighth note equals a full-value eighth note. A staccato eighth note, on the other hand, has variable duration. Its length depends on the style of performance, and its value may actually be less than half that of a legato eighth note. It can be called an eighth note only because it is immediately followed by silence which fills up the remaining time that a full-value eighth note requires. Perhaps a staccato eighth note should be called a sixteenth note, or it should bear some designation that is more precise than the label of "staccato eighth note."

Demo CD *Tracks 44–45* |

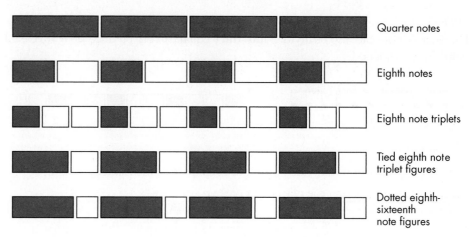

Quarter notes

Eighth notes

Eighth note triplets

Tied eighth note triplet figures

Dotted eighth-sixteenth note figures

Swing Eighth-Note Pattern

A wide assortment of eighth note durations and stresses are found in jazz styles. There are no jazz musicians who divide the beat in only one way. But there is a pattern that is more common than any other. It is a long-short sequence that is close, but not identical, to the pattern of durations found in the tied-triplet figures. The tied-triplet figure, you may remember, consists first of a long sound, then a shorter sound that is half the duration of the first sound. The two sounds together fit the duration of a single beat in the manner of a quarter-note triplet. The duration pattern most commonly employed by jazz musicians, the **swing eighth-note pattern,** falls somewhere between the tied-triplet figure and a sequence of eighth notes having identical durations. In other words, the first member of the pair is shorter than the first member of a tied-triplet pattern, and the second member is somewhat longer than a triplet eighth note. But neither member's duration is truly equal to an even eighth note, what musicians call "a straight eighth." Researcher Mark C. Ellis has found the duration ratio to range from 1.474:1 to 1.871:1, with a grand average ratio of 1.701:1. Stated differently, the ratios of long-short subdivisions ranged from approximately 3:2 to 9:5 (*Perceptual and Motor Skills*, 1991, 73, 707–713).

Demo CD *Track 43* |

The stress patterns for swing eighth-note patterns are distributed differently from player to player. Sometimes within the work of a given player, the stresses are distributed differently from performance to performance, sometimes from passage to passage. Basically, however, the first in a group of such swing eighth notes is louder than subsequent notes that occur on upbeats.

There is considerable confusion about notation of swing eighth notes. Such lack of uniformity exists in this regard that about the only accurate statement is that, when reading eighth notes, the desired choice of duration patterns usually depends upon the particular band and the style of arrangement being played. A little history might make this point a bit clearer. In countless written arrangements of jazz-oriented pieces that were published before the 1960s, dotted-eighth sixteenth figures appeared whenever the arranger wanted a swing eighth sound. (The arranger did *not* want true dotted-eighth sixteenth note patterns in which long-short meant the long member sounded three times the duration of the short one.) The notation appeared as even eighths thereafter in most arrangements, but the intention was for those notes to also be played as swing eighths. (If an arranger of this period wanted *truly even* durations, a written message appeared above the notes: "even 8ths." The musician's assumption was to otherwise play all the written eighth notes in a swing rhythm.)

Polyrhythm

To appreciate the rhythms that typify jazz, we should keep in mind the fact that several rhythms are usually played simultaneously. *Polyrhythm* (meaning *many rhythms*) is very important to jazz. When you listen carefully to a modern jazz performance, you should be able to hear several different rhythms at the same time. These include the rhythm in the melodic line, that of the bassist, the rhythm played by each of the drummer's four limbs, and each of the pianist's two hands.

Polyrhythms are often created by patterns that pit a feeling of four against a feeling of three. In other words, two measures can be played at the same time, with one being divided by multiples of two and the other being divided by multiples of three. In addition to that, the onset of one pattern is often staggered in a way which results in something less than perfect superimposition atop another pattern. Pitting three against four and staggering the placement of rhythms can project the feeling that the rhythms are tugging at each other. The resulting combination of stresses can be extremely provocative, and it can produce new syncopations in addition to those already contained in the separate patterns.

You can now understand why to say that jazz is quite rhythmic is to make an almost meaningless statement. All music has rhythm, and most music has syncopated rhythms. What sets jazz apart from many other types of music is the preponderance of syncopated rhythms, the swing eighth-note sequences, and the frequent presence of polyrhythm.

Scales, Keys, Tonality, and Modality

Understanding scales is basic to appreciating chord progressions, and an acquaintance with scales and chord progressions aids our knowledge of the rules that guide jazz improvisation. Everyone is familiar with musical scales. No one has been able to live very long without hearing a friend, neighbor, or family member practice "his scales."

Scales comprise the rudiments of beginning practice routines for singers and instrumentalists alike. Even people who cannot read music are familiar with the sequence *do* (pronounced "dough"), *re* (pronounced "ray"), *mi* (pronounced "mee"), *fa*, *sol*, *la*, *ti* (pronounced "tee"), *do*. Those eight syllables do not represent exact pitches as C, D, E, F, G, A, B, C; they are only the names of acoustic relationships. (Do not let that term, acoustic relationships, scare you. It is one of the simplest concepts in music. It means only that no matter what frequency of so many vibrations per second is assigned to *do*, the remaining seven pitches are determined by set multiples of it, for example twice the frequency, 1½ the frequency, and so forth.)

"*Do re mi fa sol la ti do*" numbers eight elements, the eighth element carrying the same name as the first, *do*. Its relationship to the first is exactly double the frequency of the first. For example, if the first *do* were 440 vibrations per second, the next higher *do* would be 880. It is no more complicated than that. That last *do* ends one sequence and begins another. The relationship between the bottom *do* and the top *do*, the first and eighth steps of the scale, is called an *octave*. The sound of two notes an octave apart is so similar that if they are played simultaneously, you can easily mistake the pair for a single tone. Most naturally produced tones contain an octave as one component of all the frequencies that combine to give a tone its own characteristic color or quality. The octave is called a harmonic or an overtone of the tone's fundamental pitch. That is the reason two tones an octave apart sound like one when they are played at the same time.

Since the interval of an eighth, from *do* to *do*, represents a doubling of frequency, you have probably guessed that those intervals between the first and the eighth must be fractions. You guessed correctly. The ratio of the fifth step (*sol*) to the first step (*do*) is ¾; that of the third (*mi*) to the first (*do*) is ¼, etc.

The seven-note scale has many labeling systems. We have already used three of them: (a) do, re, mi, fa, sol, la, ti, do; (b) first, second, third, fourth, fifth, sixth, seventh; and (c) the frequency ratios: re/do = ⅜; mi/do = ¾; fa/do = ⅓; sol/do = ½; la/do = ⅗; ti/do = ¹⅝. Next is the system that uses alphabet letters A, B, C, D, E, F and G.

Look at the diagram of the piano keyboard printed here.

↑└── an octave ──┘↑

It is constructed so that the pattern of eight white keys and five black keys recurs again and again. The distance, or interval, between the beginning of one pattern and the beginning of the next is called an "octave." The scale that beginners usually learn first is the C scale; the C scale is obtained by playing eight of the white keys in succession, starting with the one labeled C. That scale, C, D, E, F, G, A, B, C, contains the same note relationships that we know as do, re, mi, fa, sol, la, ti, do. Play the notes of the C major scale in the order in which they are numbered in the diagram.

C D E F G A B C
Do Re Mi Fa Sol La Ti Do
1 2 3 4 5 6 7 8

Look again at the piano keyboard.

The black keys are known as sharps and flats. Sharp is symbolized # (like the number sign on a keyboard) and flat is symbolized b (like the lower case b on the keyboard). The black keys derive their names from the white keys that are next to them. The black key to the right of A is called "A-sharp" because it is slightly higher than A. But it is also referred to as "B-flat" because it is slightly lower than B. If we want only a C scale, going up an octave from C to C, we use none of the black keys. But if we want scales that begin on any note other than C, we have to employ at least one (and sometimes all) of the black keys. For instance, to play a major scale on D, it is necessary to make use of two sharps, F-sharp and C-sharp.

D Major Scale

A scale may be played starting from any black or white key. Altogether there are 12 such scales. Going up (moving left to right) from C, they are the scales of C, C-sharp, D, D-sharp, E, F, F-sharp, G, G-sharp, A, A-sharp, and B. Or, naming them in descending order, C, B, B-flat, A, A-flat, G, G-flat, F, E, E-flat, D, and D-flat.

When musicians say that a tune is in a certain key, for instance, the key of C, they mean that the song is played with the notes of the major scale beginning on C.

The relationship of the notes of the major scale gives a song a particular kind of sound and structure that is called **tonality.** Although tonality is a complicated idea, it can be understood as the feeling that a song must end on a particular note or chord. A key defines a scale which, in turn, defines that key. If a piece of music has the feeling of reaching for the same note, the key note, or it seems loyal to some note more than to any other, the overall harmonic character of the piece is called **tonal.**

There is another term like the term "scale" that is not interchangeable with "key." The term is **mode.** Like a scale, a mode describes a sequence of acoustic relationships. Some modes even have the same number of elements as the scales we just explored. In fact, the C scale has a mode name: Ionian. But if we use the notes in the C scale and start the sequence on D, we produce another mode, Dorian. In other words, if we go from D to D in the key of C, we have constructed the Dorian mode (see page 493).

D E F G A B C D

Dorian mode

For each of the seven scale steps in a key, there is a corresponding mode. The major scale itself has a mode name: Ionian; beginning on the second step produces the Dorian mode; the third step, the Phrygian mode; fourth, the Lydian mode; fifth, the Mixolydian mode; sixth, the Aeolian mode; and seventh, the Locrian mode. Each has a different sound because each has a different sequence of acoustic relationships that results from starting on different steps of the scale. I urge you to find a keyboard and play these modes. The concepts outlined here mean little without the sounds they describe.

We have seen that there are 12 keys, C, C# (or Db), D, and so forth. We also know that for each key there is a corresponding seven-note scale starting on the note that bears the name of the key (C D E F G A B for the C scale). Within each key there are modes, one mode beginning on each of the seven steps. The mode constitutes an octave of its own. Scales (modes) of fewer than seven notes and greater than seven notes also exist (see pages 493–95). The most common scale constructed of more than seven notes is the chromatic, meaning simply that sequence of all the piano keys in an octave, white ones and black ones. Scale is a poor name because **the chromatic scale is actually just another way of dividing an octave into 12 equal parts.** It does not indicate a key as the C scale and the Bb scale do. *The chromatic scale is only a sequence of very small intervals called half steps.*

The chromatic scale has 12 steps: C, C#, D, D#, E, F, F#, G, G#, A, A#, and B. Unlike the modes, which have to be started on certain scale steps to guarantee their unique qualities, the chromatic scale can be started on any note, proceed through an octave and create the same identifiable chromatic quality no matter what note is chosen for its starting position. That means the C chromatic scale is identical to the C# chromatic scale (and all others). Perhaps it should be called "chromatic scale starting on C" or "chromatic scale starting on C#," specifying exactly what tone is to be the reference note.

The chromatic scale is very important because it expands the number of acoustic relations possible. Given 12 different tones in place of only seven, we have the option of raising and lowering (sharping and flatting) virtually any note we wish. Most Western European music of the past two centuries uses the chromatic scale instead of limiting itself exclusively to notes within one key at a time or, what is even more restrictive, only one mode at a time. Music was produced during the twentieth century that used all 12 tones equally and discarded the feeling of particular keys. Tonal music, you remember, is simply music that seems to be loyal to a certain note, always reaching for that note. Music without tone center is called *atonal.*

Most music has key feeling even when employing all 12 tones in the chromatic scale. This is just another way of saying that most music has tonality. During improvised music, tone centers might shift, but they usually remain long enough for their effect to be perceived. Most jazz employs tone center. It is extremely difficult to improvise without at least implying temporary tone centers and key feelings. The 12 tones are usually employed to enrich the conventional do re mi tonal orientation instead of providing a harmonic orientation all their own, one of atonality. Keep in mind that some music employs more than one key at once, but this type of music is not generally termed atonal. It is called *polytonal,* which means many keys.

If you play within the do re mi scale and enrich your melody with chromatic tones, the character of your playing can be partly described by how often you employ certain chromatic tones. Many people consider *bluesy quality* essential to jazz. A central component of bluesy quality is the frequent use of three chromatics in particular: the *flat third, flat fifth,* and *flat seventh* notes of the scale. In other words, chromatic scale tones are employed to enrich the seven tones already available.

In the key of C, the blue notes are E-flat, G-flat, and B-flat. Remember the C scale consists of C, D, E, F, G, A, and B; there are no sharps or flats (none of the piano's black keys). To create a blue note we lower the third step of the scale. In the key of C this means changing E (a white key) to E-flat (a black key). We use both E *and* E-flat in constructing jazz lines, but the E-flat stands out because it is not one of the notes in the C major scale.

| Demo CD *Track 55*

C scale without any blue notes

C scale with the flat third blue note

The second most common blue note is achieved by lowering the seventh step of the scale. In the key of C, this means changing B (a white key) to B-flat (a black key). Again we use both B *and* B-flat for our lines, but the B-flat is more distinctive because it is not in the key of C.

C scale with the flat seventh blue note (B-flat)

Note that the concepts of regular third step and blue third step are like the concepts of major chord and minor chord (the sounds of which you can demonstrate for yourself, using the following keyboard diagram as a guide to positioning your first, third, and fifth fingers).

Major chord   Minor chord

The third most used blue note is the lowered fifth. Its use was not frequent until modern jazz began in the 1940s, but thereafter it became a standard device to convey a bluesy feeling, much as the lowered third and seventh had been in early jazz. In the key of C, a flat fifth is achieved by lowering G (a white key) to G-flat (a black key).

Going up to the flat fifth (G-flat)   Coming down to the flat fifth (G-flat)

Blue Notes

The term "blue note" does not have a single, universally accepted use. Some writers use it to designate the flat third and flat seventh that were discussed above. These sounds might best be termed "chromatically lowered" pitches because they are lowered by one step of the chromatic scale, the interval known as a "half step," a "chromatic semitone." Some writers use the term "blue note" to designate any pitch that is not completely a half step below another. This makes its classification "indeterminate" because, instead of being a clearly identifiable pitch of the chromatic scale, it is a pitch we might obtain only if we could play a note from the region within the cracks between the piano keys, so to speak. Musicologists variously call such pitches "neutral thirds," "heptatonically equidistant" or "indeterminate pitches." (For a closer examination, see "Blue Notes and Blue Tonality" by William Tallmadge, *The Black Perspective in Music*, 1984, Volume 12, Number 2, pages 155–165.) These pitches cannot be produced on the piano, but that does not mean that pianists have not wanted to produce them. The recent proliferation of synthesizers in the hands of jazz-rock pianists saw the molding of numerous solos employing this second kind of blue note, apparently because synthesizers are capable of generating pitches that represent fine gradations between those found on the piano. Playing with pitches is termed "pitch bending." (See page 49, and listen to Track 58 of the *Demo CD* for examples.)

The attraction that jazz musicians have for out-of-tune thirds and sevenths might be the result of differences between European and African preferences for tuning. One origin is suggested here. The European seven-tone scale (do, re, mi, fa, sol, la, ti, do) is not based on equal divisions of the octave. It is a sequence of whole steps and half steps (the "diatonic" system) in which each half step represents about one twelfth of an octave. (The interval between C and D is a whole step, as is that between E-flat and F. The interval between B and C is a half step, as is that between E-flat and E.) A mix might have resulted between the European seven-tone approach and a West African seven-tone (heptatonic) approach in which the interval separating each successive scale tone is equal, not the unequal pattern we find in whole steps and half steps. This African "equidistant heptatonic" scale has pitches that coincide fairly closely to those in the European diatonic scale. However, the third and the seventh steps are flat in relation to their counterparts in the European scale. This means that if an African sang his own pitch in a European piece, the third and seventh steps would sound "blue" or not perfectly in-tune to the ears of a listener who was accustomed to the European scale. If African-American singers and musicians retained their taste for this particular kind of tuning, and seasoned European music to suit their tastes, then they performed European-style music in the "blue" manner we today associate with jazz.

Chords and Chord Progressions

Familiarity with the concept of scales allows us to explore the concept of chords and chord progressions, which, in turn, is essential to appreciating the harmony that jazz improvisers follow. These concepts are quite simple, but they have far-reaching applications, not only in jazz, but in all music that uses harmony.

A chord is obtained by sounding three or more notes simultaneously. Try these:

Although chords can be constructed from any tones, they are usually described in terms of scale notes and given Roman numeral names. The most common chord, one alternately described as a tonic chord, a major triad, the key chord, or a I (Roman numeral for 1) chord, employs the first, third, and fifth notes of the scale: *do, mi,* and *sol*. In other words, this chord is produced by simultaneously sounding do, mi, and sol in any key, any register, with any loudness or tone color.

Chords are named for the scale step on which they are based. A I chord is based on the first step of the scale, do; a II chord is based on the second step, re; a III chord on the third step, mi; a IV chord on fa; a V chord on sol; a VI chord on la; and a VII chord on ti. This system of naming is very handy for describing chord progressions. (See page 490 for notations.)

I chord in key of C   **I** chord in key of F-sharp

I chord in key of B-flat

A chord change is simply what it says, changing a chord. If we move from one chord to another, we have executed a **chord change.** We have moved forward, progressed, from one chord to another. In other words, a **chord progression** has been made. If the chords involved are those based on the first and second steps of the scale, respectively, we could describe the chord change as a I-II progression. If we move from a chord based on the first step to a chord based on the fourth, we create a I-IV progression. The reverse of that is a IV-I. If we move from the I chord to the V chord, and then back to the I chord, we create a I-V-I progression.

To hear the sound of a very common chord progression, the I-IV-I-V-I blues progression, find a piano, an organ, an accordion, or any other keyboard instrument and strike all the keys simultaneously, the number of counts (1234, 2234, etc.) indicated in the diagram below. You need not worry about what fingers to place on what keys. In fact, go ahead and use fingers from both hands if necessary. Try to keep a steady rate for striking the keys. If you can keep a steady rate, you may find that you are sounding

Demo CD *Track 19* | like you have heard pianists and guitarists in rhythm and blues bands sound.

1234 2234 3234 4234 (**I** chord for 4 measures)

1234 2234 (**IV** chord for 2 measures)

1234 2234 (**I** chord for 2 measures)

1234 2234 (**V** chord for 2 measures)

1234 2234 (**I** chord for 2 measures)

Chord Voicing

Most music uses chords that have been **voiced.** (For notated examples, see page 492.) The concept of voicing is a very simple concept. It involves the fact that the keyboard is a succession of repeating octaves.

└── Octave ──┘└── Octave ──┘└── Octave ── · · ·

With the resulting repetition of notes available, we can pull each chord note away from the position it holds within a single octave and spread the chord over the range of the keyboard. We can also include additional notes and/or omit some of the original notes. All these manipulations fall under the heading of "voicing."

The same chord (three notes) arranged in different positions across the keyboard.

Jazz pianists can often be identified by the way they voice chords, and characteristic preferences in piano voicing are important components of the style in almost every period of jazz. In recent jazz, for example in the work of pianists McCoy Tyner and Chick Corea, **voicing in fourths** is quite common. Voicing in fourths means that chords are made up of notes four steps away from each other. In other words, a chord voiced in fourths might contain do, fa, and ti instead of do, mi, and sol. (The interval between do and fa is called a perfect fourth. To create a perfect fourth between fa and ti, the ti must be flatted. In building a chord composed of perfect fourths, each successive note is considered do of a new scale and the fourth note, fa, in that scale is used.) You can hear the sound of a chord voiced in fourths by playing this:

Voicing in fourths

The term "voicing" also refers to how the notes of a chord are assigned to instruments in an orchestra or band. The ranges of the instruments as well as their tone colors are taken into consideration in voicing chords. Characteristic voicings serve to identify the work of different arrangers. Duke Ellington, for instance, voices chords in a manner distinguishable from Stan Kenton. Both Ellington's chords and his choice of instruments differ.

Voicing is also a term used to identify the instruments playing a melody. For example, we might say Duke Ellington "voiced the lead (the melody) for clarinet, trumpet, and tenor sax," meaning that those instruments played a unison passage in a particular Ellington arrangement.

The Blues

The term "the blues" has several meanings. It can describe

1. a sad feeling, or music that projects a sad feeling;

2. a rhymed poetic form (paired couplets in iambic pentameter);

3. a slow, funky, earthy type of music;

4. a type of chord progression, usually contained in 12 measures, that has certain predictable chord movements in the fifth, seventh, ninth, and eleventh measures;

5. any combination of the above.

Blues poetry is so common in popular music that a technical description of the positions of accent and rhyme is not necessary in order for you to recognize the form. A single, very characteristic example can serve to illustrate the structure of blues poetry:

My man don't love me, treats me awful mean. (pause)

My man don't love me, treats me awful mean. (pause)

He is the lowest man I've ever seen. (pause)

The I, IV, and V chords are basic elements of harmony used in the blues. In the 12-bar blues, which is the most common blues form, these chords are distributed over 12 measures in a particular way. Although many variations are possible, the basic form is always the same. The chords and their respective durations are shown in the following chart. Each slash (/) indicates one beat. Perhaps it is helpful for you to think of a chord played on each beat by a rhythm guitarist. Note that the principal chord changes occur in the fifth, seventh, ninth, and eleventh measures.

I				IV		I		V		I	
////	////	////	////	////	////	////	////	////	////	////	////

Although the chord relationships of the fifth, seventh, ninth, and eleventh measures usually hold, the remaining measures are the scene of countless alterations. Modern jazz blues progressions often employ more than one chord in a single measure and at least one change every measure. It is not unusual to have 10 to 20 chord changes in the space of 12 measures. Sometimes the principal chords of the fifth, seventh, ninth, and eleventh measures are also altered. When the blues is sung, the words are often distributed in a standard way over the 12-bar progression (see page 462).

A blues can be fast or slow, happy or sad. It may have lyrics, or it may be a purely instrumental piece, and its chord progressions may be simple or complex. For a piece to be a blues, the only requirement is that the I-IV-I-V-I chord progression or a variant of it be presented in a 12-measure form.

The 32-Bar A-A-B-A Tune

Another form on which jazz musicians often improvise is the 32-bar A-A-B-A tune. The 32-bar tune is made up of four eight-measure sections. The opening eight measures, called the A section, is repeated in the second section. The third part is the B section, sometimes referred to as the bridge, release, inside, or channel. The last eight bars bring back the material of the first eight. So the tune falls into what is called A-A-B-A form. Thousands of pop tunes composed during the 1920s, '30s, '40s, and '50s were 32 bars long in A-A-B-A form.

Listening for the 12-Bar Blues and 32-Bar Forms

To gain a practical familiarity with chord progressions, glance at the list of tunes on page 463. These are categorized as 12-bar blues or 32-bar tunes in A-A-B-A form. Go to a record collection and find performances of tunes on the list, and choose one of them. Listen to approximately the first 30 seconds to determine whether this rendition has an introduction or begins immediately with the tune itself. Also determine how fast the beats are passing. A clue can often be found in the bass playing. If the bass is walking, there is a bass note for every beat, four beats to the measure. Listening to that sound, you should be able to hear the pulse as though the bassist were a metronome. The sound of the drummer's ride cymbal may also be a good indication of where the beats lie.

Having listened long enough to determine the tempo, you will also have discovered whether there is an introduction, and the point at which it ends and the tune begins. If you are not sure whether the beginning of the piece is an introduction or part of the tune itself, wait a while and listen for it to recur. If it does not recur, it is probably an introduction. In A-A-B-A form, the first part, A, is immediately repeated, A-A, before a new section, B, occurs. The routine for most 12-bar blues tunes consists of repeating the entire 12 bars before beginning improvisation. Musicians occasionally use the same music for an ending that they used for the introduction. So if you hear something familiar at the end that does not seem to fit exactly in 12 or 32 bars, it may be the introduction attached for use as an ending.

By now you should know both the tempo at which to count beats and the moment to begin counting. Start when the tune itself starts (right after the introduction, in most cases). For a 12-bar blues count: "1234, 2234, 3234, 4234, 5234, 6234, 7234, 8234, 9234, 10 234, 11 234, 12 234." Listen and count until you can detect the chord changes in measures five, seven, nine, and eleven:

I				IV		I		V		I	
////	////	////	////	////	////	////	////	////	////	////	////

If your counting is accurate, you will eventually be able to anticipate these important chord changes. That should provide some insight into harmonies that the jazz musician uses in his improvisation.

Count like this for a 32-bar A-A-B-A tune:

	"1234	2234	3234	4234	5234	6234	7234	8234
repeat	234	2234	3234	4234	5234	6234	7234	8234
bridge	234	2234	3234	4234	5234	6234	7234	8234
back to A	234	2234	3234	4234	5234	6234	7234	8234."

| Demo CD *Track 33*

Listen and count over and over until you can not only hear the bridge and the repeated sections, A-A, when they occur, but anticipate them. Do not become discouraged if you find it necessary to start and stop many times. Counting beats and measures requires practice. It is very important because it may be your only clue to the tune's form once a soloist has begun improvising. Learning to count accurately may take a few minutes, a few hours, or even a few days, but it is essential to an understanding of jazz improvisation. It will be well worth the effort. You might get especially good at anticipating the B section. If you know the tune, or can learn it by listening a few times, try humming it while listening to the soloists improvise on its chord changes. This will help clarify the relationship between the improvisation and the original tune. It will also help you keep your place.

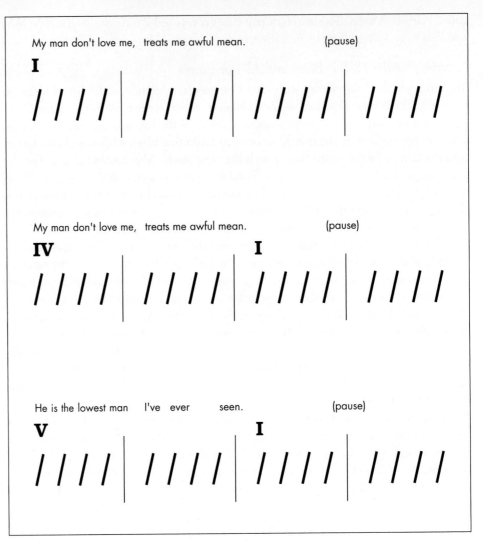

My man don't love me,   treats me awful mean.   (pause)

I

/ / / / | / / / / | / / / / | / / / /

My man don't love me,   treats me awful mean.   (pause)

IV   **I**

/ / / / | / / / / | / / / / | / / / /

He is the lowest man   I've ever   seen.   (pause)

V   **I**

/ / / / | / / / / | / / / / | / / / /

Blues poetic form in relation to the 12-bar blues chord progression. The lyrics shown are from Billie Holiday's "Fine and Mellow." Available on LP as *The Sound of Jazz* (Columbia: CK 45234, 1957), on video as *The Sound of Jazz* (Idem: 1058, 1957), on CD as *The Sound of Jazz* (Columbia: CK 6608, 1957).

Detecting Other Forms

Not all tunes fit into the 12-bar blues form or the 32-bar A-A-B-A form. "I'll Remember April" is a 48-bar A-B-C-D-A-B form. "I've Got You Under My Skin" is a 56-bar A-B-A-C-D-E-F form. Together, the 12-bar blues form and the 32-bar A-A-B-A form probably describe more tunes than any other single form, but they actually describe less than 40 percent of all tunes written between 1910 and 1960. Let us examine a few other forms.

The 12-bar blues is a particular set of chord progressions (I-IV-I-V-I) in a 12-measure package. There are 12-bar forms that are not blues simply because they do not follow the I-IV-I-V-I progression or any variation of it. For example, Richard Rodgers's "Little Girl Blue" is an A-A-B form in which each section is 12 bars long, but it is not a blues. It is also not uncommon in pop tunes to find a 12-bar section that is actually an eight-bar progression with an extra four-bar progression connected to it.

The word "blues" in a song title does not necessarily signify the 12-bar blues form. Both musicians and nonmusicians use the term "blues" to describe any slow, sad tune regardless of its chord progression. "Birth of the Blues" is a 32-bar A-A-B-A tune and "Sugar Blues" is an eighteen-bar tune. The "St. Louis Blues" is actually a 12-bar blues plus an eight-bar bridge and an additional 12-bar blues. Performers sometimes choose to repeat, delete, and reorder sections of "St. Louis Blues" when they play it.

Compositions in 12-Bar Blues and 32-Bar A-A-B-A Forms

12-BAR BLUES COMPOSITIONS

"Bags' Groove"

"Barbados"

"Billie's Bounce"

"Bloomdido"

"Bluesology"

"Blue Monk"

"Blue 'n' Boogie"

"Blues in the Closet"

"Blue Trane"

"Cheryl"

"Cool Blues"

"Cousin Mary"

"Footprints"

"Freddie the Freeloader"

"Goodbye Porkpie Hat"

"Jumpin' with Symphony Sid"

"Mr. P. C."

"Now's the Time"

"One O'Clock Jump"

"Sid's Ahead"

"Soft Winds"

"Straight, No Chaser"

"Walkin'"

"Woodchopper's Ball"

COMPOSITIONS WITH 32-BAR A-A-B-A CONSTRUCTION

"Ain't Misbehavin'"

"Angel Eyes"

"Anthropology"

"Birth of the Blues"

"Blue Moon"

"Body and Soul"

"Budo" ("Hallucinations")

"Darn That Dream"

"Don't Blame Me"

"Don't Get Around Much Anymore"

"Easy Living"

"52nd Street Theme"

"Flamingo"

"Four Brothers"

"Good Bait"

"Have You Met Miss Jones?"

"I Can't Get Started"

"I Cover the Waterfront"

"I Love You"

"I'm Beginning to See the Light"

"It's Only a Paper Moon"

"I Want to Talk About You"

"Jordu"

"Lady Be Good"

"Lover Man"

"Lullaby of Birdland"

"Makin' Whoopee"

"Man I Love, The"

"Midnight Sun"

"Misty"

"Moten Swing"

"Move"

"Oleo"

"Over the Rainbow"

"Perdido"

"Robin's Nest"

"Rosetta"

"'Round Midnight"

"Ruby, My Dear"

"Satin Doll"

"September Song"

"Take the 'A' Train"

"Well, You Needn't"

"What's New?"

"What Is This Thing Called Love?"

Some people use the terms "eight-bar blues" and "16-bar blues." Usually the tune they are describing has the I-IV movement in the first five bars and deviates from the 12-bar I-IV-I-V-I progression thereafter. Some tunes of lengths other than 12 bars sound very much like 12-bar blues simply because they contain the I-IV-I-V-I progression, but the durations of a few chords may be changed, and certain sections may be repeated. Herbie Hancock's "Watermelon Man," for example, has been called a "16-bar blues."

Unlike the 12-bar blues, the 32 bar A-A-B-A form is not always based on the same basic chord progression. Many different chord progressions have been used in the A-A-B-A form. Fats Waller's "Honeysuckle Rose" and Erroll Garner's "Misty" are both 32-bar A-A-B-A tunes, yet they have almost completely different chord progressions.

The form A-A-B-A does not always contain 32 bars nor does each section necessarily have the same number of measures. In "Girl from Ipanema," which is A-A-B-A, the A section has eight bars while the bridge has 16. In "Secret Love," another A-A-B-A tune, the A section has 16 bars while the bridge has only eight.

There are also elongated versions of the basic 12-bar blues and 32-bar A-A-B-A forms. Lee Morgan's "Sidewinder" is a 24-bar blues: each chord lasts twice as long as it would in a 12-bar blues. Another example is the 64-bar A-A-B-A form in which each section is 16 bars long instead of eight. Ray Noble's "Cherokee" and Lerner and Loewe's "On the Street Where You Live" are both 64-bar A-A-B-A tunes. Charlie Parker's "Ko-Ko" is based on the chord changes of "Cherokee"; consequently it is also a 64-bar A-A-B-A tune. There are shortened versions of the 32-bar A-A-B-A, too. Sonny Rollins's "Doxy" is a 16-bar A-A-B-A tune; each section is only four bars long.

A-A-B-A is not the only common 32-bar form for pop tunes. Numerous tunes fit an A-B-A-C form (both the C section and the B section differ from the A section). "My Romance," "On Green Dolphin Street," "Indiana," "Sweet Georgia Brown," and "Out of Nowhere" all fall into a 32-bar A-B-A-C form. In addition to the 32-bar A-A-B-A and A-B-A-C, there is also the 32-bar A-B-A-B. "How High the Moon" is an example. There are shortened versions of these, also. "Summertime" is a 16-bar A-B-A-C tune.

Hundreds of tunes fit into 16 measures. "Peg o' My Heart" is a 16-bar pop tune. Horace Silver based his "The Preacher" on the 16-bar pop tune "Show Me the Way to Go Home." Wayne Shorter has written many 16-bar tunes, including "E.S.P.," "Nefertiti," "Prince of Darkness," etc. Some chord progressions are used in 16-bar tunes almost as often as the I-IV-I-V-I progression appears in the 12-bar blues. Certain 16-bar progressions have become standard.

Verse and Chorus. It is important to note that the forms we have been examining refer only to chorus length. A large number of tunes consist of two major parts: a verse followed by a chorus. The verse traditionally differs from the chorus in tempo, mood, and harmony:

1. The chorus might be played at a faster tempo than the verse.

2. Verses are often performed freely, with accelerations and decelerations of tempo.

3. The verse might feel as though it is leading up to something, whereas the chorus usually has the stamp of finality to it.

4. There may be little similarity between chord progressions used in the verse and those in the chorus.

5. The key of the verse is sometimes different from that of the chorus.

6. Choruses are repeated, but once a verse is played, it is usually over for the entire performance.

7. The chorus is the section of the tune that jazz musicians usually choose as basis for improvisation.

Breaking into Multiples of Two. When you are listening to performances and trying to detect forms, be aware that arrangements of 32-bar A-A-B-A, A-B-A-C, and A-B-A-B tunes sometimes depart from strict repetition of those 32 bars. Arrangements sometimes contain four-, eight-, and 16-bar sections, formed by omitting or adding to portions of the original 32-bar tune. Note also that many tunes, especially pre-1930s Dixieland tunes, have long, elaborate forms similar to those of marches and of nineteenth-century European dance music (such as the quadrille). Forms for many tunes in pre-1920s jazz were derived from march music. A piece might have a series of sections consisting of multiples of eight bars. Designating each section by a letter of the alphabet, a piece might conceivably follow a pattern like this:

$$A - A - B - B - C - D - E - F - C - D - E - F$$
$$16-16-16-16-16-16-24-32-16-16-24-32$$

When listening for form, keep in mind that even in the most intricate pieces, forms can usually be broken down into two-bar segments. So if you are unable to divide a piece neatly into either four-bar or eight-bar sections, try using a few two-bar sections. "Sugar Blues" can be heard as 18 or as 8+10 or as 8+8+2. That form poses problems for the improviser because it tends to break the flow of ideas conceived in four- and eight-bar melodic units. It is like being forced to walk left, right, left, right, left, left, right. The form of the original "I Got Rhythm" is:

$$A — A — B — A + tag$$
$$8 — 8 — 8 — 8 + 2 \text{ or}$$
$$8 — 8 — 8 — 10$$

When jazz musicians improvise on its chord progression, they omit the two-bar tag. If included, the tag would interrupt the flow of the improvisations and again be like having to take two steps with your left foot before going back to an alternation of right with left. Another popular tune that has an unusual structure is "Moonlight in Vermont." It follows the form:

$$A — A — B — A + tag$$
$$6 — 6 — 8 — 6 + 2$$

Modal Forms

During the late 1950s and especially during the 1960s and 1970s, modal forms practically eliminated the "change" part of "chord change." In modal music, improvisations are based on the extended repetition of one or two chords. Those chords contain so many notes that they either include or are compatible with all the notes in a scale. The term mode is synonymous with scale, hence the term "modal music." Although this is not the definition of modal employed by classical composers and in textbooks on classical music, it is what jazz musicians and jazz journalists have come to mean by "modal." In most instances, jazz musicians also employ notes that are not contained in the mode or in the repeated chords. Some of John Coltrane's work, for example, is not strictly modal, but has the flavor of music that is.

In modal music, the entire improvised portion of the performance is often based on a single chord and scale. Usually the chord and its scale are minor, Indian, Middle Eastern, or in some way more exotic-sounding than the chords used in most pop tune progressions. Because it is based on a single scale, the music has no real chord changes, just a drone.

Sometimes a melody containing chord changes of its own precedes the improvised section of a modal performance. John Coltrane's recordings of the Rodgers and Hammerstein tune "My Favorite Things" are good examples. Coltrane played the original melody while his rhythm section played the appropriate chord changes. Then the entire group improvised only on the primary chord of the tune (and the scale compatible with that chord). Near the end of their improvisations, they switched to another chord, which lent the piece a slightly different character. Coltrane could have retained the chord progressions of the tune and used them as the basis for improvisation, but he chose not to.

Some modal music does have chord changes or "mode changes." One rich chord (or scale, depending on how one cares to conceive it) is the basis for four, eight, or perhaps 16 measures. Then a different chord is in effect for another similar duration. The Miles Davis tune "Milestones" is based on one mode for the first 16 bars, a different mode for the second 16 bars, and a return to the original mode for the final eight bars. The melody has the form A-A-B-B-A, and each section is eight bars long. Herbie Hancock's "Maiden Voyage" has a 32-bar A-A-B-A construction; here each mode lasts for four bars. The A section is based on two different modes, each lasting only four bars. The B section makes use of another two modes also lasting four bars each. If each mode were labeled by letter name, "Maiden Voyage" could be described as X-Y-X-Y-Z-W-X-Y. "So What" (on the Miles Davis album *Kind of Blue*) has a melody in 32-bar A-A-B-A form, and the use of modes corresponds to that form: there are 16 bars of one mode, eight of another, and a return to the original mode for the last eight bars. John Coltrane's "Impressions" not only takes the same form as "So What" but also uses exactly the same modes. (See pages 495–97 for modes on "Milestones," "Maiden Voyage," and "So What.")

Much jazz of the 1960s and 1970s was based on infrequent chord changes (another way of saying modal) instead of the frequent chord changes found in most 12-bar blues and 32-bar forms. Many groups abandoned both the blues form and the 32-bar forms. Some groups used complex melodies and intricate rhythm section figures, yet their improvisations were based almost exclusively on one or a small number of chords ("Freedom Jazz Dance," for example).

The Effects of Form on Improvisation

Song forms of four- and eight-bar sections tend to break improvisations into small segments of similar length. Divisions of form, in other words, can influence the flow of improvised lines. This is not necessarily a disadvantage, however. The divisions in form can frame well-chosen melodic figures, and they can provide a means of transition from one figure to another. This creates more continuity than a solo might contain without chord progressions. Forms based on single modes sounding indefinitely tend to free the improviser, enabling him to create lines that are as long or short, tense or relaxed as he desires. No preset tension-relaxation devices in the form of chord progressions are there to suggest construction patterns for his improvised lines.

Bridges. The B section of an A-A-B-A tune is called the bridge. It bridges the gap between repetition of the A sections, and it usually provides a contrast to the material in the A sections. The bridge can break up or lift the mood established by repeated A sections. Many bridges are placed a few keys higher than the A section. A key change can be a boost in any situation, but is especially effective after the repeated A sections.

The bridge is important to improvisers because a good improviser can capitalize on the bridge's natural capacity to provide contrast. Some of the greatest solo segments in jazz are those improvised over the chord progressions of a tune's bridge. The rhythm section also takes advantage of the bridge and is often especially active just before the bridge is entered and just before it is exited. Heightened rhythmic activity can announce the arrival or departure of the bridge.

Combos often use the bridge as a container for solo spots. Sometimes a tune's melody will be played for the final time in the performance, and when the bridge occurs, everyone stops playing except the drummer. It becomes his feature. Then the entire band returns precisely on the first beat of the final A section.

In some jazz tunes the bridge consists only of chord changes. Such pieces require improvisation during the bridge but return to the written melody when the final A section is reached. Sonny Rollins's tune "Oleo" is an example. Many groups also use that approach on "The Theme," a popular up-tempo number for jazz combos of the late 1950s and early 1960s.

Turnarounds. Another important part in the construction of standard tunes is the turnaround (also known as the turnabout or turnback). In many, perhaps in most songs, the seventh and eighth measures of each section are occupied by a single sustained tone or two long tones (see below). That part of the tune might be considered dead space due to the lack of melodic movement, but the jazz musician uses that space. He fills it with chord changes that lead directly to the beginning of the next section. Jazz musicians are expected to know a variety of chord progressions common to turnarounds. The manner in which they fill that space with chord changes and improvised lines is the art of the turnaround. (See page 491 for common progressions.)

The whole combo digs in when a turnaround comes up. Drummers tend to kick more and, thus, tie together the musical statements of one section and bring in the next. Those bassists who almost invariably walk are more likely to vary this pattern in a turnaround. Tension can be built during a turnaround and resolved by the onset of the next section of the piece.

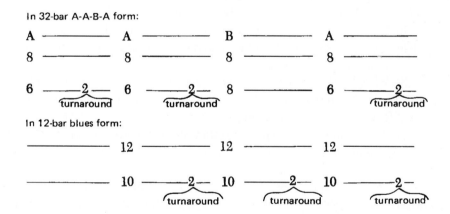

Phrasing in Relation to Form

Jazz musicians prior to the mid-1940s tended to improvise phrases that coincided with the tune structure. Most progressions consist of two- and four-bar units, and improvised solos often proceeded in phrases of similar length. Furthermore, soloists tended to make larger silences at or near the end of an A section or B section. They rarely connected tune sections by continuing phrases through the turnarounds. They stopped at or before the turnarounds, and then started anew at the beginning of the next section. They treated the eighth bar line as a barrier. Twelve-bar blues solos often contained phrases that started at the beginning of each chorus regardless of what happened at the end of a previous chorus, thus treating the twelfth bar line as a barrier.

One characteristic of modern jazz (beginning in the 1940s) and the music of the players who most influenced it was the use of phrases that began somewhere within an eight-bar section and continued into the next section without a pause. There was no lull during the turnaround.

A characteristic of some modern jazz during the 1960s and 1970s was the absence of preset chord progressions. That free approach significantly loosened the tendencies of jazz phrasing. Although players retained patterns common to preceding jazz eras, they were free to phrase with greater variety due to the lack of underlying chord movements. Some jazz of this type projects a feeling of expansiveness quite unlike the crowded feeling often projected by modern jazz of the 1940s and 1950s.

Some tunes that appeared during the 1960s, especially those of Wayne Shorter, were 16 or more bars without any repeated sections. The A section was not repeated, there was no bridge, no turnaround. These tunes were "all A." That form enabled improvisers to play with great continuity yet without the crowded, segmented feeling which sometimes characterizes improvisations based on standard A-A-B-A and A-B-A-C forms with the usual turnarounds and bridges. Sometimes a free, floating feeling could be projected by improvisers using these "all A" forms.

Tone Color

An important element of music, usually the first to be perceived, is tone quality or tone color. This element is also known as timbre (pronounced tamm' burr).

How can you tell the difference between the sound of a flute and the sound of a trumpet if they each play only one note, and it is the same note? The difference is tone color, the spectrum of frequencies generated by each instrument in its own unique way.

This definition is an oversimplification of a complex situation in which many factors come into play.

The spectrum of frequencies produced by an instrument is not fixed. The spectrum varies depending on the pitch and the forcefulness with which it is played. The ways in which a player starts and stops a note, the attack and release, also are important in determining tone color. The attack and release are accompanied by temporary changes in a tone's frequency spectrum.

Another complication arises from our tendency to associate an instrument's tone color with the aggregate effects of all the notes being played on it rather than the spectrum of frequencies present in a single note.

Finally, when sounds come to our ears, they are modified by room acoustics and by recording and playback techniques. The way our ears deal with that variability is quite involved.

Tone color varies greatly from one instrument to another, and there are also especially discernible differences in tone color among jazz musicians playing the same instrument. For example, to speak of the tenor sax tone color of John Coltrane or Stan Getz is to describe sounds so unique that some inexperienced listeners could differentiate them as easily as they could distinguish flute from trumpet. The evolution of jazz tenor saxophone playing reflects not only changes in the phrasing and rhythms, but also changes in tone color.

Tone color is a very personal characteristic of a player's style. Jazz musicians place great emphasis on creating the particular tone colors they want. A jazz musician's attention to tone color is comparable to an actor's concern for costume, make-up, and voice quality combined. Tone color is so important to saxophonists that many spend lifetimes searching for the perfect mouthpiece. They also experiment with different methods of blowing and different ways of altering the vibrating surface of the cane reeds that are attached to their mouthpieces.

Because the tenor saxophone is capable of producing an exceptionally wide variety of tone colors, it is easier to differentiate jazz tenor saxophonists by tone color alone than it is to recognize a particular trumpeter or pianist. That is not to say that differences are absent from trumpeter to trumpeter or from pianist to pianist. The differences are just more subtle.

Two pianists can play the same piece on the same piano and produce quite different sounds. No two pianos have the same tone color, and one piano can produce distinctly different tone colors, depending on how hard the keys are struck. The use of the pedals and a pianist's timing in releasing one key and striking the next are crucial to the sound. A key may be released before, after, or at the same time as the next is struck. When a note is short and ends well before the next note begins, we call it a staccato note. If one key is released after the next is struck, the two sounds overlap in time. Notes played smoothly one after the other are said to be legato. The amount of overlap influences the clarity of attack and the dimension of legato-staccato. Our ears hear sounds in combined form rather than as single tones. Whatever is left in the air from a preceding sound mixes and colors the subsequent sound. The relationship between consecutive sounds, ranging from complete separation to extreme overlapping, are resources that contribute to the personal character of a pianist's style. Count Basie's touch and tone color differ remarkably from Duke Ellington's. Perhaps you will perceive Basie's touch as lighter than Ellington's. No matter how you describe the sound, you will notice a difference if you listen carefully.

Guitarists's interest in tone color is manifested by their search for different types of picks, guitar strings, and amplifiers. Guitar amplifier dial settings are essential to the control of tone color. Bass players are also concerned with many of the same factors.

Trumpeters and trombonists explore available tone colors by experimenting with mouthpiece changes, methods of blowing, mutes, and instruments that represent different manufacturers and models.

| Demo CD *Track 63*

Trumpet with Harmon mute.
(Photo by Dan Morgan)

Straight

Cup

Plumber's Plunger

Harmon
without stem

Stem for
Harmon

Trombonist Quentin Jackson playing into plunger mute.
(Photo courtesy of John Richmond)

Miles Davis playing into cup mute.
(Courtesy of Frank Driggs)

Trombonist Dicky Wells playing into straight mute.
(Photo by William Gottlieb)

Intonation is also an important aspect of tone. Intonation refers to playing in tune, playing sharp or flat. "Playing sharp" means playing at a pitch level somewhat higher than the average pitch of the ensemble. "Playing flat" refers to playing a pitch somewhat lower than that of the ensemble. Do not confuse the terms sharp and flat with words describing actual note names such as C-sharp and B-flat. These notes are raised (sharped) and lowered (flatted) by a larger amount than is usually the case in out-of-tune playing. That is, the interval between C and C-sharp is greater than the interval between C and that of a performer playing C a bit sharper than his fellow ensemble members. Small deviations of pitch occur all the time even in the best ensembles, but larger deviations lead listeners to comment "someone is playing out of tune."

Why is intonation described in this section on tone color? Intonation affects the tone color of both the soloist and the ensemble as a whole. If a group of musicians played the same piece twice, once without listening or adjusting to each other's pitch (perhaps by pretuning their instruments and then wearing ear plugs for the performance), and then a second time, listening carefully to each other's pitch and continuously adjusting accordingly, you would hear two performances, each having distinctly different tone colors. Ensembles that lack precision tuning have a thicker, rougher sound than precisely tuned ensembles. One element of a slick ensemble sound is careful and consistent tuning.

For tone color reasons, some soloists systematically play a little "high," meaning a bit sharp. Intonation is a musical resource for them. This is common in most types of music, including symphonic, but it is especially true for jazz soloists. A tone cuts through an ensemble if it is a bit sharper than the average pitch of that ensemble. Some jazz soloists, Johnny Hodges, Stan Getz, and Paul Desmond, for instance, play at the average pitch, whereas Charlie Parker and John Coltrane, for instance, tend to various degrees of sharpness. That is another component of tone color that helps us identify a particular player's work.

APPENDIX C
Strategies for Buying Recorded Music

Minimizing Risk in Selecting Albums

One key to being a happy jazz fan is finding the right recordings. This section of the book provides guidelines and short cuts to help you.

1. **Beware of endorsements in newspapers and magazines.** They represent knowledge and understanding no greater than that of one individual. The reviewer might not be knowledgeable or perceptive. Moreover, his tastes might differ from yours. For instance, staples in the record collections of musicians are sometimes unknown by many critics, and some of these masterpieces were given only lukewarm reviews by the critics who did notice them. Albums that win Grammy awards are not necessarily outstanding, either. Usually they are merely among the albums that the largest companies want to promote. They nominate these for consideration by recording industry members who have not heard most of the jazz albums released within the preceding 12 months. (Over a thousand jazz albums are issued each year in the U.S. alone.) A parallel might be helpful. You probably remember a few Academy Award winning movies you did not find enjoyable. Conversely, you might have also found yourself liking a few movies that received bad reviews. You may have been impressed by a few movies that no one was talking about, too. Similarly, *albums receiving the most press and airplay are not necessarily the highest quality*. Extent of press and airplay is determined largely by the record company's promotional budget, luck and persistence, plus the tastes of disc jockeys and journalists. Some of the best albums never get publicized.

2. **Listen to the music before you buy it.** Try to avoid album buying as an impulse purchase. Unless you want a record for purely academic reasons or historical perspective, you might realize too late that you spent your money on something you don't enjoy. This is worth keeping in mind unless you can afford to experiment expensively. Friends, libraries, jazz courses, and radio programs can often expose you to new albums. If there is a jazz program on a college radio station near you, don't hesitate to phone and ask them to play a particular album. (College radio stations not only broadcast more jazz than commercial stations, but they are also more likely to be interested in your requests.) And when you hear something you like, you could also phone the station and ask for its album title and record company name. National Public Radio stations sometimes broadcast jazz and accept requests by phone.

3. **Use a broad sampling of recordings before forming your opinion of a particular player.** One good reason is that *few jazz improvisers are extremely consistent in producing inspired recordings*. Some of even the greatest jazz musicians have had whole strings of unexciting albums. This means that, if the only recording you hear is from an off day for that player, you derive a nonrepresentative view of his talent. You are not fair to the musician.

   Another reason for using a broad sampling is that, *if the player had more than one style period in his career, you cheat yourself if you draw a conclusion from sampling only one of them*. For instance, Sonny Rollins had a creative peak in the middle 1950s, and another in the 1990s with a different style. This means that, if you heard a few recent Rollins records and did not like them, you might not seek any mid-1950s Rollins material, even though you might have liked it. The converse would also be true.

4. **Don't accept substitutions.**   The quality and character of improvised music can vary drastically from album to album, even if made by the same band during the same period as the music you seek. So once you decide which albums you really want, don't get others first, merely because they are available and look similar.

5. **Don't wait for your desired albums to appear in stores.**   They probably won't appear. Quality of music and availability often seem inversely related. Try internet sources, and stick to what you really want.

Confusing Album Titles

Be suspicious of titles for compilations. Let's examine reasons for caution with two categories of compilations: (a) *Greatest Hits* and (b) *The Best of, The Indispensable,* and *The Essential.* **Problems for both categories often occur when the compilation comes from only one company's recordings,** and that particular company did not record the artist during his creative peak (invalidating *The Best of* designation) or during his height of popularity (invalidating the *Greatest Hits* designation). Another company did. For example, a Verve album of 1950s recordings called *The Essential Lester Young* is probably "essential" only to those Lester Young collectors who already have much of Young's creative peak represented in his 1930s Count Basie recordings, reissued by Columbia/SONY and Decca/MCA/GRP.

A second set of problems arises **when musicians have had several different styles during their careers** and a creative peak for each. They may have been recording for a different company during each important period. For example, John Coltrane made important recordings as a bandleader for three different companies (Prestige, Atlantic, and Impulse). Each company documented a stylistically different stage in his career. (And some of his best work was recorded with Miles Davis's bands for Columbia, a *fourth* record company.) This means, for example, that an Atlantic album called *The Best of John Coltrane* cannot contain Coltrane's best work from all three periods—although it could sample some of his best Atlantic sessions if the compiler knew what he was doing.

A third set of problems results **when musicians made their best recordings as sidemen in the bands of others,** not as bandleaders, yet the compilation draws only from recording sessions where they were bandleaders. For instance, Lester Young's best work was done as a sideman with the 1936–41 combos and big bands associated with Count Basie. The music on his combo recordings as leader does not sound like his music on the Basie recordings. This means that an Emarcy album called *Pres at His Very Best*, containing music from 1943–44 in which Young was bandleader, is probably not his "very" best recorded improvisations, though it might represent the best playing he recorded as a bandleader. The Emarcy album title is misleading.

Here are some other examples of the confusion arising from album titles not coordinated with varied careers. In the 1960s, pianist Herbie Hancock and saxophonist Wayne Shorter both recorded for Blue Note as bandleaders. During much of that time they were also recording for Columbia as sidemen in the Miles Davis Quintet. Most of their playing on the Davis recordings is superior to that on their own records. But since they were bandleaders for Blue Note, the Blue Note recordings, not the Columbia recordings, provide the pool for albums titled *The Best of Herbie Hancock* and *The Best of Wayne Shorter*. Hancock's and Shorter's work on Blue Note is excellent music, and it also features the outstanding composing for which Hancock and Shorter are distinguished. But when heard strictly as piano and saxophone improvising, their work on

Blue Note may not be the absolute best of either man's career, as claimed by an album title. Incidentally, a Columbia album called *The Best of Herbie Hancock* (JC 36309) contains neither his innovative playing with the 1963–69 Miles Davis groups nor his distinguished composing within the Blue Note work. The album samples a third facet: Hancock's jazz-rock material of the 1970s.

A fourth reason for approaching compilation titles with caution is that **sometimes compilers are not qualified for their task.** This means that, even if an artist recorded solely for one company during his creative peak, a *Best of* album might omit his *best* work because the person in charge of preparing the compilation was not familiar enough with all of the artist's work for that firm. The compiler might not have had sufficiently developed taste, either, or he did not realize how much he needed to call upon the taste and knowledge of consultants. This may explain why a number of single-company compilations of several jazz giants, which emerged on compact disc during the 1990s, had knowledgeable consumers wondering why so many unremarkable selections had been included while outstanding performances remained untapped in the company's vaults. It might also explain why even a few multi-company compilations have had knowledgeable jazz fans puzzled about odd choices.

Greatest Hits can be misleading as an album title because, in addition to all the previously mentioned problems, a player's best selling material might not even appear on it. For example, the largest-selling Miles Davis recording for Columbia was his 1969 *Bitches Brew* (GP 26). Yet it is not represented on the Columbia album *Miles Davis's Greatest Hits* (PC 9808). The 1964 recording of "Girl From Ipanema" for the Verve company was the highest selling recording of Stan Getz's career. Yet there is an album titled *Stan Getz's Greatest Hits* (Prestige 7337) drawn from 1949 and 1950 sessions made for the Prestige company. The Prestige material is excellent, perhaps better than the Verve material, yet it does not include his largest selling hits as the album title deceptively implies.

To avoid being misled by compilation titles, first learn about the musician's career. Then check details on the album wrapper or box insert to confirm that recording dates, titles, and personnel match what you seek. It is also wise to consult authorities to determine what companies were recording the artist during critical portions of his career and what selections are deemed outstanding.

By seeking prescreened items such as the types of anthologies discussed above, rather than making impulse purchases, you lessen risks in finding music you will want to keep. Ultimately you need to remember, however, that the main reason for buying compilations and samplers is to become familiar with a wide range of music for a small price. But also bear in mind that just because selections on the samplers are critically acclaimed or generally popular does not guarantee you will like them.

While you are pursuing this strategy, you will rarely see a desired album in the stores. Jazz fans have become accustomed to the fact that *most current jazz albums must be special-ordered, and all out-of-print albums must be obtained through special sources.* So-called out-of-print material frequently becomes available in repackaged formats, discussed below as reissues. Sources are listed on page 477.

Locating Albums

Many people think certain albums are available only in big city stores. But no matter where you live, **most albums can be obtained off the internet.** In fact, many of them will never surface in big city stores. It might be more practical to get albums by internet sources even if you live in or near a big city that has many music stores, such as New York or Los Angeles, for instance. The cost of getting there could exceed the price of an album. When you arrive at the store, the clerk may end up ordering your request by mail anyway. The main point is that *most of the jazz albums mentioned in this book will not be found in average stores.* If they are available to a store, they will probably require a special order. You therefore ought to phone ahead to determine whether traveling an inconvenient distance will be worthwhile. Some stores accept special orders over the phone. You then need only call the store periodically, and find out whether your order has arrived. Some will mail them to you, also. Keep in mind, however, that most stores are not interested in your special order business. It is an unprofitable hassle for them, though they will often fail to admit this to you. They will take forever to fill your order or never bother to notify you when they give up trying to find a particular item. Perhaps the most expedient path is to forget the stores, and go mail order. A few reliable sources are listed at the end of this section. Incidentally, out-of-print records can be obtained by getting your name on the mailing lists for jazz record auctions. You merely scan their fliers and, then bid by mail on what you want. The addresses for jazz magazines and specialty record stores on page 477 and 484 can be used to begin this process. Note that auctioneers advertise in jazz magazines.

About Reissues

When seeking out-of-print recordings, there are several things to keep in mind. Many jazz recordings which have disappeared from catalog listings return later in altered form. This includes the category known as *reissues, re-releases,* and *repackages*. Before we discuss them, here is some relevant history. Prior to the widespread use of 12-inch, 33⅓ rpm (revolutions per minute) LP (long play) records, most jazz was issued on ten-inch, 78 rpm records. Twelve-inch 33s were not common until the 1950s, so many bop and cool style bands—in addition to Dixieland and swing bands—were initially presented on 78s. Due to the size of the record and the speed of rotation, most 78s could accommodate only about three minutes of music per side. An *album* consisted of several records packaged much like a photo album. Each record had its own pocket or sleeve. The set was bound in cloth or leather. Then when the LP arrived, many of the three-minute selections originally on 78 were issued again (reissued) as compilations within 33⅓ rpm albums. This time, the word *album* meant one disc containing many selections. All the recordings in this book's premodern section and a few modern items are to be found in this kind of "reissue." Later on, LPs themselves began to be reissued, re-released, and repackaged as "new" LPs. Then when compact disc technology emerged, the contents of old LPs began appearing in CD format. Sometimes additional selections were included when the album was reissued on CD because the CD could accommodate up to about 77 minutes of music instead of the 50-minute limit that was common for LPs. Sometimes two LPs were represented on one CD. This is the altered form in which you can often find music originally available on recordings which have "disappeared" from the catalog.

Many albums that are no longer marketed by U.S. firms are available in foreign countries under the same titles they carried before they went out of print in the U.S. For instance, Japanese and European distributors have been repackaging out-of-print American albums, sometimes selling them with the original album jacket art and liner notes intact. Because of this, a list of importers and their addresses appears on page 477. More can be found advertised in jazz magazines. Relying on imports is not always dependable. So first match tune titles, personnel, and recording dates to determine whether a foreign release is the same as the American original you seek.

There is something else to consider when searching for a reissue of a particular recording. *It is common for jazz groups to record several versions of the same tunes, and some players record the same tunes with different groups.* Since you are a jazz fan, you are seeking recordings of particular improvisations, not merely the tunes they are based on. So you must find the actual performances you want. A musician's improvisations on other versions of the tune might not even resemble what you want. This consideration is essential whenever you plan to use the internet to get a given performance of one tune. Downloading services often fail to post the details you need, and often you will be confronted with a dizzying array of alternate sources once you key in the musician name and tune title. Most of the sources that are listed will not be for the particular performance you seek. They will be for other renditions of that same tune.

When you are trying to locate music from a recording that has gone out of print, you will be looking for it in new compilations of old material. For these new packages, album titles are sometimes changed, and material from the original album is scattered over several different compilations. Another common problem is that the recordings may have belonged originally to companies which later sold their material. The original company's name helps you identify reissued material. For instance, one group of important Charlie Parker recordings was originally made for the Dial record company, and its reissued form is called *The Dial Masters*. However, when record companies are bought and sold, sometimes the music is reissued intact, causing you no headaches. For example, Impulse was bought by ABC, then by MCA, then GRP, then the Verve division of the Universal Music Group, but many of the important albums John Coltrane made for Impulse during the 1960s continued to be distributed intact, though with GRP. Others became available on compact disc with additional selections and new catalog numbers.

Another key to locating material in reissued form is that it is often identified by where it was recorded. For example, the pivotal Bill Evans-Scott LaFaro music originally made at New York City's Village Vanguard night club for Riverside record company, originally issued on albums titled *Sunday at the Village Vanguard* and *Waltz for Debby*, has been reissued by Fantasy-Prestige-Milestone as *The Village Vanguard Sessions*. Recordings from an outstanding 1953 concert by Charles Mingus, Charlie Parker, Dizzy Gillespie, Bud Powell, and Max Roach are frequently identified only by recording site: Toronto's Massey Hall (*The Massey Hall Concert*).

When seeking music that you think is out-of-print, you need a complete listing of the musicians, the pieces, the recording dates, the original album title, and the name of the original record company. In some cases it also helps to have the original catalog numbers. Such information is supplied at the beginning of most listening guides in this book to help you locate the source for that selection if you want to own it, apart from its availability on the set of *Jazz Classics CDs* and/or if you want to own other tracks from the same recording session. Listening guides in this book also list the most current form that was available for the piece as we went to press.

Personnel listings can be especially useful when seeking reissued material because material is sometimes reissued under the name of a musician who was a sideman on the original recording session but has now become more significant than the leader. It is packaged as though he were leader at that original session. For example, a 1956 Tadd Dameron album called *Mating Call* was reissued under John Coltrane's name and called *On a Misty Night*. Coltrane was a sideman on it but is now in much demand in his own right. Several reissues of Joe Oliver's Creole Jazz Band have come out under Louis Armstrong's name, even though Armstrong was a sideman, not the leader, on Oliver's recordings. Much pre-1940 Lester Young material is available in reissues under Young's name, though it was originally recorded under Count Basie's leadership.

There are several ways you can keep up with what is being reissued. Reading jazz magazines is the most efficient. This will allow you to keep up with material that won't be broadcast on radio. As this book went to press, the magazines that attempted to announce most new albums and reissues were *Jazz Times* (8737 Colesville Road, Silver Spring, MD 20910-3921) and *Cadence* (Redwood, NY 13679). You can also phone or visit music stores to track listings in their *Phonolog*, *Spectrum*, or *Muze*. Several mail-order services give information and take orders by phone. (J&R: 800-221-8180, *www.jr.com*; jazzlines.com; 518-587-1102.) If you do not want to wait for an album to be reissued (and some never are), watch for it in the bins of cut-outs and used albums at music stores, garage sales, house sales, and flea markets. Amazon.com and eBay also can prove helpful. *Or contact rare record dealers and auctioneers, advertised in the back pages of jazz magazines.*

Many Versions of the Same Tune

The problem of a single tune recorded many times by the same artist increased substantially during the past 40 years. This was due to increases in: (1) legitimate reissue programs by major firms, (2) illegitimate releases (called bootleg or pirate records) by numerous small firms, and (3) the discovery, or rediscovery, of a seemingly endless variety of broadcast performances, called *air shots* or *air checks*. (Music of the 1930s and 1940s, unlike that of the 1950s and 1960s, is well documented by air checks because most jazz groups made live radio broadcasts in those days.)

Beginning in the 1960s, record companies began massive distribution of repackaged material. Hundreds of albums with new titles were introduced. Many contained music originally on 78s. Other albums had music originally available on LPs. Some of the albums featured alternate, but originally rejected, versions of tunes. These are called *alternate takes*. (Some are labeled as alternate takes, but for others, you have to hear both versions to know whether they differ. They sometimes have improvisation equal or superior to the versions originally issued.)

Albums flooded the market from companies, both American and foreign, which operated without the consent of the recorded artists (or of their estates, in the case of deceased artists). Those albums constitute the illegitimate releases mentioned earlier as *bootlegs*. The companies were small and disappeared quickly. Some of their material had appeared previously on other records, but much of it had never been available before. A lot of it came from homemade recordings of night club appearances and radio broadcasts. Many albums have incorrect tune titles. Few contain complete personnel listings and recording dates. Many display poor sound fidelity. But if you can tolerate all those weaknesses, you might be well rewarded by the music itself. It is also worthwhile to be aware of bootleg recordings because the appearance and distribution of them is very common and likely to continue. During the 1990s and the beginning of the twenty-first century, many such recordings were located by researchers, the sound was improved, correct personnel was listed, and albums containing them were issued by legitimate record companies.

With the bootleg material added to the legitimate releases and reissues, it became possible to own, for instance, more than eighty albums of Charlie Parker, or more than one hundred of Duke Ellington. The record collector might be confronted with five to ten Parker versions of "Confirmation" and "Ornithology" and just as many Ellington versions of "Mood Indigo" and "Sophisticated Lady." Keeping track of recording dates and personnel became essential to discussing particular performances of these frequently recorded tunes.

A few Charlie Parker classics illustrate the usefulness of having personnel, tune titles, recording dates, and original record company name before you begin seeking a particular recording. The much praised music that Parker originally made in the form of 78s for Dial Record Company has been sold in numerous forms, some of them offered by tiny, obscure record companies that worked without the consent of Parker's estate. Take "Embraceable You," for example. Parker recorded many different versions of it. But if you want his famous Dial recording of it, remember that he made two different versions at the same session in 1947 with pianist Duke Jordan, bassist Tommy Potter, and drummer Max Roach. Any deviation from that particular combination of identifiers will indicate that you are holding another version of the tune instead of the famous version. It is also essential to note the record company name and recording date if you want to locate Parker's famous 1945 "Now's the Time," which was made for Savoy record company with the Miles Davis trumpet solo that was later adapted and recorded by pianist Red Garland on the Miles Davis *Milestones* album. It is especially easy to become confused in this instance because another version of the same tune was also recorded by Parker without Davis in 1953 and released on a Verve album called *Now's the Time*. There are instances in which historic figures recorded only one version of a given tune, but the more you study jazz, the more you will find it beneficial to **keep track of details to ensure you're buying what you originally set out to buy.**

One final example is offered to illustrate the usefulness of having complete information about an improvisation you seek. If you have a transcription of a Miles Davis trumpet solo from a performance of "Joshua," and you want to hear the original or play along with it, you cannot just run out and buy the correct album, even if you already have the personnel listing and the year of recording. Miles Davis recorded "Joshua" at least three times with saxophonist George Coleman, pianist Herbie Hancock, bassist Ron Carter, and drummer Tony Williams. Two out of the three times were in the same year, 1963. One version was released on *Seven Steps to Heaven*, an album which was issued with two different catalog numbers: Columbia CS 8851 and CL 2051. Another version was released on *Miles Davis in Europe* (Columbia CL 2183 and CS 8983). Then Davis recorded another version in 1964 that was released in *Four and More* (Columbia 9253 and CL 2453) that was reissued on CD under a new title and new catalog number in 1992.

Rare Record Dealers, Importers, and Auctioneers

Worlds Records
P.O. Box 1992
Novato, CA 94948
800-742-6663
www.worldsrecords.com

Cadence Record Sales
Cadence Building
Redwood, NY 13679
315-287-2852
www.cadencebuilding.com

The Jazz Hunter
William Carraro
25 Aberdeen Street
Malverne, NY 11565
516-593-5975

Memory Lane Out-of-Print Records
1940 East University Drive
Tempe, AZ 85281
800-326-5343
www.memorylanerecords.com

International Association of
Jazz Record Collectors
P.O. Box 518
Wingate, NC 28174
http://iajrc.org
(Write for a membership listing, then determine who specializes in the style you seek, and write that member.)

Mosaic Records runs a broad-ranging program of reissuing hard-to-find items. Their reissue packages are prepared in a very intelligent and conscientious manner with excellent annotation. As this book went to press, Mosaic was still carrying material by Stan Kenton, Duke Ellington, Louis Armstrong, Maynard Ferguson, George Shearing, Miles Davis, Nat Cole, Don Cherry, Charlie Parker, and others. Mosaic also was running a subsidiary, called True Blue, which distributed Blue Note recordings, a source for pivotal music from the 1950s and 1960s that has become difficult to locate. Request a catalog from Mosaic Records, 35 Melrose Place, Stamford CT 06902-7533; phone 203-327-7111, *www.truebluemusic.com*.

Mail Order/Internet In-print Albums

J&R Music World
800-221-8180
www.jr.com

Amazon.Com
www.amazon.com

Ejazz Lines
ejazzlines.com

APPENDIX D
A Small Basic Collection of Jazz Videos

Gryb, Steven D. *Listening to Jazz* (Prentice-Hall, 2007) ISBN 0-13-601053-9; 800-947-7700; DVD/52 min.; demonstrations of instruments and their roles, corresponding to the audio on the *Demonstration CD for Mark Gridley*, *Jazz Styles: History and Analysis*.

After Hours [plus *Jazz Dance*] (Rhapsody, 1961; c2000); VHS/49 min.; featuring Coleman Hawkins, Roy Eldridge, Milt Hinton, and Cozy Cole.

Celebrating Bird: The Triumph of Charlie Parker (Pioneer Artists: PA-99-605-D, 1987, c1999); DVD/60 min.

Charles Mingus: Triumph of the Underdog (Shanachie: 6315, 1997, c1999); DVD/78 min.

The Coltrane Legacy (VAI: 4220, 1985, c2002); DVD/61 min.; John Coltrane performing with Eric Dolphy, Elvin Jones, McCoy Tyner, Reggie Workman, and Jimmy Garrison; interviews with Jones, Workman, Jimmy Cobb, and Roy Haynes.

Duke Ellington & His Orchestra: 1929–1943 (Navarre: 16033, c2003); DVD; film clips of the Ellington orchestra.

Duke Ellington in Hollywood (Idem: 1029); DVD; film clips of the Ellington orchestra 1929–1943.

Great Performances: Lester Young Charlie Parker Miles Davis (Idem: 1057, c2003); DVD/60 min.; *Jammin' the Blues* with Lester Young; Charlie Parker (1952 with Dizzy Gillespie and 1950 with JATP); and Miles Davis with John Coltrane and Gil Evans.

The Miles Davis Story (Sony Music: CVD54040, 2001, c2002); DVD/125 min.

One Night with Blue Note: The Historic All-Star Reunion Concert (Blue Note/EMI Video: 96008, 1985, c2003); DVD/120 min.; Bobby Hutcherson, Herbie Hancock, Ron Carter, Freddie Hubbard, Joe Henderson, Tony Williams, Art Blakey, Curtis Fuller, Johnny Griffin, Kenny Burrell, Grover Washington, McCoy Tyner, Jackie McLean, Woody Shaw, Jack DeJohnette, Charles Lloyd, Jimmy Smith, Cecil Taylor, and others.

Piano Legends (VAI: 4209, 1986, c2001); DVD/63 min.; hosted by Chick Corea; includes Earl Hines, Mary Lou Williams, Fats Waller, Art Tatum, Teddy Wilson, Bud Powell, Thelonious Monk, Lennie Tristano, Dave Brubeck, Horace Silver, Bill Evans, McCoy Tyner, Cecil Taylor, Keith Jarrett, and others.

Reed Royalty (VAI: 69072, c1992); VHS/58 min.; hosted by Branford Marsalis; includes Benny Goodman, Sidney Bechet, Benny Carter, Johnny Hodges, Charlie Parker, Sonny Stitt, Cannonball Adderley, Gerry Mulligan, Lee Konitz, Eric Dolphy, Ornette Coleman, Anthony Braxton, and others.

Satchmo (Columbia Music Video: 49024, 1989, c2000); DVD/86 min.; the career of Louis Armstrong.

The Sound of Jazz (Idem: 1058, 1957, c2003); DVD/70 min.; an unedited copy of the kinescope of the CBS broadcast with performances by Henry "Red" Allen, Count Basie, Lester Young, Coleman Hawkins, Ben Webster, Billie Holiday, Roy Eldridge, Thelonious Monk, Jimmy Giuffre, and others.

Sun Ra: A Joyful Noise (Winstar Home Entertainment: 73021, 1980, c1998); DVD/60 min.; documentary with much live music.

Tenor Titans (VAI: 69073, c1992); VHS/60 min.; tenor saxophonists: Coleman Hawkins, Lester Young, Stan Getz, Dexter Gordon, John Coltrane, Wayne Shorter, Sonny Rollins, David Murray, and others.

Thelonious Monk: Straight No Chaser (Warner Video: 11896, 1988, c2001); DVD/90 min.; live performances and a recording session; some dialog.

Trumpet Kings (VAI: 69036, c1985); VHS/60 min.; hosted by Wynton Marsalis; includes Louis Armstrong, Red Allen, Bunny Berigan, Cootie Williams, Rex Stewart, Roy Eldridge, Dizzy Gillespie, Miles Davis, Art Farmer, Clark Terry, Lee Morgan, Freddie Hubbard, Lester Bowie, and others.

The Universal Mind of Bill Evans: The Creative Process and Self-teaching (Rhapsody: 9015, c1991); VHS/45 min.; Evans talks and plays.

Note: These videos may be found in video stores, music stores, or libraries. Most of the videos listed may be available from these distributors:

Rhapsody Films
46-2 Becket Hill Rd.
Lyme, CT 06371
860-434-3610
rhapsodyfilms.com

Jamey Aebersold Jazz, Inc.
P.O. Box 1244
New Albany, IN 47150-1244
800-456-1388
www.jazzbooks.com

Music Video Distributors
P.O. Box 280
Oaks, PA 19456
800-888-0486
www.musicvideodistributors.com

www.amazon.com

Jazzland
P.O. Box 366
Dayton, OH 45401
800-876-4467
www.landofjazz.com

Cadence Music Sales
Cadence Building
Redwood, NY 13679
315-287-2852
www.cadencebuilding.com

APPENDIX E
Glossary

acid jazz usually the creation of a disc jockey who takes funky accompaniments that have been synthesized electronically and/or sampled from jazz recordings, then repeats them continuously with raps and/or jazz improvisations superimposed atop them (see Chapter 17).

antiphonal an adjective describing a common pattern of interaction between improvisers or between sections of a band, taking the form of a question and answer or a call and response.

arco the technique of playing a stringed instrument with a bow.

atonal the character and organization possessed by music that has no key (see page 454 for further explanations and illustrations).

attack the very beginning of a sound (opposite of release).

back beat strong accent on the second and fourth beats of every four-beat measure; a term usually applied to the work of a band's drummer.

ballad a slow piece (though not applied to slow blues).

big band an ensemble of ten or more players.

blue note 1. a pitch somewhere between a major third and minor third or between a major seventh and minor seventh step of the scale (see page 456).

2. minor third or seventh scale step (see page 456).

blues 1. a simple, funky style of black music separate from but coexistent with jazz; beginning at least as early as the turn of the 20th century, probably much earlier; exemplified by such performers as Blind Lemon Jefferson, Leadbelly, Lightnin' Hopkins, Muddy Waters, T-Bone Walker and Robert Johnson. It has been and continues to be an influence on jazz and rock. The majority of blues compositions employ the I-IV-I-V-I chord progression or a variation of it.

2. a piece characterized by any one or any combination of the following—
   a. the I-IV-I-V-I chord progression or some variation of it in a 12-measure package
   b. a sad feeling
   c. a slow pace
   d. poetry in the form of paired couplets in iambic pentameter
   e. many lowered third, fifth, or seventh intervals
   (see Appendix B for further explanation).

bomb a pronounced accent played by the drummer.

boogie woogie a premodern jazz piano style associated with Meade Lux Lewis and Albert Ammons. It is characterized by a repetitive left-hand bass figure that states almost every beat by dividing it into dotted-eighth sixteenth-note patterns.

bop (bebop) the style associated with Charlie Parker, Dizzy Gillespie, Thelonious Monk, Bud Powell, Dexter Gordon, and Sonny Stitt (see Chapter 9).

break 1. the portion of a piece in which all band members stop playing except the one who improvises a solo. The tempo and chord progressions are maintained by the soloist, but, because the band has stopped, it is called a stop-time. Rarely do such breaks last longer than two or four measures (see page 20 for detailed explanation).

2. the solo itself.

bridge the B part of an A-A-B-A composition; also known as the channel, the release, or the inside (see Chapter 3 for further information).

broken time 1. a style of rhythm section playing in which explicit statement of every beat is replaced by broken patterns which only imply the underlying tempo, exemplified by the 1961 Bill Evans trio with Scott LaFaro and Paul Motian.

2. the manner of playing bass or drums in which strict repetition of timekeeping patterns is not maintained, but constant tempo is; exemplified by the 1960s and 1970s playing of Elvin Jones.

chart the jazz musician's term for what is written as musical arrangement. This is distinguished from the classical musician's "score" because not all the notes are present. Many spaces in the chart are filled only by symbols indicating the chord progression that guides improvisation. Often the drum "parts" are almost blank.

chops instrumental facility.

chord progression 1. when one chord changes or "progresses" to another chord.

2. a set of harmonies in a particular order with specified durations; for example, the 12-measure I-IV-I-V-I blues progression (see Appendix B).

3. the sequence of accompaniment chords intended for a song but used instead as the basis of a jazz improvisation.

chorus 1. a single playing through of the structure being used to organize the music in an improvisation.

2. a jazz solo, regardless of its length.

3. the part of a pop tune performed in constant tempo and repeated several times after the verse has been played, usually the only portion of a tune's original form used by the jazz musician (see page 464 for further explanation).

collective improvisation simultaneous improvisation by all members of a group together.

comping syncopated chording which provides improvised accompaniment for simultaneously improvised solos, flexibly complementing the rhythms and implied harmonies of the solo line (see Chapter 3 for further explanation and Appendix G for musical notation).

cool 1. an adjective often applied to describe the subdued feeling projected by the music of Bix Beiderbecke, Lester Young, Claude Thornhill, Gil Evans, Miles Davis, The Modern Jazz Quartet, Gerry Mulligan, Lee Konitz, and Jimmy Giuffre (see Chapter 10).

2. sometimes used as a synonym for West Coast style.

3. sometimes used to denote modern jazz after bop.

counterpoint two or more lines of approximately equal importance sounding together.

Creole 1. French- or Spanish-speaking individual born in the New World.

2. a person who has both French and African ancestry and was born in the New World (also known as "Creole of Color," as opposed to the white-skinned Creole defined above).

cross-over music 1. music that has crossed in popularity from one market to another. For example, some jazz-rock fusion albums were so popular that they began selling to customers belonging to the market for pop music at large rather than only to customers primarily concerned with jazz.

2. synonym for jazz-rock fusion.

decay the very end of a sound; also known as a release. Opposite of attack (see Chapter 4 for discussion).

Dixieland style 1. Chicago combo style that was prominent during the 1920s.

2. a synonym for all pre-swing-era combo jazz.

double stop sounding two bass strings at the same time.

double-time the feeling that a piece of music or a player is going twice as fast as the tempo, although the chord progressions continue at the original rate.

Fender bass electric bass guitar, used to play bass lines instead of chords; common in jazz rhythm sections after 1970.

fill in general, anything a drummer plays in addition to basic time-keeping patterns; in particular, a rhythmic figure played by a drummer to:

1. fill a silence

2. underscore a rhythm played by other instruments

3. announce the entrance or punctuate the exit of a soloist or other section of the music

4. stimulate the other players and make a performance more interesting.

free jazz an approach associated with Ornette Coleman and Cecil Taylor, in which the music contains improvised solos which are free of preset chord progressions, and sometimes also free of preset meter (see Chapter 14).

front line musicians appearing directly in front of the audience, not blocked from view by another row of musicians. This designation is sometimes used to separate hornmen (because they stand in the front of a combo) from accompanists (who usually appear to the rear of the hornmen).

funky an adjective describing rhythms as well as melody, harmony, and tone color characteristics that evoke an effect perceived as

1. earthy or dirty

2. mean, "low down," evil, or sexy

3. bluesy

4. gospel-flavored.

fusion a synonym for jazz-rock style (see Chapter 17).

fuzak music that blends the characteristics of jazz-rock fusion styles with the characteristics of Muzak. It tends to stress electric instruments, steady funk rhythms, smooth textures, without many surprises. Used as background music during the 1980s and 1990s by listeners who liked the softer variants of fusion and funk. Often used to designate music of Kenny G, Grover Washington, Earl Klugh, and Najee (see **smooth jazz**).

growl style a method used by some trumpeters and trombonists in which by unorthodox use of mutes, lips, mouth and blowing techniques a sound is produced that resembles the growl of an animal. Despite the odd assortment of sounds that the growl includes, recognizable melodic figures can be played with this alteration of tone quality. (See Bubber Miley, Cootie Williams, and Joe "Tricky Sam" Nanton.)

hard bop the jazz style associated with Horace Silver, Art Blakey, and Cannonball Adderley (see Chapter 11 for further explanation).

head the melody or prewritten theme for a piece.

head arrangement a band arrangement that was created extemporaneously by the musicians and is not written down.

high-hat (sock cymbal) an instrument in the drum set which brings two cymbals together by means of a foot pedal.

horn general label for any wind instrument; sometimes includes stringed and percussion instruments as well (the most general term for all instruments is ax).

jam session a musical get-together where improvisation is stressed and written music is rare (jam means to improvise); may refer to a performance which is formally organized or casual, public or private, for profit or just for fun.

jazz-rock a variety of styles beginning in the late 1960s that use electric instruments, funk rhythm accompaniments and jazz improvisation; also known as fusion music; often applied to the post-1968 music of Miles Davis, Spyro Gyra, Weather Report, the Crusaders, John McLaughlin, the electric music of Herbie Hancock and Chick Corea (see Chapter 16.)

laid back an adjective used to describe a feeling of relaxation, laziness, or slowness; often describes the feeling that a performer is playing his rhythms a little later than they are expected, almost after the beat or "behind" the beat.

lay out to stop playing while other players continue.

legato a style of playing in which the notes are smoothly connected with no silences between them (opposite of staccato).

lick a phrase or melodic fragment.

locked-hands style a style of piano playing in which a separate chord parallels each note of the melody because both hands are used as though they are locked together, all fingers striking the keyboard together; also known as block chording, playing the chord notes as a block instead of one at a time. (See sections on Milt Buckner, Lennie Tristano, George Shearing, Ahmad Jamal, Red Garland, and Bill Evans.)

modal music in which the melody and/or harmony is based on an arrangement of modes. In jazz, the term can mean music based on the extensive repetition of one or two chords or music based on modes instead of chord progressions.

mode 1. the manner of organizing a sequence of tones, usually an ascending sequence of an octave.

2. the arrangement of whole steps and half steps common to scales. (See Appendix B for further explanation.)

mute an attachment that reduces an instrument's loudness and alters its tone color.

new age music that is soft and soothing, lacks variety in rhythm, loudness, and chords. It was often applied to the work of George Winston, Andreas Vollenwieder and others who recorded for Windham Hill and Narada record companies. It tends to combine characteristics of

1. the minimalist style associated with nonjazz composers Philip Glass, LaMonte Young, and Steve Reich.

2. ethnic music used for meditation.

3. music of classical musicians, including members of the Paul Winter Consort and Oregon, who improvised soft, smooth sound textures that did not swing.

pedal point low-pitched, repeated, and/or sustained tone. It usually retains its pitch despite changes in chords and improvisations occurring around it; common in the 1960s work of John Coltrane and McCoy Tyner.

pitch bending purposeful raising or lowering of a tone's pitch; usually done for coloration or expressive purposes (see pages 17, 48, and 49 for illustrations and explanation).

pizzicato the method of playing a stringed instrument by plucking instead of bowing.

polyrhythm several different rhythms sounding at the same time (see Appendix B).

progressive jazz music associated with Stan Kenton (see Chapter 10).

ragtime 1. a popular 1890s–1920s style of written piano music involving pronounced syncopation.

2. a label often applied to much pre-1920 jazz and pop music, unaccompanied solo piano styles as well as band styles, improvised as well as written music.

3. the style of music associated with composers Scott Joplin and Tom Turpin.

release 1. the manner in which a sound ends or decays (opposite of attack).

2. the bridge of a tune.

rhythm section the group of players whose band function is accompanying. This role is particularly common for pianists, bassists, and drummers, but it is not exclusive to them (see pages 23–29 for explanations and illustrations, see Appendix H for musical notations).

ride cymbal the cymbal suspended over a drum set, usually to the player's right, struck by a stick held in the drummer's right hand; used for playing timekeeping patterns called ride rhythms.

ride rhythm the pattern a drummer plays on the ride cymbal to keep time, the most common being ching-chick-a-ching-chick-a (see notations in Appendix H).

riff 1. phrase

2. melodic fragment

3. theme.

rim shot the drum stick striking the rim of the snare drum at the same time as it strikes the drum head.

rip an onset ornament in the form of a quick rise in pitch directly preceding a tone. (Listen to Bix Beiderbecke or Louis Armstrong.)

rubato free of strict adherence to constant tempo.

scat singing jazz improvisation using the human voice as an instrument, with nonsense syllables (dwee, ool, ya, bop, bam, etc.) instead of words.

sideman a designation for each musician in a band except the leader.

smooth jazz a designation for the styles of music played on radio stations subscribing to "The Wave" format of the 1980s and 1990s: a blend of Kenny G, Grover Washington, Earl Klugh, Lee Ritenour, Larry Carlton, George Benson, Bob James, and their disciples (see Chapter 17).

sock cymbal see **high-hat**

staccato brief and separated (opposite of legato).

stride 1. left-hand style used by early jazz pianists. It usually employs a bass note on the first and third beats of each measure and a chord on the second and fourth.

2. the piano style of James P. Johnson and Willie "The Lion" Smith.

swing 1. a word denoting approval—"It swings" can mean it pleases me; "to swing" can mean to enjoy oneself; "he's a swinging guy" can mean he is an enjoyable person.

2. the noun indicating the feeling projected by an uplifting performance of any kind of music, especially that which employs constant tempo.

3. the feeling projected by a jazz performance which successfully combines constant tempo, syncopation, swing eighth notes, rhythmic lilt, liveliness, and rhythmically cohesive group playing.

4. the jazz style associated with Count Basie, Duke Ellington, Jimmie Lunceford, Benny Goodman, Art Tatum, Roy Eldridge, and Coleman Hawkins, as in the "swing era" (see Chapter 6).

syncopation 1. stress on any portion of the measure other than the first part of the first beat (and, in meter of four, other than the first part of the third beat), i.e. the second half of the first beat, the second half of the second beat, the fourth beat, the second half of the fourth beat, the second beat, etc.

2. stress on a portion of the measure least expected to receive stress (see Appendix B for further explanation).

synthesizer any one of a general category of electronic devices (Moog and Arp, for example) which produces sounds or alters the sounds created by other instruments.

Third Stream a style which combines jazz improvisation with the instrumentation and compositional forms of classical music (see page 177 for further explanation).

tonal inflection alteration of a tone's pitch or quality, done purposefully at the beginning, middle, or end of a sound (see pitch bending).

tone color (timbre, tone quality) the characteristic of sound which enables the listener to differentiate one instrument from another, and, in many cases, one player from another.

tremolo 1. fluctuation in the loudness of a sound, usually an even alternation of loud and soft.

2. a manner of playing a chord by rapidly sounding its different notes in alternation so that the chord retains its character, but also sustains and trembles.

3. the means of sustaining the sound of a vibraphone.

4. an expressive technique for use by instruments in which vibrato is very difficult (flute, for example) or in which the variation of pitch necessary for vibrato may not be wanted (some styles of oboe playing, for example).

5. the rapid reiteration of the same note.

turnaround (turnback, turnabout) a short progression within a chord progression that occurs just prior to the point at which the player must "turn around" to begin another repetition of the larger progression (see Appendix B for further explanation and Appendix H for musical notation).

two-beat style a rhythm section style which emphasizes the first and third beats of each four-beat measure, often leaving the second and fourth beats silent in the bass; sometimes called boom-chick style.

vamp a short chord progression (usually only one, two, or four measures long) which is repeated many times in sequence. Often used for introductions and endings. Much jazz and pop music of the 1960s and 1970s used vamps instead of more involved chord progressions as accompaniment for melody and improvisation.

vibrato the slight fluctuation of a tone's pitch, alternating above and below its basic pitch; used as an expressive device, varied in speed and amplitude by the performer to fit the style and feeling of the music (see page 49 for further explanation).

voicing 1. the manner of organizing, doubling, omitting, or adding to the notes of a chord (see Appendices B and H).

2. the assignment of notes to each instrument.

vocalese the practice of singing lyrics set to the notes of a recorded instrumental jazz improvisation, as in lyrics composed by Eddie Jefferson for the saxophone improvisation on the James Moody recording of "I'm in the Mood for Love," released as "Moody's Mood for Love," and in lyrics composed by Jon Hendricks for Count Basie hits, performed by the singing group Lambert, Hendricks and Ross, and in lyrics set by Annie Ross to the melody and saxophone improvisations recorded by Wardell Gray for his piece "Twisted"; not to be confused with scat singing (nonsense syllables improvised by singers acting as jazz instrumentalists).

walking bass a style of bass line in which each beat of each measure receives a separate tone, thus creating a moving sequence of quarter notes in the bass range.

West Coast style the jazz style associated with Gerry Mulligan and Chet Baker during the 1950s (see **cool**).

APPENDIX F
Supplementary Reading

Biographies

ARMSTRONG, LOUIS. *Satchmo: My Life in New Orleans*. Prentice-Hall, 1954; DaCapo, 1986.
Louis Armstrong's autobiography.

BÜCHMANN-MØLLER, FRANK. *You Got to Be Original, Man! The Music of Lester Young*. Greenwood, 1990.
Analysis of Lester Young's improvisational style. Contains transcriptions of Young's important solos.

BÜCHMANN-MØLLER, FRANK. *You Just Fight for Your Life: The Story of Lester Young*. Praeger, 1990.
Summary of Lester Young's life, complements the above.

CARNER, GARY. *Jazz Performers: An Annotated Bibliography of Biographical Materials*. Greenwood, 1990.

CARR, IAN. *Miles Davis: The Definitive Biography*. Thunder's Mouth, 1999.
An intelligently written, knowledgeable biography of Davis by fellow jazz trumpeter Carr. Contains a discography as well as transcriptions of solo improvisations.

CARR, IAN, DIGBY FAIRWEATHER, and BRIAN PRIESTLEY. *Jazz: The Rough Guide*. 2nd ed. Rough Guides, 2000.
The single most intelligently written biographical reference work to be published recently. Contains hundreds of biographies of jazz musicians written by jazz musicians.

CHARTERS, SAMUEL B. *Jazz: New Orleans 1885–1963: An Index to the Negro Musicians of New Orleans*. Oak, 1963; DaCapo, 1983.
A valuable source of biographical and musical information on early jazz musicians.

CHILTON, JOHN. *Who's Who of Jazz: Storyville to Swing Street*. 4th ed. DaCapo, 1985.
Biographies of hundreds of musicians born before 1920.

DANCE, STANLEY. *The World of Count Basie*. Scribner's, 1980; DaCapo, 1985.
Covers Basie and his sidemen in profile and interview formats.

DANCE, STANLEY. *The World of Earl Hines*. Scribner's, 1977; DaCapo, 1983.
Includes reminiscences by numerous Hines associates, historical accounts in Hines's own words, an exclusive chronology of Hines's life, plus an excellent bibliography and discography.

DANCE, STANLEY. *The World of Swing*. 2nd ed. Scribner's, 1975; DaCapo, 2001.
Vignettes of swing era figures with an emphasis on interview material.

ELLINGTON, DUKE. *Music Is My Mistress*. Doubleday, 1973; DaCapo, 1976.
Duke Ellington's autobiography.

FEATHER, LEONARD. *The Encyclopedia of Jazz*. rev. ed. Horizon, 1960; DaCapo, 1984.
Leonard Feather and Ira Gitler's monumental compilation with over 2000 biographies arranged alphabetically.

FEATHER, LEONARD. *The Encyclopedia of Jazz in the Sixties*. Horizon, 1966; DaCapo, 1986.
A follow-up to the above including 1400 biographies.

FEATHER, LEONARD and IRA GITLER. *The Biographical Encyclopedia of Jazz*. Oxford, 1999.

FEATHER, LEONARD. *From Satchmo to Miles*. Stein & Day, 1972; DaCapo, 1984.
Chapters on Louis Armstrong, Duke Ellington, Count Basie, Lester Young, Charlie Parker, Dizzy Gillespie, Miles Davis, and others.

FOSTER, GEORGE MURPHY. *Pops Foster: The Autobiography of a New Orleans Jazzman*. University of California Press, 1971.
Contains numerous details of New Orleans jazz history from the turn of the 20th century plus much on the history of jazz in Chicago. The musical information in the book is indispensable to understanding the history of jazz rhythm section playing; it is not limited to the bass style of its author.

GARA, LARRY. *The Baby Dodds Story*. Contemporary Press, 1959; LSU, 1992.
Contains a peek into the techniques used by early jazz drummers; also has much on New Orleans and Chicago jazz history.

GILLESPIE, DIZZY. *To Be or Not to Bop*. Doubleday, 1979; DaCapo, 1985.
Reminiscences by Gillespie, plus interviews with his colleagues done by Al Fraser.

GITLER, IRA. *The Masters of Bebop: A Listener's Guide*. Macmillan, 1966; DaCapo, 2001.
One of the most intelligently conceived jazz history books, it includes musical and biographical discussions of Charlie Parker and the alto and baritone saxophonists; Dizzy Gillespie and the trumpeters; Bud Powell and the pianists; J. J. Johnson and the trombonists; Oscar Pettiford and the bassists; Kenny Clarke, Max Roach, and the drummers; Dexter Gordon and the tenor saxophonists; Lennie Tristano and Lee Konitz; and Tadd Dameron and the arrangers.

GOLDBERG, JOE. *Jazz Masters of the Fifties*. Macmillan, 1965; DaCapo, 1980.
A chapter each on Miles Davis, Thelonious Monk, Gerry Mulligan, Charles Mingus, John Coltrane, Sonny Rollins, Ornette Coleman, and Cecil Taylor.

HADLOCK, RICHARD. *Jazz Masters of the Twenties*. Macmillan, 1965; DaCapo, 1986.
A chapter each on Armstrong, Beiderbecke, Earl Hines, Fats Waller, James P. Johnson, Fletcher Henderson, Eddie Lang, and The Chicagoans.

HITCHCOCK, H. WILEY and STANLEY SADIE, eds. *The New Grove Dictionary of American Music*. Grove, 1986.
Contains numerous biographies as well as different jazz styles summaries.

LITWEILER, JOHN. *Ornette Coleman: A Harmolodic Life*. Morrow, 1993.

MATHIESON, KENNY. *Cookin': Hard Bop and Soul Jazz, 1954–65.* Cannongate, 2002.
Knowledgeable round-up of the key players in this period of jazz history.

MATHIESON, KENNY. *Giant Steps: Bebop and the Creators of Modern Jazz 1945–65.* Payback Press, 1999.
Well-informed summary of the major musicians in this era.

PORTER, LEWIS. *John Coltrane: His Life and Music.* University of Michigan, 1998.
Ground breaking biography with technical analyses, including ones in which the author "cracked the code" and demonstrated, for instance, that some music, previously been thought to be free-form, was carefully planned and developed according to Coltrane's own formula.

REISNER, ROBERT. *Bird: The Legend of Charlie Parker.* Citadel, 1962; DaCapo, 1975.
A biography in the form of recollections and documents.

RUSSELL, ROSS. *Bird Lives: The High Life and Hard Times of Charlie Parker.* Charterhouse, 1973; DaCapo, 1995.
A Charlie Parker biography in the style of a novel.

SHAPIRO, NAT, and NAT HENTOFF. *Hear Me Talkin' to Ya.* Rinehart, 1955; Dover, 1966.
Interviews with famous jazz musicians.

SHAPIRO, NAT, and NAT HENTOFF. *Jazz Makers.* Rinehart, 1957; DaCapo, 1979.
A chapter each on Jelly Roll Morton, Baby Dodds, Louis Armstrong, Jack Teagarden, Earl Hines, Bix Beiderbecke, Pee Wee Russell, Fats Waller, Art Tatum, Coleman Hawkins, Benny Goodman, Duke Ellington, Charlie Parker, Fletcher Henderson, Count Basie, Lester Young, Roy Eldridge, Charlie Christian, and Dizzy Gillespie.

SPELLMAN, A. B. *Four Jazz Lives.* Pantheon, 1966; University of Michigan, 2004.
Biographical interviews with Ornette Coleman, Cecil Taylor, Jackie McLean, and Herbie Nichols.

STEWART, REX. *Jazz Masters of the Thirties.* Macmillan, 1972; DaCapo, 1980.
A chapter each on Ellington, Hawkins, Henderson, Basie, Art Tatum, and Benny Carter.

STEWART, REX. *Boy Meets Horn.* University of Michigan, 1991.
Autobiography of Duke Ellington's cornetist.

SUDHALTER, RICHARD M., P. R. EVANS, and W. D. MYATT. *Bix: Man & Legend.* Arlington House, 1974.
An exhaustive biography of Bix Beiderbecke. Written by trumpeter Sudhalter from research done by Evans and Myatt, this book includes technical analyses and a chronology of Beiderbecke's life with explanations for almost every mystery surrounding it; also contains transcriptions of solos and an excellent discography.

SUMMERFIELD, MAURICE J. *The Jazz Guitar: Its Evolution & Its Players.* 4th ed. Hal Leonard, 1998.
Biographies of almost all the prominent guitarists in jazz history.

TAYLOR, ARTHUR. *Notes and Tones: Musician-to-Musician Interviews.* Perigee Books, 1982; DaCapo, 1993.
Interviews by drummer Taylor with Miles Davis, Ornette Coleman, Philly Joe Jones, Don Byas, Ron Carter, Max Roach, Erroll Garner, Dizzy Gillespie, Tony Williams, Sonny Rollins, Don Cherry, Kenny Clarke, Freddie Hubbard, Elvin Jones, Art Blakey, and others.

TUCKER, MARK, ed. *The Duke Ellington Reader.* Oxford, 1993.
A generous collection of essays, newspaper and magazine reports, record reviews, concert reviews, interviews about Ellington, his music and musicians, and a number of articles written by Ellington himself.

WILLIAMS, MARTIN. *Jazz Masters of New Orleans.* Macmillan, 1967; DaCapo, 1978.
A chapter each on King Oliver, Jelly Roll Morton, Sidney Bechet, Louis Armstrong, and the Original Dixieland Jazz Band.

WOIDECK, CARL. *Charlie Parker: His Music and Life.* University of Michigan, 1996.
An essential reference, unearths sources for Parker's style in unexpected places, thoughtful technical analyses, many transcriptions of solos.

Jazz Magazines

Cadence
(ISSN 0162-6973) 1976- .
Cadence Building
Redwood, NY 13679
315-287-2852
www.cadencebuilding.com

Coda
(ISSN 0010-017X) 1958- .
161 Frederick Street
Toronto, ON
M5A 4P3 Canada

Crescendo & Jazz Music
[previously *Crescendo International*]
(ISSN 0962-7472) 1962- .
28 Lamb's Conduit Street
London WC1N 3HQ, UK
44-207-4056556

Down Beat
(ISSN 0012-5768) 1934- .
P.O. Box 906
Elmhurst, IL 60126
800-554-7470
www.downbeat.com

Jazz Education Journal [Formerly *Jazz Educators Journal*]
(ISSN 0730-9791) 1969- .
P.O. Box 724
Manhattan, KS 66505
International Association for Jazz Education
785-776-8744
www.iaje.org

Jazz Improv
P.O. Box 26770
Elkins Park, PA 19027
888-472-0670
www.jazzimprov.com

Jazz Journal International
(ISSN 0140-2285) 1948- .
3 & 3A Forest Road
Loughton
Essex IG10 1DR UK
044 (0)20 8532 0456

Jazz Times
  (ISSN 0272-572X) 1980- .
  8737 Colesville Road, Ninth Floor.
  Silver Spring, MD 20910-3921
  888-458-4637
  www.jazztimes.com

Jazziz
  (ISSN 0741-5885) 1984- .
  P.O. Box 16357
  N. Hollywood, CA 91615
  800-742-3252
  www.jazziz.com

Jazzletter (Gene Lees)
  (ISSN 0890-6440) 1981- .
  P.O. Box 240, Ojai, CA 93023
  jazzlet@ix.netcom.com

Sources for Information About Jazz Records

ALLEN, DANIEL. *Bibliography of Discographies, Vol. II: Jazz*. Bowker, 1981.

HEFELE, BERNHARD. *Jazz-Bibliography*. Saur, 1981.

IAJRC Journal.
  (ISSN 0098-9487)
  International Association of Jazz Record Collectors
  c/o Art Zimmerman
  P.O. Box 158
  Jericho, NY 11753
  www.iajrc.org

Basic Jazz Discographies

Discographies are books that compile information about recording sessions including the formats and catalog numbers in which the recordings have been issued. They indicate how many versions ("takes") of each piece were made, the date, place, and musicians. Some list all the recording sessions for a given player or recording company.

BRUYNINCKX, WALTER. *60 Years of Recorded Jazz, 1917–1977*. Bruyninckx, 1979.

JEPSEN, JORGEN GRUNNET. *Jazz Records 1942-(1969): A Discography*. Knudsen, 1970.

LORD, TOM. *The Jazz Discography*. Lord Music Reference, 1992- .

RUST, BRIAN. *Jazz and Ragtime Records, 1897–1942*. rev. and expanded ed. Mainspring, 2002.

Note: North Country Distributors carries many discographies, rare jazz books, and imported jazz books. Write them at: Cadence Building, Redwood, NY 13679-3104; phone 315-287-2852; web *www.cadencebuilding.com*. Contact your reference librarian to locate discographies of particular musicians.

Texts for Readers Familiar with Musical Notation

BAILEY, DEREK. *Improvisation: Its Nature and Practice in Music*. Prentice-Hall, 1980; Da Capo, 1993.
  Essays and thoughts about method by a prominent, forward-looking jazz guitarist who has successfully tackled free improvisation in his performances.

HODEIR, ANDRE. *Jazz: Its Evolution And Essence*. rev. ed. Grove, 1980.

Technical analyses of various styles and recordings including an essay on trombonist Dicky Wells and one on Ellington's "Concerto for Cootie."

JOST, EKKEHARD. *Free Jazz*. Universal Edition, 1974; DaCapo, 1994.
  Technical analyses and notations of work by John Coltrane, Miles Davis (*Kind of Blue*), Charles Mingus, Ornette Coleman, Cecil Taylor, Archie Shepp, Albert Ayler, Don Cherry, the Association for the Advancement of Creative Musicians (AACM), Sun Ra, and the Art Ensemble of Chicago.

OSTRANSKY, LEROY. *The Anatomy of Jazz*. Univ. of Washington Press, 1960; Green wood, 1973.
  One of the most intelligently written commentaries on major issues in jazz.

OWENS, THOMAS. *Bebop: The Music and Its Players*. Oxford, 1995.
  Scholarly and technical examination of bebop, its origins, techniques, and the differences between styles of its players; goes all the way from Charlie Parker to John Coltrane, Freddie Hubbard, and their disciples.

SCHULLER, GUNTHER. *Early Jazz: Its Roots and Musical Development*. Oxford, 1968, 1986.
  A scholarly and quite technical examination of the earliest jazz known, its possible sources in African music and nineteenth-century American popular music. Includes detailed analyses of Louis Armstrong, Jelly Roll Morton, other pre-swing players, Fletcher Henderson, Ellington's earliest recordings, Bennie Moten, and territory bands during the 1920s and early 1930s.

SCHULLER, GUNTHER. *The Swing Era: The Development of Jazz, 1930–1945*. Oxford, 1989.
  Exhaustive sequel to the above by the most widely respected thinker in jazz history. Numerous in-depth, technical analyses and historical perspectives on the major figures. Large chapters on Benny Goodman, Louis Armstrong, Duke Ellington, Jimmie Lunceford, and Count Basie. Major sections on Art Tatum, Lester Young, and Earl Hines. Even goes as modern as Nat Cole and Lennie Tristano. Almost a thousand pages, this book and the above are basic reading for musically literate jazz fans and scholars.

TAYLOR, BILLY. *Jazz Piano: History and Development*. W.C. Brown, 1983.
  Discussion by a well-known jazz pianist and educator. Interspersed with musical notations and technical examples, the book is still useful for nonmusicians.

Technical References

BAKER, DAVID. *David Baker's Jazz Improvisation: A Comprehensive Method for All Musicians*. rev. 2nd ed. Alfred, 1988.
  A helpful instruction manual for intermediate and advanced as well as beginning jazz improvisers.

COKER, JERRY. *Improvising Jazz*. Prentice-Hall, 1964; Simon & Schuster, 1987.
  Excellent explanation of chords, chord progressions, how to swing, and how to improvise melodically.

MEHEGAN, JOHN. *Jazz Improvisation 1: Tonal and Rhythmic Principles*. Watson-Guptill, 1959.

MEHEGAN, JOHN. *Jazz Improvisation 2: Jazz Rhythm and the Improvised Line*. Watson-Guptill, 1962.

MEHEGAN, JOHN. *Jazz Improvisation 3: Swing and Early Progressive Piano Styles*. Watson-Guptill, 1964.

MEHEGAN, JOHN. *Jazz Improvisation 4: Contemporary Piano Styles.* Watson-Guptill, 1965.

Mehegan's textbooks provide a scholarly instruction series for the serious jazz student who has solid knowledge of the piano. The series is not exclusively for pianists, but any non-pianist using it must have some acquaintance with the keyboard.

REEVES, SCOTT D. *Creative Jazz Improvisation.* 3rd ed. Prentice Hall, 2001.

Textbook for budding improvisers, provides the technical basics and provides analyses of key solos from jazz history.

SUDNOW, DAVID. *Ways of the Hand: A Rewritten Account.* MIT Press, 2001.

A narrative of how one man learned to play jazz piano; filled with useful photographs and drawings of hand positions on the keyboard.

ZINN, DAVID. *The Structure & Analysis of the Modern Improvised Line.* Excelsior Music Publishing Co., 1981.

A very formal, technical instruction manual for musicians. It should also interest music theorists because it represents an intelligent analysis for the construction of melodic lines from rhythmic and harmonic perspectives.

Note: To keep up with the currently available technical references, seek the catalogs of Jamey Aebersold Jazz, Inc., P.O. Box 1244, New Albany, IN 47151-1244; phone 800-456-1388; web *www.jazzbooks.com.*

General References

BASCOM, WILLIAM R., and MELVILLE J. HERSKOVITS, ed. *Continuity and Change in African Cultures.* University of Chicago Press, 1959, 1962.

Contains an excellent chapter on African music by Alan Merriam and several other studies of African art and culture that should be helpful for readers interested in the roots of jazz.

BEBEY, FRANCIS. *African Music: A People's Art.* Lawrence Hill, 1975, 1992.

African music, its forms, musicians, instruments, and place in the life of the people; well illustrated.

BERLIN, EDWARD A. *Ragtime: A Musical and Cultural History.* University of California Press, 1980; iUniverse, 2002.

Scholarly evaluation of ragtime; includes musical notations.

COKER, JERRY. *How to Listen to Jazz.* rev. ed. Prentice-Hall, 1978; J. Aebersold, 1990.

One of the best guides to appreciating the playing of jazz improvisers; loaded with insights about how musicians develop solos. Keyed to the *Smithsonian Collection of Classic Jazz*; contains numerous, detailed analyses that often require musical background from the reader.

COLLIER, JAMES LINCOLN. *The Making of Jazz.* Houghton Mifflin, 1978; Delta, 1979.

If you can get past the author's attempts at psychoanalyzing musicians, you will find some interesting musical analyses here. The book integrates a large assortment of styles in an easy to read manner.

FEATHER, LEONARD. *The Book of Jazz.* Horizon, 1957; Dell, 1976.

An instrument-by-instrument history of jazz plus discussions of the origins of jazz and the nature of jazz improvisation. This book remains the best compact guide to jazz and summary of the perspectives of this exceedingly knowledgeable and insightful musician-journalist.

GIOIA, TED. *The History of Jazz.* Oxford, 1997.

Very readable, intelligent analysis of the field. One of the best histories on the market, it treats each style with respect and understanding, even reaching well-measured evaluation of such recent styles as acid jazz.

HARRISON, MAX, CHARLES FOX, and ERIC THACKER. *The Essential Jazz Recordings: Ragtime to Swing, Vol. 1.* Mansell, 1984; Continuum, 2000.

Informative, insightful, annotated discography that may also serve as a history of jazz.

HARRISON, MAX, ERIC THACKER, and STUART NICHOLSON. *The Essential Jazz Recordings: Modernism to Postmodernism, Vol. 2.* Mansell, 2000; Continuum, 2000.

Excellent sequel to the above.

HASSE, JOHN EDWARD, ed. *Jazz: The First Century.* William Morrow, 2000.

Lavishly illustrated collection of thoughtful, highly informative reports and essays on the major styles and issues in jazz history by some of the best writers. An impressive grasp of the field is demonstrated, and its large amount of information is conveyed in an entertaining manner.

KERNFELD, BARRY, ed. *The New Grove Dictionary of Jazz.* 2nd ed. Grove, 2002.

KOENIG, KARL, ed. *Jazz in Print (1856-1929): An Anthology of Selected Early Readings in Jazz History.* Pendragon, 2002.

Almost 2000 pages of rare articles from newspapers and magazines, spanning the time of slavery and minstrelsy to the reception of ragtime in the teens and the reception of jazz in the 1920s. This compilation should be in every respectable music library.

LOWE, ALLEN. *That Devilin' Tune: A Jazz History 1900-1950.* Music and Arts Programs of America, 2001.

A revisionist history of jazz superior to other books at demonstrating the origins of jazz in popular music and minstrelsy, then the continuation of jazz with its back and forth relation to white pop music, not just the major currents of African-American contributions. The 36 CD collection of rare sound recordings that accompanies this book illustrates stylistic connections that are routinely overlooked by most historians. This may well be the most enlightened history to be published. Pair this with the Allyn Shipton book (below), and a reader will possess what was previously known and understood only by extremely knowledgeable insiders.

This collection can be ordered by phoning 510-525-4583; emailing *info@musicandarts.com* or *ammusic@maine.rr.com*; or contacting Music and Arts Programs of America, Inc., P.O. Box 771, Berkeley, CA 94701.

NKETIA, J. H. KWABENA. *The Music of Africa.* Norton, 1974.

Nontechnical description of African musical traditions, training of performers, musical instruments; technical analyses of vocal and instrumental music; richly illustrated with music, photographs, maps and song lyrics.

PORTER, LEWIS. *Jazz: A Century of Change: Readings and New Essays.* Schirmer, 1997.

Assorted articles, some technical with musical notation, some philosophical, several serious historical inquiries, a few opinion pieces, and some reports on the reception of various jazz styles. Probably too sophisticated for novice readers, but definitely useful for musicians, teachers, and historians, notably because of its inclusion of important research and thinking by such eminent musicologists as Lawrence Gushee, Richard Rodney Bennett, Virgil Thompson, and Mark Gridley.

PORTER, LEWIS, MICHAEL ULLMANN, and ED HAZELL. *Jazz: From Its Origins to the Present.* Prentice-Hall, 1993.

One of the best jazz history books. Includes technical analyses and musical notations.

SHIPTON, ALYN. *A New History of Jazz.* Continuum, 2001.

A revisionist history of jazz, running almost a thousand pages, this volume dispels widely held myths and provides serious fresh research and thinking about what happened musically and why. The author puts musical events in perspective that have been long misunderstood or glossed over by other writers. He treats currents in jazz history from multiple vantage points. The book reaches fusion knowledgeably, even gets to such recent figures as John Zorn and Dave Douglas, and equitably positions the neo-traditionalists of the 1990s. Pair this with the Allen Lowe book (above), and a reader will understand what few teachers or scholars, and hardly any jazz journalists, understood prior to the availability of these works.

SOUTHERN, EILEEN. *The Music of Black Americans: A History.* 3rd ed. Norton, 1997.

Covers popular, classical, folk, and religious music, and jazz.

SUDHALTER, RICHARD M. *Lost Chords: White Musicians and Their Contribution to Jazz, 1915–1945.* Oxford, 1994.

Discusses the New Orleans Rhythm Kings, Emmett Hardy, Miff Mole, Red Nichols, Adrian Rollini, Bud Freeman, Jean Goldkette, Tommy and Jimmy Dorsey, Bob Crosby, Bix Beiderbecke, Frankie Trumbauer, Benny Goodman, Artie Shaw, Red Norvo, Pee Wee Russell, Bunny Berigan, and Jack Teagarden.

WALSER, ROBERT, ed. *Keeping Time: Readings in Jazz History.* Oxford, 1999.

A wide range of essays by eminent musicians and journalists. Some are factual, but most are opinion pieces. Concerned primarily with issues and controversies rather than the music itself, the collection should prove entertaining for readers who already possess comprehensive knowledge of the music and its history. It is not recommended for newcomers to jazz, however, because, for many of the essays, such readers would be unlikely to put the emotions and ignorance of the writers in perspective.

WARD, GEOFFREY and KEN BURNS. *Jazz: A History of America's Music.* Alfred A. Knopf, 2000.

An edited print-out of the script for the Ken Burns 19-hour television series: JAZZ. Like the film, this work deals more with American history of the twentieth century, the history of racism, the context of jazz, and the reception of jazz than how jazz was made and/or how to get the most out of listening to it. It is filled with alternately amusing and heartbreaking anecdotes about the musicians and their situations. Very smoothly written, illustrated with priceless rare photos, the book provides a compelling commentary for anyone who already knows the music and does not mind a narrative skewed toward gossip, stressing the sadness and struggle of its subjects.

Women in Jazz

DAHL, LINDA. *Stormy Weather: The Music and Lives of a Century of Jazzwomen.* Pantheon, 1984; Limelight Editions, 1989.

ENTICE, WAYNE, and JANIS STOCKHOUSE. *Jazzwomen: Conversations with Twenty-One Musicians.* Indiana University Press, 2004.

GOURSE, LESLIE. *Madame Jazz: Contemporary Women Instrumentalists.* Oxford, 1995.

HANDY, D. ANTOINETTE. *Black Women in American Bands and Orchestras.* 2nd ed. Scarecrow, 1998.

KOENIG, KARL. "Women Pianists in Early New Orleans Jazz." In *Jazz Research Papers,** ed. Charles Brown, 115–121. National Association of Jazz Educators, 1986.

LEDER, JAN. *Women in Jazz: A Discography of Instrumentalists, 1913-1968.* Greenwood, 1985.

MCCORD, KIMBERLY. "The Conceptualization of Women in Jazz." In *Jazz Research Papers,** ed. Charles Brown, 93–105. NAJE, 1985.

MCCORD, KIMBERLY. "History of Women in Jazz." *Jazz Educators Journal** 18, No. 2 (1986): 15.

MCCORD, KIMBERLY. "All-Women Jazz Groups." In *Jazz Research Papers,** ed. Charles Brown, 134-140. NAJE, 1986.

PLACKSIN, SALLY. *American Women in Jazz.* Wideview Books, 1982.

UNTERBRINK, MARY. *Jazz Women at the Keyboard.* McFarland & Co., 1983.

*Jazz Educators Journal and *Jazz Research Papers* are available from the International Association for Jazz Education, P.O. Box 724, Manhattan, KS 66505, phone 785-776-8744, web *www.iaje.org.*

APPENDIX G
Sources for Solo Transcriptions

There are hundreds of books filled with transcriptions of famous jazz improvisations. Catalogs and ordering information for them are available in *Jazz Education Journal*, the official journal of the International Association of Jazz Education. You can get back issues from school band directors who belong to the organization. Or you can join the organization yourself by sending them your check. It is only a small fee, and the information they distribute is well worth it. Just write International Association of Jazz Education, P.O. Box 724, Manhattan, Kansas 66502, *www.iaje.org*.

Many jazz books and magazines include notations of jazz improvisations. The Mehegan books, listed on page 486 under "Technical References," contain numerous solo transcriptions. *Down Beat* magazine, listed on page 484 under "Jazz Magazines," used to includes transcriptions or instructional aids in almost every issue. Going through back issues of *Down Beat* can reveal a treasure house of notations.

James Dapogny has transcribed several Jelly Roll Morton piano solos and added them to published works and music from the rolls of player pianos for a total of 40 numbers in *Ferdinand "Jelly Roll" Morton: The Collected Piano Music*, published by Smithsonian Institution Press/G. Schirmer.

The most dedicated of all solo transcribers is Andrew White. From him, you can order more than 700 John Coltrane solos, more than 300 Charlie Parker solos, and several Eric Dolphy solos. Write Andrew's Music at 4830 South Dakota Avenue, N.E., Washington, D.C. 20017, or phone 202-526-3666.

Jamey Aebersold distributes numerous books of solo transcriptions. One series is by David Baker, and it includes one book each for Clifford Brown, Miles Davis, John Coltrane, Sonny Rollins, Cannonball Adderley, and Fats Navarro. Aebersold also distributes transcription books by Ken Slone and Don Sickler. Slone has prepared a book of Clifford Brown solos. Sickler has one of Joe Henderson's solos. There are also some fairly elaborate books of transcriptions from a series originally published under the auspices of *Down Beat* magazine. It includes *Jazz Styles and Analysis: Guitar* by Jack Petersen (74 solos from 64 guitarists), *Jazz Styles and Analysis: Alto Sax* by Harry Miedema (125 solos from 103 saxophonists), and *Jazz Styles and Analysis: Trombone* by David Baker (157

solos). Aebersold distributes so many more such books that you ought to just write to request his catalog. When this book went to press, Aebersold was carrying books of solos by Stan Getz, Chick Corea, Louis Armstrong, Bill Evans, Horace Silver, Benny Goodman, Art Tatum, J. J. Johnson, Charlie Parker, Thelonious Monk, Bud Powell, Paul Chambers, Dexter Gordon, and others. Write Jamey Aebersold at P.O. Box 1244, New Albany, IN 47151-1244; *www.jazzbooks.com*; phone 800-456-1388.

Carl Fischer Music, Inc. has published several books by Stuart Isacoff that contain solo transcriptions, accompanied by useful analyses and comments about the styles of major players. *Solos for Tenor Sax* contains analyses of improvisations by John Coltrane, Stan Getz, Coleman Hawkins, Oliver Nelson, and Sonny Rollins. *Solos for Jazz Trumpet* contains analyses of improvisations by Louis Armstrong, Dizzy Gillespie, Miles Davis, Lee Morgan, and Freddie Hubbard. *Solos for Jazz Alto Sax* contains analyses of improvisations by Cannonball Adderley, Paul Desmond, Eric Dolphy, Johnny Hodges, Charlie Parker, and Phil Woods.

Hal Leonard Publishing Corporation has published Greg Fishman's transcriptions of nineteen solos by Stan Getz, Tim Price's transcriptions of 25 solos by Cannonball Adderley, Mike Barry and Kevin Carberry's transcriptions of 24 solos by Freddie Hubbard, Bob Leso's transcriptions of 12 solos by McCoy Tyner, Sanford Marten's transcriptions of 25 solos by Wayne Shorter, and Lennie Niehaus's transcriptions of 22 solos by Dexter Gordon. Leonard also sells the entire set of solos from the Miles Davis album *Kind of Blue*. The books may be obtained through Aebersold or directly from Hal Leonard, 7777 West Bluemound Road, Milwaukee, Wisconsin 53213; web *www.halleonard.com*.

Many solo transcriptions can be found in doctoral dissertations. These are books written to earn a doctor's degree. Most are never commercially published. However, when the doctor's degree is granted, most dissertations are automatically deposited with a company called ProQuest CSA, formerly University Microfilms, which permanently retains one copy and then makes and sells additional copies on demand. This has been occurring only since 1956, so do not contact University Microfilms for work completed before then. (Note that University of Chicago, Harvard University, and Massachusetts Institute of

Technology are among the few institutions that do not contribute to this repository.)

To get a dissertation, write ProQuest CSA, formerly University Microfilms International, 789 E. Eisenhower Parkway, Box 1346, Ann Arbor, Michigan 48106; *www.proquest.com*. Tell them the author's name (it helps to have the middle initial), the first two words of the title, the college where the dissertation was done, and the year it was completed. This information helps them identify the dissertation when you lack the catalog number. When you correspond with them, tell them your college affiliation because they extend a discount to students and faculty. You can phone them at their toll-free number: 800-521-3042. *www.proquest.com/products_umi/dissertations/individuals.shtml* They also accept credit card orders.

You will probably come across many titles of books, articles, and dissertations that you just want to glance at, not necessarily own. For that reason, it is handy to know about interlibrary loan services. If you have never used such a service, ask the staff at your college library's reference desk. The staff should have a computer that will tell what nearby library is holding the book, article, or dissertation you want. The staff can put in a request. Then you need wait only a few weeks before your library receives it for you. You can check it out just as you would check out one of your own library's holdings. Note that if you want only a single article from a periodical, your interlibrary loan staff can sometimes arrange for a distant library to copy the article and send it for you to keep. (This can be quite convenient when you want a particularly good transcription that lies in an old jazz magazine that no one in town seems to have.)

To keep up with new dissertations that are being added to the literature about jazz, you could search the music listings in *Dissertation Abstracts* that is available on-line to libraries that subscribe to the *ProQuest Dissertations & Theses Database (PQDT)*. The full database provides abstracts (summaries) of the dissertations. The company also provides Datrix, a free personalized search service that lists citations of dissertations. This is convenient if you lack access to a library subscription to the PQDT database.

The complete Stan Kenton band score and Maynard Ferguson's solos for the Robert Graettinger "A Trumpet" (available on *Jazz Classics CD2* and analyzed in the listening guide in Chapters 10) is included in the doctoral dissertation of Robert B. Morgan: "The Music and Life of Robert Graettinger" (catalog #75-00375). It was completed in 1974 at the University of Illinois.

Here are a few dissertations that have many transcriptions in them:

Charlie Parker: Techniques of Improvisation, by Thomas Owens, 1974, University of California
Catalog Number 75-1992
(Contains about 250 Parker solos)

A History and Analysis of Jazz Drumming to 1942, by Theodore Dennis Brown, 1976, University of Michigan
Catalog Number 77-7881
(Contains numerous drum solos and timekeeping rhythms as well as analyses.)

The Improvisational Techniques of Art Tatum, by Joseph A. Howard, 1978, Case Western Reserve University
Catalog Number 78-16468

Structural Development in the Jazz Improvisational Technique of Clifford Brown, by Milton Lee Stewart, 1973, University of Michigan
Catalog Number 73-24692

John Coltrane's Music of 1960 Through 1967, by Lewis R. Porter, 1983, Brandeis University
Catalog Number 83-18239

Jazz, 1920 to 1927: An Analytical Study, by Launcelot Allen Pyke, II, 1962, State University of Iowa
Catalog Number 62-4988

(Contains transcriptions of 1926 "Perdido Street Blues" with Kid Ory, Johnny Dodds, and Baby Dodds, 1923 "Snake Rag" by King Oliver's Creole Jazz Band, 1942 "Down By the Riverside" by Bunk Johnson's Original Superior Band, 1927 "Keyhole Blues" by Louis Armstrong and His Hot Seven, the 1923 Gennett recording of "Dippermouth Blues" by King Oliver's Creole Jazz Band, 1924 "Cake Walkin' Babies" by Armstrong and Bechet, 1926 "Big Butter and Egg Man From The West" by Louis Armstrong and His Hot Five, 1923 "Sweet Lovin' Man" by King Oliver's Creole Jazz Band minus Oliver, 1925 "Papa De-Da-Da" by Armstrong and Bechet, and 1923 "Southern Stomps" by Oliver's Creole Jazz Band.)

APPENDIX H
For Musicians

You have now entered the technical part of the appendix. This section is designed to give musically literate readers a chance to experience some of the musical elements discussed in the main body of the text. Keep in mind that it is possible to learn more by playing the examples at the piano than by merely reading the attached explanations. Once you have played these demonstrations yourself, the principles will be more obvious to you when they occur in jazz recordings.

Chords and Chord Progressions

One way to understand how chords can be constructed is to imagine them as being built from tones in the major scales. For instance, in the key of Bb, tones for the chords can be drawn from the notes in the Bb major scale (Bb C D Eb F G A Bb). In the key of C, they can be drawn from the notes in the C scale (C D E F G A B C). Beginning with a single tone, the chord is made by adding every other tone in the scale. In other words, the first, third, and fifth tones are used when the beginning tone is the key note (first tone of the major scale). The second, fourth, and sixth tones are used when the chord is based on the second step of the scale. The third, fifth, and seventh tones are used when the chord begins on the third step of the scale.

If a chord is based on the first tone of the major scale, it is called the "one chord," symbolized by the Roman numeral for one, I. The chord based on the second step of the major scale is a II chord. The labeling system continues through the VII chord.

The system is more involved than what we have discussed. Before you can apply chord knowledge to studying improvisation, you must become acquainted with construction of many types of chords: dominant sevenths and major sevenths; major, minor, diminished, and augmented chords; chords with added ninths, elevenths, and thirteenths; chords with added fourths and sixths, flat fifths, raised ninths, etc. You will also need to confront a collection of different chord labeling systems.

12-Bar Blues Progressions

Though basically a I-IV-I-V-I progression, the 12-bar blues may contain a huge assortment of chord progressions. Here are three possibilities for a blues in the key of C.

Turnarounds

Turnarounds are the sets of chord progressions occurring in the seventh and eighth, fifteenth and sixteenth, thirty-first and thirty-second bars of a 32-bar chord progression and in the eleventh and twelfth bars of a 12-bar blues progression. Some turnarounds occupy more or less than two measures, however. Turnarounds provide an opportunity for numerous variations, all of which depend on the preferences and era of soloist and accompanists.

Voicing

Rarely is a chord played with its tones contained in a single octave, the root on the bottom, the third in the middle, and the fifth on the top.

Usually chords are voiced. This means that the positions of a chord's tones are scattered over the keyboard; the tones may be altered, doubled, added to, or missing. For instance, instead of having the root on the bottom and the fifth on the top, a chord might have its root on top and fifth on the bottom.

Or perhaps the third is on the bottom, the fifth in the middle and the root on top.

Root of C

In some voicings, the root is doubled by being duplicated in different octaves.

A is the 6th of C

Quite frequently the sixth is added to enrich major triads.

1   2   3   4

Instead of being voiced in thirds (every other step in a major scale), some chords are voiced in fourths.

Right hand (4ths)

Left hand (5ths)

Many other possibilities are available for voicing chords. Only a few simple examples have been cited here as an introduction. Voicings are important partly because, in addition to striking force, phrasing, speed, and precision, an identifying characteristic of a jazz pianist's style is his preference in voicings. For instance, McCoy Tyner often uses an interval of a fifth in his left hand and a chord voiced in fourths in his right hand.

Modes

Though used for centuries in classical music, modes just recently became popular harmonic bases for jazz improvisation. To get a rough idea of what is meant by the term "modes," we can use the tones of the major scale to produce different modes if we play ascending sequences, starting on different steps of the scale. Each mode's unique sound is the result of its particular arrangement of whole steps and half steps. For example, in the Ionian mode (also known as the major scale), half steps occur only between the third and fourth steps and the seventh and eighth steps. (The eighth step is an octave up from the first step.)

The Dorian mode is constructed from the same tones as the Ionian, but it begins on the second tone of the major scale. The Dorian mode has half steps between its second and third and its sixth and seventh tones.

There is a mode for each step of the major scale. Each mode has a distinct musical personality because its half steps fall in different places.

Examine the following modes. Play them, and listen carefully while you play them. Find the positions of the half steps in each mode. Once you know a mode's pattern of whole and half steps, you should be able to begin it on other notes. Remember that the interval between Bb and C is defined as a whole step, as is that between E and F#. Remember also that the interval between B and C is a half step, as is that between E and F.

Diminished

Inverted Diminished

Modal Construction of "Flamenco Sketches"

The piece "Flamenco Sketches" on the Miles Davis album *Kind of Blue* follows the modal construction illustrated below. It is also available on the *JCCD2* Track 9.

mode 1

mode 2

mode 3

mode 4

mode 5

Modal Construction of "Maiden Voyage"

The original recording is available on *JCCD2* Track 8.

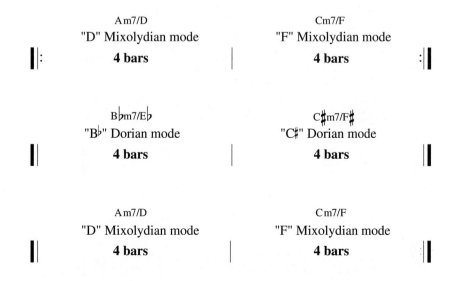

Am7/D
"D" Mixolydian mode
4 bars

Cm7/F
"F" Mixolydian mode
4 bars

B♭m7/E♭
"B♭" Dorian mode
4 bars

C♯m7/F♯
"C♯" Dorian mode
4 bars

Am7/D
"D" Mixolydian mode
4 bars

Cm7/F
"F" Mixolydian mode
4 bars

"D" Mixolydian, first mode for A section of "Maiden Voyage"

"F" Mixolydian, second mode for A section of "Maiden Voyage"

"B♭" Dorian, first mode for bridge of "Maiden Voyage"

"C♯" Dorian, second mode for bridge of "Maiden Voyage"

Modal Construction for "So What" and "Impressions"

"D" Dorian mode for first sixteen bars of "So What" and "Impressions"

"E♭" Dorian mode for bridge of "So What" and "Impressions"

Modal Construction for "Milestones"

"G" Dorian mode for first sixteen bars of "Milestones"

"A" Aeolian mode for bridge of "Milestones"

Ride Rhythms

Ride rhythms are used by drummers to keep time and propel a performance. These rhythms contribute to jazz swing feeling, accomplishing in the high register, on the cymbals, what the walking bass does in the low register. (These were all transcribed and notated by Chuck Braman.)

*NOTE: The 12/8 figures are notated from 4/4 tunes.

"Boston" or Two-Handed Stride-Style Comping (notated by David Berger)

Comping

Here are two examples of piano accompaniments, or comping, for a jazz 12-bar blues solo. Comping is accompaniment that is simultaneously composed and performed to fit the style of a piece and the directions in harmony, rhythm, and melody that are taken by the soloist. Comping usually contains pronounced syncopation.

Note that these chords have been voiced. Comping involves a seemingly endless variety of ways to voice chords, alter chord progressions, and design rhythms. But basically, comping is meant to accompany and complement the solo line by producing syncopated, unpatterned bursts of chords. Prepatterned chording, by definition, cannot flexibly enhance a spontaneously conceived solo line. Rehearsed patterns (and accompaniment figures that sound written) cannot sensitively interact with solo improvisation. The improvising soloist might just as well be playing with a big band and its written arrangements. To understand what this means, listen first to Tommy Flanagan's accompaniment work on any of the recordings he made during the 1950s and 1960s or any of the accompaniment work that Herbie Hancock did during the 1960s. Then listen to Horace Silver's accompaniment work of the 1960s with his own bands or John Lewis's with the Modern Jazz Quartet. The Flanagan and Hancock examples interact with the soloists, whereas the Silver and

Lewis examples often sound more like worked-out material, even if they were spontaneous.

Bebop-Style Comping (notated by David Berger)

Walking Bass Lines

Walking is meant to provide timekeeping in the form of tones chosen for their compatibility with the harmonies of the piece and style of the performance. Ideally, the walking bass complements the solo line.

Three choruses of walking bass are shown here. They display three increasing levels of complexity for walking bass lines for the 12-bar blues in the key of C (conceived and notated by Willis Lyman).

Rock Bass Lines

Jazz bassists of the 1970s incorporated many devices that were previously used mainly by rock and funk bassists. A number of rock and funk bass figures are notated here to illustrate the material from which many 1970s jazz bassists drew (notated by Richard Straub).

Latin American Bass Line

During performances of many jazz pieces during the 1950s and 1960s, including the first eight measures of "On Green Dolphin Street" and "I'll Remember April," bassists employed a figure like the one below. Musicians called it a "Latin bass figure."

Syncopations

The rhythms common to jazz contain many syncopations. Here are a few examples.

Comping Figures for "Rhythm Changes"

This is a typical example of piano comping for improvisations that follow the chord changes used by George Gershwin to accompany his melody "I Got Rhythm." This would also fit "Cottontail," "Shaw Nuff," "Lester Leaps In," and "(Meet the) Flintstones." Other comping examples for Flintstones can be heard on the *Demo CD*, with and without the Flintstones melody. (Comping composed and notated by Jerry Sheer.)

Jazz-Rock/Jazz-Funk Drumming

Drummers of the late 1960s learned new timekeeping patterns that resembled the materials of rhythm and blues bands as well as Latin American styles. Below is a comparison that illustrates what Herbie Hancock's drummer learned from Sly Stone's drummer. (These were all transcribed and notated by Chuck Braman.)

Andy Newmark—"In Time" from Sly Stone's *Fresh*, 1973

Mike Clarke—"Butterfly" from Herbie Hancock's *Thrust*, 1974

KEY (for this page only)

CLOSED HIGH HAT OPEN HIGH HAT SNARE BASS HIGH HAT SHARPLY
STRUCK WITH STICK STRUCK WITH STICK DRUM DRUM CLOSED WITH FOOT

INDEX

A

Aarons, Al, 155
"Above and Below," 400, 402–5
Abrams, Muhal Richard, 327, 330, 335
acid jazz, 394–98, 405, 425
  the groove, 397–98
  looping, 395
  mixers, 395
  overdubbing, 396
  rap and hip-hop, 394–95, 397, 416–18
  sampling, 395
  turntablists, 396
acoustic jazz, 422, 423
acoustic bass. *See* bass
Adams Pepper, 231
Adderley, Cannonball, 246, 265
  "Flamenco Sketches," 269–71
  hard bop, 229–30, 246, 257
  soprano saxophone work, 302
  with Miles Davis, 265–66, 268–71
Adderley, Nat, 79, 229–30, 246
African American musical traditions, 35–37,
    43–50, 51–54
  blue notes, 49–50
  the blues, 35, 36, 38, 42, 91–94
  call-and-response format, 50–51
  European-style music, 42–43
  funk, 42
  gospel, 364, 366–67
  improvisation, 44
  instrumentation, 46
  ostinato, 47–48
  overlapping, 50
  percussion, 47
  pitch alteration, 48
  polyrhythms, 48
  ragtime, 35, 39–42
  roughening, buzzing, and ringing
    sounds, 47
  syncopation, 45, 39
  vocal practices, 44
African music, 36, 41, 43, 46–47, 50, 51
African traditions, 36, 42, 44, 47
Afro-Cuban styles, 409–16
After Hours, 258
After You've Gone," 107, 109–10, 172
Agharta, 371, 373
"Ain't Misbehavin'", 70
Akiyoshi, ToshikoAlemany, Jesus, 427
Ali, Rashied, 326
Alias, Charles, 387
"Alice in Wonderland," 346
"All Blues," 268
Allen, Geri, 173, 349
Allen, Henry "Red", 60, 100, 105
Allen, Marshall, 329, 326
"All the Things You Are," 166, 266, 291
Altissimo, 413–15
alto saxophone, 102, 246
  bop, 187
  cool jazz, 206–9, 211, 217–18, 227
  hard bop, 231, 232, 246
  swing-era big bands, 101, 107–8
Altschul, Barry, 351, 439
ambient music, 392
"America the Beautiful," 44
Ammons, Albert, 73
Ammons, Gene, 157
Anatomy of a Murder, 130, 143
Anderson, Cat, 130, 135
Anderson, Fred, 330

Andy Kirk and His Twelve Clouds of Joy, 113,
  114–15
antiphonal music, 102
A.R.C., 351, 354, 437, 439
Arabic music, 426
Archia Tom, 157
arco, 25
Armstrong, Louis, 43, 60, 75–78, 83, 94, 95
  Hot Five and Seven recordings, 75, 96, 17
    "Hotter Than That," 80–82, 96
  improvisation, 75, 77–78
  movie appearances, 75
  singing and scat, 48, 76, 78, 80
  swing eighth notes, 78
  trumpet style, 64, 78
  "West End Blues," 76–77
Armstrong Lil Hardin, 60
Arodin, Sidney, 60
Arp, 375
"Arrival in New York," 376
Art Ensemble of Chicago, 308, 326,
    330–32, 337
Art Farmer-Benny Golson Jazztet, 230, 295
"Artistry in Rhythm," 208–09, 211, 213
Ascension, 292–93, 303
Ashby, Harold, 134
Ashby, Irving, 100
A-sections, 18–19
Association for the Advancement of Creative
    Musicians (AACM), 327, 330–32, 335
Astro Black, 328,
"A-Tisket-a-Tasket," 119
At the Bal Masque, 143
atonal music, 293, 309, 416
attack, 48, 314, 479
Auld, Georgie, 100Austin High Gang,
  61, 65
Autrey, Herman, 100
avant-garde, 11, 172, 307–8
  Chicago, 327–32
  popularity, 333–34
  World Saxophone Quartet, 332–33
The Avant-Garde, 292
Ayers, Roy, 397
Ayler, Albert, 308, 316–19, 333–34
  avant-garde style, 172
  "Ghosts: First Variation," 317–19
  pitch bending, 48
Ayler, Don, 326
A-A-B-A, 18–19
"*A Love Supreme*", 400

B

Bach, Johann Sebastian, 204, 221
back beats, 104, 395
Back on the Block, 376
background music, 393–94
"Bags' Groove," 176
Baker, Chet, 185, 216, 219, 225
"Bakiff," 143
Balkan music, 407
ballads, 91, 135–36, 137, 143, 191
Bangs, Chris, 394
banjo, 46, 88, 103
"Barbary Coast," 381
baritone saxophone, 136
  cool jazz, 218–19
  swing-era big bands, 101
Barnet, Charlie, 302
Baron, Joey, 406
Bartók, Bela, 351, 355

"Baseball," 430, 431–33
Basie, Count, 124, 149–60
  as bandleader, 104–5, 124
  comping, 103, 151
  "One O'Clock Jump," 52, 102, 151, 180,
    196, 376
  piano style, 19, 21, 103, 149, 151, 181
  rhythm guitar style, 103
  See also Count Basie bands
bass, 24–25, 88
  bop, 178–79
  bowing, 25, 379
  broken time, 25
  double-stops, 24
  doubling of melody lines, 354
  electric (Fender) bass, 368, 382
  free jazz, 320–24, 325–27
  funk bass, 381
  hard bop, 232, 254, 255
  jazz-rock fusion, 371
  Latin jazz *tumbao*, 411
    line, 16, 24, 179, 371
  melodic figures, 255, 346–47
  pizzicato bass with horns, 143
  solos, 103, 142–43, 381–82
  strumming, 24–25
  swing-era big bands, 103, 140–43
  two-beat style, 88, 103
  walking bass, 24, 88, 103, 381
bass clarinet, 135, 324, 329
bass drum, 28, 89, 179
bass guitar, 368, 382
bass marimba, 328
bass viol, 46, 101, 103, 368
Bauer, Billy, 205–6
Bauzá, Mario, 410
beat, 340
The Beatles, 75, 256
bebop. *See* bop
Bechet, Sidney, 60, 85–87, 95, 134, 135
"Bedspread," 321
Beiderbecke, Bix, 61, 79–85, 91, 94, 95
Beirach, Richie, 305, 356, 361
Bellson, Louis, 137–40
Belonging, 438
bends. *See* pitch bending
Benny Goodman Band, 85, 105–6, 116–17
Benoit, David, 393
Benson, George, 30, 78, 393
Berg, Alban, 355
Berigan, Bunny, 77
Berio, Luciano, 315
Bernstein, Artie, 116–17
Bernhardt, Warren, 272, 348
Berroa, Ignacio, 413–16
Bigard, Barney, 132, 134, 138–39, 143
big bands
  of the bop era, 170–71, 188, 189–90
  of the hard bop era, 254–57
  of the modern jazz era, 210–16
  of the swing era, 99–125
    bandleaders, 104–6
    block voicing, 105
    brass sections, 106–7
    call-and-response format, 102
    composing and arranging, 101–2, 113, 124,
      129, 130–32
    drumming, 104
    Duke Ellington. *See* Duke Ellington band
    hot bands, 121, 131
    improvisation, 101, 121, 123–24, 196

instrument sections, 101
piano, 47, 108–15, 124, 132, 149, 151
popularity, 121–24
rhythm sections, 101, 103–4, 108–18, 124–25, 150–51, 157
riffs, 102, 104, 151
saxophone sections, 107–8
singers, 117–21, 125
sweet bands, 121
"Big Dipper," 255
"Billie's Bounce," 167, 172
bird calls, 324
Birdhouse, 172
Birdland (nightclub), 172, 376
"Birdland," 11, 52–53, 257, 376, 380, 387
Birds of Fire, 374
Birth of the Cool Nonet, 209–10, 218, 262, 265
Birth of the Cool, 265, 266, 267
Bitches Brew, 262, 264, 265, 370, 371, 372, 375, 386, 417
"Black, Brown, and Beige," 130, 143, 146
Black, Jim, 407–8
Black Artists Group, 332–33
Black Beauty, 371, 373
"Black Bottom Stomp," 68
black codes, 37
"the black esthetic", 44
Blackwell, Eddie, 313
Blakey, Art, 257, 355
    "Cranky Spanky," 16, 25, 229, 232, 243–45
    hard bop style, 229–30, 238, 242–45
    Jazz Messengers, 243–45, 284
Blanchard, Terence, 261, 273
Blanton, Jimmy, 103, 140–43, 146, 178
Bley, Carla, 429–33, 439, 441
Bley, Paul, 308, 355
Blood, Sweat & Tears, 365, 368, 386
"Blood Count," 132
"Blue Cellophane," 137
Blue Light, 144
"Blue Horizon," 87
"Blue in Green," 268–71
blue notes, 49–50, 83
"Blue Rondo ala Turk," 18, 113, 222–24
the blues, 35, 36, 38, 42, 364–65
    improvisation, 44
    instrumental, 91
    poetic form, 462
    quality, 415, 454
    vocal, 91–94
blues chorus, 18
Bluiett, Hamiet, 332–33, 334
"Body and Soul," 21, 107, 111, 165, 192–93
bombs, 179
boogaloo, 398, 417
"Boogie-Woogie," 73
boogie-woogie, 47, 73, 113–15
"Boogie Woogie Waltz," 380
bop, 90, 134, 163–201
    bass styles, 178–79
    big band, 170–71, 188, 189–90
    complexity, 194–95
    cool jazz, 177–178, 187
    drumming, 179–80
    flatted fifths, 166
    guitar, 182
    hard. See hard bop
    harmony, 164–66
    improvisation, 164–66, 194–96, 230
    piano comping, 173–76, 180–82, 232
    popularity and success, 191–97
    reharmonization, 164–66
    rhythm sections, 178–82
    ride cymbals, 140, 180
    saxophone, 166–71, 186–88
    singers, 188–93, 194, 197

trombone, 185–86
trumpet, 170–73, 182–85
vibraphone, 177–78
whole-tone scales, 176
"Boplicity," 210, 218
bossa nova, 187, 410, 417
Bostic, Earl, 398
Botti, Chris, 393
bowed bass, 25, 379
Bowie, Lester, 330–32, 335
"Boy Meets Horn," 143
brass bands, 39–40, 41, 42, 46
brass bass, 88, 103, 368
brass sections, 79, 101, 134, 266
    See also trombone; trumpet
Braud, Wellman, 134
Braun, Rick, 393, 239, 424
Braxton, Anthony, 327, 308, 332, 335, 354, 417
Brazil, 418
Breathless, 400
break, 20–21, 80
Brecker, Michael, 253, 400–401, 402–5, 425
Brecker, Randy, 400, 402–5
The Brecker Brothers, 400, 401, 402–5
bridge sections. See B-sections
"Broken Hearted Melody," 188
broken time, 25
Brookmeyer, Bob, 224
Brown, Cleo, 220
Brown, Clifford, 185, 229, 236–38, 245, 247–50, 257
Brown, Denny, 104Brown, James, 44, 365, 368
Brown, John, 170–71
Brown, Lawrence, 106, 137, 140, 144–45
Brown, Pete, 218, 246
Brown, Ray, 122–23, 168–69, 170–71, 179, 192–93
Brubeck, Dave, 113, 218, 220–24, 226
Brubeck, Dave, Quartet, 218, 220–21, 222–24, 225
Buckner, Milt, 113, 115, 124, 182
Buckshot Lefonque, 417
The Buena Vista Social Club, 416
Burns, Ralph, 187
Burrell, Kenny, 254
Burton, Gary, 365, 368, 375, 382, 439
Butterfly, 205
buzzing sounds, 47
buzzmutes, 137
Byas, Don, 21, 107, 137
Byrd, Charlie, 187
Byrd, Donald, 235–36
Byron, Don, 406, 429

C

cadenzas, 21
Cage, John, 332, 354, 430
Caine, Uri, 349, 409
Cain, Jacki, 197
"Cake Walkin' Babies from Home," 75, 85
Calderazzo, Joey, 348
California, 203, 210, 219, 220
California style, 203, 210, 226
    See also cool jazz
call-and-response format, 50–51, 102
Calloway, Cab, 103, 418
"Candlelights," 82
"Captain Marvel," 354
Cara, Mancy, 76–77
"Caravan," 143
"Carelessly," 118
Caribbean music. See Latin jazz
The Carla Bley Big Band Goes to Church, 430
Carlton, Larry, 393
Carmen, 172
Carnegie Hall Jazz Orchestra, 422
Carney, Harry, 136
"Carolina Shout," 73

Carter, Benny, 106, 107–8, 124, 136, 211
Carter, Betty, 423
Carter, Ron, 239–42
    "Masqualero," 278–83
    "Nefertiti," 275–76
    with Miles Davis, 273–74, 285, 349, 370
"Casbah," 176
Casey, Al, 108
Catlett, Sid, 90, 183–85
Chaloff, Serge, 188, 205–6
Chambers, Paul, 254, 265–66, 269–72
"Chameleon," 257, 350, 383–84
Change of the Century, 313
Changes, 437
chants, 314, 440
Charles, Dennis, 402–5
Charles, Ray, 44, 376, 398
Charles, Teddy, 216
"The Charleston," 51, 73
Charlie Parker bands, 140
Charlie Ventura Boptet, 196–97
chart, 366–77
chatter, 90, 179
chattering, 27, 230, 325
"Chelsea Bridge," 132
"Cherokee," 166, 266
Cherry, Don, 311–12, 313–14, 333–34
Chicago, 60, 61–65, 68, 69, 75, 83, 308, 327, 330–31
Chicago avant-garde, 327–32, 334
    Anthony Braxton, 332
    Art Ensemble of Chicago, 330–32
    Association for the Advancement of Creative Musicians, 327, 330–32, 335
    Sun Ra, 327–29
Chicago style, 61–67, 94
    The Chicago School, 64–65
    piano combos, 69–72
    recordings of New Orleans style, 61–67
Chicago Transit Authority (Chicago), 365, 386
Chick Webb Band, 119
Chico Hamilton quintet, 324–25
Childs, Billy, 348
China, 46, 309
chops, 479
chord, 456–70
    change, 457–58, 465
    progressions, 18–22
        the blues, 38
        chorus, 18–19
        Coltrane's innovations, 290–91
        double-timing, 19–20
        endings, 21
        free jazz, 22, 308–9, 312–13, 314
        half-timing, 20
        hard bop, 230
        introductions, 21
        omission of the melody statement, 21
        quadruple-timing, 20
        reharmonization, 111, 124, 164–66
        rubato and pseudo rubato, 19
        solo breaks, 20–21
        32-bar A-A-B-A form, 18–19
        trading fours and eights, 19
        12-bar blues chorus, 18
    substitution, 111
    voicing, 73, 112, 255, 349
chorus, 18–19
chorusing, 438
Christian, Charlie, 106, 116–18, 125
"Chromatic Love Affair," 136
chromatic scale, 454
chromatic semitone, 456
church music, 36, 51, 143
Circle, 354
"Civilization Day," 22, 309, 311–12

clarinet, 95
 bop, 182
 early combos, 83–87
 obbligato role, 61
 ornamentation, 87
 pitch bending, 83, 87
 swing-era big bands, 132
"Clarinet Lament," 132, 143
clarinet obbligatos, 45
Clarke, Kenny, 170–71, 179–80, 197
Clarke, Stanley, 354
Classic, 422
classical music, 177, 187, 204, 218, 221
classical period of jazz, 163
clavé, 411
Clavinet, 383
Clay, James, 398
Clayton, Buck, 77, 157, 158–59
Clifford Brown-Max Roach Quintet, 247
The Coasters, 398
Cobb, Jimmy, 268–72
Cobham, Billy, 368, 374
Cohen, Greg, 406
Cohen (Copland), Marc, 348
Cole, Nat, 69, 111–12, 124, 181
Coleman, Bill, 108
Coleman, George, 239–42
Coleman, Ornette, 268, 271, 292, 308–13, 334
 chord progressions, 312–13
 "Civilization Day," 309, 311–12
 free jazz style, 292, 310–13
Coleman, Steve, 417–18
color tones, 155
Colours of Chloe, 439
Coltrane, John, 140, 288–303
 ballads, 291
 as bandleader, 173
 chord changes and sheets of sound, 290–91
 classic quartet, 293–302, 303, 372
 "Countdown," 290, 298
 "Flamenco Sketches," 269–71
 free jazz style, 292–93
 "Giant Steps," 290–91, 298hard bop style, 233,
  246, 253, 257
 impact of, 298
 innovations on saxophone, 289–93, 296–97,
  298, 372
 lead-in style, 87
 modal jazz, 291–92, 372
 pedal points and drones, 291, 296, 297
 "The Promise," 296, 297, 299–302
 soprano saxophone, 298, 302
 with Miles Davis, 265–66, 268–71, 290,
  293–94, 372
combos,early, 59–95
 The Chicago School, 64–65
 clarinet, 83–87
 collective improvisation, 61, 77, 85
 Creole Jazz Band, 64
 drums, 89–90
 guitar, 90–91
 instrument roles, 61
 New York jazz, 65
 Original Dixieland Jazz Band, 61–64
 piano, 68–75, 88–89
 recording, 61–65
 rhythm sections, 88–90
 saxophone, 85–87
 solo improvisation, 77–78, 85–87
 swing feeling, 68, 78, 85
 trombone, 87–88
 trumpet, 75–83
 vocal blues, 91–94
comping, 25, 103, 112
 bop, 173–76, 180–82
 Count Basie, 151
 Duke Ellington, 130

modern jazz, 151
 Thelonious Monk, 174
composer-arranger, 60, 67, 129, 132
compound meter, 235
composition, 23
 bop, 176–77, 197
 cool jazz, 213
 early combos, 66–67, 68, 73–75
 extended works, 130
 film scores, 130
 hard bop, 254–57
 swing-era big bands, 101–2, 113, 124, 129
 three-minute instrumentals, 130
 See also names of specific composers,
  e.g. Carla Bley
"Con Alma," 291
"Concertino for Jazz Quartet and Orchestra," 177
"Concerto for Cootie," 47, 131, 134, 143
"Concierto de Aranjuez," 267
Conference of the Birds, 327
"Confirmation," 167
conga drums, 370, 413
Connors, Bill, 354
constant tempo, 9
Contemporary Jazz, 393, 398–401
Cook, Junior, 252Cookin',265
cool jazz, 177–78, 187, 203–26, 262
 big bands, 210–16
 Birth of the Cool Nonet, 209–10, 218
 classical sound, 204, 218, 221
 composing and arranging, 204, 211, 213
 countermelodies, 204
 ECM Style, 437, 440
 guitar, 219–20
 improvisation style, 204–5
 piano, 204–7, 219, 220–24
 rhythm sections, 219–21
 saxophone, 206–11, 215, 217–19
 tone rows, 215
 trombone, 221–25
 trumpet, 209–10, 214–15, 216–17
 tuba, 210
 West Coast style, 210
"Cop-Out," 143
Corea, Chick, 339, 351–54, 358
 composing, 354
 ECM Style, 437, 439
  Elektric Band, 354
 free jazz style, 437
 hard bop style, 233
 jazz-rock and funk, 354
 Latin American music, 351, 354
 Return to Forever, 354
 solo piano work, 437, 439
 "Steps," 352–53
cornet, 79
Coryell, Larry, 365, 368, 374, 37
"Cottontail," 18, 47, 130–36, 140, 142, 143
 call-and-response format, 50–51
 instrumentation, 101, 102
Count Basie bands, 121, 149–60
 arrangements, 151
 drummers, 140
 early years, 150–57
 Jones-Smith, Inc., 157
 Kansas City Five, 157, 158–59
 later years, 157–59
 "Lester Leaps In," 158–59
 Lester Young in, 152–57
 rhythm sections, 150–51
 riff style, 151
 "Taxi War Dance," 153–54
 with Billie Holiday, 118
 See also Basie, Count
"Countdown," 290, 298
countermelodies, 46, 83, 204
counterpoint, 158, 478

country music, 364
"Country Preacher," 246
Country Roads and Other Places, 375
cowbells, 29, 46, 89, 104
"Cranky Spanky," 16, 25, 229, 232, 243–45
crash cymbals, 26
Crawford, Hank, 398, 399
Creole culture, 37–38, 42
Creole Jazz Band, 64
"Creole Love Call," 131, 132
"Creole Rhapsody," 130
The Creoles of Color of New Orleans (Haskins), 37
"Crescendo in Blue," 130
Crosby, Bing, 75, 78
Crossings, 350
cross-over music, 480
The Crusaders, 393, 398
"Crystal Silence," 354, 439
Cuba, 37, 409, 416
"Cubano Be," 173
"Cubano Bop," 173
Cuban styles. *See* Latin jazz
The Cure, 356
Curtis, King, 398
cymbals, 16, 28, 89
 crash, 26
 floor, 89
 high-hat, 26, 27, 89, 104
 in swing-era big bands, 104
 ride, 25–26, 46, 47, 90, 104, 140
 special sounds of, 28

D

Dalto, Jorge, 413–16
Dameron, Tadd, 176–77, 197
dance music, 40–41
 bop, 195
 neo-swing, 418
 ring shouts, 91
 slow drag, 42
 swing, 99, 124, 425
danzon, 411
Dapogny, James, 68
Dave Brubeck Quartet, 218, 221–24
Davenport, Cow Cow, 73, 115
Davis, Kay, 144
Davis, Miles, 182–85, 197, 260–83, 285
 acid jazz, 398
 Birth of the Cool Nonet, 209–10, 218, 262, 265
 call-and-response format, 50, 51
 compositions, 275–76
 cool jazz, 203, 211, 217, 225, 262
 echo and wah-wah effects, 264
 "Flamenco Sketches," 263, 268–71
 fluegelhorn, 266
 hard bop, 230, 233, 266–67
 Harmon mutes, 263
 jazz-rock fusion, 262, 265, 267, 283, 368,
  370–73, 386
 "Masqualero," 26, 230, 274, 275, 278–83
 medley formats, 371–72
 modal jazz, 262, 265–66, 268, 271
 overdubbing, 396
 pitch bending, 48, 263
 quintets, 262, 265–66, 275–76, 370
 rhythm sections, 272–75, 371
 smooth sound texture, 264–65
 trumpet style, 263–65, 372–73
 use of silence, 263–64, 275
 with Gil Evans, 209–10, 262, 265, 269–71, 285
 with Charlie Parker, 201
 with Wayne Shorter, 275–84, 285, 370, 371, 372
Davis, Richard, 255
Davis, Steve, 294
"Daydream," 143
Death Wish, 350
DeBrest, Spanky, 243–45

Debussy, Claude, 82, 112, 118, 276, 341, 349
decay, 48, 478
"DeeDee," 310
"Deep South Suite," 143
DeFranco, Buddy, 205–6
DeJohnette, Jack, 356
DeJohnette, John, 356
"Desafinado," 187, 197
Desmond, Paul, 217–18, 220–24, 226
Detroit, 394
Diamond, Neil, 12
diatonic scale, 456
"Dickie's Dream," 157
"Digression," 216
Dimeola, Al, 354, 374
"Diminuendo in Blue," 130
"Dinah," 88, 117
"Dippermouth Blues," 47, 64, 75, 83
Dirty Boogie, 418
disc jockeys. See acid jazz
disco, 350–51
"Dis Here," 229
"Dixie Jazz Band One-Step," 48, 62–64, 89
Dixieland jazz, 41, 419
Dizzy Gillespie Big Band, 173
    John Lewis and the Modern Jazz Quartet, 177–78
    Miles Davis in, 182–85
    "Things to Come," 170–71
"Django," 177
DJ Logic, 396
Dockery, Sam, 25, 243–45
Dodds, Johnny, 64, 66–67, 75, 80–82, 83, 95
Dodds, Warren "Baby," 64, 66–67, 90, 95
doit, 48"Dolphin Dance," 349
Dolphy, Eric, 308, 313, 324–25, 334
"Donna Lee," 381, 382
"Don't Get Around Much Anymore," 130
"Don't Get Sassy," 255
dorian mode, 453–54
Dorsey, Jimmy, 84–85
Dorsey, Tommy, 73, 106
Dotted eighth-sixteenth note pattern, 449–451
double-stops, 24, 241
double-time, 19–20, 480
Douglas, Dave, 406, 407–8, 409, 425
Dr. John, 41
Dreams, 401
Dreams So Real, 439
D'Rivera, Paquito, 412, 413–16
drones, 291, 296, 314, 438
drops, 48, 91
A Drum Is a Woman, 143
drum 'n' bass, 417, 425
drums, 25–29, 89–90, 95
    bass drum, 28, 89
    bop, 179–80, 197, 198
    chatter, 90, 179
    colorists, 29
    cool jazz, 219
    crash cymbals, 26
    Cuban timbales, 411
    early combos, 89–90
    extras, 29, 47
    feathering the bass, 179
    free jazz, 325
    hard bop, 230–32, 238–46, 255
    high-hat cymbals, 26, 27, 89
    independent lines, 89–90
    jazz-rock fusion, 368, 370, 376, 379
    kicks, prods, and bombs, 179
    modern jazz, 104
    recording challenges, 89
    ride cymbals and rhythms, 25–26, 46, 47, 90, 180
    snare drums, 26, 27
    sticks, brushes, and mallets, 28, 90
    swing-era big bands, 103–4, 137–40
    tom toms, 26

tuning, 28
wood blocks, 29, 46, 89, 104
    See also rhythm sections
Duke Ellington band, 128–29, 159
    ballads, 135–36
    clarinet players, 132
    collaborative playing, 129, 130–31
    "Cottontail," 133
    drummers, 137–40
    growl style, 131, 132, 137
    "Harlem Airshaft," 138–39
    New Orleans sound, 134
    "Prelude to a Kiss," 141–42
    recording, 129
    saxophone players, 135–37, 141–42
    Strayhorn's piano playing, 132
    string bass players, 140–43
    "Transbluency," 144–45
    trombone players, 137
    trumpet players, 132–34
    voicing across sections, 131
    wordless vocals, 131
    See also Ellington, Duke
"Duke's Choice," 321
Duotones, 400
Durham, Eddie, 157
Duster, 375

E
"E.S.P.," 278 "Eager Beaver," 211
ear, 22
"Early Autumn," 187
Eastern European music, 407
"East St. Louis Toodle-o," 132
easy listening, 393, 394
"Echoes of Harlem," 132–34, 140, 143
Echoplex, 372
ECM (Editions of Contemporary Music) Style, 436–40, 441
Eddy, Duane, 398
Edwards, Eddie, 62
"The Egyptian," 230
Eicher, Manfred, 436–40, 441
eight-bar blues, 373
eighth notes, 448–49
jazz, education, 213, 418–19, 425
Eldridge, Roy, 106, 109–10, 122–23, 124
electric instruments
    bass (Fender), 368
    guitars, 370
    jazz-rock fusion, 368, 370
    keyboards, 351, 354, 368, 370, 376
    swing-era big bands, 117–18
electric piano, 351, 354, 368, 370
Eleventh House, 375
Ellington, Duke, 11, 125, 129–46
    as bandleader, 104–5, 124, 129, 159
    composing and arranging, 129, 130–31, 143
    cornets, 79
    film scores, 130
    impact, 143–44, 145
    Latin style, 409
    piano style, 47, 130
    popularity, 124
    sacred music, 143
    three-minute instrumentals, 130
    See also Duke Ellington band
Ellington Indigos, 143
Ellis, Don, 308
"Embraceable You," 21
Empyrean Isles, 239, 350
"Enter Evening," 314
Ervin, Booker, 322–23
Escoude, Christian, 374
European musical traditions, 43–51
    call-and-response format, 50–51
    harmony, 46

improvisation, 44–45
instrumentation, 46
neutral pitches, 50
percussion, 47
pitch alteration, 48
polyrhythms, 48
syncopation, 45
"Eurydice," 381
Evans, Bill, 339, 340–48, 358
    chord voicings, 113
    ECM Style, 437
    "Flamenco Sketches," 269–71
    floating pulse, 340–41
    quartal harmonies, 341
    "Solar," 342–46
    trio recordings, 51, 346–48
    Village Vanguard session, 341
    waltzes, 346
    work with Miles Davis, 268–71, 285, 340
Evans, Gil, 209–10, 262, 265, 266–68, 285, 436
Everybody Digs Bill Evans, 340
"Express Crossing," 420–21

F
"Fables of Faubus," 322–23
Falla, Manuel de, 267
"Fantasy on Frankie and Johnny," 112
Farlow, Tal, 182
Farmer, Art, 230
Fat Albert Rotunda, 350
Fatool, Nick, 116–17
Fats Domino, 41
Favors, Malachi, 326, 330–32
feathering the bass, 179
Felder, Wilton, 398
Fender bass, 368
Fender Rhodes electric piano, 354, 376
Ferguson, Maynard, 214–15, 254–55, 256–57, 258, 376
field hollers, 36, 91
fill, 480
Filles de Kilimanjaro, 267, 274, 370
fills, 27, 51, 379
Fischer, Clare, 349
"Fishermen, Strawberry, and Devil Crab," 51, 263, 267
Fitzgerald, Andy, 108
Fitzgerald, Ella, 119–22, 125, 132, 234, 410
Fitzgerald, F. Scott, 12, 65
Five Elements bands, 418
"Flamenco Sketches," 47, 246, 263, 268–71, 291, 298, 309, 340
"Flaming Sword," 143
"Flashes," 82
flat fifth, 166, 454–56
flat seventh, 454–56
flat third (blue note), 454–56
Flintstones, 18, 183
floating pulse, 340–41
floor cymbals, 89
fluegelhorn, 134, 216–17, 266
flute, 101, 219
Folk Songs, 439
"Follow Your Heart," 374
Fontana, Carl, 221, 224–25
Foreplay, 375
Foster, Al, 372, 373
"Four" and More, 264, 274–75
Four Brothers Band, 188
"Four Brothers," 18, 101, 187, 188, 189–90, 217
"Four or Five Times," 85
Fourth Way, 365
fourth, 11–12, 46
"Frame for The Blues," 256
Franklin, Aretha, 44, 398
"Freddie the Freeloader," 256, 264, 272
"Freedom Jazz Dance," 275

free-form, 271, 308, 315, 333
free jazz, 292–93, 307–35
    Albert Ayler, 316–19
    Anthony Braxton, 332
    Art Ensemble of Chicago, 308, 326, 330–32
    bass, 325–27
    Cecil Taylor, 314–15
    Charlie Mingus, 320–24
    Chicago avant-garde, 327–32
    chord progressions, 308–9, 312–13, 314
    "Civilization Day," 311–12
    Don Cherry, 313–15
    drumming, 325
    ECM Style, 437
    Eric Dolphy, 324–25
    "Fables of Faubus," 322–23
    "Ghosts: First Variation," 317–19
    improvisation, 268, 271
    John Coltrane, 292–93
    non-European musical systems, 309
    Ornette Coleman, 308–13
    phrasing, 309
    piano, 113
    pitch and tone manipulations, 309
    synthesizers, 328
    textural density, 309
    trumpet, 238World Saxophone Quartet, 332–33
Free Jazz, 292, 308, 313
Freeman, Bud, 65
Freeman, Stan, 168–69
Free Spirits, 365, 375
French horns, 210, 213
French Impressionism, 82, 112, 118
Friar's Society Orchestra, 65
Friday Night at the Blackhawk, 272
Frisell, Bill, 434–35
front line, 88
"Frustration," 136
Fuller, Gil, 170–71
Fuller, Jeff, 413–16
funk, 182, 229–30, 246, 350–51, 364–65, 386, 392
    bass, 381
    Chick Corea, 354
    Herbie Hancock, 349–51
    jazz, 229, 232, 257
    See also hard bop; jazz-rock fusion
Funk, 389
fusion. See jazz-rock fusion
Future Shock, 351
fuzak, 393

G

G, Kenny, 369, 399–400, 405
Gadd, Steve, 368
Gambia, 91
Garbarek, Jan, 355, 438–39, 440
Garland, Red, 112–13, 265–66
Garner, Erroll, 111–13
Garrison, Jimmy, 294, 296, 299–302
A Genuine Tong Funeral, 430, 439
Genus, James, 402–5
"Georgia on My Mind," 44
Gershwin, George, 11, 51, 253
"Get Happy," 229
Getz, Stan, 187–88, 197–98
    cool jazz style, 203, 225
    Latin influence, 410
Ghana, 44
ghost bands, 422
"Ghosts: First Variation," 22, 47, 48, 317–19, 347
"Giant Steps," 290–91, 298
Gibbs, Michael, 439
Gilberto, Astrud, 187
Gillespie, Dizzy, 163, 172–73, 197–98
    compositions, 173
    flatted fifths, 166

improvisation, 172–73, 230
    Latin influence, 410
    "Shaw Nuff," 183–85
    "Things to Come," 170–71
Gilmore, John, 293, 329
Gilmore, Patrick, 40
"Girl from Ipanema," 187, 197
Gismonti, Egberto, 439
Gitler, Ira, 290
Giuffre, Jimmy, 188, 216, 217, 220, 225, 226
Glass, Philip, 392
Glen Miller band, 121
"Gloomy Sunday," 118
"God Bless the Child," 118
"Golden Cress," 137
Goldings, Larry, 431–33
Golson, Benny, 230
Gomez, Eddie, 347
Gonsalves, Paul, 136, 137, 143, 146
"Good Bait," 176
Goodman, Benny, 85, 117, 194
    as bandleader, 104–6, 116–17, 124
    "Seven Come Eleven," 116–17
"A Good Man Is Hard to Find," 82
"Good Mornin' Blues," 157
Goodrick, Mick, 375
Gordon, Dexter, 186–187, 197–98, 232, 233
gospel music, 364
"Got the Spirit," 256
Gourse, Leslie, 78
grace notes, 17
Graettinger, Robert, 214–15
Grandmaster Flash, 396
Gravatt, Eric, 377–78, 379
Green, Freddie, 103, 150, 157, 158–59
Green, Grant, 394
Greer, Sonny, 137–40
groove, 9
"Groovin' High," 173
growl style, 131, 132, 137
guitar, 46, 88, 95
    amplification, 118
    bop, 182
    chorusing, 438
    cool jazz, 219–20
    ECM Style, 437–38
    Eddie Lang, 90–91
    hard bop, 253–54
    rhythm guitar style, 103
    swing-era big bands, 103, 115–18, 125
    vibrato, 117, 118
    wah-wahs and phase shifts, 373–74
Gypsy music, 117, 118

H

Hackett, Bobby, 82
Haden, Charlie, 311–13, 325–26, 334, 355, 439
Hadi, Shafi, 322–23
Hahn, Jerry, 375
Haig, Al, 181, 183–85
Haitian revolution, 37
Haiti, 37
half-timing, 20
Hall, Jim, 219–20
Hamiet Bluiett, 332
Hamilton, Chico, 219, 220, 238, 324–25, 375
Hammer, Jan, 374
Hampton, Lionel, 106, 116–17, 439
Hampton, Slide, 233
Hancock, Herbie, 339, 348–51, 358, 386
    "Chameleon," 383–84
    composing and arranging, 349–50
    disco, 350–51
    funk, 349–51
    hard bop, 230, 233, 239–42, 257

jazz-rock fusion, 233, 383–84, 385
    "Masqualero," 278–83
    space music, 329
    turntablists, 396
    work with Miles Davis, 273–74, 285, 348, 349
"Handful of Keys," 71–72
Handy, John, 321, 322–23
hard bop, 229–58
    bass, 232, 254, 255
    big bands, 254–57
    chord progressions, 230
    chord voicings, 255
    composer-arrangers, 254–57
    drums, 230–32, 238–46, 255
    guitar, 253–54
    improvisation, 230
    piano, 234–36
    rhythm section, 232, 238–46, 253–54
    saxophone, 232, 233, 246–53
    sources, 233
    trombone, 253
    trumpet, 232, 236–38, 239–42, 255, 256–57
Harden, Wilbur, 231
Hardin, Lil, 80–82
Hardman, Bill, 243–45
"Hard Times," 399
Hargrove, Roy, 237
"Harlem Airshaft," 47, 101, 130–32, 134, 138–39,
    142, 143
harmonic improvisation, 107
Harmon mutes, 263
harmony, 22, 43, 46
Harper, Phil, 237
Harris, Bill, 106
Haskins, James, 37
"Havona," 381
Hawkins, Coleman, 107, 124
    "How Deep Is the Ocean?", 108
    improvisation style, 152–56, 165
    tone quality, 47
    "Voodte," 108
Hayes, Kevin, 349
Hayes, Louis, 235–36
Haynes, Roy, 351, 352–53
head arrangements, 151
Head Hunters, 350, 385
head, 151, 480
Heath, M'Tume, 372
Heath, Percy, 177–78
Heavy Weather, 380
Heliocentric Worlds of Sun Ra, Vol. 1 and 2, 328
Hello, Dolly, 75
Hemphill, Julius, 332–33, 335
Henderson, Fletcher, 79, 104–5, 116–17, 125, 211
Henderson, Joe, 230, 233, 246, 250, 252–53, 258
Henderson, Michael, 372
Hendrix, Jimi, 372, 381
heptatonic, 456
Herman, Woody, 210
    See also Woody Herman big band
Hersh, Fred, 349
heterophony, 45
"Hey, Jude," 256
Hi-Fi Ellington Uptown, 140
Higgins, Billy, 311–12, 313
high-hat, 26, 27, 89, 90, 104, 150, 180, 395, 411
Hill, Andrew, 329
hillbilly music, 364–365
Hindemith, Paul, 349, 351
Hines, Earl, 21, 61, 69–70, 76–77, 85, 95, 111, 115
Hinton, Milt, 103
hip-hop, 396–97, 424
hip-hop jazz, 416–18
Hodges, Johnny, 77, 107, 125
    lead-in style, 87
    "Prelude to a Kiss," 141–42

with Ellington, 132
hokum, 50
Holiday, Billie, 78, 117–19, 125
Holland, Dave, 325–26, 327, 334, 351, 439
"Honeysuckle Rose," 70
"Honky Tonk Train Blues," 47, 73
horn, 8, 21, 44, 480
horn-like lines, 69, 95, 115
hot bands, 121, 131
Hot Fives and Hot Seven recordings, 75
"Hot House," 176
hot solos, 395
"Hotter Than That," 48, 80–82, 91
house music, 394
"How Deep Is the Ocean?", 108
Hubbard, Freddie, 230, 238, 239–42, 313
"Hunter's Dance," 52–53

I

"I Can't Believe That You're in Love with Me,"
        106, 107, 136
"I Found a New Baby," 106
"I Got Rhythm," 21, 107
"I'm All Smiles," 346
"I'm Beginning to *See* the Light," 130, 146
Imitation, 418–19
Impressionism, 82, 112, 118
Impressions, 465
Improvisation, 3, 8, 10–11, 22–23, 35
    abstract nature, 195–96
    the blues, 44
    bop, 164, 230
    chord progressions, 18–22
    collective improvisation, 61, 77, 85
    Coltrane's two-chord style, 22
    cool jazz, 204–5
    free jazz, 268, 271
    hard bop, 230
    harmonic improvisation, 107
    heterophony, 45
    historic overview, 44–45
    instrument roles, 23–30
    jazz-rock fusion, 271
    listening techniques, 16–17
    modal formats, 262, 265–66, 271
    pitch alteration, 48
    preluding, 45
    recurring themes, 30
    reharmonization, 111, 124, 164–66
    rhythmic displacement, 35, 44, 91
    rules and alternatives, 30–31
    solo roles, 29–31, 77, 85–87
    swing-era big bands, 101, 121, 123–24, 196
"In a Mellotone," 136
"In a Mist," 82
In a Silent Way, 262, 370, 371, 386
"In a Silent Way," 375, 376
India, 263, 296, 309, 373, 374, 438
Indian music, 438
Inner Mounting Flame, 374
Ionian mode, 453
Inside, 314
Inside Out, 437
instrumental blues, 91
instrumentalized voice, 131
instrumental proficiency, 22, 101
instrumentation, 46
instrument roles, 23–30, 40
    bass, 24–25
    drums, 25–29
    piano, 25
    rhythm section, 24–29
    soloists, 29–30
"In the Dark," 82
intonation, 49, 50, 470
introductions, 21

"Intuition," 216
Irakere, 412
Irving, Robert, III, 373
"It's Magic," 188
Ivory Coast, 56
"I've Found a New Baby," 179
"I Want a Little Girl," 157

J

Jackson, Milt, 170–71, 173, 175–78, 198
Jackson, Paul, 383–84
Jack the Bear, 142
jam. *See* improvisation
Jam session, 480
Jamal, Ahmad, 112–13
James, Bob, 393
James, Boney, 393, 399
Jarman, Joseph, 330–32, 335
Jarreau, Al, 78, 354
Jarrett, Keith, 339, 355–59
    composing, 355
    ECM Style, 436–40
    hard bop, 233
    humming, 30
    solo piano work, 355–58, 440
    Standards Trio, 356
    "Sundial, Part 1," 357–58
    with Miles Davis, 355, 372
jazz
    definitions of, 7–12
    education, 213, 418–19, 425
    origins of , 35–54
The Jazz Age, 12, 65
Jazz Composer's Orchestra, 429–30
Jazz Crusaders, 393, 398
jazz-rock fusion, 363–87, 394–98, 401–6
    "Above and Below," 402–5
    acid jazz, 394–98
    bass figures, 371
    "Birdland," 11, 52–53, 257, 376, 380, 387
    "Chameleon," 383–84
    Chick Corea, 354
    drum styles, 368
    forerunners, 365–68, 386
    Herbie Hancock, 233, 348–51, 383–84, 385
    instrumentation, 368, 370
    Jaco Pastorius, 381–82, 387
    Joe Zawinul, 375–81, 386–87
    John McLaughlin, 373–74, 386
    Larry Coryell, 375, 386
    medley formats, 371–72
    Miles Davis, 262, 265, 368, 370–73, 386
    mode-based improvisation, 271
    ostinatos, 47
    Pat Metheny, 382–84, 386
    percussion, 376, 379
    pizzicato bass with horns, 143
    rhythmic complexity, 276, 284
    rhythm sections, 368, 371
    saxophone, 247
    solo styles, 368–69
    soul saxes, 398–401, 402–5
    "Surucucu," 377–78
    trumpet, 238
    Wayne Shorter, 283–84, 387
    Weather Report, 376–81, 387
The Jazz Singer film, 12
Jazz swing feeling, 8–11, 78, 82
Jazz-funk, 365
jazzy pop, 405–6
Jefferson, Eddie, 172
Jeff Lorber Fusion band, 399–400
Jitterbug, 418
"Jitterbug Waltz," 70
"Jive Samba," 229, 246
Jobim, Antonio Carlos, 253

Johnson, Alphonso, 381
Johnson, Bashiri, 402–5
Johnson, J. J., 106, 185–86, 229, 253, 257
Johnson, James P., 73–75, 95
Johnson, Lonnie, 80–82, 90–91, 95
Johnson, Marc, 347
Johnson, Pete, 73
Johnson, Robert, 91
Johnson, Tommy, 91
Jolson, Al, 12
Jones, Elvin, 48, 294–95, 299–303
Jones, Hank, 122–23
Jones, Jo, 104, 140, 150, 157–59
Jones, Philly Joe, 238, 245–46, 265–66
Jones, Quincy, 376
Jones, Rufus, 137–40
Jones, Thad, 79, 143, 254–55
Jones-Lewis band, 254–55
Jones-Smith, Inc., 157, 158–59
Joplin, Scott, 39
Jordan, Kent, 420–21
Jordan, Louis, 418
Jordan, Marlon, 237
"Jungle Book," 376
Jungle jazz, 398
"Just Friends," 19, 167, 168–69, 309

K

Kansas City, 114
Kansas City Five, Six, or Seven, 157, 158–59
Kansas City style, 151
Kay, Connie, 177–78
Keith Jarrett Quartet, 325, 347
Kelly, Wynton, 272
Kenny G, 393, 399–400, 405
Kenton, Stan, 208–9, 210–16, 225–26, 410
Key, 468
keyboards, 351, 354, 368, 370, 376
kick bands, 254–55
Kind of Blue, 268
    cool jazz, 217
    "Flamenco Sketches," 47, 246, 263, 268–71,
        340, 342
    "Freddie the Freeloader," 256, 272
    modal jazz, 262, 266, 268, 271
    smooth sound texture, 265
"King Porter Stomp," 68
Kirchner, Bill, 286
Kirk, Andy, 113, 114–15
Kirkland, Kenny, 422
"Kiss and Run," 16, 19, 25, 29, 48, 229, 247–50
Klezmer jazz, 406–9, 425
Klugh, Earl, 393
Knepper, Jimmy, 322–23
Koenig, Karl, 38, 40, 42
"Ko-Ko," 28
Koln Concert, 356
Konitz, Lee, 205–10, 211, 217–218, 225
Koz, Dave, 393, 399
Kral, Roy, 197
Krupa, Gene, 104, 109–10
Kyle, Billy, 181

L

"Lady Be Good," 157
"Lady Bird," 176
Lady Sings the Blues, 119
LaFaro, Scott, 313, 341–48, 346–48, 358
"La Fiesta," 354
Lacy, Steve 302
Laid back, 480
Laird, Rick, 374
Lake, Oliver, 332–33, 334
Lande, Art, 439
Lang, Eddie, 84–85, 90–91, 95
large tom tom, 26

Larkins, Ellis, 108
LaRocca, Nick, 62–64
Latin America, 36
Latin American, 173, 229, 235, 240, 241, 351, 354, 409–11
Latin American Suite, 143
Latin bass figure, 424
Latin jazz, 36–37, 351, 354, 409–16, 425
    bands, 411
    bass *tumbao*, 411
    bossa nova, 187, 410, 417
    Eddie Palmieri, 411, 412
    half-timing, 20
    hard bop, 229–30, 235–36
    Irakere, 412
    jazz-rock fusion, 368, 371
    Mario Bauzá, 410
    "Miami," 413–16
    percussion, 410
    piano *montuno*, 411
    Tito Puente, 411
"Launching Pad," 143
Lay out 478
"Lazy Afternoon," 256
"L'Dopa," 256
Lee, Donna, 381, 382
Legato, 450, 478
"Lester Leaps In," 157, 158–59
    comping, 151, 180
    drumming, 104, 179
    riffs, 102
    trading fours, 19, 21
Lewis, Jerry Lee, 73
Lewis, John, 170–71, 177–78, 197–98
Lewis, Meade Lux, 47, 73
Lewis, Mel, 254–55
Lewis, Ramsey, 257
Lewis, Victor, 431–33
Lick, 480
Liebman, David, 262, 369
Lifetime, 373, 374
Light as a Feather, 354
light jazz, 393
Lincoln Center Jazz Orchestra, 419–21
Lindy hop, 418
listening techniques, 16–17
"Litha," 354
Live-Evil, 371, 372, 373
"Livery Stable Blues," 62, 63
Lloyd, Charles, 355
locked-hands piano, 113, 124, 182
"Lonesome Lullaby," 143
Lookout Farm, 304
looping, 395
Los Angeles, 35, 210, 216, 224
Louisiana, 37
Louis Armstrong and His Hot Fives and Hot
        Seven, 75, 80–82
Louis's Children (Gourse), 78
Lovano, Joe, 430, 434–35, 441
lowered fifths, 166, 455
lowered sevenths, 166, 215, 455
lowered thirds, 166, 455
Lucia, Paco de, 374
Luminessence, 438
Lunceford, Jimmie, 104–5, 124, 159
"Lush Life," 132

M

"MacArthur Park," 256
Machito (Frank Grillo), 410
"Mack the Knife," 122
Mahavishnu Orchestra, 374
"Maiden Voyage," 29, 230, 239–42, 349, 350, 358
    double-timing, 20, 37
Mainstream jazz, 233

"Main Stem," 143
Mainstream, 422
Malachi Favors, 330–31
Mallets, 28
mambo bands. *See* Latin jazz
Mambo, 409, 411
Mangione, Chuck, 245
Manhattan Transfer, 11, 376
Manne, Shelly, 108
"Manteca," 173, 410
"Maple Leaf Rag," 39, 68
march music, 39–40, 41
Marches, 40, 45, 447
Mardi Gras, 36
"Maria," 256
Mariano, Charlie, 321
Marsalis, Branford, 417, 422
Marsalis, Wynton, 239, 420–21, 420–22, 425
Marsalis Brothers, 393
Marsh, Warne, 206
Masada, 406, 409
Mason, Harvey, 383–84
"Masqualero," 26, 230, 274, 275, 278–83, 349, 422
Maupin, Bennie, 383–84
Max Roach-Clifford Brown Quintet, 247
Mays, Lyle, 382, 384
Mazurka, 41, 42
McFerrin, Bobby, 78
McLaughlin, John, 373–74
McLean, Jackie, 229, 243–45, 321
McNeely, Jim, 348
McPartland, Jimmy, 65
Measure, 447, 448, 449
Meditations, 303
Mehegan, John, 229–30
Mehldau, Brad, 356
mellophoniums, 213
melody statements, 21, 45
"Mercy, Mercy, Mercy," 229, 246, 375, 376, 386
Mertz, Paul, 84–85
Meter, 80, 402, 446–47
Metheny, Pat, 375, 382–84, 437–40
The Metronome All-Stars, 205–6
Mexican bands, 40
"Miami," 413–16
Middle East, 309
"Milenburg Joys," 68
Miles Ahead, 266, 268, 285
Miles Davis at Carnegie Hall, 272
Miles Davis nonet, 209, 218, 220
Miles in Europe, 264
Miles Smiles, 275
Milestone Jazz Stars, 252
Milestones, 265–66
"Milestones," 217, 256, 265–66
Miley, Bubber, 131, 132–34
Milhaud, Darius, 220
military bands, 39–40
Miller, Glenn, 82, 121, 405
Miller, Marcus, 373
Mingus Ah Um, 322
Mingus, Charlie, 179, 255, 308, 320–24, 329, 334
    combo performances, 321–24
    composing work, 321
    "Fables of Faubus," 322–23
Minimalism, 392
"Misterioso," 18, 174, 175–76
"Misty," 112
Mitchell, Roscoe, 330–32, 334
Mixers, 416–17
Mobley, Hank, 235–36
modal jazz, 262, 265–66, 268, 292
    Coltrane's work, 291–92, 372
    jazz-rock fusion, 371
    pedal points and drones, 291, 296, 297
Mode changes, 466

Mode, 266, 268–70, 292, 453–54, 465, 467
modern jazz, 94, 106, 163
    big bands, 134
    bop. *See* bop
    chatter, 90
    cool jazz. *See* cool jazz
    drum lines, 104
    flatted fifths, 166
    hard bop. *See* hard bop
    piano, 111, 112, 113, 151
    pizzicato bass with horns, 143
    saxophone, 107
Modern Jazz Quartet, 177–78, 196–97, 198, 203, 225
Modes, 217, 268, 270, 292, 453–54, 465
Mole, Miff, 65
"Moment of Truth," 256
Monk, Thelonious, 163, 173–76, 197–98
    "Misterioso," 175–76
    piano style, 174–76
    rhythm-n-ing, 173–74
    whole-tone scales, 17
Montgomery, Wes, 117, 233, 253–54
Montuno, the, 411, 413
"The Mooche," 91
"Mood Indigo," 130, 131, 146
M"Moon Dreams," 265
"Moonlight in Vermont," 187, 197
Moore, Oscar, 254
Morehouse, Chauncey, 84–85
Moreira, Airto, 354, 379
Morello, Joe, 222–24
Morgan, Lee, 464
Morrow, George, 247–50
Morton, Jelly Roll, 60, 94–95
    Latin influence, 409
    Red Hot Peppers, 68
    swing style, 68
    "Wolverine Blues," 66–67
Motian, Paul, 342–48, 355, 358, 434–35, 441
Motown, 365, 368
Moye, Don, 331, 335
Mulligan, Gerry, 210, 218–19, 226, 262
multiphonics, 290, 317
Murray, David, 32–33, 334
Murray, Sunny, 317–19
"Muskat Ramble," 87
mutes, 47, 132, 137, 263, 321
Muzak, 394
Mwandishi, 350
My Favorite Things, 292
"My Favorite Things," 22, 292
My Goal's Beyond, 374
"My Lady," 20, 208–9, 309
My Song, 438

N

"Naima," 291
Najee, 399
Nance, Ray, 143
Nanton, Joe "Tricky Sam," 47, 131, 137, 146
Narada, 392
"Nature Boy," 188
Navarro, Fats, 177, 182, 185, 232, 233
"Nefertiti," 275–76, 284, 370
Neidlinger, Buell, 326
Nelson, Oliver, 231
neo-classical jazz, 418–23, 425
    ghost bands, 422
    Lincoln Center Jazz Orchestra, 419–21
    Wynton Marsalis, 420–22
neo-traditional, 239, 422
neo-swing jazz, 418
Nestico, Sammy, 255
neutral pitches, 50, 456
The Neville Brothers, 41
New Adult Contemporary format, 394

new age music, 356, 391–92, 424
New England Conservatory of Music, 406
Newman, David "Fathead," 398, 399
New Orleans Rhythm Kings (Friar's Society Orchestra), 65
New Orleans style, 37–42, 94–95
    brass bands, 39–40, 42, 46
    dance music, 40–41
    Dixieland, 41
    early combo scene, 60–61, 85–87
    free blacks, 37–38, 42
    live music, 38, 40, 42
    Mexican bands, 40
    ragtime, 39–42
    recording, 61–67
    Storyville, 40
New York style, 65, 73–75
Nichols, Red, 65, 82, 88
"A Night in Tunisia," 173
Night Music, 400
"No, Papa, No," 90
Nock, Mike, 365, 368
non-obvious pulse, 340, 341, 342
"No Figs," 20, 187, 188, 205–7
"No Line," 21
Nonet. See Birth of the Cool Nonet
Noone, Jimmie, 85, 95
notation, 23
Now He Sings, Now He Sobs, 351, 352–53, 354, 439
"Now's the Time," 167, 264

O

obbligato, 61
Oberheim Polyphonic, 376
oboe, 321, 328
octaves, 70, 72, 343, 345
octave-voiced lines, 112, 172, 343
Odyssey Synthesizer, 383
Officium, 438, 440
"Off Minor," 174
"Olé," 296
Oliver, Joe "King," 76–77
    "West End Blues," 76–77
Oliver, Sy, 444
"On a Turquoise Cloud," 143
"One Day," 47, 48, 52–53
"One O'Clock Jump," 52–53, 102, 151, 180, 196, 376
one-step, 63
On the Corner, 417
Open Sky, 305
Opera, 48
"An Open Letter to Duke," 321
Oregon, 392
organ, 256
    See also keyboards
Original Dixieland Jazz Band, 29, 61–64, 89, 94
ornamentation, 48, 87, 91
Ory, Kid, 64, 75, 80–82, 87, 95
Osby, Greg, 417
ostinatos (repetition of patterns), 47–48, 386
out music, 307
overdubbing, 396
overlapping, 50

P

Page, Oran "Hot Lips," 77
Page, Walter, 103, 150, 158–59
"Pagin' the Devil," 157
Palmieri, Eddie, 411, 412
Parenti, Tony, 60
"Pan Piper," 267
Parallel Worlds, 409
Paris Blues, 143

Parker, Charlie, 163, 166–72, 197–98
    compositions, 167
    impact, 167–72
    improvisation, 166–67, 230
    "Just Friends," 168–69
    "Perdido," 122–23
    "Shaw Nuff," 183–85
    tone quality, 167
Parker, Maceo, 398–99, 417, 424
"Parker's Mood," 172
Parlan, Horace, 322–23
Passengers, 439
Pastorius, Jaco, 381–82
Patterson, Don, 231
patting juba, 36
Patton, Charley, 91
Paul Motian Trio, 434–35
Paul Whiteman Orchestra, 82
Paul Winter Consort, 392
"Peace Piece," 340
Peacock, Gary, 317–19, 356
pedal points and drones, 291, 296, 297
Pekar, Harvey, 10, 112, 195–96, 237, 314
Penderecki, Krzysztof, 328, 332
pentatonic scales, 351
Percussionist, 29, 379, 411
"Perdido," 122–23
Perotin, 440
Peterson, Gilles, 394
Peterson, Oscar, 30, 113, 179, 181–82
Pettiford, Oscar, 108, 178–79
phase shifter, 374
"Pharaoh's Dance," 370, 375
Phillips, Flip, 122–23
pianists, 113
piano comping, 414
piano, 25, 68–75, 95, 339–59
    Bill Evans, 340–48
    block chording, 113, 124
    boogie-woogie, 73, 113–15
    bop, 173–77, 180–82, 197, 198
    Cecil Taylor, 314–15
    Chick Corea, 351–54
    chord substitution, 111
    cocktail piano, 111
    comping, 25, 103, 112, 130, 151, 173–76, 180–82
    cool jazz, 204–7, 219, 220–24
    early combos, 66–75
    electric piano, 351, 354, 368
    Fender Rhodes electric piano, 376
    free jazz, 113, 308–9
    hard bop, 234–36
    Herbie Hancock, 348–51, 383–84
    Keith Jarrett, 355–59
    Latin jazz montuno, 411
    locked-hands style, 113, 124, 182
    Miles Davis's groups, 348, 349
    modern jazz, 111, 112, 113, 151
    pedal points, 296
    quartal harmony, 341, 351
    reharmonization, 111, 124
    rhythm role, 88–89
    solos, 25
    stride style, 68, 70, 73, 89, 103
    swing-era big bands, 47, 103, 108–15, 124, 130, 132, 149, 151
    trumpet-style, 69–70, 111
    Tyner's pentatonic patterns, 295
    walking tenths, 70
    See also keyboards
Piano Improvisations Vols. I and II, 354, 437, 439
piccolo, 420–21
Pieces of a Dream, 393
Pitch
    alteration of, 48

flexibility, 49, 50
    manipulation, 48
pitch bending, 17, 48, 83, 87, 263
"Pithecantropus Erectus," 321
pixie mutes, 137
pizzicato, 25
plumber's plunger, 137
plunger-muted, 115, 323
plunger mutes, 132, 469
polite bop, 182, 204
polkas, 42
polyrhythms, 48, 451
polytonal, 454
poly-stylistic post-modernism, 429–30
Ponce, Daniel, 413–16
pop jazz, 405–6
pop music, 121
popularity of jazz, 12
    avant-garde style, 333–34
    big bands, 121–24
    bop, 191–97
    cool jazz, 225
    early combos, 94
    free jazz, 333–34
    hard bop, 257
    jazz-rock fusion, 384–86
    in the late twentieth century, 424
popular music, 12
Porgy and Bess, 51, 266–68, 372
portamento, 135
"Portrait of Bert Williams," 130
"Portrait of the Lion," 130
Powell, Bud, 69, 181, 187, 197–98
Powell, Richie, 25, 48, 247–50
Pozo, Chano, 410
Preacher, The, 464
"Prelude to a Kiss," 20, 141–42, 143, 207
preluding, 45
Preservation Hall, 94
Preservation Hall bands, 94, 419
Presley, Elvis, 365
Preston, Billy, 372
Priester, Julian, 329
Prima, Louis, 78, 418
The Prisoner, 350
prods, 179, 416
progressive jazz, 211, 481
"The Promise," 26, 47, 48, 296, 297, 299–302
Prophet synthesizer, 376
Pryor, Arthur, 40
Pursuance, 304
pseudo rubato, 19
Puente, Tito, 29, 411
"Punk Jazz," 381
Purim, Flora, 354
Puschnig, Wolfgang, 431–33

Q

quadrille, 41–42, 417, 465
quadruple-time, 20, 167, 400
quartal harmony, 341, 351
quarter note, 447
quarter tones, 49

R

Ra, Sun, 68, 308, 327–32, 333–35
race records, 364
Rachmaninoff, Sergey, 218
Raeburn, Boyd, 256
rag, 39
Ragas, Henry, 62
ragtime, 35, 39–42, 68
raised elevenths, 166
Ramey, Gene, 199
Raney, Jimmy, 182
Rank, Bill, 84–85

rap and hip-hop, 394–95, 397, 405
rasping sounds, 47
Ravel, Maurice, 82, 112, 118, 132, 276, 341,
      349, 355
raves, 394
reading, 23, 102
"Reckless Blues," 38
Recording
      acoustic, 89
      early combo scene, 61–67
      limitation on drums, 89
      Louis Armstrong's Hot Five (or Hot Seven), 75
Red Cross, 199
"Red Emma," 407–8
Red Hot Peppers, 68
Red Lanta, 439
Redman, Dewey, 355
Redman, Don, 105
reed sections, 101, 131
reharmonization, 111, 124, 164–66
rehearsal bands, 254–55
Reich, Steve, 12, 392, 440
Reinhardt, Django, 115, 117–18, 125
Relaxin', 265
release, 480
"Reminiscing in Tempo," 143
"Rene's Theme," 374
responsorial singing, 51
retro, 422
Return to Forever, 354
"Revelations," 321
"Rhapsody in Blue" (Gershwin), 11
rhumba, 409
rhythm
      back beats, 104, 395
      contrast, 45, 48
      displacement, 35, 44, 91, 118, 347
      Evans's floating pulse, 340–41
      the groove in acid jazz, 397–98
      irregular Balkan rhythms, 407
      lilt, 9
      polyrhythms, 48
      ride rhythms, 25–26, 47, 90
      swing feeling, 8–11, 68, 78, 85
      two-beat style, 88, 103
rhythm and blues (R & B), 364–68, 458
rhythm guitar, 53, 103, 133, 138
rhythmization, 47
rhythm-n-ing, 173–74
rhythm sections, 3, 24–29
      banjo, 88
      bass, 24–25, 88, 103
      boogie-woogie, 73
      bop, 178–82
      cool jazz, 219–21
      cowbells, 29, 46, 89, 104
      cymbals, 16
      drums, 25–29, 89–90, 103–4
      early combos, 88–90
      guitar, 88, 90–91, 103, 115–18
      hard bop, 232, 238–46
      jazz-rock fusion, 276, 284, 368, 376, 379
      Latin jazz, 410, 411, 412
      in Miles Davis's groups, 272–75
      percussion, 376, 379, 410
      piano, 25, 88–89, 103, 108–15
      swing-era big bands, 101, 108–18, 124–25,
            150–51, 157
      trading fours and eights, 19
      tuba, 88
      Weather Report, 276, 376, 379
Rich, Buddy, 122–23, 168–69
Richmond, Danny, 322–23
ride cymbals, 25, 46, 47, 104
ride rhythms, 25–26, 47, 90, 180
riffs, 47, 102, 104, 151

riff band, 53, 151, 158, 376
Riley, Terry, 392
rim shot, 481
ringing sounds, 47
ring modulator, 376
ring shouts, 91
rip, 81, 404, 481
ritards, 21
Ritenour, Lee, 393
"River People," 381
Rivers, Sam, 325–26, 327
Roach, Max, 140
      bop, 179–80, 197
      cool jazz, 205–6
      hard bop, 229, 238, 242, 245, 247–50
      "Ko-Ko," 28
      polyrhythms, 48
Roberts, Marcus, 349
Robinson, Fred, 76–77
rock, 20, 42, 364–65
      See also jazz-rock fusion
rockabilly, 365, 418
rock and roll, 94, 364
"Rockin' Chair," 107
"Rockin' in Rhythm," 143
"Rockit," 351, 396, 417
Rocky, 256
Rodrigo, Juaquín, 267
Rogers, Shorty, 185, 216–17
Rollins, Sonny, 229, 246–52, 257, 290, 302
roll-off, 63
Romao, Dom Um, 377–78, 379
Rosolino, Frank, 224–25
Rouder, Willa, 73
roughening, buzzing, and ringing sounds, 47
"Round Midnight," 173
The Royal Crown Revue, 418
rubato, 19
rubber plunger mutes, 132, 137, 321
Runnin' Wild, 73
Russell, Curly, 183–85
Russell, George, 308

S

"Sack o' Woe," 229, 246
sacred music, 143
"Saeta," 267
Safranski, Eddie, 205–6
salsa bands. *See* Latin jazz
Salt Peanuts, 414
samba, 410, 417
Sample, Joe, 393, 398
sampling, 395
Sanborn, Dave, 369
Sanborn, David, 399, 400, 425
"Sanctuary," 370
Sanders, Pharoah, 291–92, 326
Sandoval, Arturo, 412
Santamaria, Mongo, 350
Satchmo. *See* Armstrong, Louis
Satie, Erik, 277, 430
"Satin Doll," 146
Saturday Night at the Blackhawk, 272
      alto. *See* alto saxophone
      ballads, 135–36
      baritone. *See* baritone saxophone
      bass, 88, 101
      bop, 186–88, 197, 198
      C-melody, 82
      Coltrane's innovations, 289–93, 297, 298
      cool jazz, 206–11, 215, 217–19
      early combos, 82–83, 85–87
      hard bop, 232, 233, 246–53
      harmonic improvisation, 107
      jazz-rock fusion, 247, 370
      modern jazz, 107

multiphonics, 290
ornamentation, 87
Parker's bop, 166–72
      soprano. *See* soprano saxophone
      soul saxes, 398–401
      swing-era big bands, 101, 107–8, 135–37, 141–42
      swooping lead-in, 87
      tone rows, 215
Sbarbaro, Tony, 89
scales, 82, 176, 351
scat singing, 48, 76, 78, 120–21, 127
Schneider, Maria, 435–36, 441
Schoenberg, Arnold, 332
schottische, 41, 417
Schuller, Gunther, 177
scoop, 48, 87, 91
Scotch-Irish, 50
scratching, 396
Secret Love, 464
Senegal, 56
"Señor Blues," 37, 229, 235–36
"Sepia Panorama," 143
"Serious Serenade," 136
Setzer, Brian, 418
"Seven Come Eleven," 106, 116–17
Seven Songs, 439
Sextant, 350
Shakti, 374
"Shaw Nuff," 18, 164, 166, 179, 183–85,
            195–96, 207
Shaw, Woody, 238
Shearing, George, 112, 113, 181–82, 196–97, 204,
            225, 410
Sheldon, Jack, 185
Shepard, Andy, 431–33
Shepik, Brad, 407–8
Shields, Larry, 62
"Shoe Shine Boy," 157
Shorter, Wayne, 230, 246, 247
      composing, 277, 284
      hard bop, 233
      jazz-rock fusion, 283–84, 371
      "Masqualero," 26, 230, 274, 275, 278–83
      "Nefertiti," 275–76, 284
      saxophone style, 277
      "Surucucu," 377–78
      Weather Report, 376–81
      work with Miles Davis, 275–85, 370, 371, 372
sideman, 472
Sidewinder, 464
sight reading, 23, 102
Silhouette, 400
Silver, Horace, 229–30, 234–36, 257, 340
Simmons, John, 175–76
Sims, Zoot, 188
Sinatra, Frank, 75
singers
      "Body and Soul," 192–93
      bop, 188–93, 194, 197
      in the 1980s–1990s, 423
      swing-era big bands, 117–23, 125
      vocal blues, 92–93
      See also vocal jazz
"Singin' the Blues," 82–83, 84–85, 91
Singleton, Arthur "Zutty," 76–77, 90, 95
"Sivad," 372
sixteen-bar blues, 464
sixteenth notes, 449
sizzle, 28, 47
"Skating in Central Park," 346
Sketches of Spain, 264, 266, 267–68, 285, 372
"Skin Deep," 140
"Skip the Gutter," 90
slavery, 35–37
Slonimsky, Nicolas, 293
slow blues, 417

slow drag, 42
smear, 48, 87
Smith, Bessie, 38, 51, 92–93, 95
Smith, Buster, 167
Smith, Carl, 157
Smith, Jimmy, 254, 257
Smith, Joe, 60
Smith, Johnny, 187
Smith, Josh, 417
Smith, Louis, 237
Smith, Pinetop, 73, 115
Smith, Willie "The Lion," 115, 130
smooth jazz, 392–94, 424
snare drums, 27, 90
"Snowfall," 265
soft rock, 393
"Solar," 25, 48, 113, 342–46, 349
Sol Do Meio Di, 439
"Solea," 264, 267
"Solitude," 130
Soloff, Lew, 431–33
Soloist Synthesizer, 383
solos, 16, 20–21, 29–30
    improvisation, 29–31, 77–78, 85–87
    key changes, 111
    string bass, 142–43
Solstice, 437, 439
Someday My Prince Will Come, 272
"Someday My Prince Will Come," 346
Something Else, 313
"Something to Live For," 132
"Songbird," 400
"Song for My Father," 230
The Song of Singing, 351, 354
Son House, 91
Sonatine, 359
Sophisticated Ladies, 130
"Sophisticated Lady," 143, 476
soprano saxophone, 101, 298, 302, 370
Sorcerer, 349
soul, 365soul jazz, 229–30
    See also hard bop
soul music, 382
soul saxes, 398–401, 402–5
    David Sanborn, 400
    Michael Brecker, 400–401
Sousa, John Philip, 40
"So What," 47, 49, 256, 268–71
sock cymbal, 27
South America, 370, 373
space music, 329, 350
Spaces, 374, 375
"Spain," 354, 358
Spargo, Tony, 62
Speed, Chris, 406, 417
spirit, 9
splat, 17
Spyro Gyra, 393
"Squeeze Me," 70
Squirrel Nut Zippers, 418
St. Cyr, Johnny, 80–82
St. Louis, 232
Staccato 184
Staircase, 357
"St. James Infirmary," 90
"The Stampede," 105
Standards Trio, 356
Stan Kenton big band, 208–9, 210–16, 225–26
"Star Crossed Lovers," 132
Steamin', 265
"Steps," 25, 27, 179, 352–53
Steps Ahead, 401
Stern, Mike, 402–5
Steward, Herbie, 188
Stewart, Rex, 143
Stewart, "Slam," 21, 103

sticks, brushes, and mallets, 28, 90
Stinson, Bobo, 356
Stitt, Sonny, 187, 232, 233, 289–90
Stockhausen, Karlheinz, 315, 332, 354
stocks, 45
stomp, 417
stop-time, 63
Storyville, 40
Stone, Sly, 350, 365, 368
Story, Sidney, 40
"Straight, No Chaser," 173, 174
straight eighth, 10, 450
Straight Up and Down, 364
"Strange Fruit," 118
Stravinsky, Igor, 333, 409
"Strawberries," 48
Strayhorn, Billy, 132, 141–42, 253
"Street Cries," 48
stride, 71
stride-style, 68, 70
stride piano, 68, 70, 73, 89, 103, 130
string bands, 39, 41
string bass, 88, 142–43
    See also bass
"String of Pearls," 82
Strong, Jimmy, 76–77
"Struttin' with Some Barbecue," 83, 87
substitution, 165
Such Sweet Thunder, 143
"Suite Revenge," 350
Suite Thursday, 143
Summers, Bill, 383–84
"Summer Sequence," 187
"Summertime," 87, 464
"Sundial, Part 1," 22, 357–58
Supersax, 172
"Surucucu," 377–78
sustains, 21
Swallow, Steve, 431–33
Sweep, The, 296–97
sweet bands, 121
Sweetnighter, 380
swell, 17
swing, 3, 8–11, 47–48, 71–72, 78, 85, 90, 419
    big bands. *See* big bands
    dance music, 99, 124, 418, 425
    eighth notes, 10, 68, 78
    feeling, 8–10
    improvisation, 121, 123–24
    sweet bands, 121, 123
    style, 163–82
    vocals, 123
swinging concert music, 11
syncopation, 3, 9–10, 35, 39, 45, 118
synthesizers, 328, 354, 368, 376

T

"Take Five," 221, 222
"Take the 'A' Train," 132
Taking Off, 350
"Tampico," 213
"Tanga," 410
Tate, Buddy, 153–154
Tatum, Art, 103, 107, 108–11, 124, 165, 198
"Taxi War Dance," 50, 104, 150, 153–54
Taylor, Cecil, 113, 308, 314–15, 333–34
Tchaikovsky, Peter Ilich, 218
"Tea for Two," 165
Teagarden, Jack, 59, 87–88, 95, 106
techno, 397, 417
"Teen Town," 381
tempo
    double-timing, 19–20
    half-timing, 20
    quadruple-timing, 20
    rubato, 19

solo breaks, 20–21
"Tenderly," 346
tenor saxophone
    bop, 186–87, 198
    hard bop, 233, 247–53
    modern jazz, 107
    swing-era big bands, 101, 106–7
tenor saxophonists, 19, 82–83, 107, 108, 111, 114, 122, 137, 152, 186, 187, 276, 430
tension and relaxation, alternation of, 10, 316
Ten Wheel Drive, 365, 386
Terry, Clark, 134, 146
Teschemacher, Frank, 65
Thesaurus of Scales and Melodic Patterns (Slonimsky), 293
"These Foolish Things," 119
"Things to Come," 18, 170–71
Third Stream music, 177
Third World Music. *See* World Music
Thompson, Lucky, 107
Thornhill, Claude, 209–11, 225, 262, 264–65, 285
"Three Foxes," 256
"Three in One," 255
Three Sounds, The, 348
"Three Views of a Secret," 381
Thrust, 350
Tiberi, Frank, 422
tied triplet figure, 449
"Tight Like This," 90
timbales, 411
timbre, 468
Time Out, 221, 222
Time Further Out, 221
Tiny Bell Trio, 407–8, 409
Tizol, Juan, 122
Tjader, Cal, 410
"Toccata for Trumpet and Orchestra," 177
Togo Brava Suite, 143
tom toms, 26
tonal inflection, 481
tonal music, 453
tone center, 312, 454
tone color, 468–470
tone quality, 35, 47
tone rows, 215
Tough, Dave, 65, 104, 180
Towner, Ralph, 437–38, 439, 440
trading fours and eights, 19
traditional jazz, 233, 393–394
"Transblucency," 130, 131, 137, 143, 144–45
tremolo, 168
Tribute, 356
trills, 17
trip hop, 397
triplets, 449
Tristano, Lennie, 20, 113, 204–7, 216, 225
trombone
    bop, 185–86
    cool jazz, 221–25
    early combos, 87–88, 95
    growl style, 137
    hard bop, 253
    harmony role, 61
    pixie mutes, 137
    rubber plunger mutes, 137
    solos, 106
    swing-era big bands, 101, 106, 137
Trumbauer, Frankie, 82–85, 91
trumpet, 95
    bop, 170–73, 182–85, 197, 198
    cool jazz, 209–10, 214–15, 216–17
    early combos, 75–83
    echo and wah-wah effects, 264, 372
    fluegelhorn, 134, 216–17, 266
    free jazz, 238
    growl style, 131, 132

trumpet (*continued*)
hard bop, 232, 236–42, 255, 256–57
Harmon mutes, 263
jazz-rock fusion, 238
melody role, 61
Miles Davis's innovations on, 261, 263–65, 372–73
rubber plunger mutes, 132
solo phrases, 106–7
swing-era big bands, 101, 106–7, 109–10
tone quality, 78, 82
transition from cornet, 79
trumpet-style piano playing, 77
"A Trumpet," 214–16
tuba, 88, 210, 368
tumbao, 411
"Tune-Up," 290
Turk, Tommy, 122–23
turnabout, 467, 481
turnarounds, 164
turnback, 467, 481
turntablists, 396
Turrentine, Stanley, 399
12-bar blues chord progression, 18, 167
"Two-Bass Hit," 177, 230, 246
two-beat style, 88, 103
two-step, 40
Tyner, McCoy, 113, 295–96, 339
Coltrane's classic quartet, 292, 294–96, 299–303, 372
hard bop style, 233
hard jazz style, 230

U

Ulmer, James "Blood", 313
upbeat, 448

V

Valdés, Chucho, 412
Valente, Gary, 431–33
vamps, 21
Varèse, Edgard, 328, 329
Vaughan, Sarah, 188–93, 393
Ventura Boptet, 196, 197
Venuti, Joe, 65, 90
verse, 464
vibraphone, 106, 198, 439
vibrato, 48–49, 118
vina, 374
Vinson, Eddie, 398
violin, 383
Vitous, Miroslav, 351
bass innovations, 379, 381
"Steps," 352–53
"Surucucu," 377–78
Weather Report, 376–81
"Viva Tirado," 256
vocalese, 482
vocal jazz
blue notes, 49
pitch alteration, 48
rhythmic displacement, 44, 93, 118
rough quality, 47
scat singing, 48, 78, 120–21

vocal blues, 91–94
wordless vocals, 131
See also singers
voicing, 459, 460, 482
across sections, 131
in fourths, 351, 459
Vollenweider, Andreas, 392, 424
"Voodte," 47, 108

W

wah-wah pedal, 264, 372, 374, 420
Waldron, Mal, 173
Walker, Junior, 398, 424
"Walkin' and Swingin'", 114–15
walking bass, 24, 88, 103, 244, 381
"Walk Tall," 246, 375, 386
Waller, Fats, 70–72, 95, 418
"Waltz for Debby," 346
waltz, 48, 80, 321
Ware, Wilbur, 444
"Warm Valley," 130
Washington, Grover, Jr., 399
Water Colors, 437
"Waterfall," 381
"Watermelon Man," 349–50, 358
Watkins, Doug, 235–36
Wave, The, 392, 393
Wayne, Chuck, 343
"Weather Bird," 21, 70
Weather Report, 247, 376–81, 387, 401
"Birdland," 11, 52–53, 257, 376, 380, 387
combo improvisation style, 379–80
instrumentation, 379
Pastorius's bass style, 381–82
rhythmic complexity, 276, 376, 379
Shorter's work, 283–84
"Surucucu," 377–78
Webb, Chick, 119–20
Weber, Eberhard, 438, 439
Webern, Anton, 409
Webster, Ben, 47, 133–34, 136–37, 146
Weckl, Dave, 368
"Well, You Needn't," 173
Wells, Dicky, 157, 158–59
Wellstood, Dick, 73
"We're in the Money," 172
West Africa, 46, 91
West Coast style, 210, 226
See also cool jazz
"West End Blues," 76–77
western swing, 365
Wettling, George, 90
Whalum, Kirk, 399
"What a Wonderful World," 75
"What Is This Thing Called Love," 463
"What Love," 321
White, Andrew, 298
White, Lenny, 354
White, Michael, 365
"White Heat," 105
Whitty, George, 402–5
whole-tone scales, 82, 176
"Wild Man Blues," 68
Williams, Bert, 130

Williams, Clarence, 75
Williams, Cootie, 47, 130, 132–34, 138–39, 143, 146
Williams, Mary Lou, 113–15
Williams, Tony, 140, 239–42
hard bop, 233
jazz-rock fusion, 368
"Maiden Voyage," 29
"Masqualero," 26, 278–83
work with Miles Davis, 272–76, 285, 349, 370
"Will o' the Wisp," 267
Willis, Larry, 348
Wilson, Dick, 114
Wilson, Gerald, 254–55, 256
Wilson, Olly, 45, 48
Wilson, Shadow, 175–76
Wilson, Teddy, 69, 106, 111, 112, 124, 181
Windham Hill, 392
Winding, Kai, 205–6
"Windows," 354, 358
Winelight, 399
Winston, George, 11–12, 392, 401
wire brushes, 67, 90, 318, 347
"Wolverine Blues," 28, 66–67, 68, 83
Wolverine Orchestra, 82
wood blocks, 29, 46, 89, 104
"Woodchopper's Ball," 188
Woods, Phil, 406, 414
woodwinds, 39
Woodyard, Sam, 137–40
Woody Herman big band, 106, 187, 188, 189–90, 217
wordless vocals, 131
Word of Mouth, 381
Workin', 265
"Work Song," 229, 246
World Music, 309, 314, 334, 355
World Saxophone Quartet (WSQ), 308, 332–33, 334
"Wrappin' It Up," 105
Wright, Gene, 222–24
writing music, 23

Y

Yellow Jackets, 393
Yiddish Klezmer, 406, 425
Young, Lamonte, 392
Young, Lester, 19, 124, 152–57
cool jazz style, 211
improvisation style, 152–56
"Lester Leaps In," 158–59
"Your Lady," 297
"You've Got to Be Modernistic," 74–75

Z

Zawinul, Joe, 257, 284, 375–81
composing, 376
electric piano and synthesizer, 376
partnership with Miles Davis, 370, 375
"Surucucu," 377–78
Weather Report, 376–81
"Zodiac Suite," 113
Zorn, John, 406, 409, 425